THE GOD-IMAGE

From Antiquity to Jung

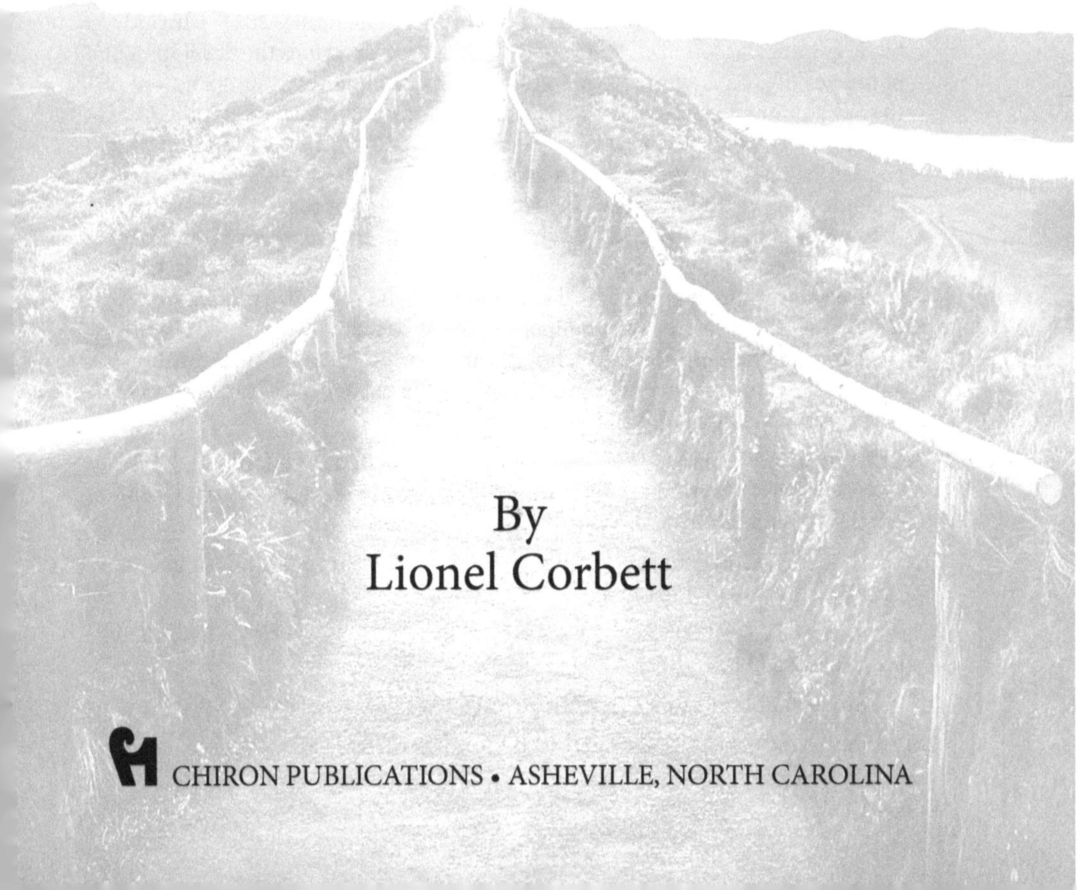

By
Lionel Corbett

H CHIRON PUBLICATIONS • ASHEVILLE, NORTH CAROLINA

© 2021 by Chiron Publications. All rights reserved. No part of this publication may be reproduced, stored in a retrieval system, or transmitted, in any form by any means, electronic, mechanical, photocopying, recording, or otherwise, without the prior written permission of the publisher, Chiron Publications, P.O. Box 19690, Asheville, N.C. 28815-1690.

www.ChironPublications.com

Interior and cover design by Danijela Mijailovic
Printed primarily in the United States of America.

ISBN 978-1-63051-984-1 paperback
ISBN 978-1-63051-985-8 hardcover
ISBN 978-1-63051-986-5 electronic
ISBN 978-1-63051-987-2 limited edition paperback

Library of Congress Cataloging-in-Publication Data

Names: Corbett, Lionel, author.

Title: The god-image : from antiquity to Jung / by Lionel Corbett.

Description: Asheville, North Carolina : Chiron Publications, 2021. | Includes bibliographical references. | Summary: "This book describes the development of images of God, beginning in antiquity and culminating in Jung's notion of the Self, an image of God in the psyche that Jung calls the God within. Over the course of history, the Self has been projected onto many local gods and goddesses and given different names and attributes. These deities are typically imagined as existing in a heavenly realm, but Jung's approach recalls them to their origins in the objective psyche. This book shows how Jung's approach avoids many of the philosophical problems produced by traditional anthropomorphic images of God and describes the myriad symbolic ways in which the Self may appear, independently of doctrinal images of God. By focusing on the empirical, psychological manifestations of the Self, Jung's approach avoids arguments for and against the existence of a metaphysical God"—Provided by publisher.

Identifiers: LCCN 2021044490 (print) | LCCN 2021044491 (ebook) | ISBN 9781630519841 (paperback) | ISBN 9781630519858 (hardcover) | ISBN 9781630519865 (ebook)

Subjects: LCSH: God. | Image of God. | Theological anthropology. | Jung, C. G. (Carl Gustav), 1875-1961. | Self.

Classification: LCC BL205 .C67 2021 (print) | LCC BL205 (ebook) | DDC 211—dc23/eng/20211102

LC record available at https://lccn.loc.gov/2021044490

LC ebook record available at https://lccn.loc.gov/2021044491

Contents

Preface / 1

Chapter 1: The Existence of God in an Age of Science / 5

Chapter 2: The God-image in Jung's Psychology / 65

Chapter 3: The God-image in Archaic Religions and Antiquity / 145

Chapter 4: The God-image of the Hebrew Scriptures and the Post-Biblical Tradition / 169

Chapter 5: The Development of the Christian Image of God / 227

Chapter 6: The God-image from the Renaissance to the Twentieth Century / 345

Chapter 7: Psychological Approaches to the God-image / 369

References / 421

Index / 445

Preface

This book contrasts the image of God in Jung's work with traditional theistic God-images. In order to place Jung's approach in its historical context, the book describes the development of ways of thinking about divinity from their earliest beginnings in archaic religions to their mature development in Judaism and Christianity. The book shows how Jung's concept of the Self, the God-image innate to the psyche, avoids many of the problems associated with traditional theistic God-images. Because Jung's approach is based on empirically available material, it avoids metaphysical speculation and by-passes traditional arguments for and against the existence of God.

Classical theistic God-images arose as part of an ancient worldview that is radically different than our own. These images are unhelpful when they are out of touch with the way we actually experience the spiritual dimension. Consequently, increasing numbers of people no longer feel attached to any of the existing theistic traditions; the era of dogmatic religions is fading. Whether or not we think these traditional religions are "true" in some sense, their God-imagery, using metaphors such as God as a supernatural shepherd or king, now seems remote. It is therefore not surprising that in a recent survey twenty four percent of Americans identified themselves as religiously unaffiliated (Jones & Cox, 2017).

I believe that Jung's approach to the Self as the "God within" is preferable to the notion of relationship to an exterior or transcendent divinity that requires the mediation of an institution and its clergy. Jung's demonstration that there is an *a priori* God-image in the psyche means that the divine and the human are seamlessly continuous with each other, in contrast to traditional notions that humanity and divinity are radically separate.

Jung suggests that because the psyche contains an intrinsic God-image and has an innate religious function, religion is an essential and inevitable aspect of human nature. Translation of the resulting religious impulse into today's language is urgently needed. However, as Tacey (2004) points out, contemporary society needs a container for spirit but does not want religion in its traditional form. The deep human longing for relationship with the transpersonal dimension can only be met by personal contact with it; our spiritual needs can no longer be met by being told what to believe. Jung's approach allows us to express our personal experience of the sacred without recourse to traditional doctrine and dogma. This approach allows us to locate the divine within our own subjectivity and alleviates the problem of meaninglessness brought about by a lack of connection to a spiritual center. The advent of Jung's psychology is particularly important at a time when many of our religious and cultural institutions seem to be failing, so that a turn to a personal, psychological form of spirituality[i] is important for many people. Jung wrote that he was addressing himself to "those many people for whom the light has gone out, the mystery has faded, and God is dead" (CW 11, para. 148).

Theology is often based on the interpretation of scripture, usually carried out in the light of pre-existing doctrines, dogmas, and creedal assertions that appeared long after the Bible was written. Because scripture can be interpreted in a variety of ways, many branches of the traditions have evolved, offering a range of beliefs that adherents are simply expected to believe. Many of these beliefs are based on stories such as the Garden of Eden, which are clearly mythic in nature. In contrast, Jung's approach is based on the direct experience of the Self, whether it appears in a traditional form or in some entirely novel manner. If we are not committed to any traditional account of how the Self should appear, we need not rely on the content of the experience as much as its powerful emotional quality and its effects on the person. We do not need to rely on a sacred text, since the direct experience of the sacred speaks for itself. The advent of depth psychology has allowed us to experience the manifestations of the sacred in new ways, consonant with our contemporary needs. It is no accident that this field emerged as the influence of mainstream religions diminished.

Although the mainstream theistic religions believe that their scriptures are eternally and universally valid, for many people they are much less relevant than they used to be. We have different concerns and a different type of consciousness than the writers of the scriptures. The images of God in the Bible are a function of the times during which they were written, and they spoke to the needs and circumstances of particular people. Depth psychology allows a further development of the God-image, which is important for those of us for whom traditional theism no longer works. We need other ways of thinking about God. A standardized religious package applicable to everyone no longer suffices. Jung's approach is an appealing alternative for the many people today who call themselves spiritual, but not religious.

A Note on Terminology

I use the word "god" in two different senses. The word is used with a lower case "g" to indicate any generic supernatural or divine being, whereas "God" with an upper-case G refers specifically to God as understood within Judaism, Christianity, and Islam. I capitalize the word God when discussing the deity of the Hebrew Scriptures, even though the image of Yhwh within the Hebrew Bible is not the same as the more sophisticated God-image of later theologians, who nevertheless insist they are talking about the same deity. I refer to God using the masculine pronouns "him" or "he" to reflect the use of these words in the traditional texts, assuming it is understood that the divine is not gendered.

I use the word "Self" with an upper-case letter S to refer to the image of the divine within the psyche, to distinguish it from the personal self, or the empirical personality. I believe that the failure to distinguish the personal self from the transpersonal Self has led to some confusion in the Jungian literature, so I have maintained this distinction throughout the text.

Various authors (Davis et al., 2013; Rizzuto, 1979) distinguish between a concept of God, which is a conscious idea based on theological descriptions that one has been taught, and a God-image, which is a subjective model of God that that may be implicit, affect-laden, unconscious, and non-verbal. One's God-image often includes qualities that reflect early attachment configurations and the quality of parental imagoes. For the psychologist, the image is more important than the concept, but they cannot be neatly separated, since early religious education affects the individual's subjective sense of the divine. In what follows, the term "God-image" is therefore understood to include both the individual's subjective sense of the divine and also his or her theology.

A Note on Dates and Biblical Sources

Many of the dates I use are controversial, so I have chosen those that are commonly accepted. The central psychological themes of the text are usually not affected by these historical controversies. All biblical quotations are from the Revised Standard Version unless otherwise indicated.

---

[i] I realize that the word "spirituality" is suspect because it is too subjective and vague. However, I have not found a more suitable word.

CHAPTER 1

The Existence of God in an Age of Science

The Existence of God

The existence of a divine being is one of the most hotly debated ideas in the history of human thought. The notion of a spiritual level of reality is often denied, and even when it is accepted, it is conceived of in a wide variety of ways. The spectrum of descriptions ranges from a supreme Personality that affects our lives, and with whom we can have a personal relationship, to an impersonal Absolute. The different textual and theological accounts of the nature of this reality conflict with each other philosophically, and we cannot prove which are correct. These conflicting accounts all agree on the existence of a spiritual dimension, nonetheless. Skeptics argue that the idea of God's existence is incoherent or cognitively meaningless because it cannot be either empirically verified or falsified. Although the existence of a spiritual reality[i] cannot be definitively proved or disproved, psychological theory can help us understand and describe the human experience of belief or disbelief in its existence, and we can describe some of the ways in which people claim to experience it.

Belief in a spiritual level of reality has several sources and a range of explanations. Some theorists see this belief as socially inculcated and reducible to human fears and needs. Jung, in contrast, believes that because the psyche contains an innate God-image, religion is inevitable.[ii] Belief may be based on claims of direct experience of a transpersonal dimension, or such belief might be due to family tradition and childhood indoctrination. Belief may also be based on reason, intuition, the authority of scripture, or on feeling. All these factors may mingle in the individual's mind. Often, people believe in the existence of God with no idea (or concern) about exactly how or why this is true, so there may be a distinct gap between the God of everyday religion and the God of theology and philosophy.

Denial of the existence of God is often a repudiation of the classical theistic[iii] God-image, which describes God using terms such as omnipotent, omniscient, immutable, ubiquitous, all-good, eternal, and a supreme spirit. Particularly in the face of suffering and evil, this image is increasingly unconvincing for many people. However, it is possible to discount the classical metaphorical descriptions of God as a king or shepherd while acknowledging the value of more sophisticated descriptions. For example, the divine has been thought of as the Ground of Being (Tillich, 1967) rather than a specific Being, as unknowable ultimate reality, as the source of design in the universe, or as the source of the moral order of the universe. In some Eastern religious traditions, divinity is thought of as pure Consciousness or pure Awareness. In this latter, non-dual view, reality is not distinguishable from our consciousness of it, or consciousness and being are indistinguishable. When the divine is spoken of as the Absolute, it is said to be beyond any kind of attribute.

If we give up the classical, anthropomorphic imagery, such as God as a loving father, God becomes increasingly impersonal and thus more difficult to relate to. This explains why Tillich's idea of God as the Ground of Being is protested at times; it seems difficult to have a personal relationship to such an abstraction which sounds as if God were a substance rather than an inconceivable spirit. On the other hand, the more we see God as a kind of personal being or a supreme personality, the more we risk falling into a God-image that is a mere projection and personification of human virtues and preferences. Anthropomorphic metaphors such as God as a divine king or shepherd may unconsciously stimulate a mental image of a large-scale person. Human ideas about God have often fallen into this trap, because we tend to think in terms of such metaphors. However, it is also possible to believe and feel that God exists without any idea of how this existence can be understood.

Traditional theists often claim that we can know something of God based on divine revelation. However, claims about the validity of revelation are controversial and require interpretation, which gives rise to further controversy. Religions that claim to be based on revelation differ in the content of that revelation even if they share a common belief in a creator God. For the skeptic, the appeal to scripture as a source of revelation is not helpful because it is circular; scripture has no source of verification outside itself. Furthermore, over the course of religious history, some of the people who claimed to have received divine revelations turned out to be false prophets or even delusional.

Science and Religion

During the Scientific Revolution of the sixteenth and seventeenth centuries, there were attempts to link ideas about God with scientific thinking. This was true of Galileo, Newton, Boyle, and other scientists of that time who believed that their discoveries demonstrated the workings of the divine mind. Thus, God was seen as a mathematician or geometer, a celestial mechanic, or the architect of the cosmos. However, it has never been clear how this kind of scientific theism is connected to the traditional moral attributes of God such as goodness and mercy, nor could the existence of many divinities be excluded based on design. Skeptics question whether there is any relationship between a scientific view of nature and nature's purported divine source, and whether the order in the universe has a cause that is in some way analogous to human intelligence. Skeptics also question whether we really need the idea of God to maintain our moral integrity. Nevertheless, many religious philosophers continue to see God as a personal spiritual agent who works by means of physical events in the world. Some of these thinkers contend that belief in the existence of God is rational and does not require evidence (Clark, 1990). Arguments for and against God's existence continue unabated, and the case for God's existence has been updated in terms of modern science (Spitzer, 2010).

In the Western intellectual tradition, particularly since the Scientific Revolution, the Enlightenment, and the Theory of Evolution, there has been a gradual decline in belief in the classical theistic God-image. This is true even though one can still find believers among contemporary scientists (Davies, 1992). Yet these tend to be exceptions. Broadly speaking, while the monotheistic traditions have taught a personal God who created the universe and cares for humanity, the scientific community typically insists that the universe is the impersonal product of energy, matter, and natural forces, and "seems pointless" (Weinberg, 1993, p. 148). Many scientists of the twentieth and twenty-first centuries assume a random universe in which life arose by chance. In these circles, talk of God is either ignored or dismissed. Contemporary scientists commonly insist that the idea of God is incompatible with scientific thinking. Natural phenomena once attributed to the deity are now explained scientifically. However, another view is that science will never be able to eliminate the essential source of religion, which is the human experience of mystery in the face of existence itself. In this view, even as we understand natural law with greater and greater accuracy, the mystery at the depths of life cannot be eliminated. The question of why the universe exists remains unanswered by science. The scientific approach to life is then only one level of discourse, and there is no authority for it to be the only one. Science explains how but not why events occur and has nothing to say about their moral qualities.

The Anthropic Principle and the Argument from Design

Some contemporary thinkers believe that science is not a barrier to religious belief, in part because of notions such as the anthropic principle, which asserts that the physical constants described by science (such as the mathematical value of the gravitational force, the strength of the nuclear forces, the speed of light, or the strength of the electromagnetic force) are exactly the values necessary to produce a universe capable of producing life. If any of these numbers were to vary even very slightly, the universe could not exist as we know it. The existence of the universe occurring by chance is improbable because the range of anthropic values is miniscule compared to the wide range of possible values that would not support life. This idea leaves room for an intelligent designer and challenges the idea that randomness could produce the high level of order found in the universe, or the chance that life arose out of a blind mechanism. The anthropic principle suggests that the universe is "fine-tuned" for the existence of life. In this view, the fine-tuning of natural constants is evidence for a creator, and the universe has been purposefully created as a home for humanity. However, this idea has been challenged for many reasons, not the least of which is that it is untestable. For the non-believer, the "anthropic coincidences" (the value of the physical constants that allowed life to develop) may eventually have conventional scientific explanations. In the skeptical view, the design argument is a tautology because if the universe were not so finely tuned and life did not exist, we would not be here to observe the fine-tuning. However, this objection explains nothing about the fine-tuning that does exist. Nevertheless, for the materialist, there is no need to explain the existence of life, and although believers insist that the universe must have a cause, skeptics deny that the universe needs any explanation.

One limitation of the argument for an intelligent mind as the designer of the universe is that this provides no evidence for the traditional attributes of the personal God of the Jewish and Christian traditions. The arguments from the design and the fine-tuning of the universe do not prove the existence of a God who is all-good. The purported designer of the world might be an evil or indifferent deity, given the level of danger, pain, and suffering in the world, or the celestial designer might be morally neutral. Another problem is that the anthropic principle does not necessarily support the theistic idea of creation ex nihilo, out of nothing, by a divine creator. Although the theory that the universe began with a Big Bang made room for the existence of a creator, Hawking (2010) wrote that contemporary physics understands the Big Bang well enough to make recourse to God obsolete. However, the claim that the mysteries of the Big Bang have been solved is contested. For theists, as Spitzer (2010) puts it, the Big Bang theory "points to a creation event as well as an ordered unfolding of the universe" (p. 14). From this viewpoint, it looks highly probable that our universe had a beginning, and it is extremely improbable that the degree of complexity in the universe arose by pure chance; it looks like life and mind were built-in from the beginning.

A possible refutation of the idea of intelligence-based fine-tuning as the source of life is suggested by the contemporary idea that a very large number of universes exist within a larger reality called the multiverse. In the view of some cosmologists, this is enough to explain the fact that at least one of them produced life. However, this is an untestable idea. Spitzer (2010) counters this argument by pointing out that although the multiverse is mathematically conceivable, "mathematical descriptions may have ontological implications, but they do not function as efficient causes, either metaphysically or materially" (p. 102).

Many materialistic scientists believe that the notions of meaning, design, and purpose behind the universe are left-over archaic thinking. Their objection to the design argument is that it assumes what it tries to prove, because the universe is all there is. Although there is design in the universe, it is unnecessary to speak of the design of the universe. Theists believe that this objection misses the point since the design argument is irrelevant to the question of God's existence. For theists, the fact that nature is intricately designed is only a feature within existence, or it describes the structures of existence, which could in principle be explained by natural processes such as evolution. The real problem is what gave rise to existence itself, not just its design. As Hart (2013) explains, "even natural selection must be bound to an ensemble of physical laws to which it could not itself have given rise" (p. 63). Hart points out that science cannot cast light on why physical reality should exist, nor can science explain why being should arise from non-being. A divine creator is one response to the question of why there is a universe rather than nothing, but Spitzer (2010) points out that science "cannot deductively prove a creation or God" (p. 22), partly because science deals with the physical universe, whereas God is not an object within the physical universe. As well, science can never be sure it has considered all possible explanations relevant to the existence of the universe.

For many people, the remarkable fact that the value of natural physical constants produced a universe that is exactly conducive to the development of life is convincing evidence of an intelligent creator. However, the classical God-image of a divine designer who pre-determines the nature of reality contrasts with scientific ideas that stress randomness and chance in the evolution of the universe. Yet there is no way to contradict the idea that the universe may have been deliberately created with an intrinsic capacity for randomness and evolution. On the other hand, order may have eventually emerged out of initial chaos without the necessity for a pre-ordained design. Skeptical biologists point out that the apparent fine-tuning in our biological nature occurred by means of natural selection, so life appeared naturally, without the need for a creator, and without invoking any kind of teleology[iv] or intelligent design. The Theory of Evolution depends on random genetic mutation to form new species, and for atheistic science the existence of humanity is a cosmic accident or sideshow in an unremarkable area of the universe. However, the religious believer points to the fact that, even given the age of the universe, it is unlikely that a succession of random biological mutations would produce a successful species, since most mutations are not successful. For believers in a creator, the chance that a protein molecule could appear by a chance combination of chemicals is infinitesimally small. For theists, the intricacies of DNA and the biological complexity of organisms are impressive enough to suggest a creator who influenced the process of evolution. This is certainly a plausible argument, but it might be countered by pointing out the sheer age of the earth, during which an enormous number of chemical permutations have occurred.

The Argument from Morality

Another theistic argument for a creator depends on the existence of our moral code. For traditional theists, there exists a transcendent moral order; God has a moral nature and is by nature loving and good, so goodness is not independent of God. However, for skeptics, the existence of such a pre-existing moral order is debatable. Morality may be a function of social evolution, or even a product of biological evolution based on the development of empathy and love, which evolved so we would look after children and our close kin, thus propagating our genes. However, the existence of a moral order cannot be proved to be explicable entirely in biological and societal terms. Theists believe that if God does not exist, objective moral values (that are independent of human opinion) would not exist, but it is widely believed that they do exist, in which case God exists. In this context, some scientists such as Gould (2002) believe that the domains of morality and science are entirely distinct and do not overlap.

Theism and the Philosophical Problem of God

Since antiquity, philosophers have attempted to explain the origins of the gods in rational terms, long before psychologists such as Freud attempted such explanations. The Greek philosopher Xenophanes (sixth century BCE) suggested that people personify their gods in their own image, so that if animals had gods, the gods would be depicted in animal form. Euhemerus (fourth century BCE) suggested that Greek gods such as Zeus were long-ago kings who were subsequently deified. Plato (in Laws Book X) claims to prove, based on reason, that gods exist. In his Timaeus he writes of a World Soul, a Mind that organizes the universe and is responsible for the movement of the heavenly bodies. Since these bodies move in an orderly way, this Soul must be rational and good. Aristotle wrote about a Prime Mover, an unmoved mover who set everything in motion. Aristotle's deity is completely transcendent—pure thought without personal connection to the world, which makes for a remote divinity. Both Aristotle and Plato seem to think of God as that which is ultimately real and true. The Latin poet Lucretius (first century CE) taught that because human beings cannot account for natural phenomena, these are attributed to the gods.

Today, not only scientists but also many contemporary philosophers are less enthusiastic than their predecessors about the traditional theistic God-image, although attempts to make a philosophical case for God's existence continue to appear (Davis, 1997; O'Connor, 2012). Many of these theists believe in the traditional God-image despite some of the intellectual difficulties associated with such belief; for example, they believe in a personal God who is at the same time transcendent, and they believe in an omnipotent God who is entirely loving even in the face of widespread suffering and evil. For these theists, the suffering that we witness can always be rationalized in terms of the mystery of God's own reasons.

For many believers, the idea of God is not capable of empirical investigation or description, because the word "God" is not the kind of word that points to a particular object, but it does indicate a special reality. Our talk about God is then different than talk about physical objects. The believer feels she does not have to be tyrannized by scientific or positivistic insistence on the use of words to refer to specific entities; she can use the word God to talk about something important to her life that cannot be rigorously defined. Then, the meaning of the word "God" is the way it is used by the believer.

Judeo-Christian theists argue that although they cannot categorically prove the existence of God, the preponderance of arguments is in their favor, because, for example, the existence of God is a rational and reasonable explanation for the existence of the universe. However, theists must address the question of why we need anything more than a purely physicalist view of the universe. They usually do so in terms of the very existence and design of the universe and the emergence of life and morality, none of which theists believe can be explained naturalistically. This area is hugely controversial; many people today believe that traditional arguments for the truth of theism are no longer compelling. In this view, theism is a matter of personal taste. The most that can be done by traditional believers is to tell their story and invite people to join in. However, important philosophical problems remain to be answered by traditional theists.

Philosophical Conundrums

Theistic philosophers are aware of the need to clarify their concept of God, because if they are unable to do so, it is not clear what it means to say that God exists. However, the typical theistic image of God is full of apparent paradoxes and philosophical conundrums. For example, the creator God is not considered to be the same as the universe but not totally removed from it—God is both immanent in and also transcendent of the world. A further paradox is that God is sometimes said to be changeless, yet he (his gender in the biblical text) appears to change his mind occasionally in stories within the Hebrew Scriptures. Despite being changeless, God is also said to be moved by prayer, to which he compassionately responds out of love. He is said to be entirely self-sufficient, and yet he also manifests himself in various revelations and is said to relate to human beings. God is said to be outside of time, space, and natural law, and so is undetectable by the methods of natural science, but somehow, even though he is pure spirit, he interacts with the physical world and affects historical events. The problem is how a perfect God can be affected by the world and respond to it, in which case he would not be entirely perfect, so it is not clear what perfection means when applied to God. In response, it is argued that when God intervenes in the world the action is only real in the world but does not change God. In other words, it has been difficult for theists to reconcile the idea of a God who is a transcendent, unchanging, and comprehensive Being with a God who takes an interest in and responds to his creation.

These kinds of apparent contradictions within the traditional God-image are sometimes approached by saying that God has different aspects. God's qualified aspect responds to human behavior, while God also has an absolute, infinite aspect that is totally unrelated to anything else. Classical theists often insist on the reality of both these aspects, even though God is a unitary being. This is a long-standing problem. The medieval William of Ockham (1285-1347) postulated a dualism in God, such that God behaves one way in his transcendent mode and another in his immanent life among human beings, especially in the Incarnation. However, this solution seems to separate the transcendent God from the immanent God, which is typical of the paradoxes raised by dogmatic assertions about God. Some process theologians see God as only absolute in some respects and still in the process of evolving (see p. 309). This idea can be compared to Jung's notion that our God-image is gradually transforming as we penetrate more and more into the unconscious. However, this transformation may only apply to the God-image as it is found in the psyche, and not to the divine itself. God is said to be pure spirit, without a physical body, but Christianity makes this assertion more complicated with its doctrine of the Incarnation, leading to a God who is both fully human and fully divine. It is difficult to see how God could incarnate while also remaining changeless and infinite.[v] However, it is always claimed that language is unable to accurately reflect the nature of God.

A further problem is that God is said to be all-good, but we do not know in what sense God is good, since there is nothing with which God can be compared. God created the world, but from an ordinary human point of view the world is obviously not only good. Thus, God also seems to be at least complicit in the fact that the world is full of evil. This raises the question of the extent to which the creator and the creation might reflect each other. Furthermore, the very notion of creation has been challenged; it is possible that endless prior states have always existed, in which case there was no beginning. For traditional Judeo-Christian theists, creation implies God's choice and will to create. Some theists believe that the world is necessary to God, while others deny that creation adds to God's perfection in any way. The problem here is that creation may imply some limitation on the part of God, since as Spinoza pointed out, a perfect being would not need to create. Some theists therefore argue that creation is a manifestation of divine love and divine voluntary self-limitation, which is consistent with the creation of creatures with free will.

Some people see God as a supreme personality, while others see this as too limiting an idea. But if not as a personality, how can God be known if God is transcendent? One view is that knowing God is like interpersonal knowing, because God makes himself known to us in some manner that is analogous to the way we know each other. In this view, we may know God as an idea, from scripture, from direct experience, or from revelation.

God is said to exist everywhere, and is said to know all past, present, and future events. However, although he knows everything that will happen, the theistic traditions believe that he does not determine human behavior since human beings are given free will, which at least to some extent is exercised independently of the will of God. However, the problem for some thinkers is that God's foreknowledge and omniscience may be incompatible with human free will. This question has been the subject of much debate.

Some philosophers believe that it is not meaningful to describe God as having thoughts or a mind, at least not in the sense that humans have thoughts. Even to describe God as conscious in the human sense of being self-aware or aware of other objects has been denied, since it implies that God's awareness could be turned in different directions, as if God has a particular point of view, rather than being ubiquitous. The notion of God's consciousness would be particularly meaningless for people who think that consciousness is a product of a physical brain. Some people think it is foolish to attribute human characteristics such as intelligence and purpose to God, since God operates on such a vast scale.

Many Christians speak of God as personal or supra-personal, and some think of God as a superior Personality, but the doctrine of the Trinity makes this latter idea complicated. Nevertheless, Christians believe that one can have a personal relationship with God. The divine nature is traditionally said to have various attributes or aspects, such as unity, eternity, righteousness, justice, mercy, and love. However, theists also believe that we cannot attribute to God these and other human qualities such as knowledge and will, because we cannot conceive what these terms mean when applied to God. In that context, these qualities may have other unknown meanings, so we do not know what we are talking about when we apply these terms to God. Furthermore, describing the attributes of God does not help us understand the essential nature of God.[vi] The theist must then fall back on the idea that reason is of no help in this endeavor. However, it is then difficult to say in what way we might know God. For many agnostics, it is not reasonable to say that we know that an unknowable being exists.

The God-image of the philosophers, arrived at by reason, is sometimes different than the God-image of revelation and the dogmatic elaborations that follow, although at times these images may overlap. It has long been held that people everywhere and always have believed in gods or a God, so the idea is often thought to be innate in the human mind. This argument is said to fail because the concept of God held by different people is so different, unless we postulate with Jung that there is an archetypal potential or readiness for the experience of God in the psyche, and the content of this potential is filled in by local beliefs. Atheists would deny any such innateness and tend to see the religious impulse as the result of our fear of death and helplessness, our sense of incompleteness, and similar feelings. For atheists, belief in God is a placebo. Such is the decline in belief in the traditional God-image, it is sometimes said that we are now living in a post-Christian age, somewhat analogous to the transitional period between the end of paganism and the beginning of Christianity. The sense that Christianity has been fading in importance since the Enlightenment is partly responsible for the desperation of some fundamentalists.

In order to deal with the kinds of questions and logical difficulties raised by the traditional God-image, theologians either fall back on the incomprehensibility of God, whose nature they insist is beyond our cognitive capacities, or they stress the need for faith. However, faith does not have to be blind, nor does it have to entail a leap. There is no reason that faith cannot be accompanied by critical inquiry, and many philosophers believe there is objective evidence for the existence of God, such as design in the universe, that makes faith rational. Faith might simply mean a commitment to the idea that the universe has a background intelligent order, without postulating any specific content or name to this order other than the way we experience it. Then, there is no need to believe that mythic biblical stories are literal history, and no need for anthropomorphic God-images.

An important branch of the theistic traditions describes God in terms of a via negativa, a negative path, which insists that, because God is infinite, God cannot have any definitive attributes, even qualities such as goodness. Thus, the twelfth century Maimonides in his Guide for the Perplexed, says: "We cannot describe the creator by any means except by negative attributes" (1:58). The idea is also found in medieval scholars such as St. Thomas Aquinas, who says that all we know of God is that we do not know him, since God surpasses human understanding. The tradition of negative theology insists that God is beyond conceptualization. Any attribution of a particular quality to God would imply limitation, since God would not have the opposite quality. The usual response to this point is to argue that each good quality is raised to an infinite level in God.

A problem with negative theology is that if God is described entirely in negative terms, it would be impossible to distinguish God from total non-existence, because having no qualities would be equivalent to not being. As well, to say what God is not must imply that we know something about what God is, or we would not be able to say what God is not. If we insist on saying that God is unlimited, infinite, and ineffable, we make the idea of God incomprehensible or inconceivable to the human mind, and this moves the theist perilously close to an agnostic position that says that we cannot know anything about God, even whether or not God exists.

Over the course of history, the word "god" has given rise to a wide range of meanings, everything from the anthropomorphic Greek deities to the omniscient, omnipotent God of Judaism and Christianity. God is sometimes thought of in abstract terms as an energetic force or power, or as simply pure potential. Sometimes gods are good, sometimes malevolent; some are objects of reverence, while some are too remote for this. Gods can be supernatural beings apart from the natural world, even beyond the limits of natural law, or they can be identified with nature, and hence immanent. Or the divine may be seen as an entirely transcendent Absolute. For these reasons it is impossible to define the word "god" in ways that would include all religious traditions. The number of religious wars in human history attests to the emotional intensity with which these differences are held. Perhaps the only point of agreement between different types of theism is that the nature of God is not fully knowable by human beings. Hence the theist uses terms such as "inexpressible." A problem arises with this usage however, because that the concept of God has no content at all, whereupon it is difficult to say in what sense God exists, just as we cannot reasonably say that we know the unknowable. Accordingly, most theists will attribute some characteristics to their God-image such as holy, eternal, and so on, while at the same time maintaining that the essence of God is beyond our understanding. This leads to the paradox that God is at the same time said to be infinite but also possessed of some qualities—which means God is not infinite, since God would not have the opposite qualities, so God would be limited. In the face of these logical difficulties, there is a tendency for the theist to retreat into notions of the incomprehensibility of God. Or, as Paul Tillich (1967, p. 236) writes, the question of the existence of God "can be neither asked nor answered," because the very notion of existence implies a finite nature, so that to say that God exists implies that God must be finite.

There are intractable philosophical problems with all the traditional attributes of God. The idea of omnipotence has been challenged on the grounds of its self-cancelling nature, for instance when we ask whether God could create a weight that he could not lift. Thus, God's omnipotence must be restricted to what is conceivable. Furthermore, the popular argument that God exists because of design in the universe has been seen as evidence against God's omnipotence, since design in nature implies that God had to employ particular means to create the universe rather than just willing it into existence. As well, if God is omniscient, and therefore knows the future, it is difficult to insist that human beings have free will, but to deny free will makes morality, praise, and blame meaningless. The idea of God's total goodness is central to Judaism and Christianity, but it is difficult to reconcile with some of God's behavior in the Hebrew Scriptures. Amos (3:6), Lamentations (3:38), and Isaiah (45:6-7) all proclaim that God is responsible for evil. The atrocities demanded by God during the occupation of Canaan are notorious: God frequently tells the Israelites to kill all the occupants of conquered cities (Joshua 6:21; Numbers 31:17), sanctions human sacrifice (Judges 11:29-40; 2 Kings 16:2-3), kills the first-born of every Egyptian family (Exodus 12:29), and sanctions slavery (Exodus 21:2-6; Leviticus 25:44-46). He commands the killing of witches (Exodus 22:18), orders death for violating the Sabbath (Exodus 31:14-15), for adultery (Leviticus 20:10), and for homosexuality (Leviticus 20:13). There are many similar biblical examples of divine brutality and vindictiveness that horrify the modern reader, although most contemporary believers simply ignore or rationalize these passages on the grounds of other principles in the Bible. Believers must construct a morality based on more enlightened sections of the text, or on modern moral standards retrospectively attributed to their God. Despite the punitive and violent quality of the God-image of the Hebrew Scriptures, Christianity insists that its God is the same God, even though the Christian God-image is said to be one of love and mercy. Despite this latter claim, at times Christian teaching has insisted that disbelievers will spend eternity in torment, because of verses such as: "he who does not obey the Son shall not see life, but the wrath of God rests upon him" (John 3:36) and other threats of punishment for disbelief. Some fundamentalist preachers still insist on a God-image that includes threats of fire and brimstone, although this idea is something of an embarrassment to liberal Christians. Liberal theologians tend to ignore uncomfortable doctrines such as hell and eternal damnation, which were of great importance to traditional Christians but are difficult to defend today. These philosophical and conceptual difficulties are entirely avoided by Jung's approach to the Self as an intrapsychic God-image.

In the last analysis, the question of whether there is a creator is a metaphysical problem that is beyond the reach of the scientific method, which should be neutral towards this question. The insistence on materialistic explanations for the existence of the universe is itself an unproven metaphysical position that remains only an ideology, just as the many suggestions of creativity in the universe are a persuasive but not conclusive proof of a creator. However, many important experiences, such as love and wonder, do not depend on proof. Despite the logical difficulties discussed here, arguments persist for the existence of God.

Philosophical Arguments for the Existence of God

Much philosophical ink has been spilled on the question of God's existence. Whether one finds these arguments and proofs convincing tends to depend on what one already believes and feels about God. It is widely conceded that there are no absolutely convincing arguments for or against the existence of God in the traditional theistic sense, and many believers find these arguments irrelevant because their faith is not based purely on reason. For them, faith is something that simply happens of its own accord, or faith justifies itself independently of reason—the doctrine of fideism.

Theists may find value in philosophical arguments that demonstrate that their belief is rational, but confirmed atheists are rarely converted by such arguments. Belief or disbelief in the existence of God often seems to have a non-rational basis that may be difficult to articulate. Perhaps direct experience of what we believe to be the divine is the single most convincing approach to this question, which is why Jung's approach is promising; it is almost entirely based on the experience of the Self and other forms of numinous experience, rather than belief.

There are traditionally three philosophical arguments for the existence of God: the cosmological, the teleological, and the ontological arguments. The cosmological argument says that everything that exists must have an explanation for its existence, which in the case of the universe is God. For the believer, the idea that the universe appeared for no reason is irrational, although the non-believer might disagree that the universe must have a reason for its existence, insisting that the question of the existence of the universe is meaningless. The cosmological argument also says that the cause of the universe must be external to it, beyond space and time, and so cannot be material. Some atheists have argued that there is no need to postulate a creator, since the universe might have had no beginning, although the Big Bang hypothesis weakens this objection since it suggests that the universe is not eternal and leaves room for a cause that brought it into being.

The main strength of the cosmological argument is that it is hard to imagine how the universe could have emerged from nothing. St. Thomas Aquinas famously developed this argument. He believed that human reason could demonstrate the foundational truths of religion even without the need for revelation. He offered five proofs for the existence of God. Everything that is moving is moved by something else, and there must be a first cause of all movement, which is God. Every effect has a cause, but nothing can be the cause of itself, so there must be an uncaused First Cause of everything. There must be something that exists of necessity, which does not depend for its existence on some other necessary existence. Since there are degrees of excellence or goodness, there must be something that is the most true and good, which is God. The very existence of goodness, beauty, and truth means that there must be an Absolute level of these attributes. Critics of these arguments point out that there is no reason to suppose that the purported First Mover or First Cause should be God in the Christian sense of the word—some entirely different being, or beings, might be responsible for these factors, with attributes entirely different than those such as the Christian Trinity. The First Mover might be entirely indifferent to human beings.

There are various other objections to the cosmological argument. The notion of a first cause is subject to the problem of infinite regress; if every effect needs a cause, then the first cause itself needed a cause, and so on. The very idea of causation is controversial; Hume pointed out that there is no universal principle of causation. We believe in causality because we see contiguous events that constantly occur one after another, such as day following night, but the assumption that one event causes another is only an inference based on habit and previous experience. We cannot assume that the same cause will always have the same effect. If we cannot rely on causation, we cannot argue for the existence of God based on causation. Kant pointed out that causation is one of the innate mental categories the mind uses to understand phenomena, but causation cannot take us beyond observable phenomena to a transcendent reality beyond what is observable.

The teleological argument is basically the argument from design, which is still defended today. This argument is based on the orderly nature of the universe, the existence of moral values, and the design of complex mechanisms such as the eye. All these are thought to infer the existence of a divine intelligence. Today, this argument often invokes the anthropic principle, which points out the fine-tuning of the physical constants necessary for life to exist. In this view, the odds that this fine-tuning appeared by chance are astronomically small, implying a designer.

The argument from design is a long-standing idea within the biblical tradition. It became very popular in the eighteenth and nineteenth centuries, well expressed by William Paley in his 1802 work, Natural Theology. Paley argued that the universe is like complex mechanism, and just as a watch implies a watchmaker, so the world must have had a designer. The implication is that God is a kind of architect. But this argument was attacked by materialists who insisted that design in nature may arise naturally without any need for a divine designer, purely on the basis of the laws of nature or by means of natural selection. Or, design may have arisen on earth by chance, given the vast age of the universe and its huge number of planets. The argument from design is also inconclusive for other reasons, partly because evidence of design does not necessarily imply one mind—there might be several intelligences at work rather than the theistic God. The design argument is also said to be an overly anthropomorphic view of the universe; although the universe seems to be designed, it may not be; we have no other universes with which to compare it. Furthermore, order is not the same as design; order is simply a necessary corollary of a stable existence. For some cosmologists, therefore, the universe is best explained by its own laws without the need for a transcendent cause. That argument is rejected by people who do not believe that the universe could cause itself. For them, there must be a transcendent cause of the high level of order in the universe. In this view, the fundamental laws of nature that are responsible for design in the universe could not have caused themselves. They could not have come about by natural selection, which itself depends on the pre-existence of the laws of nature.

An important objection to the design argument is based on the existence of evil, unnecessary suffering, natural disasters, and waste—unless the designer is careless, imperfect, or not entirely benevolent. In the end, many scientists think that the theory of evolution makes the design argument unnecessary; for materialists, evolutionary biology explains design in nature and explains features of our life such as death and pain much more convincingly. Some religious believers have sought to rescue the argument from design by attributing evolution itself to the guiding hand of divine intelligence. Then, the universe can be seen as a system that is evolving towards the development of values such as goodness. This is obviously a plausible, if unprovable, hypothesis.

The ontological argument tries to derive the existence of God by inferring it from the existence of the idea of God in our minds, without recourse to revelation or experience. (It is related to Jung's notion that there is an innate image of the divine in the psyche.) This argument was famously developed by St. Anselm, who defines God as "the being than whom nothing greater can be conceived." He means that the idea of God as a being who exists implies that God must exist, because if God does not exist, the idea would not be the idea of the greatest thing we can imagine. This proof can be re-stated in different ways. One is to say that the nature of God contains within it the necessity that God exists, or the existence of God is evident from the idea of God. The perfection of God as a perfect being must include the existence of God. Or, if one conceives of God, God exists in that understanding. Much debate has ensued about this argument, which is rarely held to be valid. (For a full discussion, seen Davis, 1997). One obvious problem is that the mere idea of a thing does not guarantee that the object exists, as we seen in the case of unicorns and witches. Another objection is that the argument presupposes the existence of a perfect being, so it is a tautology. Kant (1953) pointed out that existence is not the kind of property that can be part of the definition of a concept. If we conceive of something, such as God, and then conceive of it as existing, our concept of God is no different. The force of the idea of God is not increased by our thinking about it as existing. We cannot build a bridge from the idea of a perfect being to the actual existence of such a being. It is a logical error to affirm the being of God as if "being" or existence were a quality of God, because existence is not an additional property of an object that makes it greater than the idea of the object. Existence is not an attribute; it is a given. Before something can be perfect it has to exist. If we take existence for granted, then the ontological argument begs the question; it is like saying that if something has existence as one of its properties, then it exists—which does not prove anything. We cannot simply define God into being. Kant also thought that we could not give a coherent description of a transcendent being, and we could not say what the causal connection is between individuals and such a being. Jung pointed out that the ontological argument "has nothing to do with logic"; it is actually based on the psychological conviction that the absolute must exist, and this conviction is a "subsequently intellectualized or rationalized psychological fact" (CW 6, para. 62). He means that we have a constitutional tendency to conceive of the idea of God, so it is not surprising that the ontological argument has survived its critics and persists to this day. Another approach to this question is fideism, which suggests that religious knowledge is independent of reason, and can only be based on faith.

Kant criticized all theistic proofs for the existence of God, not because he was an atheist but because he did not believe we could have knowledge of God based on speculation or pure reason. For Kant, religion must be based on practical reason or moral grounds. Notions like God cannot be proved scientifically but neither can they be disproved by reason, so we are free to affirm ideas about God and the immortality of the soul. Without these ideas, Kant believed our experience of the moral law would not be rational. Some ethicists believe that if God does not exist, there cannot be objective moral values that are independent of human opinions. With no divine sanction against evil behavior, there would be no objective basis for moral behavior, which, for theists, is God. Many theists believe that a moral law is built into the structure of the world and built deeply into the structure of the self. For these theists, the moral law is absolute and universally valid, given by God, and not a matter of opinion. In this view, the world manifests absolute values such as complete Truth, absolute Beauty, and perfect Goodness, which are attributes of God. The contrary argument is that morality is the result of human evolution and social consensus, and requires no supernatural backdrop.

A recent argument for the existence of God was proposed by Swinburne (1979), who argues for the probability of God's existence, even though the evidence is not necessarily conclusive. Swinburne believes that the existence of the universe demands an explanation, and theism is the best available explanation. He asserts that the hypothesis of God's existence can be justified because it is the most reasonable explanation for the combination of phenomena such as the design of the world, religious experience, morality, miracles, and human consciousness. This approach is consistent with the development of scientific theories that depend on cumulative lines of evidence rather than one particular piece of evidence. For adherents to this approach, it is improbable that a universe of such complexity would exist by chance without a creator. This idea seems plausible and has the added value of simplicity, but the argument is weakened somewhat because it depends on an underlying commitment to theism. Materialists believe that theism is intrinsically implausible; Mackie (1982), for instance, believes that it is unlikely that a disembodied God exists, because our experience of persons is embodied, and the existence of the world can be accounted for by natural physical processes. Furthermore, the existence of evil counts heavily against the traditional theistic God-image. Mackie obviously begins with the opposite commitment to Swinburne, and it is typical for this difference to color a proponent's arguments about the existence of God. It is difficult to ascertain objective methods for determining whether an argument for the existence of God is plausible; this is a complex philosophical problem. The theistic God-image remains valid in the minds of many people, often based on claims of direct experience of God.

How Do People Claim to Experience the Divine?

Many people claim to have had direct experience of the divine. For these individuals, the direct experience of God is proof of God's existence and is more important than theories or ideas about God. Concepts may change, but such an experience is indelible. However, it is important to acknowledge that such claims are always open to challenge because of the difficulty of bridging the gap between an experience and knowing exactly what has produced the experience. We know that we can be mistaken; experience can be an unreliable guide to reality. We can experience illusions, hallucinations, or brain aberrations, and we cannot underestimate the power of faith, self-deception, and social pressures to affect perception. Furthermore, an experience cannot establish the truth of a metaphysical idea. Nevertheless, people have experiences that they claim result from contact with God or a spiritual presence. However, because such experiences are mediated in some way, they may not be experiences of the divine itself. Attempts have been made to account for apparently supernatural experiences in purely naturalistic terms (Taves, 2009). However, just as we never see beauty itself, but we have experiences that evoke the sense of beauty, so we have experiences that are conducive to describing the experience using the word "God." Although using this term is always an inference, if we did not have such experiences, the question of God's existence might only arise as an academic exercise. Yet, many people do have these experiences, and they can radically affect the subject's life. What follows is a description of the phenomenology of some of them. This is a pragmatic approach that follows that of William James (1982) who tried to legitimate this kind of experience without explaining it or saying what God is like. These experiences challenge a purely physicalist approach to reality.

Mystical experience, or the claim to have had direct interaction with God or with ultimate reality, is part of a long tradition. These claims are still reported. The experience occurs in a variety of ways but tends to have typical qualities. James (1982) suggests four characteristics of mystical experiences. They are ineffable, or very difficult to put into words. The experience has a noetic quality, bringing new knowledge. The experience is transient, and the subject feels passive, as if in the grasp of some kind of superior power.

Rudolph Otto (1958) stressed the emotionally powerful, non-rational aspects of a direct encounter with the holy, producing a type of experience that he believed to be the source of religion. He used the term "numinous" to describe such experiences, which produce a vivid experience of awe, wonder, mystery, dread, and fascination exemplified in the Bible by the experience of Moses at the burning bush or Saul on the road to Damascus. Moses heard the voice of God speaking to him from a burning bush, telling him to go to Egypt and persuade the Pharaoh to release the Israelites from captivity (Exodus 3:17). Saul saw a blinding light and heard the voice of Jesus saying "why do you persecute me?" (Acts 9:3-5).[vii] Otto pointed out that the subject of such an experience feels overpowered by a force that seems other than the personal self. The experience produces a "creature feeling," such that the individual feels "submerged and overwhelmed by its own nothingness in contrast to that which is supreme above all creatures" (Otto, 1958, p. 10). The experience may be uncanny, eerie, terrifying, or it may be characterized by intensely positive affect such as joy or bliss. It fills the mind with "wonder and astonishment" (1958, p. 27). The experience produces the sense that one has been addressed by the divine, or one has experienced ultimate reality. Otto believed that this type of experience is so unique that it cannot be analyzed in terms of psychological or philosophical categories; it is pre-conceptual and independent of the language used to express it.[viii] In Otto's words, numinous experience "completely eludes apprehension in terms of concepts" (1958, p. 5). Otto points out that the numinous dimension of religion is also conveyed by the images and symbols of worship services as well as the subtlety of silence and music. For Otto, the sense of the numinous constitutes the essence of holiness;[ix] its presence makes object or any place associated with it holy, and contact with it is controlled by taboos. Otto believed that various forms of archaic religion such as Totemism or the worship of demons or of the dead are explained by the attempt to rationalize the human experience of the numinous.

Jung also believed that numinous experiences are at the heart of religion. Both he and Otto believe there is an a priori predisposition in the psyche to religion.[x] Jung also agrees with Otto that these experiences are irreducible and cannot be meaningfully compared with other experiences. One can only truly understand the idea of the numinous if one has experienced it. However, although numinous experiences are central to Jung's approach to spirituality, he sees them in a different light than Otto. Otto's work was deeply rooted in his Christian heritage, so he believed that the Judeo-Christian God is the source of numinous experiences—an unprovable assumption for which he was criticized. For Jung, these experiences emerge from transpersonal levels of the psyche—an equally unprovable idea, but central to his approach to religion. Jung referred to the capacity of the psyche to produce numinous experiences as the "religious function of the psyche" (CW 11, para. 3; CW 12, para. 14). Notably, for Jung, a numinous experience may not take a traditional Judeo-Christian form; only its emotional quality is important. (Various types of numinous experiences are described in Corbett, 2006).

Jung thought that numinous experience arises within the psyche and is then projected onto something external such as a heavenly God. Otto sees the source of numinous experience as transcendent, but for Jung this source is radically immanent because it arises within the psyche and so is an intrinsic part of human subjectivity. For Jung, it is therefore not "wholly other," as it is for Otto.[xi] However, there is a level of uncertainty here, because we cannot be sure whether the numinosum is generated within the psyche or whether an external deity uses the psyche as a vehicle of transmission. Thus, we cannot be sure if a numinous experience is an experience of a transcendent God understood in the traditional theistic sense, or whether what we refer to as God is actually an experience of the transpersonal level of the psyche itself, in which case God and that level of the psyche would be synonymous.

In psychotherapeutic practice, we sometimes find that numinous experience is not entirely transpersonal because it also contains personal elements that are specific to the subject. Sometimes the connection of the experience to personal aspects of the subject's life is obvious, as it would have been for Moses or St. Paul, while at other times this connection is not obvious and emerges as a result of the subject's associations to it. The emotional power of the experience, and the fact that it often addresses some aspect of the individual's personal psychology, help to account for the transformative effect of numinous experience—what Jung refers to as its "healing effect" (1973, p. 377).

Alston (1991) points out that numinous experiences seem to occur to us in the same way as do the ordinary objects of sense perception. They have the same quality as any other perception, and they are just as trustworthy. They produce the sense of something objective appearing to us, unlike purely subjective experiences such as an insight that we might retrospectively attribute to the divine. Alston believes that when someone feels a sense of divine presence, for example, it is reasonable to assume that something may be present that does not appear through the five senses but which is detectable as a mystical perception. The content of such perception can then be dealt with as one would deal with any other source of sensory information.

Unless one is a confirmed materialist determined not to accept any notion of spiritual reality, the innumerable reports of direct experience of the holy are good if not unassailable empirical evidence for its existence. Numinous experiences are often completely convincing or self-authenticating to the subject, although they do not offer indubitable proof of the existence of God in the usual theistic sense. This doubt occurs because of debate about whether such experiences are in fact experiences of the holy, as Otto and Jung claim. There are sometimes other possible explanations for them. The awesome quality of the experience could be evoked by natural phenomena such as a spectacular sunset. The skeptic would question whether numinous experience indeed emerges from the objective psyche, as Jung claims; materialists typically reduce a numinous experience such as that of St. Paul to some form of transient psychosis, epilepsy, or an over-heated imagination. Capps (1997) believes that the experience of the mystery and power produced by a numinous experience is due to the re-emergence of a childhood experience of being terrorized by the subject's mother, which explains the dread produced by numinous experience and the feeling of being overpowered or even annihilated by it. That is, the experience is actually the return of a childhood trauma. Erikson (1977) found the origin of positively toned numinous experience in the infantile experience of recognition and affirmation by a loving mother who greets and lifts up her child. However, reductive explanations apart, the experiences themselves are irrefutable. They are profoundly meaningful events that can radically affect the subject, even changing his or her world view or beginning a religious calling. Given their quality, for many people there is no reason to doubt that they are experiences of a transpersonal reality. They certainly give the impression that they arise beyond the ego. If there is a transpersonal reality, it is probable that we would sometimes experience it. Nevertheless, the question of the actual source of any given numinous experience is often impossible to fully resolve.[xii] Some traditional religionists believe that the source of a numinous experience could be demonic, especially if when the experience contravenes their established religious teaching.[xiii]

The wide range of ways in which people claim to experience the divine is of interest, partly because God is not necessarily experienced by means of the five senses. Some people experience God as a feeling of a subtle presence. Or the subject experiences a sense of otherness, power, love, bliss, gratitude, or profound peace. At times one may experience a moment of unusually intense clarity, timelessness, or knowing that that seems to come from beyond oneself, bringing a feeling of certainty. This may appear as an opening of the heart, an inner illumination, or a sense of emotional fullness. Another possibility is the sudden realization that the world has a deeper meaning than one had hitherto grasped, or the realization that a pattern of events in one's life seems to have been determined by a background intelligence. Or, the believer might have the feeling that his or her sins have been forgiven. Conversely, for believers who are suffering, God may be paradoxically experienced as a painful sense of absence. The sense of being called to a specific vocation by something beyond oneself is another vehicle for this experience. Yet another is by means of the imagination, for example in the Spiritual Exercises of St. Ignatius or using some other form of visualization of sacred imagery. In the Taoist tradition, the movement of energy in the body known as Wu Chi or Wuji is considered to be an aspect of Tao, or ultimate reality. Eastern spiritual teachers in the non-dual tradition focus on the subjective sense of "I" or "I am," the true source of which is said to be the divine Self. For the mystically inclined, the divine is best experienced as pure silence, nothingness, or emptiness, with no form or representation. The mystics of all traditions report the sense of being gripped by a superior will (James, 1982). A sudden creative influx in an artist or writer may have a spiritual quality, because the ego cannot account for it. The skeptical psychologist might attribute most of these types of experience to nothing but an experience of the de-repressed unconscious. Jungians would respond that the divine either speaks to us through the unconscious or that the transpersonal level of the unconscious is actually synonymous with the spiritual dimension. The mythic imagery of religious traditions expresses the logic of the mythopoetic level of the unconscious rather than the logic of the ego, which is why the numinosum seems so alien.

The Pentecostal traditions stress speaking in tongues (possibly a form of trance state) and the importance of unmediated connection with the Holy Spirit. The Pentecostal emphasis on the experience of the spirit is partly based on the Gospel story of the Day of Pentecost, in which the Holy Spirit descended onto the Apostles (Acts 2). Some individuals, especially in charismatic movements, experience what they understand to be miracles or other type of saving divine intervention in their lives, often taking the form of healing or prophecy. Prayer, meditation, rituals such as the Eucharist, and reading the Gospels are other potential mediators of this experience. In the orthodox Jewish tradition, in addition to prayer and ritual the study of Torah is thought be a form of connection to the divine.

The theistic traditions all assume that God can communicate with people, either through Scripture, historical events, through the prophets, through inspired preaching, or in the form of angelic messengers. This communication may also occur in silence. Communication from God is sometimes reported to appear in the form of a voice, either heard out loud or as the experience of a thought in the individual's mind that seems to come from God because it is unusually clear or different than the person's usual thoughts. Clinicians can usually distinguish these latter experiences from the hallucinations and thought insertion of schizophrenia, if the individual shows no other signs of psychosis (Dein et al., 2007; Luhrmann, 2012). These experiences may seem like revelations or prophecy, and they may even start a novel spiritual tradition.[xiv] A delusional idea with a religious quality may be difficult to distinguish from traditional religious beliefs if the delusion is not bizarre. The cultural context of such a belief is helpful in making this distinction. Claims of supernatural experience may be consistent with the religious culture in which they arise. Ecstatic states or involuntary bodily shaking are also reported to be the result of spiritual influence on the body (Stark, 1965; 1999). This kind of intense somatic experience tends to negate radical constructionist theories that insist that religious experience is entirely constituted by the language in which it is described. All of the above are sources of what William James referred to as "personal religion," (1982, p. 29) which involves the sense of a relationship with God rather than concern with doctrine (teaching) and dogma (beliefs). Much theology and many Bible stories begin with religious experience that is subsequently formulated in terms of doctrine and dogma. However, adherence to doctrine, dogma, and ritual practices may be only forms of imitation rather than an authentic experience of the sacred.

Local cultures may color the form that the experience of God will take, since we grow up in communities that have a specific set of beliefs about God and about the distinction between what is sacred and what is profane. Nevertheless, religious experience can be entirely independent of any pre-existing theological beliefs, or it may occur in the absence of such beliefs. Numinous experiences may take a novel form that is not related to the subject's religious tradition (Corbett, 1996, 2006, 2007). Children sometimes have spiritual experiences that are independent of family and social factors (Cole, 1990).

Pious theists often expect help and guidance from God, and may anticipate divine punishment if they stray from approved behavior, albeit punishment that may be tempered by divine compassion and mercy. Such individuals see themselves as children of the divine and refer to their God as a Father who cares about them as a parent would. They may regard their personal connection to God as responsible for their success or failure in life. When they suffer, they may experience their God as absent or abandoning them. This kind of personal piety can be traced at least as far back as the religion of ancient Egypt, for example in the worship of Amen-Re, the Lord of Heaven in the twenty first century BCE (Lang, 2002).

It is noteworthy that in Hardy's (1979) account of a wide variety of religious experiences, a sense of "security, protection, and peace" (p. 26) was a common concomitant of these phenomena, as well as feelings of joy and wellbeing, sometimes accompanied by a new sense of purpose or meaning in life. Many of Hardy's subjects reported the sense of an external power or presence, which William James (1982) also noticed. When intense religious experience occurs among people suffering from low self-esteem or low levels of satisfaction with themselves, the experience tends to counter negative self-images (Spilka et al., 1993). These experiences often occur during periods of intense stress, depression, or despair, whereupon the experience tends to help the individual's sense of powerlessness. Because of such benefits, religious experiences may not be taken at face value by skeptical observers who assume that these experiences are merely defensive, hysterical, or imaginary. However, from Jung's point of view numinous experiences that support the person are examples of the healing effect of contact with the numinosum. They occur during stressful times because the hegemony of the ego and its defensive capacity are then reduced, making the personality more permeable to the unconscious.

Especially at times of crisis, such as serious illness, the individual's God-image may be called into question. An illness may be seen as a punishment, especially by people raised in traditions that stress suffering as a punishment for sin. Even when one's conscious God-image is based on sophisticated theology, as McDargh puts it, during a crisis even a theologian who thought his notions of God had been completely demythologized may be amazed to discover that he was "spontaneously evoking the God of his childhood bedtime prayer" (1992, p. 3). This happens because the individual's God-image has unconscious roots going back to infancy.

Some theologians are skeptical of the idea that finite human beings can experience an infinite God in any way other than the officially recognized biblical form of revelation, but it may not be possible to harmonize personal experience of the divine with ecclesiastical tradition. In such a case, the orthodox religious believer might protest that it is dangerous to value the unique experience of an individual when it contradicts an entire tradition. To do so might be idolatrous. For these adherents, it is particularly important to conform to traditional biblical and liturgical standards. Some traditionalists protest that faith, which for some religious authorities means adherence to dogma, is even more important than personal experience. Even traditionalists who accept the primary importance of the experience of God would agree that such experience tells us nothing about the nature of God, for which they believe we need (approved) revelation. They would not accept Jung's notion that revelation continues through the individual's experience of the objective psyche or the Self.

Materialists do not believe that events outside the natural order are possible. In this view, there are no miracles or unobservable entities such as gods or spirits. The skeptic insists on a naturalistic explanation for accounts of numinous experiences that believers claim to emanate from a spiritual dimension. However, a certain humility is important in this area, because the fact that we have no explanation for a phenomenon and no scientific means of detecting it does not mean it does not exist. The scientific method used within the physical sciences may simply be inappropriate for the study of other, non-material, levels of reality.

As evidence for the existence of God, some theists point to the experiences of the mystics of different traditions, who often describe similar experiences of contact with the divine in terms such as love, bliss, emptiness, nothingness, unity, or timelessness. Jung (CW 18) believed that all forms of mysticism are the result of contact with the transpersonal level of the psyche, so these similarities are not surprising. Although mystical experience may be colored by the imagery of the subject's personal tradition, completely unexpected numinous imagery may arise, as seen in the case of St. Nickolas of Flüe discussed on p. 76.

The Deist God-image

Deists believe that we can know about God using rational methods, an ancient idea traceable back to ancient Greek philosophers who tried to develop a rational theology that explained the origin of their gods. Deists believe that we can know truth and proper behavior when we act in accord with our rational nature, which is shared by all human beings. Because God has implanted universally true ideas in us, all reasonable people will have the same religious views. In this way, deists have tried to reconcile sectarian controversies within Christianity using reason, which was for some of them a synonym for the divine spirit within the human mind.

The deist image of God is usually monotheistic and assumes that a good God has created the world by means of natural laws that are both moral and physical. These laws require that we live a moral life. No miracles that would violate these laws ever occur. Most deists imagine God as an impersonal power who designed the natural order, set it in motion, and then left it to its own devices. This view emphasizes the transcendence of the creator and denies his immanence. Deists do not value traditional religious authority, which they see as full of error. They mistrust priesthoods, which they see as attempts to control people. Free discussion of religious matters is essential for deists, and they believe that political institutions must allow this. Deism therefore tends to flourish in societies that allow the criticism of established religions by rationalists. Deists often seemed to be thinking types.

Deism has never been very popular, partly because it lacks emotional appeal. As Europe became increasingly Christianized during the Middle Ages, deism virtually disappeared except for speculation about the relationship between faith and reason and discussion about God's attributes. Deism then reappeared during the Renaissance and the Enlightenment, with the development of the new sciences. The turmoil that these developments produced allowed new religious thought to appear, and provided the freedom for it to be expressed. In the sixteenth and seventeenth centuries, deists tended to be found among aristocrats, intellectuals, and philosophers such as Voltaire. These deists tried to find a rational ground for religion, especially natural religion[xv] not based on revelation but on the observation of nature. They denied the existence of miracles, and they believed that science was revealing the will of God in rational ways. John Locke's empiricism, for instance, tried to show that the new physics revealed God's design in nature but did not require divine intervention. Because God set the world in motion but subsequently did not intervene in its operation, deists called into question the effects of petitionary prayer. Some deists believed they had discovered the primordial faith that existed in pre-biblical times (a dubious historical claim), and early deists thought that Christianity demonstrated these universal truths. Later, deists came to see Christianity as a corruption of natural religion, even while admiring Jesus himself, whose message they thought had been corrupted by the priesthood.

Needless to say, deism produced considerable controversy and accusations of atheism, but overall, deism helped to liberalize Christianity and accommodate it to the new age of reason. In America, by the end of the eighteenth century, deism was a dominant religious attitude among the elite. It was important to philosophers such as Thomas Paine, the

American political theorist, since it justified republican politics and countered notions of the divine right of kings. Benjamin Franklin and Thomas Jefferson were also among those who promulgated the political value of deist thinking. These men wanted to put faith under the control of reason. They seemed to think that Christian ideals were universal natural truths.

Theorists who preceded the work of Charles Darwin, such as Erasmus Darwin and Lamarck, combined their ideas of evolution with deism by suggesting that God designed the universe by making evolution the mechanism by which he would execute his plan, so that no miraculous intervention was necessary. At the beginning, God had ordained the historical evolution of different forms of life, which then unfolded according to natural law.

Deism peaked and then began to falter in the eighteenth century. David Hume pointed out that the deistic, rational view of human nature was unrealistic, given the intensity of human passions and the unreasonable nature of human beings who do not have a rational religion. At the same time, materialists were developing notions about the world that did not require a creator or divinely given morality. The appeal to the importance of emotion in religion undermined the rationalism of the deists, and the importance of religious pluralism contradicted the uniformity of deist ideas.

Pantheism and Panentheism

Pantheism identifies God with the whole universe. It therefore contrasts with classical theism by making God entirely immanent in the world, removing notions of divine transcendence. Pantheism is therefore monistic, suggesting that the totality of existence is divine. Nothing exists outside of God, or nothing is independent of God. Traditional monotheists object to pantheism because it denies any personality to God, or any personal relationship with God, who could no longer be thought of as loving. The God-image of pantheism is therefore seen by traditional theists as too intellectual or austere; it removes all anthropomorphic characteristics from the divine, which becomes pure existence or being itself. Panentheism is the notion that God interpenetrates the universe, but because God is infinite and the universe is finite, the universe is contained within God but God is not limited to the universe. These ideas are both incompatible with classical theism, which insists that God is distinct from the world.

God as the Absolute

Sometimes God is referred to as the Absolute, which is an image of the divine as infinite or limitless or perfect, so that no change in God is possible and nothing is outside God. God as the Absolute is totally comprehensive and a unity. In some Eastern religious traditions, only the Absolute is totally real because only what is eternal is real. The Absolute is either eternal or it is outside of time altogether. The Absolute is self-caused, since there can be no cause outside of it, and it is self-illuminating. Some philosophers have claimed that the Absolute is morally good, while others believe it to be above all distinctions of value. Critics of the notion of God as the Absolute point to the discrepancy between such an abstraction and the personal God of the average Jewish or Christian believer. The Absolute could not be said to respond to prayer.

One way to think of God as the Absolute is found in the non-dual spiritual traditions, such as Advaita Vedanta. In these traditions, derived from the Upanishads, the Absolute is conceived of as if it were a limitless, nameless totality. Things that appear to be ontologically separate, such as apparently separate selves, are actually inseparable aspects of pure Consciousness or Awareness. The appearance of separateness, physical or conceptual, is actually an artifact born of convention, habit, language, and our perceptual systems. We see separateness and feel separate because of a misapprehension of the unitary nature of reality. In this tradition, ultimate reality is beyond image or thought. Since it is all there is or ever has been, in these traditions there is no separate creator God, an idea that is entirely a product of dualistic thought and the illusion of a separate self. The sense of self-awareness that we associate with the feeling "I am" is the transpersonal Self, before it becomes reified or arrogated by the empirical personality, which superimposes conditioned contents of consciousness onto it.

For Neoplatonic thinkers such as Plotinus (204-270 CE), the Absolute is a whole, having no distinctions of any kind, so it can be grasped with mystical intuition but not with reason. Plotinus believed that the divine emanates itself into the world with decreasing degrees of perfection as it descends into material existence. Human beings are caught in the tension between the pull towards the divine and the evils of physicality. For Plotinus, the universe is therefore a hierarchy, at the head of which is a supreme God who is unknowable, which he calls the One, who is the origin of everything. Nothing can be known or said about this level, which emanates nous, the divine mind. From this Intelligence emerges the world soul, the way the sun emanates light. This soul permeates everything. Spiritual beings then appear, until we get down to people, whose souls are trapped in material bodies. At the bottom of the hierarchy is matter, or the world we experience. The One is perfect, but at each lower level there are increasing degrees of disunity, so that material objects are separated from each other completely. The goal of life is to return to the One by the development of character, by the cultivation of reason, and by experiencing mystical union with the One in a way that leaves behind body, soul, and intellect. The One however has no desires and no needs. It does not return our love for it. Plotinus wanted to turn people away from the body towards the realm of Plato's Forms, spiritual principles such as Truth, Beauty, and Goodness, which manifest themselves in material ways. Greek philosophy influenced Christianity in this Neo-Platonic form.

Questioning the Theistic God-image

The history of our ideas about God has been a story of the gradual disappearance of God among many important thinkers and writers (Miller, 1965). Atheism either means the absence of belief in any God or supernatural being, or it means that belief in God is deliberately and consciously rejected, either because it is false or because this belief is thought to be irrational, incoherent, or even absurd. Typically, atheists think there is insufficient evidence for the existence of a deity. For the agnostic, it is impossible to say whether God exists, either because the evidence for this belief is inadequate or because it would be fundamentally impossible to provide such evidence, so we cannot know whether there is a God. Some theists believe that although there is a God, the nature of God cannot be known, which is a position that approaches agnosticism. It is noteworthy that since the existence of God cannot be finally disproved, the atheist requires faith in atheism. There is some evidence that faith in atheism is as psychologically helpful as faith in religious belief (Galen et al., 2011). The absence of theistic belief may or may not be explicit and conscious.

Atheism is often viewed with fear and mistrust by religious believers, especially those who believe that atheism inevitably leads to immorality and various forms of evil. This happens when it is (falsely) assumed that atheists deny positive values, as if atheists are somehow against goodness and virtue. Atheists contend that morality does not need to be based on the traditional God-image and evolved as a natural human competency (Pyysiäinen et al., 2010). Believers question whether morality can be developed in the absence of God, but atheists counter that it is a mistake to assume that positive values must be attributed to a supernatural realm, because morality can be developed on the basis of human understanding. Human beings invent their moral codes based on agreed-upon values and the standards of behavior necessary to uphold human welfare. Atheists object to the imposition of a moral code based on fear of divine retribution. The notion of human sinfulness is seen as a way of inducing guilt, and hence is seen as a manipulative method to control people. Atheists often suggest that human beings created God in their own image, partly because it seemed to be necessary to create a higher power to which systems of morality could be attributed. In fact, they believe that human moral behavior is developing gradually, and each advance is retrospectively projected onto the tradition's God-image as if it had been divinely given from the beginning. Atheists also point out that if God created human beings in a way that makes them prone to errors, biases, and prejudices when making moral judgments, then God cannot be a perfect being—something of the creator must be in his creation. The theistic response to this situation can only be to claim that we cannot understand the mind of God, who has his own reason for what happens.

The atheist can justifiably point to the warlike nature of many theists, not to mention the tendency towards (often autocratic) theocracy that theism has inspired and the colonialism that has often accompanied it. So many atrocities have been committed in the name of God, it is arguable that theism is responsible for more war and mayhem than for peace and brotherly love. Ever since Constantine made Christianity the official religion of the Roman Empire, institutional Churches have tended to identify with the politically powerful rather than the poor.[xvi]

Many atheists insist that the existence of unwarranted suffering and evil is incompatible with the traditional theistic God-image, which is said to be good and loving. The existence of evil and suffering has made it difficult to think of God's actions in history as entirely benevolent.

Theologians sometimes talk about the "hidden God" in these situations, but God's apparent absence in the face of evil and suffering is also an argument for atheism. A literary example is found in the words of the Grand Inquisitor in Dostoevsky's The Brothers Karamazov, who points out that what seems to be the so-called harmony of God is not worth the suffering of children. Severe trauma or loss often turns a believer into an atheist, when the erstwhile believer has been raised to believe that God is only good. The shock produced by a serious loss then seems like a betrayal. Jung's notion that our God-image must have a dark side that causes suffering and evil is obviously important here.

Another important reason for atheism is that people today often do not need the kind of comfort that religion used to bring. Religion thrives on uncertainty and fear of the future, but as our societies have become more affluent, religion-based security is less necessary. Not surprisingly therefore, countries with the best social security systems, such as those in Scandinavia, are the least religious, while poorer countries, or poorer populations within rich countries, are more religious. In the United States, the lack of universal healthcare and an inadequate social safety net contribute to the necessary pre-conditions for religion. There is often a (usually temporary) turn to religion during a national crisis and a turn away from religion as a country's economy improves. Family influences are also important; people who grow up in non-religious households are less likely to identify with a religion than those whose family was religious.

Atheists believe that various philosophical objections to the existence of God, such as the existence of evil and injustice, demonstrate that the notion of God is incoherent. Atheists dismiss all subjective accounts of contact with God as entirely explicable in naturalistic terms, so to postulate God is redundant. Atheists argue that if God exists, he ought to make his existence much more obvious, thus removing doubt, especially among people who are open to the possibility that God exists. Some atheists say they would believe in God if there were more evidence. Atheists also argue that it is impossible to maintain that God loves us, since lovers seek relationship with each other; they do not usually remain hidden. Schellenberg (1993) argues that the honest search for God often ends in failure, so that God either does not exist or choses to remain hidden. However, it is possible for the believer to counter that God is not really hidden but is omnipresent in a way that is not perceptible, since we could not tolerate the more overt presence of God. Christians sometimes insist that God appears to hide so that he will only be found by faith in Christ and not by looking elsewhere. Theists also argue that divine hiddenness is necessary in order that we might have free will, since the manifest presence of the divine would be coercive. Levinas (1979) argues that the fact of God's hiddenness makes room for human responsibility; God is to be found in our ethical behavior towards, and responsibility for, others who are suffering. Jung notes that since God acts through the unconscious, we need only look at our dreams to find the Self, a God-image, which is not hidden—although this does not prove the existence of God in the traditional theistic or metaphysical sense.

Atheists look at the story of the Garden of Eden with horror, since Adam and Eve are told not to eat of the Tree of Knowledge. This seems like a prohibition against the development of intelligence and consciousness, and a commandment to simply obey but not think. Atheists are incredulous at the idea that the behavior of two mythic individuals could condemn the entire future of humanity to a life of toil and suffering, as many Christian thinkers have believed. For atheists, this mythologem alone says a great deal about the brutality of the Judeo-Christian God-image.

Atheists see belief in God as nothing more than a comforting fable, a type of magical thinking, and a way of seeking comfort for the harsh realities of life. In response, the theist might point to the "argument from desire," which suggests that all our inborn desires correspond to objects that satisfy them, including the desire for God. The atheist might retort that we can desire non-existent objects.

Atheists point out that there are no grounds for accepting the God-image of any particular religious tradition over any other. There are several different claims of revelation, with no guarantee that one is more valid than another. In the early years of Christianity, Christians were accused of atheism because they did not believe in the Roman gods and because they would not acknowledge the Roman emperor as a god. The term "atheist" has often been used polemically, as a form of attack on people with religious views that orthodoxy considers to be heretical.

Some atheists have denied the existence of God while maintaining the value of Judeo-Christian ethical precepts. In this view, virtuous behavior such as charity and compassion does not depend on revelation from above but arises on pragmatic and humanitarian grounds and because it is part of our evolutionary heritage. There is then no need to define good and evil in terms of the dictates of religious traditions, and an approach to ethics without religion gets rid of notions of heaven and hell or posthumous rewards and punishments. Atheists also decry religions' devaluation of the body and sexuality, the relegation of women to second class status found in some traditional monotheistic societies, the often-joyless approach to life and pleasure found in some religious traditions, and the glorification of death in others.

Biblical miracle stories are not credible to many contemporary people, even to those who are not necessarily atheists.[xvii] For skeptics, assertions that the Hebrew Bible predicted the coming of Jesus, hundreds of years in the future, sound contrived. The paucity of archeological support for the Bible's historical material also casts doubt on its veracity. The belief that the Bible is the word of God is undermined by its many textual variations, its internal contradictions, its justification of abhorrent behavior, and by the innumerable amount of revision it has undergone. For these reasons, the atheist is very skeptical about the source of the Bible, which believers take to have been inspired by God. This seems unlikely to the atheist, for several reasons. Although the Bible does contain important moral teachings, in it we can also find justification for war, the inferiority of women, ethnic cleansing, slavery, and other evils. Atheists point to instructions in the Hebrew Scripture that require submission to rules that seem to be arbitrary and meaningless, at least by modern standards, even if they had some meaning at the time they were developed. These rules often lead to guilt and control by clergy who claim to speak in God's name. Examples include the biblical obsession with purity and impurity, such as laws that prohibit eating blood or having contact with menstruating and postpartum women, avoiding certain foods, not mixing garments of wool and linen, the prohibition against homosexuality, and the like. These kinds of archaic prohibitions, found in the Holiness Code of Leviticus chapters 17-26, seem to be a way of projecting and displacing any sense of personal impurity or badness onto the forbidden practice. A similar projective dynamic is seen in the primitive scapegoat ritual described in Leviticus 16:8, in which the sins of the people are loaded onto a goat that is driven into the wilderness. Christianity gave up most of these demands of the Hebrew Bible, instead insisting on proper belief. However, authorities such as Augustine maintained the tradition's anxiety about sexuality, which persists in the contemporary fundamentalists' concern with homosexuality.

For the faithful, these problems are less important than the Bible's spiritual importance, and its internal inconsistencies are thought to point to a deeper meaning behind the text. Believers often point to the authority of the canon as a coherent whole, in spite of the fact that the books consist of material written centuries apart and woven together later still, which makes the atheist skeptical about seeing it as a whole.

In recent years, a spate of books has appeared decrying belief in God. The scholarship of these "new atheists" was spoiled by their polemical tone, the uncritical assumption that the notion of a spiritual dimension is a fantasy, the authors' obvious determination to focus on the harmful dimensions of religion, and the fact that most of their criticism was only relevant to fundamentalism, which is easy to criticize. These writers ignore the tradition of historical biblical criticism and sophisticated theology, so their critique of religion feels shallow and intellectually empty. Their way of thinking about God is remarkably dogmatic and full of simplistic stereotypes and oversimplifications (McGrath, 2007). They also ignore the positive aspects of religion, such as its focus on compassion and social justice. They offer no particular suggestions for change in our cultural values, and unlike atheists such as Nietzsche, Camus, and Sartre, they offer no philosophical alternatives to religion.

The writing of the new atheists is often intolerant. Harris (2004) believes that tolerance of religion is almost as dangerous as religion itself; it is "driving us to the abyss" (p. 15), and some religious propositions are so dangerous "that it may even be ethical to kill people for believing them" (p. 52-53). One of the new atheists' main critiques is that religious faith often fosters hatred of non-believers and supports political divisions and military aggression. Thus, for Hitchens (2009, p. 56), organized religion is "violent, irrational, intolerant, allied to racism and tribalism and bigotry, invested in ignorance and hostile to free inquiry." Hitchens (p. 64) sees religion as derived from "the bawling and fearful infancy of our species." It is true that aggression and intolerance are enormous shadow aspects of religion, which often encourages tribalism, to the extent that religiously inspired violence has become a threat to civilization. A great deal of cruelty, not to mention discrimination, persecution, racism, and homophobia is carried out in the name of God. Some members of hate groups consider themselves to be Christian. However, in such cases, the valuable moral insights of the traditions are outweighed by the psychological difficulties and prejudices of their adherents, which attract them to the morally abhorrent aspects of their scriptures.

Daniel Dennett is one of the new atheists who characterize religion in a narrow manner, as if it were a danger to civilization. Dennett (2007) suggests that religious people are closed-minded and religion is an "attractive nuisance" (p. 299) that casts a dangerous spell on people, a spell that must be broken. Dennett believes that religion can be analyzed using reason and the scientific method. He expresses considerable confidence in human rationality, and refers to religion simply as if it were nothing more than a set of beliefs that have a toxic effect on society. Similarly, Dennett dismisses ideas about religion based on feelings and on religious experience, as if these are invalid. He believes that religion can and should be approached using cognitive science and evolutionary psychology. He complains that, instead of being studied critically, religion has so far been protected from scientific inquiry as if it were immune to disconfirmation. Dennett talks about religion as if we could precisely calculate its drawbacks and benefits, which is a simplistic way of thinking about religion's emotional appeal and its inordinate complexity. It is in fact doubtful that we can fully account for religion using evolutionary psychology. This approach (discussed in more detail in chapter 7) either ignores the wide range of religious experiences described above, or it is forced to reduce all religious experience to nothing but psychological defenses or brain mechanisms, revealing a prior commitment to materialism.

Atheism Among Scientists and Biologists

The French medical materialist Julien Offray de la Mettrie (1709-1751) famously developed the idea that human beings can be totally described in terms of our physical structure, and viewed as a kind of machine. He believed that all aspects of conscious life, including emotion, memory, and thought, are contingent aspects of this machine and its nervous system. This was an anti-religious philosophy, put forward as a general hypothesis for the study of humanity. La Mettrie was denounced both because his work offended religious people and also because he based happiness on the state of the body, denying the existence of the soul. For him, morality became a medical issue rather than a matter of ethics. Thus, medicine could in principle modify the mind and personality, and behavior was no longer a matter of free will. Since La Mettrie, most materialist philosophy has subscribed to the man-as-machine hypothesis, often in militantly atheistic terms. The idea bridges the gap between living and non-living things, and it experienced something of a resurgence in the nineteenth century with the increased understanding of the physiology of the nervous system. Gradually, the body was seen to be a complex physicochemical system governed by the same laws that affect mechanical systems; in contrast to the doctrine of vitalism, which insisted that life is governed by a unique vital principle. In the twentieth century, behaviorism lent weight to the man-machine idea, since behaviorists denied the importance of subjectivity and consciousness. In the materialist view, there is no soul or "ghost in the machine"; there is just the machine, whereas the religious view has always been that human beings have certain qualities, such as love and free will, that cannot be reduced to purely physical mechanisms. Today, the advent of robotics and artificial intelligence has added to the power of the man-as-machine idea. The issue persists in philosophy as the physicalist solution to the mind-body problem, which says that the mind is entirely a function of brain activity.

Atheism is common among scientists, who often believe that the universe is fully explicable on the basis of natural law, with no need for the concept of a creator. The atheist denies that the universe needs an explanation; it simply exists. The atheist concedes that there are certain facts in nature that allow the universe as we know it to exist, such as the speed of light and other natural constants, but the atheist believes there is no point in asking why they are so, and there is no need for a supernatural explanation. Atheists point out that it is meaningless to ask what caused the universe, since for something to act as a cause it must first exist as part of the universe. Many atheists celebrated a book by Stephen Hawking and Leonard Mlodinow (2010) titled The Grand Design, which postulates that the cosmos was spontaneously generated from nothing; no God was required for it to appear. The problem of how nothing could produce a universe was not addressed, because it cannot be.[xviii] Apparently if we want a proposition to be true, we can ignore its intellectual difficulties, whether we are atheists or believers. Like religious faith, atheism has its non-rational components, and such conviction may change; Mortimer Adler, an important twentieth century ethicist, rejected religious commitment for most of his life, until he was baptized at the age of 81. Some famous Christian apologists, such as C.S. Lewis, were atheists earlier in their lives.

Charles Darwin's theory of evolution proposed that human beings had evolved by a process of biological trial and error. Darwin was viewed as an atheist and a danger to the Church and the state, because his theory of natural selection meant that there was no need to postulate a divine creator.[xix] Some religious believers tried to co-opt the Theory of Evolution by suggesting that there was a background creative intelligence at work in the process of evolution. At the end of his book, On the Origin of the Species, Darwin himself suggested that natural selection was a process that the Creator had impressed on matter. Some people pointed out that Darwin only challenged the deist God-image, not the Christian image of an imminent Creator. Nevertheless, for many people Darwin's idea began the final death knell of the biblical God-image, and Darwin himself became irreligious. His theory, combined with the contributions of the geologist Charles Lyell, who pointed out that the age of the earth is much older than the Bible story allows, fostered the growing split between science and religion.

A group of modern biologists have emerged who argue that theology has become superfluous and the idea of God is obsolete. The French biologist Jacques Monod (1971) developed the view that life on earth happened by chance, as a chemical accident. For Monod, human beings are the result of random events in an impersonal universe, and evolution is incompatible with theism. Similarly, in The Blind Watchmaker, Richard Dawkins (1988) argues that there is no need to postulate a divine designer of the universe, since evolution shows that the appearance of design occurs as the result of natural selection. Dawkins believes that the religious impulse is an evolutionary mistake, a kind of side effect of the development of cognitive systems that evolved for other reasons. It may be argued that it is improbable that the random conglomeration of molecules could form complex organs such as an eye, but in Dawkins' Climbing Mount Improbable (1996) he argues that natural selection does allow the emergence of complex life forms.

For the new atheists, religious faith without empirical evidence is dangerous and irrational, since anything can be believed on this basis. For Dawkins, religious faith is one of the world's evils, comparable to a smallpox virus but harder to eradicate. In The Selfish Gene, Dawkins (1976) postulated the idea of religion as a particular societal meme or transmissible idea, analogous to a gene. A meme is said to be a unit of cultural transmission, which persists because it replicates by moving from brain to brain by a process of imitation. Memes are like mental parasites, and the God-meme is like a virus. Some enthusiasts for the idea of memes believe that the mind is largely a product of the creation of memes. However, the meme is not observable, and Dawkins has no idea about the source of memes, their properties, or their location. Furthermore, qualities such as truth, faith, and love, or notions such as free speech, are in no way simple units like genes. The concept of memes does not consider the fact that we often think about such ideas, and at times we may resist or reject them, which makes memes very unlike genes. It therefore does not seem credible that complex religious notions can be reduced to the expression of simple memes.[xx] Social evolution is entirely different than biological evolution, with very different mechanisms because of the effects of human thought, culture, and technology, which are nothing like biological mechanisms. Religion is too complex to be reduced to analogies with biological processes. Dawkins simply ignores the vast amount of experiential evidence for the existence of a spiritual domain, evidence that would usually be sufficient to suggest the reality of any phenomenon unless the observer is determined to dismiss it. When the materialist encounters phenomena such as numinous experiences that cannot be explained by physical science, he tends to deny their reality. However, it is a mistake to force-fit explanations of anomalous phenomena into existing models of reality if these phenomena need new levels of explanation.

Dawkins' selfish-gene theory suggests that the propagation of genetic material is the stimulus for much human behavior, but critics point out that this theory would not account for homosexuality, childless people, or altruism. Evolutionary explanations for religion and other forms of human behavior ignore the importance of the cultural advances we have made since our species began. Evolutionary explanations also call into question human morality and responsibility, since they imply that our actions are not free. Evolutionary psychology therefore has a jaundiced view of human nature. Faith in scientism, the notion that the scientific account of reality is the only valid one, is a fundamentalist attitude. There is, after all, no conclusive evidence for this belief, and the scientific method has nothing useful to say about the existence of God, although Dawkins insists that it does. For people of faith, belief in God is not based on logic and so cannot be disproved using logic. The arguments of the scientific atheists are irrelevant to believers.

Dogmatic scientific naturalism is the view that no supernatural forces operate in the universe and there is no creator. In this view, everything happens for natural reasons that can be investigated scientifically, and the universe has no particular purpose. Influential physicists have declared that physics has shown that the universe is meaningless, although there is no possible way to arrive at this conclusion on the basis of descriptions of matter. The irony of the physicalist position is that there is no empirical evidence for it, and it cannot be demonstrated using the scientific method. Hart (2013) points out that philosophical naturalism cannot answer three fundamental questions: why there is something rather than nothing; why reasoning is possible; and why we love. He points out that naturalism is a metaphysical system that rejects metaphysics; it claims that transcendental truth is impossible while claiming this as a transcendental truth, thus requiring "pure credence logically immune to any verification" (p. 77). Naturalism therefore remains "a pure assertion, a pure conviction" (p. 77). Adherence to purely material explanations of everything is circular thinking: "physics explains everything, which we know because anything physics cannot explain does not exist, which we know because whatever exists must be explicable by physics, which we know because physics explains everything. There is something here of the mystical" (p.77) The arguments for materialism do tend to end up saying that materialism is true because it must be true, making it sound like an article of faith. Hart suggests that atheism is actually a religion of consolation that provides "a palliative for existential grievances and private disappointments. Popular atheism is not a philosophy but a therapy" (p. 305). Ironically, this is the same argument that atheists use about religion.

Atheism Since the Enlightenment

Since the eighteenth-century Enlightenment, the classical theistic God-image has increasingly come into question. Some Enlightenment thinkers were overtly atheistic, but even those who were not atheists were critical of traditional Christianity and its God-image. These philosophers wanted to remove all traces of supernatural or mythic elements from their discourse, leaving only what could be directly experienced or proved empirically. They wished to discard all traditional beliefs that could not be validated or that had no practical utility, and they were skeptical of all metaphysical systems. Much eighteenth century thinking became increasingly secular; science and philosophy longer provided a convincing basis for the traditional God-image. Religious authorities were regarded as intolerant, and religion had caused terrible wars. Appeals to scripture and divine revelation fell on deaf ears. For increasing numbers of people, the traditional theistic God-image became either superfluous or even unintelligible.

The nineteenth century saw the increasing spread of atheism. David Strauss's *Das Leben Jesu, kritisch bearbeitet* (*The Life of Jesus, Critically Edited*), published in 1835, insisted that that the story of Jesus is mythic, and the miracles and supernatural stories of the New Testament probably did not take place. Strauss believed that Jesus represented the concept of a deity that was current at a particular time of human history. Ernest Renan's (1863) *Vie de Jésus* (*Life of Jesus*) was reverential but pointed out that the Gospels are full of legends and folk tales, and suggested that Christianity arose from the popular imagination. In 1851, Bruno Bauer, a German theologian, wrote a systematic criticism of the Gospels that argued that Jesus had never existed at all. Ludwig Feuerbach (1804-1872) believed that "theology is anthropology," meaning that people project human values and qualities onto an imaginary deity. This idea would account for the anthropomorphic nature of many God-images, and for the mixture of positive and negative traits seen in the God-image of the Hebrew Bible, who is both loving and violent. According to Feuerbach, because we are mortal and incomplete creatures, we invent a power who has the opposite characteristics; thus, humans are finite, but God is infinite, and so on. Feuerbach believed that when we talk of attributes of God such as love, we are talking about some need of human nature projected onto an ideal. Human belief in God is really belief in ourselves; we make our gods in our own image in the form of a super-human being. For Feuerbach, therefore, theology is an illusion and God is nothing more than a myth that fulfills our wish that there is such a being. With social progress, he believed that religion would eventually disappear.

Karl Marx (1818-1883) extended Feuerbach's ideas by means of his own economic and social theories. For Marx, belief in God is certainly based on the projection of human needs, but these needs are a function of social factors resulting from capitalism. Marxism therefore presupposes atheism. Marxist hope for the future is purely human. Marxists often believe that Christianity has taught resignation in the face of exploitation, because the Churches have supported social forces that have exploited workers. For Marxists, transcendence means human activity reaching beyond itself; it has nothing to do with God, who is only a comforting illusion.

Auguste Comte (1798-1857) believed that human thought and historical progress have proceeded in three stages. Early in human history, people thought anthropomorphically, explaining natural phenomena in terms of gods, demons, spirits, and miracles, proceeding through polytheism to monotheism. After the Reformation and the appearance of Newton, the universe was seen to be a machine governed by unseen spiritual forces. In the third phase, mature thinking will explain the world entirely in terms of science. In this final stage, anything that cannot be perceived will be rejected. In the fully developed rational society, according to Comte, God will be dispensed with, and people will be inspired by humanity itself. Comte thought that the third stage was imminent.

When Nietzsche announced the death of God towards the end of the nineteenth century, he was not simply referring to lack of belief in God; he pronounced the death of an entire world view, the death of the idea of a spiritual dimension of reality that many atheists saw as antithetical to human progress. Nietzsche believed that the Christian God-image denies too much of value in the world. For him, Christian morality identifies goodness with servility and thwarts the drive for excellence and self-realization. In Nietzsche's mind, Christianity has produced a morality of guilt, while the Christian emphasis on love values weakness too much. He believed that Christian theology restricts humanity, because a focus on the will of God denies human creative freedom. Belief in God offers release from sin and guilt but does so at the expense of perpetuating mediocrity. Christian doctrines of love and charity actually rest on feelings of rage and revenge directed towards qualities such as self-assertion and passion. Belief in God creates a dependency that was increasingly being eroded by science. By proclaiming that God is dead, Nietzsche wanted to move beyond conventional notions of good and evil and announce a period of freedom, responsibility, and creativity. Instead of projecting God outside themselves, people could become supreme themselves. Overall, for Nietzsche, belief in God creates a kind of sickness or dependency, and we could achieve more if we eliminate it.

Emile Durkheim (1858-1917) believed that the gods that people worship are imaginary beings, unconsciously developed by societies in order to control behavior. Whatever society needs is personified and known as God. This theory has the weakness of not accounting for morality that goes beyond the everyday needs of society, or for humanitarian religious ideas that are concerned with all people, not simply one's own group.

Despite these provocative challenges to religion, belief in God did not die out entirely during the nineteenth century. Among some people, there remained a sense of divinely inspired development or progress towards perfection. But the classical God-image had to be modified. Rather than being transcendent and hidden from the world and only knowable through revelation, the divine was seen to be immanent in nature, and in the work of Hegel it was seen in the unfolding of human history.

In the twentieth century, Jean-Paul Sartre rejected the traditional view of God, but wrote: "Even if one does not believe in God, there are elements of the idea of God which remain in us and cause us to see the world with divine aspects" (quoted in King, 2007, p. 785). Sartre realized that the desire for God is human, and we are tempted by faith, but he thought we invent the idea of God to explain the universe. He believed that human beings are condemned to futility, and he saw the classical God-image as a limitation on human freedom, so it had to be rejected. Nevertheless, it seems that Sartre struggled with his atheism and became more open to the idea of God late in his life. There are controversial reports that he became a believer as he approached death.

Albert Camus held that we suffer because our existence is not only godless but also absurd. He decided that the meaning of human life is not to be found in religions or philosophical systems but in protest against the oppression and injustice that makes people suffer. He repudiated the classical Christian image of God and struggled with the resulting absurdity of the human condition, which he felt had no ultimate meaning because the universe is not rational and cannot be rationalized by means of religion. This situation leads to despair. In The Myth of Sisyphus, he suggests that the best we can achieve is a creative confrontation with our situation; we must embrace life's absurdity, constantly commit to life and hope, and find our own meaning.

For humanists and for many existentialists, the question of the existence of God is irrelevant to the problems of daily existence and the discovery of meaning in life. They point to the fact that the discoveries of science have gradually explained many phenomena that used to be attributed to divinity, leading to the "disenchantment" of the world. However, the atheist may still regard the universe with awe at its mysteries, and many atheists try to live an ethical life without fear of divine sanction. It is also possible to see faith in ideologies such as Marxism as forms of non-theistic spirituality.

In the end, because it is impossible to conclusively verify or disprove the existence of God, atheism remains an ideology that itself requires faith. Like religious belief, atheism is not necessarily based on rational thought, and it can be subject to psychological explanation in a way that is analogous to reductive psychodynamic accounts of belief in God. Vith (2004), for example, sees atheism rooted in difficulties with a problematic or absent father figure. Another possibility is that the atheist simply cannot imagine the existence of a figure (or an internal object) that could meet all his needs.

One of the difficulties for Jung's approach to religion, which postulates the existence of the Self as an innate God-image, is to explain why atheism should exist at all, since the presence of the Self should make atheism unlikely. One possibility is that people grow up in environments in which the Self is projected onto figures such as Christ, but when the promises made by the followers of such a figure do not correspond to the individual's experience, he or she discounts the local tradition as well as the very idea of divinity. The numinosity of the Self is then projected onto other areas of culture such as art or politics.

On Faith

Given the impossibility of proving the existence of God, combined with the problem of trying to justify the theologian's descriptions of the attributes of God, many theists fall back on the importance of faith. In some traditions, faith means certainty about one's salvation, or it is understood to mean willing commitment to beliefs for which there is no unequivocal evidence. The theist may point to revelation as described in the scriptures as evidence to justify his faith, but the problem for the skeptic is the circularity of this argument; revelation pre-supposes the existence of a revealer, and so cannot be independent evidence of the existence of God.

Faith is often cited as a reason for belief in God, in contrast to belief based on reason, with the claim that faith transcends reason or allows knowledge that cannot be obtained by reason. As Jesus said: "Blessed are those who have not seen and yet believe" (John 20:29). A paradigmatic instance of this approach was given by the Church Father Tertullian (160-220 CE), who said that the story of Jesus is to be believed because it is absurd. Here, he follows several biblical passages that decry the value of reason, such as "the wisdom of this world is folly with God" (1 Corinthians 3:19). St. Paul even says that "whatever does not proceed from faith is sin" (Romans 14:23). In this vein, Martin Luther referred to reason as "God's worst enemy." According to Luther: "Faith must trample underfoot all reason, sense, and understanding" (quoted in Kaufmann, 1972, p. 307). Faith is not a response to rational argument, which for many believers is not all that important. However, to summarily dismiss reason seems to be defensive and does nothing to support the believer's claims. Preferable is the approach of St. Anselm, who spoke of "faith seeking understanding," meaning that faith prompts deeper questioning that tries to join faith with reason.

Many Christians have tried to reconcile faith and reason by suggesting that these are simply two different ways to obtain knowledge or truth, and they do not necessarily contradict each other. However, the skeptic does not believe such reconciliation is possible, because we cannot reliably demonstrate the truth of faith claims that are not based on tangible evidence. The theist replies that there are some types of knowledge that cannot be attained by evidence or reason, and reason alone is not satisfying; we need a sense of the mysterious. In this view, reason and faith accomplish different tasks for us, and we do not have the intellectual capacity to understand divine truths by reason alone. However, one must admit that it is difficult to see how faith alone can distinguish truth from falsehood, since anything can be believed on the basis of faith. It is difficult to see how faith alone can arrive at verifiable knowledge, and once knowledge becomes empirically verifiable, it no longer requires faith. Faith cannot be falsified by argument because it is not based on rational thought. Faith may crumble under the stress of adverse life events. We are not all granted the gift of faith, and the grounds for faith are not clear. Even genuine faith is often accompanied by doubt.

Whether faith is possible may depend on whether the individual developed what Erikson (1963) termed basic trust in infancy. Erikson showed that good enough care in infancy allows the development of trust in caregivers and the sense that the environment is safe and will provide what one needs. According to Fowler (1981), this childhood development is eventually transformed into mature faith in adulthood. This kind of faith is not necessarily the same as an outward adherence to a religious tradition.

Meissner (1984) points out that faith arises from a combination of subjective and objective factors. One's family, one's religious community, and also something uniquely individual play a part. Faith can be understood as a response to a kind of internal call, something within the personality that is more than the ego. The call may be thought of as an act of grace, to which we may or may not assent. However, even given such assent, one may still harbor grave reservations about traditional teachings such as the sinful nature of humanity, or one may doubt the truth of a specific biblical story. One may also have deep religious faith without adherence to any traditional religious system. For Smith (1979), faith reflects the human capacity "to see, to feel, and act in terms of, a transcendent dimension" (p. 12) and to perceive meaning in life that is more than merely mundane. Smith's approach is typical of writers who see faith as intrinsic to human nature, in contrast to those who see it as a divine gift. A more skeptical view sees religious faith as a defensive reaction to fear and an avoidance of personal responsibility.

Faith in the existence of God may arise because of direct, personal experience of the numinosum (see p. 25). This kind of faith is quite different than belief in doctrine, dogma or revelation. Religious authorities cannot command it. However, an approach to spirituality based only on personal experience may not be acceptable to conservative Christian religionists, who sometimes argue that such experience is too unreliable and may lead the individual away from the truth, which they believe requires Church authority. Traditional Thomists are not happy with the stress on personal religious experience as a source of faith, because they believe that faith means accepting that something is true on the basis of voluntary intellectual assent to the authority of Church doctrine (Stanford, 1960). This definition of faith presupposes the existence of God and the correct interpretation of biblical accounts of revelation by religious authorities. An obvious problem here is the existence of multiple authorities who disagree with each other. In practice, faith that arises because of direct experience of sacred reality does tend to be convincing, whereas faith does not necessarily arise simply because one happens to grow up in a family tradition. Faith is not necessarily instilled by routine church attendance or ritual practice.

The Church's history of violent suppression of heretics and its censorship of reason and science (Ellerbe, 1995) suggests the repression and projection of doubt or lack of faith onto non-believers, so that one's own doubt can be fought outside oneself. Culturally, this doubt is becoming more common. The steady advance of science has led to a retreat of theology into areas that it believes are beyond the reach of science. Liberal theologians such as Bultmann have responded to this challenge by trying to update and revise Christian beliefs, in his case by "demythologizing" the tradition (see p. 306). They acknowledge that many biblical stories that make supernatural claims, such as Luke's account of the virginal conception of Mary, cannot be taken literally as historical fact. These theologians are trying to arrive at the real message of the Gospels, which they believe remains valid for today. However, the risk in de-emphasizing the supernatural elements of the Gospels is that this process potentially undermines the validity of some of the historical basis of Christianity such as the Resurrection. This would conflict with assertions such as that of 1 Corinthians 15:14, which says that "if Christ has not been raised, then our preaching is in vain and your faith is in vain." However, it is possible to take the position that the literal truth of this story is not as important as the psychological and spiritual effect it has on the believer.

If there is a potential for religious faith in the human mind, the interesting question is how it got there. Jung would say that this potential is innate or archetypal, and it arises spontaneously within the psyche because of the presence of the Self. The alternative view is that religious belief is culturally transmitted, and some people are genetically more receptive to such transmission. There is some evidence from twin studies for the genetic transmission of religious belief, for example in the correlation between the level of religiosity among identical twins reared apart, which is higher than the level found among fraternal twins. Bouchard (2003) suggested that about half of the differences between people's attitude to religion could be accounted for genetically. Presumably the other half must be accounted for by environmental influences from family and culture.

Even if our sensitivity to the experience of God is innate, we may still ask whether this awareness can be justified on any other grounds. William James (1982) took a pragmatic position about God. He pointed out that even though we cannot prove that God exists, if we want to believe (or disbelieve) we are justified in doing so for psychological reasons. James rejected the argument that one should not hold beliefs for which there is no good evidence, because we may hold them for emotional reasons. Religious beliefs are an option of this type. James's famous essay, "The Will to Believe" suggests that although the concept of God cannot be decided by reason, it is reasonable to believe in God on the basis of emotion. James argues that one does not choose to believe; one just does so. However, Kaufmann (1972, p. 119) dismisses this essay as "a manual of self-deception." This is a harsh devaluation of the role that intuition and feeling play in decision-making about religion, and it ignores the role of the archetypal Self as a source of religious feeling.

Theodicy: The Justification of God in the Face of Evil and Suffering

The Christian God-image raises the question of why an all-good God would allow evil and suffering. Several critics have pointed out that if God is omnipotent and so could prevent evil and suffering, but does not do so, he cannot be all-good and totally benevolent. Or, if he cannot prevent evil, he cannot be omnipotent. This dilemma can be dealt with in various ways. One is to deny that God is all-powerful, as some process theologians do by saying that there are aspects of reality that act independently of God. Another is to assume that God is not all good, but also has a dark side, which is Jung's position and that of theologians such as Penchansky (1999) and Metzger (2009).

Other approaches, known as theodicies, try to reconcile the traditional theistic image of God with the existence of evil. A typical theodicy is the free will defense, which points out that for God to give humanity free will, there must be a choice between good and evil. Otherwise, human beings would be automata. Therefore, when people chose evil, this does not reflect on the goodness of God. However, this defense fails for several reasons. One is the enormous level of evil in the world, since there could be lesser degrees of evil or even different degrees of goodness from which to choose. Another problem is that an omnipotent, omniscient God must have designed the world with the possibility of evil within it, including the knowledge of all the atrocities that human beings inflict on each other, without preventing them. If human beings were created with the potential to commit evil because of our emotional vulnerabilities, such as fear, desperation, or because of abuse and neglect (Corbett, 2018), then the free will defense risks blaming the victim. Moreover, the free will defense does not consider natural evils, such as the suffering produced by earthquakes, tsunamis, and so on. Another theodicy invokes the notion of a world to come, after death, in which the books are finally balanced and the wicked are punished. Hence arose notions of heaven and hell. However, the appeal to an afterlife does not explain the existence of evil during our present lives. Other arguments include the idea that evil occurs for some greater good, or because it is part of God's larger plan, which we do not have the perspective to see. However, the greater good argument is of no help to the victim of evil who cannot see the greater good. Another theodicy suggests that evil will finally be defeated in a future Messianic age, an idea that simply borrows from tomorrow. Yet another theodicy is based on the idea that evil and suffering allow spiritual development, promoting kindness and goodwill between people. However, benevolence is often not present in the face of evil and suffering, which often have no observable redemptive value.

Despite these objections, notions that suffering is a test of faith or that "everything happens for a reason" die hard. None of these theodicies are compatible with the notion that God is entirely good; to the skeptic, they all sound like rationalizations. Not surprisingly, many theists have given up any attempts at theodicy; at best, evil is part of the divine mystery.

The Christian tradition on the whole prefers an idealized God-image that is entirely benevolent. Metzger (2009, p. 56) acknowledges this "predilection for a benevolent, just, loving deity" in New Testament studies, but he points out that there are, in fact, several unflattering and unsavory images of God, even in the New Testament, and religious commitments influence which texts from biblical and theological traditions are engaged or excluded. He notes God's destructive rage in Revelation, Jesus' insistence that there will be no mercy at the last judgment, and similar exhortations (Matthew 25:41-46; 13:41-42). Metzger is concerned that theologians over-idealize their God-image. He believes that the creation must mirror some of the qualities of the Creator, and we can learn something about the character of the Creator by looking at his creation, where nature is often cruel. Metzger points out that it is therefore "highly specious" (p. 69) to argue for a an entirely friendly deity who is especially concerned with human happiness and whose concept of justice mirrors our own. He points out that the tendency to exclusively highlight God's goodness shifts blame for suffering and evil to human beings, and, like Jung, Metzger believes that it would be healthier to "shift blame upwards rather than saddle ourselves unnecessarily with guilt we do not deserve," (p. 73). For Metzger as for Jung, God can be conceived of as both friend and fiend, benevolent as well as hostile.

The Holy and the Sacred: Projection or Objective Reality?

Skeptics often insist that the idea of God is based on nothing but the projection of human wishes and fears. Terms such as "holy" and "sacred" are also susceptible to this attribution, raising the question of whether the objects, texts. and places of human reverence are holy in some objective sense. For the skeptic, it is more likely that people project the quality of holiness onto them, when, in the believer's mind, they are associated in some way with the numinosum. This phenomenon is seen in religious traditions that attribute special qualities to objects such as a Torah scroll or other sacred texts that are seen to convey a divine message. Such an object carries or is imbued with the projected numinosity of the transpersonal level of the psyche, so that it seems to be sacred in itself. This form of projection is a long-standing phenomenon; in archaic religions, the world was full of spirits and demons that are now seen to be projections of levels of the psyche that were experienced as if they were parts of the objective world. Von Franz (1980) points out that whenever a new religious attitude or truth appears, previous religious ideas tend to be seen as projections, components of the inner world, whereupon the new myth supervenes. Thus, various Greek thinkers of antiquity realized that the earlier Homeric gods represented psychological powers (e.g., the god Ares personified the aggressive aspect of human nature, and so on). Jung believed that all religious imagery and ideas are projected from the mythopoetic level of the psyche, which is transpersonal and independent of individual minds. Material from this deep level of the unconscious feels holy or sacred because of its uncanny emotional power, which makes it feel "other" because of its unfamiliarity to the ego.

In archaic religions, the sacred is often associated with something taboo or forbidden, something deeply mysterious that is to be avoided on pain of a penalty. Such a distinction between the sacred and the profane or the pure and the defiled is found in several religious traditions. It represents a splitting mechanism, which allows unwanted aspects of the self to be projected or disavowed, while the goodness or specialness of the self is protected, often within a sacred enclosure. To maintain this split, a sacred object or person must not be defiled by contact with that which is considered to be impure, such as blood or corpses. Objects considered to be sacred seem to have magical power because they carry the projection of non-egoic levels of the psyche. Charismatic people in the society, who carry the projection of the Self or who intuitively sense the unconscious needs of their community, may claim to know how to direct the sacred and ritually transmit its power by means of rituals and prayers. Such an idealized person often becomes sacred himself or herself. Sometimes people in the mythic past such as the biblical Moses are retrospectively imbued with an aura of sanctity. Events in the past such as the Exodus may carry a similar quality, a phenomenon also seen in ancestor worship or the Central Australian Dreamtime.[xxi] At its best, contact with the sacred can feel enlivening and strengthening, and it is believed to consecrate the individual's life, but the notion of the sacred also opens the individual to superstition and magical thinking. The sacred dimension is also seen to be responsible for suffering, for example, in the form of divine punishment.

Over time, as early societies became firmly established, it was felt that the sacred should have its own permanent resting place where it was especially powerfully present and so could be worshipped. Hence arose temples, often constructed in places considered to be sacred because of their historical associations with supernatural manifestations. This development required the institution of a priesthood that has special knowledge of the sacred and can petition the gods in the form of sacrifice. Sacrifice is found in all religions and is thought to maintain or restore connection to the divine powers, often as a quid pro quo in which something given in return for divine favor. Sacrifice is also thought to appease the gods when they seem to be angry. The sacrifice may be burned, in which case the gods smell it, or sacrificial blood is scattered about the altar.

In the theistic traditions, the word "holy" may be used to talk about a quality of the divine itself, or it may refer to an object, text, place, or day that is hallowed by God or intimately associated with God. The Bible often refers to the holiness of God. He was thought to appear as a special presence in the Jerusalem temple, which made that site holy to that tradition. The Israelites considered themselves to be a holy people, and their land is still referred to as the Holy Land. Whether one sees these descriptions as an objective quality or a projection of the numinosity of the unconscious is entirely in the eye of the beholder.

The words "sacred" and "holy" are not exactly synonymous. At times an object or a text may be sacred to one tradition but not to others. These words are related to the notion of "mana," a term used in Melanesian and Polynesian religion to describe a special supernatural power or mystery associated with particular people or objects that carry archetypal significance for the group. This power may be good or evil. The word "taboo" has similar connotations, denoting objects that are prohibited to certain people or that may not be touched by them, since doing so would defile the object with the mundane world. Jung believed that "mana personalities" are individuals who are gripped by contact with the archetypal level of the psyche, so they seem to have a magical or fascinating effect on others. In such cases, the ego is possessed by "a dominant of the collective unconscious, the well-known archetype of the mighty man in the form of hero, chief, magician, medicine-man, saint, the ruler of men and spirits, the friend of God," (CW 7, para. 377).

In most traditions, charismatic individuals appear who have passionate dedication to their god combined with intense conviction and faith. Such people—examples are the prophets of Israel—may try to foster the moral and ethical development of their traditions. Either they attribute their own moral and ethical teachings and religious preferences to their god, or they feel inspired by contact with their god to speak for him.

Some people feel a need for an intimate relationship with the holy, to a degree that is not sufficiently provided by mainstream religions. This form of the religious spirit sometimes leads to the need to withdraw from the world in dedicated communities, such as monasteries. Innumerable religious groups have emerged, observing rituals and belief systems that include mysteries not revealed to the uninitiated. Often these individuals see themselves as elect in some way. Sometimes they gather around a charismatic, idealized spiritual teacher who proclaims a particular vision of redemption and salvation. The idealization of the cult leader is the result of the projection of the Self onto the leader by his or her followers, who are often idealization-hungry personalities.

The Perennial Philosophy: Is there a Common Essence to Religious Traditions?

Many thinkers have subscribed to the idea of a comprehensive spiritual philosophy that has survived through time. The term "Perennial Philosophy" was used in 1945 by Aldous Huxley (2009) to describe a combination of ideas from Eastern and Western religions. He suggested that all religious traditions contain a common underlying set of metaphysical truths.[xxii] According to Huxley, these truths are found among the mystics of all the world's religions. This philosophy suggests that there is a divine ground, which is the un-manifest principle behind all manifestation, and something in the soul is identical to this ground. The ground is both transcendent and immanent, and it is possible for human beings to know and love this Ground and to become identified with it. The knowledge of our one-ness with the Ground is the ultimate purpose of human life. In order to achieve this knowledge, there are divine laws that must be obeyed.

The idea of a perennial philosophy was part of a brave attempt to find the same essence within all religions, but this is clearly impossible; the differences between the theistic traditions are enormous. People who suggest that "there are many paths up the same mountain" are papering over major, incompatible opinions about what the top of the mountain looks like. When traditions use the word "God," they have very different images in mind. There are irreconcilable differences even within the same overall traditions, for example between Shia and Sunni Islam and the diversity within Christianity. When the Roman Catholic theologian Karl Rahner talks of "anonymous Christians" who will attain heaven, he offends members of other traditions who don't wish to belong to that category and find his assertion condescending. This is not to mention conservative Christians who believe that there is no salvation outside their specific Church.

God Beyond Conceptual Thought

Throughout history, human beings have created concepts and images of God that consist of a mixture of superstition, mythology, tradition, imitation, and speculation. At the same time, a long-standing view holds that no concepts can depict the divine itself, whose nature is beyond the reach of conceptual thought. That which is beyond thought cannot be described or put into ordinary language, and it cannot be circumscribed by doctrinal accounts of its nature. Krishnamurti (1992) pointed out that if we have an image of God that is based on books, tradition, and hearsay, what is created in that way "is not the eternal—it is the product of the mind…that which is not created by the mind, cannot be formulated by the mind," (p. 52). This means that the theological descriptions of God found in Judaism, Christianity, and Islam may bear little or no resemblance to the actual nature of divinity, whose nature is unknowable. These traditions are based on the accounts of their founders, which are considered to be revelations of the divine. However, the accuracy of these accounts and the dependability of their transmission over a long period of time are impossible to verify, not to mention the inevitable distortions produced by constant re-telling and by the biases of their interpreters. Herein lies the importance of Jung's notion of the Self as a manifestation of the divine as it is actually experienced by means of the psyche. For Jung, symbols of the Self arise spontaneously from transpersonal levels of the psyche and do not depend on preconceived or metaphysical ideas about the nature of the divine. We now turn to Jung's approach.

^i^ There is widespread belief in a huge range of spiritual beings, including angels of different ranks and power, demons, ghosts, fairies, and so on. Angelic messengers are important in the biblical narrative, for example in the story of Abraham (Genesis 18). Angels, demons, and other types of spiritual beings are still discussed in popular culture, in New Age thought, and among some fundamentalists. Perhaps the persistence of this belief is a way of combating the disenchantment of the world that began with the Scientific Revolution.

^ii^ Many theorists disagree with his view, instead believing that the emergence of religion is dependent on culture alone, and religious belief would not emerge spontaneously in the absence of cultural support for it (Banerjee et al., 2013).

^iii^ In the sense that I use the term here, theism is synonymous with traditional monotheism and the notion of a creator God, or a God who emanates the universe in a way analogous to the way in which the sun emits light. The God-image of each theistic tradition has unique characteristics, such as the Christian belief in the Incarnation, which distinguishes this tradition from others.

^iv^ Teleological explanations are explanations in terms of the final goal or purpose of a process. Today, most scientists are suspicious of such accounts and only accept explanations in terms of physical mechanisms.

^v^ One way the depth psychologist might deal with these apparent illogicalities is to appeal to Matte Blanco's idea that the logic of the unconscious is different than the logic of consciousness (Corbett, 2020). The unconscious is tolerant of contradictions such as a transcendent God who is also immanent. Bomford (1990) points out that the timelessness of the unconscious corresponds to the notion of an eternal deity, while the spacelessness of the unconscious corresponds to the ubiquity of God. In this view, what we call God is a way of talking about the unconscious. This idea approaches Jung's notion that the experience of the divine and the experience of the unconscious are indistinguishable.

^vi^ Aquinas believed that God's essence (*what* he is in his nature) is identical to his existence (the fact *that* he is). Unfortunately, it is difficult to understand exactly what this means.

^vii^ Saul's experience has often been discounted, for example by saying that it was the result of temporal lobe epilepsy. However, even if it was epileptic, that would not account for its elaborate content, nor could we discount the idea that the divine used the seizure as an opportunity of communication.

^viii^ A critique of this idea is that if numinous experience cannot be clearly conceptualized, it is difficult to claim that it always has the same quality. Otto assumes that the feelings aroused by the numinosum are the result of contact with the divine, which is an *a priori* assumption, so his work is not entirely empirically based—it assumes what it sets out to discover. The same can be said of Jung's idea that numinous experience arises from the objective psyche.

^ix^ Neo-orthodox theologians such as Karl Barth objected to defining the holy in terms of numinous experience, because this quality might be applied to the god of any pantheon. However, Otto was taking into account other religions beside Christianity. The influence of Otto's work declined after its initial popularity but its importance has been revived more recently (Raphael, 1997).

^x^ Both Otto and Jung rely on Kant's epistemology when they say that the holy is an *a priori* category of the mind. That is, it is not derived from the perception of the world of outer objects; it is an innate mental category that becomes conscious in a religious experience.

^xi^ Otto's approach to the holy was judged harshly and his ideas were eclipsed by the rise of notions that God is unknowable to human beings outside of direct revelation or God's grace. After the first world war, Barth was a major proponent of this approach, which rejects natural theology, the idea that knowledge of God can be gained by a combination of reason and the observation of nature. Jung's approach is to some extent a type of natural theology, since the psyche is a part of nature.

^xii^ Critics of Otto and Jung accuse both thinkers of being irrational, too subjective, and guilty of psychologism, or reducing the divine to an intrapsychic experience.

xiii Otto believed that the cruder forms of numinous experience, the "daimonic dread" and gods and spirits of animistic archaic religions, evolved into the one God of the monotheisms as human religious consciousness developed. In this process, ethical, moral, and rational components were gradually added to the non-rational experience of the numinosum, leading to the maturation of our religious traditions.

xiv An internal voice occurred to Helen Schucman, which she attributed to Jesus. This resulted in the "scribing" of *A Course in Miracles*.

xv Natural religion is based on reason and the study of nature, while revealed religion means religion based on revelation from God. Natural religion discounts anything supernatural or miraculous, including divine intervention in history, and has no place for dogma that defies reason. Similarly, natural religion does not need priests, a church hierarchy, or rituals and sacraments, which it sees as superstitious. However, Christian traditionalists believe that revelation tells us about aspects of God that cannot be derived from natural religion. Natural religion could lead to a different God-image than the traditional Christian image.

xvi The following are a few examples from recent history. When liberation theology arose, the Vatican condemned it, favoring wealthy elites rather than the struggling poor. Catholic clergy have aligned with various forms of fascism, including Mussolini, Pétain, Franco, Pinochet, South American dictators, and others. The Church signed a concordat with Hitler in 1933, said nothing about the Nuremberg racial laws of 1935 or Kristallnacht in 1938, and did not publicly condemn Hitler's attempt to exterminate the Jews of Europe, fearing that this would lead to reprisals against Catholics. The Vatican is accused of having helped to smuggle Nazi war criminals out of Europe, although Pope Pius XII is also credited with having secretly saved Jews from the Nazis. The role of the Vatican during the Holocaust remains controversial.

xvii It is often pointed out that developments in science have rendered meaningless biblical stories such as the seven days of creation. Accounts such as the story of Jonah in the belly of the whale, which are obviously not literally true, have led to an attempt to de-mythologize the tradition, getting rid of folkloric material that is not considered to be important. Some people believe that this process has clarified the true biblical message, but this approach raises question about the validity of other aspects of the Bible, such as the resurrection of Jesus, which are central to the tradition. Conservative Christians therefore do not like the process of de-mythologizing, fearing it throws the baby out with the bath water. Once this process begins, it is not easy to decide which aspects of the text are to be understood mythically and which should be seen literally.

xviii The absence of matter is not necessarily nothing if, as quantum physics tells us, there is a quantum vacuum or Zero Point Field, an underlying energy field from which particles emerge and into which they return. The notion that nothing exists is not meaningful if the word "existence" means anything.

xix Among Darwin's opponents were privileged people who criticized his idea on religious grounds as a way to rationalize their fear that his theory was a threat to establishment values, because it implied that people could improve themselves by their own efforts, which was antithetical to their elitism, based as it was on a fixed social hierarchy.

xx Although the recent spread of bizarre conspiracy theories may lend weight to the notion of memes.

xxi The term "Dreamtime" refers to an Australian Aboriginal mythic period when life appeared and ancestral figures or other culture heroes lived.

xxii There are several arguments against the idea of a transcultural perennial philosophy. It is often argued that this idea was based on a naïve reading of primary texts that were mistranslated and taken out of context. It was never proven that the mystical experiences of individuals as different as Dogen or John of the Cross were homogeneous; it was impossible to show that they were experiencing the same reality. When constructivism became popular, it was argued that all experiences are formed by the linguistic and cultural background that the subject brings to them. The received view was that there are no unmediated experiences, and no mystical experience is free of the subject's tradition. However, it is arguable that constructivism does not apply to mystical experience, or to experiences of pure Consciousness, for which a great deal of evidence exists (Forman, 1990).

CHAPTER 2
The God-image in Jung's Psychology

The Transpersonal Self as an Image of God in the Psyche

Jung believes that the notion of God is ubiquitous because the psyche contains an innate God-image, which Jung refers to as the Self or the "God within us" (CW 7, para. 399). The Self is experienced in a variety of ways; typically, it is projected onto whatever is the local name for the divine, be this Christ or any other divine being.[i] The Self also appears spontaneously in the form of numinous images of wholeness that emerge from transpersonal levels of the unconscious in dreams and visionary experiences. These images may be entirely different than traditional theistic descriptions of God, but they are recognizable because of their powerful emotional quality. An example is the following dream:

> I was surrounded by a fine mist. I sensed a presence, as if someone was coming towards me. The mist opened to reveal a gigantic blue eye, about three feet across. I felt penetrated by its gaze as I stood there in awe and fascination. The contours of the eye became red, orange, and gold. The eye came closer, until I was only aware of the round iris, which became square, then round, then square again, continuing to change in this way. The eye now seemed like a huge window or door, beyond which I could see a world of light, and into which I could now enter. I was excited by this landscape, yet also frightened by the sense of infinity, boundlessness, and eternity I saw. The light beyond the door was unlike any light I have ever seen; it was silvery and cold, but also warm, soft, and colorless. I felt as though I was falling into it.

The eye is an ancient symbol of the all-seeing divine, found in many religious traditions. The eye is also a symbolic analog of consciousness, which in the dream becomes a portal into a transpersonal or spiritual realm. The whole dream image is an extraordinary mandala, for Jung one of the classical Self symbols, representing an enclosure of sacred space and a spiritual center.[ii] It is important that there is no specific God-image at the center, just a sense of infinity—the empty center of much mystical experience, which is as Jung (1975, p. 258) puts it "the thing the archetype points to.... Emptiness in this sense does not mean 'absence' or 'vacancy,' but something unknowable which is endowed with the highest intensity."

The dreamer felt as if she had been seen by a divine eye. This dream inspired a sense of mystery, awe, and wonder in the dreamer, feelings that are characteristic of numinous experiences of the sacred or the holy. Jung believes that in terms of its emotional effect, this kind of experience of the Self is qualitatively indistinguishable from traditional accounts of the experience of the divine. The Self produces "symbolism which has always characterized and expressed the Deity" (CW 11, para. 757), so that: "For psychology the [S]elf[iii] is an *imago dei* and cannot be distinguished from it empirically" (CW 5, para. 612). However, the content of an experience of the Self may be completely novel, quite different than traditional theistic ideas about the divine. The specific imagery produced by the Self, such as the giant eye of the dream, is often related to some aspect of the subject's psychology, in this case the need to be seen, which the dream addresses.

Jung's empirical observations are based on the kind of intrapsychic God-image described in this dream. In that sense he is a phenomenologist and not a theologian. That is, he is speaking about observable psychological experiences and not about the divine as understood by theologians within theistic religious traditions. Therefore, from the point of view of psychology, he cannot say whether the God of theology and metaphysics exists; Jung can only report what emerges within the psyche, although since the psyche is real for Jung, these images are real.

The Self as Numinosum

For Jung, the Self is an "expression of the divine" (Stein, 2008, p. 309) because of the numinosity of its manifestations. The experience of the Self may arise internally as a dream image such as the one described above, or it may seem to come from the outside as a visionary experience, as in the case of Saul on the road to Damascus or Moses at the burning bush.[iv] Numinous experiences of this kind became foundational building blocks for the development of our religious traditions. Jung believes that the Self or the archetypal dimension of the psyche is the source of all such numinous phenomena (CW 12, para. 9). This level of the psyche produces a type of experience that is "unassailable by reason. We are dealing with psychic facts which logic can overlook but not eliminate" (CW 11, para. 556). There is an "authentic religious function in the unconscious" that spontaneously produces numinous imagery (CW 11, para. 3). Jung believes that because the Self and the production of numinous experiences are intrinsic to the psyche, religion is inevitable; it cannot be eradicated. The notion of a transpersonal realm of existence has been part of human thinking since time immemorial, judging by the fact that religious practices existed among our early hominin ancestors. This observation is consistent with the presence of the Self.

Jung defines religion in terms of careful attention to the numinous manifestations of the psyche (CW 11, para. 8). Jung's critics thought he was superimposing a religious point of view onto his observations of the psyche, and they disliked his thinking of the unconscious as a religiously important phenomenon. But Jung believed that the numinous manifestations of the psyche speak for themselves and are empirically observable by any observer.

The God-image described by religious traditions and sacred texts such as the Bible, which people may believe in without having experienced, might be intellectually and emotionally satisfying, but belief is not as convincing as a personal numinous experience. Such experiences can be understood psychologically without recourse to the dogma or doctrine of any specific tradition. Numinous experiences often speak to the subject's immediate psychological and spiritual state. They can be understood partly in terms of the subject's personal history, but they can also be amplified in terms of the symbolic history of humanity.

Constant attention to the manifestations of the numinosum may produce a gradual transformation of the personality, although at times (as in the case of St. Paul's vision on the road to Damascus) this effect may be dramatic and rapid (Corbett, 1996, 2006, 2007, 2011). As Neumann (1968, p. 384) notes, contact of the ego with the numinous, non-ego level of the psyche produces change that may be momentary or lasting; "it can take the form of an orderly process, or of a seemingly chaotic, directionless eruption, transforming or destroying the personality in a sudden flash; it can manifest itself as a religious experience, as love, artistic creation, a great idea, a delusion." Even a vocation may have a numinous quality and a relentless grip on the individual, since it is a call from the Self; in Jung's words, a vocation "acts like the law of God from which there is no escape" (CW 17, para. 300). What is numinous to the individual is any experience that is sufficiently fascinating, mysterious, dreadful, or awesome; the kind of experience that powerfully seizes one's attention in spite of oneself. Any experience of the non-ego level of the psyche may have the force of a religious reality, as long as the ego is surprised and emotionally gripped by the event.

Jung (1973, p. 377) believed that the experience of the numinosum has a healing effect. In a letter, he notes that "the approach to the numinous is the real therapy and inasmuch as you attain to the numinous experience you are released from the curse of pathology." Here, Jung is referring to the fact that numinous experience often addresses the subject's life situation in a helpful manner. When such experience is brought into the psychotherapeutic context, psychotherapy can become a form of spiritual practice, as the therapy helps in the integration of the experience into the person's life (Corbett, 2011). The therapeutic process fosters the experience of the Self by paying careful attention to dream material, synchronistic events, and other archetypal manifestations.

Although numinous experience may be helpful, we must also recognize that the numinosum can possess vulnerable people in an unhealthy manner. Jung (9, ii, para. 45) warned that: "It must be reckoned a psychic catastrophe when the *ego is assimilated by the Self*" (Jung's italics). He was referring to the danger of psychosis or extreme inflation that may occur as a result of numinous experience. This happens when the experience makes the subject feel specially chosen, when he or she over-identifies with the experience, or when the affective intensity of the experience is overwhelming.

The dream image of the giant eye reported above is obviously not a specifically Judeo-Christian God-image, but from the psychological point of view it is clearly a symbol of the Self because of its numinous quality and its mandala shape. It is impossible to know whether such experiences are generated by the psyche or whether the psyche acts as the medium of transmission of a divinity beyond the psyche that expresses itself by means of such imagery. Based on Kant's view, Jung (1975, p. 379) believed that we cannot know whether there is a transcendent God beyond the psyche, because we have no organ of perception that would allow us to perceive such a God. Therefore, we do not know if what we call the unconscious is identical with the divine in the theistic sense, but for practical psychological purposes this question does not matter. The fact that the psyche spontaneously generates numinous imagery helps to explain why human beings have always had a subjective sense of the divine, even though the divine is not experienced by means of the sense organs. For Jung, since the Self or the image of God in the psyche is *a priori*, not introjected, at least the *idea* of God cannot be considered to be merely an invention of human consciousness. Most importantly for the psychological approach to spirituality, numinous experiences of the Self may occur in ways that are not related to any religious tradition. Only their psychological effect—not their specific content—is important.

The Self and the God of Theism

The experience of the Self raises the question of its relationship of these images to the God of the theistic traditions. However, we cannot know whether such intrapsychic images of the Self correspond to or point to an objective, transcendent God beyond the psyche. Although Jung believed that there is a consistent psychological relationship between the God of theology and images of the Self, he thought that we cannot be sure they are identical. Jung believed that "there is an original behind our images, but it is inaccessible. We could not even be aware of the original since its translation into psychic terms is necessary in order to make it perceptible at all" (CW 18, para. 1589). However, the "psychic nature of all experience does not mean that the transcendental realities are also psychic" (CW 18, para. 1538). Jung's point is that we cannot get out of the psyche to know what is beyond it; everything we experience is filtered through the psyche. The experience of the Self "thus constitutes the most immediate experience of the divine which is psychologically possible to imagine" (CW 11, para. 396). Because we cannot know anything beyond the psyche, any image or experience of God must emerge within the psyche.[v] Even the revelations described by the mainstream theistic traditions must have originally been psychological experiences.

To insist that intrapsychic images of the Self refer to the God described by traditional theism would move us out of psychology, which is based on observable human experience, into metaphysical speculation. The most we can say is that images of the Self express a level of wholeness and unity that exists independently of the ego (CW 9, i, para. 60). Images of the Self seem to point to something transcendent even though they originate within the psyche. Thus, while Jung felt he could not prove that the intrapsychic Self and the transcendent God of the theologians are indistinguishable, he also wrote that "in practice they appear so" (Jung, 1975, p. 265). However, Jung would not commit himself definitively on this point, because he wanted to maintain the appearance of remaining an empiricist, but privately he seems to have assumed that experiences of the Self are experiences of the divine, expressed through the psyche.[vi] If that is true, the transcendent God of theology is symbolized by intrapsychic images of the Self, which is why many Jungians believe that for practical purposes the symbolic manifestations of the Self are manifestations of the divine. That is the view adopted in this book, and it is the reason that Jung believed that the Self "may perhaps be a vehicle for divine grace" (CW 10, para. 874).

Jung stressed that because all talk of God and all experiences of God arise within the psyche, we can describe the empirical God-image but we do not know whether we can infer analogies between the qualities of this image and the nature of the transcendent God described by theologians. That is, we do not know if such intrapsychic imagery tells us anything about the divine itself; the content of the experience may not be a reliable guide to metaphysical speculation about the nature of God in the traditional theistic sense. For example, the dream image of the divine eye may correspond to the sense that we are seen by the divine, but obviously there are limits to this metaphor or to the anthropomorphism involved in saying that.

Jung did not make the mistake of trying to explain religious experience entirely in psychological terms. He realized that there may well be other, metaphysical dimensions of such experience, but he believed that these cannot be explored psychologically. He was only interested in material that emerges within the psyche. He always insisted that because he was dealing with demonstrable intrapsychic material, which is the province of psychology, he was not practicing theology. Nevertheless, there are theological implications to his work on the Self if it is truly a God-image. One such implication is that revelation is continuing by means of such imagery, which is not restricted to the Judeo-Christian forms of revelation. From the subject's point of view, when something numinous arises from the depths of the psyche beyond the ego, "it is nothing less than a revelation" (CW 11, para. 534). The official Church does not trust such private revelations, because they might not conform to the authority of Church teachings. This fear is understandable, since the wealth of individual experiences of the numinosum might produce a flood of imagery that would overwhelm or even radically disconfirm official doctrine and dogma. Many traditional religious believers resist the notion of individual revelation, insisting that because their tradition is based on scriptural revelation, nothing new is needed. From this point of view, an exclusive focus on personal experience ignores the importance of scripture and the value of received doctrine and dogma. It may therefore seem arrogant to suggest that the individual may have a significant new revelation. However, the depth psychological approach to the psyche includes the idea of continuous revelation, which emerges from the unconscious. since this is infinitely creative, revelation can no longer be confined to the scriptural tradition, and it does not necessarily arise from a metaphysical domain beyond the psyche. As Jung puts it, revelation is "an essentially psychological event, though this does not, of course tell us what *else* it might be. That lies outside the province of science" (CW 11, para. 127).

Although the numinous quality of the experience of the Self may correspond to traditional descriptions of the experience of God, Jung insisted it would be a misunderstanding to accuse him of having made a "God substitute," since he was simply demonstrating the existence with the psyche of a "totality supraordinate to consciousness" (CW 10, p. 463). By "totality" he means that the Self "embraces not only the conscious but also the unconscious psyche" (CW 7, para. 274). Because the Self is the totality of the psyche, most of the Self cannot be known; the ego is a part of the Self and so could not comprehend the whole. The Self is the ultimate subject—there is nothing supraordinate to it that could know it. We therefore have no idea of the limits of the Self. Because the Self includes the unconscious, which is "inconceivable and irrepresentable" (CW 11, para. 230), we cannot form an adequate conception of it, although we experience its effects. The most we can achieve is the symbolic experience of particular aspects of the Self. Although we do not know the nature of the Self, Jung occasionally draws parallels between the Self and traditional theistic notions of divinity, for example when he says that the Self is *a priori*, "pre-existent to consciousness," and has an "incorruptible" or "eternal" character (CW11, para. 401).

God and the God-image

Jung says that he prefers to speak of a God-image "because it is quite beyond me to say anything of God at all" (1975, p. 260). He wants to avoid talking about the metaphysical God of theism and restrict himself to manifestations of the Self within the psyche. However, although in his technical writing he tries to maintain the distinction between the divine itself and its intrapsychic images, he does not always make this distinction clear. This problem is common, for example, in his *Answer to Job*, where he frequently refers to "Yahweh," without making it clear that he is talking about the biblical image of God. Jung is also not always clear about this distinction in his letters, for example when he says that God is a "strange force against or for my conscious tendencies" (p. 523), or God is an autonomous force that is stronger than the ego. In the same letter he writes that God "is the name by which I designate all things which cross my willful path violently and recklessly, all things which upset my subjective views, plans, and intentions and change the course of my life for better or worse" (p. 523). In other letters Jung suggests that "man's vital energy or libido is the divine pneuma" (1973, p. 384), or that God is a "superior deciding power to which you may give various names like instinct, fate, unconscious, faith, etc" (1975, p. 301). He also refers to God as "the supreme and ultimately decisive factor" (Jung, 1976, p. 366). Jung says that God is the "mightiest force" in the psyche (CW 5, p. 64) and that whatever wields the highest value and power in the psyche, we call God (CW 11, para. 137). These latter phenomena sound like more than simply images, although Jung is clear that the intrapsychic image itself has a powerful effect on the personality:

> From the empirical standpoint of analytical psychology, the God-image is the symbolic expression of a particular psychic state, or function, which is characterized by its absolute ascendency over the will of the subject, and can therefore bring about or enforce actions and achievements that could never be done by conscious effort. (CW 6, para. 412).

Because Jung does not always take pains to distinguish the divine in the metaphysical sense from the intrapsychic God-image, he was often accused of straying from psychology into theology or metaphysics.[vii] In response to such criticisms, Jung always insisted that he was dealing with empirically demonstrable imagery, as distinct from the metaphysical or theological speculation that gives rise to Church teachings.[viii] From the point of view of depth psychology, a good deal of such theology is speculation grounded in inherited narratives, doctrine, and dogma rather than direct experience. Theology often deals with abstract ideas or speculations about the divine, such as the Trinity, that are not necessarily grounded in the theologian's direct experience. Jung believed that doctrine itself is a symbolic expression of the psyche, whether or not it says anything real about the divine; the Trinity is an archetypal idea. But for Jung, all statements about the nature of the ultimate are "anthropomorphisms" (1975, p. 260). In fact, from Jung's point of view, the God-images of all theistic traditions are nothing more than anthropomorphisms, and he was critical of theologians who "deify anthropomorphisms, psychic structures, and myths" (p. 261).

Our images of God are the result of psychological processes that may not be the same as their putative transcendental object, to which at best the image only points. Some of these images arise spontaneously within the psyche, and some are sanctified by tradition, but in either case Jung points out that it is important to separate psychological images from their "unknowable metaphysical background" (CW 11, para. 558). Although the human image of God has changed over time, we do not know whether these changes reflect "only the concepts and images, or the Unspeakable itself" (CW 11, para. 555). We do not know the exact relationship between God-images in the psyche and the ways in which the monotheistic traditions talk about their God-image; they cannot be conflated, because the intrapsychic imagery may be entirely novel, not at all related to the theistic God-image, but recognizable by its numinosity.

Jung thinks that it would be a "regrettable mistake" to assume that an intrapsychic Self symbol of the kind in the dream described above would prove the existence of God in the theological sense, because such observations "prove only the existence of an archetypal God-image, which to my mind is the most we can assert about God psychologically" (CW 11, para. 102). Psychology cannot prove or disprove the existence of the theistic God. Jung's work deals with the way human beings describe their experience of the divine, but not with the metaphysical question of the existence of God in the theological or transcendent sense. There might be a divinity that exists beyond the psyche, but Jung felt this to be an unanswerable question because all experience is mediated psychologically. Jung by-passes the traditional theological tension between divine immanence and transcendence because what seems to be transcendence is really the experience of the non-ego levels of the psyche. Jung believed that we cannot distinguish our experience of God from the divine itself, except conceptually, because to do so "one would have to know what God is in and for himself, which does not seem to me possible" (CW 11, para. 482).

Jung was often criticized for dealing with religious material symbolically, as if this reduced a religious symbol such as the Trinity to something that is "merely" psychological, implying that it has no independent ontological status outside the psyche. On the contrary, Jung believed that the psyche is itself ontologically real, and expresses itself symbolically. He wanted to make these symbols amenable to psychological exploration and rescue them from the "sphere of sacrosanct unintelligibility" (CW 11, para. 170). This psychological approach deepens our connection to religious imagery, removing it from a purely doctrinal or dogmatic attitude that just requires belief or intellectual assent. The psychological approach does not detract from the religious value of a symbol.

The Self and the Christian God-image

Jung's position that the Self is radically immanent within the psyche is incompatible with the classical Christian God-image of a self-sufficient, transcendent deity who intervenes in history from a heavenly realm. From a psychological point of view, the experience of transcendence is produced by the sense that one is experiencing levels of the psyche beyond the ego, which are consequently entirely unfamiliar. That is, for Jung, what seems to be transcendent may actually arise from our own interiority. (This may be in part what Jesus meant by saying that "the kingdom of God is within you" [Luke. 17: 21, KJV]). Jung therefore offers a radically different myth of the relationship between the divine and the human than we find in traditional theisms, especially theologies that stress the absolute transcendence of the divine. Of course, the imminence of the divine is also stressed by theists, for example when St. Paul talks about the "Christ who lives in me" (Gal. 2:20). However, for Jung, the subjective experience of the Self may take a much wider range of forms than this one exemplar. Apart from its symbolic manifestations, the experience of the Self for Jung may also include our suffering, which is also mediated by the Self. One reason for this is that the archetypes (which are facets of the Self) are at the center of our complexes, which structure our mental life, and negatively toned complexes cause considerable suffering. Thus, Jung's approach does not split the individual's psychology from his or her spirituality.

Dream imagery may reflect the dreamer's conscious religious orientation, for example when a Christian believer dreams of Jesus. However, it is not uncommon for the imagery that arises from the unconscious to originate within a religious or mythic pantheon that is unknown to the dreamer. Furthermore, numinous experience may contravene traditional Christian doctrine. Thus, a Roman Catholic priest experienced a numinous dream of the Venus of Willendorf, an ancient pagan goddess figure (details in Corbett, 2007). Jung's childhood vision of a giant turd falling from the throne of God onto the roof of the Basel cathedral is a further example of an important numinous experience that is antithetical to traditional Christianity (Jung, 1965).[ix] Fundamentalist clergy are likely to see this kind of imagery as demonic, rather than an authentic expression of the numinosum, because they have a preconceived idea of the way in which the holy is supposed to appear. For Jung, such imagery merely proves that the unconscious cannot be Christianized, and new revelations occur that compensate for existing attitudes, both individually and collectively. This is another reason that the notion of the Self is useful; it points forward to new developments, acting as an internal spiritual guide.

An example of the way in which the unconscious might modify traditional Christian imagery, providing a personal revelation, is given in a vision Jung experienced of Christ on the Cross: "It was not quite life-size, but extremely distinct; and I saw that his body was made of greenish gold. The vision was marvelously beautiful, and yet I was profoundly shaken by it" (1965, p. 210). Jung understood this vision as an "undisguised alchemical conception of Christ as a union of spiritually alive and physically dead matter" (p. 211). The vision expressed the alchemical idea that there is a spirit (gold) in matter (green), in contrast to traditional Christianity's devaluation of matter split from spirit. Jung's vision symbolically unites them. Similarly, Jung understands the cross as a symbol of the tree of life, or nature, from which Christ had been separated and "with which he ought to be connected again to make his life or his being complete" (Jung, 1975, p. 166). The tree brings back what was lost through Christ's "extreme spiritualization," (p. 166) namely the element of the physical world. The symbol of Christ on the cross is a symbol of the union of humanity with our vegetative or unconscious life. At the same time, the cross represents the human sense of being torn between the tension of "irreconcilable opposites" (CW 9, ii, para. 79). This interpretation of the crucifixion is an example of the process by which traditional imagery can be re-mythologized or understood and interpreted in a new symbolic manner.

The Question of Interpretation

Material that emerges from the unconscious often needs interpretation because it is difficult to understand, but much theology is also based on the interpretation of revelation and scripture. This interpretation is often affected by the theologian's personal psychology combined with his prior religious commitments; it cannot be entirely objective. Thus, when the theologian tells us about the nature of God, or the preacher insists he knows what God wants of us, they are typically projecting, based on their personal priorities combined with the teaching of their tradition. The resulting interpretation of biblical passages is often highly selective. In the past, the Church has tried to impose its interpretation of scripture and its doctrinal ideas based purely on authority and canon law.

Jung's appeal to personal experience rather than focusing on doctrine and dogma is a counter to the appeal to the authority of religious hierarchies. Critics of the emphasis on individual subjectivity believe it might lead to an avoidance of critical thought about the divine as found among theologians. In this view, private truth may be misleading; personal experience of the divine requires reflection in the light of tradition, and the interpretation of such experience requires the consensus of a religious community. However, the psychologist would argue that the interpretation and amplification of a numinous image does not require reference to pre-existing theological assertions. Given the wealth of psychological theory available, there is no need for the psychologist to confine her interpretation of numinous material to traditional doctrinal correctness. This is important because it is not unusual for a numinous experience to act as a revelation that either contradicts or modifies official church teaching. In fact, Jung suggests that the Church often opposes original religious experience "because this can only be unorthodox" (CW 11, para. 903). For example, Jung (paras. 474-487) describes the experience of the fifteenth century St. Nickolas of Flüe, who experienced a terrifying vision of the angry face of God pierced by swords. This vision was heretical because it contradicted the Christian image of a loving, all-good God. To avoid the Inquisition, Nickolas had to transform his vision into an image that was doctrinally acceptable.

Belief Compared to Personal Experience of the Self

Some evangelical and charismatic Christian traditions are particularly concerned with the direct experience of the divine, while some Christian denominations focus more on correct belief in doctrine, dogma, and Scripture. However, there may be little or no connection between the dogmas of a church, which the individual is expected to believe, and her or his personal experience of the sacred. As a result, churches and temples are increasingly unable to contain the individual's spirituality. Jung rejects the primary importance of belief in doctrine and dogma because a stress on belief requires the suppression of doubt, because: "Wherever belief reigns, doubt lurks in the background" (CW 11, para. 170). He notes that: "Belief is no adequate substitute for inner experience, and even a strong faith which came miraculously as a gift of grace may depart equally miraculously" (CW 10, para. 521). This occurs because belief, such as belief in an entirely benevolent God, may crumble under the stress of adverse life events, which may call for a radical change in one's God-image. For Jung, the personal experience of the Self is sufficient, without adherence to creedal statements of the kind that many established religions demand of their adherents. By placing the divine outside the personality, in a heavenly realm, religious traditions claim to be the sole mediators of religious experience. Jung remedies this situation by finding the divine within our own subjectivity, with no need for institutional mediation.

Jung points out that sometimes at the height of a problem the Self or the archetypal level of the psyche seems to become active and take over, supplanting the hegemony of the ego, at which point "a religious-minded person would say: guidance has come from God" (CW 11, para. 534). However, Jung says he would not use this formulation because it reminds people too much of what they had already rejected.

In the psychological view, the individual who pays attention to the manifestations of the psyche is attending to the Self and living according to a unique, personal myth rather than a collective myth. According to Jung, such attention is very relevant to the practice of psychotherapy, so much so that Jung believed that among his patients in the second half of life, "there has not been one whose problem in the last resort was not that of finding a religious outlook on life...none of them has been healed who did not regain his religious outlook" (CW 11, para. 509). He was not referring to religion in the sense of a particular creed, but to a spiritual approach to the manifestations of the psyche. In this context, it is worth remembering that the Self has an important influence on the process of psychotherapy; developments that occur during this work are not exclusively the result of the personal levels of the psychotherapeutic relationship. The Self produces dreams that enter into the work, and the Self affects the relational field.

Ambiguities in the Use of the Term "Self"

There are unavoidable ambiguities in the ways in which Jung used the term Self. These arise because the Self is a transpersonal principle that is ultimately beyond conceptual understanding. Because of this ambiguity, various authors have complained that Jung sometimes described the Self as if it were an individual archetype, sometimes as the true center of the psyche, and sometimes as the totality of the psyche, which is an illogical combination. If the Self is the totality of the psyche, it cannot also be thought of as a kind of entity or as a specific structure *within* the psyche. If the Self is the totality of the psyche, it is technically incoherent to call the Self "an" archetype as if it were one among many, but this is a common usage. To add to the confusion, in some contexts the Self can also personify the unconscious in general. However, although this mixture of descriptions is cognitively unsatisfying, the Self is obviously not a concept that can be defined in a logical manner. The most one can say is that although the Self is the totality of the psyche it manifests itself in the form of discreet archetypal imagery, each example of which expresses a specific dimension of the Self.

The Need for the Self as a New God-image

The traditional forms of religion require renewal when they no longer act as a container for our spirituality. Sometimes, indifference to traditional religion occurs because the institutions are clinging to a God-image to which the individual cannot relate. The transcendent God who acts from the beyond, occasionally appearing to intervene in history or in one's personal life in mysterious ways, may not seem relevant. People in this situation need a new God-image, using new metaphors. It is noteworthy that Jung describes his work as "a language of metaphor" (CW 6, para. 428). Metaphorical references to the divine are an important part of the spiritual imagination; they help us to make meaning and give people a way of talking about God. Traditional metaphors of God as a father or as a friend and comforter, are still helpful to many believers. However, the scriptural metaphors are sometimes unhelpful or even distasteful. The imagery used to describe Yahweh in the Hebrew Scriptures no longer holds sway for many people, partly because it is so brutal and warlike, even though the prophetic tradition and subsequent more sophisticated theology has greatly modified this God-image. The Christian story is also losing its hold on our imagination because there is increasing doubt about the truth of the Gospel stories about Jesus, especially stories of miracles and casting out of demons. The validity of subsequent theological claims about him are also questionable. In contrast, images of the Self that appear as a personal experience may feel more relevant than any of the biblical imagery.

The idea of the Self as an intra-psychic God-image is an entirely different way of thinking about divinity than the God of the monotheistic traditions; the Self is not some kind of transcendent Being or heavenly Father. The Self can be seen as an intrapsychic manifestation of the Ātman of the Upanishadic tradition, which is the ground of human consciousness. It can also be seen as analogous to Tillich's notion of God as the Ground of Being (Dourley, 2011), except that the Self appears in the form of dream images and synchronistic events, and so is less abstract.

When compared to traditional theistic ideas about God, at first sight the notion of the Self may seem to be too impersonal because it does not have the comforting paternal overtones of the traditional version of God. However, in contrast to some theological notions of God, the Self has the great advantage of not being judgmental and punitive, and it gets rid of the infantile reward-punishment psychology of traditional religions. As well, as Jung says, it is unthinkable for God to be "wholly other," as the monotheisms sometimes describe God, since a wholly other "could never be one of the soul's deepest and closest intimacies, which is precisely what God is" (CW 12, para. 11, fn. 6). At a deep level, the individual psyche is co-extensive with the transpersonal psyche, an approach that is consistent with non-dual spirituality.[x]

Because the Self is the same in all of us, the notion of the Self unifies instead of divides. From this point of view, there is no need for the sometimes-murderous competition we have seen between traditional monotheisms since all religious experience arises from the same archetypal level of the psyche. Different religions are simply different forms of manifestation emerging from that level. This means that none of them are the ultimate manifestation of the Self, or the final Truth; no single tradition can exhaust the ways in which the Self can manifest itself. Unfortunately, some traditions have frozen themselves into unchanging absolutes by insisting that only their revelation is true and final, when in fact their common source is infinitely creative and continues to express itself in the form of numinous experiences. The idea that one specific revelation from a transcendent God would choose or save one group of human beings rather than any other is belied by the fact of continuous revelation emerging from the transpersonal level of psyche into the individual psyche. The Self does not manifest itself in only one way, which is fortunate for people who have become uneasy as they realize that their own tradition does not answer all their spiritual questions.

The Self in Mystical Experience

Jung often says that the Self represents the totality of consciousness and the unconscious. This union is clearly seen during mystical experience, at which times an experience of unity occurs during which the ego appears to dissolve, like a drop of water falling into a glass of wine; the human and the divine then become indistinguishable. Here, Jung draws on mystics such as Meister Eckhart, who describes a "breakthrough" when God is no longer an object but a subject that is "no longer distinguishable from the ego," which is then "reunited with the dynamic All-oneness" (CW 6, para. 430). This essentially expresses a non-dual sensibility in which the Self is the ultimate subject of experience. Then, "the original state of identity with God is re-established" (CW 6, para 431.) At the deepest level of the mystic's experience, when the ego dissolves into the transpersonal unconscious, all imagery is lost, and, as Eckhart put it, "God is nothingness" (CW 11, para. 893)—perhaps better written as no-thing-ness. This imageless experience of the divine is found among all the world's mystics. The mystics of all traditions report that the Self can manifest itself in terms of an experience of the unitary nature of reality in which there is no separation between the world and people. The following is a typical example:

> A man was walking along a road on a sunny day, near a roadside stall. Men were holding baskets of fish, while music played nearby, when:
>
> Suddenly everything was transformed, transfigured, translated, transcended. All was fused into one. I was the fish. The sun sang and the road sang. The music shone. The hands of the stall-keeper danced. All in time with the same music. They were the music and I was the music and I was the fish, the fishermen, the hands of the stall keeper, the trees, the branches, the road, the sun, the music; all one and nothing separate. Not parts of the one but the one itself (Cohen & Phipps, 1979, pp. 31-32).

Such powerful experiences of the Self as the unitary level of reality may occur because of intense spiritual practice such as meditation, or when the hegemony of the ego is attenuated, which may occur for a variety of reasons such as illness, fatigue, or severe stress. These are experiences of a unitary level of the Self that is trans-archetypal, or before the differentiation of the Self into its archetypal images. The ego does not seem to be present during states of mystical union, but somehow it retains a memory of the experience, and returns to consensual reality enlivened by it, except in the case of fragile personalities who may be unable to tolerate the experience and become psychotic.

An example of the Self as the totality occurred to Jung after a heart attack in 1944, when he was close to death, in a "state of unconsciousness" (Jung, 1965, p. 289). He describes the experience of being high up in space, seeing the earth far below bathed in glorious blue light. Then:

> I had the feeling that everything was being sloughed away; everything I aimed at or wished for or thought, the whole phantasmagoria of earthly existence fell away or was stripped from me…Nevertheless something remained; it was as if I now carried along with me everything I had ever experienced or done, everything that had happened around me. I might also say: it was with me, and I was it. I consisted of all that, so to speak. …there was no longer anything I wanted or desired. I existed in an objective form…I had everything that I was, and that was everything.

This was a non-dual view from the timeless and one-ness perspective of the Self, *sub specie aeternitatis*, from which Jung eventually returned to the limitations of the ego world. He referred to mundane reality as the "box system" because it then seemed to him as if "each person sat by himself in a little box" (p. 292).

Jung thinks of mystics as people who have had "a particularly vivid experience of the processes of the collective unconscious. Mystical experience is experience of archetypes" (CW 18, para. 218). All numinous experience of the Self is therefore a form of mystical experience, but this approach to spirituality is not stressed by contemporary mainstream religions. On the contrary, although the mystical branches of all the monotheisms describe direct, numinous contact with the divine, the mystics of all traditions tend to be marginalized by the traditions' orthodox exponents. This may be due to a fear of the immediate experience of the sacred—or of the unconscious, which in mainstream traditions is safely contained within, and restricted by, their rituals and sacraments.[xi] As well, as noted earlier, direct numinous experience may contravene received doctrine.

The Projection of the Self

Typically, human beings have unconsciously projected the Self onto purportedly external gods of all kinds such as the biblical Yhwh. Prior to our contemporary understanding of the psyche, such projection—which is instigated by the autonomous psyche—was necessary to make these deities accessible to consciousness. However, we no longer need to project the Self onto a heavenly realm. The gods can now be understood as the "personifications of psychic forces" (CW 10, para. 387). Any God-image can be experienced as an aspect of the psyche because the gods of all religious traditions arise from, or are manifestations of, the transpersonal level of the psyche. It is a startling indictment of the monotheistic traditions to suggest that they are worshipping a projected deity. Nevertheless, for Jung, all the traditionally transcendent deities, such as the biblical Yhwh, Zeus, or Shiva, are ways of talking about the Self, using local historical and traditional formulations (CW 11 para. 454). As Jung puts it, "the term '[S]elf' refers neither to Christ nor to the Buddha but to the totality of the figures that are its equivalent, and each of these figures is a symbol of the self" (CW 12, para. 20). This means that there is no single version of the Self that is the only valid one, despite the competing claims of the monotheisms to the contrary.

The Self may be projected onto a particular individual, leading to the idealization of that person, who is then seen as larger than life or particularly special in some way. This projection is actually an unconscious search for a god. This phenomenon is seen when people idealize public figures such as Princess Diana. The Self can be projected onto religious leaders such as the Pope, who seem to be invested with spiritual power. Idealization of a leader is also seen among members of religious cults who follow a charismatic leader or guru who is all too ready to accept such an idealized view of himself. In the early years of World War 2, Hitler was massively idealized and invested with quasi-spiritual qualities, so idealization is not confined to positive figures. When the Self is recognized as an internal spiritual source, such projections can be withdrawn.

Ego and Self: The Developmental Implications of an a *priori* Self

Before discussing this question, it is important to stress the understanding, emphasized in the non-dual spiritual traditions, that the ego or the personal self is not a discreet entity separate from the totality of consciousness. [xii] Neither is the transpersonal Self some kind of reified or bounded entity; we cannot know its nature or its extent, since the Self is the ultimate subject and cannot be objectified. In what follows, I use the term ego for convenience, in its conventional Jungian sense of personal consciousness. [xiii] I use the term Self in Jung's sense of the totality of consciousness and the unconscious; within this usage, the ego is related to the Self as part to the whole (CW 9, i, para. 341), and the part cannot know the whole. If the Self is the totality of the psyche, the ego must be one of its constituents.[xiv] The Self as the *imago dei* in the psyche corresponds to the Upanishadic Ātman, or perhaps the Vedantic *Ishvara*, whose nature is unknowable. The metaphysical implications here are unavoidable, but the psychologist can restrict his attention to the purely psychological manifestations of the Self. Although from the non-dual point of view there is really only one agent and one ultimate subject—the Self—at the everyday empirical level, and for the sake of clarity, we typically talk about the ego and Self as if they were different. However, the Self is the source of the ego's consciousness; just as the moon reflects the light of the sun, so the ego reflects the consciousness of the Self. Jung thinks of the ego as revolving around the Self in a way that is analogous to the earth's revolution around the sun (CW 7, para. 405), or "the ego stands to the [S]elf as the moved to the mover" (CW 11, para. 391). The Self "dwarfs the ego in scope and intensity" (CW 8, para. 430).

Jung seems to believe that the destiny of the individual, or the telos of the personality, is given by the Self. In a remarkable statement of this idea in his *Zarathustra* seminars, he says:

> So you must inquire what experiment the Self wants to make. Everything that disturbs that experiment must be avoided and everything that helps must be lived, and you will see the consequences on the spot. If you do something which disturbs the experiment you will be punished... And if you do something which rather serves your experiment, you will have the blessing of heaven and the angels will come to dance with you. You are helped along.... Mind you, it is not the ego that wants to make that experiment. Often the ego says, 'For God's sake I only hope that this thing is not coming to me!' If you have a fundamental dread somewhere, you can be sure that is just the experiment of the Self. You see, the body is meant to live; it has to be served, and your Self has a very particular purpose with it, presumably.... Inasmuch as we are individuals, our experiment is individual, and the point of life is that this particular individual should fulfill itself. (Jung, 1960, p. 403).

This means that the Self has its own agenda for the personality. However, Jung's notion that the Self determines the *telos* (ultimate goal or purpose) of the personality raises the issue of free will.

Another common Jungian perspective on this situation invokes the idea of the soul, often understood as mediator or bridge between the Self and ego consciousness. The soul can also be thought of as spirit felt in the body. The soul is an agent of the Self that has its own autonomy, which is not subject to the preferences or rules of the ego, so that the tension between the ego and the demands of the soul may produce considerable suffering. This means that many decisions and life events are not in our hands; they are determined by the Self, which is responsible for our archetypal endowment, so that our development is not entirely a function of genes and the environment.

Jung believes that the Self is the source of the ego, which emerges out of the Self during development. The Self is "an a priori existent out of which the ego evolves. It is, so to speak, an unconscious prefiguration of the ego" (CW 11, para. 391).[xv] The Self is the "Nothing out of which all may grow" (CW 10, para. 150). Consciousness of the Self, and the progressive embodiment of the Self in the form of the realization of its potentials within the personality, are goals to which the ego strives.[xvi]

During development, the ego differentiates itself from the totality of the Self, and in the process feels increasingly separate from the Self. At the same time, the ego progressively assimilates more and more consciousness of the Self during the individuation process. Edinger (1960) describes this as the "ego-Self paradox," in which the dialectical process between ego and Self leads to both greater separation and greater intimacy. However, Fordham (1985) questions this approach to the Self because he believes it confuses two conceptual levels—the Self as the totality of the psyche and the Self as "an" (individual) archetype. Logically, the Self cannot be just one archetype among others if the Self is the totality of the psyche. However, the notion of the Self as a specific archetype really refers to its individual symbolic representations, which can take many archetypal forms, but none of which could represent the whole of the Self. Any archetypal image only reflects just one aspect of the Self.

Even though the ego is actually a component of the totality of the Self, from a pragmatic, psychotherapeutic point of view, Neumann's (1959) concept of the ego-Self axis is heuristically useful; it refers to the process of communication between consciousness and the unconscious. Neumann (1959) believes that in infancy the Self is as it were externalized as it is carried by the mother, so the earliest ego-Self relationship is identical to the child's relationship to its mother. Accordingly, disturbances in the mother-child relationship, such as early childhood trauma or serious maternal rejection or mis-attunement, damage the child's relationship to the Self. The resulting sense of alienation between ego and Self leads to an inability to accept oneself, or to low self-esteem, or to the sense that one should not exist. Kohut (1977) would attribute this kind of outcome to traumatic failure of affective attunement in childhood, leading to a failure to develop a cohesive sense of a personal self. For Kohut, psychotherapy repairs and consolidates an enfeebled sense of self; from a Jungian point of view, this process also repairs the ego-Self axis. What Kohut refers to as an idealizing transference can also be seen as the projection of the Self onto the therapist, which may also be a way to repair a damaged ego-Self relationship.

An alternative developmental theory to that of Neumann was suggested by Fordham (1976). Rather than understanding the child's individuality as emerging from a primary identity with the mother, Fordham prefers to think in terms of a primary or original Self that is an initial psychosomatic unity or integrate that acts as a blueprint for psychological maturation. The original Self is pure potential with no content. It unfolds or deintegrates parts of itself to experience the environment during events such as feeding. These events allow the child to have an experience in the outer world that is then taken in and integrated during sleep. The experience then becomes part of the inner world of the developing personality. In the process, ego nuclei are formed that gradually coalesce into a center of consciousness. Fordham's ideas are related to those of Kohut, because a deintegrate of the Self has to be met by an attuned selfobject response for a stable sense of self to develop. Kohut's notion that the self has an innate blueprint for its development is consistent with Jung's belief that the Self acts as a kind of developmental ground plan for the development of the personality by providing the individual with a specific configuration of archetypal endowments.

The Incarnation of the Self into the Personality: The Individuation Process

For Jung, individuation means the fullest development of the personality. As well as the obvious genetic and environmental contributions to this process, there is an important spiritual component provided by the Self. The Self provides the individual's archetypal endowment, which begins at birth as a set of purely spiritual potentials for the individual's talents and abilities. These potentials gradually incarnate or embody themselves within the personality during the course of the individual's life. That is, the archetypal ground of consciousness is lived out within the life of a human being. For Jung therefore the incarnation of the divine is not confined to one special individual, as Christianity teaches; it happens within all of us. At the same time, during the individuation process the ego becomes increasingly conscious of the Self. Individuation is therefore a spiritual process in which the Self is progressively realized as the ego cooperates with the Self's attempt to become conscious within a personality. Jung refers to this continuing incarnation as the "Christification of many" (CW 11, para. 758). In Jung's words: "[S]elf-realization—to put it in religious or metaphysical terms—amounts to God's incarnation" (CW 11, para. 233). This process inevitably causes suffering, which is therefore not only the product of problematic object relations or environmental difficulties. For Jung, at the deepest level, one's suffering is brought about by the Self; suffering is the ego's experience of the Self as it tries to incarnate. The rationale for this statement is that embodiment of the Self occurs when we experience the affect associated with complexes. Complexes are always affectively toned, sometimes painfully so, and affect is mediated by the body. The archetypal core of such a complex embodies itself by means of affect, which is felt in the body as autonomic arousal, muscle tension, and all the other somatic manifestations of affect. In this way, the archetype is felt in the body.

According to Jung (CW 9, ii), over time the ego is radically relativized by the Self, meaning that the ego sees its own limits, for example as we confront our mortality, and the ego sees itself in a larger context, such as that provided by dreams. As this process happens, the ego "senses itself as the object of an unknown and supraordinate subject" (CW 7, p. 238). That is, we realize that the Self is aware of us, for example when we receive a dream that is precisely tailored to our personality or to our current situation. At the same time, because of the numinosity of such experiences, we realize that "the experience of the [S]elf is always a defeat for the ego" (CW 14, para. 778).

One aspect of Jung's explanatory myth about the ultimate meaning of human life involves the ever-increasing consciousness that occurs during the individuation process (Jung, 1963). Jung (1934, p. 208) refers to this process as "our mythology…a reality that is just on the boundary line of human understanding." Jung believes that the ego's activity is crucial to the process of individuation and the realization of the Self, which is the goal of the process. Without an adequate ego, the individual might either be swept away by identification with the archetype or taken over by archetypal contents of the unconscious, leading to psychosis or to political or religious fanaticism. Jung therefore relies on the participation of the ego for the individuation process.[xvii]

The Incarnation of the Opposites During the Individuation Process

Jung believes that because the Self is the totality of consciousness, the Self includes all possible opposites, such as good and evil or matter and spirit. But because the Self is an undivided unity, within the Self these are not differentiated into discreet qualities as they are within the ego. The opposites only become distinct and in tension with each other as the Self incarnates within the human ego, whereupon the individual becomes a "vessel filled with divine conflict" (CW 11, para. 233). The personality then feels torn in different directions by the tension of opposites. Jung believes that this allows the Self to differentiate itself within the ego, allowing the Self to become conscious of its internal oppositions. Jung thought that this process dignifies human suffering, gives human beings "cosmogonic significance" (1975, p. 495), and makes the development of human consciousness particularly important. [xviii] In contrast to spiritual traditions that minimize the importance of the ego, Jung credits the ego with "world creating significance" (CW 14, para. 131). Human suffering is then part of a larger process in which the Self differentiates the opposites within its own nature. At the collective level, these opposites manifest themselves as social conflicts, such as religious and political rivalry; at the personal level, the opposites within the Self appear in the form of internal conflicts or complexes.

Jung believes that the New Testament image of Christ crucified between two thieves, one of whom is raised to heaven and one who descends to hell, is a symbolic representation of human consciousness torn between divinely ordained opposites (CW 11, para. 343). The resurrection would then represent the symbolic resolution of the tension between good and evil. For Jung, good and evil can no longer be projected into supernatural or mythic realms of heaven and hell; they are part of the tension of opposites within the psyche. Jung (1973, p. 267) points out that a mythic example of this tension is the conflict between Christ's spirituality and his need for power, which appeared to him in the projected form of the devil, who tempted Christ by offering him all the kingdoms of the world if he would worship him (Matthew 4:1). The work of dealing with such opposites within human consciousness causes a great deal of suffering, but Jung believes this is the way that the divine differentiates itself. This means, according to Jung, that the individual and the collective have to suffer the tension of the opposites as a divine service. The Self needs to incarnate within humanity in order to complete itself. Somehow the oppositions within the Self have to be united and reconciled within the ego, which is one of the continuous tasks of the individuation process. This process involves a gradual increase in the individual's consciousness of the Self, combined with a progressive grounding of the ego in the Self.

For Jung, the life of Christ is a mythic or archetypal depiction of the suffering that inevitably occurs during the process of incarnation, as the Self seeks to become conscious within a human personality. This means that rather than Christ suffering on behalf of everyone else and seeing the incarnation in Christ as a unique historical event, everyone has to suffer the incarnation of the Self as it seeks to differentiate itself within human consciousness. For this reason, Edinger (1996, p. 70) believes that the task of Jungian analysis is "the reconstruction of the God-image in the individual."

The Relativity of God

Because the process of the differentiation of the unconscious transforms both the Self and the human being, it can be thought of as a process of mutual redemption or mutual completion. Not only is the individual transformed by the incarnation of the Self. If we equate the Self with the intrapsychic divine, transformation of the divine also occurs within the personality—very much in contrast to the traditional image of God as unchanging. Jung believes that as the God-image unfolds and evolves within human consciousness, the Self becomes increasingly conscious of itself, since it uses the ego as a reflecting consciousness that allows the Self to discriminate the opposites within itself (CW 11, para. 642). The Self's need for a reflecting consciousness means that not only are we dependent on God, but God also depends on humanity. This is why Jung speaks of the "relativity" of God (CW 6, para. 412), meaning that there is a kind of mutual interdependence or reciprocal relationship between God and humanity, because God becomes self-conscious within human consciousness. Therefore, the relationship of the divine and the human corresponds to the intrapsychic relationship of consciousness and the unconscious. This is a radically different image than the traditional Christian God-image in which the divine and human realms are absolutely separate from each other. The idea of the relativity of God affirms that human beings contribute to the self-realization of God, because divine consciousness and human consciousness mutually interpenetrate each other. Jung believed that an absolute God would be detached, "outside all connections with mankind...such a God would be of no consequence at all...whereas a 'psychological' God would be *real*" (CW 7, note 6, para. 235; Jung's italics).

From the classical theistic point of view, God is absolute and wholly other. However, from the psychological point of view, our experience of God results from the activation of the God-image within the unconscious. There is, therefore, a mutual and reciprocal relationship between the human and the divine, "whereby man can be understood as a function of God, and God as a psychological function of man" (CW 6, para. 412). Our experience of the divine only occurs through the psyche: "God's actions spring from one's own inner being" (para. 413). That is to say, the human and the divine are not radically separate entities; they are ontologically inseparable. This makes Jung's approach relatively monistic, since there is no radical distinction between the human and the divine, but Jung's approach is not entirely non-dual, since he wants to preserve the importance of the ego, which is much diminished in non-dual spiritual traditions.

Because the Self is inextricably linked with the human level of the psyche, as Dourley (2010) points out, the Christian doctrine of the unity of the divine and human nature in Christ, the *homoousia*, is thereby extended to everyone rather than to Christ alone. This means that the human and the divine are not as radically separate as Christianity has taught.

Edinger's Notion of the New Dispensation

Edinger (1984) has suggested that (in the West) we are entering into a new phase of our religious consciousness, which he calls a new dispensation—a new way in which divine grace enters the world. The first dispensation was the handing down of the law at Mt. Sinai; the second was centered on Jesus Christ. In the new, psychological dispensation, our sense is that we are in contact with the objective psyche or the Self, and "God is now to be carried experientially by the individual" (p. 4), and this is what is meant by the continuing incarnation. Edinger is describing Jung's idea that we now realize that the psyche has become a medium of connection to the divine. Not surprisingly therefore, Jung has been criticized for trying to start a new religion rather than developing a form of psychotherapy, although rather than seeing his work as a form of "psychology-as-religion," it is more accurate to say that he has a religious attitude to certain manifestations of the psyche, especially those that are numinous. Jung is not offering a kind of theology. (This question is discussed further in Corbett, 2011).[xix]

The Spirit of the Depths

Jung believed that we have become too removed from our source in the depths of the psyche; our culture focuses primarily on consciousness and tends to ignore the unconscious. Because the mainstream of our culture focuses almost exclusively on what can be experienced through the senses, an attitude that Jung (2009) refers to as the Spirit of the Times, our culture is ignorant of the archetypal forces of the unconscious that are the basis of religion. This ignorance of the Spirit of the Depths leads to a concomitant loss of a sense of the sacred, both in daily life and in the practice of psychotherapy. Jung believed that collective religion has become part of the Spirit of the Times, because it ignores the unconscious. By focusing on religion's historical and creedal aspects instead of its symbolic content, traditional religions foster a kind of mass-mindedness. In the process of literalizing their symbolic aspects, religious traditions have severed people from the Spirit of the Depths, from which religion originally arose in the form of numinous experience of the Self. Jung believed that much of our current social malaise results from our loss of contact with this spiritual Ground.

The archetypal dynamics of the unconscious also operate in the background of political movements such as fascism. It is often not recognized that the Nazi movement was partly driven by the dark side of the spirit. In that sense, it had its religious aspects. The Nazi phenomenon was an example of the way in which the archetypal level of the psyche may grip a whole society. Communities in conflict are unconsciously bonded together by shared numinous imagery (Dourley, 2003) such as a common faith. When a group feels specially chosen by God, or believes it is in possession of a special revelation or a special savior, it is apparently willing to behave as if it is entitled to the conquest and even the elimination of other groups, who of course feel similarly entitled to promote their particular image of God. The results have been obvious since biblical times.

Jung protested that theology "proclaims doctrines which nobody understands and demands a faith which nobody can manufacture" (CW

11, para. 285). By restricting the individual's focus within a fixed symbol system, by turning mythic stories into literal history, by insisting on the notion of an outer, transcendent deity, collective religions tend to separate the individual from connection to the depths of the psyche, which is our true source of religious experience. The extreme example of this situation is found among fundamentalists who cope with uncertainty and doubt by interpreting Scripture literally or by strict adherence to tradition. In the Roman Catholic tradition this phenomenon appeared as a resistance to the reforms proposed by Vatican 2. The alternative to these kinds of extremes is Jung's proposal, which is to pay attention to the manifestations of the Self without recourse to doctrine and dogma. However, this might be a lonely path without the kind of community found among adherents to collective religions. In a paper published in 1928, although written about 10 years earlier, Jung pointed out that "for the great majority of mankind the symbol of a collective religion will suffice. It is perhaps only temporarily and for relatively few individuals that the existing collective religions have become inadequate" (CW 8, para. 111). Since this was written, the number of individuals disenchanted with traditional religion has multiplied greatly.

God and the Psyche: God Within the Psyche

One of the central ideas in Jung's *The Red Book* is that a new God image is being born in the soul (Jung, 2009). Jung sometimes thinks of the soul as the psyche itself, and sometimes sees the soul as a component of the psyche, a "receiver and transmitter, an organ for perceiving unconscious contents" (CW 6, para. 425). In the latter sense, the soul is the bridge or mediator between the ego and the otherwise inaccessible, transpersonal depths of the psyche, allowing our connection to its spiritual dimension. For Jung, the soul allows us to perceive the divine light by creating symbols and images.

Jung (CW 11, para. 757) believes that: "It is only through the psyche that we can establish that God acts upon us." However, based solely on our experience, we cannot say whether these actions emanate from a God beyond the psyche or from the unconscious, or even whether these are two different entities. All we can say is that the God-image seems to arise from the unconscious, and the unconscious is "the medium from which religious experience seems to flow" (CW 10, para. 565). Jung is often criticized for spiritualizing the unconscious, but he uses this term to simply mean the Unknowable. For most Jungians, the unconscious is synonymous with the spiritual realm, with both its heights and its depths. Jung believes that the unconscious extends to infinity; it is "of indefinite extent with no assignable limits" (CW 11, para. 390). He refers to it as the "matrix mind" (para. 782) and the "birthplace of thought forms" (para. 782), analogous to the Universal Mind or the One Mind of the Eastern spiritual traditions. This important idea means that human consciousness has its source in, and is continuous with, transpersonal levels of the unconscious. Consequently: "In so far as the forms or patterns of the unconscious belong to no time in particular, being seemingly eternal, they convey a peculiar feeling of timelessness when consciously realized" (para. 782). For Jung therefore, transcendence refers to the experience of levels of the psyche beyond the ego, rather than a metaphysical realm.

Jung notes that when we ask what the psyche actually is, "all science ends" (CW 11, para. 533). He insists that we have no idea of the nature of the unconscious, which is only a posit, not an independent entity whose metaphysical essence we understand. The unconscious "designates only my *unknowing*" (Jung, 1973, p. 411; Jung's emphasis). "The concept of the unconscious is an assumption for the sake of convenience" (CW 11, para. 64). Jung views the unconscious as a kind of consciousness in its own right; he notes that perception, thinking, feeling, volition, and intention go on in the unconscious as though a subject were present (Jung, (CW 8, para. 362). The unconscious cannot be hypostasized; it contains many centers of consciousness (it is not a monotheistic system) and it cannot be thought of as a discreet entity or "an encapsulated personal system" (CW 9, i, para. 46) since its extent is not known. One could think of the difference between personal consciousness and the transpersonal unconscious as the difference between finitude and the infinite. Not surprisingly, many contemporary Jungians use the term "psyche" as a God-term.

Jung often points out that we cannot say anything about a possible dimension beyond the psyche, which is unknowable; the only thing we can talk about is the experience of God as a psychological state (CW 13, para. 82). That is why he insists on only talking about God-images rather than the divine itself (CW 18, para. 1615; 1975, p. 260).

Jung's approach to the psyche means that we do not need to project our religious needs onto collective symbols or onto an external savior; the divine child (an image of the Self) is born in our own soul (CW 11, para.

755), and the archetypal reality that was once expressed in religious symbols and contained by the Churches is now expressed through the individual psyche. This is particularly important, thought Jung, because: "Christian civilization has proved hollow to a terrifying degree; it is all veneer, but the inner man has remained untouched" (CW 12, para. 12). The problem is that "everything is to be found outside—in image and in word, in Church and Bible—but never inside" (para. 12). Jung was referring to the savage behavior of some Christian societies when he wrote that: a "dark paganism" remains in the soul (para. 12).

Jung believes that: "So long as religion is only faith and outward forms, and the religious function is not experienced in our own souls, nothing of any importance has happened" (para. 13). When religious symbols no longer communicate the divine presence, when such symbols are no longer numinous and doctrine does not correspond to the reality of the individual's experience, personal symbols of the Self as mediated in dreams become especially relevant. It is not surprising that dream imagery is difficult to understand, since it represents the infinite level of the psyche inserting and expressing itself within the finite mind. We see a metaphor for this process in a dream reported by Jung in a letter (1973, p. 450): "One bluish diamond like a star in heaven, reflected in a round quiet pool—heaven above, heaven below." The heavenly diamond is a Self-symbol, an *imago dei* reflected in the individual psyche, bringing to mind the ancient saying "as above, so below."

As the ego responds to this kind of imagery produced by the Self, the ego increases its contact with its source and expands its awareness. Each time the ego becomes more conscious of the Self in this work, the Self incarnates or inserts a further fragment of itself into human consciousness. This process expands the ego and helps to mature the developing personality during the individuation process, which is guided by the Self, acting as a *spiritus rector* or guiding spirit (CW 9, ii, para. 257). The Self is therefore responsible for the development of the personality into its final form. The personality that results is an expression of the Self as it manifests itself by incarnating its potentials within the individual, so that from Jung's point of view psychological and spiritual development cannot be separated. The incarnation of the Self requires a sacrifice by the Self, since it has to express itself within the limitations of an empirical personality that is bound by time and space (CW 11, para. 400).

Despite the limitations of our thought, Jung noted: "This much we do know beyond all doubt, that empirical reality has a transcendental background" (CW 14, para. 768). However, unlike traditional theologies of transcendence, for Jung what feels like transcendence emerges from a deep level of the psyche. The important implication of this observation is that the divine is not wholly "other," as the monotheisms often declare. It is an integral part of the psyche (it may even be the psyche itself), which is an aspect of our nature. Divinity and humanity exist in an intrapsychic relation to each other. Because the Self becomes conscious during the process of individuation as it incarnates within the individual: "God becomes manifest in the human act of reflection" (CW 11, para. 238). Meister Eckhart arrived at a similar conclusion in the fourteenth century when he talked about the birth of God in the soul. From a Jungian point of view this "birth" means the ego's experience of the Self. Eckhart was condemned for describing such intimacy between humanity and divinity, but Jung's psychology makes this a central idea.

Although the gods of all the pantheons arise within the psyche, they have been projected outward as if they exist in some other realm such as a heaven or the beyond. Jung believes that the development of consciousness requires the withdrawal of these projections, since now "it is not possible to maintain any non-psychological doctrine about the gods… everything of a divine or daemonic character outside us must return to the psyche…whence it apparently originated" (CW 11, para. 141). It is a "systematic blindness" and a "prejudice that God is *outside* man" (para. 100; Jung's emphasis). Religious experience is not the product of external gods and saviors. Because of this kind of statement, Jung is often accused of reducing God to nothing but a psychological reality, but he would deny that his is a reductive approach because intrapsychic material is real, and the psyche is a vehicle of the experience of the divine. Jung points out that we have no Archimedean point beyond the psyche which would allow us to know it from a position outside it, and we cannot know of gods beyond it. Humanity will not be saved by belief in a heavenly deity or a messiah or by avoiding a mythic devil. These are illusions based on projected psychological contents.

Not only is the psyche the source of religious experience, all theological ideas, including doctrine and dogma, can only be products of the psyche. At their best, these ideas express archetypal imagery; at their worst they express only the prejudices and preconceptions of their originators. Even revelation, such as the Mt. Sinai experience, must be experienced by means of the psyche. Revelation of that kind is the result of the eruption of the objective psyche into consciousness, and such revelation is inevitably reported by means of language, colored by its cultural context, and filtered through the psyche of the recipient.

The biblical God-image is sometimes seen as immanent and sometimes as transcendent, and theologians have much debated the tension between these two attributes. In its transcendent form, the classical God-image is imagined to be self-sufficient and beyond the world, entering creation from beyond it. The biblical God-image is also said to be present in history and active in worldly matters. Exactly how a transcendent God could also be immanent has never been clear. For Jung, the God-image is radically immanent since it appears in the psyche—although it also manifests itself in the outer world in the form of important synchronicities. We do not need to speculate about the relationship of intrapsychic images of the Self to a purportedly transcendent God, since the intrapsychic manifestations of the Self are sufficient for our needs. This is a radically different approach than traditions that urge us to contact the divine as if it were external to ourselves. As Jung puts it: "The world of gods and spirits is truly 'nothing but' the collective unconscious inside me" (CW 11, para. 857). The operative phrase "inside me" is particularly important. The phrase "nothing but," which he puts in quotation marks, is a slightly sarcastic allusion to Jung's critics who believe he is being reductive when he suggests that the gods all arise from the archetypal level of the psyche, without understanding that the psyche is real.

Theologians and ministers of religion are concerned with how we should listen to the voice of God; for Jung, this happens when we pay attention to the numinous manifestations of the Self, which speaks by means of the psyche. This is where the divine and the human meet. Traditional theologians used to use a spatial metaphor, thinking of heaven as "up." Once they realized that this was an inadequate word, they could only resort to words such as "the beyond" to describe the divine realm. For Jung, the Self appears as "in" rather than up. It is beyond only in the sense of being beyond the ego, but it is intimately part of the psyche.

Jung's approach does not need to be based on the Bible, in contrast to the opinion of theologians such as Karl Barth, who wanted a purely biblical theology, free of human systems of thought and reason. In Jung's approach however, no Bible is required because dream imagery is a form of direct revelation from the Self. This means that the psyche's intrinsic religious function is no longer confined to the imagery and rituals of the Church; it expresses itself freely and in novel ways in everyone. It is possible to attend to the religious function of the psyche individually, without adherence to a creed, by paying attention to the manifestations of the Self. This attitude is particularly appealing to people who have a personal sense of the sacred but who are not interested in an affiliation with any specific tradition. Indeed, for many people, such affiliation may actually interfere with the expression of their spirituality, either because traditional God-imagery is too limited, or because the tradition requires adherence to unbelievable dogma, or because of problems such as the unequal treatment of women. There is a range of ways to activate and relate to the unconscious, including dream work, individual psychotherapy, sand-play, art, and approaches through movement and the body. From the point of view of Jung's psychology, these may all be forms of spiritual practice, because they all connect us to the Self.

The Self as an Emerging Mythic Image of the Divine

The traditional theistic God-images are very much caught up in the mythological beliefs of the era in which they were written, but the Self is not; it may appear in entirely novel ways. The idea of the Self can be thought of as a new myth of God in its own right—myth in the sense of a sacred story that teaches a deep truth and adds meaning to life. Importantly, the Self can be experienced; it does not have to be simply believed in, and it does not require any insistence on correct belief analogous to the confessions of a creed. By paying attention to the manifestations of the transpersonal unconscious in one's life, one can develop a unique, personal myth that can free one from remaining unconsciously trapped in the mythic tradition in which one was raised, which is usually based in ethnicity or the religion of one's forebears. Attention to the Self is particularly important for people who do not experience the divine in the manner dictated by their inherited tradition. Some people who attend to the unconscious find renewed interest in the mythology of the tradition into which they were born by understanding its imagery at a deeper level. Others reject the tradition of their childhood because they experience the Self in entirely different ways. These individuals contribute to the emergence of a new collective myth and a new God-image.

Jung's *Answer to Job* and its God-image

Jung's usual distinction between the divine itself and the God-image of the Bible tends to get lost in his *Answer to Job* (CW 11), where Jung does not always make clear which he is talking about, although in subsequent letters he insists that this work is only about the God-image.[xx] The distinction is crucial, since if it is not maintained Jung runs the risk of treating the Job myth as if it were objective reality and making a theological statement about the nature of divinity rather than the biblical image of God.

In his *Answer to Job*, Jung suggests that in the biblical story of Job, the figure of Yhwh is unconscious of his own dark side, manifested by his cruel treatment of Job. A mixture of positive and negative qualities such as cruelty, mercy, kindness, anger, and love all exist side by side in this image of Yhwh. Thanks to the fact that Job maintains his integrity by insisting on his innocence, Yhwh is forced to become conscious of his shadow aspects, of which he was previously unaware. Jung believes that Job tries to remain faithful to Yhwh, but apparently Yhwh projects his doubt about his own faithfulness onto Job. This doubt is personified in the story by the figure of a satan,[xxi] who questions Job's piety.

Because of Yhwh's ill-treatment of Job, Jung describes the figure of Yhwh as "amoral," "too unconscious to be moral," and lacking the necessary capacity for self-reflection (CW 11, paras. 574, 600, 675). Job's moral awareness proves to be superior to that of Yhwh, because by maintaining his integrity Job behaves better than Yhwh. Of course, Yhwh has overwhelming power, but by insisting that he did not deserve his suffering, Job makes Yhwh aware that his treatment of Job is unfairly harsh. It was as if Job had superior knowledge of Yhwh that he himself did not possess. Jung (para. 575) believes that this story is a paradigm for the idea that human consciousness is necessary for the divine to become conscious of unknown aspects of itself, in this case of its dark side. It is important to point out that when he says this, Jung merges the God-image of the biblical story with the divine itself.

The notion that the divine could be unconscious of some aspect of itself is obviously controversial. For some people it is more acceptable to read Jung as saying that the God-image is in an unconscious condition within the human being. However, Jung believes that the divine itself is partially unconscious and needs humanity to act as a reflecting consciousness or even to convince himself that he exists (para. 574). Jung suggests that God would not have needed to create humanity if he were completely conscious of himself. In a letter, he notes: "Moreover it is impossible for us to assume that a Creator producing a universe out of nothingness can be conscious of anything, because each act of cognition is based on discrimination…if there is nothing outside of God everything is God and in such a state there is simply no possibility of self-cognition" (1975, p. 312). For Jung, the "rather dim consciousness" of the creator explains the "errors and impasses with the most cruel consequences, disease, mutilation and horrible fights…throughout all realms of life" (p. 312). Jung thought that the need for human beings to act as a reflecting consciousness explains why God would create conscious creatures; the creator "sees himself through the eyes of man's consciousness" (1975, p. 436). Jung believed that this is the service human beings carry out for God, and this idea became part of Jung's myth of meaning (Jung, 1963, p. 338).

The notion of an unconscious God is an extreme position that contradicts traditional theology, in part because an unconscious God could not be omniscient. Not surprisingly therefore, Jung (1965, p. 216) says that he had to overcome "the greatest inner resistances" before he could write *Answer to Job,* since he knew that the notion of a God unconscious of his own dark side would create a storm of controversy. Jung's idea that the divine uses human consciousness to differentiate itself or to become conscious of itself would also be totally alien—indeed anathema—to traditional theism, although it is not unknown among the mystics. Jung's God-image is very different than the classical idea of a totally self-sufficient, absolute and perfect God with no need of human beings and not continuous with human consciousness.

Jung seems to have had personal difficulty with his idea of the dark side of God. According to von Franz (1975, p. 174), when he was asked how he could live with this notion, Jung replied "I live in my deepest hell and from there I cannot fall any further." MacKenna (2000) points out how different is this God-image from the Christian notion that the divine creates "because it is the nature of love to be creative" (p. 177). MacKenna believes that Jung's image of a narcissistically self-absorbed God reflects Jung's own narcissistic isolation. This idea is consistent with the notion that our God-image is radically affected by our personal psychodynamics. Similarly, Jung's idea of the dark side of divinity could also be understood as the projection of his own unintegrated aggression onto his God-image.

Split-off aspects of the personal shadow and aggressive aspects of personal complexes can be projected on to a God-image that includes a dark side. However, these possibilities about the origin of Jung's ideas do not invalidate his interpretation of the Job story.

Jung points out that Yhwh's unconsciousness is partly the result of the fact that he has lost sight of his connection to Sophia, his feminine wisdom, with whom he had co-existed since the creation. Instead, he married his chosen people "who were thus forced into a feminine role" (CW 11, para. 620). This marriage was "an essentially masculine affair" because it was based on power and the need for perfection, and in his relationship with Job, Yhwh relies on brute force. Jung (para. 579) suggests that Yhwh is jealous of Job, because Yhwh suffers from the suspicion that "man possess an infinitely small yet more concentrated light [meaning consciousness] than he possesses." When Yhwh enters into a wager with the satan about whether Job will remain faithful if he suffers, Yhwh projects his doubt about himself onto Job, and this projection makes Job subject to a cruel test of his faith. This scenario is part of the narcissism within the image of Yhwh; he demands constant praise and exclusive worship, and constantly needs to be "propitiated in every possible way" (CW 11 para. 573), but these external props to his self-esteem are never quite enough, and his self-doubt is constant. In an extraordinary parallel to Kohut's concept of the selfobject, Jung notes that Yhwh "fits a personality who can only convince himself that he exists through his relation to an object. Such dependence on the object is absolute when the subject is totally lacking in self-reflection and therefore has no insight into himself" (CW 11, para. 573). Or, in Kohut's terms, Yhwh is so narcissistically vulnerable that he needs constant mirroring from humanity. As Jung puts it: "he wants to be loved, honored, worshipped, and praised as just. He reacts irritably to every word that has the faintest suggestion of criticism" (para. 604). This narcissistic problem is seen in Yhwh's demand for supremacy in the first of the Ten Commandments, which insists that "Thou shalt have no other gods before me." As the status of Yhwh's mythic image grew, all "other gods" gradually disappeared or were repressed by his followers. The parallels between Yhwh's narcissistic needs and those of humanity is striking. This parallel looks like the projection of human narcissistic vulnerabilities onto the biblical God-image.

It is the urging of Sophia, according to Jung, that moves Yhwh towards becoming human, and his increasing consciousness in the process of incarnating makes him conscious of the suffering he had inflicted on humanity. For Jung, the divine response to Job is the incarnation in Christ; by becoming human and suffering on the cross, God realizes the kind of suffering human beings experience. When Christ cries out in despair on the cross "why hast thou forsaken me?" (Mark 15:34) Jung believes "at that moment God experiences what it means to be a mortal man and drinks to the dregs what he made his faithful servant Job suffer" (CW 11, para. 647). By becoming human, the amoral image of God in the story of Job catches up with the moral level that humanity (symbolized by Job) had reached, and the image of God transforms into a God of love.

There is an important counter-argument to Jung's belief that the divine would be unconscious without humanity as a reflecting consciousness. In non-dual Eastern spiritual traditions such as Advaita Vedanta, the divine is conceived of as pure Consciousness or pure Awareness. In these traditions it would be impossible for the divine to be unconscious, since it is Consciousness itself. If the Self is Consciousness, if it is like the Ātman of the Upanishadic tradition, to suggest that the Self needs human consciousness to become conscious would be like saying that fire needs heat to become hot. The very notion of the unconscious would only apply at the level of the ego and would be meaningless at the level of the Self. If Consciousness and the psyche are indeed the same, as I believe they are, the psyche could not be unconscious of itself. In any case, Consciousness is a unity, so there is only the Consciousness of the Self—there is no other consciousness in which it might be reflected.

Jung was not enthusiastic about Eastern ideas of a non-dual level of consciousness in which the ego is totally subsumed by the Self, because he thought that there can be no consciousness without the presence of a discreet ego (discussed further in Corbett, 2016). Unfortunately, he dismisses the meditative experience of ego loss as an example of the *participation mystique* of primitives, whereas for the Eastern spiritual traditions absorption into the Self exemplifies a high level of spiritual attainment and liberation. But although Jung had a high regard for mystics, he thought that imageless consciousness was a kind of regression to unconsciousness. He could not conceive of consciousness with no content, and he rejected the idea that such states have soteriological value, as they are believed to have in Eastern religious traditions. In spite of that, he also said that he had no doubt that "the satori experience does occur also in the West" (CW 11, para. 903).

It is worth noting that, as a result of his traumatic experiences, Job had to let go of his previous God-image, which was based on the traditional notions of reward and punishment for good and bad behavior that were part of God's covenant with his people. Job had lived a conventionally pious life, obsessively observing sacrificial rituals to propitiate his God (Job, 1:5). According to the covenant, Job's piety should have protected him from evil, as his friends insisted (4, 6-7), but it failed to do so. After his tragic losses, he breaks out in boils all over his body, so that his obedience must have involved a good deal of repression of his rage in an attempt to live up to traditional standards of piety. His rage then erupted somatically in the form of a skin disorder. Having lost his children, his health, and his possessions in spite of his efforts to be good, his bitterness at feeling betrayed by God is understandable; from being a protector, God becomes an enemy. Job's idealized God-image, which was a part of his oppressive superego structure, disintegrates when he suffers intensely for no obvious reason. Job is then forced to transform not just his overly-pious, somewhat narcissistic[xxii] false self but also his naive God-image. After his numinous vision of God speaking out of a whirlwind, God is no longer a matter of hearsay but a direct experience. Job's experience is a mythic example of the experience of the dark side of the Self.

The Dark Side of the Self: Jung's Proposal

Because of Yhwh's atrocious behavior towards Job, who is allowed to suffer for no apparent reason, Jung thought that the notion of God as the *Summum Bonum* (the ultimate good) cannot be maintained (CW 11, para. 662). Jung believes that God is a paradox that represents all the qualities of creation, including its positive and negative qualities (1975, p. 435); everything that exists, including evil, is a function of its creator. Jung was concerned that if God is thought of as *only* good, then all evil must originate in human beings—and this even though the serpent was present in the Garden of Eden at the beginning of creation (p. 60). If God is only good, human beings become scapegoats for all evil, which is an overly pessimistic view of human nature. For Jung, this view does not grant evil an objective status and does not do justice to the enormity of evil. To insist that all evil is based in human behavior makes human beings feel inferior.

A God-image that is all good, such as the traditional figure of Christ, means that his devotees must carry all the darkness, making impossible demands on them, but Christian theology has tried to impose the harmful notion of intrinsic human sinfulness on the Western tradition. Traditional Christianity teaches that innate human sinfulness impedes our direct relationship with a transcendent God, who requires the mediation of Christ. This is a radically different view than Jung's approach, which sees the human soul as having "the dignity of an entity endowed with consciousness of a relationship to deity," and "the soul must contain in itself the faculty of relationship to God" because of the presence of the God-image in the soul (CW 12, paras. 11-12). That is, no mediation is necessary because human beings have an innate presence of the divine in the psyche, which is where the divine and the human meet. There is no need to think of the divine as an external, remote entity with no need for humanity, which would make it possible to have God all "outside" rather than experienced within the soul (paras. 11-12).

We have seen too much evil and suffering to have a naïve image of God. The state of the world and its depravities do not allow us to sustain the traditional notion of God as an all-good, benevolent sky-Father. Some theologians have acknowledged the problem of God's abusive or destructive qualities (Penchansky, 1995), and the question of where God was at Auschwitz remains unanswered. Yet, in spite of the evidence, the majority of traditional religionists insist on God's justice, in the face of what to many people looks like world-wide injustice. This kind of inconsistency is no longer tolerable. It is no longer acceptable to fall back on rationalizations for suffering and evil that claim we cannot conceive the mind of God, or that God has mysterious plans for us. The formulation of God as only good means that evil must be split off and projected onto the Devil or the Antichrist, although these too are a part of creation. Jung believed that an all-good God-image requires splitting of this image into irreconcilable opposites, "leading ultimately to a metaphysical dualism" (CW 9, ii, para. 76). Jung's idea of the dark side of the Self as an important source of evil and human suffering contrasts vividly with the idea found in some Christian traditions that the main reason for human suffering is human sinfulness.

Jung objected to Augustine's notion of evil as the *privatio boni*, or the absence of goodness, partly because Jung felt that if evil was not substantial, then goodness could not be, and if evil is merely an absence, what does that say about the Christian notion of the devil? Furthermore, if evil is not substantial, Jung feared that human beings would have an excuse to not take their shadow side seriously (1973, p. 541). By saying that evil is non-being or an absence, St. Augustine was trying to avoid the Manichean idea of two ultimate principles, one evil and one good. Jung addresses this issue by suggesting that good and evil are both found within the Self. The Self contains all the opposites, and the ego attributes evil to those aspects of the Self that cause suffering and destruction. To say that the Self has a dark side is not to imply that this aspect of the Self is immoral; it is simply an objective fact, based on our experience.

Jung believed that the symbol of Christ is an incomplete symbol or personification of the Self, because Christ is depicted as entirely loving and light. However, Jung pointed out that good and evil coexist in the psyche, and they are actually brothers within the Christian myth: "God had two sons, an elder one, Satan, and a younger one, Christ…if good and evil were begotten in the same way they must be brothers" (CW 9, ii, para. 103). The split into Christ and the Devil was necessary for the development of human consciousness because it helped to differentiate these opposites, allowing us to choose the good. Jung thought that this process was a service that Christianity performed for the ancient world, and our present task is to reconcile opposites such as good and evil— which are undifferentiated opposites within the divine—within human consciousness. This reconciliation is brought about by a process that Jung refers to as the psyche's transcendent function, which constellates opposites and then tries to symbolically reconcile or unify them. To the extent that we facilitate this unification we assist in the divine transformation. Exactly how this reconciliation is to be achieved is an individual matter; at the very least it means becoming conscious of one's own darkness, which is a moral demand that requires self-examination. Individuals who believe they only strive for the good tend to project evil onto others and attack it externally instead of attending to their own shadow.

A distinguishing feature of Jung's psychology is that the individual's failings and negative attributes have an archetypal component to them; they cannot be seen at a purely personal level. This is true because one's personal shadow is an incarnate fragment of the archetypal shadow, or the dark side of the Self. Thus, shadow material is an integral part of the individual psyche, but it is not entirely personal. Jung assumed that work on the individual shadow has a redemptive effect on the dark side of the Self by making it conscious within the human being. This is a very different mythic idea than the notion that good and evil will be eternally opposed to each other until a final apocalyptic battle, as described in the book of Revelation. In this book the Lamb of God turns into an aggressive ram, as the author's "long pent-up negative feelings" erupt as a result of their repression and his striving for perfection (CW 11, para. 708).

Jung's emphasis on the dark side of the Self does not correspond to the experience of many Christians who encounter a loving God. It is an essential part of the Christian tradition to say that God is love (1 John, 4:8) and evil is a rebellion against love, which is a healing factor. The idea that God might have a dark side that causes suffering, meaning that God does not simply love us, can be quite frightening. There is also concern that one could identify with the dark side of the Self, doing evil while insisting one is doing the will of God. It is also possible to be possessed by the dark side of the Self, as we see in the case of fanatically destructive or murderous religious narcissists who believe they are carrying out the will of God, which they believe coincides with their own.

Jung acknowledged that love is an aspect of the divine, and love is an ultimate mystery (1963, p. 353). However, he thought that the assertion that God is *only* love leads to an incomplete God-image that does not adequately address the problem of evil, which seems to pervade the world. The notion that the Resurrection symbolizes victory over evil is important in Christianity but does not satisfy everyone, given the level of evil in the world. In the face of this problem, in order to maintain a God-image that is all-good, Christians have had to develop theodicies, or attempts to justify God in the presence of evil (discussed in chapter 1). Jung's notion that evil results from the dark side of the divine and is not purely human avoids the need for theodicies, which, in the face of events such as the Holocaust, seem like rationalizations. Jung's approach also avoids the Christian notion that God judges the world, and Jung by-passes the Christian concern that God is sometimes hidden, since for Jung, God acts through the unconscious whose manifestations are not hidden. The emphasis on the goodness of God in the Christian tradition may have arisen to compensate for the tragedy of the crucifixion and to reassure believers, given the delay in the second coming of Christ.

Jung (1963, p. 39) had an early intimation of the dark side of God in his childhood image of a turd falling from the throne of God onto the roof of the Basel cathedral. This numinous experience gave him an immense sense of relief, and it felt like an illumination. He realized that his minister father had never had an analogous experience, but instead had relied on the Bible and on belief in doctrine and dogma. Jung was critical of believing something that we have not directly experienced; he pointed out that direct experience gives knowledge, which is more reliable than belief. In a famous interview on BBC television in 1959, when Jung was asked if he believed in God, he paused for a moment then replied: "Difficult to answer. I know. I don't need to believe, I know" (Jung, 1977). This distinction between knowing and believing produced a good deal of discussion. As he put it elsewhere (CW 18, para. 1589): "Either I know a thing and then I don't need to believe it; or I believe it because I'm not sure that I know it. I am well satisfied with the fact that I know experiences which I cannot avoid calling numinous or divine." In a letter, Jung clarified that he did not mean he knew a certain God, such as Yhwh or Zeus, but rather that he knew he was confronted with an unknown factor in himself; he knew he collided with a superior will within his own psychology (1975, pp. 525-526). He would prefer to call this factor the Self rather than give it the name of a specific deity.

According to Jung, the *Book of Job* depicts a God-image who has a double aspect; he is both a persecutor and a helper, just and unjust at the same time (CW 11). Human beings must reconcile these divine opposites within themselves through increased consciousness, since the oppositions in God have been incarnated into human beings. The reconciliation of these opposites is one of the functions of psychotherapy. This process always involves suffering. Because of Jung's recognition of the dark side of the Self, he can make the startling statement that: "Man's suffering does not derive from his sins but from the maker of his imperfections, the paradoxical God" (CW 18, para. 1681). This statement contradicts some of the moral teaching of the Western religious traditions, which tend to blame humanity for its imperfections and the suffering they produce, rather than the divine. Jung believes that "God can be called good only inasmuch as He is able to manifest His goodness in individuals. His moral quality depends on individuals. That is why He incarnates" (1975, p. 314). In other words, whether the Self manifests itself as good or evil is partly a function of human ethical choices—this, for Jung, is one reason that the ego is important.

Consistent with the idea that human God-images tend to reflect the projection of human psychology, the Hebrew Scriptures contain many mythic examples of the dark side of God. Apart from Job's experience of this dark side, there are innumerable occasions on which God promotes destruction and mass murder. Jeremiah talks about God's judgment as "war, famine, and pestilence" (28:8). Speaking through Isaiah (45:7), God says "I make weal and create woe." In the book of Psalms (e.g., Ps. 128, 109, 44), protests and laments about God's behavior are a common theme. Throughout the Hebrew scriptures, God constantly complains that his creation does not live up to his own standards, and he frequently uses these occasions to demonstrate his strength. Only the New Testament asserts that "God is light and in him is no darkness at all" (1 John, 1:5), which, given the state of the world, seems like a Panglossian level of denial. Within Christianity, the dark side of the divine is in fact acknowledged in the form of the avenging angels of the book of Revelation, but by and large, in Christian doctrine evil is seen as a corruption of God's creation, or the result of the misuse of free will. Evil is not seen as the effect of God's power. Jung's notion of the dark side of the Self is therefore incompatible with the Christian image of an all-good God and with the Christian view of evil (see Corbett, 2018 for a further discussion of this issue).

The notion of the dark side of God could imply an omnipotent but potentially malicious being who deliberately created humanity in a way that would make suffering inevitable. This idea is difficult to refute but so terrifying in its implications for humanity that it produces great resistance. Nevertheless, we experience the dark side of the Self in the forms of destruction, physical and mental suffering, negative synchronicities, and evil on a large scale such as the Holocaust, which is the kind of event that forces us to re-think our God-image. Clearly, evil of this kind is much more than the absence of goodness.

When the Self produces suffering, "one often has to accept uncertainty and persevere in patience without trying to control or explain what is happening" (Corbett, 2018, p. 106). This requires that we try to find the right attitude to the dark side of the Self, which is preferable to trying to repress or overcome it. The suffering produced by the dark side of the Self becomes a part of one's life and a part of our identity. Unhelpful responses include the attempt to drown it with substances, to convert it into a psychosomatic symptom, to deny it by desperately focusing on the positive parts of our lives, or to identify with the dark side by behaving in an evil manner.

The experience of the dark side of the Self cannot always be mollified by spiritual practices such as prayer, and may not be helped by good spiritual advice. The dark side of the Self cannot be fully overcome because it is a spiritual principle; it can only be resisted. Sometimes an entire community must be enlisted to deal with its social manifestations, such as racism. For the individual, a situation of intense suffering often requires a process of sacrifice and radical acceptance before anything will change, and: "We have to decide to live despite our suffering at the hands of the Self, as we try to relate to its dark side" (p. 106). This necessity often arises during the practice of psychotherapy, when an individual is in a situation in which the psychotherapist can only offer himself or herself as a witness or companion, hoping that the therapeutic relationship will be strong enough to support the individual through the liminal period,[xxiii] which can be seen as a process of initiation into a new level of consciousness. Working with suffering people, it is important for psychotherapists to remember that they do not know what outcome is in the individual's best interest, and the outcome is often unpredictable. (The process of acceptance, and an approach to suffering as a period of liminality, are discussed in Corbett, 2015 and 2018).

Christian theologians have objected to Jung's notion of the dark side of the God-image, when they believe it is fundamentally irreconcilable with Christian theology. They complain that Jung refuses to acknowledge the incomprehensibility of God and refuses to submit to God (Doran, 1988). Similarly, Clift (1982) believes that Jung's approach to God is based on Jung's own religious experience. Clift asserts that his own experience is of a God of love rather than a God with a dark side, and he questions the application of any psychological theory to God. For Clift, the notion of a God with two aspects is itself only an anthropomorphic projection. Jung might reply that the notion of an all-good God-image is based on a wish-fulfilling splitting defense, combined with denial of the manifest suffering and evil in the world.

Symbolic Manifestations of the Self

The Self is unknowable, even unthinkable in its totality; in Ramakrishna's felicitous metaphor, it is an ocean with no shore. Not surprisingly therefore an endlessly wide range of symbols may represent it. Common to all of them is their numinosity and their capacity to convey a sense of wholeness, completeness, and the reconciliation of opposites. [xxiv] Because of the large number of images of the Self, Jung's approach is entirely different than that of the typical monotheisms, which narrowly restrict their image of God.

The function of any symbol is to unite or bridge consciousness with the unconscious, so that the ego can find a way to connect with the Self. In Christianity the sacraments have this function. When they function as originally intended, these kinds of symbolic devices point to the transpersonal dimension and allow the worshipper to connect with it, unless the ritual has lost its true symbolic function and the sacraments have become nothing more than signs dictated by habit. The fact that there are an indeterminate number of Self-symbols reminds us that the Self is not a discreet entity and cannot be confined to a specific image; the Self is the whole psyche. Any particular symbol of the Self has a specific epistemological function; it tells us something that cannot be better said in any other way, but it only represents an aspect of the totality. The Self cannot be symbolized in its entirety, but only in a fragmentary form.

Symbols of the Self are found in all theistic traditional religions. For Jung, Christ "exemplifies the archetype of the Self" (CW 9, ii, para. 70). This archetype assimilated the human Jesus, whose life produced an image of the emergence of a new God-image into collective consciousness. However, equally valid symbols of the Self are figures such as the biblical Yhwh or for that matter Kuan Yin, or any of the innumerable gods and goddesses of existing or archaic religious pantheons, because these kinds of figures were or are able to carry the projections of the Self for their devotees. However, no single religious tradition can exhaust the ways in which the Self can appear. The existing theistic traditions have unique God-images, but they are all inevitably incomplete.

From Jung's point of view, the individual can discover his or her personal symbolic connection to the Self, which might be given in a dream or vision. There is no longer only one official, approved way to imagine the divine—at least, the divine understood as a subjective experience. The range of possible images of the Self is inexhaustible because the Self is a totality.

The Bible describes many numinous symbols of the Self, such as the vision described in Isaiah, 6:1-2: "I saw the Lord sitting upon a throne, high and lifted up; and his train filled the temple. Above him stood the seraphim; each had six wings: with two he covered his face, and with two he covered his feet, and with two he flew." Or consider Ezekiel's vision of a great cloud containing bright light and fire (1:28). The cloud contained four creatures each of which had four faces and four wings, burning like torches. He saw a wheel by each creature, and the rims of the wheels were full of eyes. Over all this was a sparkling dome, above which was a throne, on which was a human shape surrounded by a glow that looked like the glory of the Lord. The manifestations of the Self in the Bible are not always as dramatic as these visionary experiences; the Self also appeared to Elijah as a "still small voice" (1 Kings 19:11-13). Based on such numinous experiences, Jung says that the God-image is not something invented, but an experience that "comes upon man spontaneously," and just as the unconscious God-image can affect consciousness, so consciousness can modify the God-image once it has become conscious (CW 9, ii, para. 303). This idea is important because it implies that the God-image can evolve or transform when we work on it consciously. Most importantly for Jung, the psyche is an ontologically real domain, so intrapsychic images of the Self are real, not to be dismissed as "nothing but" psychological phenomena of no importance. The visions of Ezekiel and Isaiah contain imagery that is clearly culturally conditioned, but it is not unusual for numinous experiences to be colored in this way, presumably to make them meaningful to the subject.

The Self manifests itself empirically in a wide variety of dream imagery (CW 9, i, para. 315). The Self may appear in human form such as a powerful King or Queen, prophet, hero or savior figure, which represent a "supraordinate personality" (CW 6, para. 790). (Clinicians are sometimes suspicious that such figures in dreams represent projected infantile omnipotence or an idealized transference.) The Self may appear as a gigantic human being, also suggesting the Self as the greater, objective personality, or it may appear as a radiant divine child, pointing to the future of the personality. Images that seem to unite opposites, such as a winged snake or figures that are both young and old or both male and female, express aspects of the Self as a complex of opposites held together or reconciled within it, so that the opposites are seen to be complementary (CW 9, ii, para. 355; CW 9, i, para. 314-5). Jung is aware that such symbols are "mere allusions" that "hint at something…They try only to point in a certain direction, viz. to those dim horizons beyond which lies the secret of existence" (1975, p. 290).

The Self can also appear in dreams as an awe-inspiring natural phenomenon. Mountains suggest the linking of heaven and earth and an ascent to the spirit. Trees manifest the life principle and its cycle of growth, decay, and regeneration. The Self may appear as a powerful storm or wind that convey the ancient notion of the spirit of God as an impersonal presence. Animal symbolism is another possibility, sometimes taking the form of a golden, outsize creature that seems to express the instinctual level of the Self. Jung also suggests a variety of theriomorphic Self imagery, including powerful animals such as elephants, but also snakes, spiders, crabs, butterflies, beetles, and worms (CW 9, i, para. 187). At times the Self appears as a voice in a dream, and sometimes as a waking experience of the "inner light" or an "inner voice" that seems to know more than the conscious personality. The city of Jerusalem carries the numinosity of the Self for many people, acting as an *axis mundi*, a world axis or a spiritual center for several religious traditions.

Symmetrical geometrical figures that express wholeness or a totality, such as the Taoist yin-yang symbol or circles, spheres, crosses, stars, and squares are mandalas that express the Self in an abstract form. All the opposites are contained within the figure, which often has a central point that seems to hold them together (CW 9, i, para. 634; CW 6, paras. 789-791). Jung thought that mandala symbolism is a particularly important type of Self-symbol (CW 9, ii, para. 426). The mandala represents wholeness, harmony, and completion. Jung discovered that painting these figures produced a calming and centering effect. His conviction about the existence of the Self was solidified in 1927 when he had his "Liverpool" dream, in which at the center of the city was a square with a central island on which stood a magnolia tree with reddish blossoms. The quarters of the city were arranged radially around this central point, forming a mandala. The central island was blazing with sunlight. It is important that in the dream the city was dirty and sooty, it was winter and raining, and darkness surrounded the central light. This gloom must have reflected Jung's life situation at the time, but he is given an image of a numinous center that sustained him. This dream felt like an "act of grace" (1963, p. 198).

Jung suggested that mandalas are "cryptograms" that reveal the state of the Self, and that the mandala is a primary expression of the Self (p. 196). The center of the mandala represents a protected, safe space. In Eastern spiritual traditions, the center of the mandala often depicts a specific deity, but these do not seem to appear in psychotherapeutic practice, where it is more common to see dream images of mandalas in the form of symmetrical gardens or temples. Mandalas also appear composed of flowers such as the lotus or rose, stars, a cross, a labyrinth, or precious stones (CW11, para. 136).

Jung believed that mandala imagery that gives a sense of order and peace is most likely to appear in dreams when the individual is going through a period of disorientation. This imagery then seems to be a part of the self-regulating function of the psyche that tries to restore order. Such dreams represent a self-healing process. It is important to reiterate that although the Self manifests itself in these innumerable images, none of them is a complete image of the Self; they all point towards an underlying essence that cannot be imaged.

It is possible to see mandalas as defensive. Redfearn (1974) described a case in which mandala imagery defended against split-off impulses. He believed that his patient's oral sadism was defensively transformed into the idealized mandala imagery she was painting during the analysis, and that shadow impulses can be warded off by such idealized images of the Self. Mandalas with very thick walls are particularly likely to have such defensive functions. In such a situation, religious mandalas function unconsciously as amulets or defenses against evil. Perhaps this potentially defensive function contributes to the use of mandalas as a therapeutic tool, since drawing mandalas tends to have a calming effect, helping to give a sense of order while one is in a complex emotional situation.

Reminiscent of Feuerbach, Jung believes that anthropomorphic God-images or Self-symbols are a function of the human psychological constitution, which is why God is imagined as if "he" has human attributes and emotions (1975, p. 342). Thus, Jung points out that the image of God as a king (Daniel 2:44) is connected to the scourging of Jesus, who is crowned with thorns and clothed in purple robes, showing him in the archetypal role of a king who was sacrificed to benefit his people (CW 11, paras. 406-409). However, Jung points out that the image of God as king would not be useful for people with a more spiritual concept of God. Similarly, the dogmatic Christian attributes of God, such as descriptions of God as infinite or eternal, are "absolutely manmade assumptions" that reach beyond the limits of the human mind (Jung 1960, p. 927).

God-images are ubiquitous historically and geographically, which is evidence that "the idea of God" is an archetypal content of human psychology (CW 7, para. 110). This potential for the experience of the Self is filled in by the God-image of local religions. Thus, as noted above, for Christians Christ is a symbolic representation of the Self, but for Jung Christ is an incomplete symbol of the Self because it is too exclusively light and spiritualized. The Christ symbol does not include the dark side of the Self (CW 9, ii, para. 74), or the "dark son," which is projected onto the Devil or the Antichrist. The image of God as a Trinity also excludes matter and the feminine aspects of the Self, thus excluding the sacrality of a large segment of creation.[xxv] For this reason, Jung felt that a Trinitarian God-image is incomplete, and a quaternity image would be a more complete symbol of wholeness (CW 11).

Jung seemed to veer between adding the shadow or the feminine aspects of the divine to make up the missing fourth.[xxvi] Jung believed that the dogma of the Assumption of Mary, proclaimed in 1950, was an evolutionary advance in the Christian God-image because it added the feminine element to an otherwise exclusively masculine God-image. This dogma, which asserts that Mary was taken body and soul into heaven at the end of her life, is effectively a new version of the ancient tradition of a sacred marriage between the male God and the Goddess, an idea that would be unacceptable to traditional believers in the Trinity. Jung believed that the appearance of this dogma was evidence that revelation continues. In principle, this development might have served to tone down the patriarchal emphasis of the tradition.

Jung believed that among the alchemists the Christ figure was compensated for with the figure called Mercurius, who represents the cthonic spirit of the unconscious, the light of nature within the darkness of the unconscious, or the spirit within matter (CW 13, paras. 295, 303). Both Christ and Mercurius are symbols of the Self; one spiritualized and one instinctual or bodily. Jung believes that for the sake of wholeness these complementary dimensions must be brought together in our God-image. This requires a dialog between consciousness and the unconscious and avoiding a split between spirit and matter, recognizing that these are all aspects of a totality.

Although we cannot prove or disprove the existence of God in the metaphysical sense, the existence of numinous symbols of the Self is a psychological fact, and the psyche is ontologically real (CW 11, para. 751). In fact, Jung insists that the psyche is the only medium by which we may experience the divine. "It is only through the psyche that we can establish that God acts upon us, but we are unable to distinguish whether these actions emanate from God or from the unconscious. We cannot tell if God and the unconscious are two different entities" (CW 11, para. 757). We can only say that in the unconscious there is an archetype of wholeness that spontaneously manifests itself, independently of consciousness. As Jung puts it in a letter: "If God were to reveal himself to us, we have nothing except our psychic organs to register his revelation and could not express it except in the images of everyday speech" (Jung, 1975, p. 262). When we experience one of these manifestations, for example in a numinous dream, we feel as if we have been granted a personal revelation that demands attention. Because these images are so unique and tailored to the individual, in practice each person may have his or her personal God-image. Nevertheless, collective images such as the Christian Trinity are powerful and may capture the individual's imagination.

Entirely novel symbols of the Self may appear to the individual in dreams or visionary experiences. These may contain imagery from the dreamer's current religious tradition, or a numinous dream image may have no connection to the dreamer's religious affiliation. For example, a Jewish man with no conscious connection to Christianity has the following dream:

> I am the ship's doctor in a Roman galleon. Jesus is carried in, still nailed to a cross; he has just been crucified. The ship's captain tells me that since I am the doctor, I should examine him to see if he is dead or not. As I approach him, the figure on the cross rises into the air, becomes the size of a small wall crucifix, and suddenly rushes towards me and penetrates my heart.

Apparently, the psyche's innate religious function is not interested in denominational concerns. Thus, a modern-day Christian or Jew may dream of a Hindu or ancient Egyptian god or goddess. I have elsewhere reported the dream of a Roman Catholic priest who had a numinous dream of the pre-Christian Venus of Willendorf (Corbett, 2012).

It is not unusual for people with no conscious interest in religion to have a surprising dream that contains religious or archetypal imagery, as if the dreamer's spiritual life had been relegated to the unconscious and is now emerging. Since the Self is the maker of dreams, our attention to such dreams is a form of relationship with the God-image. Attention to dreams in response to a psychological difficulty is the psychological equivalent of the biblical Job asking God for help with God. Work on dreams then becomes a spiritual practice and a form of natural theology. This is not a new idea; the concept of dreams sent by a deity is found far back in antiquity. Dreams have been important in the Jewish, Islamic, and Christian traditions and in many other religious cultures (Bulkeley et. al, 2001). Although the practice of working with dreams fell out of favor among Christians for a long time, today an increasing number of pastoral counselors and spiritual directors are acknowledging the importance of dreams both in Christian history and in psychotherapeutic work (Strickling, 2007).[xxvii]

The Self in the Outer World: Synchronistic Events

The manifestations of the Self are not confined to its intrapsychic appearances. Jung also sees the Self as responsible for important outer events in one's life: "The psychological rule says that when an inner situation is not made conscious, it happens outside, as fate" (CW 9, ii, para. 126). This means we meet the unconscious in the form of outer events in our lives, which is a profound statement of the underlying unity of what seem to be separate inner and outer worlds. This unity is particularly seen in the form of a powerful synchronicity. This was Jung's term for the meaningful correspondence in time of a physical event and the subject's psychological state, even though there is no causal connection between the individual's psychology and the outer event. Synchronicity links the inner world of the psyche with the outer world of physical events, and links the material world with the world of spirit. Synchronistic events often produce a sense of something "meant to be," as if they are purposeful in some way. When we experience an important synchronicity, we realize we belong to a deeper level of reality than the ego can perceive.

Von Franz (1980, p. 177) describes a different type of synchronicity, manifested as the "social function of the Self." She believes that each person "gathers around him his own 'soul family,' a group of people not created by accident or by mere egotistic motivation but rather through a deeper, more essential spiritual interest or concern: reciprocal individuation." These relationships have objective meaning, and they are created in a mysterious way by the Self. In them we meet people with whom we belong.

Critics of Jung's concept of synchronicity point out that rare coincidences occur all around us, and they happen for no discernable spiritual or psychological purpose with no supernatural background. In the reductive psychoanalytic view, the experience of synchronicity is rooted in the projection of an internalized early caregiver onto the environment, temporarily dissolving ego boundaries between the subject and the external world. Then, the apparent sense of meaning is produced by the return of the repressed, producing an emotionally powerful experience (Faber, 1998). This kind of critique is based on a denial of spiritual reality. For those who have felt the emotional power of a synchronistic event, intellectual dismissal of such a meaningful coincidence feels unconvincing. Skepticism about synchronicity may be due to a defense against the numinosity of these events, since to acknowledge their spiritual implications would threaten an entrenched materialistic belief system. These critiques also ignore the data from parapsychological research that show that chance alone cannot explain these events.

Critiques of the Concept of the Self

Christians are sometimes concerned that it might be idolatrous to see an intrapsychic God-image as an expression of divinity if the image does not correspond to traditional theistic God-imagery. Thus, a numinous dream image of Jesus as a woman might not be considered to be authentic, especially by fundamentalists, who might even see such a figure as demonic. For Jung however, such an image simply refers to the feminine aspect of the Self in a particular symbolic rather than literally historical manner. To limit the way in which the Self can appear is to be bound by dogma that belies experience. However, traditional theists would hesitate to accept the idea that the divine might appear within the psyche in the form of a wide range of images, some of which have opposite qualities, not all of which are positive from the ego's perspective. Yet this is not surprising; if the Self is truly a totality it must include material that the ego finds unpleasant. "As a totality the Self is a *coincidentia oppositorum*; it is therefore bright and dark and neither" (CW 12, 129n).[xxviii]

A further critique of Jung's approach is that its focus on the Self does not deal with its social implications or with interpersonal relationships. Goldbrunner (1949) believes that Jung's "absolutized Self revolves around itself in self-satisfied isolation" (p. 200). Guntripp (1961) complains that the goal of individuation is narcissistic because it overlooks the essential role of relationships for the integration of the personality. Rieff (1966) complains that Jung is recommending a private form of religion "without institutional reference or communal membership" (p. 134). However, criticisms that Jung ignores relationships do not consider his comments such as: "Individuation is only possible with people, through people," Jung (1960, p. 103), and: "Relationship paves the way for individuation and makes it possible" (CW 16, fn. 15, p. 244). Individuation would not be possible without others. Furthermore, the fact that Jung believes that the Self is the same in all of us offers the potential for a deep sense of communion between people. The Self can also be seen as responsible for the archetypal levels of the interpersonal field, or for the "third thing" that happens between people at the level of the unconscious. Although personalistic psychoanalysts believe that this "analytic third" is jointly created by the therapeutic couple, from Jung's point of view the Self also participates in this interaction by adding archetypal elements to the therapeutic field in which both people participate. The Self is also responsible for synchronistic meetings that affect the course of our lives.

A trenchant critique of Jung's stress on the Self is that there may be no noticeable manifestations of the Self in a person's life. Such a person may then ask how he or she might find the Self. In this situation, intention combined with sustained attention to dreams and synchronicities usually lead to the necessary experience, but this is not guaranteed.

Transformation of the God-image

In an important letter, Jung (1975, p. 314) writes that "we are going to contact spheres of a not yet transformed God when our consciousness begins to extend into the sphere of the unconscious." Elsewhere, Jung notes that "transformations of the God-image run parallel with changes in human consciousness, though one would be at a loss to say which is the cause of the other" (CW 9, ii, para. 303.) He believes that the Self is continuously revealing itself by progressively incarnating into humanity, and our image of the Self evolves or transforms as we work on its manifestations, for example in dream imagery. For Jung, this process gives human consciousness metaphysical significance: "Individuation and individual existence are indispensable for the transformation of God the creator" (Jung, 1975, p. 314). In this sentence, Jung seems to be talking about transformation of the divine itself and not just its intrapsychic image.

Whether or not the divine itself transforms, it is certainly true that our God-image may transform as we pay attention to material that emerges from the unconscious. This prevents our seeing the Self in too fixed a manner, and links Jung's work with process thought and its focus on continuous becoming. From a process point of view, the Self affects the person and the world, and the person and the world affect the Self. In this view, the Self is "in a continuous and creative interaction with us" (Asher, 2014, p. 13).

Psychotherapy can facilitate the process of the transformation of the God-image, so that psychological development and the development of a transformed personal God-image can proceed hand in hand. An example of the transformation of the God-image is given by the following dream of a woman who was very concerned about the prospect of aging. At such a liminal period, the Self may produce a numinous dream such as the following, which initiated her into a new phase of life:

> An authoritative male voice informs me that it is going to teach me about the process of aging. A black and white illustration appears before my eyes, which represents the rejuvenated Godhead.

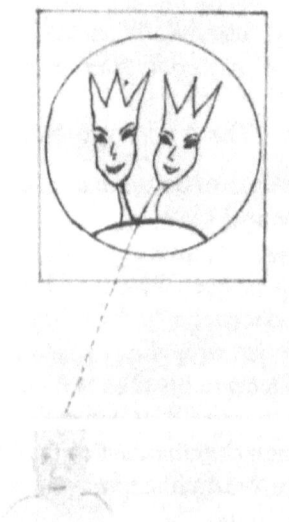

> Underneath the diagram is the living head of a very old man. A connecting line is drawn from the old man's head to the diagram of divinity, which consists of an outer elongated square

enclosing an inner circle. At the bottom of the circle is a crescent, convex upward. Out of the crescent arises two heads on almost identical long necks. I know that they share the same body which is not shown. The voice explains that this is an abstract of the rejuvenated Godhead. The right head represents the male aspect of God and the left the female aspect. The two heads are in absolute harmony with each other. They look like ethereal spirits. Their facial expression is autocratic, blithe, somewhat curious and unemotional. The tops of their heads are shaped like an indented crown with three prongs that I can see on each head. The old man looks ordinary and earthy, with reddish skin. The voice explains that we still do not understand the process of aging, which is to enable the Godhead to rejuvenate. When we are born, God is old; as we grow old God becomes younger, and when we die, God experiences re-birth. I am told that it is essential that particularly in old age we do not lose our connection to the Godhead, for otherwise we would deprive God of our share in his rejuvenation and may actually disturb the cosmic ecology. If we ignore the divine element, it sinks into itself and ceases to be conscious of itself. The voice goes on to say that belief in God constellates the inner child and thus furthers the process of divine rejuvenation. If, as we age, we lose touch with the inner child, we may simultaneously sever our ties to the divine.

This dream challenges and transforms the exclusively masculine God-image found in the tradition in which the dreamer was raised. The idea that the purpose of aging is the "rejuvenation of God" is completely unexpected and novel, and it is reminiscent of Jung's notion of the transformation of the God-image. Although the meaning of this phrase was not clear to the dreamer, it proved to be reassuring to her. She grasped the point that aging is more than a period of relentless decline towards death, since this phase of her life has a purpose. This kind of numinous experience often has a healing effect (Jung, 1973, p. 377).

This dream can be thought of as a collective or "big" dream that is relevant to many people. The dream also acts as a personal revelation from the Self, and by suggesting a personal myth it allows the dreamer to distinguish herself from the collective myth into which she was born. The dream indicates that the dreamer needs an image of the divine with both masculine and feminine aspects, and also an image that is neither masculine nor feminine, as indicated by the squared circle, a mandala that is an abstract image of the Self as a totality.

It is difficult to understand what it could mean that when we are born God is old but gradually gets younger as we age and is reborn when we die. This sounds very much like a Zen Koan. One way to look at this statement, instead of taking it as a literal account of divinity, is to see the dream as a comment on our changing experience of the Self. Early in life we tend to accept the God-image of the tradition in which we are raised, which is an old image, but as we age our God-image develops into something newer or younger. The idea of the re-birth of the Self hints at the reincarnation of a spiritual principle.

The dream stresses the importance of maintaining a connection to the inner child. In many traditions the divine appears in the form of a child, for example in the mythologies of Jesus, the Buddha, Horus, and Krishna. These divine children usually appear in dreams in the context of renewal and regeneration. We are also reminded of Jesus calling on people to become like little children if they wish to enter the kingdom of heaven (Matthew 18:3). Perhaps this means that we must cultivate trust and faith instead of a dominant ego, in the way that a child relates to a parent.

This woman's God-image has been radically transformed by her dream, which provides a good example of the way in which transformation of the God-image occurs as the Self incarnates by becoming conscious within human beings. In a letter, Edward Edinger (1987, personal communication) said: "To me the most important feature of the dream is that it informs the dreamer that she is a *partner* of God and a participant in the drama of divine transformation. This gives her suffering and sacrifice archetypal sanction and roots her in a living myth."

When we have to give up a cherished God-image because of painful life events that do not correspond to the way we have imagined God, we may need to go through a grief process during which we realize that what we were told about God is simply not so. New ways of understanding one's relationship to God then become necessary. This was the situation in which the biblical Job found himself. Jung's *Answer to Job* examines the transformation of the collective Judeo-Christian image of God, which is often seen as fundamental to the Western psyche. Jung believes that this canonical God-image was forced to change as a result of Yahweh's unconscious treatment of Job. As we see from this dream, and from the experience of Job, direct experiences of the Self are also transformative. Psychotherapeutic work on parental images may change the individual's God-image when it has been colored by parental projections.

Transformation of the God-image may require that we deal with the experience of the dark side of the Self, either in the form of our own shadow or when we struggle with collective evil. This often requires us to tolerate painful affects such as rage or hatred without denying them. Such affect-storms are often associated with negatively-toned complexes, whose archetypal cores are incarnate fragments of the dark side of the Self at the core of the personal shadow. The more we are able to understand and contain these painful states of mind, the more we are able to transform them. This means that human suffering allows the transformation of the Self, which is one of Jung's points in his *Answer to Job*. Job's capacity to tolerate and even protest Yhwh's attacks led to an increase in Yhwh's self-awareness, a transformation of Job's God-image, and also the evolution of the collective God-image. We are all in Job's position at some time in our lives.

Jung's Disagreement with the Theologians

A breakdown in the relationship between Jung and the Dominican scholar Victor White was largely due to Jung's notion of the dark side of the Self and disagreements about the doctrine of evil as the *privatio boni*.[xxix] White had hoped to reconcile or at least correlate Jungian psychology with Christian theology, and Jung hoped that White would contribute to the transformation of the Western God-image (Lammers, 1994; Weldon, 2007; Charet, 1990). However, a series of irreconcilable disagreements made their attempt at collaboration a failure. Although White (1960) could accept Jung's notion of images of God as empirical psychological facts, White could not accept Jung's notion of the dark side of the Self. White could only accept the idea that the divine could be unconscious to the ego, not that God could be an unconscious being (White, 1960). Neither could White reconcile himself to the notion that the God-image arises within the psyche, because he was committed to the notion of a transcendent God beyond the psyche, outside humanity, in contrast to Jung's notion of the Self as the "God within." White was wedded to the Thomistic[xxx] notion of an objective, remote God whose revelation and grace towards fallen humanity is mediated and interpreted by the Church. This notion is completely incompatible with Jung's approach.

White could not accept Jung's belief that Christ is an incomplete Self-symbol because it is exclusively light and excludes the dark side of the Self (CW 9, ii, paras. 76-79), or that Christ is only one of many possible symbols of the Self. White felt that Jung had repudiated the idea of divine transcendence, although in a letter Jung notes that he simply would not discuss this issue since he did not want to make theological statements that are "beyond my scope" (1973, p. 386). White was also committed to the traditional belief in a God who is entirely self-sufficient, an idea that is incompatible with Jung's notion that human consciousness is necessary for the God that acts through the unconscious to differentiate itself—what Dourley (1995) calls a process of "mutual redemption" or the "redemptive reciprocity" of the human and the divine. Jung's exclusive focus on the "God within" is a gnostic sensibility that is also unacceptable to traditionalists.

In contrast to White, Jung could not accept the traditional Christian idea of evil as the *privatio boni*, or the absence of goodness, an idea that sees evil as a kind of non-being and not substantial in its own right. This became a major source of their estrangement. White believed that this idea was a purely conceptual approach to evil that did not deny its absolute reality, which was Jung's reading of the idea. White was committed to the traditional image of God as the *Summum Bonum*, the highest good, while Jung argued that both good and evil must originate in God, or in the God-image, since everything manifest in creation reflects its creator. Otherwise, humanity alone is the source of all evil, but this would not do justice to the gravity of evil and would diminish its power and reality. Jung accuses Christianity of being dualistic by splitting the divine and the demonic, and in contrast points to the unity of the Self, which he believes contains all opposites (1973, pp. 540-541). White also wanted to view the 1950 proclamation of the Assumption of Mary as a historical event, while for Jung its archetypal significance was much more significant (see fn. 31, p. 143).

The situation was made particularly difficult for White due to Jung's occasional lack of clarity about whether he was talking about the God-image or the divine itself. Although in general Jung tried to maintain this distinction, White seemed to find it unconvincing, and he accused Jung of straying into theology, which White thought was "an infelicitous excursion of a great scientist outside his orbit" (quoted in Charet, 1990, p. 425). Hill (2010) points out that these two men had very different intellectual heritages, and he believes that personal and cultural complexes interfered with their relationship. In the Jung-White letters, Hill finds evidence of unresolved father-son difficulties as well as different visions of reality.

Although Jung always insisted that he was reporting empirically observable psychological phenomena, several critics complained that he had overstepped the boundaries between theology and psychology. Thus, Martin Buber (1957, p. 80) accused Jung of "psychologism," as if Jung thought of God as nothing but an "autonomous psychic content," or "merely a psychic phenomenon," rather than as a Being to which the psychic content corresponds. (In fact, Jung said he could not be sure of the relationship between the image and a God beyond the psyche to which the image points.) Buber also accused Jung of gnostic leanings, and it is true that Jung much appreciated the gnostic stress on unmediated direct contact with the divine. However, a major difference between Jung and the ancient Gnostics is that Jung analyzed his experiences in terms of their source in the objective psyche.

Since the human and transpersonal levels of the psyche are inextricably linked, Jung saw total intimacy between the human and the divine. In contrast, for Buber, the divine is an absolute Other, a "super-psychic Being" (p. 134) or an "extra-psychic Being" (p. 135) who is transcendent and independent of the psyche. Notably however, to refer to God as the divine "Thou" does not diminish the implicit divine-human distance in Buber's theology, which is typical of theisms but antithetical to Jung's approach.

For Jung, what Buber calls God is experienced within the psyche as the Self, but Jung could never convince Buber of the reality of the psyche and of the idea that everything we experience, including the experience of God, is mediated by the psyche (CW 8, para. 680). If the psyche is real, images of the Self are real. Buber believes that Jung's approach makes the divine too immanent, ignoring the transcendent God beyond the psyche. He accuses Jung's psychology of developing a religion of "pure psychic immanence" (p. 84). (There is some truth to this accusation.) However, as Dourley (1992) points out, Buber's critique implies that "Buber himself clearly knew where the legitimate boundaries of human knowledge of the divine lay and how the divine and human interrelate in their knowledge of each other" (p. 32). For Jung, Buber was trying to talk about a level of divinity that is unknowable. It is however easy to understand why theologians talk about the transcendence of the divine when we remember that the psyche has archetypal forces within it that grip the ego and so induce the sense of possession by something beyond it. These forces are projected onto the gods and heavens of the various religious pantheons.

Jung points out in a letter to Buber that when we talk about experiences of the Self, we cannot establish whether such a psychic content is "dependent on and determined by the existence of a metaphysical[xxxi] deity. That is the concern of theology, revelation, and faith" (CW 18, para. 1507). Even when considering direct experiences of the divine, we can only work with images "which have arisen spontaneously or are sanctified by tradition" (CW 11, para. 558). Furthermore, Jung (CW 18, para. 1507) points out that it is not clear exactly which God-image Buber is talking about when he used the word "God." The Yhwh of the Hebrew Scriptures is not the same image as the Allah of Islam or the Father of the Christian Trinity, not to mention the deities of the East. How is one to know which of these have priority? For Jung, they are all manifestations of the Self, or "an autonomous psychic content that is defined in one way by [Buber] and in another by the Pope" (CW 18, para. 1507). Jung also makes the point that an absolute God with no connection to human beings would not concern us, but a God that is psychologically available is real and can reach us (CW 7, para. 394, note 6).

Buber also criticized Jung's notion that the Self consists of both good and evil, which Buber thought could lead to immorality. This critique ignores Jung's frequent statements about the importance of personal work on the shadow, which is visible from many points of view in our dreams. This work leads to a deeper understanding of the shadow than can be provided by traditional religion, since the shadow in dreams reveals unconscious aspects of the personality, whereas religious rituals of penance and confession only deal with conscious material.

Jung's approach to religion was criticized by psychologists as well as by theologians. Erich Fromm (1972, p. 93) objected to Jung's idea that the unconscious could be a source of revelation. Fromm believed that the unconscious should be seen only as another part of ourselves "as it really is, neither with horror nor with awe." This critique ignores the capacity of the unconscious to produce awesome imagery.

Jung and the Bible

The Bible was important to Jung's life and thought (Rollins, 1995). He believed that the Bible was also of great cultural importance even if we are not committed to one of the traditions to which it gave rise. He noted: "We must read the Bible or we shall not understand psychology. Our psychology, whole lives, our language and imagery are built upon the Bible" (1976, p. 156.) He said this because he believed that Western culture has been "unconsciously stamped" with Judeo-Christian ideas (1978, p. 342). Jung reads the Bible as a product of the psyche, not primarily as a historical or religious text, taking into account the presence of the unconscious both in its authors and also in the contemporary reader. Accordingly, he is very interested in the mythic, symbolic, and metaphorical level of the text, attempting to understand its continuing power and influence.

Jung points out in a letter that he had "studied the Gospels for a lifetime" (1975, p. 359). His preoccupation with the Bible is not surprising. He was raised in a Swiss parsonage. His father was a minister, and there were many clergy in his family. However, as a child he found the theology of his father's Church too unrelated to experience; it was "stale and hollow, like a tale told by someone who knows it only by hearsay and cannot quite believe it himself" (1963, p. 43). Jung's father suffered a tragic fate. "It was the tragedy of my youth to see my father cracking up before my eyes on the problem of his faith and dying an early death" (Jung, 1975, p. 257). Jung's father struggled to remain faithful to his Church, but he was trapped by its theology, without any direct experience of God. Based partly what happened to his father, Jung was able to say that: "So long as religion is only faith and outward form and the religious function is not experienced in our own souls, nothing of any importance has happened" (CW 12, para. 13). Jung realized that simply repeating dogmatic assertions is unhelpful. Worse, an exclusive focus on the Bible and the Church may actually get in the way of contact with the divine as a personal experience. Jung believed that it is a mistake to interpose the Church and the Bible between ourselves and the unconscious—we then pay more attention to what is said about God than to the direct experience of God.

Jung realized that belief in doctrine and dogma is not sufficient, because belief may crumble under the influence of adverse life conditions, and belief is constantly beset by doubt. Traditional beliefs do not necessarily keep pace with the development of the individual's level of consciousness or with the consciousness of the time in which he or she lives. Being required to believe dogma is antithetical to the spirit of our times. Dogma may have "no basis in any experience that would demonstrate its truth" (CW 18, p. 493).xxxii However, unlike belief, direct experience of the sacred is convincing. In his attitude to religion, Jung clearly felt that he was influenced by the unanswered questions of his parents and grandparents, "as if I had to complete, or perhaps continue, things which previous ages had left unfinished" (1963 p. 233).

Archetypal themes in religions

Different religions may contain similar archetypal themes. For example, most traditions have their own versions of themes such as salvation, redemption from evil, and the idea of an afterlife. At the beginning of the twentieth century, in *The Golden Bough*, James Frazer pointed out that many religious traditions contain recurrent motifs, such as a virgin birth, the impregnation of a human woman by a god, and a dying and resurrecting god who takes on himself the sins of others. Long before Jesus, this latter theme was seen in stories of the grain gods, Attis and Adonis. Frazer's explanation for such recurrent mythological themes was the idea that these stories diffused between cultures. For Jung, recurrent motifs in different traditions, such as the notion of a divine trinity, are found in many cultures because they are archetypal and thus irreducible.xxxiii These themes, and all the gods associated with them, arise from the same mythopoetic level of the psyche.

The gods and goddesses of antiquity were suppressed and demonized with the advent of Christianity, but they can now be understood to be the personification of archetypal psychological processes, just as the biblical Yhwh and Christ can now be seen to be carriers of the projection of the Self. As von Franz (1980) pointed out, when a new religious attitude arises, previous mythic images of the divine are seen as the projection of psychological material. Consistent with her idea, we see that as the Judeo-Christian tradition fades, its mythological basis becomes clearer and we see how the Self is projected onto its God-images. Jung (CW 18, para. 1638) believed that as long as we project our God-image onto an external figure such as Christ, the Self remains in "an unconscious condition" that only wakes up when external projections are withdrawn.

The Self as the *Unus Mundus* or the Implicate Order

Jung believes there is a realm of unity and wholeness in which all events are interconnected (CW 14, para. 662). This is the absolute level of the Self, prior to its differentiation within ordinary time and space. This dimension has been given several names; in antiquity it was called the Pleroma,[xxxiv] and in the medieval era it was called the *unus mundus*, or one world. In physics, this idea has re-appeared in the form of David Bohm's implicate order, a realm of unbroken wholeness out of which emerges our world of discreet entities.

In the pleromatic dimension, all historical processes exist outside of time and space as we experience them. For Jung therefore, linear time is a relative concept that can be complemented by the idea of simultaneous existence in the Pleroma. Historical processes with underlying archetypal themes emerge from the Pleroma and incarnate within our time in an "aperiodic sequence, repeated many times in an irregular pattern" (CW 11, para. 629). Jung gives the example of the mythic theme of the hostile brothers, exemplified by the stories of Romulus and Remus or Cain and Abel. This motif is repeated in many stories the world over. That is, there are eternal, archetypal processes within the Self that incarnate in the form of processes that we experience as they participate in the events of our individual lives. Within the realm of the ego, our usual spacetime world, these events seem to be separate from each other, rather than part of the underlying *unus mundus*, a medieval term meaning one world. "Everything that happens, however, happens in the same 'one world' and is part of it. For this reason, events must possess an a priori aspect of unity" (CW 14, para. 662). Jung points out that mandala symbolism is the "psychological equivalent" of the *unus mundus*, and "synchronicity is its parapsychological equivalent" (CW 14, para. 662). That is, synchronicity is the ego's experience of the reality of the *unus mundus* manifesting itself in time and space. Any form of numinous experience is brought about by the incarnation of a fragment of pleromatic wholeness that enters into human awareness.

David Bohm (1980) coined the term "implicate order" to describe a fundamental level of reality in which everything is connected. Bohm refers to our everyday reality, which seems to consist of separately existing objects, as the explicate order. It is a short step to suggest that what Bohm refers to as the implicate order corresponds to what Jung calls the Self as the totality, which unfolds within the personality in the form of discreet archetypal processes.

The notions of the *unus mundus* or the implicate order are synonymous with the realm of the Self before it incarnates into the empirical personality. During this process it appears in the form of discreet experiences and images because its underlying unity cannot be perceived by the ego, which by its nature divides reality into parts. Our individual psyches are aspects of the universal Consciousness of the Self. The notion of the absolute level of the Self as the implicate order is also a potential link between quantum physics and depth psychology, given the relationship between consciousness and the outcome of quantum processes such as the double slit experiment, in which the act of observation correlates with the behavior of particles. Here I am referring to the view that: "The world is quantum mechanical; we must learn to perceive it as such…Nothing exists but observations…The Universe is immaterial—mental and spiritual" (Henry, 2005, p 29). This seems to be counterintuitive, but quantum physics tells us that at its fundamental level the nature of the universe is unlike the way our cognitive systems have evolved to experience and comprehend it. This approach to the Self is an attempt to address the ancient problem of the one and the many, or how to find the unity that lies behind all the apparently individual things in the universe. The unifying factor is the Self, or ultimate Consciousness, which is the underlying ground of all being. The psyche is not just "the condition of all metaphysical reality, it *is* that reality" (CW 11, para. 836).

The question of the relationship of the one and the many is relevant to a debate within Jungian psychology that Hillman has seen as a "basic ideational conflict" (1971, p. 193). Some psychologists prefer to stress the particularity of psychological contents, in the process denying the importance of a single center (Miller, 1974; Hillman, 1971). Hillman (1971) disapproves of Jung's (CW 9, ii, para. 427) comment that the Self is correlated with monotheism, because Hillman prefers to stress the multiplicity of the psyche rather than its integration. However, I suggest it is a mistake to argue that the Self is analogous to the monotheistic God. Hillman implies that Jung thinks that the Self is a single center, which is clearly not the case. Monotheism only acknowledges one god, but Jung's idea of the Self as the totality means that the Self consists of all the archetypes; it is not one thing. Jung refers to the multiple archetypal centers in the psyche as "scintillae" or sparks (CW 8, para. 338). Each of these is an aspect of the Self, with its own voice and its own demands on the personality. The Self is the process that unifies the whole system, but at certain times of life any one of these archetypal processes may take center stage and dominate the course of the individual's life. The Self is an integrative process that helps to explain why, in a reasonably healthy individual, feelings, thoughts, memories, and attitudes towards oneself and the world are relatively coherent and stable over time. Such an individual has a stable sense of identity and is able to tolerate painful affects without fragmentation. The individual feels embodied and bounded. An integrated personality is capable of acknowledging that it contains multiple archetypal dominants or centers of interest. Each of these sparks of the Self can have its due without the personality fragmenting.

The archetypal constituents of the Self can be thought of as different types of information that shape behavior and feelings, each with their own characteristics. As the ordering principle or guiding spirit of the psyche, responsible for the psyche's sense of unity, the Self is roughly analogous to the gravity that holds several planets in consistent orbits. Gravity is not an entity, and neither is the Self.

The Post-modern Approach to the Self

Some authors do not consider the Self to be *a priori* or innate. A post-modern, constructivist position suggests that the Self is not a transcendent absolute, but it is built up from the interactive field between infant and mother, within a social context (Zinkin, 2008; Young-Eisendrath,1997). The Self is also claimed to be an emergent phenomenon that arises from the development of neural networks in the brain, which is a purely materialist view (Knox, 2003). Brain-based and constructivist approaches do not see the Self or the archetypes as primarily spiritual principles. Constructivist approaches make the Self seem something almost mechanical rather than the irreducible spiritual core of the person.

I suggest that, at best, brain-based, post-modern, and constructivist theories are referring to the personal sense of self, or the emergence of personhood and the sense of being an individual, but they do not refer to the transpersonal Self. Failure to make a distinction between the personal self and the transpersonal Self is a common source of confusion. The sense of self or the ego is "only a small part of the more deeply fundamental [S]elf" (CW 13, para. 51). The personal sense of self or the ego is an emergent phenomenon that arises out of the Self,[xxxv] but if the transpersonal Self is truly "the God within us," it is not formed by human interaction, and it cannot be reduced to the brain. Essentialist views are unpopular in the academy, but it seems to me that if the Self is truly an image of the divine, at best the only features of it that could be constructed might be its collective manifestations within a culture, which partially constrains the way the Self appears by confining it within particular religious traditions. However, the Self's symbolic appearances within the individual psyche may be completely unrelated to the subject's cultural background.

A range of post-modern authors find Jung's notion of the Self too essentialist, too fixed, and too totalizing. The materialist post-modern view rejects the idea that there is anything absolute within the individual, or that human beings have a spiritual essence. However, we are not all convinced by post-modern claims that reality is mainly a social and linguistic construction or that meaning in psychotherapy is only that which is jointly constituted by the psychotherapist and patient. There does seem to be a transpersonal component to the discovery of meaning, for example that which is given in dreams, in spite of the problem of interpretation. For many of us, there are objective spiritual realities that are not simply social or verbal constructs, and the Self is one of these.

At the moment there is no incontrovertible scientific support for viewing the psyche or consciousness as purely brain-based. This view is philosophically debatable (Kelly et al., 2007); we cannot say from whence the Self or the psyche arises. As Jung puts it: "The psyche is part of the innermost mystery of life," and whether the psyche "ever 'originated' at all is a metaphysical question and therefore unanswerable" (CW 9, i, para. 187). The Self acts as if we are contained within its atmosphere, and no limits can be set to it in space or time (CW 16). It follows that, for Jung, the Self (or the psyche) is not simply a product of the brain and cannot be reduced to the genes or to a social or linguistic construction.

We have empirical evidence of mystical experiences of unity that are remarkably similar across multiple traditions and historical periods. This uniformity suggests that they point to the same underlying Absolute, which argues against a radical contextualist position. Jung would postulate that these are experiences of the unitary nature of the Self. However, the skeptic would deny that these kinds of experiences are foundational or basic in the sense of providing certain knowledge, or that they can all be attributed to the Self, because we cannot prove there is such a thing. For the skeptic, the existence of the Self is a postulate based on experiences that might have other causes. To justify belief in the existence of the Self, one can only point to the cumulative experiences of many observers who attest to its manifestations within the psyche, in the hundred years since Jung developed the idea.

Another objection to the notion of the Self is that it is an isolated mind theory, which is now unpopular in psychoanalytic circles that prefer relational approaches to the formation of the mind. However, this critique is belied by the idea that the Self or the transpersonal psyche is a field in which we are all immersed; it is therefore not an isolated entity within the skull of the individual. What seem to be individual psyches are all contained within the Self, or better, what seems to be an individual mind is one manifestation of the Self, which is a supraordinate field of Consciousness that links all apparently separate minds. Jung is clear that it is the same Self in all of us, and he insists that we should not hypostatize the Self, which he says is not an encapsulated system. The Self is simply the word we use to describe the infinite Consciousness that is the source of individual consciousness and numinous experiences.

It is reasonable to equate the psyche with consciousness itself. This equivalence would prevent our multiplying entities unnecessarily. Because the Self is the totality of the psyche, it seems plausible to equate Jung's concept of the Self with the idea of pure Consciousness in the non-dual tradition in which Consciousness and world are inseparable. Although Jung remains dualistic in his insistence on the importance of the ego, he is also able to say that "this [S]elf is the world, if only a consciousness could see it" (CW 9, i, para. 46). The contents of the human levels of the psyche are simply parts of the total manifestation of Consciousness. By linking Jung's idea of the Self to infinite Consciousness, we see that the idea of the Self in Jung is closer to the Vedantic idea of the Ātman than it is to the Christian God-image. Jung (CW 16, para. 474) wrote that the Ātman forms "an exact parallel to the psychological idea of the [S]elf," although this comparison could be questioned (Corbett et al., 2016), partly because in the tradition of the Upanishads the Ātman is not said to manifest itself in the ways that Jung believes the Self appears. However, there is no reason to assume that it does not do so. Also, linking Jung's notion of the Self with the Hindu tradition is his comment that "what is meant by the [S]elf is not only in me but in all beings, like the Ātman, like Tao" (CW 10, para.

873), which corresponds to a similar statement in the Bhagavad Gita: "I am the same Self in all beings" (IX, 29).

Jung's Approach to the God-image in Relation to Kant

Jung's distinction between the divine itself and our image of God is partly based on the philosophy of Kant. Kant's approach distinguishes between phenomenal reality, which is the world as it appears to us through the senses, and noumenal reality or the world as it is in itself, prior to our experiencing it, which he thought is inaccessible and unknowable. According to Kant, we experience the world filtered through our innate mental processes or categories such as space and time. In this view, it is impossible for us to know the transcendent divine as it is in itself, which is beyond the grasp of our mind, since the mind limits what we can experience by imposing its own categories of experience onto our perception of reality. In Jung's reading of Kant, therefore, we can only know a God-image as it emerges in our experience, mediated by means of the psyche. We cannot know the Self as such, at the noumenal level prior to its manifestation as a symbol. To be strictly true to Kant, however, since we cannot say anything about the noumenal level of reality, we could not say that the noumenal level of the Self produces images of itself within conscious levels of the psyche, which is a central idea of Jung. If the Self itself is part of noumenal reality, we could not say that it affects us causally, and we could not say that a symbol points back to the noumenal level of the archetype "as such" (CW 8, para. 417). The relationship between the noumenal Self and the personal self remains a mystery, unless we adopt a non-dual perspective in which there is no personal self that is separate from the Self.

Jung insists that his observations about religion are grounded in empirical or phenomenological observations of the psyche, avoiding "metaphysical or philosophical considerations" (CW 11, para. 2). Jung is not entirely faithful to this claim, for example when he claims that the divine uses human consciousness to become conscious of the antinomies within its own nature, or that human beings are "indispensable for the completion of creation" because people give objective existence and meaning to the world, so that humanity is a second creator of the world (1965, p. 255-256). This is an anthropocentric attitude; the perceptions of other animals beside human beings may have their own validity. We cannot know whether unknowable ultimate reality would exist without a human consciousness to witness it.

Jung's Approach to the God-image in the Light of his Early Relationships

It is possible to correlate some aspects of Jung's approach to religion with features of his personal psychology. A correlation between a theorist's inner world and his metapsychology can often be discerned (Atwood et al., 2001). In this territory, one has to remember Shamdasani's (2005) warning not to present as biographical fact what is actually a selective arrangement of historical material in a way that corresponds to a preconceived theory. This task is made more difficult now that it is known that Aniela Jaffé, the editor of Jung's "autobiographical" *Memories, Dreams, Reflections,* modified Jung's original writing or added her own material to it (Elms, 1994), leading to a good deal of misunderstanding by subsequent biographers. Nevertheless, it is impossible to ignore the work of authors such as Rizzuto (1979), who have pointed out that one's God-image is radically affected by relational dynamics in one's family of origin, and these are mentioned in *Memories, Dreams, Reflections.*

Jung writes that his parents' marriage was troubled, and both parents were unhappy. He was disappointed in his father, whom he saw as suffering intensely from trying to adhere to the religion in which he was a minister. It seemed that his father did not quite believe what he was preaching, and he was depressed, irritable, and unfulfilled. Jung also had a disturbed relationship with his depressed and frightening mother, who was absent for several months when he was three years old, which he says was deeply troubling, and it made him "mistrustful when the word love was spoken" (1963, p. 23). This early abandonment, and the stressful atmosphere at home, may account for Jung's preoccupation with the inner world and the Self, at the expense of outer relationships. He says that he immersed himself in nature "and away from the whole human world" (p. 47). For Winnicott, this attitude was a defense against the lack of personality integration that resulted from maternal failure, and he believed much of Jung's work was a search for self-healing.

MacKenna (2000) believes that Jung's failure to deal with his early trauma prevented him from developing a God-image in which love and hate wrestle but love ultimately proves to be stronger. MacKenna suggests that Jung's poorly reconciled intrapsychic splits led to his projecting his unprocessed, primitive, repressed contents onto God, and he was unable to appreciate the potential of Christian symbols to hold together opposites such as God and humanity, good and evil, spirit and matter. However, it is arguable that in fact Christianity tends to split rather than unite these opposites, by seeing God as all good and valuing spirit more than matter. The fact that Jung had intrapsychic splits may simply have allowed him to be sensitive to the fact that the Self has both a light and a dark side. The fact that Jung identified with the suffering Job, combined with the plight of Jung's father, may have sensitized Jung to the injustice that Job suffered at the hands of Yhwh. Furthermore, even if Jung's writing on religion was driven by an attempt to heal his intrapsychic splits or to help his suffering father, none of this negates his findings. To discover the source of a discovery, or the appeal to its psychological origins, does not mean that the discovery is not valid—the genetic fallacy.

Jung postulates that the Self is an innate potential to experience a divinity. This potential is colored or obscured by the superimposition of a combination of personality, cultural, and familial factors, which helps to explain why certain types of traditional God-images (benevolent and loving or angry and punitive) are more appealing to some people than to others. However, we do not know the extent to which the individual is innately endowed with a specific image of the Self that is not only a function of early object relations and cultural factors. Or, as Leavy (1990) pointed out, the divine itself may contribute to the representation of the divine in the mind, but to insist on this possibility would take us out of the domain of pure psychology.

The Emerging God-image: Jung's View

In a letter, Jung notes: "It may take many hundreds of years for certain insights to mature" (1975, p. 563), implying that his ideas would take a long time to be accepted. Resistance to these ideas is to be expected, especially by traditional religionists who (correctly) see much of Jung's work as incompatible with Christianity. However, one could also see Jung's work as offering a re-vitalization of the Christian tradition, since he interprets Christian symbols in a new way. Hillman (1975, p. 228) even suggests that "we could reappraise Jung's life-long effort to reinterpret, not so much science, philosophy, society, or even psychiatry, but theology." At the very least, Jung's work reduces the need for conflict between competing monotheisms, since they all arise from the archetypal level of the psyche, so that none can claim superiority.

An advantage of Jung's approach is that it sees the divine as located within us, not in an external heaven, whereas for many religionists the nearest we can get to the inner divine is the notion of a soul, a spiritual element made by the creator, but which is not quite the divine itself. In Jung's approach, instead of having to relate to the divine through an institution such as the Church, or by means of a covenant, we have immediate access to the Self by working with dreams and synchronicities. This approach gives us individual symbolic material that does not make us dependent on the God-image dictated to us by an institution, which may be meaningless to the individual.

The God-image has been re-imagined multiple times during human history. Who has the ultimate authority to determine which of these re-imaginings is the most acceptable? Debates about the proper way to imagine God have led to many splits within the Christian tradition, such as the division of the church into Eastern and Western branches in 1054 CE, which was partly the result of conflict about who had the power to control the tradition's way of imagining God. Historically, the "official" Church position has been imposed using force. Theologians have often insisted that their ideas are normative for everyone, exemplifying one of the ways in which narcissistic pathology can become entangled with personal spirituality. In the early years of Christianity, the dominant image of God used analogies from the power of the Roman emperor—Jesus was portrayed as a pantocrator, a powerful emperor rather than the Shepherd of the Psalms, and the Church was increasing seen as part of the divine Kingdom. The process of re-imagining God has continued, leading to the development of innumerable branches of Christianity, *pari passu* accompanied by heresy hunters.

At the very beginning of the Christian era the collective God-image underwent a radical change, as the writer of the Epistle to the Hebrews asserted: "In many and various ways God spoke of old to our fathers by the prophets; but in these last days he has spoken to us by a Son" (Hebrews 1:1-2). This idea was scandalous to the Jewish religious establishment of its day, but every new way of thinking about God leads to accusations of heresy and sacrilege. Christianity is part of a long series of human attempts to relate to the transpersonal dimension in a new way, and these attempts are always limited by the current level of consciousness. Disobedience to existing norms is sometimes a necessary precursor of the development of new consciousness. Over the course of history, human images of God have been slowly but inexorably superseded, in spite of the inevitable resistance this produces because of the belief that one particular image of God is absolute and unchanging. Jung's notion of the Self, or the intra-psychic God-image, is a further—albeit radical—re-imagining of the traditional way of thinking about God. It too has given rise to horrified objections from traditionalists, but we have to formulate our God-image in a way that is meaningful to our own level of psychological and cultural development. Now that science has displaced God as an explanation for natural processes, and heaven is no longer "above," Jung has re-located the manifestations of the divine as an *a priori* image within the psyche. Jung's distinction between God and the intrapsychic image of God is important to the debate about the existence of God. Whether or not there is a God in the traditional theistic sense, the existence of intrapsychic God-images is undeniable.

There are rational arguments for the existence of God, but none of them are universally persuasive. Jung is firmly in the lineage of empirical arguments for God's existence, because Jung's approach is based on personal numinous experience and psychological reflection on that experience. The existence of the Judeo-Christian God is endlessly debatable, but the emergence of intrapsychic God-images and other numinous material is an incontrovertible observation regularly made by psychotherapists sensitive to Jung's approach.

The validity of the religious claims of Christianity and Judaism is tied to the God-image of those traditions. Christianity depends on the truth of propositions such as the revelation in Christ, the Incarnation, and the Resurrection. Judaism depends on belief in stories such as the revelation on Mt. Sinai, the giving of the covenant, and the Exodus. Jung's approach is not burdened by the need for this kind of belief, or by the attempt to literalize or historicize the kind of mythic imagery found in the Bible. Instead, Jung depends on the notion of an objective or transpersonal level of the psyche to describe what the monotheisms might refer to as the "mind of God." God-images and numinous experiences emerge from this level, and they are all open to interpretation rather than having a fixed meaning.

For Jung, gods and devils are all part of the psyche; they do not exist in a metaphysical realm such as heaven or hell. Jung's proposal recalls all our God-images to their common source in the objective psyche, so that none is privileged. They are all projected components of the unconscious. They cannot be used to validate the literal history of a particular tribe or to claim particular territory. As long as the monotheisms each claim that their particular God-image and their sacred texts are the only valid ones, having been revealed from a metaphysical domain, conflict and tribalism are inevitable.

Resistance to Jung's approach among adherents to a specific God-image is understandable. It is difficult to let go of a commitment to a long-standing tradition. Nevertheless, throughout history, reform movements periodically arise in an attempt to revivify the traditional religious stories by revising their meaning. But even the reformed versions of the monotheistic traditions do not acknowledge that their sacred texts contain images that arose from the mythopoetic level of the psyche, and not from a heavenly deity.

The biblical stories represent early attempts to express their authors' connection to the transpersonal dimension. Inevitably, because there were no other available models, these early attempts were colored by human projections and anthropomorphic imagery. However, we cannot mature spiritually as long as this unconscious attitude continues. The process of literalizing biblical stories has had several unpleasant side effects. It has reinforced tribalism and exclusivism, and the religious impulse has become entangled with human psychodynamics, leading to pathologies of narcissism, violence, and power among religionists. However, when we withdraw our idealized projections from the traditional biblical stories, with nothing to replace this mythology, our spirituality may seem to be adrift with no anchor. Without some kind of connection to the Self we are left with an apparently isolated ego consciousness. We are then separated from the divinity in our own depths.

A further risk of being separated from conscious participation in the spirit of the depths is that this archetypal power does not go away; rather, our capacity for making religion is channeled into disguised or even perverted forms, forming "politico-social delusional systems" (CW 9, i, para. 49). That is, some kind of archetypally fueled "ism" may take hold of the person or of an entire society, as human history shows. There is then a risk of unconscious possession by forces whose religious nature is not recognized, with disastrous consequences such as political or religious absolutes.

In Jung's model, religion is not about connection to an external deity who imposes his will on people by issuing commandments, nor is it about a deity who demands a human sacrifice to redeem his own creation. For Jung, religion does not require commitment to a specific tradition or hierarchy or belief in dogma or literalism. Religion means connecting the human levels of the psyche with its transpersonal depths. This is potentially a natural process in which the experience of the Self is mediated by dreams, visions, synchronistic events, or any manifestation of the transpersonal unconscious. Jung's approach addresses the contemporary situation in which we are "keenly aware of the weakening of the Church and the precariousness of its dogmatic assumptions. To counter this, the Church recommends more faith...the seat of faith, however, is not consciousness but spontaneous religious experience, which brings the individual's faith into immediate relation with God" (CW 10, para. 563).

Jung has described the seeds of a new myth of God. This approach is largely incompatible with traditional monotheism, so it is likely to evoke considerable resistance. However, given the accelerating cultural skepticism about traditional religion, the progress of the new myth is likely to be inexorable even if it is slow. It is currently being lived out in the therapeutic situation, when the therapeutic couple study the emergence of the Self in whatever form it takes. Commonly this is achieved by working with dreams, because they emerge from the same source that gives rise to all religious experience, namely the Self or the objective psyche. Imagery from dreams allow us direct symbolic contact with the Self, in a manner that is often more emotionally powerful than traditional religious symbols, because dream images are immediately immanent. This process allows the individual to develop a personal form of connection to the Self, whereas the collective myth into which one was born may actually impede this connection, if one is unconsciously confined to received doctrine and dogma. Attention to the objective psyche has a liberating effect by allowing the development of a personal instead of a collective myth.

Jung's approach to religion is an evolutionary development in the unfolding development of the Western God-image. The multiple Canaanite deities mentioned in the Hebrew Scriptures evolved into the exclusive worship of the biblical Yhwh, who later became God the Father of Christianity. The process was followed by the appearance of Christ and the Holy Ghost, and finally "we are confronted with the aspect revealed through the manifestations of the unconscious" (Jung, 1975, p. 316). The truly radical nature of Jung's proposal is summarized in his statement that:

> We have become participants of the divine life and we have to assume a new responsibility, viz. the continuation of the divine self-realization, which expresses itself in the task of our individuation…Instead of the propitiating praise to an unpredictable king or the child's praise to a loving father, the responsible living and fulfilling of the divine will in us will be our form of worship and of commerce with God. (1975, p.316)

If one has experienced the Self in one of the ways Jung describes, one does not need to "believe" in the classical theistic descriptions of the divine. One has been given an irrefutable experience that may be entirely different than the traditional imagery. However, traditional questions about an afterlife or the existence of an objective moral order are not addressed by Jung's approach.

Jung's stress on a wide range of images of God implies an unknowable reality or spiritual source from which they arise. The fact that the Self can appear in so many ways means that none of them is a definitive expression of the Self, which is beyond image. The nature of this source is unknowable, but having experienced it, one may have faith in the source simply because one is aware of its presence without any particular image being central or ultimate. Because of this, our spirituality retains a sense of mystery.

i An analogy might be the acquisition of language by children; we all have this ability, but the local language is the one that is learned.

ii Based on the comparative iconography of many traditions, Jung believed that circles and spheres are ancient symbols of infinity, completion, heaven, or the divine (CW 11, para. 418) because they are perfect shapes with no beginning and no end. Symbols of quaternity or fourness, such as squares and cubes, are incarnate or earthly symbols of stability and wholeness (para. 101) because they refer to the earth's four directions, four seasons, four winds, four elements, and so on. The square implies limitation, structure, and form, unlike the endless circle. The dream motif of alternately squaring the circle implies the mutual reciprocity of heaven and earth, or their union in a higher synthesis.

iii The editors of Jung's Collected Works chose to use the lower-case letter "s" to avoid the implication that Jung was writing about religion. I have added the upper-case S to indicate that he was not referring to the personal self.

iv Visionary experiences such as those of Moses or St. Paul are psychological processes that escape their internal containment and appear to come from outside. Perhaps their affective intensity is responsible for this externalization. Thus, Moses's vision of the burning bush might represent the projection of his intense spiritual passion. Alternatively, at the level of the experience there is no inside-outside distinction.

v Jung even goes so far as to say that: "Not only does the psyche exist, it is existence itself" (CW 11, para. 18). He also sounds like a philosophical idealist when he says that "we know of matter only in so far as we perceive psychic images mediated by the senses" (ibid., para. 16).

vi According to Heisig (1979, p. 208), von Franz believed that Jung was "personally convinced that God was an objective reality transcendent to the psyche." Jung based his statements about God on Kant's notion that we cannot know God or noumenal reality directly, because of the limitations imposed on us by our mind, which imposes its own categories on our perception of reality. Therefore, metaphysical certainty is impossible. Accordingly, Jung thinks we cannot experience the Self except as it appears by means of the psyche, but this does not deny the possibility of God as an ontological reality beyond our capacity to perceive.

vii Jung believed that "everything men assert about God is twaddle, for no man can know God" (1975, p. 377). Instead, he proposes that "we take all talk of god as mythological" (p. 262). In order to understand religious imagery, Jung felt that today, a psychological approach is preferable to a theological approach. His project was in part to take religious forms of thought "that have become historically fixed, to try to melt them down again and pour them into molds of immediate experience" (CW 11, para. 148).

viii It is, however, true that in his private correspondence, Jung does make metaphysical speculations, for example when he refers to archetypes as "organs (tools) of God" (Jung, 1976, p. 130).

ix This experience looks like an image of the repudiation of the church. It has been interpreted as an attack of Oedipal rage against Jung's father or his father's institution, since his father was a minister (Rieff, 1966). Tacey (2010) believes that this Freudian reduction is "a cheap attack" on Jung's vision, because "instead of seeking to murder the father, he seeks to redeem the father by going beyond him" (p. 132). As many of us do, Jung tried to address his father's unsolved problems with religion.

x Jung approaches but does not embrace the non-dual religious traditions that see Consciousness as primary and see God and humanity as a unity. He expresses a non-dual sensibility when he says that "God is Reality itself and therefore last but not least man" (CW 11, para. 631), and when he says that "this Self is the world if only a consciousness could see it" (CW 9, i, para. 46). However, he is unwilling to relinquish the importance of the ego, which he sees as essential for consciousness. (See note xiii below.)

xi For example, the Roman Catholic tradition provides a fixed mythic context with its own rituals but discourages any departure from this imagery. This tradition requires obedience to only one form of spirituality. The Protestant tradition has removed much of its ritual and mythic imagery but does not encourage a mythic or a personal symbolic sensibility.

xii There is an almost inevitable tendency in the psychological literature to reify the ego. Non-dual philosophy has clearly revealed the fallacy of this tendency, showing that the ego is not a discreet entity; it is an aspect of the Self conditioned by individual circumstances. However, the term "ego" is useful for clinical and heuristic purposes as a shorthand term for what *seems to be* individual consciousness.

xiii Jung (mistakenly) believed that there cannot be consciousness without an ego. Thus, he insists that ego functions such as "exclusion, selection, and discrimination are the root and essence of everything that lays claim to the name 'consciousness'" (CW 9, i, para. 520). I think he errs in assuming that consciousness must be identified with ego-consciousness, since the Self is Consciousness. Exclusion and selection are simply the result of differences within a totality.

xiv The Jungian literature often uses the term "ego-Self axis" in a manner that treats ego and Self as if they were different. However, if the Self is the totality of the psyche this cannot be the case. It is also a mistake to think of the Self as "an" archetype among others; the Self is supraordinate. As Colman (2006) points out, the fact that the Self appears in personified or symbolic form does not mean it is a separate personality in conflict with the ego. That would mean that the "inexpressible mystery of the All is scaled down into something more like an internal object relationship" (p. 163). Colman makes the important point that treating the Self as a separate consciousness is the result of conceptual confusion. The Self is an unknown "other" only from the point of view of conscious experience.

xv In *Memories, Dreams, Reflections*, Jung describes two dreams that suggest that the unconscious or the Self "is the generator of the empirical personality" (p. 324). One is a dream of a UFO that projects Jung's existence, clearly showing that the ego emerges as a manifestation or emanation of the Self. The other is the dream of a yogi who is meditating Jung's existence; Jung is the dream of the Yogi. However, if the Yogi represents the Self, the dream suggests that the Self is conscious of the ego, which tends to contravene Jung's notion (discussed later) that the Self requires the ego to become conscious of itself.

xvi Neumann (Jung & Neumann, 2015, p. 134) wrote that: "The incarnation is already pre-existent in the ego-Self unity in which the numinous ego-nucleus of the ego has the capacity for consciousness." However, even given that this is true at the very beginning of ego development, for Jung the incarnation of the Self is a continuous process over the course of one's life.

xvii Jung's stress on the importance of the ego for individuation contrasts with Eastern ideas that the ego is an obstacle to enlightenment. This difference makes it clear that the concepts of individuation and enlightenment reflect different processes and goals that cannot easily be conflated.

xviii This idea is found in the work of mystics such as Jacob Boehme (Dourley, 2001).

xix There are several ways in which Jungian work is not a religion in any organized or traditional sense. This work values individual attention to material arising from the unconscious but does not pay much attention to community or to practices such as ritual and prayer, except in the form of active imagination and the rituals of psychotherapy. Jungian work makes values and morality largely a matter of personal choice rather than the dictates of a transcendent divinity—although Jung felt that the Self does have an innate moral function. In Jung's model, religion tends to become private, with no ordained authority.

xx It is important to note that Jung always insisted that in *Answer to Job* he was talking about the God-image and not the divine itself (1975, p. 260), but it is difficult to remember this distinction when reading the text, which uses the words "God" or "Yahweh" much more often than the phrase "God-image."

xxi At this stage of the tradition, a "satan" is a member of the heavenly court, not the Satan of later theological speculation.

xxii Job had various indicators of significant narcissistic pathology, seen for example when he lists all the ways in which he was very important in the community, where he "sat as a chief/ and I dwelt like a king among his troops" (Job. 29:25). Job's suffering transformed this grandiose aspect of his personality. (The psychology of *The Book of Job* is discussed in more detail in Corbett, 2007).

xxiii The term "liminal" refers to the most difficult, middle period of a process of transition, when the subject is being initiated into a new level of consciousness (Corbett, 2015).

xxiv From a non-dual point of view, the ego can only reflect the consciousness of the Self, so paradoxically the Self is the ultimate Subject that experiences its own symbolic manifestations.

xxv Although the body and the feminine are making a cultural come-back, the notion of the dark side of the God-image has not yet captured the imagination of the public even though theologians are aware of it (e.g., Penchansky, 1995).

xxvi It is unfortunate that Edinger's (2015, p.102) discussion of the transformation of the Trinitarian God-image into a quaternity by the addition of Mary includes the idea that symbolically "she brings the attributes of matter, flesh, and humanity—sinful humanity." He thereby hints at the patriarchal attitude that equates matter with sin. Obviously, the recognition of matter or a feminine aspect of the Godhead does not need to imply that these have any necessary association with evil. To add both the principle of evil and the feminine to the Trinity would constitute a symbol with five components rather than a quaternity model.

xxvii In the Hebrew Bible and in early Christianity, dreams were considered to be important sources of divine (or demonic) revelation. The Hebrew patriarchs were often given direction or prophecies in dreams, although the wisdom literature, such as Ecclesiasticus, warned that dreams may be the instruments of false prophets. One reason that attention to dreams faded from the Christian tradition was that in about 375 CE, while translating the Bible into Latin, Saint Jerome had a frightening dream in which he was punished for preferring pagan authors to Christian literature. As a result, he translated the prohibition against fortune telling in Leviticus 19: 26 and Deuteronomy 18: 10 as a prohibition against working with dreams. Jerome's translation was generally accepted for the next 1500 years, so the use of dreams for the purposes of spiritual guidance fell out of favor (Kelsey, 1991). Dreams are still important in contemporary Islamic life, where "true dreams" carry religious significance.

xxviii The term *coincidentia oppositorum* means the coincidence or union of opposites. According to Henderson (2010) Jung appears to have misunderstood or oversimplified Nicholas of Cusa's idea of the *coincidentia oppositorum*; for Cusa, God was beyond the coincidence of opposites. Jung sometimes mistakenly attributed the term "*complexio oppositorum*" to Cusa. The notion of the tension of opposites such as matter and spirit, and the problem of how to unite such opposites, was a life-long preoccupation for Jung. He states that conflict is an essential aspect of the experience of the Self, or "the way to the Self begins with conflict" (CW 12, para. 259). This happens in part when the Self makes contradictory demands on the person, pulling the ego in opposite directions.

xxix The Christian doctrine of *privatio boni* asserts that evil is not substantial but is only the absence of goodness. Jung thought this idea was merely a philosophical invention. In his mind, the idea does not give due weight to evil, which cannot be attributed solely to human beings, since the Self has a dark side. However, the notion of the dark side of God is antithetical to Christian theology that sees God as entirely good.

xxx Thomism refers to the work of St. Thomas Aquinas, who synthesized Christian thought and Greek philosophy in the thirteenth century. Until Vatican 2, Thomism was widely regarded as the official philosophy of the Roman Catholic Church.

[xxxi] By "metaphysical" Jung means ideas for which empirical, objective evidence in the scientific sense cannot be obtained.

[xxxii] Jung believed that dogma expresses and mediates the archetypal level of the unconscious in symbolic and mythic form, but the imagery of dogma is often not relevant or meaningful to the modern individual. Dogmas lose their symbolic importance if they are taken too literally. The 1950 dogma of the Assumption of Mary, according to Jung, should not be interpreted simply as a historical event but as a symbolic or mythic statement about the elevation of the importance of the archetypal feminine, which illustrates the "compensatory activity of the living archetype forcing its way into consciousness" (1973, p. 567-568). This dogma compensates an exclusively masculine God-image by integrating the feminine principle into it.

[xxxiii] Examples are the Sumerian Anu, Bel, and Ea, the Babylonian Sin, Ishtar, and Shamash or the Egyptian Osiris, Isis, and Horus.

[xxxiv] The word Pleroma means fullness. It is used in the New Testament and among the Gnostics to mean the realm of divine perfection. Jung used the word to refer to a dimension beyond time, space, and causality, a state of absolute unity or potential out of which anything might arise. He also refers to God as the Pleroma in *The Red Book*, (p. 348), where, in the *Seven Sermons to the Dead*, he says that "In the Pleroma there is nothing and everything…The Pleroma penetrates the created world as the sunlight penetrates the air everywhere" (p. 347).

[xxxv] Psychoanalytic self-psychologists think of the personal self as an intrapsychic structure that is built up in development and endures through time. They distinguish this conceptual structure from the self in the ontological sense, thought of as if it were an entity, whose existence is hard to prove. This level is the self as experiencer or agent that is "more than simply a content, structure, or experience within the mental apparatus" (Suler, 1993, p. 41). This ontological level is not analyzable and might be closer to Jung's notion of the Self, which is *a priori* and not purely personal. (For a discussion of some differences between the self in Kohut and Jung, see Corbett, 1989).

CHAPTER 3

The God-image in Archaic Religions and in Antiquity

The Development of Early Religion

Archaic forms of religion developed with the very beginning of the human species, which emerged about 300,000 years ago. Life was precarious for early hominins,[i] who were vulnerable to natural forces such as storms, disease, or the availability of food. Their need for harmony with nature was therefore particularly important. We can imagine that they were deeply concerned with the mysteries of climate, life, death, and fertility, and we can understand their amazement at the capacity of life to regenerate and renew itself. It is not surprising that they would sense an uncanny, supernatural order behind this ability, and that they were concerned with their relationship to the powers of this unseen dimension, which could be helpful or destructive. Over the course of human history, this sense or intuition of a mysterious background to life evolved into a wide range of god-images. This development became important enough for McNamara (2009) to suggest that belief in the existence of gods is one of the features that most differentiates *Homo sapiens* from our early hominin ancestors.

There is a range of explanations for the development of our belief in gods. Diel (1986) suggests that religion arose because early humans felt helpless in the face of nature, a state of mind he refers to as sacred fear, which he believes they tried to overcome by spiritualizing it, leading to the development of myths and religion. For Diel therefore, God is "the personified symbol of the mystery of creation" (p. 126). The materialist view is that spirituality was purely a function of the development of the brain (McNamara, 2009), while Jung would suggest that the notion of a sacred power is intrinsic to the psyche by virtue of the presence of the Self, so the development of religion was inevitable.

Evidence for the existence and nature of religion among our prehistoric ancestors arose from various sources. Prehistorians use ethnological parallels, or similarities between archaic religions that still exist, and Paleolithic (Stone Age) practices. This approach assumes that the practices of surviving hunter-gatherer or foraging cultures are similar to those of the remote past, although this assumption does not allow for development within the surviving cultures and ignores the influence of missionaries and other forms of contact with modernity. Nevertheless, in recent times, hunter-gathers in different areas of the world have been shown to have much in common; they live in similar size groups of up to 150 people and move from place to place at different times of the year in search of animals. Specialized members of the group may enter altered states of consciousness, using a variety of means such as local psychoactive plants or ritual practices. These shamanic practitioners become expert at contacting helpful animal spirits, either to heal the sick or to discern the movements of animals for the hunt. Because these practices seem primitive to moderns, it has been assumed that people living in early pre-technological societies were more intellectually limited than we are. However, since their brains had evolved to the same state as ours, this is probably not the case.

The theory of Naturism, proposed by Max Müller (1823-1900), suggested that early religion arose from the personification and worship of phenomena such as lightening, the sun and moon, and other manifestations of nature's power. It would be a short step to imagine that destructive natural forces such as disease are the result of retribution when these forces are seen as gods. Müller, a philologist, also traced the origin of religion to an innate sense of the divine in the human mind, a kind of consciousness of the infinite. Müller believed that the local names for the gods could all be traced to their origin in human languages; thus, if the sun was worshipped and the word for sun was a masculine noun in a particular language, the sun-god was then thought of as a male being with the necessary supernatural powers.

Müller's Naturism fell out of favor because it was thought to oversimplify early religion. In 1871, the anthropologist Edward Tylor (1832-1917) published his influential *Primitive Culture*, which suggested that the original or primordial form of religion was Animism, the idea that a spiritual or animating principle explains the difference between a live and a dead body. This principle also explains the movement of natural phenomena such as trees, wind, and rain, which seem to be endowed with vitality. Even inanimate objects may be inhabited with spirits or souls. At times, natural phenomena were not worshipped in their own right, but they were considered to point to a background spiritual force. Tylor believed that in this way early religion tried to explain phenomena that are common but difficult to explain. Tylor saw dreams as a major source of religious ideas; dreams seemed to be evidence of the existence of a spiritual realm. The dream of an ancestor indicated that the ancestor still existed, so there had to be a realm of the spirits or an afterlife where the ancestors lived. This provides evidence for the immortality of the soul. Tylor thought that archaic religions had many spirits but no specific god-image. He suggested that the notion that an object such as a tree has a spirit gradually evolved into the notion that a forest god collectively controlled all trees, leading to early polytheism. This theory does not account for the cultural spread of phenomena such as religious ritual and beliefs, but it is otherwise consistent with some contemporary accounts of religion. There remain religious traditions that believe in a world inhabited by spirits.

In all early religions, people believed that the spirits that populate the world may produce physical effects, bringing good or bad fortune. Over time, stories about the effects of particular spirits, reputed to have brought success in the harvest or in war, became magnified with repeated telling until they were thought of as gods, acquiring more and more power. To understand such belief in spirits, Herbert Spencer (1820-1903) developed his Ghost Theory of religious belief. This suggests that people have a spirit identity, which may leave the body during dreams and leaves the body permanently at death. The spirits of ancestors, medicine men, and famous tribal leaders appear in the form of ghosts, which eventually came to be worshipped as gods. Ghosts inspire fear, which inspires religious belief. Spencer thought that ancestor worship is the root of religion. Eventually the Ghost Theory was seen to be too simplistic and lacking in evidence; it was difficult to prove that prehistoric people thought in this way, and the leap from ghosts to gods was based on conjecture.

Related to Animism is the theory of Totemism, developed by W. Robertson Smith in the late nineteenth century. This theory suggests that before the emergence of anthropomorphic gods, groups of human beings felt a kinship with a specific animal. This animal was treated as if it were a relative of the members of its particular clan. Each clan or sub-group within a larger tribe is identified with its own animal, a totem that is considered to be sacred. It may be killed and eaten only on specific religious occasions for ritual, sacrificial purposes. This theory, too, was shown to have little empirical evidence, though it became important to Freud's *Totem and Taboo*. Totemism is absent from many archaic religions, and although some theorists believed that Totemism would sustain social cohesion, in practice it is found to divide groups with different totems as much as it unites their society.

All these early theories of the development of religion now seem to be oversimplified, because they ignore the human psychological need to believe and various evolutionary and societal factors that affect the development of religion. But there is no doubt that early people had some kind of religion, represented for example by the extraordinary Paleolithic cave paintings of animals found in France, Spain, and Indonesia. The earliest images have been dated (with some uncertainty) to about 44, 000 BCE, although there are estimates that some images were made 66, 000 years ago by Neanderthals (Appenzeller, 2018). These images are found in caves that reach deeply into the earth and are very difficult to access. There is a range of explanation for them. The simplest is that these images are entoptic, meaning that they are subjective visual phenomena that originate within the eye, because being in darkness predisposes the individual to see imagery. Another prevailing theory (Clottes, 2008) is that these caves were essentially temples, used for ritual purposes by shamans who found that the caves' darkness allowed sensory deprivation and disorientation that predisposed to trance states. The shamans may have identified with the animals of the hunt, or they may have petitioned whatever they believed to be controlling the herds they hunted. The animals in these paintings often seem to hang in the air rather than being grounded, so they may represent animal spirits, while some of the figures seem to be dancing. In the Caverne des Trois Frères in Ariège, France, a horned anthropoid figure seems to be clothed in the skin of a stag, and wears antlers. The figure's eyes are large, furry, and penetrating, and it has a long tongue or beard. He seems to be holding a musical instrument and is surrounded by animals. He looks as if he is performing a ritual dance in which he mimics the movement of an animal. He is often referred to as the Dancing Sorcerer.[ii] One of the important implications of such images is that our early ancestors had a symbolic capacity that allowed them to feel connected to the spiritual realm.

THE GOD-IMAGE IN ARCHAIC RELIGIONS AND IN ANTIQUITY | 149

By Clottes, J.Y. & D. Lewis-Williams, Public domain, via Wikimedia Commons

Since various cave paintings depict people dressed in animal skins, perhaps early people employed a form of sympathetic magic to influence the hunt. This means that they acted out or mimicked the hunt they wished to have, or this seemed to be a way to renew the supply of animals. Perhaps they were attempting to influence the spiritual forces they believed to be operating. The caves seem to have functioned as a sacred space for ritual practices, and the images give the strong impression of an underlying mythology, but what that might have been remains an enigma. There are alternative theories about Paleolithic cave art; rather than having religious significance it can be seen as nothing more than early art for the sake of art, or early attempts at abstract representation of the world. However, this idea is not consistent with the frequency of images found in the most inaccessible parts of the cave, which required immense effort to reach, using primitive lamps, suggesting that they were more than merely decorative. Bone flutes have also been found in these caves, suggesting that music was involved in ritual practices. The fact that these caves were so deep and dark may have given rise to the notion of an underworld, which is found in many religious systems.

There is also evidence, albeit controversial, of the worship of bears among Neandertal and Paleolithic populations. Bear skulls on top of stone blocks that look like altars have been found in the Chauvet cave. Bears may have been sacrificed to a deity. Skulls and long bones of cave bears have been found enshrined in stone chests or wall niches in caves around Europe. Perhaps bone symbolized existence after death because it is lasting, so the preservation and worship of bear bones may have been thought to generate new bear life.

Some of the earliest evidence for religious belief is found in ancient burial practices among *Homo sapiens* and Neanderthals of the Middle and Upper Paleolithic period.[iii] Careful burial of the dead was practiced between 40,000 and 130,000 years ago. Belief in an afterlife is suggested by the practice of burying food, jewelry, shells, mammoth ivory beads, animal bones, animal skins, utensils, or stone tools with the body. These artefacts must have taken time and effort to produce, and such elaborate burials imply that these early people believed they would be of use in an afterlife. It seems to have been assumed that a man who hunted during his life would continue to hunt in the afterlife. The body was sometimes placed in a posture of sleep or in a fetal position, as if it was returned to the womb, often in an east-west orientation, perhaps suggesting belief in the possibility of survival after death or rebirth. Sometimes the body was painted with red ochre, which presumably had symbolic associations to blood, life, and animating power. One burial site at Sungir, in Russia, dated to about 34,000 years ago, contained spears, figurines, and the hollowed-out shaft of a woman's femur packed with red ochre (Trinkaus et al., 2014). The occasional decapitation of the body, or the placement of heavy stones upon it, suggest belief that the spirit might return. Some nomadic hunters carried with them the skulls of their departed kin, perhaps believing that the skull represented the seat of life.

The fact that people were buried within residential areas among Paleolithic populations suggests continuing concern for the dead or the wish to stay connected to them. This practice is also suggested in Paleolithic practices such as burial under the floor of the cave in which people lived, as if the dead were still part of the family, still existing in spirit form. It may have been assumed that the ancestors could intercede on behalf of the living. Some of these ancestors may have evolved into deities. Veneration of ancestors has long been practiced by hunter-gatherer societies and continues in some contemporary religions.

The French philosopher Lucien Lévy-Brühl (1857-1939) suggested that early people used a kind of pre-logical thinking. He believed that the main feature of archaic religion is the absence of any sharp boundary between the natural world and the spiritual world. He suggested that early human beings did not clearly distinguish themselves from their environment, a phenomenon he referred to as *participation mystique*. Thus, inanimate objects might be seen to have intentions, so this phenomenon is closely tied to projection. This theory was criticized by anthropologists who denied that early people think differently than moderns. Lévy-Brühl later retracted the theory and it has remained controversial. The idea remained important to Jung (CW 10), who believed that individuals may sometimes have an unconscious, projected sense of identity with an object in the world, such a holy object, or with another person—a mechanism that is now referred to as projective identification. In this way, we color our experience of the outer world with our inner world.

Hunter-gathering gave way to agriculture and settlements in the emerging Neolithic period, between 10,000-12,500 years ago, varying with the geographical area. This development led to the domestication of plants and animals. The reason for this change is not clear; it may have been due to an increasingly warmer and more stable climate following an ice age. One of the effects of the agricultural revolution was to change religious thinking. Agriculturalists became concerned with the spirit powers that affected the growth of their crops, so the development of farming may have promoted the development of religion. An alternative theory is that farming developed because of the necessity to feed communities who were building ancient megalithic ceremonial sites such as Göbekli Tepe in Turkey (see note v).

The development of agriculture, farming, and animal husbandry changed people's religious attention from concern with the hunt to the importance of crop cycles and the seasons of nature. These concerns led to the appearance of mythologies of grain gods who die in the winter and are resurrected in the spring. Inevitably, given the human tendency to anthropomorphize, to project human traits onto the gods and imagine that the gods think and feel as we do (a Theory of Mind[iv]), these gods were assumed to have human characteristics, both good and bad.

The concept of dying and resurrecting grain gods such as the Phrygian Attis, the Assyrian Adonis, and the Sumerian Tammuz suggests the belief that because plant life comes from a spiritual source, one could partake of the divine life by eating the body of the god in the form of grain. This notion became important in Christianity. The cycles of nature gave rise to the religion of a mother goddess, an archetypal figure of the divine feminine (Sjöö & Mor, 1987; Neumann, 1963), for whom the earth was a womb from which life arose again and again. Settled agricultural villages gave rise to organized societies with a division of labor, including religious specialists who it was believed could talk to the gods on behalf of the community. Temples were built in which to house the gods.

It is not surprising that early agriculturalists would develop a notion of life after death, given the fact that crops appear to die but reappear at a later time. In India, this reappearance may have given rise to the notion of reincarnation. With the rise of agriculture, planting and harvesting festivals (or rituals) became important to ensure the continuity of life cycles. Sometimes, the fertility of the fields seemed to require a blood sacrifice, as if this would replenish the life and fertility within the soil. Sacrifice to the gods seemed to be necessary because it was assumed that the gods needed some reciprocity for their gifts to humans, or the gods needed to be placated or implored to send a good harvest.

Megalithic structures such as Stonehenge and Avebury in England or Göbekli Tepe in modern Turkey were first built in the Neolithic period.[v] Similar large stone structures can be found throughout Europe. There are many theories about the reason for their existence. They must have been of great importance, since they required immense labor and organization to construct. These megaliths may have been early temples, places of sacrifice, tombs, monuments to the ancestors, or astronomical observation devices that would indicate propitious times for planting. The imperishable nature of stone must have been very suggestive and impressive to these builders; stone is so different than flesh that stone seems to be associated with eternity, immortality, power, lack of change, the absoluteness of being, and hence divinity. Thus, Eliade (1957) shows how stones may act as hierophanies, or manifestations of the sacred, and the worship of sacred stones is found in many religious traditions. Standing stones are often thought to be endowed with the ability to confer fertility. Egyptian pyramids are part of the archetypal connection between death, divinity, immortality, and stone. The building of huge cathedrals is part of that tradition.

Archaic religion was also associated with early metallurgy, which may have begun with metal found in meteorites, which must have been awe-inspiring to early humans since meteorites seem to come from the heavens as a divine gift (Eliade, 1978). Early people made tools from this metal, which was so fascinating to them that it seemed to have a sacred power, and a cluster of myths, taboos, and rituals developed around metal and those who worked with it. Each metal was attributed with its own qualities; gold became a symbol of divinity and immortality because of its indestructible nature and its resistance to corrosion; iron was thought to protect against demonic forces or the evil eye, and so on. Accordingly, smiths and metallurgists had an important place in the community, and gods of metals and metallurgy appeared in many pantheons. Metals seemed to be gestated within Mother Earth. "A common background theme was that heavenly or volcanic fire impregnated Mother Earth, causing her to bear metals" (Carmody, 1981, p. 48). All metals were thought to eventually turn into gold if left alone to gestate in the earth.

The civilizations that began in Mesopotamia between about 6000 and 3000 years ago had a strong religious foundation, for example in Sumer (present day Iraq). These cities may have originally begun as religious centers. Pictographic and cuneiform writing developed among the Sumerians, along with artistry in wood, metals, and jewelry. The plough, the wheel, and the chariot appeared. An influential priestly class arose, and the temple became very important in the local economy, leading to an intertwining of religion and politics. The king of the city was often imagined to have a semi-divine status, since he was considered to be a descendent of the gods and goddesses of the city. The Sumerian pantheon included hundreds of gods, and the function of the temple was to serve them. They were organized into a hierarchy that mimicked the political hierarch of the city. These deities and their associated mythology provided some of the background for biblical mythology.

Early Goddess Traditions

The notion of a deity is often said to have begun with belief in a great goddess or earth mother who was the source of life, birth, and death (Stone, 1976; Sjöö & Mor, 1987). The precursors of the worship of the goddess or the Great Mother are thought to be found in stone and clay carvings of female figures about 25,000 years old, such as the Venus of Willendorf. There are many similar figurines, which typically emphasize the maternal aspects of the body such as large breasts and hips, but none have any specific facial features. They have been found in regions as far apart as Spain, Germany, France, Austria, and Russia. They may have been objects of worship or simply fertility icons. Imposing female figures that may represent a mother goddess have also been found in a Neolithic site at Çatalhöyük in Turkey, which, beginning about 7400 BCE, may have been a cult center or a shrine for the worship of ancestors. Because of the agriculturalist's stress on the goddess as the source of life, women often had political power in goddess-worshipping societies, which were often matrilocal (couples settled in the woman's home) and matrilineal (the line of descent was through the mother).

As goddess religions emerged in the ancient Near East and the Indus Valley, the goddess became a cosmic parent figure who created the universe and ruled heaven. She created life, and she ruled the natural world and qualities such as fate, time, wisdom, justice, healing, and fertility. She was regarded as both life-giving and death-dealing. As agriculture and cattle-raising developed in Mesopotamia and Egypt, goddesses such as Ishtar, Ashtoreth, and Isis appeared, becoming the Queen of Heaven. Isis was a cow-goddess who nurtured people with her milk, and she was the goddess of the dead. She was revered as the inventor of agriculture, a lawgiver, and a healer. The primeval Sumerian goddess Nammu was said to be the mother of humanity. In prehistoric Upper Egypt, the goddess known as Nekhebt was symbolized as a vulture, while in Lower Egypt the Goddess Ua Zit was worshipped in the form of a cobra. The goddess Nut ruled the sky, while her brother-husband Geb ruled the earth. The oldest recorded story of creation is a Babylonian text, the *Enuma Elish* of the twelfth century BCE, which names the goddess Tiamat as the mother of the gods in that tradition. The god Marduk killed her, split her body into two, and out of it created heaven and earth. Babylonian mythology influenced the later Hebrew tradition.

In the Greek civilization that arose in Crete during the middle of the third millennium BCE, the maternal principle was personified as either a single great mother or as multiple goddesses with specific roles, such as the warrior goddess Athena. The goddess was also represented as the snake-goddess of Minoan Crete or as the Mistress of Trees. The goddess was often called the Lady of the Beasts, because, like Artemis of the Greek pantheon, she controlled or hunted animals. Sometimes each animal species was ruled by a specific deity. (In some places, the Lord of the

Animals was male, as we see in the Bible [Lang, 2002]). The Greek earth goddess Gaea created Uranus the sky god. In other creation mythologies, creation arose out of an egg, which symbolized the womb of the goddess.

In ancient Greece, the Cult of Eleusis, a matriarchal tradition based on the goddess Demeter and her daughter Persephone, flourished for almost two thousand years, beginning in the fifteenth century BCE. This religion declined with the advent of Christianity in the fourth century CE, during which time the Emperor Theodosius closed the temple of the goddess at Eleusis and the Emperor Constantine closed the ancient temple of Ashtoreth/Astarte and suppressed her worship. In Athens, the Parthenon, sacred to the goddess since 1300 BCE, was converted into a Christian church in 450 CE, and the temples of Isis were converted into Christian churches by the Byzantine Emperor Justinian in 535 CE.

Over time, the goddess sometimes acquired a son-lover or brother, who was her consort. They united in a sacred marriage, which was ritually re-enacted by a marriage of the high priestess, a representation or incarnation of the goddess, with a lover. This consort was often ritually killed in his youth, leading to an annual period of grief and lamentation. Many of the priests in the tradition of the goddess castrated themselves (Kramer, 1969). There are controversial accounts that at the beginning of the new year, the king of Sumer would have intercourse with a priestess who represented the Goddess Inanna, in a ritual in which the king represented Dumuzi, Inanna's consort. The goddess was clearly the dominant partner. This ritual would ensure the fertility of the crops for the following year by releasing divine energy onto the fields. These rituals very much angered the Hebrew prophets.

When, after the Sumerians, the Babylonian empire became the dominant power in Mesopotamia, the goddess was known as Ishtar, and her dying son-lover was Tammuz. Ritual mourning for the dying Tammuz is reported in the book of Ezekiel (8:14). The sacred marriage theme appeared in classical Greece in the form of the goddess Aphrodite and the shepherd Adonis, whom the goddess took as her lover. In Rome, during the ritual of the mother goddess Cybele and her son-lover Attis, the son in effigy was tied to a tree and buried, rising from the dead three days later, bringing salvation at his re-birth. Presumably, the early Christians were influenced by this mythology. As James Frazer reported in *The Golden Bough*, vegetation gods such as Attis, Adonis, Osiris, and Tammuz were associated with the annual cycle of the apparent death and rebirth of the crops in Mediterranean agrarian cultures, which Frazer claimed to be parallel to the story of Jesus' death and resurrection. Frazer also connected the Christian story of Jesus' atonement on the cross to ancient Roman and Scandinavian myths of Gods who died on a sacred tree to save others. Frazer defined religion as the "propitiation or conciliation of powers superior to man which are believed to direct and control the course of nature and of human life" (1922/2009, p. 50).

There is controversy about the way the goddess was supplanted by male gods. One theory (Gimbutas, 1973) is that, during the Bronze Age (about 3000 BCE), religions and mythologies of the goddess began to be transformed and suppressed by waves of invasion by Indo-European patriarchal warrior societies, Kurgan nomads from southern Russia. These groups brought with them the kind of androcentric cultures found in the Hebrew Bible and ancient Greece. The invaders insisted on the superiority of their male sky-father gods, who were often storm gods. Gradually the male gods became dominant, even though the goddess survived despite all efforts to eliminate her. According to Lerner (1986), the transition to patriarchy occurred gradually over a period of 2500 years. Ultimately, the functions of the goddess were taken over, repressed or subordinated by the advent of masculine god-images such as the biblical Yhwh. Partly because Gimbutas' theory bridges between archeology, religion, linguistics, and mythology, and partly because she relies on intuition, her claims about pre-Indo-European, Neolithic, egalitarian, woman-centered, pacifist civilizations based on goddess worship have been strongly challenged by contemporary archeologists with an empirical bias. These theorists believe such claims to be largely ideologically based (Davis, 1999).[vi] Another possible reason for resistance to Gimbutas' ideas is that they demand that we question our entrenched beliefs in hierarchies of dominance and gender, the inevitability of warfare, and a masculine God-image.

An alternative explanation for the demise of the Goddess is given by Leonard Shlain (1998), who believes that the invention of writing had important consequences for culture because it reinforced the more masculine left side of the brain at the expense of the right side. Shlain suggests that the shift to alphabetic writing and literacy led to the dominance of linear, masculine modes of thought, which are based in the left hemisphere, and a devaluing of images and holistic approaches that are based in the right hemisphere. In his view, this shifted the balance of power between men and women and initiated the devaluing of the goddess and the decline of the status of women.

In Judaism, the goddess disappeared except for the notion of the Shekinah, the feminine presence of God, and Sophia, a feminine wisdom emanation of God. In Christianity, the light side of the goddess was preserved in the figure of the Blessed Virgin Mary, but the dark feminine was suppressed, although she still appears in the form of images of the Black Madonna, who is widely revered. She is an archetypal representation of the dark side of the goddess that patriarchal traditions have not been able to eliminate.

Rivkah Kluger (1995) believes that the Judeo-Christian tradition, because of its male sky-God imagery, freed people from what had been total immersion in the great mother archetype and led to the differentiation of consciousness and the unconscious. However, the problematic aspect of the advent of the patriarchal sky gods was the split that developed between spirit and body, combined with the devaluation of matter and the feminine.

Polytheism

As agriculture developed, and as societies became more complex and settled, the notion of multiple, formless spirits and powers gave way to the idea of a multitude of gods who would, if treated properly, respond to social needs. It was assumed that the divine world somehow mirrored the hierarchies and roles of the human realm, so the gods of polytheistic traditions each developed specific spheres of influence and had particular attributes. The Egyptian Ra and the Babylonian Shamash were sun-gods. In ancient Greece, the center of family life was personified as Hestia, the goddess of the hearth. The god Apollo was in charge of oracles, prophecy, healing, and the sun. Some goddesses such as Aphrodite and Demeter were connected to natural processes such as fertility. Men who seemed to have special powers, such as the hero Heracles or Asclepius the physician, were elevated to the level of divinities or demi-gods. Even archaic or primitive religions sometimes acknowledge a high god who is the creator of the universe who rules over the lesser gods, but this figure was often seen as remote and uninvolved in daily human activities (Smart, 1984).

Ancient Egypt was unified about 3000 years ago, on a religious foundation, especially belief in divine kingship and the importance of the afterlife. Divine law and order were thought to pass to humanity through the pharaoh, who had the title of the son of Re, the sun god. The pharaoh was thought to be a manifestation of the divine, and after his death he could mediate with the gods, which is perhaps why the Egyptians went to some lengths to preserve the pharaoh's body by mummification and by providing very elaborate tombs. The notion that some kind of physical (rather than purely spiritual[vii]) existence continues after death is suggested by the provision of furniture, servants, boats, and other implements in Egyptian tombs. Instructions for how to behave after death were also provided. After the pharaoh's death, he was thought to be able to travel with the gods in the sky, perhaps beginning the notion of a heavenly sphere. He was also identified with the god Osiris, who descended to the underworld after his death, modeling the notion of an afterlife. Osiris represented the dying and resurrected grain; the death and burial of Osiris was held to be responsible for the fertility of the land, as if his body was a fertilizer. He was also responsible for the annual flooding of the Nile, which allowed fertility, because he was thought to be in the mud that enriched the land. Interestingly, in Egyptian mythology, the earth was considered to be masculine, ruled by a male god, while the sky was feminine. The creation of human beings was imagined to have arisen from the tears of the sun god Re, or from the words of creator god Ptah, or by the work of the god Khnum who made people on a potter's wheel and placed the person in the womb.

In ancient Egypt, gods were personified in a very wide range of images, from celestial objects such as the sun and moon to animals and insects. Some gods represented abstract ideas such as truth. The gods were often portrayed in mixed animal and human forms, sometimes having human bodies and animal heads. The gods had the power to judge, to give life or death, assure fertility, and maintain cosmic order. The characteristics of these gods often evolved; some who were initially thought of as terrifying gradually took on more compassionate qualities. The god Osiris was particularly interesting for our purposes because he had died and been resurrected—an early concept of a savior who dies and lives again that reappeared in Christianity. Osiris and Maat, the personification of truth and justice, were responsible for judging the individual after death, by weighing the deceased's heart against a feather. Osiris promised his followers a happy afterlife if they had behaved well. The mythologem of a dying and resurrecting deity was also found in stories of the Mesopotamian god Tammuz, the Phrygian Attis, and the

Syrian Adonis, who were vegetation gods whose death and resurrection was associated with the dying and reappearance of the grain. Sometimes the goddess, such as Demeter, was held to be responsible for allowing or withholding the growth of the grain. The images of the gods took on new qualities in response to the needs and interests of their worshippers and their societies.

The gods of Mesopotamia behaved like human beings with supernatural abilities. They formed a hierarchy that governed different aspects of the heavens, earth, and sea. There were thousands of gods, who participated in all aspects of life—there were gods in charge of activities such as farming, writing, and accounting, as well as deities in charge of the planets and the natural world. There were gods of animals, disease, weather, the household, fertility, and motherhood. The Sumerians imagined these gods as if they behaved and organized themselves like human beings, except that the gods were immortal. Each of the major cities had its own patron deity. There was usually a single chief god, and at different periods in ancient Mesopotamian history different gods took control of the pantheon, in the process absorbing the power of other gods. (This process may have been a step towards monotheism.) Humanity's purpose was to support the gods by building temples in which they could live, where a statue represented the god. Such idols had exaggerated human characteristics, such as multiple limbs, or additions such as wings. It was important to sacrifice to the gods because everything that happened depended on their activity, and the possibility of offending them could lead to a poor harvest, floods, or an epidemic, causing great anxiety. Over time, the kings of each Mesopotamian city-state became deified themselves, leading to an early mingling of politics and religion. In the city of Ur, Mesopotamian kings were found not only buried with valuable grave goods for use in the afterlife, but also with human and animal sacrifices. One of the interesting differences between Mediterranean religion and Christianity is that the afterlife for Mesopotamians was situated in a miserable and dark underworld. Early Mesopotamian religion had a concept of judgment after death, by Utu the sun god and Nanna the moon goddess, who decided the fate of the dead based on their behavior during life.

Mesopotamian religion did not have a moral code in the Judeo-Christian sense, based on proper behavior towards other people. Good behavior required pleasing the gods, which required meticulous, often complex ritual processes. People were constantly on the lookout for signs that a god was angry and needed to be placated with the appropriate ritual and prayers, indicating how easy it is to imagine one's god as a kind of super-parent. Misfortune was a sure sign that a god was angry. Indications of the will of the gods were found in the stars, in dreams, or in the scrutiny of animal entrails or organs such as the liver, which was regarded as a place in which the gods could write messages. (This kind of divination was later forbidden in the book of Leviticus [19:26]).

Common to many of Mesopotamian god-images is the idea that the deity is the life-giving principle, so the search for divinity appeared in the projected form of the gods of agriculture and fertility, or as the power of the sun. It was widely assumed that the presence of the gods was necessary to prevent the universe descending into chaos. Often, gods and religious beliefs of different cultures merged together, sometimes as a way of forging alliances, sometimes as a result of conquest. Because the gods were at the center of Mesopotamian politics, at times gods would merge with each other in an attempt to unify diverse regions, while at other times conflict over the gods incited wars. The image of a god or goddess might develop as local gods were assimilated to the gods of invaders, for example when Babylonians absorbed the older Sumerian gods.

Conflict between cities was common, and success was attributed to the victor's god over the god of the defeated people. The Babylonian god Marduk was considered to be the ruler of the whole world as he assimilated the powers of lesser gods in the second part of the second millennium BCE, although he never quite became the only god. In Egypt, in about 1340 BCE, the Pharaoh Akhenaten (early in his reign known as Amenhotep) tried to introduce the monotheistic worship of the sun god Aten, and declared that other gods were his manifestations. However, this attempt to universalize one god failed after a few decades. (Freud thought this may have been one of the sources of the appearance of monotheism in ancient Israel.)

There are some interesting parallels between the mythology of ancient Babylon and that of the Hebrew Bible.[viii] The goddess Nintu (also called Mama) makes men and women from clay, mixed with the flesh and blood of another god. She also establishes the marriage bond, endows humanity with the power of procreation, and establishes the length of a pregnancy. Because humanity multiplies rapidly and make so much noise that people disturb the gods' sleep, the gods send a flood that covers the face of the earth. One man, Utnapishtim, is forewarned and told how to build a boat in which he and some animals survive. The boat comes to rest on a mountain, and as the waters recede, birds are sent out to find dry land. The biblical writers adopted such well-known mythic imagery to promote their own God-image, so the biblical reason for the flood became human wickedness and disobedience to God.

In ancient Mesopotamia, the gods were thought to meet each new year and decide what was to happen in the following year; their decision was inscribed on tablets of fate.[ix] Professional diviners tried to discover these pre-ordained events, and similar diviners are mentioned in various parts of the Hebrew Bible (Isaiah 47:13; Daniel 5:11-12; 2 Kings 21:6). Other aspects of Mesopotamian mythology were also incorporated into Hebrew mythology, such as the story of Moses receiving the ten commandments in Exodus 34, which describes how Moses's face shone with light—or, according to a different translation, he grew horns. Lang (2002) relates this story to the same theme found in Mesopotamian stories in which a leader or king is transformed into an angelic being or a god.

Sometimes the gods of different societies were easily matched with each other, as in the case of the Greek Zeus and the Roman Jupiter, whose attributes were very similar. At other times there were no counterparts and various gods merged into one god such as Serapis, who had a mixture of Greek and Egyptian origins. Religious syncretism of this kind was common in antiquity. Gradually, the functions of many gods were subsumed under the name of one greater god with different aspects, perhaps because the function of the lesser gods, such as those in charge of the growth of crops, became better understood and more under human control.

Ancient Iranian religion was polytheistic until the advent of Zarathustra[x] about 1200 BCE. He was originally a priest in the traditional religion of Central Asian Iran. As a result of a vision of a hitherto unknown god, which turned him against the traditional pantheon of gods of ancient Iran, he announced that the true god was the cosmic creator, Ahura Mazda, who represented the principle of goodness. He was opposed by a principle of evil, Ahriman. These were cosmic principles of equal status who had always existed and were eternally in opposition to each other. This dualistic notion of competing supernatural forces became influential in several subsequent traditions such as Gnosticism, Manichaeism, and some aspects of Christianity and Judaism. It was a useful idea because it helped to explain the existence of evil. Needless to say, it was assumed that ultimately good would win, and Ahriman would be defeated. Zarathustra believed that if people followed Ahura Mazda the world could be brought to a state of perfection. Zarathustra believed in the advent of a messiah born of a virgin, and, like the ancient Egyptians, he believed in judgment after death based on one's behavior towards others.

Karl Jaspers (1953, 1960) pointed out the interesting fact that many founders of the world religions lived between the 8th and the 3rd centuries BCE, especially in the 6th century. He referred to this period as the Axial or Pivotal age, during which the Buddha, Zoroaster, Confucius, Lao-Tzu, the Upanishads, and the Israelite prophets all appeared. During this time, Jaspers claimed that people became particularly interested in finding meaning and developing greater self-awareness. The idea of an all-encompassing, transcendent reality grew at this time. Religions became more universal. One possible explanation for this mysterious phenomenon is the diffusion of religious ideas between different countries. Religious believers might see this phenomenon as the result of different forms of revelation, while for Jung it would represent the synchronistic worldwide emergence of archetypal themes, at a time when the cultural settings and human cognitive abilities allowed such themes to appear.

The pagan gods were worshipped partly because they were politically important; participation in public worship was evidence of a citizen's loyalty to the state. Apparently, such civic worship was not entirely satisfying, so many people turned to the mystery traditions such as the Eleusinian mysteries and the cults of Attis, Adonis, or Dionysus. Mystery religions all aimed at some type of salvation based on closeness to the divine. They offered sacred secrets and a sense of security that allowed devotees to break out of an otherwise difficult existence.

The God-image of the Ancient Greek Philosophers

The ancient Greek concept of divinity had both philosophical and religious components. Greek god-images are found in epics such as the *Iliad* and the *Odyssey*. In this pantheon, Zeus was the chief among a hierarchy of goddesses and gods who presided over the world and produced phenomena such as earthquakes and lightening. The gods often behaved capriciously in their dealings with humans, and the effects of human actions were often thought to depend on divine support or opposition. Humans seemed to be helpless in the face of the gods' actions, and their favor often seemed arbitrary, but they certainly had human favorites. The Greeks had no concept that apparent injustices in this life would be balanced by judgment in the afterlife.

Xenophanes, of the sixth century BCE, attacked the notion that the gods were anything like mortals. He pointed out that if animals had a god-concept and could paint, they would depict their gods in the form of animals. He developed an early account of the divine nature, saying there is one great god who is not like mortals either in form or in thought. This god governs the universe without effort; he is without beginning or end, and he does not intervene in human affairs. Xenophanes is often regarded as one of the first monotheists, although he may have believed in multiple other gods as well as a supreme god. Since this god is the whole of nature, Xenophanes is also seen as a pantheist, believing that everything in the universe is god. He is sometimes seen as a precursor to Spinoza. In about 450 BCE, Anaxagoras shocked his fellow Athenians by declaring that the sun was a red-hot stone, which meant it could not be a god. About 300 BCE, Euhemeris of Messene taught that the gods were originally great kings of remote antiquity who were deified by subsequent legends. This mechanism actually operated in various religions; thus, Imhotep, the builder of the Step Pyramid in about 2700 BCE, was over time transformed into a healing god in Greco-Roman Egypt. (Euhemerism reappeared in Herbert Spencer's theory that religion arose as a result of ancestor-worship).

Early Greek philosophers attempted to account for the existence of the world without recourse to the gods, although the philosophers themselves often believed in the gods. Philosophers such as Aristotle and Plato had an important influence on medieval Christian and Jewish thought. At the core of Plato's work was the search for what is permanent behind the flux of daily experience. He postulated the existence of eternal "Ideas" or "Forms" that are the spiritual essence of things. He believed that these eternal truths are innately present in the soul and can be recalled by the intellect. Plato sometimes writes as if his idea of the gods was traditional, but at other times he suggests the existence of a supreme god who rules the universe and who is perfectly good. In his *Timaeus*, Plato's image of god was the eternal Demiurge, a kind of architect or craftsman who took raw matter that had always existed and used it to form the universe based on the eternal Ideas. He then put mind or soul into this matter. The Demiurge was responsible for the existence of evil, while a higher god was far removed from humanity. The Platonic God does not have much interest in people, but gives order to the universe, which has a plan behind it. The notion of the Demiurge became important for the Gnostics, who believed that the world had been created by this inferior deity and was a prison for the spirit.

Epicureans were polytheists who believed that the gods were shaped like people, although much more attractive, with bodies of light. They did not create the world and they were not interested in people. Nor did they interfere with the world in any way. They lived a carefree life with none of the worries that affect human beings. Epicureans held that the world is made of atoms that produce all natural phenomena, so that everything that happens has natural causes. At death, the atoms that constitute a person entirely disperse, so he or she ceases to exist—there is no immaterial soul. The main competitors of the Epicureans were the Stoics, who believed in a god who had an extremely refined body. This god or *logos* is the divine spark of life or spirit within all things, related to the world as the soul is related to the human body, as a force that penetrates everything. This god is the father of everything, takes a minute interest in the world, and rewards and punishes people according to their behavior. This philosophy had some influence on later Christian thinking, although Christianity preferred to think of God as the creator of the world rather than a divine spark within everything. The Skeptics attacked the Stoic idea of god, denying that human reason can know god at all, or even know whether god exists. The Cynic philosophers of ancient Greece wanted to live a virtuous life in accord with nature, often becoming ascetics or mendicants who opposed conventions and rejected conventional ambitions for wealth and power. Some historians have pointed out similarities between their teachings and those of Jesus. For Aristotle (384-322 BCE), god was the timeless and space-less Prime Mover who was the first cause of everything, on which creation depends. This god is the ultimate cause of all motion but does not move itself, and it is not affected by events. For Aristotle, god is the source of truth, goodness, and pure intelligence. Greek philosophical ideas were very appealing to medieval Christian theologians who tried to integrate them with Christian doctrine, albeit with some difficulty when it came to comparing Plato's Demiurge or Aristotle's Prime Mover with the God of Genesis.

The Latin poet Lucretius (first century BCE) was an early exponent of the idea that religion stems from human fears and needs—an idea later to appear in the work of the eighteenth-century philosopher David Hume. Lucretius believed that because men could not explain natural phenomena, they ascribed them to the gods, who actually had no contact at all with the world or with humanity.

Monotheism

Andrew Lang (1844-1912) was an anthropologist who found evidence for the origin of religion in the attempts of early people to rationalize their experience of the mysteries of the natural world. His book, *The Making of Religion* (1898), suggested that archaic religious belief included a supreme being, a creator god or "All-Father." Later research showed that this supreme god of early religions was actually only one among many gods, so this was in fact a form of polytheism. A traditional view supposes that the attributes of all the spirits and gods that were thought to inhabit the world were eventually gathered up into the one deity of the monotheisms. Typically, the most important deity of a pantheon gradually assimilates the qualities and powers of the lesser gods, and their images merge. Henotheism, meaning the elevation of one god to a special position among other gods, is thought to be an evolutionary step in the development of monotheism. However, why monotheism became more appealing than polytheism is not clear. Perhaps it is more satisfying or more intimate to have a single, all-powerful divinity than a multitude of gods, each with limited jurisdiction. Perhaps one god among all of them seemed to be particularly powerful, and this one became more and more unique until it became the only one. However, polytheism often seems more democratic, more inclusive, less totalizing, less likely to lead to violence, and less rigid than monotheism. Needless to say, if there is only one deity, it would be important that this one is considered to be omnipotent, moral, and loving. Monotheism seems to be related to human political hierarchies that allocate power to one person at the top.

The contemporaries of both the pharaoh Akhenaten and the prophet Zarathustra rebuffed both these early attempts to make monotheism dominant. Such opposition to monotheism partly occurs because the negation of all other gods makes monotheism too exclusive, leading to resistance from devotees of particular gods. Furthermore, intolerance is one of the typical side effects of monotheism; polytheism allows other people's gods to exist, but monotheism insists on their elimination, sometimes violently. Given the human tendency to anthropomorphize god-images, some of the resistance to monotheism may arise because it is difficult to imagine how one god could contain all the attributes of all the other gods, including being both masculine and feminine, good and evil, maternal and paternal, and so on. The term monolatry is used to describe a situation in which a group worships a specific god that is the only one worthy of worship, even if other gods exist. Many early people preferred to worship one high god who ruled over a pantheon of lesser gods, to whom one might turn on specific occasions such as war. This type of henotheism is found in many cultures whose gods reflect their hierarchical political, social, and family structures. The idea of an underlying unifying principle led to non-duality in the Eastern spiritual traditions. This idea teaches that there is only one ultimate reality from which nothing is separate.

i The word hominin refers specifically to the human line of evolution that developed into *Homo sapiens*, while the word hominid refers to all great apes, including the human line.
ii The degree to which this drawing accurately reflects the original image, and the question of whether the image depicts a shamanic practice, have been challenged, but the image seems to indicate a cult object.
iii The Lower Paleolithic period was between 2.5 million and 200,000 years ago; the Middle Paleolithic Period between 200,000 and 40,000 years ago, and the Upper Paleolithic Period between 40,000 and 10,000 years ago, at which time the Neolithic period began.
iv The Theory of Mind refers to our ability to imagine what others are thinking. It is thought to have evolved because it offered survival advantages. This ability also allows people to imagine what the gods are thinking and what the gods think humans are thinking. A Theory of Mind may therefore be essential for belief in gods (Bering, 2012). Bering notes that because of the ability to conceive of other minds, our ancestors probably believed that they were being watched and judge by a supernatural audience.
v Stonehenge was built in stages from about 3000 BCE until about 1500 BCE, while Göbekli Tepe is at least 7000 years older. This site covers more than 20 acres and contains huge pillars and carved figures, both humanoid and animal. Its function is unknown; it may have been a temple or ritual site.
vi Davis (1999) points out that contemporary cultures that worship goddesses such as the Hindu Kali or the Shinto Amaterasu are not utopian; they practice a caste system and other forms of violence. He also notes that the notion of a matriarchal society devoted to the worship of a goddesses and based in agriculture dates back only to the work of Bachofen in the mid-nineteenth century, during an occult revival and the development of neo-paganism that may have been a reaction to the Enlightenment. The idea was continued in James Frazer's famous *The Golden Bough*. Robert Graves's *The White Goddess* (1947) described an idyllic image of pre-historic times when the Triple Goddess (virgin, mother, and crone) was the only deity, and women ruled societies that were in tune with nature. Eller (2001) points out that the notion of a utopian, egalitarian, peaceful, goddess worshipping matriarchal society attuned to nature actually reinforces gender stereotypes. She points out that too many prehistoric objects or drawings have been taken as evidence of universal goddess worship; it is inherently difficult to reconstruct prehistoric societies based on the physical objects that have survived.
vii The Egyptians did not have a body-soul dualism; what they referred to as the *ba* was not the soul but a form that the body took after death.
viii Needless to say, traditionalists would object to the description of biblical stories as mythic, because they believe that they are literally true. However, these stories are clearly myths in the broader sense of the word, meaning sacred stories.
ix This notion survived in the Jewish tradition that at the beginning of the new year, God decides who will be "inscribed in the book of life," or live for another year.
x Zarathustra's dates are uncertain; estimates range from the sixth century BCE to 1000 BCE.

CHAPTER 4

The God-image of the Hebrew Scriptures and Post-biblical Judaism

Historical Aspects of the Biblical Text

In their attempts to explain the behavior and nature of their God, the authors of the Hebrew Bible drew upon existing Near Eastern religious, literary, and cultural traditions. The biblical authors modified the mythology of their neighbors' polytheism in the light of the authors' monotheistic God-image. For example, in earlier Mesopotamian religion, Shamash was the sun god, or was the sun itself. However, in the Hebrew Bible, divinity was no longer seen as the personification of the forces of nature. Instead, the biblical authors conceived of their God as transcendent of nature, although he is said to create natural phenomena as an act of will.

The Hebrew Scriptures were written by multiple authors and editors over a long period of time, often after a prolonged period of oral transmission, beginning perhaps as early as 950 BCE (Davis, 2007). Earlier texts and traditions were periodically modified and re-written in the light of changing historical and cultural circumstances. The order in which the books are presented in modern bibles is not the sequence in which the books were written, so the text cannot be read as if it were chronologically meaningful. There is no consensus about when the canon (the authoritative collection of texts) was finalized—which was sometime between 200 BCE and 200 CE—but eventually many works had been excluded, some of which later appeared in the Dead Sea Scrolls. The final canon according to the Jewish tradition consists of twenty-four books, which expand to thirty-nine in the Protestant version of the text[i].

The books that constitute the Hebrew Bible seem to be coherent texts, but they all contain material written at different times by different authors, so each text is the result of the compilation of several documents and a great deal of editing. Differences in language and style have been smoothed out by modern translations. Thus, the first part of the book of Genesis was written later and by a different author than the second part, and the second part of the book of Isaiah was written at least a hundred years after the first part. Each text has been copied and redacted repeatedly, often by scribes who were able to insert or remove material according to their preconceived ideas about what should be in it, and according to how these editors imagined events. The Hebrew Bible therefore contains many voices and opinions that describe the history of the people of Israel over a long period of time, always from the point of view of particular authors' ideas (projections) about God's intentions and preferences.

Parts of the biblical text contradict other parts. There are various repetitions and discrepancies in the text, such that the same story is sometimes told with different details, suggesting different perspectives or a wish to preserve different accounts.[ii] These discrepancies, and the amount of editing, make it very unlikely that the text is literally "the word of God." However, apologists point out that the Bible is primarily an inspired religious text, of spiritual importance to its believers regardless of its historical accuracy, with a consistent overall message. For those who accept its authority, the Bible explains how God operates in the world and describes his relationship with the people of Israel, while acknowledging that his behavior can be difficult or impossible to understand.

Biblical stories reflect the God-image of their editors, who eliminated what they did not approve of and emphasized what was important to them. The views of many generations have therefore been blended in these books. Nevertheless, traditionalists and fundamentalists see the text as having special authority. They tend to ignore the fact that a long historical process took place during the formation of the final text, with a gradual evolution in the text's God-image. One example of this development is that early on, the biblical Yhwh[iii] was thought to be solely the God of one people, but later it was asserted that he was the God of all nations. As well, the tradition gradually developed from polytheism to monotheism; the Hebrew Bible is full of warnings not to worship other gods, of whom Yhwh was "jealous."[iv] Many but not all of these references to early Hebrew polytheism have been edited out, and Smith (2001, p. 157) suggests that what remains is only the "tip of the iceberg."

Some of the books of the Hebrew Bible contain historical material, but this is not necessarily reliable history. The historicity of the Bible is a controversial topic. Accounts of the appearance of God to individuals such as Abraham are of no help in confirming biblical history. For scholars who are skeptical of the historical value of the text, there is little written or archeological evidence outside the Bible for the existence of biblical personalities such as David or Solomon (Finkelstein, 2002).[v] Many of the biblical stories were written down long after the events they describe, and contemporary material was sometimes retrospectively inserted into earlier text to make it seem as if it were prophecy, or to fit with the theology of the later authors. For example, although there is controversy in this area, some biblical archeologists doubt that there was in fact a violent conquest of Canaan by the Israelites in the twelfth or thirteenth centuries BCE, as described in the books of Joshua (5-11) and Judges (1-2).[vi] The Israelites may have been indigenous to Canaan itself, one of several Canaanite tribes rooted in Canaanite traditions and worshipping El, their chief deity, among several others. Perhaps a Canaanite cult that worshipped Yhwh was a splinter group. Or, the Israelites may have immigrated and assimilated in a peaceful manner over a long period of time, while over centuries of re-telling the story became embellished into a national epic and retrospectively attributed to divine intervention. Archeological evidence of destroyed cities does not tell us who caused the destruction, which may have been the result of internal revolutions within Canaanite society rather than conquest by the people of Israel.[vii] The later development of distinct tribes among the Israelites may have occurred as a function of the natural division of the land into different areas (Coogan & Chapman, 2017).

The story of the Exodus from Egypt is also a problematic story from a historical perspective. There is little documentary or other evidence that the Israelites were enslaved in Egypt or that an Exodus occurred as described in the text.[viii] If there was an Exodus, the number of Hebrews[ix] who left Egypt was probably much smaller than the six hundred thousand men mentioned in the biblical account (Exodus 12:37). If we add the number of women and children who would have accompanied them, this implies an enormous number of people (and their animals) wandering in the desert, requiring food and water and leaving burial sites, which have not been found. There is also debate about whether the biblical Moses actually existed, even though he is a very important figure in the stories.

The early accounts of his life were edited and embellished by later monotheists who wanted to grant him divine authority. Despite these difficulties, conservative religionists tend to believe that biblical history is essentially accurate, and the necessary archeological evidence has not yet been found. In any case, for the believer, these books are not simply historical texts; they are a record of the fulfillment of the divine promise. Many biblical stories are clearly legendary or mythic, such as the creation story in Genesis or the story of Moses in the bulrushes, which is an archetypal motif of the birth of the hero found in many cultures.[x] These kinds of stories are mainly of interest when we try to understand their spiritual or psychological significance, or when they tell us about their authors' beliefs and assumptions.

For skeptical readers, the Hebrew Bible only represents what the tradition *believed* to have happened to figures such as Moses, based on the projections of many pious authorities about their God's behavior. The biblical authors are not shy about telling the reader what God was thinking or intending at a given moment. (Contemporary preachers do the same thing, based on their own preconceptions and projections.) Fundamentalists in particular often ignore the historical context of the text, whose teachings they interpret and apply to modern circumstances the original authors could never have imagined. Some biblical material is so violent and cruel that it is abhorrent to modern sensibilities, so the Bible is always read and quoted in a very selective manner, usually with an agenda in mind.

The biblical stories were clearly influenced by pre-existing Mesopotamian traditions. Many of the mythic themes of the Hebrew Bible are found in earlier Sumerian and Babylonian stories, for example, a tree in a garden of immortal life, the making of humanity out of clay, and the stories of the flood and the Tower of Babel. However, there are important differences between these earlier sources and the biblical stories, in which the earlier stories are re-told to reflect the values of the emerging monotheistic God-image. For example, in the earlier Babylonian creation myth, several gods argue and fight among themselves, while in the Genesis story there is only one God who knows what he is doing. He creates order amid chaos, through the power of his voice. In the Babylonian stories, humanity is created to serve the gods, but in Genesis humanity is created in the divine image, apparently endowed with some of the same qualities as its creator. Even though there are conceptual connections between earlier creation myths and the creation account in Genesis, an important difference between them is that in some creation myths the world emerges from a prior state such as an egg, or from water or diffuse darkness, which exists before the gods. Kaufman (1972) refers to this initial state as a metadivine realm. He denies that this realm exists in Genesis, where God brings into being everything that exists. A further difference is that the pre-biblical pagan gods are associated with the forces of nature and have no moral character, but the biblical God transcends nature and is depicted as good and moral. Many authorities insist that the biblical accounts of the personal relationship between God and humanity are unlike anything found in earlier Mesopotamian traditions.

The Traditional Biblical Story

A core narrative has shaped the identity of the Jewish people. The tradition says God revealed himself in a variety of ways, beginning when God told Abram to leave his home in Ur and move to Canaan. This event is often dated around 1800 BCE. God changed Abram's name to Abraham, and made a covenant or contract with him according to which, in return for his obedience, God (whom Abraham worshipped as El) would care for Abraham's successors and give them the land of Israel. Abraham, his son Isaac, and his grandson Jacob lived in Canaan for a while, but later Jacob's sons were forced by a famine to move to Egypt. Eventually, the Egyptians felt threatened by the Israelites' numbers, and they were enslaved about 1500 BCE. Yhwh did not explain why he allowed this to happen, and there is no account of his presence during their oppression. Thanks to divine intervention, Moses eventually led the people out of Egypt.[xi] They wandered in the desert for forty years and arrived in Canaan around 1200 BCE, which they eventually conquered with the help of God. While they were in the desert at Mount Sinai, Yhwh gave them the Torah,[xii] the Law or teaching. The orthodox tradition teaches that an oral law was also given at Mt. Sinai along with the written Torah. The oral law was codified in the form of the Mishnah and Talmud, which provide a series of rabbinic interpretations and commentaries on the Torah, claiming to clarify its deeper meaning. This tradition, completed between 200-500 CE, established religious practices and further transformed the image of God found in the Torah.

At the same time as the Torah was given, God made a second, Mosaic covenant. (Later, another covenant was made with King David, in which

God promised that David's dynasty would last forever). The covenant[xiii] God made with the Israelites (Exodus 24:3-11) required their promise to be faithful to him, ignoring all other gods and only worshiping him. They were expected to keep his law, circumcise their male children, keep the Sabbath as a day of rest, and offer temple sacrifices. In return, Yhwh promised he would protect his people and grant them fertility and prosperity. In the eighth century BCE, prophets such as Amos and Hosea further refined the tradition's God-image by stressing morality while diminishing the importance of ritual sacrifices. This change of attitude began the process of allowing the tradition to be practiced anywhere rather than being tied to one physical place, which became essential after the Romans destroyed the Jerusalem temple in 70 CE.[xiv] Subsequently, every time tragedy struck, in order not to lose faith in Yhwh, national disasters had to be (and sometimes still are) explained in terms of the people's failure to live up to the covenantal agreement. Military success or failure were seen as a reaction to the nation's behavior in relation to the will of God. When the nation suffered defeats and exile at the hands of nearby nations, the prophets explained the nation's suffering as the result of Israel's apostasy. Much of the account of the relationship between Yhwh and his people is based on this psychology of reward and punishment.

After the destruction of the Jerusalem temple, sacrifices were no longer possible. They were replaced by a focus on prayer, atonement, adherence to God's law, relationship with God, and the hope for a Messiah, an idea that had arisen within Zoroastrianism. To sustain the tradition without a temple, the rabbis had to develop a God-image that focused on history and revelation, stressing the direct experience of important people such as Moses, Abraham, Isaac, and Jacob, and the testimony of the prophets. Earlier stories were modified to fit this approach.

Yhwh's Relationship to his People

The religion of Yhwh was originally an ethnic or nationalistic religion, concerned with the relationship of Yhwh and his particular people, which he chose to be special to him (Exodus 6:7; Deuteronomy 14:2).[xv] He wanted them to be separate, so he ordered restrictions such as dietary laws that kept members of his people from being too intimate with outsiders. He was very biased in favor of his people; he promised to "bless those who bless you and curse him who curses you" (Genesis 12:13). Why God chose this particular people is not known, except that he loves them, and he wants them for himself, as his "own possession" (Deuteronomy 7: 6). He makes them holy as he is holy (Leviticus 21:8), as if he needs a reflection of his own holiness, which is one of Yhwh's most important characteristics. It seems as if possessing a unique people with a holy vocation helps Yhwh to feel unique among the other gods, just as being selected by their God helped his people feel special. It was important to Yhwh that the people always remember that he was the one who brought them out of Egypt, a story that he often reminds them about. The price that the people pay for being chosen is obedience to his law, or being a spiritual teacher of the nations, or being God's servant (Isaiah 42:1). According to tradition, the choice of Israel was the fulfillment of a promise made to the Patriarchs (Deuteronomy 8:1). Needless to say, skeptics would say that the people projected this choice onto their God, in effect choosing themselves to be chosen, to compensate for their weak political and economic position in relation to the great powers of Egypt and Babylon who surrounded them. The sense of being chosen may have been a defense against envy of stronger powers to whom the people were subject. Since they had been enslaved, making the gods of the slave-masters worthless by stressing the superiority of their own God would have helped the people's self-esteem, and this would be further helped by making themselves as different as possible in their dietary habits and other customs. In a clear parental projection, the tradition teaches that because Israel is precious to God, he is saddened or angry when his people disobey him and pleased when they return to him.

Although Yhwh sometimes acts in a helpful way to protect his people, at other times he ignores their prayers, and he justifies their suffering by saying: "My thoughts are not your thoughts" (Isaiah 55:8). This attitude is used to rationalize multiple episodes of persecution such as the Holocaust, when God appeared to ignore the covenant. The Holocaust raises the perennial problem of maintaining a relationship with a God who permits or causes suffering and evil. A good deal of important biblical literature, such as the *Book of Job*, tries to address this question.

Polytheism in the Israelite Tradition

A scholarly debate has arisen about the sources and development of the God-image of the Hebrew Scriptures. The orthodox Jewish tradition describes the exclusive worship of Yhwh by Abraham and Moses, but despite the way this tradition has been handed down, the early Israelites were not monotheistic. Later editors and translators partially obscured their polytheism, but in the text itself the Israelites are often accused of worshipping Canaanite gods, so that the exclusive worship of Yhwh was clearly not universal. For example: "And the people of Israel did what was evil in the sight of the Lord, forgetting the Lord their God, and serving the Ba'als and the Ashe'roth" (Judges 3:7). In Genesis 35:2, Jacob says to his household: "Put away the foreign gods that are among you."

It was probably hard to imagine an invisible God, compared to the ready availability of statues of pagan gods. Because Yhwh was a war-god, he was worshipped preferentially during wartime, for example during the threat from the Assyrians, but afterwards people turned back to the worship of their local and family gods. Lang (2002) suggests that: "Temporary monolatry[xvi] in times of war can be considered the prototype or embryonic form of the Yahweh-alone idea and thus the precursor of monotheism" (p. 187).

Many scholars believe that the biblical image of Yhwh developed out of existing Middle East religious traditions, beginning as one of many local gods. For example, according to Lang (2002) there is some evidence that Yhwh was originally a weather and mountain deity of the Edomites, a people who were said to be descended from Esau and one of the traditional enemies of Israel. A multiplicity of available gods is suggested by biblical phrases such as: "Who is like thee, O Lord, among the gods?" (Exodus 15:11). In other words, the biblical Yhwh was initially one of many gods of the region. Monotheism was a later development, retrospectively inserted into the Bible by editors who re-wrote the earlier stories in the light of their beliefs. The famous phrase "Hear O Israel: The Lord our God" (Deuteronomy 6:4) may have referred to our specific God as distinct from the deities of other people. The commandment to have "no other gods before me" (Exodus 20:3) does not preclude the existence of other gods and may have only meant that Yhwh should be the most important one. There are many warnings in the Bible about the dangers of worshipping these other gods (Joshua 23:16); Yhwh is said to be jealous[xvii] of them (Exodus 34:14). The Deuteronomic law commands that even brothers, sons, or daughters who worship "other gods" should be killed (Deuteronomy 13:6-10), indicating the degree of pressure exerted by the followers of Yhwh.

A common consensus among biblical scholars is that the God of the Hebrew Bible began as one of the gods of a local desert tribe, perhaps a deity of storms and war, who was later credited with having freed his people from bondage in Egypt, then handing down the law at Mt. Sinai (Gerstenberger, 1996; Smith, 1990). However, there is a minority opinion that the development of devotion to Yhwh was not the result of the evolution of previous god-images. In Kaufman's (1972) view, Yhwh appeared spontaneously as an original creation of the Israelites, who had an insight about God that was quite different than the gods of the pagan traditions. For Kaufman, Israelite monotheism was a radically new God-image that was not an evolutionary development of earlier polytheism; monotheism was a revolutionary break with the past based on a different world view. Kaufman believed that Yhwh cannot be understood in ordinary mythic terms because the Israelites conceived of God in a way that was qualitatively different than the gods of their neighbors. However, although there is a range of views about when the Hebrews adopted belief in a single God,[xviii] the predominant view is that strict monotheism did not arise until the Babylonian exile in the sixth century BCE (Smith, 1990), when a large proportion of the people of the kingdom of Judah was deported to Babylon. It may be that they developed the idea of monotheism from their exposure to the Zoroastrian religion during their time in Babylon.[xix] Some of the exiles embraced Babylonian gods, while others remained faithful to Yhwh and believed that although the exile was a punishment, eventually their land would be restored. They believed that the land had originally been given to them by God as a promise to the patriarchs, or perhaps the land was granted by God to the people who left Egypt on condition they obeyed the Mosaic Law.

The biblical God has many names (Lang, 2002 lists 40), some of which may have originally referred to gods other than the Hebrew God. The multiplicity of divine names may also be the result of the merger or assimilation of the gods of different religious traditions, which was a common practice in the ancient world in order to form political alliances. Candidates for this merger of gods include Yhwh, who was a local warrior-god (Smith, 1990; Day, 2000; Lang, 2002) combined with features of the Canaanite gods El and Baal (Miller 2000). El was the patriarch or chief god of this pantheon and a god of wisdom. Most of the Canaanite gods were involved in the control of the natural forces of nature, personifying phenomena such as storms or fertility. Rituals in the gods' service tried to bring these natural forces into balance. The social order of this pantheon mirrored the social structure of ancient Near Eastern city-states (Handy, 1994).

In Canaanite mythology, El created and ruled the entire universe, but he was seen as remote. He delegated various responsibilities to his family, which he produced with his female consort, Asherah. Baal, a son of El, was a god of storm, war, and fertility, and was king of the other gods, but he was not a lawgiver. There is a range of theories about the relationship between El and Yhwh (de Moor, 1990; Cross, 1973). Some authors (Smith, 1990) see El as the original main God of Israel, which adopted Yhwh later. It is possible that two religious traditions merged, one in the north that worshipped El and one in the south preferred Yhwh. Over time, El and Yhwh blended into the same deity. Yhwh took over some of the qualities of El, and El became one of the names of Yhwh as Yhwh's people became more powerful.[xx]

At one time, Yhwh and Baal were rivals, but eventually Yhwh assimilated most of the attributes of Baal, for example when Yhwh became the source of storms, using thunder and lightning as weapons (Psalms 144 and 29). He was also a weather-God who controlled rainfall and the harvest (Jeremiah 5:24) and manifested himself by means of earthquakes and volcanic action (Exodus 19:18-20), as demonstrations of his power. When he was displeased, "the earth reeled and rocked; the foundations of the mountains trembled and quaked, because he was angry" (Psalms 18). He also controlled the sea (Exodus 15:8,19). However, the worship of Baal included ritual sex and sacred objects such as pillars and trees, which did not find their way into the cult of Yhwh. The Israelites adopted some pagan practices such as the burning of incense and the offering of baked cakes to the Goddess, practices condemned by the prophets (Isaiah 17:8; Ezekiel 6:4: Jeremiah 44:15-19). Canaanite religion practiced child sacrifice at times of crisis, and it is possible that the Israelites did so as well (Judges 11:30-39), but this practice was later forbidden by the prophets and by the law code of Leviticus and Deuteronomy. Another important difference between the Israelites and their neighbors was that Yhwh was not allowed to be depicted in the form of an image (Exodus 20:4)[xxi] in contrast to local gods who were commonly represented in the form of statues and paintings.[xxii] However, the biblical text frequently uses bodily metaphors to describe Yhwh. For his followers, idolatry was a particularly heinous sin.

Animal sacrifice was as important for the Israelites as it was for other Canaanites, since God was thought to enjoy the aroma of burning animal flesh (Genesis 8:21; Leviticus 1:9). Sacrifice was believed to return to God the life that he had given. Sacrifices were also intended to atone for sin, petition for aid, ask for blessings, and maintain God's presence in the temple. The spilling of blood seems to have been of particular importance to the biblical God. At his command, Moses threw blood on his altar and on the people, as a sign of their covenant (Exodus 24, 5-8). Blood was also thrown about when priests were inaugurated (Exodus 29, 1-46), and King Solomon slaughtered 22,000 oxen and 120,000 sheep as a peace offering to Yhwh (1 Kings 8:63). Blood seemed to symbolize the transfer of life and power from the worshipper to God, or it was a food offering. To the psychologist, this behavior looks like the projection of the worshippers' own bloodthirstiness onto their image of God.

Most scholars agree that the ancient Israelite religion was initially a form of monolatrism, meaning that other gods were acknowledged but one was preferred, and it took some time before the biblical Yhwh was considered to be the only God. The worship of Baal by the Israelites is described in the book of Judges (6:25-31). Baal must have been popular, given the number of times he is attacked in the Bible, leading to Yhwh's punishment of people who turn from him, typically by defeat in battle (Judges 3:7-8).[xxiii] Other deities were also important in ancient Israel; during the exile in Babylon, the prophet Ezekiel (8:14) complained that he had seen women weeping for the god Tammuz at the temple in Jerusalem. Although the Israelites worshipped various deities, Yhwh was apparently considered the most powerful (Smith, 1990; Gerstenberger, 1996). Over time, to expand the characteristics of Yhwh, the tradition borrowed attributes from mythic images of the Egyptian Amen-Re, the creator god Marduk of Babylon, Ashur, the head of the Assyrian pantheon, and Ahura Mazda, the Zoroastrian deity.

The Hebrew word *Elohim* is a plural noun that is typically translated as God in the singular. Although this word probably refers to many deities, it might refer to the many aspects of the same God. Another important plural term is found in Genesis 6, which says that the "sons of God" took human wives, implying that these sons may have been spiritual beings or even gods of some kind, although the phrase may refer to human rulers. The Bible occasionally talks of a divine council, for example in Psalm 82: "God has taken his place in the divine council; in the midst of the gods he holds judgment." Here the term "gods" is usually rationalized to mean local human authorities or angels. According to a Qumran (Dead Sea) scroll, the original translation of Deuteronomy 32:8 said that the supreme God divides up the nations of the world according to the number of other gods, giving a nation to each god. This apparent recognition of other gods led later editors to change the wording of this text to read "according to the number of the children of Israel." Genesis 1:26 begins with the phrase: "Let us make man in our image," and when Adam eats the apple Yhwh says "the man has become like one of us." The use of the plural terms "our" and "us" suggests traces of an original polytheistic Canaanite religion.[xxiv] Later monotheists try to rationalize the use of these plural terms in various ways. The plural pronouns may imply the royalty of God, or the plural terms may refer to the divine beings around God. Christians have suggested that the plural terms refer to the Trinity, but this seems unlikely, given that the rest of the text consistently uses the term "he." Christian fundamentalists have assumed that the term "us" is used to include Jesus, who is said to have been with God at the beginning.

Smith (1990) believes that the emergence of Israel as a distinct people coincided with the emergence of Yhwh as their chief deity. Lang (1983) suggests that in ancient Israel there was competition between a group of Jerusalem priests who would only worship Yhwh and a competing faction that worshipped many deities of which Yhwh was the main one. Just before the destruction of the first Jerusalem temple in 586 BCE, the prophet Jeremiah had warned the people about worshipping other gods, threatening them with the coming destruction that would be a punishment for worshipping the goddess in addition to Yhwh. However, not until the painful destruction of their temple and their exile in Babylon did the Israelites turn to the exclusive worship of Yhwh. Then, as Smith (1990, pp. 193-194) puts it, "the old head-god of monarchic Israel became the Godhead of the universe." The Israelites who returned from the exile came back with a renewed commitment to monotheism and the suppression of all traces of polytheism and goddess worship. The renunciation of the worship of the divine mother was partly emphasized by strictly separating men and women during worship and by erecting other taboos against women.

Worship of the Goddess in Ancient Israel

There is textual evidence that the ancient Israelites worshipped both masculine and feminine deities (Gerstenberger, 1996; Smith, 1990). There is controversial evidence that the biblical Yhwh had a female consort (Patai, 1990). In this view, the divine pair were known as Yhwh and his Asherah and were sometimes worshipped together.[xxv] Asherah, a mother goddess, was also the wife of El, and was clearly one of the female deities worshipped by the early Israelites (2 Kings 13:6). Early Hebrew polytheism also included other powerful female deities including Asherah's daughter Anath, a bloodthirsty goddess of love and war, who was the sister and consort of Baal (Patai, 1990), and Astarte, who was identified with fertility rites. The Canaanites believed that the fertility of their fields depended on the sexual fertility of Baal and Anath. There is a controversial theory that this had to be mirrored by human sexuality, so that "sacred prostitutes" were associated with Canaanite temples. According to one reading of texts such as Deuteronomy 23:18-19, Hosea 4:14, and 1 Kings 14:24, this practice was abhorrent to the Hebrews. However, it should be noted that the term "prostitute" was used by scholars and archeologists who were biased by their adherence to the monotheistic biblical tradition. As Stone (1976) pointed out, in their own context these women were not prostitutes in the modern sense; they were regarded as sacred or holy women who represented the goddess.

Goddess worship had flourished in the Near and Middle East for many thousands of years before the arrival of Abraham. Although many scholars agree that the early Israelites worshipped a queen of heaven (Day, 2000; Coogan et al., 2012), this idea is vehemently denied by some orthodox Jewish religious authorities. Nevertheless, the prophet Jeremiah (44:17) complained that the women of his day worshipped the goddess Astarte instead of Yhwh, so the cult of the mother goddess was popular at least as late as the sixth century BCE. The book of Proverbs contains some of the oldest biblical literature. The first nine chapters describe Sophia, a wisdom figure who is portrayed in language redolent of goddess imagery. She reports that she was present at the act of creation "like a master workman" (Proverbs 8:22-30). Eventually, just as most traces of female divinities were obliterated, this divine figure was demoted by monotheistic revisionists to nothing more than a poetic personification of a feminine aspect of Yhwh (Lang, 2002). Yet in the text, she is a teacher and counselor: "She is a tree of life to those who lay hold of her" (Proverbs

3:18.) In the book of Sirach (24:3,9), Sophia's divinity is clear: "I came forth from the mouth of the Most High...from the beginning, he created me." Although worship of the goddess was suppressed, and the Asherah was split off completely, remnants of the feminine aspect of the divine survived in the tradition in the forms of Sophia, the personification of divine wisdom, and as the Shekinah, the divine presence on earth. [xxvi] Perhaps the tradition's emphasis on the land of Israel represents an unconscious need for a feminine element, so that the land became a containing, maternal presence. Psychoanalysts see the renunciation of the mother goddess among the Jews, or the absorption of her qualities into the figure of Yhwh, as an attempted solution of an unconscious oedipal problem or an incest taboo. The Jews' insistence on an invisible, non-material God, combined with the loss of animal sacrifices after the destruction of the temple and the prohibition against making images of God, all contributed to the spiritualization of the tradition.

The Image of God in the Hebrew Scriptures

To imagine what was going on in the mind of their God, the biblical authors projected human psychological dynamics onto their concept of God. For example, it seemed impossible to them that there was no guiding hand behind their victories and defeats. God oversaw history, so a defeat had to be a punishment, part of a divine plan, while a victory obviously meant that God was on their side. In other words, the image of God in the biblical text is based on the authors' projected idea of how they assumed any given situation looked from their God's point of view. Eventually, as Yhwh's adherents became more spiritually evolved, their projections onto this image changed. Over time, the God-image of the Hebrew Scriptures became more sophisticated, reaching a high level in the prophetic tradition, *pari passu* with the development of human morality, which the prophets attributed to their God. Thus, originating as a superior personality who walked and talked in the Garden of Eden, God gradually became an infinite, omnipotent, heavenly being. As this image developed, his immediate presence faded from the biblical text, although he was and still is assumed to be personally involved in human affairs. His image becomes increasingly compassionate in the rabbinic tradition, which amplified the biblical text, but as Gellert (2018) points out, this God-image does not reach its most evolved characteristics until the appearance of the Jewish mystical tradition.

THE GOD-IMAGE OF THE HEBREW SCRIPTURES AND POST-BIBLICAL JUDAISM

The image of God in the Hebrew Scriptures is often anthropomorphic, although it is usually clear that God is being described in ways that are metaphorical and analogical rather than literal. The anthropomorphisms were probably intended to allow early worshippers to grasp ideas that otherwise could not be talked about. The character of God is portrayed in the text as if he were a personality with traits that are typically found in human beings, including violent shadow aspects that are painful to read. These latter traits are particularly relevant to Jung's notion of the dark side of the God-image. The tension of co-existing opposite qualities is very striking in the biblical descriptions, which often treat the biblical God-image as a character in a story.

God is described as having a face and a right arm (Psalm 89:13) and walking in the Garden of Eden (Genesis 3:8). He makes promises (Isaiah 40:29-31) that he does not always fulfill. He changes his mind or repents, for example, when he regretted making Saul king (1 Samuel 15:11), or sometimes in response to appeals from Moses (Exodus 32:12-14) or Abraham (Genesis 18:16-33). He has emotions such as jealousy (Deuteronomy 4:24), grief (Genesis 6:6), and anger (Exodus 15:7). He condemns and blesses according to his judgment of human behavior, which can be harsh. When he is disrespected, or when the people complain about him, his anger leads to devouring fire (Leviticus 10:2), plague (Numbers 11:33), earthquakes that swallow people up (Numbers 16:32), and poisonous snakes (Numbers 21:6). He sees and hears everything that is happening. He sometimes responds to prayer (Jeremiah 29:12), but sometimes he is unforgiving (Lamentations 3:42-44). He grants people children (Psalms 127:3) and economic and social success (Deuteronomy 29:9). He is a triumphant, divine warrior (Exodus 15:3), and like many deities of the ancient world, he assists his people in battle (Joshua 5:13-14). He defines war as holy, and expresses his will in terms of military victory. He is then particularly ruthless, commanding the killing of civilian captives (Deuteronomy 20:10-17; Numbers 31:1-18), behavior that is never explained but sounds as if it is due to envy of the fact that the conquered people worshipped other gods. Intolerance and vengeance seem to have been components of his insistence on monotheism. One of his tactics is to use Israel's enemies, such as Assyria or Babylon, as agents to punish the people when they are disobedient (Jeremiah 51:20-24). The prophetic tradition not only sees Yhwh as a God of battle but also as a great king with a throne in heaven and the earth as his footstool (Isaiah 66:1).

Yhwh requires the death penalty for a range of offenses, including worshipping other gods (Exodus 22:20), a persistently rebellious child (Deuteronomy 21:18-21), a child who hits or curses his parents (Exodus 21:15,17), working on the Sabbath, adultery (Leviticus 20:10), pre-marital sexual intercourse (Deuteronomy 22:13-21), and male homosexuality (Leviticus 20:13). He sends plagues to Israel's enemies, on one occasion killing a 185,000 Assyrians by means of a plague (2 Kings 19:35). Yhwh's followers also did a great deal of killing in battle, at his command: "I will make my arrows drunk with blood" (Deuteronomy 32:42).

Yhwh demands submission, obedience, and a high standard of behavior from his people (Deuteronomy 30:16), but never acknowledges that they may be resentful because of his demands. He reacts strongly to the way his people behave towards him, sometimes with attacks of murderous rage, for example when he orders the death of three thousand people after they worship a golden calf (Exodus 32:28),[xxvii] or when he kills twenty-four thousand men who consort with the priestesses of a Canaanite god (Numbers 25:1-9). These atrocities seem to justify mass killings on behalf of God, with well-known historical consequences. He is very sensitive to affronts to his prophets; when in the name of God Elisha curses a group of children who make fun of him because he is bald, God sends two bears to attack forty-two of them (2 Kings 2:23-24). Although Yhwh is said to know the future, in return for a guarantee of victory he allows Jephthah to promise to sacrifice whatever meets him when he returns home from battle; in the event Jephthah must sacrifice his only child (Judges 11:28-40). Yhwh kills Aaron's two sons as a punishment during a ritual sacrifice, for a mistake that is not specified (Leviticus 10:1), and then says that he did so to "show myself holy" and be glorified before the people (Leviticus 10:3). Despite this violent aspect of his personality, he is also said to be "slow to anger and filled with kindness and truth" (Exodus 34:6-7), and also "merciful…and abounding in steadfast love" (Psalms 103:8). However, his rage—which sounds like vengeful, narcissistic rage—takes so long to calm down that he visits the iniquity of the fathers upon their children and their children's children (Exodus 34:6-7). He has an amazing capacity to bear a long-standing grudge, for example when he swears to eliminate the Amalekites "from generation to generation" (Exodus 17:16) because they attacked Israel on the way to Canaan. Much later, God orders King Saul to kill all the Amalekites, including women, children, and animals (1 Samuel 15:2-3). He gets angry when David takes a census of the fighting men of the people (2 Samuel 24:1-17), and 70,000 people are killed as a result—the reason is not given, but it may be that taking a census implied ownership, which was rightfully God's. Many of the Psalms are full of such violence and vengeance, although some suggest divine mercy and renewal.

Yhwh murders the innocent first-born children of the Egyptians (Exodus 12:29) because Pharaoh will not let Yhwh's people leave Egypt. In an appalling demonstration of his power shadow and his narcissism, Yhwh first hardens Pharaoh's heart, making this massacre of children more likely, so that Yhwh can "get glory" for himself (Exodus 14:6). In this behavior Yhwh mirrors the behavior of Pharaoh, who had ordered the mass murder of Israelite baby boys at the beginning of the story (Exodus 1:16). Yet, the biblical text also promises that, despite all his violence, eventually Yhwh will bring about such peace that: "The wolf shall lie down with the lamb" (Isaiah 11:6-8).

Yhwh is also depicted metaphorically as a husband or wife, a bridegroom (Isaiah 62:5), a father (Hosea 11:1-4), a mother (Isaiah 42:14), a redeemer, and a shepherd who guards his flocks (Isaiah 40:11). He reveals his will on a large scale, sometimes in "mighty acts" such as the Exodus from Egypt. He may also appear to individuals in the form of dreams (Genesis 28:12; 1 Kings 3:5) or in numinous visionary experiences such as his appearance to Moses at the burning bush. At times his spirit may possess people (1 Samuel 10:1-6), and he may send an evil spirit to afflict them, causing melancholy or rage (1 Samuel 16:14; 18:10). He makes human beings in his own image (Genesis 1:26-27), although he does not say why he does so and it is not clear exactly how we are created in his image, since we do not know what God is like. However, this idea became particularly important in later theology and has been much discussed. Perhaps it refers to the fact that human beings are creative, just as God is, or the idea implies that humans are the summit of creation, only "a little less than God," (Psalms 8:5), with dominion over what God has created. Or the notion of being created in God's image might mean that human beings have the same values that God has, or that we have endowments such as love, intelligence, the capacity for relationship, and a moral sense.

Yhwh oversees animals and birds (Psalms 50:10-11), but he gives human beings authority to eat them (Genesis 9:2-3), just as he delegates authority over nature to humans (Genesis 1:28-29). The God of the Hebrew Scriptures is also a legislator and a lawgiver, which is not surprising since the religion of early Israel was influenced by Mesopotamian gods such as the Babylonian sun god Shamash, who was responsible for the administration of justice at the time of Hammurabi. Yhwh often behaves as if he is a paternalistic personality who cares for his people, but this attribute is inconsistent. He can be loving, faithful, forgiving, and compassionate, but he also brings and heals diseases (Exodus 15:26). The ambivalence of his image is further seen in the fact that he is the creator of heaven and earth but also "a devouring fire" (Deuteronomy 4:24). He breathes life into Adam but then rather petulantly destroys most of humanity and the earth's animal life with a flood (Genesis 6-9).

Yhwh is vengeful when his 613 commandments, which regulate all aspects of people's lives, are ignored. His commandments, such as dietary laws, are said to render holy those who abide by them, in imitation of Yhwh (Leviticus 19:2). The commandments were also a means by which Yhwh's people could set themselves apart from others (Leviticus 11:43-45) and feel special. Any place in which Yhwh appears is holy, and anything or any place that has a relationship to him, such as his altar and utensils, becomes holy, meaning the object is set apart from ordinary use and is only for his use. The most holy object of all was the Ark of the Covenant, and when this was touched by Uzzah simply to prevent it falling, God killed him (2 Samuel 6:6-7). Before anything can be considered to be holy, it must be purified. Ritual impurity is contagious; it arises from contact with birth, death, genital discharges, and skin diseases. According to Klawans (2014), because God is eternal and does not die or have sex, by avoiding these contaminants the people were able to separate themselves from what was least God-like. According to the Holiness Code in Leviticus, holiness requires physical health. Any disabled, blind, lame, or disfigured person is considered to be impure and is not qualified to be a priest. He must not be allowed to approach the altar (Leviticus 21:16-23).

There is no clearer example of the projection of human personality traits onto the divine than that provided by Yhwh's demands to be mirrored and praised forever. His narcissistic vulnerability is suggested

THE GOD-IMAGE OF THE HEBREW SCRIPTURES AND POST-BIBLICAL JUDAISM | 187

by statements such as "You shall have no other gods before me," or "I am the Lord and there is none else" (Isaiah 45:5-7). This insecurity is also indicated by his demands for loyalty, his sensitivity to abandonment or rejection, and the harsh punishment that results even when an offense is caused inadvertently (2 Samuel 6:6-7). His narcissistic rage and need for vengeance are seen when the Israelites follow other gods, whereupon he hands his people over to their enemies as a punishment (Judges 2:14). He then appoints leaders to save his people from their enemies, but the cycle of rebellion, punishment, and redemption keeps recurring. He makes grandiose pronouncements, announcing that he will do "wonderful and marvelous" things (Isaiah 29:14), although most of these promised marvels never materialized. Incidentally, not until Isaiah (40:3) do we see sentiments such as: "Comfort, comfort my people...Speak tenderly to Jerusalem..." One suspects that this development in the God-image is the result of a development within the prophet who announces it, so that he becomes able to project caring rather than dominion and power onto his concept of God. However, despite the often-violent nature of the biblical God-image, this image showed occasional spurts of moral growth and tolerance, for example in the book of Ruth, who was a foreigner but was well treated after she proved her goodness and loyalty to Yhwh.

Yhwh has no physical body, although he was very concerned with reproduction and sexuality in the form of rules about cohabitation and menstruation; he determined that menstrual blood and semen cause pollution (Leviticus 15:16-19). However, there is no hint in the Bible of his own sexuality. Perhaps this is to stress the idea that he is one of a kind, not reproducible, or he is above such human concerns. He often uses metaphors such as infidelity, fornication, and prostitution to complain about his people's behavior towards him (Jeremiah 13:27; Ezekiel 16:25, 35-41). He enjoys the smell of burnt offerings (Genesis 8:21), but as Miles (1996) points out, there are few other allusions to divine delight or pleasure in the Bible, and although the people are told to rejoice in God, he does not express joy at their joy. Neither does he show much pity; indeed, he often advises against it: "Your eye shall not pity; it shall be life for life, eye for eye, tooth for tooth" (Deuteronomy 19:21). The effects of this ruthless mythic image can still be detected.

Yhwh's mixture of attributes, and the fact that he clearly has a dark side that causes evil and suffering, still cause a certain amount of anxiety among his devotees, not least because he can be unpredictable. He inspires some ambivalence in his followers, sometimes promising through the words of Isaiah 25:8 to "wipe away tears from all faces," while also threatening that: "Terror, the pit, and the snare are upon you, O inhabitants of the earth" (Isaiah 24:17). Yhwh abandons his people periodically, although usually the people are blamed for this. He can be remote even when he is needed; thus, the Psalmist (10:1) cries: "Why O Lord, do you stand afar off?" Because he is omnipotent, he is the author of both good and evil; thus Isaiah 45:7 says, "I make weal and create woe." [xxviii] Such an ambivalent image suggests the biblical authors' parental projections onto their God-image. When innocent people suffered and the wicked prospered, the tradition usually invokes the notion of deferred punishment in the world to come, or simply divine mystery.

There is nothing to which Yhwh can be compared (Isaiah 40:18). At the same time as he is infinite, he is also immanent. Yet sometimes his glory is seen, although a kind of fiery envelope or cloud surrounds him when he reveals himself, because human beings cannot tolerate seeing him directly; "for man shall not see me and live" (Exodus 33:20). Thus, at Mt. Sinai, the people were not allowed to touch or even approach the place of revelation (Exodus 19:10-12). This event can be seen as a numinous eruption from the objective psyche, projected as if it came from the outer world. Presumably the people were in a state of emotional upheaval for this to have occurred. Why this revelation seemed to be focused on the figure of Moses, we cannot know. If there was such an individual, he must have been particularly permeable to the archetypal levels of the psyche.

Emphasizing both his administrative ability and his ability to judge his people, Yhwh keeps a record of people's behavior in the book of life and threatens to blot out the names of those who sin (Exodus 32:31-33). Some people are resurrected into everlasting life, while others are destined to a place of "shame and everlasting contempt" (Daniel 12:2).[xxix] He does not forgive without repentance. Yhwh sometimes appears to act in inexplicably unjust ways, for example when, purely on the basis of a wager with a satan,[xxx] a member of the heavenly court, God makes Job suffer by testing his piety for no obvious reason. This story makes God seem either unfaithful, sadistic, insecure, or unable to see the future. He offers no explanation for his ill-treatment of Job, other than to say that his ways are beyond human understanding. This was not a new problem; Jeremiah (12:1-4) had already asked why the "way of the wicked prospers."

Yhwh was assumed to be both just and omnipotent, so that the inexplicable suffering of the innocent and the prosperity of the wicked became a problem reflected in texts such as the *Book of Job*. In that book, God's response is that suffering has to be seen in the context of creation as a whole, playing a role that humanity cannot understand. God cannot be questioned by human beings. This response to the suffering of the innocents satisfies few people, however, and it remains a central problem for traditional theists, made more acute by the Holocaust. The problem of apparently unjust suffering was eventually addressed during the rabbinic era by invoking the notion of a world to come, by belief in the resurrection of the dead, by belief in a Messiah, and with the hope that Yhwh would eventually vindicate the suffering of his people and punish their oppressors.

The God of the Hebrew Bible is a creator, but in a different sense than the mother goddesses of matriarchal religions. The biblical image of God was obviously influenced by the experience of people who were used to occupations like farming or pottery, for example when God is described as making a man from dust (Genesis 2:7), and people are in his hands like the hands of the potter (Jeremiah 18:6). Unlike the nurturing earth mother goddess who produces humanity out of her body, the implication is that the biblical God conceives of his creation in his mind. Whereas the goddess nurtures and grows plants and animals from the soil, Yhwh tends to appear on the scene as an eruption from an unknown realm. In Genesis, God's breath gives life, so that he creates out of his spirit rather than his flesh, by means of his word, by speaking things into existence, for example when he commands "Let there be light" (Genesis 1:3). In such a case, the body and matter are much less holy or important than the mind, and creation is not a part of the creator as it was in the earlier goddess traditions. Unlike the divinities of those traditions, Yhwh was seen to be outside the forces of nature, although in control of them. He sometimes seems to be alienated from the natural world. He mainly uses the forces of nature to demonstrate his power over them (Genesis 19:24; Leviticus 9:24). When he gives the law, he engraves his words onto stone tablets, perhaps as a way to imprint his word onto matter, which is then only a receptacle.

Although God rests after having created the world and initially sees it as good, he regrets his creation afterwards, as if he is dissatisfied with what he had made. He realizes that his creation has a defective nature:

"For the imagination of man's heart is evil from his youth" (Genesis 8:21). This exemplifies one of the paradoxes in the biblical God's character, which is that he does not always seem to foresee the results of his actions. Thus, because he is dissatisfied with his creation, he is capable of world-destruction, as we see in the story of Noah and the flood.[xxxi] However, his compassion eventually overrules his anger, so by keeping Noah alive he does not entirely destroy his creation.

Yhwh's image is not always fiery and stormy; he is also experienced in more subtle ways, for instance as a "still small voice," alternatively translated (in the NRSV) as "a sound of sheer silence" (1 Kings 19:12). As the biblical story unfolds, the appearances of Yhwh become less and less dramatic. Early on he walks and talks with Adam and Eve in the Garden of Eden,[xxxii] talks to Abraham at the trees of Mamre while taking on human form (Genesis 18:1) and appears to Moses in a burning bush and on Mt. Sinai. However, gradually, he seems to stop talking and almost disappears, becoming more and more transcendent, so that Isaiah (45:15) complains: "Truly, you are a God who hides himself." The traditional reason for this aloofness was human sinfulness, but another suggested reason for God's hiddenness is that it makes people actively search for him. Perhaps his increasing transcendence made him seem even more powerful. Friedman (1995) disputes the common assumption that God's increasing hiddenness in later books of the Bible results from the increasing sophistication of later writers. Friedman believes that the disappearance of God from the Bible occurred because the biblical narrators themselves did not witness miracles—they only knew stories about them, so they assumed that God's interventions "belonged to a bygone age" (p. 89).

Different biblical writers stress different aspects of their God-image; Amos stresses his justice while Hosea focuses on his love and forgiveness. It is however difficult to know how any particular biblical writer actually conceived of God, except in terms of the writers' metaphors, which reflect the way they imagined him. These metaphors are important because they take us beyond cognition and the limitations of language in powerful ways. Yet, the problem with attributing even metaphorical attributes to God is that if God has a nature and characteristics, he is necessarily limited. Not surprisingly, the nature of God, apart from descriptions of his attributes, is never given in the Hebrew Bible. In contrast to the gods of many mythological traditions, the Bible says nothing about the origin of the biblical God; he is simply said to have always existed; he was not created, and before he created the universe, he was alone since eternity (Psalms 90:2).

In the book of Daniel (7:9-12), Yhwh is depicted as an Ancient One with snowy white clothing and hair like pure wool. Over time, as the tradition developed, the image of God becomes less anthropomorphic or metaphorical. Yhwh becomes increasingly more abstract or formless, and the tradition eventually forbad the speaking of his name, which was considered to be sacred. As the tradition evolved, its way of talking about the divine became more and more detached from the physical world, leading to the notion of an invisible god who cannot be detected with the ordinary senses. God came to be thought of as a Supreme Being, one of a kind. As the moral behavior of his devotees gradually improved, so their image of God had to change to keep up with changing social values. Accordingly, the God-image gradually matured from a moral point of view, reaching a high level among the Hebrew prophets, who attributed their own values to their image of God.

Psychological Aspects of Biblical Anthropomorphic Projections

The God-image of the Hebrew Scriptures changed markedly from the earlier to the later books of the Bible, and this image continued to evolve in the post-biblical Jewish tradition. Although it is often claimed that we cannot describe God in terms of human characteristics, throughout the Bible God is depicted as if "he" has qualities that are obviously human projections. So anthropomorphic are these descriptions that many of the ways God behaves would be pathological if they belonged to a human being. These characteristics are clearly the projection of elements of human psychology onto a God-image. The text describes the image of a deity who suffers from affective instability, moodiness, and narcissistic fragility that leads to lethal rage attacks. He suffers from envy of other gods, constantly insisting that he is the only deity worthy of worship. He can never be quite sure about the reliability of his people's tie to him, as if he has insecure attachment. He seems to need his people, as if he is lonely or suffers from abandonment anxiety. His insecurity is visible on many occasions, for example when he allows terrible suffering to be inflicted on Job just to see if Job is truly faithful to him, in the process betraying his own lack of faithfulness. He tries to force his people to love him, partly through threats and promises and partly by regulating all aspects of their lives. He can be impulsive, paranoid, and defensively inflated. He is prone to all-good and all-bad splitting, leading to large scale, ruthless massacres. The clinician will immediately see that this deity behaves like a human being with a borderline personality disorder. Since this diagnosis is obviously meaningless in terms of the divine itself, we can see the truth of suggestions by Feuerbach and Freud that the classical idea of God is based on the projection of human personality traits. However, these writers were only half-correct when they developed this idea; the fact that human beings color their God-image with human traits does not mean that God does not exist. It means that many descriptions of God are relatively unsophisticated and consist largely of projections and fantasy. Perhaps it has been true that the only way to talk about God is by means of metaphor and anthropomorphisms, but Jung's notion of the Self offers an alternative.

Development of the God-image Among the Prophets

Beginning in the eighth century BCE, and for the next 320 years, a group of important Hebrew prophets arose who critiqued their society and reminded people what they believed God really wanted of them. The prophets thought they were speaking in the name of God, or that God spoke through them. They spoke with a missionary zeal and with drama and urgency that gives the impression that they suffered from intense inner turmoil and pressure. They prophesized disasters as a divine punishment for what they saw as the cultural shadow, such as the idolatrous worship of gods other than Yhwh, especially when this was carried out by the kings of Israel.

The prophetic tradition is not simply about predicting the future; it is largely about the importance of turning away from evil and apostasy, and the importance of repentance. The prophets insisted that God required a virtuous life and a just society. They developed the moral and universal qualities of the God-image of their day, under seriously adverse political situations such as the threat of invasion. They saw morality as a divine attribute. (There is scholarly debate about whether they originated the tradition's stress on morality or whether they were referring to long-standing traditions.) Under their tutelage, the people's image of God evolved from that of a tribal war-deity to an ethical God who cared more for good behavior than for military conquest or cultic rituals.

The prophets displayed anguished emotional reactions to the behavior they saw around them, which they saw as corrupt. They projected these feelings onto their God, as if he was feeling what they felt. The prophets' main function was exhortation about what they imagined were God's wishes, motives, and intentions, about which they claimed to have special insight. Typically, they denounced too much emphasis on ritual, insisting that God really wants authentic prayer, justice, and morality. This was a radical idea for its time, but it had the benefit of freeing the religion from the confines of a specific place or time period, since these are universal, permanent values. This development, combined with the loss of their temple, contributed to the Jews' capacity to live and practice their religion anywhere.

During hard times, the people would often turn to the worship of local nature gods and goddesses, practices that the prophets believed would incur the anger of Yhwh. The prophets would then speak of the people as an unfaithful bride or an adulteress (Eze. 16). Nevertheless, the prophets promised that the people would eventually be reborn, when God would adopt a maternal role: "As one whom his mother comforts, so I will comfort you" (Isaiah 66:13). Some of their prophecies came true. Amos and Hosea warned the northern kingdom of Israel that it would be destroyed because of its king's infidelity to Yhwh, and in 722 BCE the Assyrian army invaded and the prophecy came true. There are several similar examples, but some of these are suspect because anonymous authors, translators, and editors inserted material to the prophetic texts after the predicted event had happened. Because Deuteronomy 18:21 insists that if a prophecy does not come true it was not the word of God, prophecies that did not materialize may have been deleted from the prophetic material. Ezekiel (14:9) acknowledges that a prophet may be deceived by God: "And if the prophet be deceived…I the Lord have deceived that prophet." Later Christian authors borrowed heavily from the Hebrew prophets, especially the messianic prophecies in the book of Zechariah (3:8; 6:12-13; 9:9), which were retrospectively attributed to the coming of Jesus.

It is not clear exactly how the prophets knew God's intentions or how they distinguished the divine will from their own preferences and intuitions. Typically, the biblical text says that "the word of the Lord came" to the prophet (Jeremiah 1:4), but it is not known if he actually heard a voice or whether this term was always used metaphorically, perhaps to indicate the sense of an interior illumination or an "inner voice." [xxxiii] For example, the prophet Ezekiel (11:5) says that: "the spirit of the Lord fell upon me, and he said to me, 'Say, Thus says the Lord.'" Or "The Lord made it known to me and I knew" (Jeremiah 11:18). Sometimes the prophets had visions, or something was shown to them (Amos 7:1-7; Isaiah 1:1). Some prophets experienced ecstatic states, or God's intention was conveyed when they performed a miracle. Dreams or visionary experiences were also important vehicles of divine transmission; the book of Numbers (12:6) says: "If there is a prophet among you, I the Lord make myself known to him in a vision, I speak with him in a dream." Sometimes the prophet felt an irresistible call or a sense of inspiration, while sometimes the medium of transmission is not given.[xxxiv] For the psychologist, it seems that they were seized by material from the objective psyche, which they interpreted as sent by God. In whatever manner the information was received, the prophets believed they could speak for God or speak from God's point of view. Because of this, their criticism was directed not only to ordinary people but also to kings and priests, or wherever they saw reprehensible behavior. They sometimes put their message into behavioral metaphors, as when Jeremiah (27:2) wore a yoke as a sign of the people's impending captivity or when Isaiah (20:2-4) walked naked and barefoot as a sign of what happened to Egypt.

The prophets were extremists, but they clearly believed they were divinely inspired. Inevitably, their religious message was intertwined with domestic policy and relationships with surrounding nations. Their rejection of the gods of other nations was a form of nationalism that may have also attempted to consolidate domestic political power.

The prophets typically asserted that wickedness would be punished and righteousness and obedience to the law would be rewarded, but this claim was not always convincing to their contemporaries. The prophets all complained passionately about social injustice, and they castigated the people in almost cosmic terms. The prophets promised divine rage, retribution, and destruction because of the nation's guilt when it contravened the covenant either morally or by means of idolatry. The people of the time valued wealth and strength above all things, but the prophets were iconoclastic and decried these attributes and the pretensions of the affluent: "I abhor the pride of Jacob/And hate his strongholds" (Amos 6:8). What people regarded as wisdom, the prophets denounced: "The wise men shall be put to shame…and what wisdom is in them?" (Jeremiah 8:9). At times the prophets denounced orthodox religious practices on behalf of God, realizing that the priests were fraudulent: "Your burnt offerings are not acceptable, /Nor your sacrifices pleasing to me" (Jeremiah 6:20). To their contemporaries, the prophets' decrial of sacrifice must have been shocking or blasphemous, since the importance of any god at the time was reflected in the greatness and power of his cities, temples, and shrines. The prophets announced that God would use the people's enemies as instruments of his power, so that Assyria is called "the rod of my anger" (Isaiah 10:5). Amos may have sounded treasonous when, in the name of God, he threatened to "send a fire upon Judah, / and it shall devour the strongholds of Jerusalem" (2:5), but he must have felt tremendous internal pressure to communicate such a dire message. Prophetic messages were often contradictory or mixed, using the most extreme language. Amos says: "The end has come upon my people Israel" (8:2) but then says: "I will restore the fortunes of my people Israel" (9:14). Hosea (13:9) has God say, "I will destroy you, O Israel," but a few lines further he says, "I will love them freely, for my anger has turned from them" (Hos. 14:4).

The prophets typically imagined that although people are rebellious and sinful, God cares about them and is saddened when they forget his rules. The prophets pointed out that God's punishment can be severe, but they also taught that there is a way back to him if people repent; they all brought messages of hope and reconciliation with their censure. The prophets expected that they would be ignored, which they often were. Perhaps because their behavior was provocative and disrespectful of the secular and religious authorities, their contemporaries sometimes reacted angrily, and the prophets were often persecuted. They were sometimes treated as troublemakers by those in power, and they were accordingly attacked or driven away. Jeremiah complained that people invented charges against him (18:18, 23) and called for his death (26:11). Amos was banished (7:11). Nevertheless, their words became of great historical importance to the tradition, radically coloring its God-image.

It is important to understand the historical context in which the prophets spoke. A united monarchy had developed during the reigns of Kings Saul, David, and Solomon, between about 1050 BCE and 930 BCE, during which time the first temple was built. Originally a powerful empire, around 930 BCE it divided into two weaker states, Israel in the north and Judah in the south. By 750 BCE, both the northern and southern kingdoms of Israel were being threatened by the Assyrian Empire, which was expanding rapidly in a rapacious manner. The Assyrians were brutal and murderous, and they conquered and annexed the northern kingdom in 722 BCE. In 586 BCE, the Babylonians conquered Jerusalem, destroyed the temple, and exiled the Israelites to Babylon. The Persian empire conquered the Babylonians in 540 BCE and allowed the Israelites to return to Jerusalem and rebuild their temple.

Amos

Amos, the first of the main prophets, appeared in the northern kingdom at the time of King Jeroboam II (circa 780-746 BCE). Amos was a farmer and shepherd who felt that God had forced a mission of prophecy onto him (Amos 7:14-15). At this time, the northern kingdom of Israel had reached the heights of its power and prosperity, and the threat from the Assyrians was underestimated. This was also a period of increasing social injustice and inequality, when affluent people afflicted, ignored, and exploited the poor. Judges were corrupt, and there was only lip-service to religious tradition with an over-emphasis on empty liturgy. Amos was therefore angry; it seemed to him that success had become an end in itself, and the wealthy and powerful had perverted justice and lacked compassion. He was very sensitive to the suffering of his people. As well, he believed that the people had rejected the Torah of the Lord and were not keeping his laws (2:4). Amos (5:21-22) insisted that God was not interested in religious ceremonies for their own sake and would not accept their burnt offerings if at the same time people behaved in unjust and cruel ways. He reminded them of their history, and predicted disaster and defeat by an enemy acting according to God's direction. This harsh preaching was offensive politically and militarily, and Amos was accused of sedition and ordered out of the country. Many of the people preferred the gods of the Canaanites, who still flourished in Israel, but Amos had a concept of a God who is universal and was not just a local tribal god. Amos believed that God morally judges all nations but had a special covenant with the Hebrew people, and this covenant made particular demands on them for moral behavior rather than only observing cultic practices. For Amos, injustice was a particular sin: "let justice roll down like waters, / and righteousness like an ever-flowing stream" (5:24). Amos believed that the nation would inevitably come to grief because of its sins. The last few lines of the book reverse this dire prognosis, but these are often thought to be later editorial additions intended to soften Amos's judgment.

Hosea

In the face of the Assyrian threat, beginning in about 740 BCE, the prophet Hosea, a younger contemporary of Amos and also a native of the northern kingdom, preached a radical idea. Rather than trusting in human leaders or in foreign alliances, Hosea insisted on trust in Yhwh, otherwise the people would be breaching their covenant with Yhwh. Speaking on behalf of Yhwh in threatening ways, Hosea railed against the moral and religious laxity of his time, and especially condemned idol worship or the worship of gods other than Yhwh, which was common at the time. He does not deny the existence of other gods such as Baal.

Hosea compared Israel with a wife who betrays her husband, because Israel had betrayed Yhwh by worshipping pagan gods (3:1). Hosea compared the worship of other gods to sexual promiscuity (4:13-14) that would be punished by Yhwh as if he were a jealous husband. Hosea was told by God to marry a prostitute, who was unfaithful to him. She was initially sent away, but God told him to bring her back home and renew his love for her "even as the Lord loves the people of Israel, though they turn to other gods" (3:1). Hosea's marriage was renewed, making the analogous point that God will not abandon Israel even though she is faithless. Apparently, the difficulties within his own marriage, followed by its reconciliation, allowed Hosea to empathically understand the divine capacity for forgiveness.

At this time, the demand for the exclusive worship of one God was radical, since people worshipped different gods for different life exigencies, but Hosea promised them divine protection by Yhwh if the people devoted themselves exclusively to him. Hosea may have believed that devotion to one God would unite the people against the Assyrian threat. His anxiety about the Assyrians may have inspired his religious ideas.

Hosea has an image of God that is more compassionate and merciful than that of Amos. Hosea teaches the knowledge and love of Yhwh rather than formal religious practices: "For I desire steadfast love and not sacrifice, /the knowledge of God, rather than burnt offerings" (6:6). For him, knowledge of God means awareness of God or intimacy with God; otherwise, the people are "destroyed by lack of knowledge" (4:6). According to Hosea, the motive driving God's behavior in the course of history is God's love for Israel: "When Israel was a child, I loved him" (11:1). Hosea strikingly imagines an internal dialog within Yhwh, a soliloquy in which God thinks about withdrawing and delaying his judgment on his people as he waits for Israel to acknowledge her guilt and return to him (5:15)—but God realizes that there is little hope of this. Hosea takes the side of God in his harsh threats of punishment for Israel's faithlessness: "Give them a miscarrying womb/And dry breasts" (9:14).

In the event, despite these prophetic warnings, the Israelites did not abandon their polytheism. In 722 BCE the Assyrian King Sargon II invaded the northern kingdom and deported most of its population, who dispersed and became known as the Ten Lost Tribes of Israel. Their subsequent identity remained a matter of historical curiosity for a long time. The southern kingdom of Judah managed to survive by paying tribute to the Assyrians. The defeat of the northern kingdom was attributed to delayed punishment for the idolatry of wicked kings.

Josiah's Reforms

Despite the fate of the northern kingdom, the southern kingdom of Judah remained polytheistic. In about 640 BCE, Josiah became King of Judah. In 622 BCE, he was presented with a book that was said to have been found during the restoration of the Jerusalem temple. This book claimed to contain the laws of Yhwh as given directly to Moses. The book demanded that the Jews accept Yhwh as their only God. The book survived in the form of parts of the book of Deuteronomy (sections 12-26), which gave lists of rules and regulations which, if followed, would ensure victories and the blessing of Yhwh, but if ignored would lead to punishment by him. No one is sure of the authorship of the book, whose discovery is told in 2 Kings 22:8. It may have been written in Josiah's court, but it is quite likely to have been a version of Hosea's demands that were brought south a century earlier by refugees from the northern kingdom, who worshipped Yhwh exclusively. This book, which forms much of the legal core of Deuteronomy, is sometimes seen as a pious fraud, because it endorsed the reforms that Josiah wanted to impose for political reasons. If that version of events is correct, Josiah invented the biblical story of Israel by re-working the earlier texts in order to unify the people under his leadership, partly to unite the kingdom against the Assyrian threat. He made Jerusalem his capital and invented a new theology. Josiah decreed that only Yhwh could be worshipped. The shrines and altars of other gods were destroyed. Some of these gods may have been foreign, while some were members of a pantheon of gods worshipped by the Israelites. Josiah also confined the worship of Yhwh to Jerusalem rather than other sites, which consolidated Josiah's political power. Only the prophets of Yhwh were tolerated; the prophets or worshippers of other gods were to be killed (Deuteronomy 13:6-11).

The Deuteronomists who wrote the book "discovered" in the temple also rewrote the early history of Israel,[xxxv] and they added, revised, and updated earlier laws. They enhanced earlier narratives in a way that gave more prominence to Moses and the Exodus story. Deuteronomy emphasizes social justice and care for the oppressed and weak, so here the biblical God-image became more humanitarian, emphasizing responsibility to others. The text also stresses the love of God for the people, while their reciprocal loyalty to his law is required.

Josiah's reforms were eventually ignored, and polytheism supervened again, until a new disaster appeared. The Babylonians defeated the Assyrians in 612 BCE, and in 597 BCE the Babylonians under King Nebuchadnezzar invaded Judah and installed a puppet king, Zedekiah. In an allegiance with surrounding states, he revolted against the Babylonians. In response, in 587 BCE the Babylonians laid siege to Jerusalem, an event that the prophet Jeremiah regarded as the will of God. The Babylonians destroyed the temple to Yhwh in Jerusalem and deported most of Judah's elite to Babylon, leaving behind the poorer people. The Babylonian exile was a major blow to the worship of Yhwh, since it implied that Marduk, the god of the Babylonians, was more powerful than Yhwh. Many of the exiled Israelites began to worship Babylonian gods.

The Judeans blamed themselves for this disaster. Jeremiah told them it occurred because they had broken Yhwh's laws and worshipped other deities such as the Queen of Heaven (Jeremiah 44:25-27), although a competing faction believed that the trauma of the exile had occurred because they had stopped worshipping her (44:17-18). Eventually the devotees of Yhwh became dominant, but the Israelites were forced by their exile to re-evaluate their theology, to question whether God's covenant was still operative, and to ask whether Yhwh was truly the God of history. While it was usually assumed that a military defeat meant that the god of the victorious nation was stronger than the god of the defeated nation, in this case the followers of Yhwh rationalized their defeat by assuming that Yhwh had used the Babylonians as an instrument to punish the Israelites for their infidelity to him, thus turning their military defeat into a kind of theological victory for their deity.

While in exile in Babylon, some of the people finally adopted Hosea's radical monotheistic teaching. After the exile, they re-wrote their earlier scriptures to reflect the exclusive worship of Yhwh, assuming as Hosea had taught that Yhwh would protect them if they were obedient. As part of the re-write, the Exodus story was enlarged to include the story of the giving of the Law on Mt. Sinai. Meanwhile, many of the people who had stayed in Judah remained polytheistic.

Jeremiah

Jeremiah began to preach about a hundred years after Amos, in the year 627 BCE, during the reign of King Josiah. Jeremiah believed he had been destined from the womb to be a prophet (1:5). He responded to this call by saying he did not know how to speak because of his youth (1:6), but Yhwh "touched his mouth," putting words into it. Despite his conflict over his vocation, Jeremiah preached when it became clear that in spite of Josiah's reforms Israel was not free of polytheism. Jeremiah saw the Babylonians who captured Jerusalem in 586 BCE as the agents of God's punishment.

Jeremiah was unusual in that he revealed some of his inner life. He was very unhappy about his role as a prophet: "Cursed be the day on which I was born!" (20:14). However, he was remarkably courageous, despite the fact that he was disliked and mistrusted by his fellow citizens. He was distressed that the wicked prosper (12:1-3), and he wanted revenge. His preaching was harsh: "You have polluted the land with your vile harlotry. / Therefore, the showers have been withheld, and the spring rain has not come" (3:1-3). He devalued the importance of temple sacrifices (7:22), strongly denounced religious apostasy in Judah, and condemned the worship of idols and worship of the goddess (7:18-19). Like other prophets, Jeremiah used the image of Israel as a faithless wife who has been promiscuous, promising however that if Israel would return to God, God would be forgiving. Jeremiah saw King Jehoiakim as fraudulent: "Do you think you are a king because you compete in cedar?" (22:15). Because of his hostility to the king, he had to put up with a good deal of scorn and persecution (15:15) by his fellow Judeans, who saw him as a traitor. He was imprisoned and flogged (20:1-6) and his life was threatened. He sometimes felt abandoned by God: "I sat alone, because thy hand was upon me" (15:17), He was obviously lonely, hopeless, and afraid on many occasions, even though God promised to make him "a fortified wall of bronze" and reassured him that "they will not prevail over you" (15:20). But Jeremiah's anguish is very clear: "Woe is me, my mother, that you bore me, a man of strife and contention to the whole land! I have not lent, not have I borrowed, yet all of them curse me" (15:10). He goes on: "Why is my pain unceasing, my wound incurable, refusing to be healed?" (15:18). "I have become a laughingstock all the day; everyone mocks me" (20:7). He felt surrounded by people who plotted against him (18:18), and even his family turned against him. Of course, he asked God "Why does the way of the wicked prosper? / Why do all those who are treacherous thrive?" (12:1). He felt deceived by God (20:7). Nevertheless, he preached a new covenant between God and the people of Israel (31:31-34), even though they largely ignored him.

Ezekiel

About 559 BCE, the Persian king Cyrus became the major power in the region. His rise inspired the prophet Ezekiel, who preached during the Babylonian exile. There is controversy about both the date of the composition of the book of Ezekiel and its authorship. The prophet's call began with an extraordinary vision that is difficult for us to imagine (1:4-28). He saw a cloud of light, with lightening flashing within it. In the cloud were what looked like four figures with human forms, each with four faces and four wings. The noise of their beating wings was like the sound of an army. Each had the face of a man, a lion, a bull, and an eagle. There was a wheel beside each figure, and the rims of the wheels were full of eyes. Whenever the beings moved, the wheels moved with them. Over them was an expanse of crystal, and above that was something resembling a throne with the figure that had the appearance of a man but was surrounded by fire and radiance. It appeared to Ezekiel to be the glory of the Lord, so he fell on his face. A voice told him to speak the word of God to the rebellious people of Israel, even if they refused to listen to him. He was given a scroll (perhaps describing his commission) and told to eat it, and it tasted as sweet as honey (3:3). His vision is often seen as the descent of God in a chariot, surrounded by angels, and it became a source of inspiration in the Jewish mystical tradition. (It has also been suggested that he saw a UFO). For Jung, this was a direct experience of the Self. The vision is amplified in detail by Edinger (2000). Ezekiel has been accused of being epileptic or psychotic because of some bizarre behavior. At various points in the book, he is told to lie on his left side for 390 days to symbolize the number of the years of the exile, then forty days on his right side to symbolize the length of Judah's captivity. He is commanded to bake his bread using dung as fuel, his tongue is tied by Yhwh, and he is told to shave his head with a sword. These are symbolic acts to announce the coming disaster, because the Babylonians are on the way to destroy Jerusalem.

The destruction of Jerusalem and Yhwh's temple in 586 BCE had raised the question of how to reconcile such a devastating event with the goodness and omnipotence of God. Ezekiel felt that the destruction was deserved because of the peoples' failure to observe the law of God. Exiled with many of his compatriots, he preached doom and the necessity for repentance, complaining that Israel had "played the harlot" with false gods (16:15). Because of the people's "abominations," some of Yhwh's threats spoken through the mouth of Ezekiel are extreme: "fathers shall eat their sons…and sons shall eat their fathers…A third part of you shall die of pestilence and be consumed with famine" (5:10-12). The book of Ezekiel clearly acknowledges a God-image that is both benevolent and potentially dangerous. Ezekiel rejects the earlier biblical view that God punishes children for the sins of their parents, or punishes people collectively; instead, each person will be judged individually (18:3-4).

After news of the destruction of the temple was received, Ezekiel announced that the Israelites had paid enough for their earlier sins, and their relationship with God would be restored. He predicted that the people would be cleansed of their impurities and would return to their ancestral homeland and rebuild their temple. As it happened, events evolved as he predicted. In 539 BCE, the Persian King Cyrus captured Babylon and the exiles were indeed able to return home. Cyrus decreed that the Jews should rebuild the Jerusalem temple that the Babylonians had destroyed. A high-ranking priest named Ezra rebuilt the temple and became deeply involved in reforming adherence to the law of Moses, which had become lax. Ezra prohibited inter-marriage with pagans, because Israelites were "holy seed" and non-Israelites were not (Ezra 9:2). He made his people renew their promise to observe the conditions of the covenant, a renewal that seems to have restored the people's spirit. Jewish tradition credits Ezra with establishing which books of the Hebrew Scriptures became canonical.[xxxvi] Nehemiah, an official in the court of the

Persian King Artaxerxes 1, became the governor of Judah and supervised the re-building of the city walls of Jerusalem.[xxxvii] It looked as if the predictions of the prophets had been fulfilled, since history seemed to turn in their favor as the exiles turned to the exclusive worship of Yhwh. Yhwh was given the credit for Cyrus's victory; Isaiah referred to him as "God's anointed...whose right hand I have grasped" (Isaiah 45:1)—although Cyrus himself attributed his victory to the god Marduk. However, the peace that the prophets had promised did not materialize; Judah was subsequently occupied by several foreign powers, from the Hellenistic Seleucid empire to the Romans.

Isaiah

The book of Isaiah is a composite work of several authors, divided into three sections. The first 39 chapters are traditionally attributed to an individual (First Isaiah) who was a contemporary of Amos and Hosea. He lived in the late eighth century BCE, in the southern kingdom of Judah, at a time when Assyria had destroyed the northern kingdom and was the dominant power in the region. Assyria was intimidating Judah and its other neighbors, who lived in constant fear of destruction.[xxxviii]

The second section of this book, chapters 40-55, is attributed to one or more authors (Second Isaiah) who lived and preached in Babylon during the Babylonian exile, about two hundred years later, when Cyrus, the king of Persia, was the dominant power in the region. The sections may have been brought together because the first Isaiah preached judgment while the second preached consolation, forgiveness, hope for the future, and the promise of "everlasting salvation" (Isaiah 45:17). Second Isaiah is thought to have been one of the first people to not only preach ethical monotheism but also to explicitly insist that Yhwh is the only God (44:6) and God of the whole earth (54:5). This God was said to bring justice to the nations (42:1) and to have made the people of Israel "as a light to the nations" (Isaiah 49:6). This seems to represent a change in the God-image, which now has a benevolent view of other nations that were previously enemies, but it implied the superiority of the Israelites and the expectation that other nations would serve them (45:14.) The third section of the book of Isaiah, chapters 56-66, is thought to have been written just after the return from the exile, before reconstruction had begun. At the end of the book, the prophet announces a message of consolation. He promises the nation's eventual reunion with Yhwh and a new heaven and earth (66:22).

Isaiah (9:6-7) prophesized a mysterious savior of the people, a Messiah whom later Christians identified as Christ. Apparently, the promise of such a figure was necessary to focus the hopes of the people in very troubled times. As a result of their defeat by an alien power and subsequent exile, the people had suffered a grievous narcissistic injury and a crisis of self-esteem. The exile was a considerable challenge to the idea that Yhwh was indeed the God of history who had made a covenant with the patriarchs and with David. A messianic vision for the future helped to enhance the people's sense of national significance and restore their narcissistic equilibrium. The people could look forward to a new age of fulfillment in which they would be dominant again. These dynamics are discussed by Meissner (1978b) and Gruenwald (2004).

Isaiah (6:1-7) had a vision of God sitting on a throne surrounded by seraphim with six wings. He was terrified by this experience and filled with a sense of his own sinfulness.[xxxix] One of the seraphim took a burning coal from an altar, touched his mouth with it, and told him his sin had thereby been forgiven. The text continues in a puzzling way, when Isaiah is told by God to say to the people: "Hear and hear, but do not understand;/see and see, but do not perceive" (6:9-10). That is, Isaiah is told that God will prevent the people from seeing, hearing, understanding, converting, repenting, and being healed "until cities lie waste...and the land is utterly desolate." The image of God here seems to stress God's justice and punishment rather than his mercy. Apparently, people during the reign of King Uzziah (783-742 BCE) felt self-satisfied, since the kingdom of Judah was prosperous, and people felt blessed by their God. They felt unique and chosen, so that even though Isaiah felt he had to preach, he realized that destruction was inevitable. His preaching was useless because the people were blind to their faults and would not take his warnings seriously. Isaiah accused them harshly, saying "your hands are full of blood" (1:15). He accused Jerusalem of being sinful, a harlot, a city of murders (1:21) and likened Judah to a diseased body. Accordingly, Isaiah told them that God would no longer accept their prayers and sacrifices and promised a day of doom (2:12) and divine retribution, although he does promise that in the end universal peace will be attained (2:2-4).

In the book of Isaiah (52-53) the people of Israel are depicted as a Suffering Servant, suffering without reason as an atonement on behalf of others (53:3-5). This servant figure is a righteous man who is chosen by God to carry God's law to all nations. Even though he is attacked, he does not resist, and the text says that God will eventually vindicate him. He bears all this suffering on behalf of others, as a scapegoat who takes responsibility for evil he has not committed, and he is put to death to save others. There is controversy about the identity of the Suffering Servant. The Jewish tradition believes this figure represents the people of Israel, who, at the time, had been exiled to Babylon and were mourning the loss of Jerusalem in 587 BCE. The prophet known as "Second Isaiah" is trying to encourage them, by saying that although they are miserable and seem to have been abandoned by God, they have a bright future. His people are required to become an example to others in the spreading of God's law. This sounds like a way to rationalize their suffering and support their self-esteem. Christian commentators believe the story of the Suffering Servant refers to the coming of Jesus Christ (Matthew 12:17; Luke 2:32) or to the Christian people. Skeptics assume that the story of the story of Christ was deliberately written in a way that matches the Servant Songs. However, unlike what happened to Jesus, the Jewish concept is that the Messiah will be a powerful figure who will enforce God's will in the world, which is close to what Jesus actually preached.

It seems clear that the prophets hoped that Yhwh would avenge Israel's defeat by the Assyrians and the Babylonians, again demonstrating his military power as he did when he defeated the Egyptians. However, this never happened. Israel was not restored to the glory it reached during the time of King David. The temple of Yhwh was not restored after its destruction in 70 CE. The revolt against the Romans in 60-73 CE and the disastrous defeat of Bar Kochba's rebellion against the Romans in 136 CE [xl] left the people feeling hopeless. It was obvious that Yhwh was not going to intervene to save his people. The God-image of the people thus had to change from that of a military leader to a God of wisdom who demands piety, minute observance and study of the Torah, and patient waiting for the advent of the Messiah.

Much of the prophetic imagery is based on promises of reward and threats of punishment and is therefore strikingly redolent of parental material and a tyrannical superego projected onto a God-image. The believer will justifiably complain that such a psychological approach to the prophets ignores their religious message and their social context, and it is in fact impossible to judge their psychology at this historical distance. However, the driven quality of the prophets' behavior, and the fact that they sometimes risked their personal well-being in response to their call, demand a psychological explanation. Jeremiah for instance suffered agonizing internal conflict about his call; he was beaten, placed in the stocks, and mocked (Jeremiah 20-30), but the irresistible intensity of his vocation made him persist.[xli]

It is difficult to account for the intensity of the prophets' conviction about their mission and their influence on others. They seemed to have been charismatic individuals, sometimes with an aura of grandiosity, so they could claim to be speaking for God. The way we see the prophets is very much a function of the lens we use. One could see them as speaking out of their direct contact with the Self, able to see and communicate a transpersonal level of reality. A skeptic would see the prophets as narcissistically inflated, while a traditional believer sees them as truly possessed by the divine. Another possibility is that the prophets' conversations with God were actually a form of active imagination in Jung's sense of that term. Given the emotional intensity of prophetic language, we could also see these men as possessed by powerful complexes that erupted in the form of prophecy. We can only guess at the sources of their emotional turmoil.

Stirred up by the prophets Haggai and Zechariah, the temple of Yhwh was eventually rebuilt in the year 515 BCE, albeit in a much more modest way than the original temple of Solomon, and monotheism took over. New religious strictures were implemented, such as dietary rules, which were described in the book of Leviticus. A renewed sense of national identity emerged, based on religion rather than country. It is not clear why the monotheistic worship of Yhwh persisted, given that the surrounding nations remained polytheistic. Perhaps the worship of one deity helped the people to stay unified politically.

The covenant that existed between Yhwh and his people was said to protect them if they were faithful. However, the people suffered a series of disasters, culminating in the Babylonian Exile in 598/7 BCE, following the conquest of the kingdom of Judah. Many Israelites believed that this was the result of the people's faithlessness to Yhwh, so that the exile was the determining factor that began the exclusive worship of Yhwh (Gerstenberger, 1996). When the priestly elite who believed in Yhwh alone returned from the exile, they were placed into positions of power and were able to impose their monotheistic beliefs and suppress the worship of the Asherah. The power to grant fertility was transferred from her to Yhwh, and references to her worship and that of Baal were condemned. The time of the nation's greatest defeat was transformed by the prophets into proof of the need for greater faith in him. National disasters had always been interpreted as the result of punishment for apostasy, but as this idea became less tenable in the post-exilic era, an apocalyptic eschatology developed that assumed a coming messianic era. In this new world order, the enemies of the people would be overthrown and evil would be judged and punished. Yhwh's final vindication of Israel would mean the eventual overthrow of demonic powers that were associated with the gods of Israel's oppressors.

The God-image of the Post-biblical Jewish Tradition

Theologians in the Jewish tradition used metaphors to talk about God, knowing that they could not grasp his essence, leading to a tension between God's unknowability and the descriptions of him in the biblical and post-biblical texts. A further problem for theologians was that, if God is absolute and eternal, how does he relate to humanity and the temporal world? The theologians had to affirm the idea of divine rewards and punishment, to be consistent with the scriptures, but a God who behaves in that way must be a changing being and thus not absolute. For the pious, however, these philosophical problems are irrelevant, and only adherence to ritual and one's relationship with God is important.

In the first century CE, Philo of Alexandria identified the God of the Old Testament with the deity of the Greek philosophers and tried to synthesize biblical theology and Greek philosophy. Thus, in the words of one scholar (Goodenough, 1986, p. 10), Philo "read Plato in terms of Moses, and Moses in terms of Plato, to the point that he was convinced that each had said essentially the same things." To deal with the problem of how a transcendent God could interact with the world, Philo invoked the Greek notion of the Logos, which was a common term among the Greeks, with a range of meanings such as word, order, and reason. In modern terms it could be thought of as natural law, such as the laws of physics. Philo conceived of the Logos as God's instrument of creation during the six days in which the earth was created—the Logos was a kind of blueprint for creation. For Philo therefore, there is a distinction between

God's essence and his power expressed in the world. This power is the source of creation and order. The Logos is the interface or place of contact of humanity and divinity; it gives history a moral direction and guides humanity. The Torah given by Moses is part of the Logos, which is also the wisdom of God. Philo believed that the mind is the divine element in humanity, and at its higher levels the human mind is an extension of the divine Mind. Philo tried to cope with the Bible's anthropomorphic depictions of God—his "right arm," his emotions, or the "six" days of creation—by assuming that these are all allegorical, merely serving pedagogical purposes. Philo believed that we cannot know what God is, because he is too far above humanity, but we can be sure he exists. He is the source of everything, and he is absolutely good. Descriptions of God in scripture indicate his existence, even though his essence is inconceivable.

The enormously influential Maimonides (1135-1204) was the most important Jewish philosopher of the Middle Ages. His influence has been incalculable. His *Guide of the Perplexed* was written for people whose faith had been shaken by contemporary philosophy, in an attempt to explain why they should adhere to traditional Judaism. He tried to show that the anthropomorphic biblical imagery has spiritual meanings besides its literal meaning. Maimonides believed that the emotions attributed to God are really the human emotions evoked by God's actions.

Maimonides tried to do for Judaism what Christian scholastics were doing for Christianity, by making traditional beliefs rational and subject to philosophical investigation. Like the Christian scholastics, he does so by combining Aristotelian thought with biblical revelation. In this way, he tries to make reason compatible with revelation. Maimonides insists that nothing can be said about God other than his existence; we cannot attribute any positive attributes to God, even to say that God is good. God is not subject to change; he cannot be influenced; and he has no positive qualities, so that he consists of nothing but his essence—he is nothing like his creatures or any kind of finite thing. At the most, attributes applied to God such as omnipotence and omniscience can only be interpreted in terms of action, so if he is said to be merciful, that means he acts in a merciful manner. Essential attributes must be seen negatively, so that if God is said to exist, that means he is not non-existent.

Maimonides tends to reject the idea that God can be personal. He accepts the traditional notion that God is omnipotent, omniscient, eternal, the cause of all things, incorporeal,[xlii] perfect, a unity, and so on, but Maimonides believes we have no idea what these attributes mean when applied to God, who is completely incomprehensible. God is only known through his effects. In this, Maimonides was articulating ideas that had long been a part of traditional Judaism. Following the esoteric tradition, Maimonides wrote in an enigmatic manner, deliberately making contradictory statements about the same topic in different parts of his book. For example, in one place he asserts that the world was created *ex nihilo,* which is perhaps his real belief, while in another place he says the world is eternal, with no beginning. He leaves it to the reader to decide which were his true opinions. He is therefore sometimes difficult to interpret. One of his main emphases is on the love of God, and this idea contributed to the development of the Hasidic movement in the eighteenth century, which stresses devotion to God, often in ecstatic union.

The Jewish mystical tradition is known as the Kabbala. The name comes from a verb meaning to receive. The tradition has it that the Torah and the Kabbalah are different aspects of the same whole, but the Kabbalah is a kind of inner core of the Torah, revealing what has been hidden. The most elaborate text of the Kabbalah is the *Zohar*, whose authorship is controversial but is often attributed to Rabbi Shimon Bar Yohai, who was said to have been taught by Elijah or even by Moses. It first appeared in Spain in the thirteenth century, published by Moses de Leon. Kabbalists believed that the reason for the existence of the world is that God wished to behold God; he wanted a mirror of his existence. As discussed on p. 98, Jung asserts almost the same idea. It is difficult to know whether Jung derived it from the Kabbala.

The Kabbalists wanted to deal with the apparent contradictions between a God who is both transcendent of his creation and a total unity, with no attributes or qualities, while at the same time asserting God's actions in the world. Accordingly, the idea developed that there is a level of God hidden in the depths of his own being, but also a way in which he reveals himself. Therefore, the Kabbalistic tradition conceived of God as having a transcendent or absolute aspect, of which nothing can be said, and ten attributes or emanations that describe how God is in contact with the world. The unknowable level is the *Ein Sof*, or the endless world, which has no beginning or end, and no time, space or motion, where God is entirely beyond human comprehension. However, God desired to let us have knowledge of him, so he withdrew or contracted the *Ein Sof* to allow space to appear in which creation could occur. From the Endless Light of the *Ein Sof* a beam of light or divine will emanated in the form of ten manifestations or vessels, known as the *Sephirot*. These are thought of as divine attributes, or facets of the revealed God expressed in the world. The first is *Keter* or crown, which is an intermediary between God and the lower Sephirot. There follows Wisdom, Understanding, Kindness, Severity, Beauty, Eternity, Splendor, Foundation, and Kingdom, or the presence of God in matter. These attributes are said to underlie the whole of existence. Isaac Luria (1534-72) developed a form of Kabbala with its own creation myth, in which the seven lowest Sephirot were unable to contain the flow of God into them, so they shattered, and this splintering is responsible for the presence of evil. The work of the Jews is to repair this damage on behalf of the world.

Most Jewish thinkers see God as personal, in the sense of a supernatural presence, a process, or a force that can be directly addressed and experienced. God is seen as an agent who knows everything and has the unlimited ability to control events. However, since he gives people free will, in this way he seems to limit his own power, but he also makes people responsible for their actions, which leaves room for human independent action. At the same time, he seems to have purposes and desires for people. God commands that human beings should love him (Deuteronomy 6:5), although being ordered to love sounds like an oxymoron. The text also calls for total surrender to God (Deuteronomy 18:13), while in return grace is given by God, since "in thy presence is fullness of joy, / in thy right-hand are pleasures for evermore" (Psalms 16:11). There is also an element of fear in this relationship: "The fear of the Lord is the beginning of wisdom" (Psalms 111:10), and the human duty is to fear God (Ecclesiastes 12:13), although the Hebrew word for fear is also translated as reverence.

Of central importance in the traditional descriptions of God is the balance between his anger and his justice, righteousness, mercy, and loving kindness. All his benevolent attributes were challenged by the Holocaust.

The Post-Holocaust[xliii] God-image in Jewish Thought

It has always been important within the Jewish tradition to insist that God both plays a part in history and also reveals himself in history. The

Holocaust therefore presented a special problem for the tradition and acted as a catalyst for new ideas about the traditional benevolent God-image. The intensity of the trauma produced by the Holocaust produced a wide range of responses, some of which challenged the fundamentals of the faith (Katz et al., 2007). How could God remain silent and not intervene at Auschwitz? Is the covenant with God still relevant? The covenant was supposed to provide security, so does the Holocaust mean that God has abandoned his people and broken his promise, or was the Holocaust a form of divine retribution for a failure to live up to the terms of the covenant? Any God-image, Christian or Jewish, now must be tested in the face of the victims of Auschwitz.

There has been no complete psychological, historical, or theological explanation for the Holocaust, which was an event of major religious importance. Attempts at explanation often seem hopelessly inadequate, even disrespectful of the Holocaust's victims. Therefore, an important line of thought insists that the Holocaust is incomprehensible psychologically, theologically, and philosophically; it is essentially a mystery, and attempts to develop some kind of narrative of redemption ignore the severity of the trauma it inflicted. Yet, for some thinkers, this is a council of defeat, since it is clearly important to keep trying to understand what happened from the point of view of the relevant disciplines.

Some survivors gave up on the idea of God altogether, becoming atheists. Some fell back on the idea that God's ways are not our ways. Others decided that God had abandoned them, or that God is so distant and transcendent that he had nothing to do with the Holocaust. For others, God was seen as limited, not omnipotent, and was thus unable to prevent it. Still others adopted a stunned silence. A popular argument invoked the free-will defense; it is fundamental to Judaism that God gives people the choice of how to behave and does not restrain people from committing evil. This argument surely fails, if only in the face of the million children who were murdered, whose deaths seem like a grotesque price to pay for free will. Writers such as Levinas deny that any such theodicy[xliv] is possible after Auschwitz, although in a way theodicy is at the heart of the problem, acknowledging that some attempts at theodicy are the result of the unbearable emotions stirred in us when witnessing the accounts of survivors.

The response of some orthodox Jews to the Holocaust was to blame secular Zionism, since they believe that it violates the will of God to try to bring salvation through human effort. For them, only God can end the exile and restore the State of Israel. Other orthodox Jews take the opposite view, believing that it was important to found the State of Israel so as to hasten the advent of the Messiah. Many in the orthodox community simply believe that the Holocaust was an impenetrable mystery. Some see it as a test, an ordeal of purification, or a punishment for lack of observance of the law, invoking passages such as: "The Lord will send on you curses, confusion, and frustration in all that you undertake to do, until you are destroyed and perish quickly, on account of the evil of your doings, because you have forsaken me" (Deuteronomy 28:20). This line of apologetics insists on the righteousness of God, and makes the victims somehow in the wrong, because God is entirely just. The Nazis were then an instrument of God, just as God had used the Assyrians as "the rod of my anger" (Isaiah 10:5). The suffering of the pious and observant Jews was compared to the binding of Isaac (Genesis 22:1-19), or they were like the Suffering Servant of Isaiah 53, which suggests that the righteous suffer vicariously to atone for the wicked. Or, the Holocaust was part of the birth pangs of the advent of the Messiah. The fact that God needed six million victims for this purpose is glossed over. However, the idea of divine retribution for deviation from the law is consistently found in the Hebrew Scriptures, especially among the prophets (Hosea 13:7-15; Amos 3:2). However, the intensity of the suffering produced by the Holocaust makes this kind of simplistic reward-punishment approach almost obscene, and makes us ask what kind of God would require such retribution. As Wiesel (1968, p. 6) writes, "perhaps someday someone will explain how, on the level of man, Auschwitz was possible; but on the level of God, it will forever remain the most disturbing of mysteries."

Not surprisingly, some Jewish theologians took a "death of God" approach to the Holocaust. Writers such as Rubenstein (1966) seriously questioned the concepts of divine justice and mercy. For Rubenstein, the only honest response to the death camps is to reject the traditional idea of God altogether, and recognize that our existence is meaningless, with no transcendent purpose; we have to create our own meaning and values. There is no divine intervention in history and the traditional image of God as a supreme king or creator or judge is no longer viable. For Rubenstein, theological rationalizations of the Holocaust are meaningless and must be de-mythologized. The entire Jewish system of theology, and the notion that the Jews were chosen by God, must be rejected; there is

THE GOD-IMAGE OF THE HEBREW SCRIPTURES AND POST-BIBLICAL JUDAISM | 213

no covenant with God. In his view, all that is left are the people of Israel as a national community. Rubenstein prefers notions of God as the ground of being, or even as nothingness, "which is at the beginning and end of creation" (p. 221), here referring to the *Ein Sof* of the Kabbala. In his later work, he spoke of God in a more deist manner.

Some Jewish authors continued to defend the traditional God-image after the Holocaust. Berkovits (1973) pointed out that after each catastrophe in Jewish history, God did something new with his people; thus, rabbinic Judaism arose after the destruction of the Second Temple in 70 CE, and from the people who survived the Holocaust arose the state of Israel. For Berkovits, the Holocaust was an example of God's hiddenness, which allows human freedom and the possibility of ethical human behavior. Here, Berkovits invoked the tradition that for some unknown reason, God sometimes hides his face from humanity and is absent from history, and this was one of those occasions.[xlv] Berkovits also suggested that God voluntarily withdraws his omnipotence from the world in order to make space for human freedom of choice. The Holocaust was therefore an example of the misuse of free will. For more skeptical observers, such defenses of the traditional God-image sound like painful rationalizations.

Greenberg (1988) believes that the Holocaust has ushered in a new era of the Jewish covenant with God. For Greenberg, the first era was the biblical period, with an asymmetrical relationship between God and Israel, since God was clearly in charge. The second phase began with the destruction of the Second Temple by the Romans in 70 CE, which led the rabbis to believe that the covenant had been renewed in a new way, such that the people had to take a more equal role with God, who would be manifest in a different way than he had been in the temple; through study and prayer rather than sacrifices. Greenberg suggests that the Holocaust introduces a new major cycle in Jewish history. The covenant made at Sinai is clearly in ruins, and a new covenant must take its place. Morally speaking, God must now repent of the covenant because he gave his people an unbearable task without protecting them. Greenberg asserts that because the original covenant is now clearly untenable, God can no longer have any claim on the Jews; therefore, the new covenant must be voluntary.

Cohen (1981) refers to the Holocaust as the *Tremendum*, a reference to Rudolph Otto's description of one of the terrifying manifestations of

God. For Cohen, the Holocaust forces a new God-image because the traditional image of a providential, benevolent God who interferes in history is clearly no longer applicable. Cohen adheres to a process theology perspective that denies that God is always a direct causal agent in human history; God lacks this power. This view emphasizes that God is in the process of becoming and lacks the traditional divine omnipotence. In this vein, as Jonas (1967) suggests, God is a suffering God, in contrast to the biblical God-image. God's own being is affected by what happens in the world. He is a caring God, but he has left some things unfinished for others to complete.

Raphael (2003) adopts a feminist perspective by suggesting that the correct way to understand God after the Holocaust is through the model of God as mother rather than father. The patriarchal model clearly does not work, given the death camps, but one could see God as a caring maternal presence who is not omnipotent. This God sustains the world through her care.

Fackenheim (1970a) maintained that Auschwitz is evil for the sake of evil, with no purpose and no possible long-term compensation; it would therefore be blasphemous to attach meaning to it, although a response to it is essential. Fackenheim therefore urged the Jewish people to maintain their commitment to Judaism to avoid granting Hitler a posthumous victory. He believed that the people were forbidden to despair of humanity and the world and forbidden to despair of the God of Israel. He was convinced that the traditional image of God had been destroyed by the Holocaust, but there is now a mandate to restore a new divine image through dedication to Jewish survival. In the past, the existence of God ensured the survival of the Jewish people, but after the Holocaust, the continued existence of the people ensures the existence of God. The redemption of the God of Israel is expressed in the existence of the State of Israel.

An important thread found among the work of these writers is that the traditional Jewish God-image, or notions such as a divine "plan" for history, look naive in the face of the Holocaust. A new God-image is required that does not promise divine intervention in history; in the future, if the people are to survive, it is up to them. However, a different school of thought insists that God was not involved in the Holocaust, which was a purely human affair. The fact that God allowed it to happen is not explained. These writers do not acknowledge Jung's notion of the dark side of the God-image, which is clearly relevant to Holocaust studies. Jung's view that the Self has a dark side (see p. 215) is particularly relevant to the problem of God's behavior when it is inexplicably destructive.

Christian Theological Responses to the Holocaust

Christian thinkers have asked themselves what Christianity, especially its God-image, history, and theology, contributed to the Holocaust. Protestant and Roman Catholic Church leadership was often silent or indecisive while the Holocaust was going on, with notable exceptions such as pastor Dietrich Bonhoeffer and those Christian families and religious institutions that sheltered Jews. Although some influential Christian theologians ignored the Holocaust, for many Christians, the Holocaust was not only a problem for Judaism, but it also represented a spiritual and moral crisis for Christianity, one that took some time to address (Ruether,1974; Oldenhage, 2002). The Holocaust has been seen as a specifically Christian phenomenon because the hatred of Jews is part of the essence of Christianity (Maccoby, 1984). In this view, Christian anti-Semitism prepared the way for the Holocaust because of the anti-Jewish indoctrination of Christians by their leaders, for example by emphasizing the Jewishness of Judas, which inculcates a hatred of Jews beginning in childhood Sunday school. Some Christian theologians acknowledge that Christianity must take some responsibility for the Holocaust because of the Gospels' anti-Judaism. There are many such examples; one is the comment in Matthew (10:5-15) that the "lost sheep of Israel" deserve a fate worse than the fate of Sodom for rejecting the Kingdom of God.[xlvi] Hostility to the Jews continued in the work of notables such as St. Augustine, St. John Chrysostom, the later work of Luther, and many Christian monarchs and popes. This long-standing murderous hostility provided fertile soil for Nazi persecution, which took advantage of traditional Christian stereotypes of Jews.

There has been a long-standing Christian mission to convert Jews as part of the notion of supersessionism, which teaches that Christianity has replaced or supplanted Judaism.[xlvii] This idea may have contributed to the silence or active collusion of many Christians during the Holocaust. Some Christians have expressed distress that Christians and Christian institutions cooperated with the Nazis, or that these institutions were silent, especially in Germany (Ericksen et al., 1999). This collusion did not occur because Christianity lacks the necessary moral teaching but because this teaching was either ignored or not properly understood or implemented during the Holocaust. Because Christians who participated in the Holocaust betrayed their own mandate to "love one another" (John 13:34) or to "Love your enemies" (Luke 6:27), it has been suggested that the Christian tradition may need to restructure or revise itself in some manner (Littell, 1975). It is difficult to maintain traditional Christian certainties, such as the faith that redemption has occurred, given the level of evil that persists in the world. Of course, it is possible to insist that God is not responsible for such evil, but if God is involved in history, the Holocaust had to be permitted as a part of divine providence.

Some Christian theologians have interpreted the Holocaust in terms of Christian theology. The Holocaust has been understood as a kind of purification by suffering, or even as a redemptive process analogous to the crucifixion, with the astonishing implication that Jewish suffering in the Holocaust was somehow connected to Christ's suffering on the cross, despite the radically different circumstances of these events. In this way, there has been an attempt to Christianize the Holocaust by identifying the suffering of the victims with the suffering of Christ (Soelle, 1975).

Some writers have tried to distance Christianity from any involvement, or they have tried to exonerate the Churches. This latter tactic fails; as Fackenheim (1970b) pointed out, if masses of Christians would have worn yellow stars, "there would today be no doubt or confusion in the Christian churches, no talk of the death of God" (p. 568). At the extreme, some Christians have seen the Holocaust as a punishment for the Jewish rejection of Jesus (Lewy, 1964). These Christians have an image of a God who is willing to wait two thousand years and then wreak vengeance on millions of people who were not present at the time of Jesus. A more enlightened response has been the suggestion that Judaism and Christianity represent two different, but valid, covenants (van Buren, 1983; Wallis, 1997). These Christians are calling for an affirmation of the Jewish people, seeing their eventual survival as a validation of God's faithfulness to them, although it is hard to see mass slaughter in that light.

How Sacred are the Hebrew Scriptures, Given God's Destructive Behavior?

There are many passages in the Hebrew Scriptures that are horrifying to modern ears. The obvious biblical examples that suggest a dark side to the God-image are those such as exhortations to genocide (Joshua 6:21;

Deuteronomy 20:16-17),[xlviii] the approval of slavery,[xlix] and commandments such as: "If a man has a stubborn and rebellious son...Then all the men of the city shall stone him to death" (Deuteronomy 21:18-21).[l] Penchansky (1999) has pointed out several other instances in which the Hebrew Bible's God-image can appear to be vindictive, malevolent, abusive, and morally questionable. Crenshaw (1984) is also willing to face the dark side of the biblical God-image without using theological interpretations to justify it. He points out that the believer may feel a sense of betrayal and outrage as a result of God's destructive behavior, but Crenshaw acknowledges that despite this, people will not abandon their God. From within the Jewish tradition, writing in the context of the Holocaust, Blumenthal (1993) also acknowledges the abusive attributes of the biblical God-image, and he insists that the texts that show this trait must not be censored.

Is it reasonable to believe that God really says, as Hosea (13:16) insists, that when people rebel against God "their little ones shall be dashed in pieces, /and their pregnant women ripped open"? God's inexplicably callous behavior, such as the killing of innocent Egyptian children, is so problematic that, although some scholars of the Hebrew Bible address it, this problem is often either ignored or rationalized, for example by saying that the Bible's moral content can only be judged contextually and in terms of its intended audience, who may have been at a low level of development by our moral standards. Nevertheless, Breuggemann (1997, p. 275) describes God's negative behavior as "endlessly problematic for theology."

God's destructive behavior in the Bible is rationalized in various ways. Breuggemann tries to transform Yhwh's negative traits into something positive by suggesting that God's power is always used righteously, for the sake of his people. Eichrodt (1967) suggests that God's wrath is never malicious, capricious, envious or Satanic; it is merely a manifestation of God's displeasure and so is above human conception. God's apparently irrationally harsh punishment, for example when Uzzah is killed for touching the Ark simply to prevent it tipping (2 Samuel 6:6-7), is typically understood to be the result of sin that is not mentioned in the text. Other authors use examples of God's harshness as examples of God's justice, using the authors' theology to justify God's anger based on his holiness and the need to punish whatever interferes with the divine plan. In this view, which is a kind of father-knows-best theology, Yhwh's negative attributes are transformed into examples of his goodness. Another rationalization suggests that images of divine ruthlessness and cruelty are merely residues of the Israelites' early, more primitive God-image, perhaps incorporated from the god-images of the Israelites' neighbors such as the Babylonians. The Bible's dark images of God are then only historical remnants. In contrast, God's positive attributes such as his goodness, righteousness, love, and faithfulness are said to represent a historically later, more sophisticated God-image. It is true that Yhwh's loving characteristics gradually became more prominent than his ruthlessness, especially among the prophets: "I have loved you with an everlasting love" (Jeremiah 31:3). However, the negative portrayals of Yhwh are particularly problematic for people who believe that the entire text is an authoritative revelation, in which case God's abusive behavior is impossible to reconcile with depictions of him as compassionate. The dark side of God's behavior raises the question of whether the text could really have been given or inspired by a God who is said to provide an absolute moral standard. This is important, not only because the dark side of the biblical God-image raises major theological questions, but also because, as Miles (1995) pointed out, biblical stories have deeply affected Western culture and behavior. Miles interprets God's negative attributes as part of the development of the complexity of his personality, progressing from action in the early books to speech through the prophets to the silent Ancient of Days. Miles approaches this evolution from a literary point of view, but process theologians actually believe that the metaphysical nature of God includes the evolution of his character (Pinnock, 1994).

It is true that commandments such as the order to show no mercy to defeated opponents (Deuteronomy 7:2) or the approval of public stoning (Deuteronomy 20:16-18) coexist with humanitarian commandments of which we do approve, such as the need to care for poor people (Leviticus 19:9-10), orphans, widows, strangers (Deuteronomy 10:19), and the aged (Leviticus 19:32). At the same time, the commandment in Exodus 22:28 to "not permit a sorceress to live" has been responsible for the deaths of many innocent women accused of witchcraft. The imposition of the death penalty for adultery (Leviticus 18:20), the right of parents to execute a rebellious child (Deuteronomy 21:18-21), the forced marriage of a rapist and his victim (Deuteronomy 22:28-29), and the acceptance of slavery (Exodus 21:2-6) are abhorrent to us. But if we are the arbiter of sections of the Bible that are valuable and those that are not, the entire text cannot be sacred or authoritative. Because of its immoral passages, the text has to be interpreted according to contemporary moral standards. Human moral standards have gradually improved, and believers consistently attribute their personal morality to the ancient text. Passages that are irrational or abhorrent by our standards tend to be ignored or explained away by pious believers, who pay selective attention to some commandments while ignoring others. Contemporary apologists for the genocidal, abusive, and cruel dimensions of the biblical God-image argue that he has the authority to take or give life; he had to be firm with the Israelites to convince them of the importance of following his commandments. In this view, the Canaanites that the Israelites massacred "must have been" wicked and so deserved to be exterminated. Or, it is argued that although the Israelites were behaving the way they believed God wanted them to act, this behavior does not reflect God's love, mercy, and justice. However, it is not surprising that the invocation of the name of God continues to inspire violence.

Adding to the problem of overtly immoral behavior, several of the stories in the biblical text were borrowed (although modified in the light of monotheism) from earlier pagan mythology such as Babylonian and Egyptian stories and Hammurabi's code. These sources further cast doubt on the notion of divine inspiration. From this point of view, the text does not teach absolute truth and is only sacred by virtue of human projections onto it. We have no idea to what extent the descriptions in the text reflect the nature of divinity. That question lies in the realm of faith.

Many conservative religionists believe that the biblical text accurately reflects the divine intentions and will. In contrast, I subscribe to the idea that nothing at all can be said about the nature of the divine, which cannot be encompassed by means of conceptual thought and language. Therefore, the biblical depictions of God's actions are *only* a reflection of the psychology of the writers of the text. For skeptical modern readers, the stories of the Hebrew Bible are mythic images combined with legend, folklore, and ancient traditions which people created to explain important events. This approach helps to account for the evolution of the God-image over time, from the God who walked and talked in the Garden of Eden and thundered on Mt. Sinai to the God of the prophets. As the human understanding of nature became more sophisticated, miracles such as the parting of a sea seemed to occur less often.

Although traditional religionists still believe that God intervenes in history, we are now more concerned with the subjective experience of divinity. Armstrong (1994) suggests that one reason religion seems irrelevant today is that "many of us no longer have the sense that we are surrounded by the unseen" (p. 4). However, this does not take into account Jung's proposal that we may find the divine image by looking inward rather than by reliance on external sources.

[i] The reason for the difference in number is that in the Jewish Bible various books are combined that are separated in the Protestant text. There are forty-six books in Catholic editions. The extra seven are mostly Greek texts that were not accepted into the Jewish canon because they were considered too late to qualify. It is noteworthy that the books of the Hebrew Bible and those of the Christian New Testament are organized in a different sequence. Miles (1996) and Gellert (2018) describe the historical and theological reasons for these differences.

[ii] There are two biblical accounts of creation that contradict each other, and there are two versions of the flood story with different accounts of its duration and other discrepancies. The second creation story (in Genesis 2) is older than the first (Genesis 1), which arose after the Babylonian captivity. Presumably the people who compiled the text did not want to lose either account, either because both seemed important to them or because they could not decide which was correct. These stories complement each other in a way that could not be achieved with either account individually.

To form the final text of the Pentateuch, the controversial documentary hypothesis (first published in 1878 by Julius Wellhausen) suggests that at least four traditions were sewn together from different time periods. These documents are termed J, E, D, and P. (Here I rely partly on Friedman, 1987). The oldest is J, written in the southern kingdom, about the time of King Solomon or King David—the date is debated. This focuses on personalities and behavior such as Noah's drunkenness or the deceitful way that Jacob steals his father's blessing. The God of the J source is approachable, and uses the name Yhwh, while the E source, written between 922 and 722 BCE, uses the term Elohim. J has an anthropomorphic God-image, for example when God "walks" and "talks" in the Garden of Eden. The E source wrote a similar story for the northern kingdom, and after that kingdom was destroyed by the Assyrians in 722 BCE, the two stories were combined. J and E use different names for the same places and people, such as Mt. Sinai in J or Mt. Horeb in E. E is very interested in ritual and tends to depict God acting through angels and dreams rather than directly.

In 621 BCE, during the reformations made by King Josiah, the Deuteronomic or D source appeared, and was added to the combined J and E material in about 550 BCE, forming the book of Deuteronomy. The Deuteronomist source tends to be liturgical, containing important prayers. P, or the priestly code, appeared in the court of King Hezekiah between 722 and 609 BCE (Friedman, 1987). It combined elements of both J and E material, alternating the use of Yhwh and Elohim, apparently trying to merge these two deities into one. The P source contains genealogies from creation to the entrance into the Promised Land and describes the covenant between God and the people. It includes details of the functions of the priests in the temple, sacrifices, and the importance of holiness, purity, and meticulous observation of the law. The God-image of the P source is relatively abstract and transcendent. These texts were woven together by another source, known as the Redactor, who wanted them to be read as a unitary document. Friedman believes that the final redactor was probably Ezra, a post-exilic priest in Jerusalem in the mid-fifth century BCE.

Although most scholars agree that the text has been heavily edited, the documentary hypothesis has been widely debated and much criticized, and it is no longer universally accepted in its original form. None of its proposed sources have been found independently of each other; they are reconstructions. One of the criticisms of this hypothesis is that alternative accounts of the same events are merely literary conventions of the time, where different names are used for the same thing. The final text is sometimes seen to be too disparate to be reduced to the work of only a few sources, so that there are alternative explanations for the composition of the Pentateuch. One is that it is a compilation of many small fragments of text, while another describes a single document supplemented by pieces added from several sources, put together by final editors who added material of their own.

It may only be accurate to speak of a J or P tradition, transmitted over many centuries, rather than specific documents. Some scholars argue that everything in the Pentateuch is post-exilic.

iii The name Yhwh probably means something like "that which causes to be." When Moses asks God who he is (Exodus 3:14), Yhwh replies, "I am who I am," alternatively translated as "I will be what I will be."

iv To describe God as jealous is obviously a projection of the authors' jealousy of the fact that other tribes worshipped other gods.

v An inscribed stone referring to the House of David was discovered in the Israeli city of Tel-Dan in 1993. It gave rise to considerable controversy. No other artifacts have been excavated that mention King David or King Solomon. Some revisionists believe that David and Solomon might have been local tribal chieftains rather than major rulers.

vi Excavations at Jericho and Ai suggest that both towns were destroyed two centuries before the time of the conquest of Canaan, so the miracle story of Joshua bringing down the walls of Jericho is not historical.

vii The historian Josephus thought that the Jews were descendants of the Hyksos, who had originally been enslaved in Egypt but then ruled Egypt from about 1640 BCE until they were expelled about 1550 BCE. There is speculation that the story of the Hyksos evolved into the story of the Exodus. There is some evidence that the Pharaoh of the Exodus story was Ramses. There is scholarly debate about whether the ancestors of the Israelites were a group of people known as the Habiru, who were a group of outsiders of inferior social status who lived in Egypt. This theory has it that they were the slaves who escaped from Egypt and developed their own settlements in Canaan.

viii There is no archeological evidence of encampments in the Sinai desert. The Exodus is often dated to about 1250 BCE, but Finkelstein and Silberman (2002) suggest that the story was actually written at the time of King Josiah, in the late seventh century BCE, as a political manifesto or a work of propaganda intended to unite Israelites against the rival Egyptian empire. Of course, the mythic image of divine intervention has had a powerful effect on subsequent generations. Today, the story of the conquest of Canaan is tangled in political considerations about who owns the land of Israel.

ix The term "Hebrews" is used in various senses. One is to refer to people of the patriarchal era before God's promises to Moses, after which the term "Israelite" is preferred. The word "Hebrews" may also simply refer to those who spoke Hebrew.

x There are analogous stories about King Sargon of Akkad, the English King Arthur, the Persian King Cyrus, and the Roman Romulus. In mythic traditions, the birth of a hero such as Moses is always unusual, often involving dangerous circumstances.

xi The people are initially referred to as Hebrews, later as Israelites. We do not know if these are the same people, or whether they represent two different groups with different names for God. We do not know whether the people who came to Egypt with Joseph were the same people as those who were led out of Egypt by Moses, or whether they truly were the descendants of Abraham. The story of the covenant with Abraham may have been added by later editors.

xii In order to stress the importance of the Torah, the rabbinic tradition teaches that it existed before the creation of the world, it was the blueprint according to which God created the world, and the study of Torah is one of the reasons God created humanity.

xiii There is scholarly debate about whether the covenant was made at the beginning of the Exodus from Egypt or whether it occurred at the culmination of the war against the Canaanites. It is also possible that the idea originated during the seventh century BCE, as part of the reforms of Josiah, in an attempt to retrospectively explain the origins of the people.

xiv Temple worship consisted of the sacrifice of various types of animals to express thanks, to atone for sin, and to maintain a proper relationship to God. This practice had been commanded by God. After the destruction of the temple, the rabbinic tradition decided that acts of compassion for others, prayer, and the study of Torah would substitute for temple sacrifices and allow Israel to keep faith with God.

[xv] Hayes (2012, p. 182) suggests that the idea of being chosen "may be rooted in the ancient Near Eastern political sphere in which sovereigns singled out vassals for the status of special property." The notion of being chosen has been minimized by many members of the Reform Jewish tradition, who fear the accusation of hubris associated with it. Hayes points out that the writers of Deuteronomy were aware of the danger that election might foster a feeling of superiority, so the Israelites are admonished not to assume that they were chosen by virtue of their own merit; they were chosen as an "act of spontaneous love for the patriarchs" (Hayes, 2012, p. 183).

[xvi] Monolatry is the notion that although the existence of many gods is acknowledged, one of them is a particular tribe's chief deity. Yhwh was thought of as the strongest deity during war time. Monolatry seems to be a way-station in the evolution of a god-image between polytheism and monotheism.

[xvii] The Jewish Publication Society translates this word as "impassioned" rather than jealous.

[xviii] Some scholars believe that Hebrew monotheism began with Abraham and the patriarchs; others date this development to Moses and the Exodus, others to the age of the Classical Prophets (e.g., Amos, Hosea, and Micah) (Carella et al., 1988). Many people believe that monotheism took hold during the exile in Babylon.

[xix] Zoroastrianism also teaches the idea of a savior who would periodically appear, leading to a Day of Judgment. This tradition also teaches that a savior would be born of a virgin from the semen of Zoroaster, when she bathes in a lake in which it has been stored. According to this tradition, Zoroaster's mother was a virgin who conceived him by means of a ray of light, or the Divine Reason.

[xx] In the sixth chapter of Exodus, God says that his name is Yhwh, but he appeared to Abraham, Isaac, and Jacob as El Shaddai.

[xxi] The fact that no image of God was allowed to be made turned him into a purely spiritual presence, which in turn allowed for the progressive development of the idea of God within the tradition.

[xxii] Idol worship is frequently condemned in the Bible, but it is unlikely that the people of the time worshipped the actual piece of wood or stone; they probably believed it pointed to an invisible reality, analogous to the use of icons.

[xxiii] A famous victory by Elijah over the priests of Baal (1 Kings 18-27) was important politically. In this story, they competed to see whether Yhwh or Baal would ignite a sacrificial fire. Only Elijah's invocation of Yhwh was successful.

[xxiv] Ugarit was an important Canaanite city in northern Syria that was destroyed in about 1200 BCE. A library of Ugaritic documents was found at Ras Shamra in 1929, which helped to clarify the relationship between Israelite and Canaanite religious practices, showing that during the second half of the second millennium BCE, there was little distinction between them until the worship of Yhwh became dominant. Many Ugaritic elements are found in the Hebrew Bible.

[xxv] Most ancient Near East pantheons were headed by a divine couple. Archeological evidence suggests that during the monarchies of Judah and Israel, about 975-586 BCE, a divine couple was worshipped as a source of fertility. Inscriptions on pottery suggest a king and queen of heaven. Many female figurines have been found from this period but it is not known if they were statues of fertility goddesses.

[xxvi] In the Zohar, a thirteenth century Kabalistic book, the notion appeared that God has both masculine and feminine characteristics, and the union of God the mother and God the father produce creation. The Zohar emphasizes the Shekinah as the feminine aspect of God, obviously responding to a religious need for a loving and motherly deity who would remain with the people throughout their suffering until their redemption.

xxvii The golden calf may have been a representation of El, the deity the people originally worshipped before Moses persuaded them to worship his preferred deity, Yhwh. The text tries to reconcile the tension between these two divinities by having Yhwh state that he appeared to Abraham, Isaac, and Jacob as El Shaddai rather than as Yhwh (Exodus 6:2-3). The two deities gradually merged, with Yhwh absorbing the qualities of El, taking over his role of heavenly king as well as the attributes of Baal, the storm god.

xxviii In context, this comment of Isaiah was intended to make it clear that his God, not the Babylonian god Marduk, was responsible for the victory of the Babylonians. The prophets always assert that Israel's suffering is the deserved result of the people's apostasy. There are many other examples of the dark side of God in the Hebrew Bible; for example, Yhwh afflicts the people with a plague when they disobey him (2 Samuel 24:15), an "evil spirit from God" afflicts Saul (1 Samuel 16:14), and Amos (3:6) asks: "Does evil befall a city, unless the Lord has done it?" For a fuller list, see Penchansky, 1999.

xxix The same kind of eschatological judgment is found in the New Testament in Matthew 25:34-43, and in Revelation 20:11-15, when those whose names are not in the book of life are thrown into a lake of fire.

xxx This satan is not the same as the Satan of later Christian and Jewish thought, who becomes an enemy of God.

xxxi The biblical story of the flood echoes an earlier Babylonian story found in the Epic of Gilgamesh, the details of which are similar to the account in Genesis. In the original creation myth from about 2000 BCE, Tiamat, the primordial sea-Goddess, is defeated and killed by her grandson Marduk, a storm god, who then creates the world out of the body of the goddess. In the Genesis story there is no violence or retribution, only a sense of divine generosity.

xxxii The fact that Adam was created first and woman as a helpmate was used to justify the tradition's stress on male domination of women and fostered the tradition's patriarchal image of God. The serious damage that arose from an exclusively male God-image has been pointed out by feminist theologians (Daly,1973; Plaskow, 1990; Christ, 1992). Biblical tradition imposed many degrading restrictions on women, who were typically regarded as subservient to men. The biblical authors often seem to regard women as dangerously seductive, or sometimes as harlots or witches. Women were excluded from the priesthood and the temple sacrificial rituals. Ironically, it has been suggested that the Yhwist (J) author was a woman (Friedman, 1987).

xxxiii The inner voice is not the same as Freud's superego. It is more akin to the voice of God or the Self manifesting itself subjectively.

xxxiv Similarly, the Bible does not say how God told Noah to build his ark, or how God spoke to Abram as told in Genesis 12.

xxxv In 1943, the biblical scholar Martin Noth suggested that the books of Joshua, Judges, 1 and 2 Samuel, and 1 and 2 Kings were all composed during the period of the Babylonian exile, and not at the time of the events they record. This theory suggests that the Deuteronomistic editors used these books to explain that God appeared to have abandoned the Israelites to the Assyrians and Babylonians because of the Israelites' idolatry. This theory is controversial.

xxxvi Another tradition fixes this decision to the council of Jamnia in 90-100 CE. However, some of the prophetic books had not yet been completed at that time.

xxxvii Ezra and Nehemiah probably did not work at the same time, but later editors give this impression by combining their work in the books of their name.

xxxviii Edinger (2000) points out that this constant anxiety about invasion by the Assyrians may have been responsible for the activation of Isaiah's unconscious.

xxxix The skeptic will see this episode as hallucinatory, perhaps the projection of Isaiah's superego.

xl The revolt led by Simon Bar Kochba against Rome was triggered by the Roman attempt to build a temple to Jupiter on the Temple Mount. Bar Kochba was initially regarded as the messiah by many Jews of the time, who hoped he would restore Judean independence. Large numbers of Jews were killed during the revolt, which was brutally suppressed. As a result, messianic expectations were spiritualized and Bar Kochba was considered to be a false messiah.

[xli] Edinger (2000) makes the interesting suggestion that Jeremiah might have written the Book of Job.

[xlii] The insistence on an incorporeal God was a response to accusations that the Jews believed in a God with a body, because of scriptural passages that describe God using anthropomorphic imagery such as having a "right arm."

[xliii] The Greek word *holocaustos* means "completely burned."

[xliv] Theodicy is the attempt to justify God in the presence of suffering and evil, for example by saying that God has his own mysterious reasons for allowing evil, or that goodness eventually comes from evil.

[xlv] The notion that God is hidden is common in the Hebrew Scriptures, for example in Isaiah 45: 15: "Truly, thou art a God who hidest thyself." He only reveals himself when and in ways that he chooses. Various Psalms assure us that God is only hiding temporarily but will eventually show himself (Psalm 86). In the face of the gravity of the Holocaust, the idea that God "hid his face" because of people's sin is extremely objectionable to many people.

[xlvi] This is the kind of comment that makes it difficult for skeptics to believe that the Gospels are entirely the word of God.

[xlvii] Some Christian theologians saw the historically difficult situation of the Jewish people as evidence that the original covenant had been annulled, and it was passed on to the followers of Christ. The Jewish response has always been to point out that they have a relationship with God that cannot be measured in terms of social success or failure.

[xlviii] It is sometimes claimed that God did not command these mass killings and the Israelites were simply mistaken when they assumed that God ordered them. This argument would raise problems about the authority of the text, such as the extent to which the people misunderstood God in other ways. These atrocities have also been rationalized as God's necessary judgment because of the sinful behavior of the Canaanites. It seems more likely that the Israelites' bloodthirsty characteristics were projected onto their image of God, so they did what they wanted to do and attributed their behavior to their God's instructions.

[xlix] The Hebrew Bible's approval of slavery, combined with St. Paul's insistence that slaves should "obey your earthly masters with respect and fear...just as you would obey Christ" (Ephesians 6:5) had a dampening effect on the emancipation movement in the United States, since slavery was considered to be divinely ordained.

[l] This commandment is so incomprehensible that rabbinic commentators say that it was never implemented and was never meant to be implemented; it is the kind of law that was only intended to be studied (*Babylonian Talmud*, 71a). It is a good example of the need to apply contemporary moral standards to an ancient text, and it is one of the sources of doubt that this text is truly sacred.

CHAPTER 5

The Development of the Christian Image of God

There are innumerable Christian denominations and religious orders. The differences between them are based on different ways to understand God and on different interpretations of Jesus' life and teachings. The books of the New Testament[i] are subject to a multitude of interpretations. The resulting controversies between different branches of Christianity have taken on considerable importance, leading to a great deal of conflict during the history of the tradition. This chapter discusses some aspects of the Christian God-image that are controversial and some that are generally agreed upon, with special reference to the figure of Jesus, who is considered to be the divine made flesh, having both a divine and a human nature.

Central to Christianity is the idea that humanity is alienated from God, but this situation has been healed through the saving death of Jesus. His story has captured the imagination of untold numbers of people, a fact that requires a psychological explanation in addition to its theological importance. The appeal of Christianity seems to depend on the powerful notions that the individual is saved for eternity by a personal redeemer, while at the same time we are cared for by a loving God who acts justly within world history.[ii] The offer of universal salvation from a God who cares so much that he is willing to sacrifice his own son is enormously moving. As well, Christianity claims to interpret the meaning and purpose of human life in the light of divine revelation. At a deeper level, Jung believed that the reason people perceived the "light shining in Christ" and seized upon it so passionately was because there was a correspondence between the image of Christ and the unconscious need for a Redeemer. For Jung, the "archetype of the God-man" (CW 9, ii, para. 283) projected onto Jesus was more important than the historical figure.

The Christian Story

The Christian story begins with the account in the Hebrew Scriptures in which God created the world and placed Adam and Eve in the Garden of Eden. God initially found the world to be good, but the first couple was disobedient. People became alienated from the creator because of their sinfulness, which some Christians consider to be intrinsic to human nature. But God so loved the world that he sent his only son to redeem and save the world from sin. The Father incarnated as the Son, who was killed because of human sinfulness, but he was raised from the dead. Belief in him is essential for redemption. The problem of why a loving God would create human beings in such an imperfect way that this terrible sacrifice became necessary remains a troubling question for many people.

The Traditional Christian God-image

The traditional Christian God-image depicts a personal deity who is unchanging, omnipotent, omnipresent, omniscient, loving, righteous, and good. The early Church Fathers regarded God as eternal in the sense of being outside of time.[iii] God is said to have created the universe as an act of overflowing love. According to the tradition, although God is infinite, God both causes finite reality to occur and also enters into human history without changing his essential nature. Although God's nature cannot be understood, he can be known by means of his revelations, by direct experience, and in a relationship with him. God is the source of all beings, or for some theologians God is Being itself, or that which sustains reality. Love is typically seen as God's essence in the New Testament, although he tends to favor those who believe in him, and the Letter to the Hebrews warns that: "It is a fearful thing to fall into the hands of the living God" (10:31). This and similar passages caution believers that God is not only loving and merciful but can also be judgmental, although there is a distinct preference among Christian writers to see an idealized image of God who is always benevolent. There is however a tendency for the New Testament writers to show burning anger against those who are not among the elect, promising "the wrath of God" for the disobedient (Ephesians 5:6). In the book of Revelation, God's rage promises devastating consequences for disbelievers.

The idealized attributes of the divine are important for many people in order to maintain the idea that God is worthy of worship, and these attributes are not too different than previous Jewish ideas about God. The fundamental change in the God-image produced by Christianity was the understanding of God as incarnate in Jesus Christ. That doctrine is common to all branches of the tradition, but over the course of Christian history a controversial range of other concepts of God developed. For example, there are arguments within the tradition about how transcendent or immanent God is. Extreme immanence leads to pantheism, which says that the world is itself the body of God, and there is no God apart from the world, which would not be acceptable to Christians. Neither is the opposite view, that God is absolutely other than the world. More traditional is a middle view that sees God as operating in the world and ordering it, but more than the world. In that view, transcendence does not mean remoteness from humanity; God is somehow present personally but transcendent at the same time. If God were to be conceived of as completely transcendent, God would thereby be excluded from direct human experience and the human imagination, and would become foreign to human concerns. This is one reason that Jesus as the incarnate divine is so important to Christian philosophy; as Christ, God is not outside human experience.

The Historical Development of the Christian God-image

Both Judaism and Greek philosophy influenced the Christian concept of God. Most Christians have assumed that the God described within the Hebrew Scriptures is also their God. The early Christian image of God also fused with partly compatible elements in Greek thought, such as Aristotle's notion of a Prime Mover, the initial cause of all the motion in the universe, or Plato's Idea of the Good, which is the source of values and virtues such as truth and justice. Christian apologists attempted to join these Greek traditions with their own, for example by teaching that the Prime Mover was the divine source of the universe, and he is good and eternal. The Gospel of John (written about 100 CE) shows the influence of Greek thought on Christianity; it begins with the doctrine of the Logos, which in Greek thought was a kind of world spirit that emanates from the divine to create and organize the world. This idea became necessary for Christian thought because if God is perfect and unchanging, an additional factor such as the Logos was necessary to account for creation. In the Gospel of John, the Logos became an aspect of God but partly distinguishable from God. John claims that this Logos manifested itself on earth in the form of Jesus (John 1:1; 1:14). This usage radically changed the meaning of the Greek term, in a way that would have been unacceptable to Greek thought. Christian philosophy differed radically from Greek thought in some other important ways, for example, because Christians believed in the revelation of divine law, given to Moses by God.

In the first two centuries CE, Christians were sporadically persecuted by the Romans, and this became systematic under the emperor Decius in 250 CE. The shrines of martyrs became places of pilgrimage. However, the emperor Constantine promoted Christianity in the fourth century CE, because, according to the historian Eusebius, just before an important battle, Constantine had a heavenly vision of a cross bearing the inscription *"In hoc signo vinces,"* which means "in this sign you will conquer." With this development, the pagan gods of the Greeks and Romans began to be suppressed, initiating a long decline of paganism. Because this was a time when traditions were evaluated in terms of their age, Christian thinkers adopted the Hebrew Scriptures[iv] as a part of their own lineage, thus establishing the idea that their religion began with the creation of the universe. This meant that they had to maintain continuity between the God of the Hebrew Scriptures and Jesus. They did this in various ways, often by insisting that Jesus fulfilled the prophecies of the Hebrew Prophets. For example, at the Feast of Pentecost, the book of Acts (2:14-36) reports that Peter preached that the prophecy of the prophet Joel was being fulfilled, and Jesus was a descendent of King David and had been raised from the dead by God, who made Jesus "both Lord and Christ."

The group that eventually became the mainstream tradition viewed the God of Israel as the Father of the human Jesus, whom they also saw as divine. But the problem of how this combination of humanity and divinity was possible while remaining monotheistic troubled Christian thinkers for a long time, producing major theological disputes and schisms. Many different opinions appeared about the exact relationship between God the Father and Jesus. For example, as discussed below, some people believed that Jesus had two natures, one divine and one human. Others decided that God the Father, Jesus, and the Holy Spirit were the same person, so that there are three aspects of the same God, or one God appeared as three persons. Others believed that Jesus was a human being who was adopted by God.

The Gospels

The New Testament consists of 27 separate texts. There is a great deal of scholarly controversy about where, when, and by whom they were written, and about the details of the source material preceding them. The four Gospels were named after Matthew, Mark, Luke, and John, but their actual authors are unknown.[v] The Gospels were written within communities of faith, and they express the beliefs and prejudices of those communities. As Helms (1997, p. i) puts it, the Gospels may "tell us more about the situations of their origin than about their subject." The writers often shaped their stories to match their theology. Thus, the story of Jesus' death was informed by the Gospel writers' beliefs about the meaning of his death. Sometimes these writers clearly tried to match their account to fit the prophecies of the Hebrew Scriptures that they believed refer to the coming of Christ.

The Gospels were not the work of eyewitnesses; instead, they rely on the memories of people who passed on stories about Jesus.[vi] These stories were repeated again and again, orally transmitted over several decades before they were written down, so that it is difficult to know how accurately they were transmitted and how much was invented or exaggerated (Ehrman, 2016). The need to preserve the oral tradition about Jesus and make sense of it in terms of an emerging theology led to the development of the written Gospel tradition. Each Gospel tries to give a different impression of Jesus and was written for a different audience.[vii] There is some debate about the extent to which the Gospel writers were influenced by the earlier work of St. Paul (Smith, 2011).

A series of Church Councils decided on the composition of the New Testament as we have it today, beginning in the fourth century with the Councils of Rome and Carthage, ending in the seventeenth century with the Westminster Confession of the Calvinist tradition, which became central to its theology. The motivations for deciding which books were authoritative or canonical[viii] were both religious and political. The choices were affected by the struggles with heresies and by the need to develop a unified church to help consolidate the power of the Roman Empire. Many controversial books that circulated among the early Christian churches were eventually not included in the canon because they were not universally accepted as scriptural. Some of the books that were included were rejected as heretical by some of the early Church leaders. The decision to include or exclude a text was made on the basis of whether it had a connection either to Christ or to the Apostles or to one of their immediate disciples. The text also had to conform to orthodox Christian teachings. The final product, which emerged in 393 CE at the Synod of Hippo, was the result of a great deal of debate and conflict, representing the diversity of the early Church.

The books of the New Testament were written in Greek by at least sixteen authors with a range of literary styles. The letters of Paul were written about 20 years after Jesus' death, while the Gospels were composed between about 70-100 CE, up to 70 years after his death. These are controversial estimates, but it seems certain that the books were finished before 120 CE. Because of the time lag between the life of Jesus and the writing of the Gospels, it may be that none of the writers knew him personally, in which case their knowledge of him is entirely based on oral and written transmission.

No copies of the Gospels can be definitively dated before the end of the second century CE. Importantly, we do not have the original manuscripts of the Gospels, only copies made later, and sometimes only copies of copies. Some of these manuscripts contain either mistakes or intentional alterations, which may affect our interpretation of the text. Some of the differences between these versions of the Gospels are significant, so that interpretations, as well as problems with translation, have been unavoidable. The differences between the manuscripts give rise to questions about the accuracy with which the texts were transmitted. Because there are thousands[ix] of Greek manuscripts (or fragments of manuscripts) of the New Testament, many of which differ from each other, all modern bibles are the result of editorial opinion.

Despite the uncertainties surrounding the Gospels, many committed Christians believe that the New Testament is an accurate and reliable account of the story of Jesus. It is however difficult to know how many of Jesus' reported teachings are authentically his, and how much material was retrospectively put into his mouth by his followers in order to persuade readers of the followers' views of him.[x] Some of this material seems too polemical and sectarian to be authentic.[xi] Even given this difficulty, the teachings and parables in the Gospels that have an authentic ring are often compelling and sometimes sublime.

The Gospels are typically read as history and biography, although much of the story of Jesus' life has a mythic quality, for example when he raised the dead child of Jairus (Matthew 9:18-26), calmed storm winds

(Mark 4:35-40), cast out demons (Matthew 8:16), raised Lazarus from the dead (John 11:1-44), and turned water into wine (John 2:1-11). The Gospel story of Jesus' resurrection has been monumentally important for his followers, leading to the expectation that he would come again soon "to judge the living and the dead" (2 Timothy 4:1).

After Jesus' death, an oral tradition developed that was presumably greatly affected by the spiritual and psychological needs of his followers and their communities. The Gospel of Mark was written around 70 CE and may be the most reliable source of information about Jesus' life. Mark's account is less mythologically tinged than the later Gospels, which contain increasingly impressive and miraculous stories about Jesus, suggesting that the collective memory of him became increasingly idealized over time. Subsequent writers added more material to Mark's story, each with his own interpretation, emphasizing particular theological points about Jesus and adding to his mythic status. This culminated in the Gospel of John, in which Jesus makes remarkable claims about himself, such as: "I am the light of the world" (John 8:12); "I and the Father are one" (John 10:30); "I am the bread of life" (John 6:35); "I am the way, the truth, and the life" (John 14:6); and "He who has seen me has seen the Father" (John 14:9). This Gospel is very much a depiction of the Christ of faith. To the non-committed reader, it sounds more like interpretation and testimony than history, while to the believer it demonstrates an unfolding revelation. The Gospel of John is less concerned with what Jesus did and said than with who he was. It is arguably the only Gospel that unequivocally equates Jesus with God. Although this point is debated, many scholars believe that in the earlier Gospels Jesus does not make such claims about himself; rather, this belief was projected onto Jesus by his followers. For example, the Gospel of Mark depicts Jesus as a human being who was made divine by an act of God, while the Gospel of John sees Jesus as divine by nature, as a pre-existing divine figure who became human. Ehrman (2014) points out that in ancient mythologies there is a continuum or overlap between the human and the divine realms, such that gods may become temporarily human and humans may become gods. In the Hebrew Scriptures, God appears in human form on various occasions (Genesis:18:1-33; 16:9-13). However, the claim that Jesus was God is crucially important to Christian theology. Ehrman (2014) believes that if Jesus had not been thought to be divine, his followers would have remained a small sect within Judaism.

The Gospel stories were clearly written in order to convey the very special nature of their subject, using familiar, widely available mythic or archetypal themes such as the virgin birth, which can be found in a range of pre-Christian religions and mythologies. Over time, the Gospel stories were accepted as history. Later writers copied and recopied each other, adding or subtracting what was important to them. A theological superstructure was built onto the original story. The details of this structure were decided by Church councils, beginning during the fourth century CE, and their opinions became received truth. In this way, the voice of the official Church added more and more of its own coloring to what Jesus actually said.[xii] Subsequent theologians tended to project their own moral and religious convictions onto Jesus.

The Bible has always been seen by Christians as the true word of God. However, its meaning is not always clear; it has been a long-standing tradition that the human ability to understand the truth of the revelations in the Bible is limited, and God accommodates his message to our level of understanding. This, of course, leaves open the potential for misunderstanding and misinterpretation, complicated by the fact that there are differences between different Gospel accounts that cannot be reconciled. One of many examples is that the stories of Jesus' birth in Matthew and Luke are inconsistent with each other.[xiii] Some stories about Jesus are in all the Gospel accounts; others are in only one of them. There are well-documented historical inaccuracies in the Gospels[xiv] including different family trees for Jesus in Luke and Matthew. The four Gospels' account of Jesus' trial differ, and there are other problems that make it difficult to believe the historicity of the Gospel. One example is that the Gospel of John says the Last Supper took place before Passover, but the story in Mark 14:12 says the Last Supper was a traditional Passover meal followed by Jesus' trial. However, it seems unlikely that the Jews of the time would have held a trial during a major festival, since doing so would contravene Jewish law. During this meal, Jesus is said (by St. Paul) to have instituted the Eucharist. The reader familiar with the strict Jewish prohibitions about eating blood (Leviticus 7:26-27) finds it surprising that Jesus would symbolically offer his own blood in the form of wine (Matthew 26-28), or that he would violate the Jewish taboo against even symbolic cannibalism.

For skeptics, the differences between the Gospel accounts undermine the sense that all the Gospel stories are factually credible. In particular, the miraculous stories in the Gospels, and especially the story of the Resurrection, are seen by skeptics as a reflection of the faith of Jesus' early believers rather than the historical Jesus.

The Continuity of the Hebrew Scriptures and the New Testament

An important early controversy during the apostolic age centered on the question of the continuity of the Hebrew Scriptures with the emerging new tradition. Some early Christians wanted to abandon the Hebrew Scriptures completely, while others wanted to assert its continuing validity. Eventually, it became important for early Christians to claim that Christianity was a continuation and culmination of the tradition of the Hebrew Scriptures. In this view, Christianity worshipped the same God, so that when Jesus spoke of the Father, he meant the God of the Hebrew Scriptures. Accordingly, the writers of the New Testament often called on the Hebrew Scriptures to legitimate what they were saying, sometimes inventing stories to make them fit with the Hebrew prophetic texts. For this purpose, Christians pointed to passages within the Hebrew Scriptures that were read as if they were referring to the coming of Christ, who they believed fulfilled these prophecies. (Deuteronomy 18:15). Some scholars believed that Paul (1 Corinthians 1:24) identified Christ with the figure of Wisdom in Proverbs 8, who was present at the beginning of God's creating the world. Psalm 110:1 invites a lord to "Sit at my right hand," and Paul applies this to Jesus at his resurrection, as if at that moment Jesus was exalted to heaven and made divine (Acts 2:32-36). Jesus is frequently identified with the Son of Man in Daniel 7 (Matthew 13:37) or with the Suffering Servant of Isaiah 53.

The process of re-working the earlier Hebrew text to apply it to Christ has the potential for distorting its meaning, for example, when the King James translation of the Gospel of Matthew (1:23) quotes Isaiah 7:14 as "a virgin shall conceive and bear a son." This is now understood by many scholars to be a mistranslation; contemporary scholars render the verse as "a young woman will conceive." Another misleading statement is found in Matthew when Jesus' family flees to Egypt to escape Herod's attempt to kill Hebrew children. Matthew 2:15 says: "This was to fulfill what the Lord had spoken by the prophet, 'Out of Egypt have I called my son.'" This line was taken from Hosea 11: 1, which says: "When Israel was a child, I loved him, and out of Egypt I called my son," referring to the exodus of the

Hebrews from Egypt, where the word "son" obviously means Israel. Typically, such misinterpretations are rationalized by saying the texts have a double meaning, one for their own time and one for the future.

The Gospels often describe Jesus using metaphors originally used in the Hebrew Scriptures; thus, he is called the "true vine," a name used to describe Israel in Isaiah 5:7. Jesus is also referred to as the true bread, true manna, living water, and the lamb of God, all imagery that was important in the Hebrew Scriptures. His body is described as the new temple (John 2:20), which was understood to be the place in which dwells the divine glory. The Hebrew Scripture's mythic imagery was also re-interpreted in terms of Christian dogma. For example, in the book of Revelation (1:14), there is a description of Jesus as a stern judge with snow-white hair and flaming eyes, which is clearly intended to remind the reader of the description of God as the Ancient of Days in the book of Daniel (7:9). Jesus is seen as a High Priest who was foreshadowed in the figure of Melchizedek, a priest of unknown provenance who blessed Abram in the book of Genesis (14:14). The sacrifice of Christ was seen as an analogy of the sacrifice of the paschal lamb, whose blood was painted on the doorposts of the Israelites during the tenth plague that killed the first born of the Egyptians. The blood of Christ saves his followers, just as the blood of the original lamb saved the Israelites in Egypt, so that the story of Christ can be seen as a second Passover. Moses was seen to prefigure the advent of Christ, who was believed to have fulfilled the Mosaic Law and the prophetic promises. The Sermon on the Mount is an analog of Moses giving the Law from Mt. Sinai. The manna from heaven that fed the Israelites during their time in the wilderness was seen to foreshadow the consecrated bread of the Host during the Mass. The *Song of Songs*, which the Jewish tradition referred to as an analogy of the relationship between the Israelites and God, became a metaphor for the relationship between Christ and his Church. Using the imagery contained within this poem, the Blessed Virgin Mary was referred to as the Rose of Sharon or the Lily of the Valley. The story of the wise men (Matthew 2:1-12) who visit the baby Jesus bearing gold and frankincense was derived from prophesies in Isaiah 60:6 about journeys to Jerusalem by kings. The transfiguration of Jesus, when he became radiant on top of a mountain and "his face shone like the sun and his garments became white as light" (Matthew 17:1-8) as he spoke with Moses and Elijah, is said to be analogous to the ascent of Moses up Mount Sinai, when Moses's face became radiant. The association to the presence of Moses in this scene links Jesus with the giving of the law, while Elijah associates him with prophecy (see Spong, [1998], for a fuller account of these sources). There are many similar examples of instances from the Hebrew Scriptures being adopted for Christian purposes. This process unified the old scriptures with the new and allowed the Bible to be seen as history. The apparent analogies between the two traditions seemed to be visible signs of the truth of Christianity, although to skeptics these analogies seem forced. Furthermore, it is very unlikely that the early followers of Jesus would have subscribed to the description of him in the Nicene Creed, just as it is difficult to imagine that he would recognize himself in these descriptions. The notions of Jesus' divinity and Jesus as an incarnation of God were developed much later than the period of his life. Since then, a huge theological edifice has been built by interpreting and re-interpreting the Gospel stories, leading to doctrines that are not found in the Gospel texts themselves. Institutional and clerical superstructures and political views also developed that often seem to be removed from Jesus' original values. These structures were often based on the work of St. Paul rather than Jesus.

Some of the Hebrew Scriptures' mythic imagery became essential for Christian theology; in this context, the Fall of Adam described in the book of Genesis is particularly important. In this myth, God created Adam by breathing his breath or spirit into the dust of the earth, so that God resides in the body as the soul. Initially, Adam was perfect, and lived in complete harmony with his surroundings, in a reflection of heaven on earth. Eve was then created as a companion for Adam. However, although Adam and Eve were endowed with freedom, they chose to disobey God's will by eating of the Tree of Knowledge (Genesis 2:16-17) at the prompting of the serpent, who is often considered to represent Lucifer. This made God angry, and he cursed the primal parents and cast them out of the Garden. Adam was condemned to hard labor in order to grow food, and Eve was condemned to deliver children in pain. In the Christian tradition, this story was understood to have resulted in a fall from divine grace. The tradition assumed that the disobedience of Adam and Eve condemned the human race to be born into a permanent state of sin that required the advent of Christ for its redemption. It is however noteworthy that the story in Genesis is actually said to bring mortality to humanity, not a state of unredeemed human sinfulness, which is a theological superimposition onto the myth.[xv]

Traditionally, the Tree that produced death became the Tree of the Cross, which became the Tree of Salvation.[xvi] Thus, Christ is thought of as the second Adam (1 Corinthians 15:45), and Mary as the second Eve. Later, in a kind of second creation story, the tradition decided that the Spirit conceived the Word in human form within the womb of the Blessed Virgin Mary. Based on this kind of material, various authors have point out that Christianity created a "speculative, confessional, mythic system, reified as objective mundane and transcendent reality" (Ellens, 2004, p. 13). This body of myth was subsequently treated as if it were "historically warrantable" and ontologically real (pp. 13-14). That is, in the skeptical view, the mythic aspects of the biblical stories have been read as actual history. From that perspective, theologians have spent much ink on metaphysical[xvii] interpretations of the myth, as if the events it described happened in literal reality. It took some time for the spiritual or symbolic meaning of the biblical stories to become clear and to be incorporated into Christian doctrine. Each generation used its own approach to explain the stories' meaning. For many contemporary people, the Christian story is best appreciated metaphorically as a source of spiritual truths. However, the boundary between myth and literal history has often become blurred, as we seen in the story of Satan.

Satan

In Christian mythology, God created the angel Lucifer, the Light Bearer, who believed himself to be the crowning glory of God's creation, so that he resented God placing humanity at a higher level than him. Filled with malice, envy, and pride, he rebelled, and refused to surrender to the will of God, whereupon he was cast out of heaven. Because of his pride, the love of self rather than the love of God became an ultimate sin within the tradition.

The origin of the Lucifer myth is found in Egyptian and Canaanite gods of the morning star, and in the mythology of an Assyrian lightening god, imagery that re-appeared in Isaiah (14:12, KJV) in the form of Lucifer. Jesus equated Lucifer with Satan by saying "I saw Satan fall like lightening from heaven" (Luke 10:18), a repeat of a Zoroastrian myth in which the god of light cast the evil god Ahriman out heaven into the underworld. After being expelled from heaven, Satan fled to the Outer Darkness, or Hell, and with his angelic followers he did everything possible to frustrate God's creation. God is said to allow Satan to function in this way, without condoning it. In the Christian tradition, Satan is a real power of darkness and evil, unlike the Satan of the Hebrew tradition who ministers the wrath of God but is not so autonomous. Jesus himself was reported to be very concerned with overcoming the power of Satan (Acts 10:38), so that his healings and exorcisms were seen as battles with Satan or with "unclean spirits" (Mark 5:2-13). The New Testament writers were concerned about the "prince of the power of the air, the spirit that is now at work in the sons of disobedience" (Ephesians 2:2) and the "spiritual hosts of wickedness in the heavenly places" (6:12). Augustine and Aquinas had the same concern, as did Luther and Calvin. In medieval Europe, biblical references to Satan combined with ancient pagan anxieties about evil spirits contributed to the persecution of witches.

For Christianity, Satan does not have equal standing with God, so this is not an absolute dualism like the good and evil powers of the Manichean tradition. Nevertheless, Christians are still warned to be constantly on their guard against Satan, who they believe tries to lead people into sin. Only the grace of God protects people from him. The Christian tradition finds it difficult to accept the Hindu or Jungian notion that the divine can have a dark aspect. Nor could Christian doctrine accept the idea that God is beyond good and evil, because the essence of the Christian God-image is entirely good and loving. The Continuity of Christianity with Earlier Mythic Traditions

Early Christian thinkers in the tradition that evolved into mainstream Christianity adopted the pre-existing Hebrew scriptural image of God as a heavenly Father. But Christianity also transformed the Hebrew image of God in some important ways. In the teachings of St. Paul, the God of the Hebrew Scriptures became a God of sacrificial love, a suffering God, and a Son rather than only a Father. In this way the new tradition humanized the more remote God of the Hebrew Scriptures and made him more accessible. This process probably made it easier to gain converts in the Greco-Roman world, since there were some ways in which the new God-image was more similar to pre-existing pagan divinities than the Hebrew God, who was transcendent and invisible. In the Christian view, God was thought to have come "down" from heaven and to be incarnate among humanity. The visibility of God in Christ may have helped to account for the attraction of Christianity among people who otherwise experienced God as remote or absent. But this idea could only be understood and interpreted in terms of a first century worldview, so that the Christian writers' challenge was to make the shift from their inherited Jewish concept of God as an infinite heavenly being to a God present as a man. For this purpose, they drew on pre-existing sacred traditions and texts.

Religious cultures at the time of Jesus typically associated worship of the gods with blood sacrifices, so the Christian message of the sacrifice of a son resonated with surrounding pagan traditions. Other themes found in existing mythologies also made the Christian story sound familiar; the notion of a virgin birth, impregnation of a woman by a god, miraculous portents at birth, apotheosis into the ranks of the gods, and miraculous healings were all characteristic of earlier religions.[xviii] The extent to which these parallels influenced early Christianity is very controversial, but there are many of them. Although skeptics often exaggerate claims about the similarities between the story of Jesus and the mythology of pre-Christian gods, some of these parallels are suggestive. For example, it is possible that the notion of a divine child may have originated in the Egyptian myth of Horus, the son of Isis. Jesus was thought to judge those who have died, like the Egyptian god Osiris, who also offered his devotees eternal life. There are elements of the Mithraic tradition—an early rival of Christianity—that were incorporated into Christianity, but the extent of this influence is not clear because Mithraism was a mystery religion whose sacred texts have not survived. Several of the mystery religions of the ancient world were designed to "take the candidate through the gates of death" (Godwin, 1981, p. 34) and assure eternal salvation. Frazer (1922/2009) believed that the story of Jesus offering his body in the form of bread was a continuation of the archetypal theme of dying and rising grain gods of earlier traditions. This idea was disputed by later scholars (Parrish, 2006) and defended by others (Mettinger, 2001). Campbell (2001) pointed out that the traditional animals of the Christian nativity scene, the ass and the ox, were symbols of the Egyptian gods Set and Osiris, and the Magi were priests of Mithra. The implication of their presence is that these earlier gods are recognizing Christ for who he is. These mythic elements provided some continuity between Egyptian and Graeco-Roman religions and the emerging Christian tradition, offering analogs that made people receptive to the new religion. The recurrence of the same archetypal motifs in many traditions point to levels of meaning beyond the literalness of the fundamentalists.

At the time of Jesus, it was not unusual to believe that an ordinary man could be deified; Roman emperors and Egyptian pharaohs often insisted they were divine. In the book of Acts (14:8-18), when Barnabas and Paul healed a man, the crowd shouted: "The gods have come down to us in the likeness of men." The crowd thought that Barnabas was the god Zeus and Paul was the god Hermes. The crowd was prepared to offer them sacrifices. In such a milieu it is not surprising that Jesus might be thought of as a divine being. One of Jesus' boldest claims about himself, "before Abraham was born, I am" (John 8: 58), sounds as if he saw himself as divine, since this is an allusion to Exodus 3:14 in which God says to Moses "I am who I am." However, it is implausible that the writing of St. Paul and the other three Gospels would not have mentioned that Jesus called himself God, had he actually done so. In this view, the Gospel of John is making a theological point rather than a historically accurate claim.

There is some debate about when Jesus achieved the status of the Son of God. The Gospel of Mark says the spirit descended on Jesus at his baptism, which is when he became the Son of God. Matthew and Luke say that Jesus became the Son of God when he was born, while John says that he was the Son of God before creation. This Gospel is the only one in which Jesus is reported to unequivocally refer to himself as the Son of God (John 10:36). It seems unlikely that Jesus thought of himself as the "only" Son of God as John 3:16 claims that he was. In this context, is also not clear exactly what Jesus meant when he referred to God as his Father.

There were several aspects of the emerging tradition that were attractive both to pagans and Hellenized Jews. These include the relaxation of Jewish laws such as circumcision and dietary restrictions, the promise of the salvation of the soul, paradise after death, eventual resurrection, and the moral and social benefits of belonging to a community that preached and practiced love and concern for others, at least for other Christians. The relaxation of legal requirements to become a follower of Jesus was a radical change from the very national religion of the Jews, and it widened the growing gap between the Jewish community and Jesus' followers. However, given Jesus' traditional Jewish background, such extreme relaxation of the law might have been disconcerting to Jesus himself.

The Expansion of the Appeal of Christianity

The God of the Hebrew Scriptures had originally been a national or ethnic God of Israel, whereas the God of Christianity eventually developed into a God for all nations. In Jesus' own mind, his teaching may have been primarily intended for his fellow Jews, at least if we judge by his instruction to his Apostles (emissaries or delegates) to go to "the lost sheep of the house of Israel." According to Luke 22:30, Jesus was expecting the Apostles to "sit on thrones judging the twelve tribes of Israel." Another such indication is the episode in Matthew (15:22-28), when he initially refused to help the child of a Canaanite woman until she submissively demonstrated her faith and he relented.[xix] Here, he metaphorically referred to foreigners as "dogs." In the Gospel of Mark (12:29-31), Jesus stressed the importance of the commandment to love God and to love one's neighbor, but in his mind this love may have been restricted to fellow Israelites, as it probably was in the original Hebrew text. In John 5:46, Jesus is reported to have said that Moses "wrote of me," and in Matthew 5:17-18 he says that he has not come to get rid of Mosaic Law. Given these comments, it is possible that Jesus' idea of salvation was really about the salvation of his own people in the same tradition as Isaiah. However, as the emerging tradition was expanded by St. Paul, it became an inclusive, multicultural and multiethnic religion.[xx] After the destruction of the Jerusalem temple in 70 CE, pagans were increasingly admitted into the new faith. Paul's teaching of justification by faith meant that one could become part of the Body of Christ through baptism rather than circumcision; baptism represented a new birth and the end of one's old life. St. Paul claimed that those who are baptized in some sense become a part of Christ (1 Corinthians 12:12). It is as if they had been adopted by him (Ephesians 3:6), and like him they have overcome death (1 Corinthians 15:22).

For some time after the death of Jesus, the new movement was predominantly Jewish or Judeo-Christian, in the sense that many of its followers conformed to Jewish law and attended the temple in Jerusalem. The Jewish Christians differed from the rest of the Jewish population who did not believe that Jesus was the promised Messiah. Antagonism between them and gentile Christians gradually increased. Jewish Christians were rejected by mainstream Judaism and became increasingly marginalized by other Christians. Most of them died out by the fifth century CE, but there are still Jewish individuals who consider themselves to be followers of Jesus.

The Advent of Jesus

For the Church Fathers, for medieval Christians, and for many contemporary Christians, the appearance of Christ was the center point of history, which was understood with him as its focus. During the development of Christianity, it was assumed that with the coming of Christ a new covenant had been reached between God and humanity, replacing the old covenant between God and the people of Israel (Hebrews 1:1-3). This change was justified in various ways; for example, the Letter to the Hebrews quotes God's promise to Jeremiah (31:31) that he would establish a new covenant with Israel (Hebrews 8:8-9). This promise is then applied to Christ, who is said to bring the new covenant, since his death was said to redeem people from the "transgressions under the first covenant" (Hebrews 9:15). Later, Protestant reformers such as Calvin developed this idea into covenant theology, in which the first Adam failed, so God made a second agreement with Christ, who obeyed God perfectly. Christ therefore replaced Adam. The notion that the Jews forfeited their covenant with God because they rejected Christ led to the idea that Christianity has superseded Judaism, and this idea has contributed to Christian anti-Semitism.

Jesus' main mission was to preach the love of God, the imminent coming of the Kingdom of God, and the idea that repentance is necessary for those who wish to enter the Kingdom (Matthew 4:17). He may not have been referring to a physical kingdom, since he made comments such as "the kingdom of God is in the midst of you" (Luke 17:21), and "unless one is born of water and the Spirit, he cannot enter the kingdom of God" (John 3:5). Whatever Jesus meant by this phrase, he apparently thought this Kingdom was to arrive so soon (Mark 9:1) that earthly goods were not important (Luke 18:22), and it was even necessary to forsake family and home. He anticipated the imminent destruction of the temple by the Romans, promising to rebuild it in three days (John 2:19). He seems to have attributed the function of the temple—connection to God—to himself, which was blasphemous to most of his fellow Jews. Jesus stressed faith and taught that divine reward would accrue to those who followed precepts such as humility (Matthew 6:18), while punishment and severe judgment would be meted out to those who would not obey the words of the Apostles (Matthew 10:14-15). Whether Jesus actually made such harsh pronouncements is a matter of debate.[xxi]

Jesus had a concept of himself as fulfilling a divinely appointed mission: "the works which the Father has granted me to accomplish… bear me witness that the Father has sent me" (John 5:36). Some of Jesus' teaching was simply a stress on pre-existing Jewish precepts—for example, the command to love God with one's whole being (Deuteronomy 6:4). The Golden Rule (Matthew 7:12), "whatever you wish that men would do to you, do so to them," is found in the teaching of Rabbi Hillel, Jesus' contemporary. Jesus' admonition to "love your neighbor as yourself" (Matthew 22:39) is taken directly from Leviticus 19:18. His prohibition against anger (Matthew 5:22) is found in Leviticus 19:17, and there are other similar examples, indicating that in some ways Jesus did not deviate much from traditional Judaism. He explicitly connected his own ministry with the ancient prophecies by making comments such as "the time is fulfilled" (Mark 1:15). Yet Jesus' personally flexible approach to traditional Sabbath restrictions, dietary laws, and his contact with marginalized people made his contemporaries suspicious of him, even though he taught that "not an iota, not a dot, will pass from the law until all is accomplished" (Matthew 5:18). However, although he said that he had not come "to abolish the law or the prophets" (Matthew 5:17), he called for a variety of changes based on his own authority (Matthew 5:27-28; 31-32; 43-45). He was apparently much more concerned with human welfare, social justice, healing, and forgiveness than were many of his contemporaries. He obviously cared more for sincere spirituality, charity, and love of neighbor than adherence to rules. Like the prophets of the Hebrew Scriptures, he was attacked by many of his contemporaries.[xxii] His own family was concerned that he was "beside himself" (Mark 3:21).

Gradually, the image of Jesus becomes more and more colored by mythic and archetypal accretions. The Gospels report about thirty-five occasions on which Jesus performed miracles, or "acts of power." He heals the sick, raises people from the dead, casts out demons, and demonstrates power over the natural world. The early Christians see these actions as proclamations of the Kingdom of God, and they reinforce the Christian belief in Jesus. Like the Buddha and Zoroaster, Jesus was able to withstand the temptations of the devil.[xxiii] He was said to be seated at the right hand of God when he ascended to heaven (Ephesians 1:20-23), where he has divine authority. He will judge the living and the dead on the day of the Last Judgment (Matthew 25:31-33). He is also a divine warrior, ruling nations and carrying out God's vengeance "with a rod of iron." In the book of Revelation (19:13) he is depicted as "clad in a robe dipped in blood" with a sharp sword issuing from his mouth, distributing "the fury of the wrath of God the Almighty." (Revelation 19:15). He "judges and makes war," (Revelation 19:11) and he is a victorious "King of kings and Lord of lords" (19:16).

The Crucifixion and Resurrection

Immediately after Jesus' death, it probably looked as if his movement had failed, but instead the notion of his resurrection became a central idea that rescued the movement. The crucifixion was emotionally painful for Jesus' immediate circle, and theologically awkward for his early followers. They managed this psychological disaster by turning it into a symbol of God's sacrificial love for humanity, and by insisting that Jesus had been resurrected, an idea found in the book of Daniel (12:2). This claim turned Jesus' apparent defeat into a success. The resurrection was a turning point; it meant that Jesus was no longer dead, but alive at the right hand of God, and it seemed to mark the beginning of the events leading to the End Times. Belief in Jesus' resurrection was a major reason for his followers' claims that he was divine, rather than seeing him as a human teacher or prophet. The resurrection was seen to herald a reconciliation with God and a new start for humanity. People who believed in Jesus' resurrection expected that they too will be resurrected from the dead when Jesus returns (1 Corinthians 15:21-23), and: "whoever believes in him should not perish but have eternal life" (John 3:16).

The Resurrection is the foundation on which Christianity rests. Although the reported details surrounding the event vary in the different Gospels, the basic evidence for Jesus' resurrection was twofold; an empty tomb, and, according to Mark and Matthew, after Jesus' death Mary Magdalen and his mother Mary saw him. He was later seen by the apostles. In Paul's first letter to the Corinthians (15:4-8) he says that Jesus appeared to more than five hundred people after his resurrection. At the same time as Jesus was resurrected, "the tombs also were opened and many bodies of the saints who had fallen asleep were raised" (Matthew 27:52), but nothing more is said about the fate of those people.

Rationalists describe the Resurrection as at most a metaphor, meaning that Jesus re-appeared in the minds and hearts of his followers. Believers assert that the fact that Jesus was seen after the crucifixion is proof that the resurrection literally happened. More skeptical readers point out that it is difficult to know if accounts of these appearances were pure fiction or were the result of visions, dreams, or apparitions of Jesus that became exaggerated with repeated re-telling.[xxiv] In that case, his apparent post-mortem appearance was based on the intensity of the expectation that he would return There are skeptical theories that Jesus did not really die on the cross, because it was possible to survive a crucifixion.[xxv] It is noteworthy that the early manuscripts of the Gospel of Mark do not mention the Resurrection; they end with the story of the empty tomb at 16:8. Later manuscripts do have a story of Jesus appearing after his death (16:9-20), but this material was added 200 years later by scribes who were shocked that Mark himself did not mention the resurrection. Modern English translations of this Gospel acknowledge this later addition by adding a footnote, noting that ancient texts end at verse 8.

Some early Christians believed that after his death, Jesus appeared in the form of a spiritual body (1 Corinthians 15:44), which could pass through locked doors (John 20:26). Other Gospel stories, such as that of Doubting Thomas (John 20:24-28), suggest that Jesus was resurrected physically, since Thomas could put his finger into the wound in Christ's side. Luke 24:51 and Acts 1:9 say that Jesus was carried up to heaven as the Apostles watched. Once this had happened, as Ehrman (2014) points out, it was a short step to believing that Jesus was a divine being by nature, he had always been a divine being, and he was not divine simply because God had exalted him.

Jesus' followers turned to the Hebrew Scriptures to find passages that explained his painful death, such as the story of the Suffering Servant of Isaiah 53, which the followers interpreted as a prediction of Jesus' suffering. Jesus was also said to fulfill Isaiah's prophecy that God's servant would bring justice to the nations as a "bruised reed…and a dimly burning wick" (42:3). Perhaps for this reason, the Kingdom of God was associated with small things such as yeast in flour (Luke 13:20-21), a small pearl of great value (Matthew 13:45-46) or a mustard seed (Mark 4:30-32). Jesus renounced worldly power and recommended a position of humility, although he also promised to return "in his glory, and all the angels with him, then he will sit on his glorious throne" (Matthew 25:31). After Jesus' death, his followers began to insist that he would return, and the development of the Eucharist was a way of emphasizing his living presence.

Within the tradition, the idea grew that Jesus' death was divinely ordained with God's purpose in mind, which was to save others. This idea dealt with the huge problem of why Jesus had to die; it meant that his apparent failure was in fact part of the divine plan—a line of thought that skeptics see as a rationalization. Along these lines, Paul decided that God's power is "made perfect in weakness" (2 Corinthians 12:9) rather than by means of any outward successes, so God's weakness is actually a strength. This attitude became one of the great Christian paradoxes, in which strength is achieved by means of apparent weakness that ultimately triumphs over evil. Belief in the Resurrection spread after the Crucifixion, and many believers suffered martyrdom in support of the belief that Jesus was the promised Messiah of the Hebrew Scriptures. Over time, stories about him gradually enhanced his importance more and more, as he accrued archetypal projections as a God-man and as a sacral king.

Messianic and Apocalyptic Expectations

There has been a long-standing debate about whether Jesus saw himself as the expected Messiah.[xxvi] He may have participated in a messianic movement that was begun by John the Baptist, expecting the Kingdom of God to be established as predicted by the Hebrew Prophets. Jesus does quote directly from the messianic prophecies in the book of Isaiah, which he applied to himself (Luke 4:16-21; 7:18-23). Whether or not he saw himself as the Messiah, there is no doubt about the messianic projections onto Jesus by his followers, evidenced by many Gospel passages (Mark 8:29; Luke 2:11). In order to understand these messianic projections, it is important to understand the political situation of the day. At that time, the Roman empire was still strong, but was beginning to decline. First-century Palestine was under Roman occupation. There was political instability, even chaos at times, and its people were suffering great unrest. It seemed possible that the "last days" and the Kingdom of God predicted by the Hebrew Prophets were imminent. People wanted a savior who would free them from Roman rule, but the national aspirations of the Jews were being firmly suppressed by the Romans. The need for the fulfillment of the Hebrew Scripture's promise of a coming Messiah seems to have been intensified by the Jews' subjugation.

At the time of Jesus' ministry, although there was a good deal of messianic expectation and fervor among the Jews, there was not much agreement on the form that the coming Messiah would take. Based on prophecies in the Hebrew Scriptures, he was typically expected to be a righteous king and a descendent of King David (Jeremiah 23:5-6). Jesus may have grown up knowing that he was a male heir of this royal line, and if he did think he was the Messiah he would have been guided by these scriptural passages. Some people thought the Messiah would be a heavenly being, others thought he would be a priest, while still others believed he would be a warrior who would begin an age in which Israel's enemies would be triumphantly defeated. Many people expected someone who would carry out God's will by establishing God's kingdom on earth, in which the Jews would be favored. No one expected a suffering Messiah who would be crucified by the Romans, who were the oppressors that the Messiah was supposed to defeat. If Jesus were truly the expected Messiah, his death would imply that the nation and its national God had been defeated, contrary to the promises of the Hebrew prophets who had promised the national supremacy of the Jews and the victory of the Jewish God over all other gods. The prophet Isaiah had promised that the Messiah would bring a kingdom of peace (11:6-8), and Micah had also predicted that when the messiah came, nations would "beat their swords into ploughshares, / and their spears into pruning hooks;/ nation shall not lift up sword against nation" (4:2-4). Ezekiel had promised that when the Messiah came the community would be secure and free of enslavement and fear (34:27-28). Jeremiah (23:5-6) had announced that a "righteous Branch" would rule as a king, and Malachi predicted the return of Elijah (4:5). Zechariah (6:12-13) said that there will be a priest or a "Branch" who would "rule upon his throne" and "build the temple of the Lord." The fact that Jesus did not appear in any of these expected ways contributed to his failure to be accepted by many of his Jewish contemporaries. It seemed to many of them that Jesus' humiliating crucifixion meant that he could not possibly have been the one they expected. The radical change in the Christian concept of the Messiah was not simply to see him as sent by God but to be God himself, and to direct prayer to him.

One of the extraordinary aspects of the story of Jesus is that, given the expectations of his followers, the story does not represent him as a military leader who exerts power. Instead of entering Jerusalem triumphantly with an army, Jesus entered the city "sitting on an ass's colt" (John 12:15). He did so because of a prophecy in Zechariah (9:9) that a king would arrive in this way. Jesus' supporters must have understood the reference. He was tortured and cruelly executed, demonstrating vulnerability in a manner very different than the usual portrayal of God as omnipotent and sovereign. It is remarkable that God incarnate would allow himself to suffer a painful death, a fact that has led some commentators to describe his death as a suicide. His death certainly inspired later Christian martyrs. St. Paul derived a theology of salvation from Jesus' death that radically separated it from any political and nationalistic ideals, helping the new sect to avoid appearing to challenge the Roman occupation.

Some of Jesus' followers were expecting the incipient end to the world as it was, with the creation of an ideal world; messianic expectations are often combined with apocalyptic imagery.[xxvii] Jesus told his followers that there are "some standing here who will not taste death before they see that the Kingdom of God has come with power" (Mark 9:1; 13:30) or "the kingdom of heaven is at hand" (Matthew 4:17). People will know it has arrived because "the sun will be darkened, and the moon will not give its light, and the stars will fall from heaven" (Matthew 24:29). The idea of the coming of the day of the Lord is taken from the prophets Isaiah (13:9-11) and Zechariah (14). After Jesus died however, no such dramatic event happened, so that Luke (17:20-21) announced that the kingdom is not coming in terms of observable things but is "within you" or "among you" (translations of this phrase vary). Or, St. Paul said that the Kingdom would only come after death, because "flesh and blood cannot inherit the kingdom of God" (1 Corinthians 15:50). Again, to the skeptic, these latter ideas seem like rationalizations to deal with the failure of his prophecy.

The view of Jesus as primarily an apocalypticist is not universal, but those who see him this way believe he was trying to prepare his followers for the establishment of the Kingdom of God, which it was widely assumed would mean the end of Roman rule and the re-establishment of the kingdom of Israel. The Romans therefore considered Jesus to be guilty of sedition, for which they had no tolerance. Many contemporary Christians believe that Jesus' idea of the Kingdom, and the meaning of messiahship, was actually not political but was about deliverance from sin and evil.

Eventually, St. Paul's version of Jesus as a savior eclipsed Jesus' apocalyptic teaching. Instead, his death was interpreted as the fulfillment of the prophecy of the Suffering Servant described in Isaiah 53:3-5, and the story of his life was retrospectively magnified accordingly. To deal with the failure of the Kingdom of God to appear on earth, as Jesus had promised, it was (and still is) assumed that God's timing is different than human timing, and the end times will occur at some point in the future. The notion of an afterlife with Jesus in heaven (John 14:2-4) was also an important development that helped with the disappointment caused by the failure of the Kingdom to appear.

Jesus' Values

Jesus' compassion for the sick, the poor, and those on the fringe of society is striking; he was more concerned with humanitarian behavior and human welfare than overt piety and adherence to the law. His spiritual path was one of love, and for many people this teaching outweighs the historical difficulties of the Gospel stories. It is important to note that Jesus' ideas about kindness, generosity, equality, forgiveness, and humility, combined with comments such as: "Blessed are the poor in spirit" (Matthew 5:3), were very different than the system of values among the Greeks and Romans of his day, who did not consider altruistic qualities to be virtues. The emergence of Christianity therefore allowed a radical departure from attitudes such as that of imperial Rome, which was dedicated to power and wealth. Jesus' teaching was also radical because his approach to what is religiously important was different than the orthodox religious teaching of his day. His sense of personal authority and his uncompromising opinions contributed to his conflict with the religious authorities. He famously welcomed into his movement people from the margins of society, offering them solace. These individuals probably found accounts of a revision of the existing world order particularly appealing, for example when Jesus told them that the meek would inherit the earth (Matthew 5:5) and the lowest would become the highest (19:30). Jesus often challenged the conventional wisdom of his day. When he dined with sinners (Mark 2:15-17), he was denying the importance of traditional Jewish codes of purity, or at least he was making relationship and compassion more important. He taught the importance of forgiveness (Mark 2:5) and insisted that humility and penitence are essential to approach God (Luke 18:9-14).

Despite his largely benevolent attitudes, Jesus occasionally seemed to demonstrate unusual harshness. He is reported to have been hard on non-believers, as in Luke 19:27: "But as for those enemies of mine who did not want me to reign over them, bring them here and slay them before me." Or, if someone denied him, "that person I also will deny before my

THE DEVELOPMENT OF THE CHRISTIAN IMAGE OF GOD | 251

Father who is in heaven" (Matthew 10:33), and for those who did not believe in him "the wrath of God rests upon him" (John 3:36). Jesus consigned to a furnace of fire in Hades those who did not believe in him (Luke 10:15; Matthew 13:42, 50), and he made it clear that he expected people to follow him even if that meant ignoring or abandoning their family (Luke 14:26-35). Jesus also recommended the beating of recalcitrant slaves (Luke 12:47-48). He said that "whoever blasphemes against the Holy Spirit never has forgiveness" (Mark 3:29) and that "he who is baptized will be saved; but he who does not believe will be condemned" (Mark 16:16). He refers to his enemies as children of the devil (John 8:44). He tells a man whose father has just died not to bury him (Matthew 8:22), which would have caused extraordinary pain because this contravenes a long-standing tradition. However, these latter teachings, and Jesus' comments about the fires of hell, are not consistent with the tradition's image of Jesus as loving and forgiving. They are so different than Jesus' typical attitudes, expressed for example in the Parable of the Prodigal Son, that they may not be authentic. Perhaps they simply represent the eruption of his shadow, but it is more likely that they were inserted by second century followers who did not understand him, in order to frighten people into joining their movement. If these bitter statements are sectarian later insertions, they may represent a splitting defense on the part of the Gospels' authors, who divide the world into those who believe in Jesus and those who do not. Similar splitting is seen in eschatological texts such as the Book of Revelation, in which non-believers will be harshly and violently dealt with. In this context, it is important to remember that Jesus' teachings were delivered in the context of his apocalyptic thinking. Jesus assumed that the end times were about to appear, and it was important to prepare for them because only those who lived according to his moral standards would be admitted to the Kingdom of God. This may have referred to an enlightened state of consciousness rather than a literal future time.

A great deal of good has been carried out in the name of Jesus, but his values have often been applied selectively by Christian churches, which tend to follow some of his teachings while ignoring others. We tend to see him in the light of our own values. Thus, few churches or Christian leaders today practice or recommend his admonition in the Sermon on the Mount not to resist evil or to turn the other cheek. The modern Christian stress on the family is belied by Jesus' own hostility to his family members, whom he virtually disavows (Mark 3:32-34). His stress on the importance of poverty has been turned on its head by the prosperity gospel,[xxviii] despite his warnings such as: "Woe to you who are rich" (Luke 6:24). Another aspect of Jesus' ministry that is often ignored by contemporary liberal Christians is that he seemed to think that illness, including mental illness, could be the result of possession by demonic spirits, and he often stressed his battle with Satan during his frequent healings and exorcisms (Acts. 10:38). These were an important aspect of his ministry.[xxix] One gets the sense from these accounts that he felt he could be a bridge between this world and the spiritual world, which for him included demonic forces as well as divine goodness.

The early Christians practiced and embodied Jesus' gentle values in their daily lives, at least towards other followers. Their kindly behavior towards others helped to spread the word. However, the tribal quality that we see in the Hebrew Scriptures continued in the Christian tradition, which gradually took over the notion that God was especially on its side. A cultural revolution followed the conversion of Constantine. Subsequent Roman rulers systematically and harshly eliminated non-Christian groups by killing their followers and demolishing their shrines and temples, turning them into Christian churches.[xxx] As Christianity became institutionalized it became increasingly politicized, militaristic, and often murderous, for example during the Crusades and in the struggle with heretics. The image of Jesus as compassionate and loving also changed into an image of him as a holy warrior (Revelation 19:11-16) and the leader of the Church Militant that struggles with the Devil. Over time, the spiritual and the political became harder to distinguish. Christian political leaders have often claimed divine authority for their actions. Today, liberal and conservative wings of the tradition selectively quote Jesus to emphasize their personal political views and values. Conservatives ignore Jesus' teachings about justice for the poor, while liberals tend to de-emphasize Jesus' harsher teachings about the judgment of unbelievers.

Jesus' Non-dual Sensibility

When Jesus says, "I and the Father are one" (John 10:30) and makes other "I am" statements such as "I am the light of the world" (John 8:12), he is speaking in a way that is consonant with the non-dual spiritual tradition, which sees no distinction between humanity and the divine. His comments such as: "as you did it to one of the least of these my brethren, you did it to me" (Matthew 25:40) also reveal a non-dual sensibility. These were the types of claim that led to his conflict with the Jewish establishment and accusations of blasphemy, whereas in the Eastern religious traditions he would be thought of as an enlightened or God-realized soul or an avatar of the divine. Many of his teachings, such as the admonition to turn the other cheek, are directed against personal ego concerns, an attitude that is very much in keeping with non-dual spirituality, which minimizes the importance of the ego.[xxxi]

Jesus and Judaism

Although Jesus was Jewish and deeply embedded in first century Jewish culture (Vermes, 1981), as Christianity developed the signs of Jesus' Jewishness were more and more effaced, denied or ignored, contributing to millennia of hostility between these traditions (Levine, 2006). Nevertheless, it was important for early Christians to establish the continuity of the new religion with the Hebrew Scriptures, in part because the Roman Empire allowed only members of ancient traditions to be exempt from worshipping the state gods. At the same time, to establish the priority of the new religion, Christians had to undermine the primacy of the Jewish tradition. For this purpose, passages from the Hebrew Scriptures were used to reinvent Judaism in the form of Christianity. Christians argued that Jews had forsaken their God by killing his son, so their covenant with God no longer applied. The Law of Moses was seen as only temporary. The destruction of Jerusalem by the Romans in 70 CE was seen as deserved because of the execution of Jesus, which was only the latest of the Jewish refusals to listen to the prophetic word of God.

The early Jewish followers of Jesus did not think of themselves as separate from their tradition. However, increasingly they struggled with their relationship to traditional Judaism, and they eventually parted company from it (Galambush, 2006). This may have been partly for political reasons; it was important for the new sect to distinguish themselves from people in conflict with the Romans. The Gospel writers gradually divorced their movement from Judaism and emphasized the novelty of the Christian message, in part by contrasting its emphasis on spirit rather than law. These early writers harshly criticized the Jews who rejected Jesus, and later Christian theologians saw this early criticism as a rejection of Judaism in general. There are many openly anti-Jewish passages in the Gospels; Jesus himself is said to have described the Jews as being "of your father, the devil" (John 8:44). (Since he was Jewish himself, it is hard to imagine that this statement is authentic.) The Jews came to be seen as adversaries. However, the Gospel stories that describe a Jewish crowd insisting on Jesus' death were written two generations later, when relations between Jesus' followers and the Jews who did not follow him had become very strained, and these accounts may not be accurate. However, there are many statements in the New Testament that make the Jews entirely responsible for Jesus' death (1 Thessalonians 2:14-16), planting the seeds of later Church anti-Judaism and cultural anti-Semitism. The Gospel of John, the latest to be written, can be and has often been read in a way that puts Jews in the worst possible light, possibly to distance the Christians from any taint of sedition against Rome by making the Jews the villains in the story of Jesus. According to the Gospel of Matthew (27:25), a Jewish crowd cried "His blood be upon us and our children," and demanded Jesus' death. These kinds of comments allowed church authorities across subsequent generations to transfer what they saw as the historical guilt of the Jews to the Jews of their own time, culminating in polemical Christian anti-Judaism based on the fact that the Jews had rejected Jesus. Two thousand years of massacres, persecutions, and pogroms followed, exacerbated by anti-Jewish polemics from Christian authorities such as John Chrysostom, Aquinas, and Martin Luther. This behavior seriously undermines Christian claims that they follow a God of universal love. Not until the second Vatican Council in 1962 did the Roman Catholic Church affirm that the Jews had not been rejected by God.

The extent to which the Jewish authorities were involved in Jesus' death has been extensively debated (Boys, 2013), and it is a sensitive issue because the New Testament account has been used to justify anti-Semitism. Jesus did offer an unconventional interpretation of Jewish law, he accused the Pharisees of hypocrisy, and he seemed to be threatening the Temple (Mark 13:2), which is why the high priest Caiaphas arrested him. However, when describing his arrest, some authors minimize the involvement of the Sanhedrin, the Jewish religious court, or they suggest that the Gospel account of its involvement is fictional (Winter, 1974). This view is partly based on the fact that the Gospel story contradicts the Jewish juridical procedures of the time, and the depiction of Pilate as a merciful judge contradicts his historical reputation for cruelty. Pilate may have been concerned to prevent an outburst of anti-Roman feelings in a city crowded with Passover pilgrims. The Sanhedrin probably resented Jesus' success, but more importantly was concerned that if Jesus was not silenced and the Romans thought he might instigate rebellion, there would have been mass slaughter, since the Romans exacted serious reprisals for such disturbances. Given the political situation at the time, it is likely that the Romans were responsible for the death of Jesus as a punishment for sedition. Aslan (2013) promoted the view that Jesus was a zealot who wanted to wrest control of his people's land from their Roman occupiers, and he was crucified because the Romans saw him as a military insurgent who had declared himself to be the king of the Jews. According to Aslan, his followers later changed his message to one that advocated love and forgiveness. The budding new Christian sect did not want to be associated with what to the Romans seemed to be a political rebellion.

Saint Paul's influence on the Early Christian God-image

The success of the Jesus movement was in large measure due to the way in which Paul of Tarsus fostered and embellished Jesus' image, beginning about 20 years after his death. Without Paul's influence, it is less likely that Christianity would have separated from Judaism. Much Christian theology is based on Paul's teaching, sometimes more so than on the words of Jesus. The work of St. Paul is particularly important because there was nothing in Jesus' Jewish tradition that would have seen his death as an atoning sacrifice for sin. This way of thinking about Jesus began with Paul, who is therefore often thought of as the founder of the Christian Church.

Paul was initially a fundamentalist Jew, a strict observer of the Torah or the law of Moses, who had participated in the oppression of Jesus' followers. The book of Acts (9:3-9) reports that he had a major conversion[xxxii] experience on the road to Damascus, during which he was blinded by a "light from heaven" and heard Jesus' voice saying, "why do you persecute me?" He then began a long period of proselytizing all over the Mediterranean. Paul's visionary experience remains controversial; either it was a genuine mystical experience, or it was hysterical or epileptic,[xxxiii] depending on the reader's metaphysical commitments. However, in whatever way one conceives of Paul's experience, there is no doubt of its importance for the subsequent history of Christianity. Like Jeremiah (1:5), Paul wrote that he was called by God to preach, "set apart before I was born," (Galatians 1:15), and he believed that he received his apostolic commission directly from Christ and God (Galatians 1:1). However, he remained somewhat isolated from the other Apostles, who never seemed to fully accept him as an equal (1 Corinthians 9:2; Acts 9:26), perhaps because they remembered his earlier persecution of them. According to Galatians 2:9, it was agreed that he would preach to the Gentiles and the others "to the circumcised."

Paul abandoned the political and nationalistic aspirations of the Jews who wanted to overthrow Rome, so he did not threaten Roman authority. Instead, he emphasized a theology of personal salvation. He stressed the importance of a personal relationship with Jesus Christ, whom Paul saw as "the man of heaven," (1 Corinthians 15:48), divine before his birth, who had come to transform the existing world. Perhaps this is why Paul said little about the personal life of Jesus such as his birth or his family. Paul saw the human aspects of Jesus as unimportant. For Paul, Jesus was an entirely spiritual figure, in whom "the whole fullness of deity dwells bodily" (Colossians 2:9), and his advent represented a turning point in history. Paul depicted Jesus as "the image of the invisible God, the firstborn of all creation" (Colossians 1:15). However, Paul's God-image is different than that of Jesus, whose God-image was that of a loving father. Paul changed this image to that of a strict father who demands atonement and human sacrifice. Paul also shifted the emphasis from the historical Jesus to a mythic image of him. For example, Paul wrote that when Moses struck the rock to bring forth water for the Israelites in the desert (Numbers 20:11), "the Rock was Christ" (1 Corinthians 10:4)—meaning he must have existed at that time. Paul rarely quoted Jesus directly; Paul made Jesus himself central, rather than Jesus' teachings. It seems clear that Paul projected his own ideas about Jesus onto him, and this radically affected Paul's theology.

Paul's Theology

Paul believed that traditional Jewish law is unable to save people; salvation could only be attained through faith in Christ, who represented the final goal of the Jewish tradition. Paul believed that the God of Israel had finally done what he promised he would do,[xxxiv] by sending a Messiah, albeit in a manner that was totally unexpected. Paul had been rooted in his Jewish tradition, but he believed that the Temple and the Torah were not the final realities the tradition had imagined them to be; they were only way-stations pointing to Jesus. Whereas traditional Judaism taught that humanity can only know God through the Torah, for Paul, humanity can only know God through Christ. Paul believed not only that the law of Moses does not free people from sin (Acts 13:38-39); in fact, this law actually increases sin (Romans 5:20), whereas the cross of Christ had defeated the force of evil and death. The evidence for this was the Resurrection, which proved that Jesus was the Messiah even though he had been crucified.

Paul thought that living by the Torah had only been a temporary necessity, at best a protection against sin until Christ appeared (Galatians 3:24). Christ would establish a new world order. Now that Christ had come, God's promise to Abraham had been fulfilled by Christ, who is the heir to the promise God made, as are all Christ's followers who are united in baptism (3:25-29). Accordingly, there was no longer any need to keep the law of Moses; in fact, "if justification were through the law, then Christ died for nothing" (2:21). Christ's atoning death fulfills the Mosaic law and then ends it. The original covenant with Abraham and his descendants had now been superseded by a new covenant that God had made with all people by means of Jesus Christ. Paul claimed that exclusive faith in Jesus was essential for salvation; only believers were to have eternal life. Paul was convinced that we are justified by grace through faith; this grace, revealed in Jesus, is freely given by God (Romans 3:24) and is not dependent on human virtue.[xxxv] The doctrine of justification—being righteous and acceptable to God—became central in Christianity.

Paul was preoccupied with the notion that humanity had been condemned by the Fall of Adam, as a result of which God had decreed death for all mankind (Romans 5:12), but Jesus atoned for this sin.[xxxvi] For Paul, the world is helpless because of the power of sin and death. Sin controls people, and sin even uses the law for this purpose. Paul insisted that Christ was sent to redeem humanity from its sins (Romans 8:2-3), and only he can rescue people from sin. Paul clearly had an anguished view of the human condition, for which Jesus was a solution.

For Paul, after Adam's disobedience, the death of Jesus brought the world back into a reconciled relationship with God, just as the sacrifices in the Temple had kept the peace between humanity and God. Jesus therefore fulfilled God's original intention for humanity. It is of interest that Paul placed little emphasis on Jesus' actual teachings, and even contradicts some of them.[xxxvii] Paul also differed from Jesus in the sense that Jesus was forgiving and seemed to think that God's love was more important than his justice, but Paul stressed a more punitive image of God.

Paul believed that to be saved it was only necessary to trust in the atonement provided by Jesus, and this was applicable to all people, not just the Jews. Paul therefore extended Jesus' stress on love to include all nations, but only to people who accepted the new message; otherwise, if anyone were to preach a contrary gospel, "let him be accursed" (Galatians 1:9). The scriptural basis for Paul's mission to the Gentiles is found in his letter to the Romans (14:11) where he quotes Isaiah's (45:14) promise that Egyptians and Ethiopians "shall come over to you and be yours.... they shall come over in chains and bow down to you. They will make supplication to you..." That is, Gentile nations will submit to Israel's God or to Israel's Messiah. Accordingly, Paul wants to "win obedience from the Gentiles" (Romans 15:18). When the Jews rejected Jesus because they could not tolerate the idea of a crucified Messiah, Paul saw himself as called by God to be an apostle to the Gentiles (11:11-13). Apparently however, even some Gentiles believed that his claims about an executed criminal sounded foolish (1 Corinthians 18-23). To encourage converts, Paul facilitated the process by saying there is "neither Jew nor Greek" (Galatians 3:28) and by abolishing the requirement to follow Jewish dietary laws and the need for circumcision, which was no longer important because there is now a "new creation" (Galatians 6:15). This, of course, alienated many Jews because these requirements are vital parts of the Hebrew Scriptures, but this move facilitated ethnic inclusion, which was also fostered by Paul's stress on brotherly love. Paul offered his Gentile listeners participation in an ancient tradition that promised a powerful, loving God who was about to transform the world and reverse the status of the poor, who could feel saved even if they were not rich. Pride and ostentation became sins rather than virtues, as they were among the Romans. Belief in Jesus as the Messiah made one part of a new family that would reflect a new way of being in the world, part of a new covenant with God. In these ways, Paul radically revised the religion of Jesus.

Not surprisingly, Paul was harshly rejected by most of the Jews to whom he preached that Jesus was the expected Messiah, because the image of a defeated Messiah was nothing like Jewish messianic expectations, and the Jews had had previous experiences with failed messianic movements. Paul therefore had to find a way to prove that Jesus had not been defeated but was in fact triumphant. Paul also had to reconcile the tortured death of Jesus with the idea of a loving, divine providence.

The fact that Jesus died on a wooden cross is important, because in Deuteronomy 21:22-23, God pronounced a curse on anyone who was hanged on a tree. But a cursed man could not be God's Messiah, which is partly why Paul initially persecuted Jesus' followers. However, after he became an Apostle, Paul decided that since Jesus was resurrected, he must have been righteous, so he must have been punished for the sins of others. Given the stress on sacrifice in Paul's Jewish tradition, where blood sacrifice was necessary for atonement and expiation, it made sense to him that Jesus' death would save others.

Paul saw the person as composed of body, soul, and spirit, using the term "spirit" to mean the higher nature of human beings. However, he sometimes seems to devalue the body, writing that the desires of the flesh are opposed to the Spirit and "the desires of the Spirit are against the flesh" (Galatians 5:16). (This is not a Jewish idea, nor is it found in the Hebrew Scriptures, so it may have to do with Paul's personal psychology.) In contrast, he also wrote that the "body is a temple of the Holy Spirit within you." Paul (or whoever wrote in his name) also sounds as if he struggled with his sexuality or had some antipathy to it. Paul praised chastity and, celibacy, and only reluctantly consented to marriage, preferring the single status (1 Corinthians 7:8-9). Why he had this attitude is open to debate; it may have been because "the appointed time has grown very short" (1 Corinthians 7:29) before the world would pass away and Jesus would return. Whatever the reason, this attitude, in combination with the work of writers such as St. Augustine, was responsible for the later Church's attitude to sexuality as nothing more than a vehicle for procreation.[xxxviii] Eventually, celibacy and other forms of self-denial became the particular province of professional religious.

Paul's attitude to women has caused controversy, and he has often been accused of misogyny. In one of the letters attributed to him, which he may not have written,[xxxix] he told wives to be "subject to your husbands...for the husband is the head of the wife" (Ephesians 5:22-23). In another letter often believed to be pseudepigraphal, Paul (Titus 2:5) says that young women should be trained to be "domestic, kind, and submissive to their husbands." Paul directed women to be silent in churches (1 Corinthians 14:34-35), although this is not consistent with the fact that women often appeared in leadership positions in the early

Pauline Church (Acts 17:4), and Paul commended this leadership (Romans 16). He assigned women and men equal rights and responsibilities in family situations (1 Corinthians 7:3-5) and admonished husbands to "love your wives" (Ephesians 5:25). He also says that "there is neither male nor female; for you are all one in Christ Jesus" (Galatians 3:28). He writes that "a man....is the image and glory of God; but woman is the glory of man" (1 Corinthians 11:7), but it is not clear what this means. He seemed to hold women in high esteem, so that his apparent silencing of women is often understood to be a later insertion that was in keeping with women's social position at the time.[xl] The fact that women (perhaps Phoebe and Priscilla)[xli] played a significant role in the early Church made the new movement attractive to women, who had a subordinate role in Roman society. (It may be significant in this context that Paul completely ignores any details about Jesus' mother.)

Paul has been criticized by progressive Christians for appearing to support slavery (Ephesians 6:5 and Colossians 3:22-24—letters he may not have written), and in Romans 1:26-27 he seems to condemn homosexuality. In Romans 13:1-2, he instructs his followers to obey the governing authorities, which raises complaints among contemporary political activists. They point out that while Jesus criticized the status quo, and was radically accepting of people, Paul's letters stressed building up the church as an institution and rejected unbelievers. Supporters of Paul point out that he was trying to develop a cross-cultural mission in a highly stratified Roman Empire.

Paul may have been an apocalyptic thinker before his conversion. He can be read to believe that the end of the world could occur at any moment: "For the form of this world is passing away" (1 Corinthians 7:31). However, it is difficult to know whether Paul's messianic eschatology was referring to a catastrophic end of the entire world or to the destruction of the Jerusalem Temple, which Jesus had predicted, according to Mark 13:2. Apocalyptic eschatology was common among Paul's Pharisaic contemporaries, who believed in a coming Messiah, a final judgment, the resurrection of the dead, and a time when God would restore the world to its proper state. The Jewish tradition also believed that because of prophesies such as that of Zechariah (8:22-23) and Isaiah (2:2-3), when God establishes his kingdom, the Gentiles will turn to the God of Israel. Paul appeared to believe that it was his mission to help establish this kingdom by preparing people for the return of Jesus. He wrote that when this happened, Jesus would descend from heaven, and the dead will rise: "then we who are alive, who are left, shall be caught up together with them in the clouds to meet the Lord in the air" (1 Thessalonians 4:17).[xlii] Paul placed great stress not only on Jesus' resurrection but also on the eventual resurrection of all the faithful: "For the trumpet will sound and the dead will be raised imperishable" (1 Corinthians 15:52). This was a powerful claim of everlasting life to believers.[xliii] Since Paul believed that the kingdom would be heavenly rather than earthly, the complete Roman suppression of Jewish nationalism made this idea attractive.

Paul also claims that Jesus instituted the Christian Eucharist by saying: "This cup is the new covenant in my blood. Do this, as often as you drink it, in remembrance of me" (1 Corinthians 11:24-25). The traditional explanation for this act is that Jesus shares his blood, representing his life, with his people. However, as noted earlier, it seems extraordinary that, given the Hebrew Scripture's strict prohibition against eating blood (Leviticus 17:13-14), Jesus would nevertheless encourage his followers to do so, even symbolically. It may be that Paul derived this ritual from similar practices among Hellenistic mystery cults in which meals of various kinds were eaten in identification with a god, not simply to remember the god.

Paul presented Jesus as sent by God for the salvation of humanity by means of his incarnation, death, and resurrection, which Paul believed was a divine plan to save humanity from eternal damnation. Given this idea, Jesus' death was no longer pointless. It is however unlikely that Jesus' Jewish followers regarded him as God incarnate, since it would have been difficult for them (as it has been for many people since) to imagine that the infinite creator God of the Hebrew Scriptures could appear as a human being. When Paul referred to Jesus as the son of God (Galatians 4:4), Paul may have been using the term "son" in a metaphorical rather than literal sense. He may not have believed that Jesus was himself divine, but that he had a special closeness to God, he revealed God's spirit and activity in the world, and he had replaced the Torah as the manifestation of God in the world. But Paul clearly believed that Jesus was the promised Messiah, and that Jesus was adopted by God or was designated as the Son of God at his resurrection (Romans 1:4), which was an early view of him.

Paul's God-image in Relation to his Personal Psychology

It is important to try to understand how Paul's personal psychology affected what he was trying to do, and in particular what drove him to keep repeating behavior that led to his being ill-treated and derided. We would like to understand what drove his relentless travelling, writing, preaching, and his ability to maintain and restore hope and faith in the face of great hardship and periods of despair. However, the psychologist faces the problems of the historical distance combined with disagreements about the authorship of the Pauline corpus among specialists in the field. We do not know how accurately the events in the texts have been conveyed, and how much of the texts have been distorted by the biases of Paul's followers and later editors. Although for these reasons our conclusions must be tentative, because of Paul's overwhelming influence on the Christian tradition, it is worth using his writing to try to discern the relationship between his psychological makeup and his personal God-image, which hugely affected that of Christianity. Paul's writing contains hints about his personality that point to some well-known character traits. Given the limitations of psychohistory and psychobiography, I hope it is clear that these are possibilities based on the textual evidence alone, and from this we can only infer Paul's state of mind. Inevitably, we bring to bear contemporary psychological theory, raising the question of the extent to which it applies to a very different culture.

Paul's letters suggest that he suffered from internal tension and conflict, combined with a sense of personal badness. For example, in Romans 7:15-16 he says that he does what he doesn't want to do, he does what he hates rather than what he knows is good, and that there is a "law of sin which dwells in my members" (7:23). (This may refer to his sexuality. It has been speculated, without evidence, that he may have been homosexual.) Paul describes himself as a "wretched man" who needs to be rescued from his "body of death" (7:24). Typical of such intense self-criticism and his tendency to splitting, he writes: "I of myself serve the law of God with my mind, but with my flesh[xliv] I serve the law of sin" (7:25). In the grip of his self-criticism, which at times verges on self-loathing, it is not surprising that he feels that only divine grace and not human effort can remove human evil. Before he became an apostle, he may have obsessively used ritual practices to try to alleviate his sense of guilt, but these practices only have a temporary effect, so it must have been a huge relief to him that belief in Jesus would justify him before God even if Paul remained sinful.

Paul's preoccupation with sin makes him ignore the many places in the Hebrew Scriptures that teach that God forgives sin (Psalm 103:10-12). Paul's rigidity and his aggression are seen in the fact that he curses anyone, even an angel from heaven, who preaches a different gospel message than his own (Galatians 1:8-9), beginning a long tradition of Christian intolerance, exemplified by comments such as: "He who believes and is baptized will be saved; but he who does not believe will be condemned" (Mark 16:16). Currents of severe paranoid anxiety and aggression appear in Paul's apocalyptic idea of a "day of wrath when God's righteous judgment will be revealed" (Romans 2:5) and angels in "flaming fire" will take vengeance on the non-believers (2 Thessalonians 1:7). He even blinds a man he considered to be a false prophet (Acts 13:11), and he wishes that "those who unsettle you would mutilate themselves" (Galatians 5:12). (This phrase is sometimes translated as "castrate themselves.") These vindictive attitudes and sadistic fantasies suggest a good deal of rage towards his adversaries, perhaps worsened by narcissistic vulnerability that did not allow him to tolerate disagreement.

Even before his Damascus Road experience, Paul had been intolerant of heresy (Galatians 1:13) and had persecuted unbelievers in a "raging fury" (Acts 26:11). This kind of fanaticism often serves to deny doubt, which is projected onto non-believers and attacked externally. Paul's radical division of humanity into the saved and the damned reveals a marked capacity for splitting and projection, such that his adversaries are seen as wicked rather than simply wrong. He makes a sharp distinction between people who believe in Christ and those who do not, whom he believes will perish (2 Corinthians 2:15). He consigns non-believers to eternal damnation, insisting that only believers will enjoy eternal life. For him, the world seems to be divided between those who will and will not be saved. He projects a great deal of negativity onto pagans and onto Jews who did not believe in Jesus, whom he calls "enemies of God," while at the same time acknowledging his own Jewish origins (Romans 9-11). He also writes to the Romans that the Jews supply the root onto which the Gentiles have been grafted, and it is "the root that supports you" (11:18). He adds that the Jews are "beloved for the sake of their forefathers" (11:28). This mixture of admiration and hostility towards his own people seems to produce depressive anxiety and guilt that he experiences as "great sorrow and unceasing anguish in my heart" and the wish to be "accursed" (9:2-3) for the sake of his Jewish kinsmen. It is noteworthy that Paul's negative writing about the Jews has been used to legitimate their persecution ever since the fourth century, while his positive comments about them have been used to combat anti-Semitism.

Paul's capacity for splitting is also seen in the drama of his conversion. Before he became a follower of Jesus, he was scrupulous and "extremely zealous" (Galatians 1:14) about following Jewish law, even though he felt he could never fulfill it completely. He violently persecuted Jesus' followers, encouraging their death (Galatians 1:13; Acts 26:11), or he dragged them off to prison (Acts. 8:3). After his conversion, Paul became a devoted follower of Jesus, feeling responsible to bring him to the Gentile world. What happened to change him has been the subject of a great deal of speculation, ranging from divine intervention to purely psychodynamic factors.

There are several factors that contributed to Paul's radical change of heart, in addition to his encounter with Christ on the Damascus Road, which was certainly the main catalyst. Here I should note that New Testament scholars sometimes insist that Paul's conversion experience cannot be analyzed psychologically because it was a divine revelation, although a plausible psychological explanation for religiously motivated behavior and experience does not rule out its religious significance. Psychological interpretation is not necessarily reductive or iconoclastic.

Seeds of Paul's change of heart may have been sown by the calm and confidence in the face of death he saw among Christians such as Stephen,[xlv] a Jewish convert who was martyred for his faith in Christ, who died saying "Lord, do not hold this sin against them" (Acts. 7:60). Given his personal emotional turmoil, Paul may have been deeply affected by such events, which may have instilled doubt in him about his attacks on Jesus' followers. He saw in them the kind of peace that he needed. During his numinous experience on the road to Damascus, he heard Jesus' voice say: "It hurts you to kick against the goads" (Acts 26:14). Goads were used to force the direction of oxen in fields, so this metaphor, usually understood to mean that Paul had been trying to resist divine will, may also imply that prior to this experience he had been struggling against a secret attraction to Christianity. Perhaps he used his fury at Jesus' followers to drown out this fascination. The fact that he was able to preach immediately after his Damascus Road experience suggests that he was very familiar with early Christian ideas. However, he points out (1 Corinthians 1:23) that the idea of a suffering, humiliated messiah was impossible for Jews to accept, which tends to argue against his having any consciously positive feelings towards Jesus before his Damascus Road vision. He presents his conversion as a sudden event entirely due to this experience. The believer therefore has a case for divine intervention.

The skeptical psychoanalyst, determined to find a naturalistic explanation for Paul's conversion, will point out his need to rebel against Jewish law and against the authority of the Sanhedrin, both of which represent the Jewish Father-God, with whom at the same time he also wanted to be reconciled. Paul assumes that the strict way he judges himself is the way that God judges everyone. A punitive God-image of this kind typically results from the projection of a harsh, self-critical conscience onto God. Obsessional people typically experience conflict between a need to conform and a need to rebel against authority. Paul's writing suggests conflict between a need to surrender to the Father-God and rebellion against him by revoking Judaic law, which Paul said could not give life (Galatians 3:21). With rather tortured logic, Paul accused this law of inciting sin (1 Corinthians 15:56) because it was impossible to fulfill. He may have felt a sense of failure because he could not keep up with the demands of the law, or because obedience to the law was not alleviating his oppressive sense of guilt or anxiety. Eventually his intense ambivalence about obeying the law became intolerable, leading to an emotional crisis that finally forced him to join the Christians. Paul's constant emphasis on sin suggests that he suffered from a tyrannical superego, and it must have been a relief to him when he decided that his burden of guilt was alleviated by Jesus' sacrifice, which atoned for human sins. His personal need for such comfort played a large part in his theology.

Paul seems to have intensely identified with Christ, for example by saying: "it is no longer I who live, but Christ who lives in me" (Galatians 2:20). This identification is also shown by Paul's idea that the Church is the body of Christ. Paul did not simply transmit Jesus' teachings; he turned Jesus into the figure that Paul needed him to be; he greatly enlarged Jesus' image to the point that he saves all humanity. This seems to have been based on a need for an idealized figure, someone who provides wisdom, soothing, and strength with which the self can merge and which it can aspire to emulate (Kohut, 1977). Paul's rage at non-believers may have been in part a reaction to any threat to this intense need. A striking feature of Paul's movement was his insistence on ideological control of his followers' beliefs. Again speculating, this may have been due to an intense twinship need, the need to share experiences with others who are like oneself. Intense twinship needs can lead to the perception that differences are bad. According to the Gospels, Jesus also required dedication from his followers, and the early Church became particularly intolerant of deviation from official doctrine. This form of religious narcissism became characteristic of many subsequent Christian leaders.

Paul takes pride in suffering "weakness, hardship, insults, persecutions and calamities... for when I am weak, then I am strong" (2 Corinthians 12:9-10). He says often went without sleep, food, shelter or clothing (11:24-27), and he lists the times he suffered flogging, scourging, stoning, drowning, fasting, and imprisonment. He seemed to glory in this kind of ill-treatment, and he also inflicted discomfort on himself: "I pommel my body and subdue it" (1 Corinthians 9:27). He asked others to do likewise. These ascetical attitudes and a variety of ascetical practices became firmly ingrained within later Christian teaching, producing a curious tension between its stress on the Incarnation and a devaluing of the body.[xlvi] The usual rationalization for such asceticism is that denial of the body brings one closer to God, but religious asceticism is sometimes difficult to distinguish from characterological masochism. Asceticism is consistent with intense guilt and the need for self-punishment. The notion of unconditional divine love and acceptance would be irresistible to a person with these dynamics. Consciously, Paul's tolerance for suffering and persecution may have been motivated by the story of the Suffering Servant in Isaiah 53.

Although Paul sometimes sounds intolerant and prone to extremes, one also has to admire his courage, energy, passion, devotion, his outspokenness for his beliefs, and his powers of persuasion. His extraordinary praise of love in 1 Corinthians (13:1-13), and his list of the fruits of the Spirit as love, joy, peace, patience, kindness, goodness, faithfulness, gentleness, and self-control, reveal a profound spiritual intelligence. I suspect that this list also reveals what he personally craved or coveted.[xlvii]

The Early Controversies About Jesus' Divinity

Early Christians had to address the question of how to worship Jesus as God and remain monotheists, since although Jesus was God, he also prayed to God (John 17:1-26). The prophet Isaiah (45:22-23) has God say, "I am God, and there is no other," but Paul had to equate Jesus of Nazareth with the God of Israel, and eventually this became a standard Christian belief. However, early disagreement arose about the divinity of Jesus. Questions emerged such as whether Jesus was born divine or only became divine later. A variety of solutions were proposed. Controversy ensued between those who asserted that Jesus was entirely divine (the doctrine of monophytism), those who believed he had both a human and a divine nature, and those who believed he was completely human but was adopted by God either at his baptism or his resurrection. It was difficult to find a formula that would allow one of these positions to be correct without completely denying the others, and these competing groups argued with each other for many years. Eventually, the dominant opinion became the idea that Jesus was God and always had been God, but in the process of developing this majority opinion, various heresies had to be dealt with. Heresy has always been a problem for the Christian tradition; all dissident factions believed that their teachings were in accord with what Jesus taught. What was regarded as orthodox for one period was sometimes condemned as heretical by another. A wide range of heretical beliefs evolved that differed from those that came to be regarded as acceptable (Christie-Murray, 1976).

Docetism was an early heresy based on the idea that if Jesus was truly divine, he must have only appeared to have suffered and died. Therefore, Jesus' body was not a real one but a phantom of immaterial origin that only appeared to be real. One of the early docetists was Marcion of Sinope (85-160 CE), who could not accept the idea that the bloodthirsty, angry Yhwh of the Hebrew Scriptures could be the same God that Jesus referred to as his Father. Accordingly, Marcion decided that there are two gods; the creator God of the Hebrew Scriptures, which Marcion rejected, and a loving, merciful God, the eternal Logos who revealed himself in the form of Jesus. Out of kindness, this God sent Jesus to free humanity from the creator God of the Hebrew Scriptures and sever Christianity from Judaism. This was, in part, an attempt to explain how a good God could allow evil. One possible source of this idea was suggested by Lang (2002), who pointed out the existence of two deities within the Hebrew tradition. In this view, "the Most High appoints a second god, delegating to him certain tasks or even the complete authority over all creation" (p. 197). Lang believed that without this pre-existing Hebrew mythology of two deities it would not have been possible to attract Jews and Gentiles to belief in Jesus. However, the notion of two Gods was eventually overshadowed by an insistence on monotheism, partly for political reasons, to maintain the authority of the Bishop of Rome. According to Pagels (1979), the sovereignty of one God corresponded to the idea that there should be one bishop in charge of the church—the earthly hierarchy had to mirror the divine realm.

The Ebionites, Jewish Christians, believed that Jesus had been conceived and born in the usual way, and because of his righteousness God had chosen him as his son when he was baptized in the Jordan river. They tried to be both Jewish and Christian in their practices, following Jesus while practicing Jewish dietary laws and circumcision. They rejected the authority of the Pauline letters, maintaining that salvation occurred by "works" as well as by faith, as the Letter of James insists. According to Ehrman (2003), the Ebionites' view of Jesus was probably closer to Jesus' view of himself than the image of him that eventually developed.

These kinds of internal conflicts within the developing tradition prompted the Emperor Constantine to insist that an agreed-upon doctrine about Jesus should be decided. It is usually believed that Constantine did so partly because the Christians were becoming numerous enough to become a political threat, and partly try to unify a socially diverse and divided empire by using the umbrella of a single religion. Hence arose the council of Nicaea in 325 CE, where Christ was proclaimed to be coequal and coeternal with God the Father. Everything else was created out of nothing, but Jesus was begotten by God (with no mention of a mother). It was decided at this Council, which consisted of 317 bishops, that Jesus was of the same essence or substance as the Father, not just like the Father.[xlviii] Athanasius of Alexandria (ca. 296-373 CE) believed that Christ was begotten,[xlix] not made, by the Father, and he shares the full nature of the Father. Jesus was henceforth declared to be both fully divine and also uncreated, a doctrine that was enforced by imperial decree. This idea suppressed the human dimension of Jesus, preserved the unqualified divinity of Christ, and at the same time maintained his distinct status as the Son of the Father. The Nicene Creed became foundational for Roman Catholic, Eastern Orthodox, and some (but not all) Protestant churches.

The Council of Nicaea had to deal with the competing opinion of Arius of Alexandria (256-336 CE), who believed that the Son was subordinate to the Father, who had existed before the Son, who therefore could not have the same essence as the Father. In this view, Christ was more than human but not fully divine—he was a kind of perfect spiritual figure, but he was not God, since there must have been a time when he did not exist. Arius insisted that since there is only one God, who existed from eternity and was indivisible, it was impossible for Jesus to be God himself. Arianism was condemned as heretical at the Council of Nicaea, in part because it meant it would be idolatrous to worship Jesus if he was not fully God. Athanasius pointed out that Christ had to be fully God in order for him to redeem humanity, which was the position adopted by the Council. The conceptual transition from the human Galilean teacher to the incarnate divine was then complete. The doctrine that the Son and the Father were of the same essence or substance, or in Greek *homoousios*, became the official doctrine within mainstream Christianity.

The Doctrine of the Trinity

At the First Council of Constantinople in 381 CE, the Holy Spirit was added as an aspect of the divine, distinct from Father and Son, leading to the concept of the Godhead as a Trinity, which has persisted to the present day. The trinitarian notion of God maintains that although God is three persons, each of whom is divine, there is only one God, or one divine substance or *ousia*. This essence belongs equally and fully to each of the three persons of the Trinity. To justify this somewhat counterintuitive idea, Christian theologians point to various biblical verses that talk about God sometimes as Father, sometimes as Son or Holy Spirit. Or, the notion of the Trinity is based on the appearance of God to Abraham in the form of three figures (Genesis 18). At this Council, the idea that Jesus was conceived of the Holy Spirit and the Virgin Mary was added to the original Nicene creed. Later, at the Council of Chalcedon (451 CE), the idea developed that Jesus had two natures, one fully human and one fully divine. (Exactly how this is possible has never been explained.)[1] The one who is of the same essence as the Father is also the one who was born of Mary, so he is begotten from the Father in his divine nature and born from Mary in his human nature. Jesus is wholly God but not the whole of God, which includes Father, Son, and Holy Spirit. The one Godhead is a trinity of three co-equal persons or aspects of the same nature, defined by their internal relationship to each other. Given that Jesus was raised in a traditional, monotheistic Jewish culture, it is difficult to believe that he would have recognized himself in this complex description, even though the creed says that Jesus himself taught it. He and his Jewish followers might have found the notion of the Trinity either incomprehensible or even antithetical to their monotheism.

According to the dogma of the Trinity, God the Father, who is the "I am that I am" of Exodus 3:14, has eternally existed, and in a deeply mysterious way he was always the three Persons of the Trinity even before the advent of Christ. That is, Christ co-existed with the Father from eternity, before Jesus' physical birth. The Son was always in the process of being begotten by the Father, and the Holy Spirit was always proceeding from the Father and the Son. Therefore, before his incarnation, the "only begotten Son" was not yet the son of Mary; he was the Word of God or he spoke the Wisdom of God. The Son was the object of the Father's love, and the Holy Spirit was the Love that passed between them. Another understanding of the Holy Spirit is that it represents the divine presence in the world. Later, for Augustine, the Son is eternally generated as an object of thought in the divine mind, while the Holy Spirit proceeds eternally in the form of love by an act of divine will. Augustine and subsequent theologians typically said that the Trinity represents three manifestations of divine unity. One way to think of the Trinity is to see the Holy Spirit as God in his immanent aspect, while God the Father is transcendent, and Jesus is the means by which the transcendent becomes immanent. A competing notion was Modalism, which maintained that all three persons of the Trinity are actually a single God who has revealed himself in three successive modes of being, as the Father, as the Son, and as the Holy Spirit. These three are not distinct from each other, but the same God in different modes of existence at different times. This contrasted with the Trinitarian doctrine that God is one being or essence, eternally co-existing as three distinct, co-equal persons, so that Modalism was condemned as a heresy.

The doctrine of the Trinity is considered to be a revealed truth, but it led to passionate debates about the nature of the relationship between the three aspects of the Trinity, such as whether the Father and Son are equal, and whether the Holy Spirit arose from just the Father or from both Father and Son.[ii] However, the Trinity is a mythic or archetypal image that cannot be conceived of in ordinary logical terms. The idea was an attempt by Church councils to describe something unknowable. The Christian tradition is largely committed to the idea that God and the Trinity are both incomprehensible, although some people believe the

Trinity can be grasped intuitively, or as the result of mystical experience. During the Middle Ages a great deal of effort was expended trying to philosophically justify this doctrine, while during the Enlightenment it became an embarrassment.

The idea of the Trinity often seems as if it was contrived in an attempt to settle the theological disputes of early Christianity. The idea has various difficulties, including gender bias. One can see the Trinity as a hierarchy in which the Father is primary since he is the source of the Son, and the Holy Spirit also proceeds from the Father. The Trinity has often been depicted using masculine imagery, consonant with a male Church hierarchy. This gender bias and literalism are just two of the reasons that the doctrine of the Trinity is difficult to relate to for many people, and it is often thought to need reformulation. Various attempts in this direction have been made, summarized most recently by Bourgeault (2013). She believes it would be a mistake to try correct the gender imbalance within the Trinity by envisioning the Holy Spirit as feminine, or as identical with Sophia, the feminine wisdom of God. Bourgeault regards this theology as shortsighted from a metaphysical point of view. Instead of thinking of the Trinity in terms of "persons" with fixed identities who manifest the unity of God, which is the Church's theological position, Bourgeault sees the Trinity as the process by which God moves from one state to another. This process unfolds according to an ancient metaphysical principle known as the Law of Three. Whereas, in binary systems, opposites such as masculine and feminine are in balance, according to the Law of Three a third force emerges as the necessary mediation of two opposite forces, generating a synthesis at a new, higher level. This process tries to explain how the fullness of the unmanifest divine manifests itself in multiplicity and diversity, expressing itself in a new dimension. Appealing to the metaphysics of Jacob Boehme,[lii] who also tried to describe how the unity of God could flow into multiplicity, Bourgeault suggests that within the eternal unity of the divine a manifesting principle (the Logos or the yearning of the divine for self-awareness) breaks the symmetry of divine stillness, giving rise to an outward impetus to manifestation. These two forces evoke a reconciling third force that expresses, in a new dimension, what the inner being of God looks like. The hidden ground of love is thus made visible in time and space.

Bourgeault prefers a trinitarian system to Jung's notion that the Trinity could be converted into a quaternity by adding a feminine dimension, because she sees the quaternity as only a double binary system of balanced opposites. For her, this would stabilize the system but weakens the necessary asymmetry of the Trinity that produces a new dimension. Bourgeault believes that the missing fourth must be found at the new level of the dynamic interplay of the three.[liii] An advantage of Bourgeault's idea is that it does not freeze the members of the Trinity into fixed genders. The disadvantage is that the notion that the divine has yearnings is not meaningful except as a human projection.[liv]

The notion of a trinitarian God is found in many religious traditions. In Jungian terms, the trinity is an archetypal symbol of unity in diversity or the uniting of opposites, which helps to account for its numinosity and its attractiveness. Such archetypal images emerge spontaneously from the objective psyche, often in visionary states or in meditation. The Trinity is then not a mere theological contrivance but a deep spiritual structure, which arose when social conditions allowed it to do so.

The paradox of how the infinite God of the Hebrew Scriptures could also be Jesus took a few hundred years to resolve, and was partly achieved by means of the doctrine of the Incarnation. However, this solution raised new problems, such as how a transcendent, perfect, unchanging God could incarnate and suffer a painful death without ceasing to be eternal, which is an essential Christian belief. The question of God's impassibility, or whether he can suffer, has been much debated. One solution, proposed at the Second Council of Constantinople in 553 CE, was that the Father does not suffer in his divine nature, but God suffers in his humanity.

In summary, as Christian thought evolved, the same divine substance was said to take the form of the Father, the Son, and the Holy Ghost, and all three were said to have eternally existed. Yet certain problems remained. Exactly how the Father and Son could be the same has been a persistent problem; how can the infinite God be involved in human life and death without being less than the eternal, transcendent God? Is God divisible? Do the Father, Son, and Holy Ghost have equal amounts of the divine substance? Did the Father appear first, so the Son was dependent on the Father? In the end, the believer simply has to accept the paradoxes and questions involved in the notion of the Trinitarian God-image. The divinity of Christ became the official teaching of Christianity, even though this raised the question of how to maintain the basic principle of monotheism that Christianity had inherited from Judaism. Today, there is considerable focus on Jesus' divine nature.

The Role of Mary

The feminine aspect of the divine appeared in the Roman Catholic tradition as the worship of Mary, who took on the *de facto* role of Queen of Heaven for many Christians. She gained this status even though the early Church went to some lengths to stress that Mary was mortal and only a receptacle for the Holy Spirit. However, her role was crucial, since without her there could have been no Jesus. She represents complete receptivity to the divine. Because she consented to the incarnation, she became the essential bridge between humanity and God, allowing the miracle of redemption. Hence, she became the "mediatrix of all graces," as she is referred to in the Roman Catholic tradition. She is seen in her full glory in the Book of Revelation (12:1), where she appears "clothed with the sun, and the moon under her feet, and on her head a crown of twelve stars." This mythic image seems to represent her as a moon goddess shining by the light of the sun, crowned by stars. Mary has long taken the place of the mother goddess in the hearts of many Christians, an idea that was confirmed in the 1950 Dogma of the Assumption of Mary, which teaches that after her death she was taken bodily into heaven.[lv] Jung believed that this dogma was an important development, since it returned the missing feminine element to the Christian image of God. For most Protestants however, any suggestion of the worship of Mary would be anathema.

The worship of Mary as the mother of a divine being is a continuation of earlier divine mother-son traditions such as Isis/Horus or Cybele/Attis, although Mary was not regarded as particularly significant in the early years of the Christian tradition, perhaps because of this potential association with early pagan goddess traditions. Consequently, the exaltation of Mary took some time to emerge. The earliest feminine imagery in the tradition was Jerusalem as a mother figure or the Church as the bride of Christ (implied in Ephesians 5:22-33). However, Mary's position gradually became increasingly important, especially in the folk tradition, and beginning in the early Middle Ages she was worshipped in her own right. She officially became the Mother of God (after some controversy) at the Council of Ephesus in 431 CE. This role implies that she is the source of Jesus' human nature. Mary became the second Eve who undid the disobedience of the first Eve. Within the tradition, Eve came to symbolize matter, and through her women were cursed, but Mary represents the divinizing of matter, and through her women are blessed (Heiler, 1968).

In the fourth century CE, temples of several pre-Christian goddesses were re-consecrated to Mary. Medieval cathedrals were dedicated to her, and these churches sometimes portrayed Mary as the central figure in their mosaics. The fifth century development of Monophytism, the doctrine that Jesus only had a divine nature and not a human nature, made Mary of particular redemptive importance, since this doctrine separated Jesus from the rest of humanity, so that many people turned towards Mary as a representative of redeemed humanity. By the sixth century, her importance was enhanced by the popular belief that she had either not died or had been resurrected and admitted to heaven.[lvi] People turned to her as a mediator or intercessor and a source of salvation. Sometimes her merciful and forgiving nature was contrasted with the image of Jesus as an apocalyptic warrior or with the judgmental Father God. Mary became a particular object of devotion for many Christian ascetics and celibate priests, and at her shrine at the Basilica of our Lady of Guadalupe she is honored by some local people as much as the Father and Son.

The dogma of the Immaculate Conception of Mary (proclaimed in 1854) teaches that she was conceived without inheriting original sin, from which all other human beings suffer.[lvii] This idea was necessary because if Jesus had been conceived naturally, he would have inherited original sin. The notion of Mary as perpetually virginal began in popular piety very early in the tradition. This idea is archetypal; in the Greek pantheon several goddesses were virginal, referring to an essential purity that is complete in itself, without needing the masculine, and not affected by fate. Being born of a virgin mother was often part of the mythology of heroes and saviors such as Heracles or even the Buddha. In all mythologies, to be born of a virgin implied the special favor of a heavenly figure and endowed the individual with charisma and with followers. However, the theme that Mary was pregnant by means of the Holy Spirit or that she was a virgin is only alluded to in two of the Gospels (Matthew 1:18; 25 and Luke 1:27), suggesting that the other Gospel writers were not aware of the idea. They usually describe Jesus as the son of Joseph or the son of a carpenter. Some Christian theologians denied the idea of the virgin birth, and it is unlikely that Jesus' immediate followers imagined some kind of divine impregnation. Mary's role has remained important among Roman Catholics but is more restricted among Protestants.

The Gnostic God-image

Gnostics believed that redemption and salvation are achieved by direct knowledge of the divine, or gnosis, rather than by adherence to faith and belief. Many Gnostics believed they had secret knowledge that was the key to salvation. This esoteric knowledge was passed on by instruction and ritual initiation, so they believed more in private spiritual development and self-discovery than public witness.

The Gnostics produced a variety of traditions and mythologies, although these had some common features, such as attempts to reconcile the presence of evil with the goodness of God. One gnostic solution to this problem is that since God is good, but the material world is evil, the world was not created by the high God but by an inferior divinity. Typically, the Gnostics believed that the true God or First Principle created the Pleroma, or fullness, which contains a number of spiritual beings. The final one was Sophia, who bore the Demiurge, a lower, imperfect deity who either created the physical world himself or who was the father of the lesser, malefic god who created it—sometimes equated with the Yhwh of the Bible. Either the supreme God did not prevent this creation, or he did not know about it, but the result was that the world is corrupt and evil. Not only does this idea explain why creation is so flawed, it also meant that Jesus was not responsible for the violence perpetrated by the Yhwh of the Hebrew Scriptures.

Although the Demiurge created the material part of human beings, Sophia infused some of her spiritual essence into them, so that (some or all) humans contain a spark of the divine. This spark is trapped in the prison of the earthly body, from which it has to be freed so that the person may enter the realm of pure spirit. Gnostics tend to see stories such as the virgin birth and the Resurrection not as historical events but as symbolic pointers to deeper understanding.

In the Gnostic system of thought, Christ came to bring people to gnosis, or knowledge of the divine, by means of his secret oral teachings, which were not written down. According to some Gnostics, Jesus was a man who was possessed by a divine being sent from heaven at his baptism. This divinity left Jesus at his crucifixion. Gnostics largely rejected the idea of the Resurrection. They believed that Jesus was sent to teach people how to find the divine spark within themselves and how to escape from the evil Demiurge. This idea rendered the official Church almost irrelevant to salvation and abolished the authority of the bishops. The threat this made to the mainstream tradition is obvious, so that Gnostics inspired a large volume of hostile critics among the mainstream authorities, which presumably meant that Gnosticism was attractive to many people. Gnostics were either suppressed as heretics or they were ignored. Pagels (1979) pointed out that the gnostic idea of women as close confidants of Jesus (which is seen in the Gospels) questioned the exclusively male character of the priesthood. The Gnostics had their own Gospels, such as the Gospel of Mary, arguing that Jesus continued to appear to those who are prepared to receive him through gnosis. This view challenged the authority of the orthodox Church, which taught that Jesus bestowed spiritual authority only on his Apostles, establishing a line of succession from Peter to the generations of bishops to follow.

There remain areas of Gnostic thinking within Christianity. Because many Christians believe in the literal existence of the Devil, some Christian thinking is as dualistic as Gnosticism in terms of the split between good and evil. Christians also make a sharp distinction between matter and spirit. This split has continued a devaluation of the body and the feminine in some strands of the Christian tradition.

Some contemporary Christians still see Gnostic thought as a threat to Christianity. Gnostic ideas are still promoted by progressive voices as a contrast to the dogmatism or exclusiveness of mainstream Christianity. Controversy continues in this area, but it may not be possible to reconcile the idea of salvation arising from an external savior with the idea of salvation arising through self-knowledge and personal experience of the sacred. These seem to be different approaches to the divine-human relationship, although they may not be mutually exclusive. Jung's approach is firmly in the gnostic tradition that values direct experience of the holy more than doctrine or dogma.

The Need for Atonement by Bloodshed, and the Alternatives

In most traditions of antiquity, animals or human beings were sacrificed to the gods. In the Hebrew Scriptures, blood sacrifice was used for consecration, atonement, purification, and atonement for sin (Leviticus 16:14 & 19). In contemporary pagan traditions, child sacrifice to Canaanite deities such as Moloch was well known, although the idea of a deity sacrificing his son to save humanity was very unusual. However, the necessity of blood sacrifice was still operative at the time of Jesus, so that "under the law almost everything is purified with blood, and without the shedding of blood there is no forgiveness of sins" (Hebrews 9:22).[lviii] The theme of blood sacrifice is common throughout the New Testament (1 John 1:7; Revelation 1:5; Colossians 1:20), and entered Christian liturgy and hymns with phrases such as "washed in the blood" or "saved by the blood" of Jesus. The Gospels draw on Isaiah's comment "with his stripes we are healed" (53:5), which, at the time it was written, referred to the Jewish people but was appropriated by Christian theologians to refer to Jesus. The idea developed that Jesus' suffering and death atoned for the sins of humanity, leading to the salvation of humanity. This notion of atonement has been central to Christianity, and it is one of the features that makes Christianity distinct from other religions. However, why Jesus had to suffer terribly and die for the sins of others, and how this atonement leads to salvation, is not clear, and has been the subject of controversy. Many people believe that there is absolutely no evidence for the idea, and it seems like an avoidance of personal responsibility. From a psychological point of view, the Christian idea that atonement for sin requires bloody sacrifice looks like the projection of human violence onto the divine.

The rituals of the Jewish temple had included blood sacrifices intended to reconcile the people with God because of their sins, and Jesus' death is often seen as a continuation of this kind of sacrifice for the sake of the redemption of humanity from sin—hence the idea in Mark (10:45) that Jesus gave his life "as a ransom for many." As the Christian tradition developed, the need for animal sacrifices of the kind found in the Hebrew Scriptures disappeared, because this need was seen to have been fulfilled by Jesus' sacrifice. It was replaced with symbolic participation in Christ's sacrifice by means of the Eucharist.[lix]

The medieval St. Anselm believed that humanity owed God the Father a ransom of satisfaction because of human sin, but human beings did not have enough to offer. Humanity's sin against the infinite God required an infinite satisfaction that could only be offered by an infinite being, the Son of God in the person of Christ. Eternal damnation would have been unavoidable except for the grace bestowed on us by Christ, who suffered as an acceptable substitute on behalf of humanity. In this view, Jesus cancels the debt humanity owes to God because of humanity's sinfulness. One problem this raises is to determine who benefits from Jesus' sacrifice—perhaps everyone, or perhaps only Christians, or only Christians of a certain type. A further problem that arises here is our horror at the idea that an offended father requires the death of his own son to satisfy the father's outrage. There is a certain logical problem in the idea that God killed God in order to save mankind, so that later Christian theologians went to great lengths to find alternatives to these ideas.

The notion of atonement requiring Jesus as a substitute sacrifice has fallen out of favor with some theologians, for various reason. It sounds too legalistic, it ignores the importance of a personal relationship with Jesus, and it has a threatening tone in which the Church offers the only way out. The idea that salvation must require sacrificial suffering seems to glorify or legitimize suffering, death, and scapegoating. The central image of Christ on the cross as a redemptive act seems to suggest that the suffering of a child in obedience to the will of the father is somehow justified (Brown et al., 1989). The idea that Jesus has to die to pay the price for human sin is a brutal God-image. Traditionalists deal with this by pointing out that since Jesus was also God, he reveals his compassion in this self-sacrifice. Alternatively, Jesus' death can be seen as an example of selfless service to others and obedience to the divine will, and "you should follow in his steps" (1 Peter 2:21). Some authors prefer to see the story of Jesus in terms of liberation from oppression rather than redemption from sin. Another alternative is to focus on Jesus' love for humanity and our love for him. The love of God for humanity is understood to be his recognition of human need and God's desire to answer this need by offering Christ. The love of humanity for God means the soul's desire to be united with God. However, the focus on love has its own problems, such as minimizing the problem of sin and trying to command someone to love. Furthermore, the image of a God who has his son killed to satisfy his displeasure with humanity seems more punitive than loving. Needless to say, this debate also has political implications. For some Evangelicals and for right wing politics, the stress on individual morality requires the notion of sin and punishment, while left-wing or liberal politics stresses Jesus' compassion in its support for issues such as LGBTQ rights.

Some strands of the Christian tradition have emphasized the idea that sin has permeated creation, which was originally intended to be good. This emphasis leads to the idea that human beings are radically alienated from God. Humanity is totally condemned and judged, and there is nothing one can do about it, except by believing in the redeeming and atoning power of Christ. Psychologically this looks like the projection of a "naughty child—angry father" approach to the divine. This doctrine takes advantage of the fact that many people grow up with an internalized sense of personal badness as a result of harsh parental criticism. They are therefore vulnerable to being told they are intrinsically sinful, which confirms their negative self-image and resonates with internal persecutory objects or a harsh superego. Psychoanalysts also detect an underlying strain of sadomasochism in the insistence that redemption and atonement require suffering.

Early Developers of the Christian God-image

Irenaeus (130-200 CE), the Bishop of Lyons, was one of the main intellectual defenders of Christian orthodoxy against contrary opinions and heresies, which he believed were a threat to the truth of the Gospel message that the faithful had transmitted to his generation. He believed that true Christian belief was progressively revealed to believers, and the best custodians of correct belief were the churches founded by the Apostles. He was hostile to innovation and too much questioning of religious belief. Irenaeus rejected Gnostic material and stressed the authority of the Gospels and their unity with the Hebrew Scriptures.

Origen (185-254 CE) was one of the most original early Christian thinkers. He believed that the scriptures are inspired, and they provide the answers to life's mysteries, but the scriptures cannot always be understood literally. They have different levels of meaning and they must sometimes be interpreted allegorically, morally, and spiritually. Origen saw God as unknowable and inconceivable except to the Son, who is the Word of God. God has communicated to humanity through the Son and through Moses and the prophets. Origen taught a theory of continuous creation, in which God holds the universe together. Origen believed that God had partly revealed his divine Logos to the prophets, but Christ possessed the whole Logos, and he acted as medium for the union of the Logos with humanity. Origen placed great emphasis on free will; the fact that God requires human beings to behave well proves they have free will and are responsible to God. The fact that demonic powers try to interfere with good behavior proves the need for God's help. Although Adam's Fall destroyed an original unity, Origen was sure that eventually God would restore the whole human race to unity in God, so that evil will no longer exist. As a Christian Platonist, Origen was sure that human beings have an innate knowledge of the divine that could potentially be remembered, and the soul could ascend to God, freeing itself from the prison of the body to become spirit. However, this idea implied that Jesus was not necessary for salvation, so in the ninth century some of Origen's ideas were condemned as heretical.

St. Augustine (354-430 CE) was one of the most influential of all Christian thinkers. His image of God idealizes all the qualities that people consider to be good; for him, God is perfectly good, omnipotent, wise, the source of everything, and eternal. For several centuries, the picture Augustine painted defined the traditional Christian image of God. Augustine saw the world in terms of a hierarchy, in which God was on top. Good angels lie just below God, while the souls of good people are just below them. At the bottom of the hierarchy lie physical objects, so there are degrees or gradations of being. Augustine interpreted God saying to Moses "I am that I am" (Exodus 3:14) to mean that God is the most real Being of all, while other creatures are less fully real. Creatures can change, but only God is immutable. Creatures have parts to them, but God is a unity with no parts. God is the supreme good, and everything else on the hierarchy is good to lesser degrees. Logically for Augustine, if the degree of goodness is the same as the degree of realness, pure evil would have no goodness at all and so cannot be real. Evil is therefore the absence of the goodness that ought to be present—the doctrine of *privatio boni*. By promoting this idea, Augustine wished to avoid any hint of Manichean dualism[lx] that might be implied if evil had independent existence. Augustine believed that creation is essentially good, having been created by God, so that evil cannot have its own, separate, being. Evil is entirely the result of human free will, and God knows all things without undermining human free will. According to Augustine, God originally arranged the world properly, but human beings and fallen angels are responsible for disorder and evil. The paradox produced by the existence of evil in a world that God created and declared to be good was never resolved.

Augustine believed that God created matter out of nothing, and the forms that God impressed on matter had been in his mind since the beginning of time—or even before that, since God existed prior to or outside of time. The notion that God creates out of nothing was a remarkable change from earlier beliefs that animals, plants, and human beings arose from an earth goddess. In the archaic view, the world is a living system of which the gods are a part, but with the advent of a transcendent God who creates *ex nihilo*, divinity is no longer an intrinsic part of the world, and seems remote. This doctrine also suggested a God who was an omnipotent King with obedient subjects, which is hard to reconcile with the image of God as love, sensitive to his creatures.

According to Augustine, with the grace of God, the most we can do is to make some progress in the direction of perfection, which Jesus (Matthew 5:48) had commanded by saying "You, therefore, must be perfect, as your heavenly Father is perfect."[lxi] The British monk Pelagius challenged Augustine's interpretation of this phrase, on the grounds that God would not order us to do something that lies beyond our ability. To argue that we need special help from God to improve ourselves is to destroy moral effort, but Pelagius believed that since we are given free will, our moral development is up to us. In his view, original sin did not taint humanity, and we are capable of living without sin. Pelagianism was condemned at the Council of Carthage in 417 CE, and it became official doctrine that people cannot perfect themselves without divine help.[lxii]

Augustine believed in the doctrine of predestination, the idea that God has chosen some people for salvation through Christ, and all others are damned. This means that the individual has little or no power to influence his or her fate; only God's grace is effective, and grace is a gift of God. Tension remains between the doctrines of divine predestination and human free will.

Augustine believed that human will is corrupted by original sin, which we have inherited from the sin of Adam, which is why babies need baptism. Therefore, the notion of original sin and the need for a Savior hinge on the reality of the story of Adam, since if there was no such person there is no need for Jesus' mission.[lxiii] Accordingly, Augustine took the story of Adam and Eve literally and taught that all human beings must pay for the sin of this original couple, whose sin was passed on through sexuality. Because of this sin, Augustine believed that all human beings deserve to be condemned, and they are only rescued by an act of God's grace. This idea further established what developed into an indelible connection between sin and sexuality, and meant that people could not save themselves. (Echoes of Augustine's personal difficulty controlling his sexuality can be heard here.) Augustine believed that God had been offended by Adam's behavior, and a debt of restitution was owed to God, which is why Christ is essential, since he paid the ransom due to God. Consequently, the tradition of the virgin birth became important to Augustine; the Savior himself could not be the product of Adam's sin. His Father was the Holy Spirit. The idea developed that God had intended creation to be perfect, but humanity had fallen because of Adam, and this Fall had to be overcome so that the world could be restored to its originally intended perfection. Jesus was the one who would achieve this.[lxiv] Human beings were considered to be alienated from God by the nature of their being, even though this nature was given to them by God. Augustine's argument appeared to justify the imposition of Church authority as essential for salvation.

At the turn of the sixth century, a mysterious figure named Pseudo-Dionysius the Areopagite appeared. He claimed that his work had been written by the Dionysius who heard St. Paul preach in Athens, as described in Acts 17:33-34. The inauthentic nature of this claim was not established until the late nineteenth century, but during the author's lifetime his claim gave his work considerable authority, and it had an important influence on subsequent Western thinking about God. Pseudo-Dionysius pointed out the limits of language when talking about God; when we describe God using terms such as good, we only give the impression that we know what God is like. But God is not good in the ordinary human sense. Nothing we can say about God conceptually is meaningful, and we can only approach God by negations, not by affirmations, and even the negations must eventually be negated. Divine silence, darkness, and not knowing are all that are left in this *via negativa*. In this view, God is beyond both affirmation and negation.

The medieval term "cloud of unknowing" belongs to this kind of theology, which describes God as unknowable and incomprehensible. This is a different notion than the Augustinian view that sees God as the most real and the most intelligible being of all. In this view, even though God is incomprehensible, we can encounter God as a beatific vision (an individual experience of God) or an illumination. Augustine believed that the human mind is designed to see the light of divine truth, even though our sinful hearts prevent this.[lxv] The problem was to explain how there could be a beatific vision if God is incomprehensible. These two views of God could not be reconciled, and they existed side by side throughout the Middle Ages. Thomas Aquinas tried to reconcile this difficulty by teaching that although we cannot understand God with the intellect, divine grace may allow us to do so.

After Augustine and the fall of the Roman Empire in the fifth century CE, the West entered into what is now thought of as one of the darkest periods in Western history. Not much original thinking appeared, with exceptions such as John Scotus Erigena (815-877 CE), who tried to show that the traditional theory of the creation of the universe out of nothing was reasonable, and that God created the world "out of himself." Before he did so he had a complete plan of the world in his mind, whereupon the world radiated out of him. The universe is therefore an expression of God's thoughts, but it is only a small revelation of God, who is more than the universe. We can know something about God by studying the universe, but we will thereby only learn a little about God, who is unknowable.

The Christian God-image During the Middle Ages

Medieval scholastic theology[lxvi] tried to combine Christianity with Aristotelian philosophy, which had been rediscovered by Western scholars in the twelfth century. The translation of Aristotle into Latin, combined with translations of Jewish and Arabic philosophy, provided a new impetus for the development of Christian theology. At this time, there was tension between people who believed that Christian belief and the philosophy of Aristotle were compatible and those who saw too many contradictions between these systems. Agreement was only possible in some areas because Aristotle had no concept of a God in the Christian sense.

Medieval Christian theologians assumed that the pagan gods of Greece and Rome were inventions of the devil, that Islam was a heresy, and that Christianity had superseded the original covenant of Israel with God. The Hebrew Scriptural commandment to offer animal sacrifices was considered to be no longer effective, since the only offering that could restore the human connection to God was the sacrifice of Jesus on the Cross. In the new covenant of the Christian dispensation, the temple sacrifices are replaced by the crucifixion; Jesus offers people what they would previously have obtained by going to the temple. The Law given to Moses was thought to be impossible to obey, but this Law had been replaced by the mystery of divine grace. For medieval thinkers, God lived in heaven but created the earth and then became immanent by incarnating as Jesus Christ. The presence of God in the world was thought to be mediated by means of the Church, which linked heaven and earth, just as the soul linked the body with God. During the later Middle Ages there was a consolidation of the power of papal authority, and a considerable growth in the number of religious orders such as the Franciscans and Dominicans. The Church demanded unquestioned obedience to its doctrines, enforced by the Inquisition. Christian theology tended to have an Augustinian view of humanity, focusing on St. Paul's opinion that all men are sinners (Romans 3:9-12; 5:12-21), the depraved nature of human beings, and fears of divine judgment after death. Mortification of the flesh was the recommended remedy for these problems.

The Church was the most prominent single institution in the West during the Middle Ages. People were assumed to be dependent on the Church for their relationship to God. God was very much a father and lord, corresponding to the feudal system of the time, and his anger at the disobedience of Adam and Eve had to be appeased by the death of Jesus. There was considerable medieval focus on the passion of Jesus and his redemptive suffering. This gave people an opportunity to re-work the long-standing paradox of how Jesus could be both human and divine, and to address the paradox of how an immortal God could suffer and die on the cross. This problem could not be solved, but it provided an intense subject for meditation, music, and poetry.

One of the major debates among medieval Christians was between two philosophical doctrines, Realism and Nominalism. Realists believed that ideas such as the Trinity are concepts or Universals that exist independently of actual things and experiences, and they are not created by experience. Universals are ideas such as "motherhood," which are as real as particular instances of motherhood. In contrast, Nominalists believed that individual things are the only reality, and so-called universals are only names—there are no universal qualities independent of things. Ideas are the result of experiences and otherwise would not exist.[lxvii] Roscelin (ca. 1050-1125) applied the doctrine of Nominalism to the Trinity by saying that the Trinity refers to three distinct persons or substances, three Gods equal in power. The three persons of the Trinity are only nominally one. This denied the official doctrine of the Church, which taught that the Trinity was one substance, so in order to preserve the official version of the Trinity the Church adopted the Realist position that Universals are the only real things, and individuals are particular forms of universal ideas. This became the dominant position of the Scholastics, and much Christian thinking was based on it, for example by insisting that the bread and wine of the Eucharist are truly the body and blood of Christ, and baptism is a real union with Christ. The Church can claim to teach universals, such as a moral code, because these were revealed by God. For later Protestant traditions, nominalism became more popular, holding that the sacraments are only a memory or a spiritual reality in the mind of the participant. In the nominalist view, Church doctrine has no special authority since it is purely a human creation, so that morality is not based on a spiritual realm.

Saint Anselm of Canterbury (1033-1109)

Anselm wanted to make Christian teaching rational and intelligible. He saw his task as faith seeking understanding. He was interested in finding necessary reasons for the truth of Christian doctrines such as the Incarnation and the Trinity, without simply appealing to scripture or to the authority of the Church Fathers. He hoped that people could be led to faith through the use of reason.

Anselm thought that the idea of God was innate. He developed a famous ontological proof of the existence of God. In brief, Anselm suggested that even to deny the existence of God first implies the idea of God, and the fact that we can imagine God as the greatest conceivable thing implies the existence of that greatest thing. As discussed on p. 22 this idea has been rejected by most philosophers, in part because we can imagine witches and unicorns that do not exist.

Anselm addressed the issue of why God would become man. He believed that people were originally created by God to be happy, but Adam sinned, and because of this sin, humanity must be punished in proportion to the gravity of the sin. But only the death of a God-man could render sufficient satisfaction to save the whole of humanity. Therefore, out of his mercy, God took on human nature and died on the cross.

St. Bernard of Clairvaux (1090-1153)

Bernard of Clairvaux has had a major influence on Christian thinking. He believed that the aim of human life is to free oneself from false and unnecessary pursuits, so that we may be brought to union with God by recovering our lost likeness to him. He insisted that intellectual curiosity, or the knowledge of external things, is sinful; only self-knowledge is worth seeking, and this may be had without technical training. If we were to truly know ourselves, we would be humble and fear God. When we know God, we are filled with love and hope; without knowledge of God, we might despair. If we stop seeking the illusory and ephemeral, the image of the divine in us is restored. The soul is naturally simple and free in its essence, but these qualities can be covered over by duplicity and sin. We become like what we desire, and our freedom is chained by our desires; if we were to desire nothing, but simply love God, we would remain free. The union of one's will with the will of God produces the highest simplicity, and we would only have the wishes of God, which is the ultimate realization of human potential. For Bernard, a pure conscience and faith are enough to win salvation.

John Duns Scotus (1265-1308)

The Scottish philosopher Duns Scotus wanted to maintain the truth of Church teaching at all costs. He was a critic of the notion that we cannot say anything meaningful about God, since he believed that we could develop some positive ideas about God from our knowledge of creatures; the difference is one of degree, since God is more perfect than creatures. He argued that we cannot know what God is not unless we first know what God is.

St. Thomas Aquinas

Aquinas became one of the most famous theologians of the High Middle Ages. For many generations he was the official philosopher of the Roman Catholic Church, exerting a huge influence. He was one of many people at the time who wanted to justify the beliefs of the Church using reason. For Aquinas, although the human mind cannot know the nature of God, the existence of God can be demonstrated from the effects of God in the world. Aquinas attempts a series of logical arguments (his "five ways") that he thought would reinforce our belief in the existence of God.

Based on Aristotle's notion of an Unmoved Mover, the initial cause of all motion in the universe, Aquinas argued that since everything is in motion, there must be something that set everything in motion but is itself unmoved, and this is God. Furthermore, nothing can exist as the cause of itself, and there must be something outside the sequence of causal events that accounts for this sequence, and that is God. Aquinas intends this to mean that God is first in the hierarchical sense, not in the temporal sense, because we cannot prove that the universe had a beginning in time. Human beings and things in the world are contingent and eventually perish, so that over a long period of time everything would cease to exist. However, since things do exist there must be a non-contingent, necessary being that never ceases to exist, on which the world order rests. This being is God, who is the reason that there is something rather than nothing. As well, things in the world exist in a gradual scale from the lowest forms of life to greater and greater perfection, so there must be something perfect at the very top. There are different degrees of perfection and goodness in the world, and our ideas of what is more or less perfect imply a best or most perfect Being whose goodness is the cause of the relative goodness of other beings. This Being can only be God. Finally, the fact that we see teleology in nature and order in the world presupposes an intelligent ordering principle that governs the world. God creates this order at the same time as he maintains his perfection and unity. These abstract, intellectual proofs are not convincing to atheists (Siniscalchi, 2018),[lxviii] but they do give theists some reason to believe God exists.

Aquinas saw a radical discontinuity between the natural realm and the divine realm. For him, God was absolutely transcendent, beyond the human capacity to experience. Aquinas maintained that God is pure form, meaning he is not composed of anything. We cannot describe what God is like; we can only say what God is not. However, because of revelation, we can speak about God by analogy to human experiences such as love, but God is much more than human love. He is changeless, transcendent, infinite, and immanent in the world without being changed by this. God's essence is identical to and inseparable from the being of God, or it is the essence of God to be. This makes God unlike ordinary creatures whose existence and essence are distinct. Creatures receive their possibility of being from God, who is existence itself, and God confers existence on other beings. For Aquinas, it is pure love that leads to creation.

Aquinas believed that God has both a divine nature and a human nature; the divine nature is primary and beyond change. In Christ, the human nature is united to the divine nature, and the human nature is an instrument of the divine nature. Jesus is said to have been united with God from the moment of his conception in the womb. Aquinas believed that Adam's fall from grace, and the resulting transmission of original sin, made the incarnation in Christ necessary, since this was the only way that humanity could restore its lost connection to God, through the sacraments of the church. The church's insistence on original sin transmitted by an original couple in the Garden of Eden makes baptism[lxix] essential and helps to explain the church's opposition to the theory of evolution until the middle of the twentieth century. The church wanted to hold onto a literal reading of the creation of an original couple, not the appearance of humanity as the result of evolution.

Aquinas's thinking, or Thomism, preserved a very traditional God-image and was the dominant Roman Catholic philosophy until the mid-twentieth century. It was enforced by canon law. In its classical form it was often regarded as anachronistic, but a range of new interpretations of Thomism arose in the twentieth century that are much more receptive to modern thinking. For example, whereas Aquinas believed that faith had access to higher truth than reason alone, Neo-Thomists believed that both human reason and science are applicable to Christian theories of human nature, but the supernatural order is restricted to the domain of theology. A typical critique of Thomism is that of Dourley (2010, p. 97), who believes that Thomism splits the supernatural and the natural orders of being, as if "an objective God revealed himself from beyond." This meant that grace has to come from without, in contrast to Jung's emphasis on the Self as a subjective experience found within the psyche rather than in a heavenly realm.

In 1277, the Church hierarchy condemned a series of theological teachings, including some of those proposed by Aquinas, because of a fear that Aristotelian physics tended to limit the power of God, as if God had to conform to natural law. At the same time, scholastic theology had become so dry that the intellect became suspect as a path to God. Instead, intense affective states were increasingly valued, especially by mystics, since these states were thought to indicate direct experiences of the divine. For the mystics, who despaired of understanding God by means of reason, it was most important to directly experience God by means of contemplation and meditation. These individuals were often impatient with philosophical speculation and were skeptical about systematic theology.

St. Bonaventure (1221-1274)

The Scholastic philosophers of the medieval period looked at the universe through the eyes of their religion; for them, the universe bears witness to the existence of its creator. Bonaventure exemplified this attitude. He interpreted Plato's notion of the Ideas or Forms as thoughts in the mind of God. Unlike Aquinas, Bonaventure was profoundly suspicious of Aristotle. He thought that Aristotle had made a mistake when he rejected Plato's Ideas, and Bonaventure pointed out several other ways in which Aristotle is incompatible with Christian teaching. For example, Aristotle believed that the world was eternal, without any beginning or end, but Christian dogma teaches a moment of creation out of nothing. Aristotle denied the immortality of the soul, which meant that there cannot be reward or punishment after death, as Christianity teaches. Bonaventure was a traditionalist; he believed that innovations in doctrine were errors, and the wish to introduce new doctrines is a sign of bad character. There can be no truth that is not related to Christ in some way; Christ is the source of all exemplars. For Bonaventure, this world is like a mirror that reflects its creator in its existence, but God can be seen even more clearly through the image he implanted in the soul. The outer world is an exterior book through which the creator can be read, while the mind is an internal book for doing so.

Meister Eckhart (1260-1327)

Eckhart was a dominant voice in the medieval church, and he has had a wide and long-lasting influence. For him, the ground of the human soul and the ground of God are the same, so that we can find union with God within ourselves. God cannot be known rationally, but can be known through immediate mystical experience, which culminates in the human reunion with God in the depths of the soul. For Eckhart, this means the birth of God or the birth of the Son of God within the soul, so that the soul again becomes one with God. This union is the ultimate goal of the human being and the height of spiritual experience, but it is ineffable. The key to this process is detachment from the importance of material things. Eckhart believed that beyond God as Father, Son, and Holy Spirit lies the Godhead itself, which is the ground of God beyond any image. In these ideas, Eckhart was trying to reconcile or synthesize the Neoplatonic notion of God as Pure Being or eternal Form with the Christian Trinity. He also tried to reconcile the notion of the eternity of the Forms with the Christian teaching of God as creator, and he had to reconcile the Platonic notion that the soul is uncreated with the Christian notion that God creates the soul. Not surprisingly his solutions led to charges of heresy, which he denied.

Before leaving the medieval period, I should note that all these erudite discussions about the nature of God during the eleventh to the thirteenth centuries had little effect on the actual behavior of Christians; between 1096 and 1099, on their way to conquer Jerusalem, Crusaders killed tens of thousands of Jews and Muslims, all in the name of God. Violence and looting of conquered cities were common throughout the period of the crusades, which continued to the end of the thirteenth century.

The Christian God-image During the Renaissance

Compared to attitudes in the Middle Ages, the Renaissance (between the fourteenth and seventeenth centuries) encouraged a much broader outlook on life and the natural world, with an emphasis on human abilities, knowledge, and creativity that had hitherto been attributed to God alone. Theology and science started to part company. Traditional religion became increasingly unsatisfying. People began to want a more immediate or personal form of faith than that provided by the dry scholasticism of the medieval period. During that period, the individual's life choices had been largely confined within the structures of a feudal society and the individual's position at birth, but during the Renaissance there was increasing interest in self-discovery, personal awakening, autonomy, the role of the individual within society, and the person as a rational agent. Society was increasingly centered in cities. A new merchant class gained power, and people's mobility increased. Popes and emperors struggled to differentiate their power. New religious movements emerged and religious literature in vernacular languages appeared. During the fourteenth century, for about fifty years the bubonic plague, or Black Death, ravaged Europe, and this was widely regarded as the result of the wrath of God. There was an emphasis on the absolute power of God as the only source of help. The will and power of God became major themes, except among the mystics. Their focus was on the direct experience of God, often as love, rather than on the details of theological speculation about God. Indeed, sometimes mystics had experiences that tended to contradict received doctrine; for example, Julian of Norwich spoke of Christ as a Mother. Because mystics searched for God in the soul, much mysticism became heretical, since to seek direct contact with God means that one does not need the mediation of the Church, although most Christian mystics continued to receive the sacraments.

Modern concepts of God began to emerge during the Renaissance, when the recovery of classical Greek philosophy widened the range of available ideas. People started to free themselves from domination by the Church's thinking, and they became aware of inconsistencies in the thought of the Scholastics. New forms of biblical interpretation and theology combined with disputation rather than silent acquiescence to Church authority, all increased.

Nicholas of Cusa (1401-1464) believed that we can have an immediate intuition of God, and this solves some of the difficulties that appear if we try to conceptualize God. He talked of God using mathematical analogies, and thought of God in terms of infinities such as an infinitely long line, or what he called the absolute maximum. God's relationship to entities in the universe is then analogous to the way in which an infinite line can contain and generate any defined lines, triangles, circles, or any other geometrical figures. Nicholas referred to God as the reconciling unity of all opposites as well as their source, but at the same time he pointed out that God is beyond the *coincidentia oppositorum,* or the coincidence of opposites.[lxx] This means that God is undifferentiated. God surpasses all things because he includes all things without their restrictions and oppositions. Yet such analogies cannot penetrate the divine mystery, because God is also incomprehensible. Nicholas therefore referred to his mathematical analogy as a form of learned ignorance, meaning that we must be aware of the limits to our knowledge, and we need both reason and a non-rational understanding of God. Nicholas added that although God is unknowable, he is also the cause of the pluralities and differences in the world, so we can name God as the not-other-than-not-other. God is the source of all things and is therefore the can-be, the principle that gives patterns and shapes to all forms of being. (This sounds very much like Jung's notion of an archetype as an ordering principle.) In this tradition, Jacob Boehme (1575-1624) also taught that God is the union of all opposites in the universe, and through the objects of the universe God becomes conscious of himself.

Marsilio Ficino (1433-1499) was an important advocate of Neo-Platonic and Platonic ideas, which he believed to be part of an ancient tradition that was divinely inspired. In this model, God is the source of all being, and God is at the summit of a hierarchy of perfection. Borrowing from Plotinus, Ficino believed that everything in the cosmos is a progressive emanation from the divine, emerging from the heavenly sphere with lesser and lesser degrees of perfection down to earth, with the immortal soul somewhere in the middle. The soul was therefore the connection between divine things and mortal life. Although God is entirely benevolent, the world of matter is evil.

During the Renaissance, the classical philosophy of Greece and Rome experienced a rebirth and a reinterpretation, partly because the Crusades had brought Christians in contact with Arab philosophers who had preserved the work of Greek writers. Some aspects of this thinking were antithetical to the traditional theology of the Scholastics, and the thought of Plato and the Neo-Platonists began to combat the dominant Aristotelian thought of the academy. The Renaissance humanists of the fifteenth and sixteenth centuries were antagonistic to Church authority. They were however deeply religious people, and they did accept the basic assertions of Christianity, but they were dissatisfied with the attempt to find answers to religious questions within the dogmatic confines of scholastic thought. These humanists believed that subjective convictions and feelings are much more important to religion than metaphysical arguments. The humanists believed that theology should be simplified, and people should be required to believe only the minimum of dogma that is essential to salvation. Humanists believed in the harmony of faith and reason, including harmony between the truth of Christianity and what they learned from philosophy. They argued for religious toleration, syncretism, and freedom of thought, and they were particularly distressed at the Church's vicious persecution of heretics, since they believed that faith cannot be coerced. Attempts were made to demonstrate the basic harmony of all religions, and the doctrine of the Trinity was sought in religions beside Christianity.

Desiderius Erasmus (1466-1536) was interested in revitalizing Christianity in the spirit of the movement known as *devotio moderna*, a reform movement that began in the fourteenth century as a result of dissatisfaction with the behavior of priests and the state of the church. Its proponents taught the importance of piety, humility, obedience, and a simple life. Erasmus disliked scholasticism. He believed that faith is inward and simple, and only requires assent to a few basic propositions. He believed that we cannot be certain about any concept of God, and he had an aversion to dogma. Human beings were seen to be at the center of a great chain of being,[lxxi] free to rise to union with God or to fall away from him, without the intervention of a savior. Since all religions derive from the same God, there should be peaceful coexistence between religions. He believed that the best way to reform the church was by going back to its original sources in the Hebrew and Greek Bible. His production of a Greek

New Testament in 1516 allowed scholars to compare the original text with the later Latin Vulgate translation.

Erasmus attacked abusive secular and religious authorities and he criticized corrupt clerics who were warlike and mainly interested in money and prestige. His satirical critique of the corruptions of the Roman Church was so powerful that his writing was included in the *Index of Forbidden Books*. He thereby laid the foundation for the subsequent Protestant Reformation. He preached moderation, compassion, generosity, and tolerance, in the face of a great deal of superstition, bigotry, blind adherence to doctrine, and superficial piety. He stressed the importance of human concerns rather than a focus on the supernatural. For him, Christ is the model for pious Christians, and Christ is the exemplar of humility, patience, and love, which we may all imitate. Erasmus, therefore, believed that human beings are perfectible. His was a philosophy of the heart, not a speculative theology.

Giordano Bruno (1548-1576) also combined classical and medieval sources with his own notions about God and the universe. He thought of the universe as both infinite and divine. He believed that everything is contained in God, who is the only substantial reality in the universe, since the infinite cannot have anything external to itself. For Bruno, if God is infinite, the universe he created must also be infinite; there must be an infinite number of worlds, surrounded by planets and moons and inhabited by intelligent beings. Everything we experience is an expression of the divine nature or change within the being of God. The transcendental remoteness of God is thereby abolished, and matter is divinized. All souls are essentially identical with the divine world soul, which is totally immanent to the universe and fills every event with a spark of the divine. Bruno was charged with heresy, and in 1600 he was burned at the stake for denying central Church teachings, although it is not certain whether his belief in many worlds was part of his heresy.

During this period of Christian Europe, very few people would have doubted the existence of God, but there was also a feeling during the Renaissance that we cannot understand God in any sense. Many thinkers and skeptics of this time believed that all human notions about God are nothing more than personal opinion, and there is no way to check the assertions of faith. Consequently, some skeptics preferred to resort only to the scriptures to understand the self-revelation of God, ignoring rationalistic concepts of God.

At this time, God was often assumed to be on the side of conquering armies, so that when the English defeated the Spanish Armada in 1588, this was seen as a defeat for the Catholic version of God at the hands of the Protestant version. When European colonialism began in the fifteenth century, it was assumed that domination of other cultures was the will of God. The European wars of religion in the sixteenth and seventeenth centuries forced people to try to find ways to avoid conflict over their different images of God.

The Christian God-image During the Sixteenth Century Reformation

Drastic changes began to appear within Christianity during the Protestant Reformation, which produced a strong reaction against medieval thought. Earlier attempts at reform of the Church had failed, but Martin Luther (1483-1546) radically changed Western Christianity, leading to very different conceptions of how a person should respond to the divine. Luther articulated a spiritual revival based on personal faith, which had begun during the Renaissance.

In Luther's day, there was widespread criticism of the clergy. The worldliness and wealth of the Pope was being severely criticized, and it was widely thought that such worldly churchmen should be deposed. There was an obvious need for greater spiritualization of Church practices, and many pamphleteers were demanding reform of abuses of the Church such as indulgences[lxxii] and dispensations. These were used as a way of making money, needed to pay for the building of St. Peter's church in Rome. There was agreement that the reform of the Church should be the work of God himself, acting through the right people, but there was disagreement about which members of the Church should lead authentic reforms or what the best method of producing reform would be. To understand the intensity of these arguments, it is important to bear in mind that at this time religion was desperately important to many people, who were concerned with the prospect of hell and who believed that only the correct form of religion could save them.

Luther was preoccupied with the Gospel of Luke passage where Jesus is asked "what shall I do to inherit eternal life?" (10: 25). Luther grew up with an image of God as a harsh judge of sinners. Luther therefore struggled with the tension between good and evil, the demonic and the divine, and he suffered from anxiety about his own salvation. He believed that the root of human sin lies in human nature, and he had a terror of death and God's judgment. He did not believe that a person could be loved by God because of the person's own worth or because of his or her good deeds. Luther also suffered greatly from the sense that God could hide himself. For Luther, God's revelation occurs through hiddenness or by means of opposites, so that God is hidden in suffering or is revealed in what seems to be weakness. What looks like the scandal of the crucifixion is actually a triumph or a hidden revelation. For Luther, God has to be hidden in order to make room for faith.

In his youth, Luther had been particularly tormented, worrying that, because God is punitive, God might attack the individual directly and become the enemy. He was therefore very conscious of the dark side of God. Luther sounds as if he suffered from a tyrannical superego, and he projectively incorporated his punitive God-image into his theology. Luther decided that all forms of atonement and penance for sin were ineffective, since we are justified not by works but by faith alone (*sola fides*), or by grace that is gratuitously given by the mercy of God. Here, faith means complete trust in God. For Luther, faith is essential because human merit and good works are not enough to attain salvation. Luther insisted that redemption is a divine gift, but the Vatican believed that Christians had to pay for their sins through acts of penance. In opposition to Luther, traditional Roman Catholics argued that both faith and works were necessary, pointing to the Epistle of James (2:17) which says: "So faith by itself, if it has no works, is dead." Luther was openly opposed to this Epistle, which he thought contradicts the teachings of St. Paul, who said we are justified by faith apart from works (Romans 3:28).

Luther believed that Adam's fall had left humanity in a state of permanent, wicked rebellion against God, and we are in a state of original sin, the result of which is death. Although God could have condemned humanity because of this sin, he chose out of love to redeem sinners; this love manifests itself fully on the cross, which brings humanity into a right relationship with God, since Christ is punished in place of sinful humanity. In Luther's theory of the atonement, there wasn't a complete reconciliation between God and humanity based on God's acceptance of Christ as a substitute for humanity. In fact, this sacrifice was a mysterious decision on God's part, because God's love for man is completely unmerited. Luther sees faith as the work of God and received from God; for him, human beings contribute nothing to salvation; righteousness comes from God alone, while human corruption remains. The alarming consequence of Luther's stress on faith alone is its implication for people who have not received the biblical message, so its proponents have been accused of exclusivity and intolerance.

For Luther, the main vehicle of God's saving word is the Bible. Luther believed that although human beings are natively equipped with some knowledge of God, this knowledge, or knowledge of the universe, will not save them. We must turn to the scriptures to guide our lives and to be saved. But the Roman Catholic Church of his day rejected this notion of *sola scriptura*, (scripture alone), on the grounds that the Bible is complex and needs an interpreter, even as Luther was sure that the text interpreted itself. He repudiated the medieval idea of the Church as the only channel of divine-human interaction. For him, each person stands alone in a personal encounter with God. All baptized Christians are priests; the "keys of the kingdom of heaven" (Matthew 16:19) do not belong to the Pope but to the community of believers. Luther felt that the establishment of canon law and Church tradition had become oppressive, and he made a sharp distinction between God's commands, found in the Bible, and the ordinances of councils and theologians. Luther denied that Church tradition had evolved as an expression of divine will, and he saw the traditional system of sacraments as an invention of the Church to enhance its power.

During the Reformation, the Roman Catholic doctrine of transubstantiation became controversial. Luther believed in the real presence of Christ in the Eucharist but gave up the idea that the bread and wine actually changed into the body and blood of Christ, because this idea was not scriptural. He believed that the true sacrament is the word of God, which is communicated through baptism, penance, and the Eucharist. In his churches, ritual became less important than it had been, and the Eucharist became a symbol and a way of remembering, no longer identical with its transcendent reality. Statues and icons were largely abolished. The reformers believed that priests should be able to marry, and they wanted to conduct services and read the Bible in local languages rather than Latin, so by 1534 Luther had translated the Bible into German.

In 1521, Luther was excommunicated by Pope Leo X. He was called to defend his theology before the Holy Roman Emperor, Charles V, where he defiantly refused to recant. However, he was protected by powerful secular political forces, local princes who shielded him from Church authority. Another ingredient in his success was that his ideas appealed to people of all social classes. The invention of the printing press allowed the quick spread of both the reformers' ideas and the arguments of their opponents. Both groups were forced to refine their theology and their interpretation of the tradition. Protestantism gradually evolved into a large number of denominations, each based on its own interpretation of the Bible, each insisting on proper belief, each insisting that it alone had the truth, and often intolerant of other groups.

John Calvin (1509-1564)

Calvin became the center of an international reform movement with widespread influence. His theology drew from both Luther and Augustine. He believed that neither philosophical reasoning nor direct religious experience, apart from biblical revelation, would allow knowledge of God. Human sinfulness prevents us from seeing God as he really is. Although God's nature is incomprehensible, some knowledge of God can be found through God's self-revelation in both the Hebrew and Christian scriptures, which indicate the divine will. Biblical revelation of God's will and God's law should be applied to the affairs of society.

According to Calvin, only an elect portion of humanity is able to receive knowledge of God, and only God decides which portion. The notion of predestination can be found in the work of Augustine and Luther, and in Paul's letter to the Romans (8:29), which talks of those who are "predestined to be conformed to the image of his Son." This letter goes on to say that God "has mercy on whomever he wills, and he hardens the heart of whomever he wills" (9:18). Calvin took the idea further by declaring that not all are saved. Although we all deserve damnation, some people are predestined to salvation while others are predestined to condemnation and damned according to God's decree, regardless of their condition and their behavior. This doctrine of predestination means that salvation depends on God's initiative, not the behavior of the sinner, and only some are chosen. This decision is eternal and unchanging. Interestingly, many Calvinists believed that affluence was a sign from God that they had been selected to go to heaven, so they worked hard to achieve wealth. This attitude was a precursor to what became the Protestant work ethic.

Calvin believed that, because of Adam, all of humanity is affected by sin, so that any ability to restore the individual to a right relationship with

God is completely lost. Calvin would not answer the question of why a loving God would hold people responsible for a sin they cannot deal with, and for which they have no responsibility. In his view, we can only discover that God acts a certain way, as revealed in scripture, but not why. Calvin dogmatically insisted on this interpretation of scripture. It is worth noting that Calvin suffered the death of his mother at age four and was subsequently rejected by his father. It is hard not to see in this biography a connection between an angry God-image and a sense of hopelessness.

Calvin taught that only Christ can bridge the gap between sinful humanity and God. We are united to Christ by membership in the true Church, which is marked by correct interpretation of the Word and the correct administration of the sacraments of baptism and the Eucharist. For these reformers, redemption through Jesus Christ is necessary because the human situation is one of fallenness. Humanity cannot help itself, but the atoning work of Christ provides redemption; he is the sole means of reconciliation with God for those who are elected to be redeemed. Salvation is gained by communion with Christ, and this is established by faith alone, which means trust in God's goodness and Jesus' sacrifice. This faith is itself a gift of grace, given as a matter of God's choice with no regard for the state of the recipient.

By the middle of the seventeenth century, Calvin's ideas had spread to England and Scotland, from where it was later carried by the Puritans to New England.

The Roman Catholic Church responded to the Reformation with a Counter Reformation, led by Ignatius Loyola. This response was based on decisions made at the Council of Trent between 1545 and 1563, which clarified Catholic doctrine about sin, salvation, and the sacraments, and condemned what the Vatican considered to be Protestant heresies. The Vatican tried to maintain its authority, insisting that the Bible needed to be interpreted and clarified by the judgement and consensus of the Church hierarchy. Protestants believed that the notion of a magisterium (the teaching authority of the Roman Catholic Church) was an affront to the authority of the Bible. Roman Catholics insisted that too much confusion and disagreement occurs if we appeal to the Bible alone, so that we need the teachings of the Church and the authority of the Pope to settle such debates. The Catholic Church emerged from these debates somewhat along the model of a monarchy, strengthening the power of the pope and the hierarchy and attempting to enforce dogmatic beliefs.

Luther and Calvin were mainly concerned with the reform of doctrine, but other groups, such as the Anabaptists and the Evangelicals, were even more radical.[lxxiii] Christendom fragmented even further after the Reformation, and faith often became synonymous with correct belief. Part of the fragmentation of the tradition had to do with the difficulty of interpreting some passages of scripture. Much of this interpretation was based on prior education within a particular tradition. Animosity grew between Protestants and Catholics, resulting in civil wars in England and France. The bloody Thirty Years war, a religious conflict that involved several European countries, began in 1618.

One of the legacies of Protestantism is recurrent rebellion against religious authority and a distrust of tradition when it seems dogmatic, instead preferring to focus on personal experience or the Bible as a source of certainty. Protestants in general insisted on a personal relationship with God mediated by scripture. They regarded the worship of saints and Mary as idolatrous.

Following the Reformation, one of the main dissenters was George Fox (1624-1691), the charismatic founder of the Quaker movement. He was distressed by the superficiality he saw among both the clergy and laity of his day. In 1646 he began to experience a series of "openings" or revelations, which told him that only the spiritually reformed are true believers, that God does not live in buildings, and that only Christ could explain the scriptures. He felt he had found the truth, and he began a preaching mission in England against what he considered to be superficial religion. He behaved somewhat like a prophet, attracting large numbers of people, arousing suspicion, hostility, and accusations of blasphemy by saying that he was directly inspired by Christ. At the center of his teaching is the idea that the light of Christ is in everyone. Every human being must be respected because there is "that of God" in all of us. The availability of this inner light means that human beings are radically equal. This light is the source of our knowledge of God, and the light shows us correct behavior and judges whatever is contrary to God. Worship can take place anywhere and does not require any of the traditional trappings. There is no distinction between clergy and laity, since we can all know God directly. Fox separated from Calvin by teaching that the inner light confers the possibility of human perfectibility before death.

During the seventeenth century, both Protestant and Roman Catholic theologians appealed to the authority of the Bible to justify their theology. Religious conflicts made religion look dangerous and intolerant. Scientific discoveries seemed to be much more certain than traditional religion, while theology lost much of its prestige. Part of the problem became how to relate the Bible to the teachings of a specific Church and also to reason and science. This question became even more acute during the Enlightenment.

The Effects of the Enlightenment on the Christian God-image

The Enlightenment, an intellectual movement beginning in the late seventeenth century and continuing during the eighteenth century, marked the transition to the modern period. At this time, the role of God in philosophical and social thought gradually became less important. People became more tolerant of different God-images, and the God-image in the Bible came under increasing scrutiny. Enlightenment thinkers refused to accept traditional ideas about God based solely on ecclesiastical authority; belief had to be based on reason, which became the final judge of truth. Many Enlightenment thinkers were opposed to any form of metaphysical speculation. Kant pointed out that there is no way to establish the existence of God in the same way we can establish the existence of a physical object; God exists beyond the world of sensory experience. For Kant therefore, belief in God is a matter of faith. Kant thought that we can form ideas about God, but we cannot prove them, even though they may be of practical value for our moral framework. God's existence is a necessary presupposition for making objective moral judgments that go beyond relative, moral preferences.

Until the eighteenth century, most thinkers had agreed that God existed as a supernatural being endowed with will, intelligence, and benevolence towards his creatures. However, the eighteenth-century Enlightenment saw the flowering of atheism as a cultural movement, combined with harsh criticism of the traditional God-image. Society became increasingly secular. Because of the rise of science, nature became more and more stripped of any supernatural elements. Many eighteenth-century philosophers and scientists focused on material reality and avoided any metaphysical speculation or attempts to prove the existence of God. They had become tired of religious wars, religious intolerance, claims of clerical privilege, and unexamined superstitions. Human beings were increasingly seen to be autonomous and the final measure of truth.

Typical of the eighteenth century rise of skepticism towards the traditional God-image is the work of Thomas Paine (1737-1809), a defender of human rights, intellectual freedom, and political independence during the revolutions of late eighteenth-century America and France. Paine hoped that these political revolutions would be followed by a religious revolution. Well known as an important catalyst for the American colonies to become independent of Great Britain, he also attacked institutional Christianity, especially its dogmas, which he saw as a weapon of control that restricted the individual's discovery of God. For Paine, free thought and liberty go together. Paine was a skeptic who said that his own mind was his church. He was a deist (see p. 32) who believed that God communicates through nature, not in the form of revelation by means of words. His deism was an attempt to apply Enlightenment principles to religion. He realized that the authority of the Bible is tenuous, and he pointed out that the Hebrew Scriptures contain a great deal of brutality and wickedness. For Paine, we can use reason to discover God, who is the first cause, and theology is only the study of human opinion regarding God. Reliance on stories of miracles and prophecy obscure the knowledge of God we can perceive through reason. Thomas Jefferson, the third president of the United States, was another deist luminary of that period. He believed that Jesus was a reformer and an important teacher of moral behavior, but nothing more. For Jefferson, none of the miracles reported in the New Testament actually happened.

The Christian God-image in the Nineteenth Century

During the nineteenth century, several new religious movements appeared, especially in America. These include various forms of Millennialism, or the thousand-year reign of Christ. This belief describes the immanent destruction of the present world order and the establishment of a new order that reverses the status of the oppressor and the oppressed.

Among believers, important changes in the God-image developed in the nineteenth century. Transcendentalists such as Emerson imagined God as a kind of cosmic Oversoul or a divine spark within nature and humanity that connects everything. This essence can be discovered through intuition and by listening to one's own inner voice, so one can be independent of organized religion. Friedrich Schleiermacher (1768-1834) agreed that philosophical speculation cannot establish the existence of the biblical God, nor do biblical and ecclesiastical authority provide any basis for religious doctrines. He wanted to address the Enlightenment criticism of religion by rationalists, using a different approach. Schleiermacher denied Kant's notion that the basis of religion is only to be found in morality. Schleiermacher based religion not on thought but on intuition and feeling, which he thought produce a pre-rational awareness or "taste" for the infinite within the finite (Schleiermacher, 1996/1799, p. 23). Schleiermacher believed that such a predisposition was common to all human beings, but life circumstances may or may not allow it to fully develop. This approach removes religion from comparison with science, because religious feeling is not an object that is amenable to scientific study; this feeling is purely subjective. By "feeling" Schleiermacher did not mean any kind of emotion, but the powerful effect produced by our experience of the universe. Schleiermacher understood the Christian God to be the source of this unique feeling, so that talk about God is really talk about the ground of religious feeling. In a later work, Schleiermacher (2011/1821) suggested that religion is based on the consciousness of being absolutely dependent on God as the ground of the world. The feeling of absolute dependency on something greater than ourselves is the same as being conscious of existing in relationship to God. People are religious to the extent that this feeling predominates in their lives. The self consists partly of a consciousness that seems to be self-caused, but the self also has the sense of having come into existence as a result of something that is not self-caused, and this something is God. That is, the self becomes aware of itself in relation to the presence of a divine Other.

For Schleiermacher, nothing can be said about God other than what we derive from experience, which is the basis of piety. Only what we can derive from religious experience is valid talk about God; speculation and religious authority do not tell us anything about God's nature. Schleiermacher believed that we cannot attribute to God traits of personality such as will and thought. He conceived of God as the timeless ground of all causation; as immanent in life, rather than as a transcendent supernatural being who intervenes into a fallen world. God and the world are one, and the world cannot be without God, who is the creative force of the universe and the source of life. Like many liberal theologians, Schleiermacher did not focus much on sin or human alienation from God. He saw the Bible as a record of human religious experience rather than a historical account. Schleiermacher's focus on direct experience rather than authority or speculation became very important. He has been called the father of modern theology.

Biblical criticism had begun in the seventeenth and eighteenth centuries with the work of people such as Spinoza, Hobbes, and Thomas Paine. This approach to the Bible gained speed in the nineteenth century as scholars focused on the history of biblical texts, their sources, their social context and background, their composition, their possible authors, the reasons they were written, and their intended audience. Historical criticism of the Bible insists that these factors are important in determining the meaning of a text. Taking such material into account, many nineteenth century biblical scholars concluded that the Bible, including much of the story of Jesus, was written by human beings rather than by God, so it was not necessarily historically accurate. The historical-critical approach to the Bible is often criticized because it is seen to have a vested interest in undermining the authority of the Bible.

The nineteenth century saw the spread of atheism as well as new religious movements. When Nietzsche (1844-1900) proclaimed that God is dead, he meant that the existence of God could no longer be taken for granted by modern people, as it had been for people in earlier times. Modernity had done away with God. Nietzsche saw that although nineteenth century Europe was still dominated by belief in the Christian God, Christianity was much less strong than it had been, for a variety of reasons. Advances in science and technology had reduced dependence on God. In the face of continuous, unmerited human suffering combined with philosophical attacks on traditional theology, the notions of God's goodness and omnipotence were under attack. A new trust in human ability and the possibility of progress through human effort was developing, making God less important. Although many people professed belief in God, according to Nietzsche, this was a habitual response and lacking in depth, although most people did not realize the significance of this development and were not ready to confront its implications.

The demise of the traditional Christian God-image during the nineteenth century is typically expressed in a mournful poem by Thomas Hardy titled "God's Funeral," an event he imagines himself witnessing. Hardy expresses the idea that the traditional God-image is entirely a "man-projected Figure...whom we can no longer keep alive." Hardy believed that religion had to be divorced from dogma, and a new form of religion was needed.

Darwin showed that human beings evolve by means of natural processes and do not occupy a privileged place in creation. There is no need to postulate any divine purpose in natural forces. The geologist Charles Lyell showed that the biblical myth of creation does not fit with the geological evidence. If anything, creation is continuing to evolve and is not a finished product as the Bible said. It looks as if there never was an initial state of perfection, so there is no need for an external savior to restore it. Furthermore, if people have evolved from animals, it is not clear what the Bible means by saying that we are created in the image of God.[lxxiv] The Church tried to resist this emerging assault on its traditional God-image, but theology did not have the power it had in medieval times and it could not silence this development.

During the nineteenth century, believers were in a dilemma; the advances of science and the work of historical biblical criticism had cast considerable doubts on traditional religious certainties, making it difficult to maintain traditional beliefs while maintaining intellectual integrity and a modern mind. Accordingly, liberal Protestants tried to modernize their Christianity in a variety of ways. They applied it to the social problems of the day, such as poverty. They looked at Scripture symbolically rather than literally, and they saw the hand of God in the process of evolution. The reaction to this Modernist movement contributed to the development of fundamentalism. In the Roman Catholic Church, a Modernist movement arose that tried to reinterpret traditional teachings rationally, in the light of the new knowledge, thus allowing for the evolution of Church doctrine. For example, Ernest Renan suggested that Jesus was nothing more than a remarkable man, and Alfred Loisy suggested that the Christian religion was more of an ethical system than the result of divine revelation. This movement was condemned and ruthlessly suppressed by the Roman Catholic Church at the turn of the twentieth century, but the Second Vatican Council vindicated some modernist attitudes.

The Christian God-image in the Twentieth century

During the twentieth century, the Church tried to move towards Christian unity through the Ecumenical Movement, eventually leading to the World Council of Churches, which includes a wide range of Christian denominations. At the same time, textual and literary criticism of the Bible continued to undermine many traditional Christian beliefs about its authorship. The image of God as a supernatural parent figure continued to be viewed as less and less viable. It was increasingly argued that philosophy could not help theology in its quest to understand God. New concepts of God were urgently needed, but Christian theology became a fragmented discipline. The twentieth century brought a failure of confidence in nineteenth century notions of progress and humanity's goodness and perfectibility. This failure was the result of the horrors of World War 1 combined with the rise of industrial cultures that had little regard for the individual. Instead of history revealing the unfolding of the divine spirit, history seemed to be demonstrating injustice, exploitation, and cruelty. The optimism of earlier generations was shattered by the devastation produced by the war, which made it difficult to think of God as immanent in the world. Accordingly, it seemed that if there was to be hope for the despair of humanity, help had to come from the transcendent divine. Accordingly, after World War 1, a new image of God appeared. Theologians such as Karl Barth began to stress divine transcendence. He denied any understanding of God based on anthropological descriptions (Barth, 1958). He believed that God is completely distinct from human ideas.

The neo-orthodox or neo-Reformation position of theologians such as Barth rejected the liberal theology of the nineteenth century. Liberal theology had wanted to recast Christian belief in the light of modern knowledge, because the supernatural origin of scripture had been undermined by historical-critical biblical research. In contrast, neo-orthodox theologians felt that since humanity is sinful and fallen, and unable to know anything of the transcendent dimension, all true knowledge of God is based on revelation alone, which occurs through the Word of God, communicated through the history of Israel and in Jesus Christ. God is so remote that we can only know him by means of faith in Jesus Christ. No proofs of God are possible or relevant to faith, and no metaphysical speculation can discover the attributes of God. In the neo-orthodox view therefore, philosophy is irrelevant to faith, so that the God of Christianity has to be the creator God of the Bible. He is the divine Thou who meets people in a personal encounter. In this view, because the God of Christianity is the God of the Bible, whatever is said about him must be based in the Bible. For Barth, Christian faith is independent of history. God is a personal being who acts and speaks; he is involved in history, and he shows his will there. He is loving, he judges sin, redeems, and promises salvation. Barth believed that outside of Christianity, any other way of knowing God is impossible.

In the theology of Rudolf Bultmann, it was only possible to see God in terms of revelation, not as an object of human thought, so that almost no theological doctrine of God was possible. Bultmann said that God could speak though the preaching of the Gospel, but we cannot objectify God by speaking of him or we are in danger of mythologizing what is transcendent. He believed that the New Testament was a collection of myths that had to be interpreted to reveal its underlying message, a process he referred to as "demythologizing." Stories such as the virgin birth, supernatural healings, and Jesus' ascension into heaven are mythological, and should be understood in terms of their existential meaning. Bultmann was concerned that the mythological world view of the Gospel writers would interfere with the modern reader's appreciation of the Gospels. Bultmann did not think that the historical study of the New Testament was necessary, because the facts about the historical Jesus are not as important as his message. For him, the central message of Christianity was the revelation of God's love as revealed through Jesus, and submission to God frees us from our existential anxieties. Some subsequent writers have rejected Bultmann's Christian existentialism, which stresses the need to make choices in order to be authentic. Religious existentialists often agree that metaphysical language about God inevitably distorts and obscures our experience of God. They prefer to talk about God in subjective terms and in terms of faith and commitment.

During the twentieth century, liberal theologians thought we could turn to science to explain nature, and we can stop seeing God as responsible for all events, including wars and other disasters. Many in the liberal wing of the Christian tradition gave up the notion that God wills some people to eternal condemnation and others to salvation. It became increasingly unclear what it means to say that God speaks, acts, judges, or saves. Some twentieth-century theologians were not happy with classical claims about God, such as his self-sufficiency and changeless eternal nature; instead, they emphasized his personal characteristics, such as his judgment and love. Others believed that no theological doctrine of God is possible. Some philosophers fell back on the idea that religious belief simply means being prepared to behave *as if* God is real.

Various twentieth century theologians suggested that the Bible is simply the human interpretation of the actions or the word of God. In this view, the Bible is only a human document, or a medium of revelation, and may not all be literally true. In the light of twentieth century approaches to texts, it became clear that no one reads the Bible with an objective or neutral stance; theologians are situated in historical, cultural, psychological, and linguistic contexts that affect their beliefs. All readers have presuppositions and commitments that affect their interpretations of a text. Therefore, the underlying meaning of the Bible is open to interpretation that is in accord with our contemporary situation. While many traditionalists continued to maintain that the Bible is the main form of revelation, what mattered for other theologians was a personal encounter with Jesus.

Strongly influenced by religious existentialism, partly as a result of his experiences during World Wars I and II and his encounter with human despair, Paul Tillich (1964, 1967) radically questioned the traditional God-image. He tried to make Christianity understandable to skeptics from a non-religious background, and he argued that existential theology could bridge the gap between Christianity and modern culture. Influenced by Heidegger (see p. 365), Tillich emphasized the immanence of God as Being itself,[lxxv] as ultimate reality, as the ground of finite beings, and the source of personhood. For him, "nothing can be said about God that is not symbolic" (1967, p. 239). God is not an object like other objects that may exist. God cannot be an object of cognition and, although the content of divine revelation does not change, the way we experience it does change. Tillich did not think in terms of a God who intervenes within human history (1964); he rejected belief in a personal God. Rather, God is the depth in which human existence and human personal life have their origin and fulfillment. Unlike the notion of a transcendent God who is separate from finite life, an idea that Tillich thought was a kind of idol, for him God is the ground of natural processes, the spirit within ourselves that provides a sense of significance and value. Tillich believed that human beings cannot fulfill themselves without connection to these divine depths through revelation and through faith. For Tillich, to be self-conscious of the human condition is to be anxious. He grounds our existential anxiety on the basis of our removal from our divine essence.

At the other wing of the Christian tradition, a small group of Roman Catholic and Anglican theologians continued to develop classical notions of God based on the work of Thomas Aquinas. This Thomistic view values natural theology, or philosophical arguments for the existence of God based on reason and on our experience of nature.[lxxvi] In this view, we can formulate and theologically elaborate what is known by intuition and revelation. These theologians understood God in traditional terms as self-sufficient, perfect, changeless, and the redeeming source of grace. God should be spoken of as Being and the creative cause of being, which is the basic way God relates to the world.

Thomistic theologians clung to a God-image that is the source of salvation by means of the Incarnation, the Church, and the sacraments, but this approach seemed to be anachronistic to many people because of its medieval quality. However, those who reformulated the Thomistic concept of God, while agreeing with the neo-orthodox that revelation is necessary to understand God's nature, believed that philosophical theology is a way of establishing the existence of God rationally and objectively, and it can formulate what is received by revelation. Natural theology, or knowledge of God based on observable facts and experience rather than revelation, was seen as a way of talking about God using language employed in ordinary life, so theology can be related to ordinary experience. Otherwise, we do not know what we mean when we use theological language.

During the twentieth century, because of the advances of science, some religionists retreated to traditional Christian principles such as the sinfulness of human beings, the divine as transcendent of humanity, and faith understood to be cognitive assent to doctrine and dogma. To the influential Roman Catholic theologian Karl Rahner (1904-1984), this attitude was mistaken since he believed that God wants to communicate with human beings within their daily lives as an act of grace. Rahner believed that there is an *a priori* or given capacity within all human beings that allows them to receive God's grace, which is found in the depths of human existence, the ordinary things of life, and in everyday reality (Rahner, 1978). This *a priori* ability in people allows them to grasp metaphysical objects such as God (Vass, 1985). Faith is an acceptance of or an openness to God, not a matter of conformity to dogma but based on a sense of an internal presence. We are open to transcendence, and transcendence is an aspect of the human condition. Rahner wanted to re-interpret the meaning of God for modern people, and he wanted to make theology philosophically respectable. He believed that we are constituted to question who we are, and this mystery leads to the mystery of God. At the center of our nature is a longing for knowledge of God. He wrote of

God as the Holy Mystery or the Infinite Horizon of human consciousness. God is incomprehensible except as he communicates himself to the world, which he did in the historical incarnation in Christ. Rahner is part of the long apophatic tradition that teaches that the divine itself is beyond all images and concepts.

Rahner developed a famous theory of "anonymous Christians." Because all people are open to God's self-revelation, even those who are not members of the Church have the possibility of a saving relationship with God, and so they are anonymous Christians. (Members of other traditions are not always comfortable with this appellation.)

Several twentieth century theologians pointed out a fundamental lack of awareness of God in Western society, because of the disparity between its scientific orientation and the manner in which the Christian message had traditionally been expressed. This disparity acted as an intellectual barrier to accepting Christianity. Accordingly, instead of stressing miraculous divine interventions, these theologians believed that the Christian message had to be recast. Instead of the traditional emphasis on Jesus' sacrificial death and victory over sin, he is better thought of in terms of the disclosure of God that he revealed through his ministry—he made people newly aware of the presence and love of God, and he empowered people to express this in their own lives.

Some twentieth century theologians questioned the notion that God can be identified with Being or grasped by any other concept. However, concepts about God are stubbornly persistent, perhaps because they are learned very early in life, and they give people a way of connecting to God or a way of making sense of an experience of God.

The God-image in Process Theology

A radically new approach to theology appeared in the early twentieth century in the form of process theology, which was based on the process philosophy of Alfred North Whitehead. This approach valued a philosophical basis for talking about concepts of God, and wanted to translate religious claims into modern language. Most of this approach was based on natural theology; God was seen as a spiritual force within both historical and natural processes.

Process theologians radically opposed the traditional God-image (Hartshorne, 1984). Their idea was that although there might be a transcendent, unchanging aspect of God, God is also constantly in the process of changing and becoming. God fulfills his own being through the gradual perfecting of the world. God has reciprocal relationships with human creatures—God is affected by what happens, in contrast to the traditional notion of God as immutable. This God-image is not omnipotent, self-sufficient, or omniscient, and he is not the source of everything that happens in the world. He is one among many factors in an all-inclusive process; there are forces in nature that are independent of God. He works in everyone to actualize their potentials, but although he is loving and has the power of persuasion, he does not always have final control over events. He is not judgmental about sin, and he does not redeem the world from it. God did not incarnate exclusively in Jesus but is incarnate in the lives of all people when they act in accord with God. A Darwinian quality is seen in the idea that reality and God are constantly evolving or progressing as part of the entire cosmic process.

A traditional critique of process theology is that because God is no longer seen as omnipotent, the power of God is severely limited, to the extent that God would not be worthy of being worshipped. The response from process theologians is that the traditional, power-drenched concept of God is itself not worthy of being worshipped. The image of God as a divine King supports militarism, and if he is seen as a heavenly Father this could lead to escapism. For process theology, it is preferable to see God's power as relational rather than tyrannical, whereas the classical Judeo-Christian image of God has been as an almighty regal power. Of course, God's love is also a kind of power, but very different than the kind of power associated with kingship and domination.

Christian Fundamentalism in the Twentieth Century

A series of books titled *The Fundamentals* were published between 1910-1915, which claimed that liberal theologians were abandoning some of the fundamental doctrines of Christianity. The authors were conservative Protestants who rejected nineteenth century historical criticism of the Bible because this approach was prejudiced against its historical accuracy and against belief in miracles. Much to the distress of the fundamentalists, some liberals had repudiated belief in the inerrancy of scripture and the Second Coming of Christ, and they had suggested that belief in the virgin birth was unnecessary. After the Scopes "Monkey Trial" in 1925,[lxxvii] fundamentalism became alienated from mainstream Protestant denominations, but it flourished in the latter part of the twentieth century. Most fundamentalists are opposed to the kind of liberal theology that avoids emphasizing miracles and instead focuses on the work of God in history and in the life of the Church. Fundamentalists believe in the resurrection of Christ, the virgin birth, and the historical reality of Christ's miracles. They argue that the Bible is the word of God, or at least it is inspired by God, and it is never in error; if it seems to say something incredible it must mean something allegorical, hidden, or something other than the obvious meaning. Thus, the "six days" of creation mean six long phases or eons of time. Carried too far, this approach forces meaning onto the text that is not present. Fundamentalism is often seen as a desperate attempt to cope with the frightening sense that God is absent, hidden, or non-existent, which was a dominant theme in the twentieth century following the rise of science and the secularization of society. Because of the rise of fundamentalist-inspired terrorism, fewer people today describe themselves using this term, instead calling themselves conservative evangelicals. However, some that identify with this term do not consider themselves to be fundamentalists.[lxxviii]

Most, but not all, fundamentalists are Dispensationalists, meaning they believe that history can be divided into a series of periods or dispensations, an idea based on various numbers in the prophetic books of the Bible that are thought to indicate future events. Each dispensation represents a distinct covenant between God and humanity. Many fundamentalists are also premillennialists, believing that Christ will return at the end of the present dispensation to inaugurate a thousand-year period of peace, during which the Jews will regain their earthly kingdom and convert to belief in Christ. Before the tribulation that will precede all this, which they believe is described in the Book of Revelation,[lxxix] some fundamentalists believe they will be taken up to heaven (the Rapture) to spare them any suffering.[lxxx] In this final book of the New Testament, large numbers of human beings are destroyed, reminiscent of the destruction of humanity described in the story of Noah's ark. This ending contradicts the notion that the biblical God-image has progressed from a God of war to a God of love. However, for believers this book promises the ultimate victory of good over evil.

Fundamentalism is partly a reaction to an unconscious sense that the grip of traditional belief systems is loosening, so they must be held onto ever more tightly. This is especially important when a tradition serves to provide a source of structure, identity, certainty, and safety that would otherwise be lacking. Fundamentalism is partly a defense against the grief produced by the loss of the traditional God-image; some of the anger expressed by fundamentalists against non-believers is partly derived from their unconscious grief. Fundamentalist insistence on a set of dogmatic beliefs is a form of religious narcissism, with all the underlying emotional vulnerability that implies. (The psychology of fundamentalism is discussed in Corbett, 2018).

The Continuing Debate about the Christian God-image

Until about the middle of the twentieth century, the debate continued about whether to talk about God in terms of revelation or in philosophical terms, and about whether God is transcendent and changeless or immanent and in process. Theologians who emphasized revelation regarded philosophical thinkers as too oriented to human wisdom, too unrelated to the biblical God, and speculating about God even to the point of idolatry. Philosophical theologians such as the Thomists saw in their opponents a rejection of the traditional attributes of God such as his omnipotence, his self-sufficiency, and his changelessness. The process theologians saw the neo-orthodox tradition as too similar to classical theism with a God-image that is not meaningful to modern people because it is too transcendent and too independent of humanity. They wanted a God-image that is immanent, related, and developing. As these groups debated with each other, all of them struggled with the contemporary increase in atheism and diminishing church attendance in some denominations.

By 1960 the traditional view of God was under severe strain, to the extent that theologians themselves began to raise the question of whether God really exists or whether God could be spoken about at all in that secular age, which had increasingly lost any sense of the sacred in the traditional Christian sense. The old certainties were seen to have crumbled in the face of world events such as the horrors of World War II. A group of radical "God-is-dead" theologians appeared, some of whom rejected the very idea of God, at least in the traditional theistic sense of an oppressive, transcendent deity (Altizer, 1956). This revolution did not last long. Other theologians felt that traditional God-language was no longer adequate, and instead it was important to renew focus on the ethics taught by Jesus without thinking in terms of a personal God (Van Buren, 1966). In the 1980's a movement known as the Sea of Faith promoted the idea that religious faith is a human creation; what we call God is the sum of our values and has no independent existence apart from the human mind, language, and culture (Cupitt, 1988). Rather than God creating humanity, humanity created God. In this view, talk about God might have value, but it is really about human spiritual ideals and emotions, or about practicing a religious form of life, without implying the existence of God. (These ideas are similar to the projectionist theories of Feuerbach and Freud.)

As a result of these developments, by the mid-twentieth century, among some Christian theologians there was disagreement about whether they could speak of God in any certain way. The question was *how* to speak of God, whether through revelation, philosophical speculation, faith, or in some other way. In the later part of the twentieth century, many theologians were forced to radically assess their views. Some of them began to use linguistic or phenomenological approaches to religious experience. Towards the end of the twentieth century, theology became a hermeneutical discipline, emphasizing meaning and personal experience rather than objective truth. The reaction to the death of God movement gave rise to a theology of hope in writers such as Teillard de Chardin, who saw the universe in the process of evolving towards the final divine unity of the world. For him, Christ was the goal of evolution. This idea to some extent revived the ancient notion that the world has a divine designer.

The Changing Image of Jesus in the Twentieth Century

During the twentieth century, the image of Jesus continued to evolve in response to the ways people felt they needed him. Many twentieth century theologians interpreted Jesus in the light of Western liberal values, seeing him as a support for human rights and equality. They related his teaching to contemporary culture. What these theologians had in common was an insistence on the continuing need for Jesus, although as Schweitzer (2005/1906, p. 397) had long since noted, individuals tend to "find their own personal standpoint in regard to him." Modern liberal Christianity rebelled against the classical teaching that Christ is only to be thought of as the unique and complete expression of the fullness of God; instead, they saw Jesus as a mystic, a prophet, an enlightened teacher, or a revolutionary. Some writers spoke of "Christ consciousness" as a universal principle found in all traditions.

Some twentieth century theologians saw Jesus mainly in terms of his moral influence, which was an idea that had begun in the twelfth century.

In this view, Jesus saves people from a lack of moral concern for others and a lack of love. Jesus moves people to seek justice, resist evil, and behave and relate to others in conformity with God's wishes. He gives people a new sense of values and inspires people to live out these values in their own lives. In these new attitudes, there was less concern with soteriology and more concern with social evils like racism, an approach that continued the ancient theme of the struggle with evil.

Writers such as St. Augustine had seen the crucifixion as a campaign against the devil. For these early Christians, a major way of understanding the atonement that Jesus achieved had been in terms of victory in the conflict between God and evil. God had achieved this victory by means of Jesus' death and resurrection, which was said to promise a final defeat of evil and was thought to empower people in their struggle against it. In this vein, some twentieth century theologians linked their work to movements seeking radical social change, social justice, and the environmental movement. Liberation theology imagined God as the power of freedom and hope against the forces of oppression and exploitation. In that tradition, God was seen as preferring the poor, because in God's eyes "many that are first will be last, and the last first" (Matthew 19:30). Liberation theologians pointed out that there is more in the Gospels about poverty and social justice than there is about people being saved from sin (Luke 4:18). The crucifixion represented the evil in the world, but because of the resurrection the crucifixion could be seen as an expression of God's love in which Jesus accomplished something of saving significance for humanity. Jesus' work was seen as essentially about liberation from dehumanizing ideologies such as racism. African Americans have seen Christ as an example of standing up to abusive authority, and they see him as suffering with them and for them. In this view, salvation includes deliverance from social injustice and liberation from poverty. Jesus' resurrection gives hope that in the end justice and reconciliation will prevail. There are also twentieth century approaches to the Bible from the point of view of ecology, gay liberation, and Asian and Black theologies. The days in which the Church could impose its own agenda on the meaning of the Bible are past. The postmodern understanding was that the interpretation of a text such as the Bible can be an act of domination by those in power. Furthermore, the meaning of a text such as the Bible is derived from the interaction between the text and the reader; the text is not autonomous. Or, the biblical text has no fixed meaning; its only meaning is based on the reader's personal perspective and his or her perception of the text. In either case, the contemporary reader may have a different understanding of the text than its ancient authors. These attitudes undermine the traditional Christian authoritarian approach to the Bible.

A further development in the twentieth century was a renewed reaction against the traditional idea that Jesus' death was required by God for the forgiveness of sin. This idea had often been criticized as contrary to the idea of God as love. Feminist theologians argued that the theological glorification of Jesus' suffering as salvific supports the idea that women should accept abuse, and also sustains a culture of abuse. For some contemporary Protestants there is an aversion to focusing on the crucifixion and a preference for emphasizing relationship to God. However, in the liturgy the crucifixion remains central.

Some twentieth century theologians continued to insist that Jesus' suffering and death had special saving significance, and they asserted the traditional idea that Jesus is the only way to salvation. Others rejected this idea, believing that because Jesus reveals the presence of the divine in human life, adherents of other traditions can encounter him through their own practices. As a source of truth, he transcends the Church. However, while acknowledging that salvation can be found outside Christianity, some theologians insisted that when this happens it is nevertheless secondary to the saving significance of Jesus. A pluralistic strand has also emerged that asserted that each religion has a partial vision of the truth, because the same God transcends all of them. In this view, religions have to recognize the truth claims of other religions while holding on to their own truth.

Wink (2004) believes that "something has gone terribly wrong in Christianity" (p. 209). For him, Jesus' original impulse has been "buried under the detritus of routinized religion" (p. 211). Wink is disillusioned because the churches often do not continue Jesus' mission; Wink cites the churches' anti-Semitism, their collaboration with oppressive political regimes, their hierarchical power structures, the paucity or absence of women in senior leadership positions, the churches' abandonment of radical egalitarianism, and the rule of patriarchy in the church. Wink has his own list of Jesus' important teachings. He believes in particular that Jesus condemned all forms of domination, including the domination of women and the economic exploitation and impoverishment of all classes of people. Jesus condemned power arrangements that disadvantage the weak, he condemned the subversion of the law by privileged people, and he condemned racial superiority, ethnocentrism, and belief in sacred violence and sacrifice. Wink acknowledges that there cannot be an objective reading of the Gospels and makes the important point that: "No scholar can construct a picture of Jesus beyond the level of spiritual awareness that he or she has attained" (p. 216).

After Jesus' death, each successive generation added something new to the question of who he was, leading to a more and more elevated or divinized status until he became God himself. The process of the enhancement of the image of Jesus continues. In the work of Teilhard de Chardin: "The mystical Christ has not reached the peak of his growth" (2004, p. 307). Chardin developed a theology of nature, which he describes as a "divine milieu" because the sacred exists in nature. Chardin places Christ at the center of the divine milieu: "Christ reveals himself in each reality around us, and shines like an ultimate determinant, like a centre, one might almost say like a universal element" (2001, p. 125). Chardin believed that in addition to his human and divine qualities, Christ has a third nature consisting of universal or cosmic attributes. The cosmic Christ is a universal being that pervades and drives all creation. The goal of creation is the Omega Point, which Chardin thought was Christ as the culmination of the evolution of divinized matter, or the universe as the transfigured body of Christ.

Chardin believed that God created the world by means of the process of evolution. However, when Chardin was writing, such ideas were a threat to traditional Roman Catholic teaching, which could not tolerate de Chardin's correlation of traditional theology with the theory of evolution. A 1950 papal encyclical (*Humani Generis*) regarded evolution as unproven and insisted on the doctrine that all humanity had descended from an original couple, which is the only theory "compatible with inherited original sin" (Dourley, 2015, p. 100). After de Chardin's death in 1962, the Vatican issued a warning against his work because it offended Catholic doctrine. There is some debate about whether the Church was suspicious of him because of his belief in biological evolution or because of his theological and philosophical speculations. The warning was reaffirmed in 1981 and has not been withdrawn (Dourley, 2015). Barnhart (2008, p. 186) has continued in the spirit of Chardin by asserting that "history is itself an unfolding of the event of Christ." That is, the trajectory of history is a creative expression of the path of Christ.

In the late twentieth century and early twenty-first centuries, theologies of emergence arose that see God as involved in the process of evolution, which is seen as an emerging divine process. Even the divine itself has been seen as an emergent phenomenon. Peacocke (2006) sees the incarnation of Christ as an emergent new reality; Christ is the highest point of evolution, a new type of humanity arising as a result of a long natural process of creation. This approach tries to minimize supernatural claims about Jesus and replace them with naturalistic approaches. However, this view seems to imply that matter is primary, rather than seeing the universe as contingent on an immaterial God. (Leidenhag, 2016, has articulated several other theological objections to the theology of emergence.)

The Search for the Historical Jesus

In the early years of Christianity there was no distinction between the Christ of faith and the historical figure of Jesus. Nevertheless, as long ago as the eighteenth century, scholars have been trying to separate theological accounts of Jesus' life from what can be known about him historically. Enlightenment thinkers such as Hermann Reimarus, a deist, suggested that Jesus derived his understanding of himself and his mission from contemporary beliefs that God would send a messiah to liberate them from Roman occupation, thus casting doubt on the degree to which the Christ of faith bore any relationship to the Jesus who existed 2000 years ago. In this view, events frustrated Jesus' ambitions, and the idea that Jesus' death led to the forgiveness of sins and that he was resurrected and would return in glory were simply contrived by his disciples.

The New Testament is the only real source of information about Jesus, since there is very little reliable historical confirmation for the Gospel story of Jesus, and the reports of his miracles give rise to considerable skepticism. The search for the historical Jesus is sometimes motivated by the wish to make him purely human and to discredit traditional supernatural claims about him, such as the virgin birth and the resurrection. This search has also been carried out to modernize our image of him or to focus on his ethical rather than his apocalyptic teachings. However, for some people, the drawback of the historical search is that it takes the figure of Jesus too literally, instead of seeing him as a mythic figure of symbolic importance.[lxxxi] Of course these are not incompatible views; an actual historical figure may also carry symbolic and spiritual importance. Although skeptical historians may question whether Jesus actually existed, the Gospel stories, and the fact that his early followers preached his message in the face of the threat of death, are compelling enough evidence of his existence for many people.

An important counter to the historical approach is the assertion that no reconstruction of the historical Jesus is relevant to Christian faith or practice. Faith must be based on the figure of Christ as he is depicted in the Bible, not on a reconstruction of the historical figure, which is unnecessary. Schweitzer too believed that the historical Jesus is irrelevant, and only the Christ of faith is important; what matters is the effect he had on his followers. Johnson (1996) points out that many important qualities, including values and meaning, cannot be captured by the historical approach, which does not provide the only form of truth worth considering. For him, the writings of the New Testament do not allow an adequate reconstruction of the history of the movements that produced them, but they do help us define the nature of these movements. Johnson is concerned that the historical approach might undermine faith, since he believes that even the best historical account cannot express who Jesus really was.

There have been at least three phases in the search to understand the historical Jesus (McGrath, 2017). The nineteenth century, influenced by the Enlightenment, sought to portray him as an enlightened moral teacher, minimizing the idea of Jesus as a supernatural redeemer. Numerous nineteenth century "lives" of Jesus appeared in an attempt to remove the accretions of faith from a man whose life could be understood in ordinary human terms. These accounts were surveyed by Schweitzer in his famous *Quest of the Historical Jesus,* first published in 1906. The second period of the search began in the middle of the twentieth century, with the realization that there is a discontinuity between Jesus' actual preaching and the subsequent preaching about him. Here, the Christ of faith came to be different than the earthly Jesus. In the later part of the twentieth century, the focus shifted to the continuity between what Jesus said about himself and what the early Church said about him. Later writing focused on the relationship between Jesus, first century Judaism, and the politics and cultural background of that period. Jesus' teachings were contrasted with Jewish practices (Meyer, 1991). These investigations all cast little or no new light on the story itself. One of their main effect in recent years has been to emphasize Jesus' Jewishness, which many earlier Christians had ignored.

The search to ground the story of Jesus in history has always faltered because of a lack of adequate data. Outside the New Testament, there is not much physical evidence for the existence of Jesus. There is one mention of him in the Babylonian Talmud, and references to him by the historians Suetonius and Tacitus and by the writer Pliny the Younger. The Jewish historian Josephus refers to Jesus twice, but copies of Josephus's work were made by Christian monks some centuries after the original documents were written, so their reliability is not clear. There is no other contemporary documentation of his story, which is rather surprising, and no definitive archeological evidence of his existence. Skeptics are dubious about reports of Jesus' miracles, so the historical credibility of the biblical account has been called into question by scholars who only see the justification for any belief in terms of evidence. However, Evans (1996) points out that an alternative strategy for Christians to have faith in Jesus is not necessarily based on the need for evidence. Jesus' contemporaries believed in his capacities, and there was a consensus from early on that Jesus had been raised from the dead. This testimony is important for believers today. The approach of the critical historian is therefore not the only approach; we might have true beliefs that cannot be justified on the basis of evidence. Believers claim that their faith in Jesus is God-given; for them, reliable knowledge can be given by faith. For these believers, evidential information about Jesus as a historical figure is not relevant to Christian faith. This is a kind of tacit acknowledgment that the mythic or archetypal or psychological levels of the story are more important than the historical level. For many contemporary Christians, the historical Jesus has been gradually transformed into an almost entirely divine figure, thanks to the archetypal projections onto him.

Childs (2000) pointed out that one of the problems with all historical research is that we can never escape our subjectivity or the myth-making aspects of our perceptions, which are an inevitable aspect of the way we understand the events of the past. Even the Gospel writers, who wrote relatively soon after the death of Jesus, were influenced by a set of circulating memories, stories, and archetypal projections that met important ideological and psychological needs. Childs believes that today we can only reinterpret the available documents, but we cannot reconstruct the past or decide what really happened. What we call history may become colored by its mythic dimensions, especially when there are gaps in the historical record. Then, at best, history is an interpretation.

Given that the interpreters of the Gospels have all had different agendas, it is not surprising that no consensus about Jesus has been reached. The disputes about Jesus that began with the early Church councils have never been fully resolved. Many writers have found a historical Jesus who suits their ideological and personal needs combined with the writers' prior religious commitments. Many for instance have not been comfortable with Jesus' apocalyptic teachings, and instead they have projected their own values onto him, imagining that he taught what the authors thought was good and holy.

There are many images of Jesus, and some of the historical research has become politicized. Nevertheless, some historians have tried to look for the historical Jesus on the basis of available evidence, without superimposing the perspective of faith onto him. Considerable effort has been made to discern what Jesus actually said and did, as distinct from what the evangelists and others reported him to have said (Chilton et al., 1999 a & b). The historical method studies all the available manuscripts, compares this imagery with other Near Eastern material, considers multiple translations and oral transmissions of the text, and where possible includes the archeological evidence. The search for the historical Jesus is therefore distinct from the Jesus of the theologians and those who venerate him.

Contemporary scholarship places Jesus in the context of the turbulent political atmosphere of first-century Palestine, in which Jews suffered from Roman oppression, occasionally tried to revolt, and desperately hoped for a promised Messiah. Jesus has always been seen in specific historical contexts, for example as a triumphant king during the Middle Ages or as the Holy Infant of the Baroque era. However, sometimes the twentieth century historical search went to extreme lengths, for example when Jesus was seen as the creation of early Christians under the influence of psilocybin mushrooms (Allegro et al., 2009). Jesus has also been seen as a magician (Smith, 2014), as a priest of the Qumran sect (Thiering, 1993), as a wisdom teacher and holy man (Borg, 1994), as part of a non-violent social protest movement (Horsely, 1987), as an ardent Jewish nationalist misrepresented as a pacifist (Brandon, 1968), as a great Galilean rabbi, part of the Jewish prophetic tradition (Vermes, 1981), or as a marginal Jew and an itinerant evangelist and wonder-worker (Meier, 1994). According to Tabor (2007), Jesus saw himself as the founder of a worldly royal dynasty, destined to restore Israel and guide it through an apocalyptic upheaval that would result in the Kingdom of God on earth, with Jerusalem as its capital. This was to happen during the time in which he lived, not in some future period. Jesus also has his appearances in popular culture, such as his depiction in various movies. Needless to say, doubt about the very existence of Jesus continued throughout the twentieth century, for example in texts such as Bertrand Russel's 1927 *Why I am not a Christian*.

The search for the historical Jesus was boosted by the scrolls found in 1945 in Nag Hammadi in Egypt, and in 1947 near the Dead Sea, which provided new information about the environment in which Jesus lived. Since then, Jesus' Jewishness has come to the fore. Vermes (1981) pointed out that Jesus' behavior was similar to other Jewish Hasidim of the time who also healed the sick and cast out demons.

Psychological Approaches to Jesus

An important twentieth century approach to Jesus was the attempt to understand him psychologically. This work was initially unpopular because of a scathing 1913 text by Albert Schweitzer, *The Psychiatric Study of Jesus*, which showed how some nineteenth century and early twentieth century psychiatric studies of Jesus were grossly misleading. These studies represented Jesus as fanatical, delusional, paranoid, or hysterical, because he saw himself as a Messiah who would return on clouds of glory (Mark 13:26; Matthew 24:30), not to mention the fact that at one point Jesus' family thought he was "out of his mind" (Mark 3:21). However, Schweitzer believed that Jesus was entirely sane. Schweitzer pointed out that these psychiatric studies did not consider Jesus' social context and the way people thought at the time, which are important factors when evaluating a possibly delusional idea. Furthermore, the early studies were based on material that is not proven historically. Although, judging from the Gospel texts,[lxxxii] it seems possible that Jesus thought of himself as the coming Messiah, or at least thought highly of himself, this does not prove that he was mentally ill. His contemporaries did not seem to think so, even if they disagreed with his claims, and he would not have inspired followers if he had been overtly unhinged. Schweitzer's famous *The Quest of the Historical Jesus* (2005/1906) suggested that Jesus saw himself as an apocalyptic prophet who believed the end of the world was near and who thought he could bring about the Kingdom of Heaven.[lxxxiii] According to Schweitzer therefore, the way doctrine and dogma portray Jesus is not entirely accurate. However, when Jesus talked about the end of the world, he may not have meant it in the modern sense; he may have meant the end of the present age and the advent of a new age. In any case, Schweitzer's account is no more provable than those he discounts.

Many biblical scholars have been resistant to psychological approaches to the Bible, pointing out that psychologists tend to be ignorant of biblical scholarship and the historical-critical method of biblical study. Psychological studies often did not consider the ways in which multiple editors affected the literary shape of the text. As well, theologians have been concerned that psychological approaches to the Bible might reduce it to "nothing but" psychology, ignoring the divine revelations within the Bible and the reader's encounter with biblical history. Some psychological approaches are purely speculative, for example when Jesus' post-resurrection appearance is attributed to a mass hallucination. Nevertheless, in the last few decades of the twentieth century, psychobiographical attempts to understand Jesus appeared, and psychological approaches increasingly gained acceptance within the mainstream (Rollins, 1999; Kille, 2001). Psychological theory has evolved considerably since Schweitzer's time, and can now give us some understanding of the minds of the biblical authors, the Bible's symbolic material, and the effect of the Bible on the reader (Theissen, 1987; Wink 1973).

A typical psychological study is that of Miller (1997), who tries to show that because Jesus lost his father at a young age and was estranged from his family, he achieved peace by finding a heavenly father. Capps (2000) believes that because Jesus was illegitimate, he was a melancholic individual who turned to belief in God the Father to deal with his melancholia. Haley (1986) suggests that Jesus was trying to gain control and power over his social environment, and Witwicki (quoted in Citlak, 2019) also believes that striving for power was an important motivator for Jesus' behavior, perhaps in an attempt to overcome a sense of social rejection.[lxxxiv] However, although it would be of great interest for us to understand Jesus' psychology, we must acknowledge that this kind of psychobiography makes many assumptions that are difficult to substantiate for a variety of reasons. They usually involve major theoretical projections onto the Gospel stories about Jesus, not to mention the psychologist's personal projections onto him. Furthermore, psychologists are rarely competent to evaluate the historical tradition, so they may use historically dubious or unsubstantiated material to bolster their theories. Thus, without knowing the social and cultural conditions of the time, it is difficult to assess the impact of Jesus' illegitimacy on his claim to have a heavenly father, on his apparent coolness towards his mother (Matthew 12:46-50), on his conflict with the religious authorities, on his search for an identity and a mission, and on his concern for social outcasts. Perhaps his illegitimacy[lxxxv] gave him a special sensitivity to marginalized people, but when making such claims the psychologist has to make it clear that he or she is only commenting on the Jesus depicted in the text, not on Jesus himself. The psychologist can usefully comment on the symbolic material in the text, on the effect of the text on the contemporary reader, on the ways that the typology of the reader affects his interpretation, and on the consensus of the faithful about Jesus. We can talk about the psychodynamics of biblical personalities as they are depicted in the text, and we can develop a hermeneutic approach to the meaning of biblical stories, but we can only speculate about unconscious factors in their authors. Overall, the usefulness of the psychologist's comments depends on the validity of his theoretical assumptions, and many biblical stories can be interpreted from multiple psychological perspectives, which continue to evolve. However, it is not clear to what extent our current psychological theories apply to very different historical and cultural contexts. Despite this caveat, the massive idealization of Jesus by his followers is consistent with Jung's notion that they project the Self onto him, thereby meeting an intense psychological need.

If it is true, as Paul says, that the Christian message is essentially Christ crucified (1 Corinthians 1:23), then trauma, despair, a sense of abandonment by God, and brokenness are at the heart of Christian theology and the Christian God-image. Intense suffering is a central feature of this God-image because Jesus atones for human sin by sacrificing himself. Unfortunately, there is a psychological danger that such theology will somehow justify the essential presence of trauma and violence in the Christian image of God, as if there is an inevitable correlation between suffering and the divine. Jesus was supposed to be the ultimate scapegoat who atones for and redeems evil, but given the subsequent violent history of Christianity, his sacrifice had little redemptive effect on the behavior of many of his followers. The skeptical psychoanalyst sees Jesus' voluntary self-sacrifice as an example of moral masochism,[lxxxvi] originating in a problematic connection to his mother (because of his illegitimacy) that he could only express by means of self-sacrificial suffering. Indeed, it has been claimed that moral masochism is at the heart of Christianity. In this view, Jesus' painful death was not redemptive but masochistic, and "deemed purposeful only by guilty Christian believers after the fact" (Rancour-Laferriere, 2003, p. 13).

Jung on the Life of Jesus

In response to the theologian's suspicion of psychology, Jung would reply that scripture is permeated through and through with numinous, archetypal imagery, and this level has to be acknowledged in any hermeneutic approach to the text, which cannot be understood purely historically. The fear of psychological reductionism—suggesting that the text is "only" psychological with no transpersonal referent—is however understandable. Jung warns that in the realm of religion: "A psychological approach is permissible only in regard to the emotions and symbols which constitute the phenomenology of religion, but which do not touch upon its essential nature" (CW15, para. 98). Because of its numinous underpinnings, scripture cannot be approached as a purely intellectual exercise; it has to be approached with a sensitivity to its underlying archetypal or spiritual meaning.

Jung pointed out that the life of Jesus has an archetypal character, as we saw in the parallels between the traditional biographical details of his life and mythological motifs from earlier traditions. Because of these connections, according to Jung, the Gospels would lose their wholeness "if one tried to separate the individual from the archetypal with a critical scalpel" (CW11, para. 146). Jung believed that the life of Jesus was "completely overlaid, or rather smothered, by metaphysical conceptions: he is the ruler over all daemonic forces, the cosmic savior, the mediating God-man" (CW11, para. 228). His life reveals the attributes of mythological heroes: "improbable origin, divine father, hazardous birth, rescue in the nick of time, precocious development, conquest of the mother and of death, miraculous deeds, post-mortem effects (reappearances, signs and marvels, etc.)" (CW 11, para. 229). For Jung, the historical figure disappeared under the weight of these kinds of expectations and archetypal projections onto him. It was as if the archetype of the redeemer had determined the destiny of the man. In

Jung's words: "the archetype fulfills itself not only psychically in the individual, but objectively outside the individual" (CW11, para. 648). The search for the details of the historical Jesus might be unconsciously motivated by a search for the numinosum that he revealed. For many people, the biblical images associated with Jesus are very powerful, irrespective of their historical truth, because they convey archetypal or spiritual truths that resonate emotionally.

Over time, the archetypal role of divinely-sent Messiah was increasingly projected onto Jesus, to the point that it has proved difficult to separate the historical Jesus from the mythologized image of him as a God-man, based on the accretion of dogma about him. Jung (1975, p. 89) pointed out that because the Gospels tell of "the life, fate, and effect of a God-man," we cannot account for Jesus' historical effect by assuming he was nothing but a great teacher, mistaken in his messianic expectations. In Jung's view, Jesus' effect on his early followers cannot be explained using the methods of rational, historical, or literary criticism, because these approaches ignore the power of the archetypal process at work in the psyche of the individual and the collective. Because of the archetypal projections onto Jesus, the folkloric stories and legends about him have often been as influential as the accounts of him in the scriptures, making it impossible to find the "real" Jesus.

Feminist Critiques of the Masculine Christian God-image

Although the Hebrew Scripture's image of God as a kind of cosmic, male sovereign has been abandoned by sophisticated Christian theologians, the use of masculine pronouns to refer to God persists within popular piety, homiletics, hymnology, and liturgy. The original Christian God-image was male, since, according to St. Paul, Jesus is the visible image of the invisible God (Colossians 1: 15) and a second Adam (1 Corinthians 45-49). This male imagery became firmly rooted in the tradition. It originated in a patriarchal culture that legitimized the subordination of women, until it was challenged by feminist theologians who pointed out that the traditional domination of men over women is not divinely or biologically ordained (Ruether, 1996). Various feminist authors (Brown et al., 1989) have published devastating critiques that revealed the complicity of Christian politics in acts of violence against women and children, whose suffering and abuse was theologically justified and silenced for centuries. However, the Christian tradition is more complex than these specific critiques would suggest. Some feminist theologians believe that feminism is compatible with Christianity, and they have developed their own images of Jesus, in ways that are relevant to their own experience (Grant, 1989). The emphasis on the divinity of Sophia as co-creator, and the realization that Jesus behaved well towards women and was related and vulnerable, has also helped to neutralize some of the emphasis on his maleness.

Feminists have pointed out many problems with the male God-language and the misogyny that persists in the Abrahamic traditions, which is largely a residue of the cultural milieu in which these traditions began. Feminist writers have pointed out many instances in which the Bible demeans or belittles women (Gaylor, 2004). Women in the Hebrew Scriptures were not usually in positions of authority, and there were no female priests in the Jerusalem temple. Patriarchy was well established by the time the gender of God was taken for granted. The masculine God-imagery of the Nicene-Constantinopolitan Creed was adopted in 381 CE. This is still the accepted ecumenical statement of many Christian denominations, although it was developed at a period of history with a very different collective consciousness than ours. It describes God as the Father Almighty, while Jesus is the only-begotten Son of the Father. However, for many contemporary people, the notion of God as a father is very dated; it is androcentric, limited, and suggests a Baroque-era image of God as an old man beyond the sky. This image has been used for a long time to imply the lesser status of women, reflecting the quality of gender-relations in patriarchal societies. According to the mainstream tradition, there were no women among the Apostles, although St. Paul includes the woman's name Junia on his list of apostles in Romans 16:7. However, this is a controversial reading of the text because the Greek word is ambiguous. There clearly were some first-century church leaders who were women, such as Phoebe and Priscilla (Romans 1:1-5).

Feminists sometimes object to the notion that God is perfect, since this seems like a very patriarchal concept of God. As Anderson (2014, pp. 12-13) puts it: "this patriarchal ideal ensures the dominant authority of men who remain blinded by their vision of perfection, unaware of the implications for the 'rationality' of their beliefs concerning women as well as non-patriarchal men." Daly (1973) points out that the image of God as a divine Father who rules his people leads to the notion that masculine superiority is the divine plan. Plaskow (1982) believes that masculine

God-imagery and God language have led to women being marginalized and discriminated against, and justifies the restriction of religious authority to men. Christ (1970) also argues that the image of God as Father legitimizes the political and social authority of men in society.

The description of God as "almighty" in the Nicene creed has also given rise to a great deal of criticism. It implies that God is omnipotent, which raises the question of why there is so much evil and suffering in the world, since an omnipotent God could presumably mitigate evil. There are obviously times when God chooses not to use his power to prevent evil, which raises questions about his absolute goodness. Many feminists have objected to the idea that God has absolute power, since this can be seen as a destructive trait:

> An all-powerful deity lends itself to the drive for power. Moreover, idealizing omnipotence contains the belief that absolute power is an absolute good…in glorifying divine omnipotence, human beings—or rather human rulers—are similarly encouraged to seek after such power…We only have to consider human history to see the legacy of thinking of power in this way…consideration needs to be paid to the effect that this glorification of power has on human relationships. (Clack, 2015, p. 9)

However, omnipotence does not necessarily imply that God's power is misused. Yet, it is true that the Hebrew Scriptures often depict God as if "he" were a warrior king who exerts his power by demanding the complete destruction of his enemies.

Feminists have dealt with such traditional androcentric imagery by emphasizing elements such as Sophia, the feminine wisdom of God, or by focusing on the Shechinah, the feminine presence of God in the Jewish tradition, or by remembering the pre-Christian traditions of the goddess. While these are understandable correctives, in the long run it may be preferable to use neutral terms such as "the divine" rather than masculine or feminine language.

McFague (1988) points out that traditional images of God are "triumphalist, monarchical, patriarchal" (p. xi). Furthermore:

> The primary metaphors in the tradition are hierarchical, imperialistic, and dualistic, stressing the distance between God and the world and the total reliance of the world on God. Thus, the metaphors of God as king, ruler, lord, master, and governor,

and the concepts that accompany them of God as absolute, complete, transcendent and omnipotent permit no sense of mutuality, shared responsibility, reciprocity and love (except in the sense of gratitude). (p. 19)

McFague believes that although this imagery has been deconstructed, there has not been much new construction. "If, however, metaphor and concept are as I believe, inextricably and symbiotically related in theology, there is no way to do theology for our time with outmoded or oppressive metaphors and models" (p. xi). In an attempt to re-mythologize the relationship between God and the world, she describes a variety of alternative metaphors for thinking about God, including God as mother, lover, and friend. She acknowledges that most theology is a fictional elaboration of such key metaphors and models, and she calls for a thought experiment with new models commensurate with an evolutionary and ecological sensibility. Needless to say, Jung's notion of the Self is such a new model.

In a later work, McFague (2008) points out the difficulties with some other traditional models of God. She rejects the deistic model, which denies any kind of supernatural revelation and relies on reason. In this model, after the workings of the universe were created, God withdrew and was no longer involved in the world. To McFague this seems sterile and impersonal and separates God and the world too much. She also rejects the view of God as an all-powerful king who controls his subjects, in return for which they offer him loyal obedience. This makes him distant from the world and does not focus on creation apart from his "realm." The dialogic model focuses on the relationship of God and the individual, especially on sin, guilt, and forgiveness, but it is indifferent to the natural and social worlds. It is therefore too narrowly individualistic. She points out that liberation theologies insist that God's relationship with the world must include the political and social dimensions as well. She also objects to the traditional idea that God is an agent, a kind of "person," who acts in history and oversees the world. This model seems to conflict with scientific accounts of the world and has been marginalized accordingly. She prefers to see God as both spirit and matter, so that the world is infused with and given life by God.

McFague believes that the classical theistic model of God exacerbates the problem of global warming, since it privileges human life above all other forms of life and worships a God who is remote and transcendent.

In her view, the tradition has become too focused on salvation in the next life. A model of God as a "super-being" who lives apart from the world, "who creates and judges the world but otherwise is absent from it," implies that "I will conduct my affairs largely without day-to-day concern about God" (p. 31). That is, it is dangerous to see God as remote, which does not fit with the tradition's emphasis on incarnation, which means that God is "with us in the flesh" (p. 34). She prefers to think of the world as within God or the world as God's "body." She denies that this is a pantheistic model, which would identify God and the world; rather, God is to the universe as each of us is to our bodies, so that God and the world are not identical. She does not make it clear in what way the world is the body of God. For traditional theists, God cannot be identical with the world because the world is contingent and had a beginning, whereas God had no beginning and exists necessarily.

God and Time

The traditional image of God as eternal raises the issue of God's relationship to time; does God transcend time in some way or exist outside of time? In the view of classical theists such as Augustine and Aquinas, God is the maker of time and he exists beyond time and beyond temporal change, in a kind of eternal now, knowing past, present, and future simultaneously. After all, if God were not timeless and changeless, he would not be perfect. If God exists in time, he would not be independent of time and could not have created it. However, it is not clear how the idea of a timeless God can be reconciled with the notion of God creating the world, acting in history, and eventually judging the nations of the world (Isaiah 2: 4). If God is doing these things in a temporal sequence, he must have some relationship to time and history. This problem can be rationalized by suggesting that although God's actions changed the temporal world, what God did "was not itself a temporal willing on the part of God, and God's inner being never changed" (Taliaferro et al., 2016). Or, God is both temporal and atemporal at the same time, so to speak. Taliaferro points out that if time began with the Big Bang, then:

> God did not exist "before" the Big Bang, because that would be to exist in a temporal relation. Rather, God "changelessly existed" in a mysterious way beyond the Big Bang ("changelessly existed" because there were no temporal events beyond the Big Bang, for if there were then time would not begin at the Big

Bang). Subsequent to the Big Bang, God entered into temporal relations with the creation. (p. 113)

Taliaferro and Meister also ask: if God both knows all things and is sovereign, how can human beings have free will? If humans are free to choose their actions in a manner that is not determined, then their actions may not be what God would have chosen, so how does God maintain sovereign control? Their response is that God's power is persuasive rather than coercive.

The Question of Biblical Inerrancy

Many Christians believe that the Bible is inspired by God, or at least that God influenced its choice of words, partly (using circular logic) because 2 Timothy 3:16 says: "All scripture is inspired by God." However, even among people who see the Bible as divinely inspired, there are debates about the meaning of the word "inspired." Liberal Christians understand this to mean that although God influenced the writers of the Bible, the text may nevertheless require interpretation at times, taking into account the circumstances in which it was written and the humanity of its authors. The potential for human error in translation and transmission of the text is another problem, so it is not clear whether our copies of the text represent the original. However, perhaps as a result of threats to the tradition by the Enlightenment and by the historical-critical approach to the Bible, there have been fundamentalists who took the notion of inspiration to mean that the text was virtually dictated by God. Today, most proponents of biblical inerrancy would say that God's inspiration guided the Bible's authors to accurately convey his message. Accordingly, the book must be without error and must be completely trustworthy (Geisler et al., 2012), although it might be allegorical at times or its meaning might be hidden. Fundamentalists believe that the apparent inaccuracies and inconsistencies in the Bible actually reveal its divine origin and mean that God intended some parts of the Bible to be difficult as a test of faith. There is considerable debate over the doctrine of perspicuity, or the degree to which the meaning of the Bible is clear and able to be understood by the average reader. The Roman Catholic tradition asserts that Scripture needs the interpretive framework of the Church; Protestants believe that if the Bible is approached in faith and humility, God's overall meaning can be grasped even if there are particular points of difficulty. Postmodern readings focus more on the subjective meaning of the text to the reader, rather than trying to discern the originally intended meaning, which may be unclear.

For skeptics, the notion that the Bible is inerrant and infallible is challenged by the genocide, misogyny, and other truly horrifying material in the text, such as the commandment to burn to death the daughter of a priest who "profanes herself by playing the harlot" (Leviticus 21:9). The notion of inerrancy ignores the vituperative hatred of the Jews found in the New Testament (Matthew 23:23-31) as well as its references to obedient slaves (Ephesians 6:5) and silenced women (1 Corinthians 14:34). The notion of biblical inerrancy defies the fact that the text is inconsistent with modern science in areas such as the age of the earth. Some conservatives insist that modern scientific explanations that contradict the Bible are wrong, and the Bible is right, despite the evidence.

Fundamentalists suggest that there must be an explanation for the Bible's inconsistencies that we do not yet understand. Another rationalization is that the original text did not have any errors but these were introduced by copyists. So intensely are these kinds of defenses maintained that they look as if they are based on fear that acknowledgement of any error would invalidate the entire Bible, which acts as a soothing (even maternal) selfobject for fundamentalist devotees. It has long been observed that one can find justification for a wide range of beliefs in the Bible, and people tend to find whatever corresponds to their own preferences. Religious texts are inevitably colored by unconscious psychological factors in their authors, and these also operate in the readers and interpreters of the texts.

Since the nineteenth century, the Bible has been seen in its historical perspective, supplemented in modern times by a social science perspective, a psychological approach, and a focus on the Bible as a literary text. Archeology has also made contributions to this field. As a result of this scholarly scrutiny, only fundamentalists continue to see the Bible as the literal word of God. It is important to reiterate that the Christian claim that the Bible is the word of God is only grounded in the Bible itself. For skeptics, the Bible reflects the way the tradition sees God; there is nothing to justify the claim that the Bible is the word of God.

There are many sectarian disputes about how to interpret the Bible. Liberal Christians point out that the Bible was written over a long period of time by fallible people who were affected by the beliefs and prejudices of their time. In this view, the literal accuracy of the biblical writers is not as important as the actions of God they describe or the overall biblical message. Conservative Protestants came to depend on the authority of the Bible, but although they sometimes believe that only the correct reading of Scripture is salvific, there is no agreement on what is correct. As well, the Bible's authority has been undermined by textual or historical biblical criticism. This results in an ever-greater emphasis on belief in doctrine and dogma. The results of modern textual criticism and biblical research are not often described from the pulpit, partly because it may be difficult to maintain the faith of parishioners in the face of a de-mythologized text.

Christian God-images in Art

The second of the Ten Commandments forbids the making of graven images. This prohibition was taken seriously until the end of the second century, when Christians began to express their faith artistically, often as funerary decorations that typically depicted the resurrection.

Art can be a powerful medium of religious expression, and often reflects cultural values and popular God-images. Changing God-images have been reflected in the art of each period of Christian history. Early Christian art used a complex symbol system to promote the Christian message. Some of these images were abstract, while some were human or animal. Doves symbolized peace, while the fish symbolized Christ, since the letters that form the Greek word for fish, ἰχθύς, lead to an acrostic that says "Jesus Christ Son of God Savior." Early mosaics depicted Jesus as a Good Shepherd carrying his sheep. A favorite image was the orans, a figure with hands lifted in prayer. God was represented as a globe, a circle, a triangle surrounded by rays, a triangle enclosing an eye, an anchor, a hand, or an empty throne. Imagery from the Hebrew Scriptures such as Adam and Eve, Jonah and the whale, or New Testament themes such as the baptism of the Lord or the raising of Lazarus, were commonly used by Christian artists. The Last Supper, the Annunciation, the Crucifixion, the conversion of St. Paul, and the Madonna and Child are other major themes in Christian art. After the conversion of Constantine, when churches became public buildings, Christian symbols provided rich material for mosaic art, and by the fifth century portraits of Christ and the saints were widespread. The mosaics of Mary found in early churches are artistic evidence of the independent importance accorded to her.

By the time of the Renaissance, God the Father was often depicted in fully human form, in images such as Michelangelo's painting of God on the ceiling of the Sistine Chapel. In some art of this period, just the right hand of God was shown, or God the Father was depicted as the Ancient of Days, an old man crowned with a kind of papal tiara. He typically holds the Son, while the Holy Spirit is depicted as a dove radiating light. Sometimes Christ is depicted as a Holy Child or lamb. Paintings of Jesus in the first three centuries CE depict him with dark features, but after Christianity became Romanized his portraits become lighter. In the Baroque era (beginning around 1600) and the Reformation period, artists continued to depict God as a cosmic father figure. Interestingly, just as the importance of God tended to fade during the Enlightenment, so did images of God in Christian art forms. But they reappeared in the nineteenth century work of William Blake and other visionary and Romantic painters.

The Spread of Christianity

Christianity spread widely for a variety of historical, social, theological, and psychological reasons. Traditional explanations for this diffusion include the idea that pagan ideas had become increasingly unbelievable, and Christianity had superior moral and ethical standards. The Christian doctrine of existence after death was attractive, and the miracles reported by early Christians, the "signs and wonders" (Romans 15:19) that Paul spoke of, were convincing demonstrations of the power of their God. The witness of Christian martyrs, who accepted death for the sake of their faith, and the practice of Christian charity for members of the community, also played a part. The Gospels promised divine grace, the remission of sins, the conquest of evil, and the promise of immortal life, all of which were a balm to many people who lived in a fearful world. Christians were zealous for the rightness of their beliefs and instituted an effective social organization to promote them. The fact that Christians believed that women and men were equal before God, the injunction that husbands should treat their wives with consideration, and teachings about the sanctity of marriage may have made Christianity particularly successful among women. Ehrman (2018) points out that to become a Christian meant the exclusive worship of the Christian God, meaning that one had to abandon the worship of one's pagan gods, so that every Christian convert meant one less adherent of a pagan deity. Other religions were not so exclusive. Ehrman believes that many pagans were henotheists, believing that one deity was superior to all the others, and this paved the way for the Christian insistence that there is only one true God. Furthermore, new converts were able to worship God without the restrictions imposed by Judaism, such as dietary laws and circumcision. Christian evangelism was a further important factor, especially when it insisted that God would soon judge the world and only those who believed in Christ would be spared from punishment and would live in a heavenly utopia. Jesus was expected to return from heaven in a vengeful, flaming fire, and those who were not believers in the Gospel would suffer God's vengeance and "eternal destruction" (2 Thessalonians 1:8-9). For Christians, therefore, to love others meant saving them from eternal torment. This "combination of evangelism and exclusion proved to be decisive for the triumph of Christianity" (Ehrman, p. 125).

The threat of eternal damnation in the afterlife has been partly responsible for the Christian stress on correct belief, even more so than on correct practices, although that attitude is changing of late. In the past, there has been an assumption among Christian theologians that their tradition is particularly privileged and the most valid approach to the divine. The Church has denied that other religions can save one from sin, leading to various forms of Christian imperialism based on texts such as "there is no other name under heaven given among men by which we must be saved" (Acts 4:12) and "no one comes to the Father, but by me" (John 14:6). For a long time, the grandiose notion that there is no salvation outside the Church was taken for granted in both Roman Catholic and some Protestant denominations. Such ideas are now increasingly challenged in the face of attempts to be more inclusive, although this attitude has not entirely disappeared. For many contemporary people, the idea of absolute ecclesiastical authority is now meaningless, and scriptural authority is limited. Given world events, the classical Christian idea of God as a transcendent, perfectly good and loving Being looks increasingly untenable.

THE DEVELOPMENT OF THE CHRISTIAN IMAGE OF GOD | 335

ⁱ The word "testament" arose from the Latin word for a will and the Greek word for a covenant or agreement. For Christians this means that Jesus' death brings a new covenant (Luke 22:20).

ⁱⁱ Dr. Mark Gundry pointed out that there are less individualistic factors in the Christian story that are compelling. He sees the Cross as a kind of mirror that reflects the reality of human violence. The Incarnation gives us a God-image that is willing to suffer with its own creation, while the Resurrection offers embodied hope for suffering creation.

ⁱⁱⁱ God had to be outside of time because if he had existed within time there might be something outside of God that he had not created.

^{iv} I use the term "Hebrew Scriptures" following Levine (2006), who points out that the term "Hebrew Bible" is misleading, because different Christian denominations accept different books in a different sequence than the collection of texts used by Jewish communities.

^v There were many other Gospels circulating in the early years of Christianity, such as the Gospels of Peter and Thomas. These were rejected by the emerging mainstream Christian community because they contained material considered to be heretical or Gnostic.

^{vi} There is a possibility that an unnamed disciple mentioned in John 21:24 was an eyewitness.

^{vii} Luke is thought to have written for a gentile Hellenistic and Roman audience, to which Luke tried to explain the new religion in a way that would reduce anxiety about its political implications for Rome. Matthew wrote for a Jewish-Christian audience, trying to bridge the gap between the Old and New Testament, to show what Jesus had to offer Jews as an alternative to the rabbinical tradition. Mark wrote for Roman Christians who were suffering from persecution by Nero. Matthew's main source was Mark, but Matthew consistently edits Mark to reflect Jesus' increasingly enhanced status. The process of enhancement continued; the Gospel of John was an attempt to use Jewish literature to show that Jesus was the fulfillment of the Law and biblical prophecy. Subsequent Church councils further enhanced Jesus' image.

^{viii} The word "canon" comes from a Greek root meaning a rule or standard.

^{ix} There are about 3,000 copies or fragments of copies of the New Testament, and about 10,000 early Latin translations. There are also several thousand early manuscripts in other languages such as Syriac, Coptic, Armenian, and others. Working with these texts, combined with quotations from the writing of early Christians, textual scholars have tried to reconstruct the most likely form of the original texts. Variations in the texts were inevitable.

^x For example, in Matthew 16:24, Jesus says that anyone who wants to follow him should "take up his cross," but it is dubious that this phrase could have been meaningful in its present sense before the crucifixion.

^{xi} For example: "He who believes and is baptized will be saved; but he who does not believe will be condemned" (Mark 16:16). This sentence is almost certainly a later addition to the original text. Jesus' typical stress on forgiveness, which was obviously important to him, is also contradicted by Mark 3:29: "but whoever blasphemes against the Holy Spirit never has forgiveness but is guilty of an eternal sin." Another example is Jesus' condemning the cursed to "the eternal fire prepared for the devil and his angels" (Matthew 25:41). These kinds of fantasies of revenge do not sound like the Jesus who recommends that we love our enemies and bless those that curse us.

^{xii} It is difficult to determine what Jesus actually said and what was added by the early Church. Several criteria are used for this purpose. The criterion of multiple attestation states that if a certain story is found in more than one independent Gospel, it is likely to be true. Another is the coherence of a story with others like it. A third is that a story is likely to be true if it does not correspond to what would be expected from Jesus' background and the early Church.

^{xiii} There are many examples of this problem (Green, 1999). The Gospel of Mark (11:15) says that Jesus overturned the tables of the moneylenders in the last week of his life, while

John (2:15) says it was at the beginning of his ministry. There are different accounts of the story of Jesus' resurrection, different accounts of Jesus' last address to his disciples, and differences in the stories of the number of women who went to the tomb and the time of day they went. Mark, Luke, and John say the tomb was already open when the women arrived; Matthew says it was closed but opened in their presence. There are variations in the time and place of Peter's denials of Jesus, differences in Jesus' genealogy, and disagreement about the date of Jesus' death. The Gospel of Mark depicts Jesus in despair at the end, saying to God "why has thou forsaken me?" (Mark 15:34), while the Gospel of John has different final words that show no sign of despair; here, Jesus expresses concern for his mother, says he is thirsty, and finally says: "It is finished" (John 19:30), which makes it sound as if Jesus was in control.

Micah 5:2 says that the Messiah would be born in Bethlehem; the Gospel of Mark says that Jesus came from Nazareth, but Matthew says his parents lived in Bethlehem but had to flee to Egypt and then settled in Nazareth. Luke says Jesus' parents went to Bethlehem for a census and returned to Nazareth after his birth. While Mark does not pay much attention to Jesus' origin, Matthew presents the idea that Jesus was conceived by the Holy Spirit. Luke is quite concerned with Mary and recognizes Joseph. The important question is whether these discrepancies and textual differences are really significant. The fact that there are differences and errors of transcription between copies of the text does not necessarily deny their divine inspiration. (The Hebrew Scriptures have many analogous discrepancies, some of which change the meaning of the text.) There are also striking similarities between the synoptic Gospels, which often use the same wording. There have been a range of explanations for these similarities. One is that they copied from each other. Another is the two-Source hypothesis, which suggests that Matthew and Luke borrowed material from both Mark and a postulated Q source, from the German word *Quelle*, meaning source. This has not been found.

[xiv] For example, the Gospels link the birth of Jesus to the time of King Herod, who in fact had died some years earlier. Luke's (2:1) account of a worldwide census and taxation is also historically inaccurate (For details, see Fox, 1991).

[xv] The story does not need to be taken literally; it can be understood symbolically or metaphorically to depict the idea that suffering is the price we pay for the development of discriminating consciousness and the capacity for self-reflection. This requires that we are cast out of a paradisiacal state of primal but immature wholeness, in which the opposites are undifferentiated. Freudians would see in this story an Oedipal rebellion against God the Father.

[xvi] Tree symbolism is found in many earlier traditions. Archetypally, the tree standing in the center of the Garden of Eden represents a kind of *Axis Mundi*, the sacred center of the world or the place of connection between earth and heaven. In Christian folklore, the cross on which Jesus was crucified is sometimes said to have been made from the wood of the tree of Eden.

[xvii] By metaphysical I mean the attempt to say something definite about a level of reality that cannot be described in ordinary physical terms, because it transcends what we can know.

[xviii] There are several mythological instances of human women being impregnated by a god. Zeus fathered divine children such as Aphrodite and Athena, human children such as Perseus, and semi-divine figures such as Heracles. Asclepius, Heracles, and Romulus were humans who became gods after their death. The story of Apollonius of Tyana, a contemporary of Jesus, is remarkably similar in many details to the story of Jesus. The Hindu deity Krishna was said to have had a virgin birth, which is also a common theme in Egyptian and other mythologies.

[xix] This is the version of the story as it is given in Matthew. In the Gospel of Mark (7:29) Jesus does not mention her faith; it seems that he relents and helps her daughter when she admits her lower status.

[xx] For example: "There is neither Jew nor Greek…for you are all one in Christ Jesus" (Galatians 3:28).

[xxi] The Jesus Seminar consisted of a group of scholars who met to decide the authenticity of the reported actions and sayings of Jesus. They saw him as an itinerant Jewish sage-healer. They denied that he expected the apocalypse, as Albert Schweizer and many others had believed. In the view of the Seminar, Jesus did not refer to himself as the Messiah, nor did he see himself as a divine being sent from heaven to die for the sins of the world. Such claims were made about him by people in the early Church. The work of this Seminar has been controversial among some New Testament scholars who believe that its scholarship is shallow (Johnson, 1996) and who question the qualifications of some of its members. Johnson (1996) believes it is a mistake to smuggle in a theological agenda under the rubric of the search for the historical Jesus; historical knowledge is not normative for faith. Whereas the Jesus Seminar avoids discussing historical evidence about Jesus outside the Gospels, Johnson argues that the Pauline corpus and the Gospel narratives describe a consistent story about the death of Jesus.

[xxii] He was accused of being "born of fornication," (John 8:41) and of "having a demon" (John 7: 20). Attempts were made to kill him (Luke 4:29) or stone him (John 8:59).

[xxiii] A powerful demon tempted Zarathustra when he lived in the wilderness, and the demon Mara tempted Buddha.

[xxiv] We are in the same position when we try to assess the modern-day visions of the Blessed Virgin Mary. There is no need to question the sincerity of those who make such claims, but there is also no proof of their veracity.

[xxv] It may be that the story of the Resurrection was designed to bring in new converts. Another possibility is that there was competition for the leadership of the movement, in which case the story of the resurrection was a political device to promote the leadership of the people to whom Jesus was said to have first appeared. One of these was Peter, and the Roman Catholic Church is based on the idea of apostolic succession following Peter, thus establishing its authority. There is a theory that Jesus survived the crucifixion and went East to India or Kashmir.

[xxvi] The word Messiah is a Hebrew word; the Greek equivalent is Christ. It means the anointed one, typically referring to an anointed king specially chosen by God. To refer to Jesus as "Jesus Christ" is therefore to conflate his name with his title. If Jesus did think of himself as a king, he may have meant that this would apply within the coming Kingdom of God, not in his contemporary political sense. Some texts that suggest that he believed this about himself are Mark 8:27-31, where Jesus asked his disciples "Who do men say that I am?", and Peter answered, "You are the Christ," whereupon Jesus told them not to tell anyone about him. In his response to the high priest Caiaphas's question "Are you the Christ?", Jesus says: "I am, and you will see the Son of man seated at the right hand of Power and coming with the clouds of heaven" (Mark 14:62). Here, it is not certain that Jesus is talking about himself as the Son of Man. This term was commonly used in the Hebrew Scriptures, especially in the book of Ezekiel. Usually it means a human being, except in the book of Daniel, where God as the "Ancient of Days" gives dominion to a Son of Man, a supernatural being who protects the "people of the saints of the most high" (7: 27), which probably refers to the people of Israel. When Jesus uses this term, it is not always clear whether he is referring to himself or to the figure in the book of Daniel, although the Church assumed that this phrase refers to Jesus himself because of Mark 8: 31, which predicts that the Son of Man will be killed and rise three days later.

[xxvii] Apocalyptic thinking is ancient, going back at least to post-exilic Judaism, and it was common among early Christians. It sees the world as fallen, perhaps under the control of Satan or cosmic powers of evil, and it always has a mythic cast. Apocalyptic literature suggests that the world cannot redeem itself; the only hope is for direct intervention by God, who will destroy the powers of evil after a period of great suffering. Believers in the apocalypse always seem to think these end times are about to happen, and there have been

several such predictions. They are always wrong, leading to constant revision of the date of the End Times. Helms (1997) points out that the failure of Jesus to appear in the clouds as Mark's Gospel predicts was one of the reasons that Matthew and Luke had to revise Mark's writing. Apocalyptic thinking is often accompanied by anxiety about the future combined with aggressive and paranoid projections about who will be the elect and who the saved. The apocalyptist is always one of the saved, revealing a narcissistic element. Apocalyptic and Messianic thinking is probably based on anxiety about the future combined with the difficulty of living an ordinary life. Notions of renewal or resurrection after a final destructive battle may be related to the denial of death. Apocalyptic fantasies tend to be seen among powerless, enraged, oppressed people hoping for justice, revenge, and the defeat of evil. Apocalyptic ideas are still important to many Christians.

[xxviii] The prosperity gospel teaches that God rewards faith with financial blessings. It is regarded as heretical by many Christians, for whom it contradicts Jesus' teachings about the importance of poverty.

[xxix] The story of Jesus curing epilepsy and mental illness by exorcising unclean spirits (Mark 5:8 & 9:25) offends our modern ideas about these problems. Many contemporary liberal Christians tend to ignore this aspect of his ministry, although major Christian theologians, including Augustine, Aquinas, Luther, and Calvin also spoke about the importance of being free from the devil. Many fundamentalist Christians today see the world as under the control of the devil until God's final victory.

[xxx] In the fourth century CE, the Emperor Constantine destroyed the temple of Ashtoreth, the Canaanite Queen of Heaven, and suppressed goddess worship throughout Palestine. Theodosius closed the temple of the goddess at Eleusis and the temple of Artemis at Ephesus in 380 CE. In the fifth century CE, the emperor Justinian converted the temples of Isis into Christian churches.

[xxxi] Various attempts have been made to develop a non-dual approach to Christianity. Bede Griffiths (1989) believes that because Jesus does not say "I am the Father," he maintains a unity with a distinction, or a mutual interpenetration that combines unity and distinction, and this distinguishes Jesus from the Hindu who can say "I am Brahman" or "Thou art That." Barnhart (2007) suggests that Incarnation is a non-dual event, and baptismal initiation is an experience of the divine-human identity at the core of the person. In his view, the unity of God and humanity is transmitted in baptism. Baptism is a participation in the baptism of Jesus and in this initiation the believer is identified with Jesus himself. Baptism is then "an awakening to the divine non-duality" (p. 66). Barnhart believes that in the Christ-event: *"Nonduality has become a human being"* (p. 176, emphasis in original). However, this is a radical misunderstanding of non-duality, which would not agree that the "Christ-event is the *incarnation of nonduality,*" (p. 110, emphasis in original), since from a non-dual point of view there is no "event" of incarnation since there never was and cannot be any divine-human separation. Non-dual divinity does not "become" embodied; it is eternally embodied. Meister Eckhart is probably the closest exponent of Christian non-duality, for example saying that "God's ground and the soul's ground are one ground" (cited in Colledge & McGinn, p. 42). However, most contemporary Christianity is distinctly dualistic; God is beyond the self rather than one with our intrinsic being as the non-dual traditions teach. Jung's notion of the Self tends towards a non-dual sensibility when he says that it is the same Self in all of us, and when he speaks of the Self as the totality of the psyche.

[xxxii] There is some debate about the meaning of the word "conversion," and whether it truly applies to Paul. Those who deny that Paul was converted point out that Christianity did not yet exist, so Paul did not really change religions. William James (1982) sees conversion as the process by which a person struggling with guilt and low self-esteem becomes regenerated and unified as a result of a religious experience. This definition fits with Paul's experience. I use the term "conversion" to mean Paul's radical change of heart, before and after he abandoned his traditional Judaism and became a believer in Jesus. It may be

preferable to refer to this experience as his call to be an apostle. In Acts, the Damascus Road experience is described three times, and it is mentioned in other places in Paul's letters, so it must have been important to early believers, perhaps as a hoped-for model for the future conversion of many.

xxxiii Paul's experience does have some of the hallmarks of an epileptic aura, including temporary blindness and loss of muscle control. It is possible that the "thorn in the flesh" he reports (2 Colossians 12:7) refers to periodic temporal lobe seizures, which are known to produce experiences with a religious quality. He reports various other episodes that sound like ecstatic or visionary states (2 Colossians 12:1-7). However, it is important to add that a seizure might only be responsible for opening the subject to a transpersonal dimension that is otherwise inaccessible to a normal brain. Most of the proponents of the idea that Paul was epileptic are eager to find naturalistic explanations for his numinous experience. However, against this diagnosis is the fact that most epileptics cannot recall much of what happened during a seizure. Nevertheless, there may be some connection between Paul's putative epilepsy and his personality. Ramachandran (1998) points out that during the periods between seizures, people with this disorder sometimes become obsessively preoccupied with religious and moral issues. Such people tend to be self-important and sometimes maintain elaborate diaries (epistles). Some become argumentative, angry, pedantic, and egocentric. These traits could be seen in Paul's rage and violence towards Christians before his conversion, and in his zealous anger against non-believers after his conversion.

The fact that Paul describes his experience on the road to Damascus in Galatians 1:16 using the Greek term "in me" rather than "to me" has been understood to imply that the experience was entirely subjective rather than external. But the three accounts of the experience in Acts sound as if at least some of it was shared by his companions. Acts 9:7 says that the others heard a voice but saw no one; Acts 22:9 says they saw the light but heard no one; Acts 26:14 says that the witnesses all fell to the ground. These accounts are in the same category as events such as the glorification of Moses at Mount Sinai, the transfiguration of Jesus, the vision of Ezekiel, and the like. For the non-believer they have a mythic quality; for the believer they carry spiritual authority.

xxxiv After the exile, God had promised through the prophets to return in glory (Ezekiel 11:14-20; Jer. 10:14) but had not yet done so; Paul thought Jesus was the fulfillment of this promise and the promise to Abraham.

xxxv One of the critiques of Paul is that the notion that sin is forgiven by faith in Jesus has a magical ring to it.

xxxvi Why Paul believed this is an interesting but unanswerable question. It seems that he took the Garden of Eden story literally. In the Eastern Church, Adam's fall was seen in terms of human mortality, while the Western Church understood it mainly in terms of inherited guilt and the corruption of humanity.

xxxvii There are several examples of Paul contradicting Jesus. For example, Jesus confirmed the validity of the Torah "till heaven and earth pass away," (Matthew 5:17-19), but Paul insists in several places that the law has ended for followers of Jesus (Romans 7). Jesus says that salvation occurs through repentance (Matthew 18:25-35), but Paul says one is justified through faith alone (Romans 4:4; Ephesians 2:8-9). Jesus says that if we forgive others, God will forgive us (Matthew 6:14), but Paul says that we are only redeemed through the blood of Jesus (Ephesians 1:7).

xxxviii The warning that "everyone who looks at a woman lustfully has already committed adultery with her in his heart" (Matthew 5:28), which is related to a similar comment in Proverbs 6:25, has had a profoundly guilt-inducing effect on subsequent believers, and in some fundamentalist circles still leads to the repression or suppression of normal sexuality.

xxxix The problem raised here is to discern what he actually wrote and what was added later by others writing in his name. Although there are thirteen letters attributed to St. Paul in the New Testament, according to modern scholarship he probably wrote only seven of them (1 Thessalonians, Galatians, 1 and 2 Colossians, Romans, Philippians, and Philemon) Other letters are often thought to have been written by his followers who wanted to continue his legacy by applying his teaching to new situations. These letters, such as Ephesians, Colossians, and 2 Thessalonians, are contested on the grounds of style and content. However, other authorities defend Paul's authorship of these letters; it is possible that he dictated them, which might account for their differences in style.

[xl] 1 Timothy 2:9-15 forbids women from teaching or having authority over men, but this letter was probably not written by Paul. It is noteworthy however that many Southern Baptists still assert the subjugation of women because they believe that the Bible is the inerrant and infallible word of God.

[xli] Phoebe was a servant of the church (Romans 16:1-2). Priscilla worked to help Paul develop churches.

[xlii] It is difficult to say whether this was meant literally or was a metaphor for what we would call another dimension of being. Or this may have been a metaphor for the uniting of heaven and earth.

[xliii] It is not clear how the resurrection of the body and the immortality of the soul are related to each other. Perhaps the soul maintains the identity of the individual after the body is resurrected. These ideas are important components of Christian hope.

[xliv] By "flesh," Paul means "fornication, impurity, licentiousness, idolatry, sorcery, enmity, strife, jealousy, anger, selfishness, dissention, party spirit, envy, drunkenness, carousing, and the like" (Galatians 5:19-21). In contrast, the fruits of the spirit are "love, joy, peace, patience, kindness, goodness, faithfulness, gentleness, self-control" (5:19-21; 22-23).

[xlv] Stephen had spoken in a synagogue about the way in which God's revelation cannot be tied down to a particular people or holy place. He reminded the congregation that their ancestors had persecuted the prophets and they had now killed the Righteous One. By saying that the resurrected Jesus was sitting at the right hand of God (Acts 7:55), Stephen breached the notion of pure monotheism. This offended an enraged a mob who stoned him, while Paul watched and consented to this (Acts 7:58). The experience probably affected Paul deeply, leading to intense guilt.

[xlvi] St. Augustine continued a devaluation of the body and physical pleasure. Some later strands of the mainstream Christian tradition continued to mistrust the body or even taught that matter and bodies are fundamentally evil, despite the idea that the body is "a temple of the Holy Spirit within you, which you have from God" (1 Corinthians 6:19). Women's bodies have been a particular problem for the tradition, since they were often seen as temptations to sinfulness. It is noteworthy that Jesus himself did not devalue the body, but frequently healed it.

[xlvii] Paul singles out "all kinds of covetousness," usually understood as the wish to possess what belongs to another, as a personal trait about which he feels guilty (Romans 7:7-8). Here we are in uncertain territory because we do not know what he coveted or what he meant by this word. It may indicate some kind of painful emptiness or yearning for something.

[xlviii] In those days, reality or the essence of things was considered to be made of a substance. The Church fathers used the Greek philosophical term *homoousios*, meaning of the same being, to say that the Son and the Father were of the same substance.

[xlix] The word "begotten," which is found in John 3:16, does not necessarily imply physical procreation in the ordinary sense. It is a translation of the Greek *monogenes*, meaning unique or one and only, implying Jesus' unique relationship with God. This word could mean generated by God, but that meaning would imply that Jesus was created, and so cannot be divine. Instead, the word begotten is taken to imply an eternal relationship as distinct from an ordinary birth.

[l] Bourgeault (2013) suggests that the two natures of Christ are different phases of the unfolding of the Trinity, which is a seven-stage process of divine self-disclosure. Initially there is a phase of the unified Godhead, followed by the divine manifestation as the Logos,

while the third phase appears as the visible universe. A series of such trinitarian processes then unfold which in turn produce the human Jesus, the Spirit, the Kingdom of Heaven, and the fullness of reality. This is really speculative metaphysics.

[li] In the Eastern Orthodox Church, the Trinity is said to be composed of three distinct essences, with the Father as the source. The Eastern church disagreed that the spirit proceeded from both the Father *and* the Son. This difference has not been resolved. Christianity split into the Roman Catholic and Orthodox traditions in the Middle Ages. At that time, arguments developed about whether Church authority should be centralized, as the Roman Church wanted, or decentralized as the Orthodox preferred. In 1054, emissaries of Pope Leo IX excommunicated the Patriarch of Constantinople, and the Patriarch retaliated by excommunicating the emissaries.

[lii] Boehme also believed that in the undifferentiated unity of God there is no self-awareness or capacity for self-reflection, and the yearning for divine self-consciousness drives the impetus to manifestation. Jung picks up this idea in his notion that the divine needs human consciousness to become conscious of itself (see p. 98).

[liii] Here we are reminded of the alchemical Axiom of Maria, which Jung used as a metaphor for individuation: "One becomes two, two becomes three, and out of the third comes the one as the fourth." This is a way of talking about a process of the differentiation of unconscious wholeness into the tension of opposites, followed by a potential resolution leading to a transformed state of consciousness or wholeness.

[liv] As well, Dr. Mark Gundry pointed out to me (personal communication, 2019) that by introducing the idea of process, Bourgeault introduces change and temporality, hence implying that God is only relatively transcendent and not transcendent of time.

[lv] There has been some debate about whether Mary died and was then the first person after Jesus to be resurrected bodily, or whether she did not actually die. The doctrine of the Assumption of Mary was declared while invoking the prerogative of Papal infallibility. Protestants do not believe that anyone can be required to believe Mariological doctrines, such as this one or her Immaculate Conception.

[lvi] An iconoclastic reaction emerged in the eighth century, initiated by the Emperor Leo the Isaurian, when many such images were destroyed by those in favor of the traditional prohibition against idolatrous images of the divine. But such icons had become very popular, much valued, and an aid to devotion. Icons were finally restored in the Orthodox church in the ninth century by the Byzantine empress Theodora.

[lvii] In the Eastern church, Mary was considered to have been cleansed of original sin rather than born without it.

[lviii] The need for blood sacrifice to the gods is found in so many religious traditions that it seems to be an archetypal pattern. The underlying idea may be that sin can be transferred to the sacrificial animal whose death takes the place of the worshipper, removing his guilt. The Letter to the Hebrews seems to regress, in the sense that it makes the human sacrifice of Jesus more important than the animal sacrifices of the Hebrew Scripture. It also seems to valorize violence and makes violence necessary to avert the wrath of God. In the Hebrew Bible, when God demands that Abraham sacrifice his son, a ram is substituted; in the Letter to the Hebrews, Jesus is a human sacrifice who is substituted for the animals sacrificed at the Temple. The psychology of sacrifice is discussed in more detail in Corbett (2015).

[lix] Some theologians have denied that Jesus instituted the Eucharist at the Last Supper. There has been considerable controversy among Christian theologians about the meaning of the Eucharist. For some, Jesus was asking his disciples to remember that he will return as the Parousia, the second coming. Augustine thought the gathering together of many grains of bread in the Host symbolizes the union of all the members of the body of Christ.

[lx] Manichaeism, a third century Persian religion, taught that a divine power of goodness was eternally opposed by an evil power.

[lxi] This sentence has also been translated to mean that we should become as we were designed to be. The word "perfect" is also translated as merciful, or it may refer to truth or sincerity.

[lxii] Aquinas tried to settle this issue by distinguishing the state of humanity before and after the Fall. Before the Fall, human beings were uncorrupted, and did not need divine grace to perform ordinary virtues, although we did need special grace to perform actions purely out of the love of God. After the Fall, we need "healing grace" to perfect ourselves from mortal sins but we cannot avoid venial sins. Absolute perfection only comes in Eternity.

[lxiii] From a psychoanalytic point of view, the notion of the Fall has been seen as a form of Oedipal rebellion against the Father God, whereas Jesus has been seen as a model for the removal of the Oedipal structure by loving God, by renouncing sexuality, and by being radically obedient to God; Jesus is then the "anti-Oedipus" (Vitz et al, 1984). This theory has been challenged by Bridgman et al. (1989) who believe that narcissism is the original sin, which is best understood as a manifestation of the "pre-oedipal drive towards omnipotence found in Freud's concept of primary narcissism," (p. 3), which is more fundamental than Oedipal theory. In the view of these authors, Jesus is better understood as the "Non-Narcissist," (p. 7), given his surrender to the will of God.

[lxiv] There remain a small number of people, especially mystics, monks, and ascetics who continued to believe in the perfectibility of humanity. In the twentieth century, Teilhard de Chardin developed a metaphysical scheme in which we can perfect ourselves by cooperating with nature in our progress towards a loving society. In his vision, eventually we will be gathered up into the body of Christ and attain final perfection.

[lxv] This reveals a typological preference for thinking over feeling.

[lxvi] The theology of the universities or schools.

[lxvii] Jung believes that the debate between nominalists and realists was based on their typology; he thought that nominalists are extraverted and realists introverted (CW 6, paras. 54-55).

[lxviii] David Hume pointed out that there is no reason to assume that God is the first cause; there may be a different first cause.

[lxix] Infants who die unbaptized were traditionally thought to go to Limbo, where they are not damned but cannot merit the beatific vision, the direct communication of God to the individual. This idea never became an official doctrine of the Roman Catholic Church.

[lxx] Jung's slightly mistaken appropriation of Nicholas's term is discussed in footnote fn. xxviii, p. 142

[lxxi] The idea of a Chain of Being suggests that the universe is ordered as a series of gradations, in a hierarchy extending from the lowest creatures up to the divine realm. The idea of grades of perfection was transmitted from antiquity into the work of Christian thinkers such as Augustine, who also believed in the principle of plenitude, which said that God is inexhaustibly productive. The idea of a Chain of Being was challenged by philosophers such as Voltaire, who pointed out that it makes life immobile and static; if every level is filled, there is no room for movement. Kant pointed out that the notion is not empirically verifiable; it is just a way of talking about order in nature. Another problem with the idea is that it is too dualistic, as if spirit and matter are widely divided. The theory of evolution finally put paid to the idea.

[lxxii] Indulgences are based on the idea that Christ and the saints had built up a store of merit on which the Church could draw to pay the penalty required by original sin. This penalty was owed both by the living and also by the dead in Purgatory, who were being purged of their sins. Any outstanding penalty could be paid for by indulgencies.

[lxxiii] Anabaptism centered on the idea that only people who make a personal profession of faith should be baptized. Evangelicals rejected the idea of a state church and the sacrament of infant baptism.

[lxxiv] There have been many interpretations of this idea. It has been taken to mean that the human body in some way mirrors the divine, or that the human mind represents the divine, or that human beings are the lords of creation or that we have attributes that reflect

the divine. Modern interpretations suggest that it refers not to a particular quality but to our capacity for relationship with each other and with God, and our capacity for love in human relationships. Alternatively, the idea refers to a divine essence within the person, something that is like God.

[lxxv] The problem with identifying God with Being is that it makes God somewhat of an abstraction. Some people object to Tillich's idea if it means that God is impersonal. Tillich is trying to avoid the idea of God as a big Person in the sky; personality is a characteristic of beings, not of Being itself. For Tillich, God is not exactly personal but cannot be entirely impersonal and is the ground of personality.

[lxxvi] Natural theology based on reason and the experience of nature is distinguished from revealed theology based on scripture.

[lxxvii] The Scopes trial was a legal case against a high school teacher, John Scopes, who was accused of teaching evolution in violation of a state law. He was found guilty, but the verdict was overthrown.

[lxxviii] Evangelicals who are not fundamentalists tend to speak of the Bible as inspired but not necessarily infallible; they accept the principles of biblical criticism. Many evangelicals are more accepting of modernity than fundamentalists.

[lxxix] The Book of Revelation was probably written towards during the rule of the Roman Emperor Domitian, who persecuted Christians and demanded to be worshiped as a god. The book was a polemic against the Roman Empire; it was not about today's politics.

[lxxx] The idea of the Rapture is based on an interpretation of 1 Thessalonians 4:16-17, which describes how Christ will descend from heaven and the resurrected dead and the living will ascend into the sky.

[lxxxi] The Christ myth theory suggests that Jesus was not a historical figure at all; accounts of his life are largely mythic in nature and cannot be confirmed historically. Obviously, this is entirely in contrast with the mainstream Christian view.

[lxxxii] For example, after reading from the book of Isaiah about a promised servant of God who would save Israel, Jesus added: "Today this scripture has been fulfilled in your hearing" (Luke 4:21).

[lxxxiii] For example, Jesus said: "The time is fulfilled, and the kingdom of God is at hand," (Mark 1:15); and "there are some standing here who will not taste death before they see that the kingdom of God has come with power" (Mark 9:1). Jesus refused to commit himself about exactly when the end would come (Mark 13:32). Because the kingdom did not arrive, the assumption grew that it would appear sometime in the future. When Jesus said that "the kingdom of God is in the midst of you" (Luke 17:21), he may have been referring to a state of consciousness rather than a political entity.

[lxxxiv] The evidence for saying that Jesus was interested in power is that he competed with the educated elite and the establishment and offered his own interpretation of the Torah. He was argumentative and aggressive at times, provoking conflict. He tried to make his listeners feel guilty by telling them to suppress their anger and sexual feelings. It is also alleged that when he healed the sick or the possessed, he desired domination, and he helped people on condition they humiliated themselves and accepted his superiority. This view sees him as possibly driven by messianic fantasies.

[lxxxv] During an argument, Jesus' opponents say to him: "We were not born of fornication" (John 8:41). The not-so-subtle implication is that he was illegitimate.

[lxxxvi] Moral masochism means the willingness to suffer for the sake of a greater good, because of unconscious guilt. Some moral masochists unconsciously provoke negative reactions in authority figures, or painful experiences are actively pursued because of unconscious guilt. Often, the child feels like a burden to a self-sacrificing parent, rather than a source of pleasure, so that the child feels responsible for the parent's unhappiness. Attachment is then associated with painful feelings. The individual feels compelled to surrender his own needs to the wellbeing of others, in an identification with a miserable parent. Another possibility is that the individual attempts to repair severe injury to his self-esteem by achieving mastery or self-cohesion through suffering. The potential connection of moral masochism to religious martyrdom is obvious.

CHAPTER 6

The God-image From the Scientific Revolution to the Twentieth Century

The God-Image of the Early Scientists

From a strictly scientific, physicalist point of view, the world is like an enormously complex machine that behaves in a deterministic manner, following mathematical principles and the laws of physics. At the same time, the theistic traditions all believe that God cares for humanity, intervenes in history, and guides human lives. Therefore, if God exists, one of the main problems for the dialog between science and religion has been to explain how God acts on or is related to the world. This question has a long history.

Early modern scientists such as Copernicus, Kepler, and Galileo were deeply religious people who believed that the universe had been designed by God using mathematical principles. In their day, there was no distinct separation between science and religion; in fact, it seemed that these disciplines could inform each other, because science seemed to reveal the details of God's design. This scientific theism allied the scientists' image of God with their discoveries. They saw God as a celestial architect, and the mechanics of the universe were metaphorically compared to a gigantic clock.

Nicolaus Copernicus (1473-1543), a canon of the Church, developed a model of the solar system that placed the Sun rather than the Earth at the center of the universe. This idea had been proposed by the Greek astronomer Aristarchus in the third century BCE, but it was rejected early in the Christian era in favor of the astronomy of Ptolemy and Aristotle. This model taught that an immobile earth was at the center of the universe, surrounded by planets and stars that moved around the earth in circles. The heliocentric idea contradicts various biblical passages,[i] so Copernicus upset the reigning Christian opinion by suggesting that the Earth and the other planets revolve around the Sun. Both Catholic and Protestant clergy were very hostile to his ideas, which implied that impersonal physical forces rather than divine intention were moving the planets.

Johannes Kepler (1571-1630) is an example of an early scientist whose work was grounded in his Christian faith. His discoveries represented a fundamental advance over the earlier system of astronomy. Kepler postulated the existence of a force, now known to be gravity, which links the movements of the planets, keeping them in elliptical orbits. He believed that his discovery was a gift of divine providence. For Kepler, it was as if geometry was the language of God, and the study of mathematics and geometry was a study of God's work. God did not create the universe randomly; he is a divine architect and mathematician.

Galileo Galilei (1564-1642) was working at a time of extreme religious intolerance, when the Roman Catholic Church was feeling threatened by the Protestant Reformation and was willing to harshly punish dissenters. Galileo confirmed the findings of Copernicus, but he also believed that his research did not deny the Bible or the truth of Christianity. He believed that God is a divine geometer who is the author of the Book of Nature as well as the Book of the Bible, and both are true. For him, science and theology are two different disciplines that do not contradict each other. Galileo upheld the traditional distinction between divine perfection and imperfect, human knowledge. Nevertheless, Galileo's work was placed on the Church's *Index of Forbidden Books*. He was found guilty of disobedience to the Church and forced to recant.

The findings of the sixteenth and seventeenth century astronomers were a considerable threat to the traditional notion of God as a celestial king, because if the universe works according to mathematical principles and natural laws, the need for constant divine intervention is reduced. As well, as astronomical knowledge advanced, it became difficult to imagine how God could send fire down from heaven (1 Kings 18:38) or how Jesus could ascend to the sky after his death (Acts 1:9-11).

Robert Boyle (1627-1691) was one of the founders of modern chemistry and the scientific method. Personally pious, he believed that science provides evidence for the existence of God and God's involvement with the world, and he was a strong supporter of Christianity. He was one of several important scientists of the time who believed that the new science would not lead to atheism but would reveal God's providential design in nature. However, he believed he could never be quite certain about his scientific conclusions because of the limitations of human abilities, and because it is possible that God might miraculously change the course of nature as soon as we formulate a scientific law.

Isaac Newton (1642-1726) is not usually thought of as a theologian, but he had firm belief in and theories about the actions of God, and he wrote various tracts dealing with the interpretation of the Bible. He believed that the movements of the sun and planets are so mathematically precise and orderly that they must have been designed by God. He thought that the physical forces and laws of motion of the universe are manifestations of God's actions, and the intricate design of the universe revealed God's existence. In contrast to the attitude of theologians such as Aquinas and Augustine who did not believe that nature could tell us anything about God, Newton believed that science is the best way of understanding God.

Newton believed that religion had become corrupted with superstition. He regarded the doctrines of the Trinity and the Incarnation as false; he wanted his religion to be as rational as possible, and he wanted to prove the existence of God scientifically. Newton was concerned to show how God worked in the world according to physical principles—nature was a book that contained the word of God that he was deciphering. However, Newton's scientific God-image is rather remote and impersonal, quite different than the personal God-image of Christianity. Nevertheless, many of Newton's contemporaries, worried about the rise of atheism, used his scientific approach to religion as evidence for the existence of a divine engineer or designer, to counter religious skeptics. However, to postulate a designer is to say nothing about the other traditional attributes of God such as his justice, mercy, and goodness, which cannot be inferred from the argument from design. Neither can the possibility of polytheism be excluded on this basis.

Francis Bacon (1561-1626) was an important proponent of the new seventeenth century science. He was one of the founders of modern empiricism and the scientific method. He is typically seen as an early defender of the separation of science and religion and as a protagonist of the secularizing ideas of the Scientific Revolution. Bacon is sometimes portrayed as preferring faith in human rationality to faith in divine providence, although in fact he believed he was guided by divine providence, which he thought would restore both the knowledge of nature and the knowledge of God. He distinguished scientific knowledge that is acquired by reason from religious knowledge acquired by faith. He was a strong defender of Christianity, and he identified religion as the foundation of civil society. He believed that his era was "one of apocalyptic transformation of the human condition that restores humanity to its prelapsarian state" (McKnight, 2007, p. 463). Utopian perfection, or an ideal society, could be achieved by a combination of right religion and the proper study of nature. At a time when the witch hunt was at its height, Bacon presented his new approach as the opposite of such superstition.

As well as his important contributions to science, Bacon divided theology into a natural and a revealed form. Natural theology means inquiry into the attributes of God without appealing to revelation or scripture. This tradition asks questions about God, or tries to prove the existence of God, using human faculties such as reason and introspection, taking into account the evidence of history, science, and the observation of nature. Believers would say that anything more than that we must learn from revelation and we have to be guided by the Church. For traditional theists, one of the major drawbacks of reliance on natural theology alone is that it says nothing about divine grace and not enough about the limitations of human reason in its understanding of divinity.

The Renaissance had seen the revival of the ancient Greek notion of a world soul, the *anima mundi*, a cosmic spiritual principle that seemed to be infused into the material universe. In the early seventeenth century, the Catholic philosopher Marin Mersenne (1588-1648) saw the dangers of this idea, which seem to suggest that matter could be imbued with life, and hence God could be identified with nature. This, Mersenne feared, would legitimate magical practices and lead to heresy. If the natural world could be imbued with inherently active powers, as Renaissance naturalism had suggested, the role of God would no longer be necessary. It was therefore fundamentally important to Mersenne that matter should be passive, so that the distinction between the natural and the supernatural domains could be maintained. This view of matter was elaborated by the emerging science and made central by Descartes.

The God-image of the Seventeenth- and Eighteenth-Century Philosophers

During the seventeenth century, many philosophers made God important within their systems of thought. Several of these thinkers made major contributions to the ongoing conversation about the Western God-image.

The idea of God was of major significance to Descartes (1596-1650), for whom God was personal and very present in human affairs. Descartes felt he could be sure that the world is real because God would not deceive him when he perceived the world. He believed that the world runs like a mechanical piece of clockwork that was begun and sustained by God, with mathematical perfection.

Descartes offered a series of attempted proofs for the existence of God. The first was based on the fact that Descartes had innate ideas in his mind, such as the idea of truth and the idea of a supremely perfect being. He believed that such innate ideas must have a source apart from his own mind. God is that source, because the cause of the idea of a perfect being must be as real and as perfect as the idea itself, so Descartes himself could not be the source of this idea since he was not perfect. Another attempted proof was based on God as the cause of Descartes' own existence; he had proven to his own satisfaction that he exists, because he can think, but he could not have created himself—if he had, he would have made himself more perfect. Another proof is based on the idea that a supremely perfect being must contain within itself the necessity of its own existence. Otherwise, it would not be a supremely perfect being.[ii]

Thomas Hobbes (1588-1679) also tried to develop a rational form of religion as part of his philosophical system. For Hobbes, since only matter exists, there is no such thing as a purely spiritual being; God is a kind of invisible but corporeal spirit. Hobbes believed that processes such as thinking and memory are the result of material motion inside the brain. However, the idea that the mind or even the soul could be embodied was a considerable challenge to traditional religion. If the mind or the soul are material, they can be studied by doctors; they are no longer the exclusive province of theology. What is more, if the soul were material it could die. Hobbes was skeptical about religion in general, attributing it to fear, ignorance, and the attempts of rulers to control their subjects. His attitude was characteristic of a time when the traditional certainties were becoming much less certain.

John Locke (1632-1704) believed that it was inconceivable that unconscious matter could have produced thinking, intelligent human beings, not to mention the order and beauty in the world. He could not have existed without a creator. Reason therefore leads us to belief in God, who gave people the capacity to think. God must have the capacity for thought, since mind and matter are distinct and matter could not produce mind, so the existence of God is the only good explanation for the development of thought in a material world. Locke thought that we form complex ideas about God by enlarging to infinity ideas such as existence, duration, power, and knowledge. The idea of God was the result of reflection on the idea of infinity based on numbers, which can be expanded infinitely. This results in our idea of God as a being that possesses an infinite cognitive ability and infinite attributes. Locke believed that although God is omniscient and omnipotent, he gives people freedom to act. God also gave us moral behavior and reason, which allows everyone the right to their own conscience in matters of religion. Although Locke believed we do not know the nature of God, Locke frequently appealed to the role of God in explaining the processes of nature, even though we have no idea how God makes material objects behave the way they do. This ignorance restrains our pride and motivates us to seek God. For Locke, since the natural world provides evidence for the existence of God, there is no further need for revelation or superstitious doctrines. For Locke and for many other rationalist Protestants of his time, Christianity mainly served as an ethical system that Jesus taught.

During the seventeenth century, a group of thinkers at Cambridge University selectively Platonized Christian thinking. The Cambridge Platonists had a kind of mystical theology, such that wherever is found beauty, love, harmony, or wisdom, there one finds God. They tried to justify a religious approach to the world in order to deal with the increasing tide of material explanations for the universe based on the emerging science. They also wanted to counter the influence of Hobbes's materialism. The Enlightenment eventually rejected these writers, but they had an important effect on Isaac Newton and other subsequent philosophers.

Henry More (1614-1687), a contemporary of Descartes, believed that a reasonable person could be convinced of the existence of God, partly because of the nature of the idea of God and partly because of the wisdom and design in nature. He objected to purely mechanical or material causes for motion and resisted the idea that the world could be explained without divine intervention. More believed that the world consists of both inert matter and active spirits, created by God, which are indiscernible but which interpenetrate all physical objects. Spirits, God, and matter all operate in cosmic harmony. For some years, More worked with Isaac Newton in an attempt to decipher the symbolic meaning of the biblical books of *Revelation* and *Daniel*. More was an ardent exponent of the new science, which he felt was compatible with his spiritual metaphysics. For him, the behavior of the material world needs a spiritual explanation. This attitude was lost as Enlightenment materialism began to dominate thought.

Another erudite Cambridge Platonist, Ralph Cudworth (1617-1688), was also engaged in the attempt to combat materialism and atheism. He believed in the existence of an ancient wisdom, a *prisca theologia*, a single theology given by God that exists as a common thread through all religions. Cudworth was sure that trinitarian Christianity is the best expression of this ancient revelation. He thought that this wisdom was transmitted by people such as Moses and Hermes Trismegistus,[iii] but their teachings have become obscured and diluted by the variety of different religions that have arisen over time. Cudworth was sure that the number of religions points to an original pure religion that is incorporated into Christianity. He pointed out that although we cannot form an adequate concept of God, this does not give us reason to doubt the existence of God and we can form a limited concept of him. Cudworth also believed that because we are imperfect, we could not have created the idea of a perfect being out of nothing. He believed that God had built the world for the good of humanity. God continues to contribute to the world and orders it by means of spiritual powers that make things happen. Cudworth argued against the prevalent ideas that religion was merely based on superstition and fear, or that religion was simply a set of beliefs used by politicians to make people behave. To Cudworth it seemed unlikely that people everywhere at all times could have been deceived in these ways.

Blaise Pascal (1623-1662) was a child prodigy and one of the greatest intellects of the seventeenth century. He made mathematical and scientific discoveries at a young age, but among his major preoccupations were the painful state of the human condition and the possibility of salvation from it. The notion of a mechanical universe was meaningless and frightening to him, even if God was its designer. Pascal believed that to achieve happiness one has to get beyond rational thinking and depend on divine revelation. One can only achieve certainty through the heart, not by means of the mind or by philosophical argument. Pascal realized that there are several traditions to choose from, and only God can give the grace that makes one believe in the true religion, which for Pascal was Christianity.

Pascal presented a famous wager based on a choice between two possibilities; God either does or does not exist. Rationally, we cannot decide which is true, but it makes a huge difference if God does exist, while if God does not exist, we are simply left in our hopeless situation. According to Pascal, it would therefore be prudent to bet on religion, since one then has nothing to lose and everything to gain. If God does exist, it would be dangerous to be an unbeliever, but if God does not exist it does not matter what we do. Furthermore, we have to place a bet, since not to bet is to bet on God's non-existence. The usual response to this wager is to point out that Pascal minimizes the sacrifices of time, energy, and resources that are required if we choose belief. Pascal's argument seems to be partly based on the threat of damnation for non-believers. However, it is not clear that one can simply decide to believe or make oneself believe in God based on this kind of argument, which sounds as if it is based more on self-interest than on true faith. A further problem is that Pascal takes for granted that God is the Christian God, but if the God of Judaism or Islam is the true one, the gamble might be risky.

Gottfried Leibniz (1646-1716) believed that the world consists of an infinite number of monads, which are like metaphysical, indivisible, self-contained points that do not occupy space. They are the building blocks of the universe, arranged in a continuous series of increasing clarity; at the highest extreme is God, the most perfect monad, who directs all the others. Each human soul is a monad. God created all the other monads that make up the world, and each is given a unique nature. Each monad has its own inbuilt history and its own perspective on the world, but there is no interaction between them, although they are aware of each other. Since all monads are created by God, everything that happens is prepared by God, part of a vast design. Individual events are each the effect of a greater cause, which is God, who is the necessary ground of their existence but also independent of them. The monads are correlated with each other by what Leibniz calls pre-established harmony. The apparent interconnection between events is therefore not due to causality but results from this harmony. (This idea seems to be a precursor to Jung's notion of synchronicity.) This harmony also accounts for the coordination of the soul and the body; God ordained at creation the principle that the actions of the soul would coincide with the movements of the body. Leibniz believed that God determined each individual's nature as well as possible in terms of the harmony of the whole universe.

Leibniz is famous for his *Theodicy*, which tries to justify God in the face of the existence of evil, a problem that was central to Leibniz's thought. Leibniz believed that God permits moral evil for the sake of free will, so God is not responsible for evil. All created things are necessarily imperfect, and this imperfection is the source of all error and evil. Evil must be judged teleologically, in terms of the best possible outcome; evil is used to achieve greater goodness than would otherwise be possible, and evil is eventually overshadowed by goodness. For Leibniz, God is deeply involved in human affairs, but God is not the author of sin; God only permits moral evil but does not will it. God can permit sin without any detriment to God's perfection, and since nothing comes from God that is not good and just, some evils must be necessary. Evil is partly the result of God's plenitude, since the world contains the maximum number of possibilities, so a world with evil and suffering is better than one without these problems.

Leibniz believed that God is perfect and had an infinity of choices when he created the world, and because he always acts for the best, God must have created the least imperfect world that could possibly have been created. Therefore, this is the best of all possible worlds. This idea raises the obvious question of how we can be condemned for being the way God created us. Leibniz's idea was later attacked by Voltaire and by others, since the presence of evil is the greatest objection to the notion of a benevolent God.

Voltaire (1694-1778) was one of the most influential thinkers of the Enlightenment. In his satirical novel *Candide*, he attacks any kind of spiritual optimism by pointing out the hardships and horrors in the world. This novel was written just after the Lisbon earthquake of 1755 had killed thousands of people, leading to questions about whether there is any possible explanation for the problem of evil. Voltaire tried to show the futility of Leibniz's notion that this is the best of all possible worlds. Voltaire believed that we cannot judge the world because we do not know enough about it. We can only suffer, submit, and die. He believed that biblical religion is one of the sources of the ills of humanity. The Bible worships a man-made deity, and theology has rationalized and institutionalized this ancient religious view, using it to control people. Voltaire aggressively attacked Judaism and Christianity, believing that both should be eliminated. In his mind, the rational paganism of Greece and Rome would be a better basis for European thought and morality. Yet he was not quite an atheist; he advocated deism, the notion that there is a cosmic force that runs the world, a force that is entirely transcendent and may have no moral qualities. The evidence for this is the design in nature that Newton had discovered. But Voltaire found no connection between this designer and the God-image of Christianity; he pointed out that even if there is an intelligent order to the universe, we cannot infer morality from that order. For Voltaire, reason is the natural basis for morality and justice. He is remembered for suggesting that: "If God did not exist, man would have to invent him."

Benedict Spinoza (1632-1677) insisted that philosophy should begin with the idea of God. Spinoza questioned the Mosaic authorship of the Bible and asserted that the Bible does not offer rational knowledge of the divine. Rather, the Bible's laws were directed towards teaching the notion of the superiority of God and the promise of reward for obedience and punishment for disobedience. Spinoza criticized the claim that rational truths should be set aside if they disagreed with the Bible. For him, the Bible consists of parables, and it is a mistake to assent to anything in the Bible that is contrary to reason, which is the highest divine gift. Religion is best understood as moral teaching rather than philosophy. Spinoza pointed out that a God who created the world would have been imperfect before that creation, because a perfect being would not need to create. For Spinoza, the world must be the same as God because there can only be one infinite, divine substance[iv] that comprises all of reality, and this substance is God. This substance is self-caused and self-determined. God and nature are identical; God is not transcendent to nature and also not other than nature. Nature is a series of modifications in the divine substance; every event in the universe is a consequence of the divine nature. What we perceive as a world of separate creatures and objects is actually nature as a whole, which is the same as God. God produces the entirety of finite things as a result of the infinite perfection of the divine attributes. Reality is an eternal cosmic unity. For Spinoza, mind and body are not distinct; they are two different modes of the same substance, which is God. When something happens in the body it also happens in the mind, since they are two aspects of the same substance. Spinoza would therefore not distinguish between spirit and matter as if they were qualitatively different.

God is self-determined, but God determines human beings, and since the entire order of nature, including human beings, is predisposed to behave as it does, there cannot be free will even if we experience freedom. Our hopes and fears are in vain, since we cannot affect nature, so that emotions of despair at failure or happiness at success are not warranted, since everything is determined by causes outside us, and every event in the universe is the result of the divine nature. We can only choose to act as we have to act. All objects in the universe form a chain of causes; everything was caused by something else, all flowing by mathematical necessity.

Spinoza believed that God has no personality traits; Spinoza therefore rejected the idea of a personal God, and he thought that the idea of the immortality of the soul is an illusion. The appreciation for the natural scheme of things is a form of the intellectual love of God, since God and Nature are one. The mind's intellectual love of God is the same thing as God's love for people; it is the expression of God's self-love using the medium of human thought. Therefore, every time we understand ourselves, we take a step towards union with God.

Spinoza's ideas about God and his approach to the Bible were completely unacceptable to the Jewish community in his native Holland. Some people believed he was using the word God simply as a way of talking about the universe, in which case he could be seen to be an atheist. As a result, the rabbinical authorities of Amsterdam excommunicated him, and his work was also branded as heretical by the Christian community. However, if he is read as saying that when we talk of nature we are really talking about God, he can be seen as deeply religious. He can also be seen as a pantheist, or as saying that the world is totally divine, which one could see as a religion of nature. As he puts it: "Whatever is, is in God" (*Ethics* 1, prop. 15). However, for many people, the invocation of an idea as abstract as "nature" was not as satisfying as the traditional personal God-image. Impersonal God-images do not respond to prayer.

Bishop Berkeley (1685-1753) believed that much atheism and materialism would be abolished if he could disprove the independent existence of matter. Berkeley therefore argued that things only exist because they are perceived, so that mind is the deepest reality; matter does not exist outside of consciousness. The properties of objects, such as solidity or color, have no existence outside our perception of them. In fact, everything that exists, everything we believe to be material, is only known as an idea in the mind, or in the mind of God. God is a supreme spirit, and God is the cause of all our sensations and our ideas. Objects continue to exist in the mind of God when no person is perceiving them.

By the end of the seventeenth century, there was a great deal of agreement about the existence of God, especially since it seemed that the century's greatest scientists, such as Newton and Boyle, had demonstrated the existence of a creator. As well, the most important philosophers of the period, such as Descartes, Leibniz, and Locke had made the question of God central to their thinking. There was also general agreement about the attributes of God as a transcendent, all-powerful, all-good being. Most people at the time agreed that God could be known, and he was the source of hope. This attitude radically changed in the eighteenth century, during the Enlightenment, when thinking and reason dominated ideas about God. At this time, many people either became atheists or at least were radically critical of traditional Christian concepts. The general tenor of the eighteenth century wanted to limit science to the study of matter, avoiding the seventeenth century attempt to correlate science with theology to try to prove the existence of God. Enlightenment philosophers became increasingly skeptical about traditional notions of God; morality and social thought in general became increasingly secular. The Enlightenment attitude in general militated against all traditional forms of authority, including religious authority, and disliked anything that smacked of superstition or appeals to divine revelation. Ideas during this period emphasized personal experience and autonomy. Even for religious believers, because the new sciences had shown that the universe provide evidence for a creator in its design, there was less need for Church authority in arguing for the existence of God. The notion that the mind was really a bodily process gained ground, supporting an increasing emphasis on reason and lessening the emphasis on the soul.

There were many contributions to the religious debates of the time, including some at each extreme of theism and atheism. The mathematician Christian Wolff (1679-1754) proposed a rational theism that tried to base religious truths on the mathematically certain evidence provided by science. He attempted an abstract analysis of the meaning of God as a perfect being. Wolff argued that revelation and belief in God are not necessary for moral development, and this idea had important repercussions for the remainder of the 18th century. Baron d'Holbach (1723-1789) was a dogmatic materialist who wanted to replace religion with science. He denied that there is any grand design to the universe, and he derided religion. d'Holbach believed that there is no need for the God of Newton, because nature contains its own energies and achievements, and religion is a product of fear and superstition. d'Holbach insisted that the material world is the only reality, and it can only be understood scientifically.

David Hume (1711-1776) tried to show that reason cannot demonstrate the nature of God, and all previous attempts to prove the existence of God were faulty. Hume was a critic of the notion that design in the universe implies a divine designer.[v] He pointed out that this argument depends on an analogy between God, the world, and objects in the world that have been designed by human beings. However, for Hume, this analogy does not work because the human designers of objects in the world and the supposed divine designer of the world are not comparable. The universe is not like any man-made object, and we do not know if the universe has been made in a way that is analogous to human productions. Some other kind of process might be responsible for the world. The argument from design also fails because if design requires a designer, then something must have designed God's intelligence, leading to an infinite regress. As well, if the analogy of God as a designer means that God's mind is like human minds, his greatness is sacrificed, whereas if we stress God's infinite nature, we weaken the argument that he is a designer. Furthermore, as well as the benevolent aspects of nature, God's design would include disease, disorder, and evil, which would be evidence of malice, incompetence, or impotence in the designer. If there is a creator of order in the universe, we cannot say anything about the creator's moral qualities. If God has infinite power, goodness, and wisdom, we cannot explain the existence of evil. The arguments designed to prove the existence of God are therefore inconclusive, and only suggest that something was a first cause, but that is not necessarily God in the Christian sense. For Hume, the only proposition we can assert is that the cause of order in the universe probably bears some remote analogy to human intelligence, but order in nature may be the result of natural processes; the world may be the cause of itself. For Hume therefore, we can only fall back on belief in God, and this belief comes from our desire for happiness and our fear of death. Because of these feelings, we construct our belief in God and then try to rationalize it by means of reason. Later theologians, such as Kierkegaard, argued that Hume's critique of religion is so powerful that only faith and revelation can be the basis of religion.

Immanuel Kant (1724-1804) also looked at the traditional arguments for the existence of God, and decided that all of them fail. Kant therefore agreed with Hume that we cannot know anything about supernatural entities such as God, but Kant believed he could justify belief in God as a matter of faith. For Kant, God is the highest idea we can have, the idea of the highest unity that encompasses everything. We cannot think of this unity without it becoming an object, so we make an entity of the idea, then we personify it and call it God. However, although we cannot know God through reason, at the same time reason can acknowledge God as a necessary unknown. Concepts like God stimulate science, since the world created by God must be constructed rationally and so would reward scientific inquiry. However, Kant pointed out that science could understand how nature works, but not why it works.

Kant believes we cannot know God because we can only know the phenomenal world as it appears through the prism of our minds, and we have no access to the metaphysical realm. Kant's approach to religion was therefore through morality rather than in terms of metaphysical speculation. He believed that although we cannot prove the existence of God, we need this idea as a foundation for our ethical principles. Morality also demands the truth of the immortality of the soul, even though that too cannot be proved. This moral argument is not a proof of the existence of God in the ordinary sense; it is based on practical reason, something we can believe to support our moral law, which it is our duty to fulfill.

One of the reactions to eighteenth century materialism and reductionism was Romanticism, a movement that wanted to include imagination, feeling, and intuition as well as reason as valid ways of understanding the world. Romantics rejected deterministic science and the idea of human beings as machines; they embraced the importance of human creativity, emotion, and freedom, especially in literature and ethics. This attitude was epitomized by Schelling, the founder of the school of *Naturphilosophie* or the philosophy of nature. He believed that "nature and spirit both sprang from the absolute and constituted an indissoluble unity" (Ellenberger, p. 202). Schelling believed that nature is visible spirit and spirit is invisible nature. There is an essential unity of humanity and nature; "human life was regarded as a participation in a kind of cosmic movement within nature" (p. 203). The material universe and human consciousness arise from a common spiritual principle, a World Soul. Nature is a form of the revelation of this absolute ego, so that nature becomes self-conscious through spirit. Therefore, nature cannot be understood only in terms of physical principles but "must be understood in terms of the underlying spiritual laws" (p. 203). Schelling believed that God can be understood as a creative energy that is the ground of everything. Since this is the soul of the universe, this idea is close to pantheism.

The God-image During the Nineteenth Century

Despite the development of both atheism and biblical criticism in the nineteenth century, God remained important for many people. However, the notion of a transcendent God only known through revelation, metaphysical speculation, or religious authority, became increasingly suspect. For example, Albrecht Ritschl (1822-1889) believed that metaphysical, doctrinal, and ontological ideas about God were irrelevant; God is only known as a loving personal God, in human history and especially in the moral development of humanity, which is more important than theological correctness.

Some nineteenth century thinkers saw the presence of the divine in the unfolding processes of human history. Hegel (1770-1831) agreed with Kant that we could not know a transcendent God, so that the divine must be immanent and universal to be relevant to every form of immediate human experience. For Hegel, reality must be the creation of a rational spirit, but Hegel's God is impersonal. Hegel suggested that the Absolute, or Absolute Spirit, is the basis of reality, and everything that exists is an actualization of spirit. In this view, since the Infinite is the ground and unity of life, God must be changing as life and history change. Hegel therefore sees God as present in the entire process of evolution, past, present, and future. For Hegel, God knows himself through human consciousness, which is God's self-consciousness. God is incarnate in all people, in the history of humanity, and in everything finite, since the finite world is only one moment in the dialectical development of the nature of God. God is revealed in the world, and as the world develops God becomes self-conscious, or comes to know himself more fully.[vi] God reaches his clearest self-consciousness in humanity. Thus, human intellectual history is the externalization of the mind of God within human thought. For Hegel therefore, God was radically immanent and dynamic rather than transcendent and changeless, and Jesus was not so much important as an individual but rather as a symbolic representation of a period of history when humanity became conscious of its unity with God.

William Blake (1757-1827) believed that religions have made their God-image in the image of humanity. He resisted the tyrannical God of the theistic traditions who compels human beings to serve him; this for Blake is satanic. He famously questioned established values and the limitations of established religions. He realized that life could not be fully described using the rational philosophy of the Enlightenment, using quantitative measurement, or by means of Newtonian science. Like many Romantic writers, Blake believed that too much rational thinking enslaves the imagination. For him, the infinite imagination is the divine being within people.

God was an important preoccupation for Søren Kierkegaard (1813-1855), and he constantly struggled with religious questions. He reacted strongly against Hegel's image of an impersonal God; for Kierkegaard, God is intensely personal and requires a personal commitment. Kierkegaard also objected to Hegel's belief that Jesus Christ has no individual religious value because God is incarnate in everyone. For Kierkegaard, the Incarnation in Christ is a unique and decisive event in history, because only through relationship to Christ can one develop an intimate relationship with God. By means of the Incarnation in Christ, the Absolute becomes known to mankind. Although the incarnation is logically impossible, Kierkegaard believes that through faith the believer acquires certainty about its truth.

Kierkegaard accused the established Church of being lifeless because it believed that baptism and confirmation were sufficient evidence of being a Christian, without acknowledging the difficulties of true faith, which must make a difference in a person's life beside attending church on Sundays. Kierkegaard also criticized the Church for making faith too easy, too respectable, and too lacking in commitment. Kierkegaard believed that Christians did not realize the difficulty of the claim that the infinite creator had come down to earth in the form of a man. He believed that the self only becomes a self when it is in relationship with God, who may place us in demanding situations where we have to make painful choices as a test of faith. The authentic Christian is one who does not try to escape from this burden by doing what everyone else does. Kierkegaard believed that if the existence of God could be proved, there would be no virtue in this belief.

For Kierkegaard the central feature of faith is the relationship of the individual to God, which can only occur as a leap of faith that cannot be rationally justified to non-believers, and no justification is necessary for believers.[vii] By making a leap of faith, what used to seem absurd is now understood as the highest truth. However, Kierkegaard's emphasis on the individual's relationship with God raises the problem for traditional religionists that intermediaries or churches become less necessary. A stress on the subjective or personal level of the relationship also raises the question of whether God has an independent existence, since no evidence for God's existence in the outer world is then necessary. The existence of God becomes a matter of personal choice.

The tradition of scientific believers such as Newton did not die out in the nineteenth century; the physicist and psychologist Gustav Fechner (1801-1887) believed that God is a world soul, related to the world as the human soul is related to the body, so that nature is the body of God. However, during the nineteenth century it became less fashionable to make God the center of philosophical and scientific speculation. The idea of God became superfluous or even unintelligible for many thinkers. The culture had become more secular, and it was impossible to interpret the advent of the Kingdom of Heaven in terms of social progress. Atheism became quite popular under the influence of Marx, Darwin, and Nietzsche.

Auguste Comte believed that attempts to get to the essence of the universe are symptoms of human mental immaturity. He thought that we will give up attempts to discover God and focus on what can actually be discovered when humanity reaches the developmental stage of positivism, the theory that only information arising from sensory experience and interpreted by reason allows certain knowledge. Also typical of the nineteenth century critics of institutionalized religion was William Godwin (1756-1836), who saw Christianity as a purely man-made system. For him, the God of scripture is a tyrant, and the doctrine of original sin with its rewards and punishments creates servitude. The notion of an afterlife of retribution shackles the mind with fear. Christian doctrine is intolerant and leads to controversy and war, while the church hierarchy simply amasses wealth. In Godwin's view, religious systems must be dissolved so that humanity can fully realize its natural reasoning powers.

The sociologist Emile Durkheim (1858-1917) dismissed the importance of God almost entirely, since for him the main aspects of religion are rites and rituals, which arouse powerful emotions and bond societies together. He rejected the idea that religion arose in an attempt to explain the mystery of existence. For him, people may have a God-image in mind, but they are really worshipping their society. He thought of God as playing a minor part in religion, which is mainly a sociological process; essentially, God only represents society, or God represents human endeavors to objectify social forces (Durkheim, 1995). In this view, which seems dubious, religious activity is purely a social function. Durkheim's approach has not withstood scrutiny, partly because of the circularity involved in defining religion as a set of practices that unite the community and then finding that religion creates social solidarity. From an evolutionary point of view, kinship is probably a more powerful means of social cohesion than religion.

Charles Darwin (1809-1882) stimulated a new orientation in both biology and psychology. His hypothesis that humanity was descended from lower forms of life enormously weakened the idea that human origins were the result of divine creation, and also diminished the notion that nature had a spiritual dimension. The theory of evolution offered a convincing alternative to the argument that the world must have had an intelligent designer. Natural selection took the place of divine design as a way to account for the complexity of living organisms. This theory does not need any form of teleology; evolution is dependent on chance variations in the environment, rather than the environment having been created for the sake of life forms, as the Bible claims. The notion of survival of the fittest is not compatible with a benevolent creator. Furthermore, if evolution is going on, creation is not finished.

Darwin speculated that religious belief may have developed as the human brain evolved. The best response theologians could make to Darwin's ideas was to suggest that God guides the variations that produce natural selection, although Darwin himself was skeptical about the existence of a divine designer. The notion that a divine force guides evolution was popular for a time in the early twentieth century but was abandoned by most biologists in favor of natural selection as a non-purposive, random mechanism. However, the idea that the human moral sense had evolved through natural selection alone was offensive to many people who believed that this faculty was divinely given.

Among religious believers, the general trend in the nineteenth century was to modernize the concept of God by talking about traditional theism in terms that made sense to contemporary people. Human beings were increasingly thought to be the measure of reality and truth, and the immanence of the divine in the processes of nature and in human history became an important religious motif. The traditional theistic notion of God as transcendent and all-loving was called into question, except for people in the Roman Catholic tradition who continued Thomistic thought. Otherwise, the notion of a supreme being hidden from the world and only knowable by scriptural or religious authority increasingly seemed to be irrelevant or even superstitious.

By the end of the nineteenth century, although it was still possible to think of God as the spiritual force that accounts for evolution and historical progress, this meant that God was not necessarily as absolute, omnipotent, self-sufficient or changeless as the classical concept taught. Instead, God could be thought of as part of an unfolding process of becoming, moving towards perfection. This idea, prominent in the form of process theology (see p. 309) is quite a different image than the God who is complete in himself, in no way dependent on the world.

The God-image Among Twentieth Century Thinkers

Confidence in the nineteenth century idea of the progress of history and the perfectibility of humanity waned in the twentieth century, because of the eruption of world wars and other evils. It looked as if culture was threatened with collapse rather than gradual progress. If the divine spirit was manifesting in history, it was appearing in the form of violence, cruelty, injustice, and exploitation, as well as fulfillment. For many twentieth century philosophers therefore, speculation about God became irrelevant or even unintelligible. No transcendent reality seemed necessary, given the progress of science. To more and more people, religion seemed nothing more than a source of conflict, and therefore more trouble than it is worth. Philosophy moved away from speculative metaphysics towards a focus on direct experience, deconstruction, post-modernism, and the philosophy of language. Secular existentialism was largely atheistic, emphasizing human despair in a meaningless world, while religious existentialists believed that metaphysical talk about God obscured God. Talk about God was increasingly seen as a purely personal language of faith and not suited to philosophical reasoning, so that philosophy is no help to theology. Even some theologians began to ask whether there really is a God, and a proportion of priests saw religious doctrines only as guiding myths or ways of talking about proper behavior. Postmodern philosophy mistrusts the idea that a single vision, such as that of one religion, could be the absolute truth.

During the twentieth century, philosophers became concerned that theological or metaphysical statements might be meaningless or were not actually saying anything we could experience—as if we were to say that there is a unicorn in a certain forest. Between 1924 and 1936, a group of logical positivist philosophers and scientists rejected all metaphysics. They decided that we can only make meaningful statements about matters that can be tested and verified empirically. Therefore, the concept of God had no meaning, because it cannot be tested; it simply expresses a vague feeling. Even atheism is incoherent, since there is nothing about which we can be atheistic; metaphysical statements cannot be verified in principle. In this view, it is not clear what it actually means to say that Jesus loves you—how would you show that? Such theological assertions are not falsifiable, and theologians do not allow anything to count against statements such as "God is love," because such statements can be justified whatever is the state of affairs.

In this view, at best, theological statements can be seen as expressions of moral commitment or expressions of one's personal attitude. Or, a statement such as "God loves you" has meaning as an expression of faith, and faith is independent of reason (the doctrine of fideism). Perhaps talk of God is just talk about human mental states. Another approach is to appeal to Wittgenstein's idea of language games and different forms of life. This approach suggests that language is used differently in different areas of life, and the rules for using language in science are different than the rules used in theology. Thus, theological language does not have to meet the same standards as science does; religion has its own rules. But the question of whether we are actually talking about anything real when we talk about God is not settled by these attitudes, not to mention the problem that different religions are referring to radically different concepts when they talk about God. Some theologians are talking about the personal God of Judaism and Christianity. Others, such as Tillich, do not refer to God as an entity, while Heidegger rejects traditional metaphysical notions of God and sees Being rather than a particular being as the ultimate reality.

After the Second World War, especially after the Holocaust, it became impossible for many theologians and philosophers to speak about God in the traditional ways. Both theology and philosophy were unable to explain the Holocaust. Its grotesque cruelty and disastrous loss of life shattered any hope of relating the traditional God-image to everyday life, and the doctrine of divine providence no longer seemed tenable. The Holocaust proved to be a grave challenge, not only to the Jewish God-image but also to Christianity, whose teachings failed to prevent the Holocaust and, in some cases, even encouraged it.

Martin Heidegger (1889-1976) exemplified the difficulty that arose when speaking or thinking about God in the twentieth century. He rejected metaphysical notions of God, and in fact dismissed the whole of metaphysics as ontotheology, a word that means speaking about God in metaphysical terms, or attempts to explain the being of God, for example as the First Cause of everything. Heidegger wanted to abandon the God of philosophy, which he thought was dead, in contrast to the God of faith. Heidegger complained that theologians had made God an object, or a being among other beings, even if theology puts God at the top of the hierarchy. However, God cannot be objectified or thought about in this way, so the Christian God-image is not the real God, who is beyond the God of the Christians.

In his *God Beyond Being*, Heidegger stresses the unknown and mysterious nature of Being, a word that partly means that which makes possible the existence of beings. Being and beings as entities are not the same, but Being should not be thought of as a metaphysical something beyond beings; Being is always the being of an entity. For some time during the Christian tradition, God was understood as Being because of Exodus 3:14, in which God says: "I am who I am." For some twentieth century theologians, Being became synonymous with God even though Heidegger (1947) insisted that Being is not God in the traditional theological sense. Being is vaster than individual beings, and however God might exist he is not a being among other beings (Vedder, 2007).

Perhaps it is no accident that the relative absence of God in twentieth century culture is mirrored by the fact that twentieth century artists such as Paul Klee, Jackson Pollock, and Mark Rothko tended to express spiritual themes through abstract compositions, in highly personal ways, not based on any specific traditional concept of God. At the same time, the proportion of people regularly attending Sunday services dramatically declined in the twentieth century, more so in Europe than in the USA.

The development of quantum theory in the twentieth century challenged several pillars of classical physics. It made untenable the reductionism of classical mechanics, which tried to explain matter entirely in terms of the predictable interaction of ever-smaller entities. Determinism, the view that all events are completely determined by previous events, is undermined by quantum mechanics, which points out the unpredictability involved in the measurement of quantum particles. Quantum theory also challenges metaphysical realism, the doctrine that things exist whether or not anyone is thinking about them, since the results of some experiments at the quantum level are affected by the consciousness of the experimenter. The development of quantum theory allowed a new dialog between physics and theology to emerge. According to some accounts of quantum theory, the universe can be seen holistically, arising out of a hidden dimension of the wave function and dependent on consciousness for its materialization. This offers an argument against physicalism and reductionism, which are important opponents of belief in God, and it gives particular value to human subjectivity and its effect on our perception of reality. Quantum physics makes us realize that there are aspects of reality we simply cannot talk about in ordinary language. Our scientific descriptions of reality are now known to be incomplete, leaving room for belief in a transcendent background or a spiritual dimension, which may be the same as the impersonal quantum energy field. This is sometimes thought of as a fifth dimension. That is, quantum theory allows us to think about divinity in a way that is entirely different than the traditional Judeo-Christian God-image. However, one of the difficulties of this idea is that the quantum realm seems to operate randomly, and is only predictable statistically, not at the level of individual events. It is however possible that God designed the universe to operate by means of randomness, or perhaps God acts by means of quantum uncertainty, but we have no way to discern whether or how divinity affects natural processes. We cannot tell whether apparent randomness or indeterminacy is masking underlying divine intervention, and quantum uncertainty may not be relevant to the macroscopic world, although macroscopic quantum phenomena are now being observed. Furthermore, there are deterministic approaches to quantum mechanics.

The discovery of the Big Bang allowed theologians to suggest that God was the source of this event, which indicates a beginning, and theologians were able to claim that God designed the laws of nature that emerged from it. In this view the universe has an uncaused Ground, which is inaccessible to our understanding. This Ground explains the existence of the universe, which, it is argued, could not have arisen from nothing. This Ground is inseparable from the universe, leading to a kind of pantheism or even non-duality. However, these kinds of arguments remain inconclusive, since it is impossible to prove or disprove that there was a creator of the Big Bang, and even if there was such a creator, this might suggest a deist model rather than a Judeo-Christian model of God.

During the twentieth century, the relationship between science and religion tended to boil down to one of two approaches. The conflict model sees them as completely divergent with no valid connections between them. The convergence model sees religion and science as essentially expressing the same truths, even though they rely on very different methods.

The Return of the Goddess in the Twentieth Century

One of the feminist alternatives to traditional patriarchal theism stresses goddess symbolism. Many twentieth century feminists point out that there was a goddess long before there was a male sky-God and phallocentric Christianity (Stone, 1976). For some of these writers, the suppression of the goddess by patriarchal religion has resulted in the cultural dominance of masculine concepts of power and aggression rather than feminine qualities. Some authors believe that the return of interest in the goddess offers new models of the divine, especially in response to the needs of women, because goddess-centered spirituality legitimizes female power as beneficent and independent, instead of the devalued and submissive depictions of women in the Western religious traditions (Christ, 1982). Goddess imagery also affirms the value of the female body, and understands time as cyclical rather than linear. Goddess worship recognizes the earth as a nurturing mother who brings forth life, although the goddess is also the Queen of Heaven. However, the traditional association of the feminine with nature and the material world—in contrast to the association of masculinity with mind and spirit—has been challenged because it seems to legitimize a social order that has been constructed by patriarchal consciousness.

[i] For example, a biblical passage (Joshua 10:13) says that with the help of God, Joshua stopped the movement of the sun and moon so that he could finish a battle in daylight.

[ii] These arguments are generally not considered to be successful proofs. The problem is that we have no idea of the nature of the infinite being that Descartes postulates, and the fact that we can imagine such a being does not mean the being actually exists. Furthermore, there is no proof that God put the idea of God into us; this idea may be a human creation. Nor can we be sure that God is the reason we exist.

[iii] Hermes Trismegistus is a mythological figure who combines the Greek Hermes and the Egyptian Thoth, both gods of writing and magic. During the Renaissance he was described as if he was a real person and the founder of various occult traditions, including alchemy.

[iv] For Spinoza, a substance is something fundamental that does not depend on another substance from which it was formed.

[v] There is an ancient argument that the world is so intricately organized that it must have a designer. This idea became prominent in 1802 as a result of the work of William Paley, who believed that the world was a mechanism designed by God. This idea was persuasive until it was replaced by the theory of evolution.

[vi] This may be one of the sources of Jung's idea that the divine uses human consciousness to become conscious of itself.

[vii] Many subsequent theologians with an existentialist orientation, as well as Barth, Bultmann, and Tillich, also try to free Christianity from too much metaphysical speculation and emphasize the relationship between humanity and God.

CHAPTER 7
Psychological Approaches to the God-image

Reductive Psychological Approaches to Belief in God

In contrast to Jung's view that an innate God-image in the psyche predisposes us to belief in God, there is a range of reductive explanations for this belief. These approaches either lead to atheism or they are based on a prior commitment to atheism. Reductive theories of the origin of religion typically assume that religions persist because, by answering questions about human existence, religion creates meaning, comfort, and order in a world that otherwise seems arbitrary and frightening. Religions also help us cope with death and offer the possibility of influencing our environment through prayer and ritual, thus relieving anxiety. However, reductive explanations that dismiss the reality of a spiritual dimension are typically directed at God imagined in the classical form of an anthropomorphic, benevolent celestial protector and provider. They are much less relevant to Jung's approach, which is based on direct experience of the numinosum or the Self.

The most simplistic attempt to explain away belief in God is to see such belief as a residue of the baby's feeling of being cared for by a loving mother. This emotionally powerful experience is thought to leave traces in the unconscious, or even in the structure of the brain, which account for later belief in God. In this view, the feeling of being watched over and cared for by a God of love is really based on our unconscious memories of parental love in infancy. Along these lines, according to Faber (2004), prayer represents our deep desire for mother to come and comfort us, and the apparent efficacy of prayer is based on the evocation of early experiences of being helped. This means that when we believe we feel the presence of a helpful deity, we are really retrieving early experiences of a good maternal provider. Psychoanalysts often believe that strong religious commitment is the result of identification with, or yearning for, such an early lost object, which is turned into a deity. This approach suggests that because deeply embedded psychological structures from childhood drive our wish for a deity, human beings develop images of their deities that are like parents; protective, compassionate, and forgiving even if morally demanding. Implicit, unconscious memories from childhood are transferred onto religious figures such as gods, spirits, and angels, which are thus illusory.

However, this naturalistic[i] approach to religion, which dismisses it as infantile, is clearly inadequate. Numinous experiences and images of the Self are not always traceable to infantile residues, and they may not have a parental quality. Spiritual practices such as prayer, pilgrimage, meditation, and ritual, are more complex than merely asking for comfort. Furthermore, many atheists have had good mothering but feel no desire for a deity, while people with poor early maternal care may nevertheless be religious. It is true that some aspects of religion address primitive needs and fears, and it seems reasonable to suggest that parental love may form a template for the love of God. However, even if this approach casts light on the reason that so many people think of the divine in terms of parental metaphors, it does not explain many other aspects of religion. The assertion that religion stimulates infantile symbiotic experiences would not explain the selfless concern for others or the personal sacrifices demonstrated by religious people, unless all this was nothing but an identification with early caregivers. The religious emphasis on charity, compassion, and morality would all have to be similarly reduced in a simplistic manner. The assertion that religious experience is an illusory attempt to re-create an infantile situation would not explain the destructiveness of religious violence, when religion becomes pathological.

It is still common to assume that religion is mainly deployed to alleviate anxiety, to soothe fear of the unknown, to calm our fear of death, and to allow us to anticipate life after death. However, religion probably causes at least as much anxiety as it alleviates when it is characterized by accusations of sinfulness and a fear of eternal punishment. It is true that religion fulfills important needs, such as our need to believe that life is meaningful, our need to explain the existence of good and evil, and our need to believe in a moral order and pro-social behavior. Yet, it cannot be shown that these needs explain the origin of religion; perhaps the satisfaction of these needs is mainly an effect of religion.

Our images of God are partly based on the human capacity to imagine another mind, this time much larger than our own. Because we tend to anthropomorphize God-images, the theistic traditions have often imagined the divine as if it were a super-human being who watches over us. As Feuerbach (1851/2004) pointed out, the traditions exaggerate or compensate for human characteristics, so that God is thought of as infinite rather than finite, immortal rather than mortal, omnipotent rather than fragile, and so on. In other words, we have created a God-image that reflects some of the characteristics of humanity but without human limitations. That is, whatever people assert about God is at the same time an assertion about some aspect of human psychology, writ large. In this view, the way we think about God is inextricably connected to the way we think about ourselves and the human condition. We need to explain our experience and be comforted when life is difficult. Consequently, even irrational religious beliefs persist when they help us make sense of the world. However, reductionist accounts such as this seem to be imposing the author's personal metaphysical convictions onto religion. These accounts insist that religion is a human construction, but do not take into account the complexity of religious faith and religious life in general. Nor do these accounts do justice to the psychological sources of the individual's God-image such as direct experience of the Self and the effects of early social influences. To understand religious believers in-depth requires complex levels of explanation. There are several of these available, some of them reductionist, some antireductionist, some based on brain processes, others purely cognitive or psychodynamic.

Evolutionary, Biological, and Cognitive Theories About Belief in God

There is a range of theories about the ways in which belief in a spiritual dimension emerged among our hominin ancestors during the course of human evolution. The continuance of this belief to our own time puzzles atheists because of its apparent illogicality, since the spiritual realm is not perceptible through the senses. Furthermore, science has explained much that used to be the province of religion, so there is less and less need for religious explanations of natural phenomena.

Evolutionary biologists and psychologists wonder whether religious belief appeared and survived because it had adaptive or reproductive advantages during the evolution of our species. However, it is not easy to see how belief in a spiritual realm, and notions such as survival after death, could have offered survival advantages to our ancestors during the Pleistocene era. The idea of an unseen spirit seems to be counterfactual and counterintuitive, and spiritual practices require the sacrifice of energy and costly resources that might have been in short supply for our early ancestors (Atran, 2002). Nevertheless, there are suggestions that religion evolved and persisted because the responsible genes conferred an evolutionary advantage to the group as a whole. In this version of events, the functional disadvantages of religion are offset by various adaptive advantages. For example, religious beliefs may have evolved because they foster the ability of members of a community to trust and support each other, which would have been necessary for survival when small bands of early hominins faced dangers. A common religion would have helped in the cohesion of social groups and supported moral and altruistic behavior, which probably enhanced the possibility of the group's survival and reproduction. The sense that one is being watched by the gods may moderate asocial behavior. The willingness to sacrifice oneself or even die for the ideals of the group may confer selective advantage on a group, compared to groups that lack religion.[ii] However, many studies suggest that religion does not necessarily have much effect on human moral behavior. The gods of Mesopotamian, Egyptian, and ancient Greek religions were brutal, capricious, and not at all good moral exemplars. Even the God of the Hebrew Bible sometimes behaves in morally questionable ways, and religion is notorious for starting wars and ill-treating dissenters.

Although some evolutionary psychologists see religion as the direct result of natural selection, as an adaptation that fostered survival of the species, other theorist deny this, seeing religion as a "spandrel,"[iii] a design phenomenon within the brain that is an incidental by-product of human evolution. Evolutionary explanations for the origin of all aspects of human psychology point out that the human brain evolved over a long period of time, developing neurological systems that allowed our hominin ancestors to cope with problems such as avoiding predators, finding a mate, protecting children, and other contingencies. Torrey (2017) suggests that religion appeared about 40,000 years ago, when the brain had evolved sufficient complexity to develop autobiographical memory, so that we could imaginatively project ourselves backwards and forwards in time and therefore think about the inevitability of death.

Evolutionary psychologists believe that the idea of a god or gods is a function of cognitive processes that are common to all human brains. These psychologists take it for granted that the mind is a function of the brain. In their view, neural schemata have evolved that allow for a range of human behavior, including social functioning and death anxiety. Such brain systems are thought to provide basic assumptions about reality, acting like mental templates. Although some brain systems evolved for reasons that were not originally about religion, religious ideas may activate them (Boyer, 2001). That is, religion is a by-product of the evolution of the brain because religious ideas resonate with neurological structures in the human brain that evolved for other reasons. Thus, when a person thinks of a god, the brain activates the brain's template for a person, which is why the God of the Bible acts like a person with extra-special qualities such as omnipotence. Boyer thinks that templates with unusual properties are particularly memorable, as long as these properties are only minimally counterintuitive, meaning different enough to interest us but not different enough to reject altogether. A man with apparently special qualities who is sufficiently anomalous or different than ordinary men becomes particularly important in this context, leading to the idea of a godman. Feierman (2009) suggests that humans have evolved a brain program that allows them to make themselves lower, smaller, or vulnerable in uncertain situations, and this program is evoked during petitionary prayer or whenever we submit to a higher power. This attitude is related to the behavior seen among many mammals to indicate submission in order to deter attack. Religion also taps into psychological mechanisms such as the need to seek protection from authority figures (Kirkpatrick, 2005; 2013).[iv]

Consonant with Feuerbach's theory that God-images reflect human traits, Guthrie (1993) argues that all religion is based on the attribution of human characteristics to natural processes. Thus, because of our childhood association of pain with punishment, we readily interpret random accidents and natural disasters as punishments, and because we are pattern-seeking organisms we see human faces in clouds. Such anthropomorphic explanations of natural phenomena happen for evolutionary reasons; to survive in a perceptually ambiguous environment, in order to be safe, early humans had to develop perceptual strategies that assume that a given object might be alive rather than inert. All kinds of natural phenomena can then be assumed to be intentionally caused by human-like gods or spirits, which we imagine must have thoughts and feelings that are similar to our own. This approach helps to explain why biblical God-images are so anthropomorphically colored.

According to cognitive theorists, human beings have an innate predisposition to believe in the supernatural because the human brain's cognitive systems can misinterpret information given by the senses. These mechanisms are hardwired into our brains. The ability to assume purposeful behavior when we see movement in the environment was important for the survival of the species during our evolution, so that we could detect predators using a postulated agency detection device. Several lines of research suggest that human beings have an innate tendency to assume that whatever happens in the world is the result of the action of an agent rather than the result of a random mechanical process (Culotta, 2009). We prefer purposeful or causal explanations for events; we like to ask why things happen and we sometimes personify the responsible cause—hence the belief in spirits. However, sometimes we detect agency in the environment when none is present, because for our early ancestors this would have been safer than to under-detect the presence of a predator. This is not important if we can correct our mistake easily, but we are prone to notice false positives, leading to the belief in (unobservable) supernatural agents or gods around us. The human tendency to assume that these agents are like us in some ways leads to the idea that the gods have personalities. They must be placated, and they need food and shelter just as we do, so we build temples for them and sacrifice to them. By projecting these anthropomorphic characteristics onto the gods, human beings eventually developed religions. In other words, while very early humans projected divinity onto natural forces such as weather, later traditions projected human traits onto the gods. In the course of our religious history, when things went wrong it was a short step to assume that we had offended a god, and hence arose many religious rituals and sacrifices.

From the evolutionary perspective, because our brains have evolved to detect patterns and the movement of agents that might signal danger, the misapplication of this kind of cognitive process makes it easy to anthropomorphize a natural phenomenon such as the wind by calling it a spirit. This leads to animism, the belief that there are invisible supernatural forces all around us. Religion is then partly a side effect, or a by-product, of the architecture of the brain. The brain makes us pattern-seeking animals because the detection of patterns is important for learning and decision making. However, the brain may see patterns in the world even when none exist, in order for us to feel some understanding and control of our environment; we are uncomfortable with chaos (Shermer, 2008). For reductionist theories of religion, this proclivity makes us see the hand of God in our lives. This idea is related to Gould's "spandrel" theory of exaptation, the idea that a trait that developed in evolution for a particular function may eventually come to serve another function. For example, bird feathers may have originally evolved for warmth but eventually evolved into wings. This dual-inheritance theory suggests that belief in supernatural entities is a byproduct of the evolution of the brain's cognitive abilities that were co-opted to motivate pro-social behavior. Or, religious emotions such as awe and wonder evolved for other purposes but are co-opted by religion; they did not evolve primarily to produce religion. (This view tends to undermine claims that emotions such as awe are fundamentally religious). From this perspective, when we feel we are in touch with a personal God, we are actually calling on brain structures that evolved for other reasons. For many evolutionary psychologists, even the human sense of morality, which makes us behave well towards others, is based on brain processes that are the result of natural selection, since cooperation with others evolved to foster survival. Similarly, according to Boyer (2001), an emotion such as disgust that evolved to make us avoid hazardous food may contribute to the notion of ritual pollution found in various traditions. There may also be aspects of the human mind that evolved to allow credulity in situations when survival depends on group thinking rather than thinking independently, a phenomenon known as conformity bias. Another important evolutionary development is the human ability to imagine that other people have minds that function like our own, so that we can anticipate the actions of others and make sense of their behavior—the Theory of Mind. It is then possible to imagine a divine mind, not connected to a body. Because we cannot conceive of having no mind or not existing, the notion of an afterlife is appealing.

Evolutionary accounts of religion can be used in these ways to try to disprove the validity of religious belief, but they are all based on the assumption that purely biological or physical explanations are sufficient to explain religion and its cultural transmission (Feierman, 2009). They therefore take a metaphysical position about the primacy of the brain. However, it seems likely that cultural phenomena such as religion are too complex to be solely explained by evolutionary theory, which is basically a biological theory. When trying to understand the origin of religion we also have to consider cultural evolution and the social transmission of beliefs, rituals, texts, and other aspects of religion that are more than biological. From Jung's point of view, the origin of religion results from the presence of the Self in the psyche and cannot be reduced to a purely biological mechanism.

A sociological approach to religion argues that spiritual beliefs are simply acquired within a culture and transmitted to each new generation. For example, belief in reincarnation is much more common in Asia than in the USA. Such beliefs have been shaped and re-shaped over a long period of time. Apparently, some religious ideas are particularly acceptable to human beings. Whether this is the result of the structure of the brain or it occurs for some other reason, such as an archetypal predisposition, is hard to say. It may well be that we have evolved to conform with others and to believe what the people around us believe, because these strategies foster survival by increasing group cohesion and thus safety. However, evolutionary processes that developed the necessary brain regions may have been guided by a spiritual principle, which may use the brain as an organ of its expression. The fact that the brain has systems that correlate with religious phenomena does nothing to dismiss the objective reality of such phenomena. The brain may have evolved to allow us to detect the spiritual dimension.

Religion and the Brain

The question of why some people are religious and others are not became more complicated when, in 1997, neuroscientists claimed to have discovered a "God-module" in the temporal lobes of the brain. For some scientists this discovery implied that there is a neurological substrate for religious faith, so that some of us may be more hard-wired for it than others. This was not the first attempt to find a neurological explanation for religion. Jaynes (1982) made a strong claim about the origin of religion in the brain. He believed that self-reflective consciousness did not arise until about 1000 BCE, and until that time, humans possessed a bicameral mind, or a mind that was divided into two chambers. The experiences of the right hemisphere of the brain were the source of auditory hallucinations that were perceived by the left hemisphere to be the voice of gods or spirits. These hallucinatory voices would appear whenever the individual encountered a problem that could not be managed based on custom or habit. Novel or stressful situations were likely to trigger such experience. Jaynes suggested that because characters in early works such as the *Iliad* and the early books of the Hebrew Bible (ca. 1000 BCE) lacked introspection or self-consciousness about their own behavior, the gods took the place of such self-awareness. People seemed to be moved about by the gods rather than their own initiative. Not until the later *Odyssey* (ca. 750 BCE) did the characters in the story feel as though they made their own decisions, suggesting a more evolved consciousness. Jaynes believed that in our time the right hemisphere is suppressed in favor of the left hemisphere. We also have a different form of consciousness because of historical and cultural changes, so we no longer hear these voices. Jaynes believed that religious ecstasy and schizophrenia are contemporary expressions of the old form of consciousness, and religion is an expression (or a relic) of our thirst for the old bicameral experience that used to warn people and give advice. Janes thinks that the loss of our bicameral mind answers the question of why the gods have left us. Jaynes's book was criticized for making sweeping assertions, such as the idea that early peoples were not as self-conscious as we are. It is now understood that many functions of the brain are distributed and linked across the whole brain and cannot be neatly localized into discrete right and left sided areas.

Contemporary neuroscientists still make claims for the neurological basis of religion. Various areas of the brain have been implicated in the genesis of religious experience (Newberg, 2018). Joseph (2001, p. 107) suggests that "the essence of 'God' and of our living soul may be slumbering within the depths of the ancient limbic lobe that is buried within the belly of the brain." Persinger (1987) believes that particularly the temporal lobes of the brain are the source of religious experience, which is triggered by psychological factors such as stress and loss. He (2010) suggests that the sense of self is maintained by the left hemisphere of the brain, which is normally matched by corresponding parts of the right hemisphere, but if the right and left hemispheres become uncoordinated, the left hemisphere interprets the right hemisphere as another presence, perhaps as angels or the divine—meaning that the sense of God is illusory. However, religious experience and practices are so complex that it seems unlikely that one area of the brain will account for them; religious belief is probably related to several neural networks.

It is not surprising that spirituality involves the brain, because all experience does, but this says nothing about the source of spiritual experience. Reductionist neurological explanations for religion ("neurotheology") are not convincing, because rather than generating religious experience, the brain may only be the organ that allows us to have it. Just as the eyes are designed to allow us to see, so the brain may be designed to help us connect to the spiritual dimension. The fact that we have evolved brain pathways that predispose to religious belief says nothing about the reality or truth of those beliefs. The skeptical counter to this argument is to point out the existence of folkloric figures such as Bigfoot.

Although cognitive and neurological theories of religion often claim that religion is nothing more than a side effect of the way the brain works (Visala, 2016), these theories do not answer the important question of why religion is so emotionally important that people are willing to kill or be killed for their beliefs. Neither do such theories explain religious awe, unless this emotion evolved as a response to anything that is totally overwhelming.

Psychoanalytic Theories About Belief in God

Psychoanalysis as a discipline was explicitly atheistic in its early years, and it became an important source of the secularization of western culture in the twentieth century. Atheistic psychoanalysts typically view belief in God reductively, for example believing that the wish for a relationship with God unconsciously expresses the need for union or reunion with early objects or attachment figures. In this view, the infantile need for a figure who provides safety and love is never outgrown. Religion is therefore an inevitable product of infantile human needs. This kind of psychoanalytic reduction implies that because we can understand the origin of religion psychologically, we cannot trust its veracity. If this attitude were correct, it would undermine the value of a variety of cultural achievements.

Freud developed a spectrum of ideas about religion. He perceived a similarity between religious rituals and the private rituals carried out by people with obsessional disorders. Accordingly, in his 1907 paper "Obsessive Actions and Religious Practices," Freud suggested that religion was a form of universal obsessional neurosis that we would eventually outgrow. In *The Future of an Illusion*, Freud (1927/1964) says that religious beliefs are illusions motivated by the wish to make the world better and safer. Religious illusions are the "fulfillments of the oldest, strongest, and most urgent wishes of mankind" (p. 27). These illusions can be turned into subjective truths that resist evidence that contradicts them; in fact, religious beliefs become so strong that the believer does not care whether they can be verified or not. Religion for Freud has some psychological value because it is soothing and comforting, but he considered the need for God to be infantile and regressive, something we must outgrow.

Freud believed that religion is an achievement of civilization because it is a way of controlling instinctual drives such as aggression and sexuality, making the burden of civilization tolerable. Religion has therefore served us well so far, but it is now time for it to be superseded by the advance of science. Freud did not think the notion of God could be of any real help in dealing with human suffering. Rather, he believed we should strengthen the ego in order to cope with reality without this illusory support. For Freud, belief in God is a way of coping with human insecurities, helplessness, and our fear of death. Therefore, belief in God is essentially a defense, which helps to account for the irrational level of anger and threats of eternal damnation that believers have directed towards non-believers.

Freud believed that belief in God is fundamentally based on the child's relationship with his or her father; thus: "A personal God is, psychologically speaking, nothing other than an exalted father" (Freud, 1910). According to Freud, the child's image of his father is internalized during the resolution of the Oedipus complex, which forms the nucleus of the superego.[v] God-images therefore have Oedipal roots, because in the mind the father is replaced by the superego, which is why religion always has components of fear and guilt. The child's father image is repressed, and the quality of the original relationship with the child's father is reproduced and projected into the heavens in the form of a Father-God. However, God-as-Father is an ambivalent image, consisting of a mixture of love and fear, since although God is protective, he also prohibits certain desires and punishes those who disobey his laws. (For many observers, this idea points to Freud's ambivalence towards his own father.) Freud's emphasis on God as a Father suggests that obedience to the law of God, however that is understood, contains a mixture of submission, hostility, and rebelliousness that is characteristic of people with domineering fathers. Freud does not take into account religious traditions such as Hinduism that worship a goddess and do not exclusively stress a father-god. Furthermore, although the God of the Hebrew Bible is very much an Oedipal father in his omnipotence and moralism, it is noteworthy that the story of Christ leads to a very different God-image that cannot be reduced to an Oedipal theme. Freud (1927) was scornful about abstract theological notions of God, which he dismissed as vague and insubstantial.

Freud's 1913 *Totem and Taboo* attempted a historical and anthropological approach to religion. He combined the theory of Totemism (see p. 147) with his Oedipal theory, which for a male child describes the desire to eliminate the father and forbids incest with mother. *Totem and Taboo* is a psychoanalytically oriented myth, in which Freud described a scenario in which early humans lived in small groups that identified with a totem animal. The group was dominated by a powerful, jealous male who kept the women (mothers) for himself and drove off all rivals, including his own sons. One day, the sons rebelled and killed their father. By then devouring him, they identified with him and acquired his strength. However, this action filled the sons with remorse. To deal with their guilt, they forbad the killing of the totem animal, which Freud believed represented the murdered father, and they gave up their claim to their mothers, leading to the prohibition against incest. Freud believed that Totemism begins a developmental process in which the place of a totem animal is eventually taken by an anthropomorphic God. The repressed memory of the primal father reappears in the form of this God, who is initially experienced with awe and devotion, although eventually hostile feelings towards him also appear. The Oedipus complex, according to Freud, lives on in all later religious practices because each successive generation inherits the sense of guilt produced by the initial killing of the father, or even from having the fantasy of doing so. The evidence that the totem animal represents the father is partly that the tribe believes it is a descendent of the totem animal. As well, young children sometimes have a phobia of a particular type of animal that they have never seen before, which Freud attributes to a displaced fear of the child's father, who represents the totem animal.

Because Christianity teaches that humanity was redeemed from sin when Christ was crucified, and Christ reconciles us with the Father, Freud infers that the original sin was the murder of the primal father. The Christian ritual of confession and atonement for guilt acknowledges the original primal deed. The idea that Christ becomes God and replaces the father as the center of religious devotion, represents the ambivalence of the son towards the father. (Freud misunderstands Christianity here; in Christian doctrine, the son does not replace the Father—they become one, or the Son sits at the right hand of the Father.) The ancient totemic meal is repeated in the Eucharist, which symbolically repeats the eating of the body of Christ, which allows identification with him and eliminates the Father once again, repeating the early guilty deed. For Freud therefore, religion enacts a defense that allows the easing of guilt while also allowing the disguised expression of forbidden wishes.

Twenty years after the publication of *Totem and Taboo*, Freud produced a sequel in his *Moses and Monotheism*, which also assumed an analogy between the psychological life of a society and the dynamics of the individual psyche. In the later book, Freud assumed that the Israelites had killed Moses during a ritual re-enactment of the same kind of primal murder he had described in *Totem and Taboo*. Freud speculated that Moses was in fact an Egyptian aristocrat, or perhaps a priest in the court of the pharaoh Ikhnaton, who had instigated the monotheistic worship of the sun-god Aten. When the king died however, the people returned to their ancient polytheism. In his disappointment, Moses turned to the Jews, instructed them in the religion of Aten, and introduced them to the Egyptian practice of circumcision. Moses postulated a deity even higher than the sun, who was invisible, omnipotent, and omniscient. With a group of followers, Moses led the people out of Egypt. However, his religion was too spiritualized for the people, who overthrew and killed Moses. But his teachings were preserved, and later the people were influenced by the worship of Yhwh, a local volcano god. The Midianite leader of this religion was also named Moses. Eventually, Yhwh was credited with liberating the people from Egypt and the story was told in a way that substituted the original Egyptian Moses for the Midianite Moses. In order to make it seem that Yhwh had always been the god of the Jews, the legends of Abraham, Isaac, and Jacob were invented. In this way, the religion of the original Moses gradually returned and became dominant. Hence, according to Freud, arose the Jewish notion of a single almighty God. But the people also carry the burden of the repressed memory of the original father murder in their totemic past, and their remorse over this act leads to the wish for a Messiah, who would represent the return of the murdered father.

Both *Totem and Taboo* and *Moses and Monotheism* are based on a hypothetical reconstruction of historical events whose veracity has been rejected by most anthropologists and historians. Freud's notion of a primal horde that killed and ate an original father is now seen as pure conjecture. Furthermore, Totemism is not universal, and where it does exist Totemism rarely entails the killing and eating of the totem god-animal. Freud's ideas about Moses are not generally accepted; the existence of a Midianite Moses is widely denied, and so is the idea that the religion of Aten is the source of Moses's monotheism. Freud's idea that guilt over the putative murder of a primal father is transmitted to subsequent generations is impossible, because knowledge of an ancient event could not be transmitted biologically to subsequent generations.[vi] However, Freud rejected anthropological and historical criticisms of his theory; he saw these criticisms as a defense against the fact that the Oedipal situation "must" have been a factor in the origin of religion. Evidence contradicting this theory "must" be based on repression among the anthropologists reporting this evidence. Another important critique of Freud's approach to religion is that he selects only certain aspects of religion, such as belief in a Father-God and the practice of religious rituals, and he treats them as if they represent the entirety of religion. He thus ignores religion's complexity. Freud takes the huge step of transforming metaphysical beliefs into psychological realities. However, Freud realized that his psychological explanations of the origin of religion do not refute its truth claims. It is also worth noting that while Freud thought that religion is infantile, a great deal of subsequent research has demonstrated its value in terms of both mental and physical health, such as reduced levels of suicide and drug abuse among religious people (Green et al, 2010).

Despite Freud's negative opinion, some early psychoanalysts spoke favorably about religion. Ian Suttie (1932; 1935) was positive about the value of religion, which he saw as a form of psychotherapy. He felt that the drive to restore or substitute for mother's love as it was experienced in infancy is important in the development of religion. He noted the importance of matriarchal religions that cannot be explained by Freud's focus on the father image. He found in matriarchal traditions the projection of pre-Oedipal elements, while in patriarchal traditions he found the projection of Oedipal material. Harry Guntrip (1956) believed that religious experience is an expression of human nature. He pointed out that religion provides a good object relationship to which the anxious individual can turn for refuge, and this belief strengthens the individual if other forms of healing are unavailable. He also thought that the sense of a cosmic connection has its earliest roots in a good infant-mother relationship. Guntrip pointed out that religion may become contaminated by the individual's psychological difficulties. Schizoid people cannot tolerate the emotional and relational aspects of religion, and so tend to intellectualize it. Depressives who consider themselves to be sinful find some relief from their self-punishment by attacking the sins of other people. Troubled people yearn for religion's promise of salvation, and even disturbed people may be stabilized by religion. Emotionally healthy people need communion with others and with the divine; so much so that, for Guntrip, full maturity involves "an essentially religious way of experiencing life" (1956, p. 198). Erik Erikson (1950) also finds the roots of religious experience in the individual's early relationship with mother, who provided a source of religious images of nurture, care, and trust (Zock, 1990). For Erikson (1993), believers are nostalgic for a "hallucinatory sense of unity with a maternal matrix" (p. 26), although Erikson resisted entirely reducing religion to infantile origins and he maintained that religion in its mature form is valuable for psychological development. Erikson (1964) believed that the infantile experience of being responded to whenever the baby is distressed develops basic trust, which allows the child to develop hope, which ultimately leads to mature faith. Religion has thus "shrewdly played into man's most childlike needs" (p. 153). The formation of basic trust, according to Erikson, affects the individual's capacity to experience the world as loving, and thus influences the individual's God-image.

Donald Winnicott talks about religion in terms of his concept of transitional space, which is an intermediate area between the child's subjectivity and the outer world. It is therefore not fully outer and not fully inner; it has meaning within the child's imagination. In this psychological realm are found fantasy, play, creativity, reverie, and religious belief. Winnicott's idea of a transitional object suggests that the infant invests a toy or blanket with special meaning. This object has a soothing capacity, since it stands in for mother's presence and defends against the anxiety that would be produced by mother's absence. The transitional object is more real than a hallucination but not entirely objectively real. A transitional object is a kind of illusion that eventually helps the child towards reality and towards mature relationships, rather than being a flight from reality.[vii] Meissner (1978b) and Rizzuto (2013) both see the God-image as a kind of transitional object in Winnicott's sense. However, unlike typical transitional objects such as teddy bears, the God-image is not forgotten; it remains available throughout life and is called upon during times of crisis. Rizzuto believes that parents suggest the idea of God to the child as a way of explaining causality, and this gives the child the idea of a power beyond people. Pointing out that the projection theory does not solve the problem of God's existence, Winnicott (1989, p. 205) asked: "If God is a projection, even so is there a God who created me in such a way that I have the material in me for such a projection?"

Psychoanalytic self-psychologists believe that figures such as God or Jesus are imagined or experienced as unfailing, idealized selfobjects,[viii] entirely reliable, totally empathic, powerful and soothing, providing goals, values, and a sense of direction in life. For the self-psychologist, belief in God, and the search for mystical experience, are ways to cope with narcissistic vulnerabilities resulting from failures to find an adequate selfobject in childhood (Rector, 2001). Gruenwald (2004) suggests that for Christians Jesus took over the empathic role previously occupied by the God-image of the Hebrew Scriptures. In fact, because Jesus was human, he was felt to have an increased capacity for empathy. Rituals of baptism and the Eucharist may also be seen in terms of a twinship transference or an unconscious participation in the life of Jesus. Within Judaism, study of the scriptural texts, combined with prayer, ritual, obedience to the law, and messianic expectations, became idealized selfobjects. The intense importance of religion when it is used as a selfobject can be seen in the behavior of religious people when their faith is challenged, which has often led to war, bigotry, and phenomena such as the Inquisition. In all these approaches, whether using Freud's original formulation or later psychoanalytic theory, the individual's representation of God is seen to be derived from human emotional needs, ignoring the possible influence of the divine itself and the role of the experience of the Self.

Very gradually, instead of these reductive accounts, contemporary psychoanalysts are beginning to recognize something in the psyche beyond the personal level, analogous to the Self in Jung's work. Here we think of Bion's "O," his term for the ultimate reality from which the inner world arises, and Winnicott's sense of a sacred core in a person that is private, silent, and incommunicado, that must not be violated. Bollas

(1999) speaks of an intelligence that moves through the mind and which creates its objects. He says: "If there is a God, this is where it lives" (p. 195).

As well as exoteric or mainstream religion, mystical experience has also not fared well in the hands of the psychoanalysts. The mystic's report of union with God is often interpreted as a return to an infantile merger with mother, as a regression to an early infant-mother symbiotic relationship (Lewin, 1950), or as an imagined pre-genital paradise (Pollock, 1989). Rolland Romain described the mystic's "oceanic feeling" as a state of being limitless and eternal or at one with the universe. Freud regarded this state of mind as a regressive state of lost primary narcissism that occurred prior to the development of a differentiated ego. Mystical states have also been thought of as a type of transitional phenomenon, employed for the sake of self-soothing. It has also been assumed that emotional distress may lead to mystical experience as a way of coping. Kakar (1991) suggests that visionary experiences are attempts to lessen the agony of separation from early objects. Mysticism is also said to be a way of dealing with grief, because many mystics have experienced early losses. This line of thought substitutes pre-Oedipal, maternal accounts of religious experience instead of Freud's Oedipal and paternal explanations for religion.

It is striking how often psychoanalysts tend to view mysticism, or states in which the individual experiences union with the divine, as a regressive return to an infantile state of mind. This attitude assumes that ego-consciousness is the highest achievable state of consciousness. The meditative and mystical traditions would dispute this claim; union with the divine might not be a regressive return to blissful union with mother but the experience of a much larger, infinite Consciousness.

Working therapeutically with religious people, it does sometimes appear that a relationship with God or the Church may substitute for either a missing father image or for missing maternal containment. There may be an obvious relationship between attitudes to the Church and attitudes to the individual's mother or father. Needless to say, however, such psychological parallels do not affect religions' truth claims. The source of the sense of God or the experience of God may be the divine itself, unrelated to psychodynamic factors, which may only color one's God-image. Going beyond the idea of God as a transitional object, Spero (1992) believes that we might be able to form a God-image that is objective rather than purely subjective, because God actually exists as more than a mental representation. This assertion obviously takes us into areas of faith rather than psychology, but it is relevant to believers.

The fact that we may color our image of God with parental projections does not mean that there is no God onto which the projections land. Just as belief in God can be understood through a psychodynamic lens, so too can atheism, which might result from unconscious ambivalence towards early caregivers, from an Oedipal desire to get rid of the father (making death-of-God theology a manifestation of the Oedipus complex), or just from sheer narcissistic unwillingness to submit to anything larger than oneself. One gets the sense from narrowly reductive account of religion that the writer is searching for evidence to confirm a pre-existing bias. Reminiscent of dogmatic religion, some of the attempts to dismiss religion show little intellectual humility.

The Influence of Family Dynamics on the Development of God-images

The dynamics of early relationships in childhood radically color our projections onto our God-image, or they affect the representation of God in the mind. This mental image includes both ideas and feelings, some of which may be unconscious. The quality of this image may be more important to the individual than the teachings of the religious tradition that he or she follows. One might be able to converse with this internal image, or one may be afraid of it or dislike it. Rizzuto (1979) believes that atheists have an image of God in which they do not believe. Unlike Freud, Rizzuto thinks that the God-image can be useful in the development of the personality and can be a part of healthy psychological functioning.

Several authors (St. Clair, 1994; Rizzuto, 1979; Vergote, 1969; McDargh, 1983, 1992) have pointed out that children develop a rudimentary image of God based on a combination of the ways in which people behave in the child's family of origin and the God-imagery the child is taught during his or her religious education. This image continues to evolve throughout the course of the individual's life and is colored by experiences that tend to either confirm or deny it. The infantile core of this image of God might be punitive and angry or benevolent and loving, depending on the child's early relational experiences, or this image might try to compensate for parental shortcomings. It may be difficult for the individual to reconcile her personal God-image with that of her religious tradition.

Religious ideas are transmitted in often unconscious ways by the child's culture and family, so the growing child is exposed to preconceived notions about God that are taken for granted (Vergote et al, 1981). These ideas are internalized as felt truths. As well, Rizzuto (1979) believes that one's mental representation of God is influenced by the (largely unconscious) mental representations of early objects, or one's primary caregivers. Her study was based on the religious ideas of 20 people, based on in-depth, structured interviews. Unlike Freud's exclusive emphasis on the child's father, Rizzuto and other writers have pointed out the important influence of the child's mother and grandparents in the formation of a God-representation. It has often been suggested that the yearning for God is reminiscent of the yearning for the pre-oedipal mother, and several writers have pointed out that the individual's God-image may more closely resemble characteristics of the child's mother than his or her father. Hutch (1990) suggested that the center of sacred authority in life is a powerful mother-imago. He believes that this early psychological experience leaves a residue that is the psychological origin of "all religious myths, rituals, doctrines, communities, and ethics" (p. 85). Early experiences of mothering may be unconsciously evoked, for example, when singing hymns about the love of God in church.

In most cases the parent that is most emotionally important to the child has the largest effect on the child's God-image. Since parental imagoes may be positive or negative or ambivalent, the God-representation follows suit. Whether the family child-rearing practices are harsh and punitive or loving and forgiving radically affects the individual's God-image. Thus, a punitive, angry father is projected onto the image of a dangerous God. Rizzuto believes that the God-image is formed from a combination of the actual parents, the wished-for parents, and the parents who are feared in the individual's imagination. Rizzuto points out that there may be a direct opposition between the characteristics of one's God representation and the experience of one's parents, for example when God is idealized while parents are frustrating. That is, some aspects of one's God-image may correspond to the properties of parental objects while others compensate for it. These experiences in the family are eventually combined with the creedal influences to which the child is exposed. Rizzuto believes that throughout the course of one's life, one's God-image is continuously modified as it is affected by life experiences that interact with the God-image of the individual's religions tradition. Accordingly, people may have a very private God-image that consists of a combination of theological teachings and childhood residues, some of which are unconscious.

Once the God-image has formed, Rizzuto thinks it cannot be made to disappear: "it can only be repressed, transformed, or used" (1979, p. 90). As spiritual development occurs, the individual's God-image usually becomes more sophisticated. If the God-image of childhood does not change it may eventually be experienced as irrelevant or meaningless as the individual matures. Meissner (1984) points out that the God-image expresses itself differently at different stages of life and different levels of development. A primitive image of God is said to be in place by the age of three (Hyde, 1990).

One of the critiques of Rizzuto's idea is that it makes God nothing but the sum of early object relationships and does not leave enough room for the reality of the divine as a contributor to the representation of the God-image (Leavy, 1990). Or, as McDargh (1983, p. 245) points out, "God may be a source for the sense of 'God,'" a view that is consonant with Jung's idea that there is an innate or a priori God-image in the psyche that is not the result of introjection. While this potential is certainly colored by local influences such as family and culture, clinical experience suggests that there are aspects of the individual's God-image that are not exclusively the result of these influences. Dreams occur in which the Self appears in ways that are not necessarily related to parental imagoes.

Cornett (1998) points out that demanding, narcissistic parents might foster a narcissistic God-image, expressed in a commandment such as "you shall have no other gods before me" (Exod. 20: 3) This type of God-image sets high standards and demands absolute obedience, which may correspond to a style of child rearing. When children must meet their parents' need for affirmation, when love and acceptance are conditional, accompanied by the constant threat of parental withdrawal or abandonment, the resulting God-image produces anxiety and insecurity about the state of the relationship. One's God-image is affected not only by this kind of early relationship but also by one's psychopathology. People suffering from severe psychopathology often have negative images of God; either God is seen as detached and passive (among schizoid and paranoid people) or (among obsessionals) as a harsh, punitive judge (Schaap-Jonker et al, 2002). People who have had early trauma or abandonment, or whose parents were detached and cold, tend to experience God as irrelevant, distant or punitive (Schaap-Jonker, 2002). Unconsciously repeating the pattern of their early object relations, such individuals may assume that God is an angry judge and that they have to live up to high expectations. Such a God-image may be reinforced by religious education. The individual's long-standing God-image may become untenable because of a traumatic life event that contradicts the teachings of the individual's tradition. One's notion of an entirely loving God may be destroyed by serious trauma, and with it an important buttress to the stability of the self and its sense of identity may be lost.

The patriarchal God-image of an imperial, triumphant war God who hands down law that must be followed may appeal to people whose father fit this description, to whom the individual had to submit. Images of hell found in medieval religious iconography either terrify the individual into conformity or allow him to enjoy watching rebellious individuals suffer. Such a punitive God-image might be related to a punitive superego that results from harsh parenting. A person whose parents were constantly critical may consciously or unconsciously believe that God is constantly looking over his or her shoulder, ready to criticize. Or, the individual may be preoccupied with the need to be religiously scrupulous because conformity pleased his parents. The transformation of such a God-image may be seen in psychotherapy as the parental imagoes are explored, and religious beliefs based purely on projection are discovered.

The induction of excessive guilt and shame in children predisposes them to a God-image or an overall theology that makes the individual feels particularly sinful, or it makes people predisposed to belief in a savior who relieves them of guilt. People are drawn to God-images that reflect their psychological structures, so that a person afflicted with guilt and shame for developmental reasons may adhere to a theology that stresses divine censure. The Judeo-Christian tradition has fostered the idea that suffering is a punishment for sin. In the Hebrew Scriptures, drought, famine, and death occur when God's commandments are disobeyed (Deuteronomy 11:15-17). The prophets said that the nation of Israel was conquered by invaders because they were unfaithful to God (Jeremiah 2:14-17), the Psalms teach that sin makes the body sick (Psalm 32:3), and Jesus warns about the wrath of God being turned against the wicked (Matthew 13:41-42). These threats are ways of controlling people, and they all take advantage of unconscious guilt, fear, and shame that may have developmental roots. We see parental metaphors in the Bible when God is said to punish the people of Israel for their iniquities because God loves them (Amos 3:2), or when God disciplines us "for our good" (Hebrews 12:10), or God's anger is always contained within his compassion (Lamentations 3:31-33). These biblical comments are examples of the kind of "for your own good" rationalizations used by abusive parents. One can understand the ambivalence felt by a child towards such a parent, just as one can understand the theist's ambivalence towards a punitive God who is also supposed to be a shepherd (Psalm 23) who protects the innocent and poor (Ezekiel 34:11-16) and saves the oppressed (Psalm 146:7-9). The Christian tendency to blame all evil on human sinfulness begins with the Christian interpretation of the story of Adam and Eve and continues throughout the Bible (Romans 5:12). The assertion of universal human sinfulness is central to Christian teachings. Among believers, this attitude worsens the low self-esteem of individuals who were raised with guilt-inducing parents. These kinds of psychological structures are often more important determinants of the individual's God-image than the teachings of the individual's religious tradition. Because of the influence of early relational dynamics, people who belong to very conservative religious traditions may nevertheless develop a benevolent God-image, and people from liberal traditions may develop a punitive God-image. Although the promise of eventual salvation or eternal life allays anxiety, a punitive God-image may at times create the very anxiety it purports to alleviate by promising divine punishment for sin. Although God-images may be based on the superego, in which case they are characterized by power and an emphasis on obedience and guilt, over time the individual's God-image may change as he or she matures, often becoming more loving.

Various other individual psychodynamics are projected onto the God-image; thus, notions of a Judgment Day (Acts 17:31) may be unconsciously connected to fears of parental judgment. Belief in an afterlife may be related to extreme death anxiety. Notions such as the End Times may have developed to satisfy the need for ultimate retribution, justice, reward and punishment, and the destruction of evil.

There is a significant correlation not only between the individual's God-image and parental imagoes but also between this image and the individual's self-image (Meissner, 1994; Laurence, 1997; Vergote et al., 1981) and self-esteem (Greenway, 2003; Francis, 2001). Loving God-images tend to be related to the individual's positive sense of self-worth, while threatening and punitive God-images are related to a negative sense of self. If one can accept oneself, one has a more accepting God-image (Benson and Spilka, 1973). Not only do we project our own psychology onto our God-image, we also identify with the idealized qualities of our preferred God-image, and these qualities become part of our own self-image. This process may affect personality development.

Individual numinous experience can radically transform the individual's God-image, as we see in the biblical story of Job (Corbett, 1996, 2011). One's God-image may also be affected by the political and social situation of the times. It is very common for people to project culturally desirable qualities onto their God-image and imagine that God approves or disapproves of certain behavior, based on their own preferences. Since different societies have different preferences, "holy" wars based on different God-images have been common. Broadly speaking, as human morality has evolved, the idealized moral qualities that people project onto their God-image has also improved *pari passu*.

Attachment Theory and the God image

Traditional theists assume that their deity will always be available as needed. Attachment theorists argue that the need for such an attachment figure and belief in its constant availability are fundamental dynamics underlying theistic religion. Attachment needs explain why faith in God provides emotional security that is always present for believers. In a similar manner to the object relations theory of the God-image, attachment theory suggests that the quality of one's God-image is formed on the basis of the quality of attachment one has had with one's primary caregivers. God, the Blessed Virgin Mary, or Jesus are perfectly reliable attachment figures that are available for protection in the event of danger (Kirkpatrick, 2005). One's style of attachment to one's God-representation may correspond to or reflect the way one was attached to early caregivers, or it may contradict or compensate for one's early attachment style. The correspondence style means that we attach to God in a way that is similar to the way we were attached to an early figure. The compensatory model makes God a substitute attachment figure because the early caregivers were not secure, in which case the relationship with God compensates for parental failures. When compensation predominates, people whose early relationships were distant or unavailable may develop an image of God as loving and totally available. People with secure attachment styles tend to see God in a benevolent light, as caring and loving, and they see themselves as worthy of God's love. People with insecure attachment styles are more likely to see God as angry, demanding, and punitive, but these individuals may find in their relationship to God a more secure attachment figure than they have been able to achieve in human relationships. Anxious/ambivalent attachment styles are correlated with the idea that God metes out punishment inconsistently. Dismissive/avoidant attachment correlates with the sense that God is remote. That is, based on the individual's early attachment history, God can seem to be loving or hateful, constantly present and a safe haven, or abandoning. Based on these attachment styles, the individual can either rebel against God or be obedient. He or she may trust in God or deny God's existence.

There is evidence that belief in a loving God increases the likelihood of having a sense of meaning, direction, and purpose in life (Stroope et al., 2013). These factors are important for both psychological and physical health (Levin, 2010). The sense of a loving God-image provides confidence that one is cared for and helps to alleviate suffering. The individual's sense of a loving relationship with God exerts a protective effect that allows the individual to cope with adversity (Levin, 2002). The individual with this kind of God-image feels that God's purpose is being served by the individual's life situation, and this provides consolation during difficult periods. Such a loving image of God supports self-esteem. For Roman Catholics, the image of Mary is a powerful image of maternal love.

Behavioral Approaches to Religion

Behaviorists explain religious behavior in terms of learning theory. Atheists in this tradition such as Vetter (1958) reject all spiritual notions such as soul or spirit because they do not have an observable referent, nor is there empirical evidence of their existence. In this view, notions of divinities are meaningless; they arose because of the assumption that events around us are the result of animistic agents. Based on the work of Skinner, Vetter sees religion as superstitious behavior analogous to the behavior of pigeons whose behavior was rewarded intermittently, in a manner that had no relationship to the bird's actual activity. The result was that whatever behavior the bird happened to be doing when the reward appeared was reinforced. Vetter suggested that this behavior is a prototype of human religious behavior, which becomes a habit that is rationalized with religious explanations. Vetter believes that religious ideas about gods are a function of the way we learned to behave towards parents.

In his view, religions are perpetuated because of social approval of behavior such as prayer and rituals. This reinforcement conditions behavior, much of which is emphasized by self-serving clergy. This skeptical position is also held by other behaviorists such as Skinner (1974), who believes that once rituals are learned, myths are invented to explain and perpetuate them. For him, faith is simply a way to account for persistent religious behavior when we do not realize it is being reinforced by environmental events. For behaviorists therefore, notions such as sin and morality are simply behaviors that are shaped by social pressures and reinforcements. Religious institutions and doctrines about heaven and hell are merely instruments of control.

Although these behavioral views of religion are simplistic, it is striking how the behavior of deities, such as the God of the Hebrew Bible, is often interpreted by their devotees in terms of reward and punishment. However, the typical behaviorist critique of religion is largely based on a critique of fundamentalism, and only takes into account a limited range of observable religious behavior. The interpretation of religious belief in strictly behavioral terms ignores human subjectivity, the influence of the unconscious, and the complex sources of human intentions, goals, and feelings, none of which are publicly observable behavior. Faith too is very subjective and not necessarily observable. Behaviorism cannot deal adequately with psychological phenomena such as love, desire, and human ideals that are central not only to religion but also to our humanity and our lived experience. The complexity of our societies adds another factor that undermines the behaviorist account. In particular, the behaviorist cannot explain numinous experience, except reductively.

Religious Role Taking: The Social Origins of Religion

The Swedish psychologist Hjalmar Sundén (Capps, 1987) suggests a social constructivist approach to religion. He believes that religious experience could not occur in the absence of a socially-learned religious ideas. Religious traditions and texts teach people specific roles, which are organized models of performance related to particular life situations in which we are expected to behave in a certain way. This view sees religion as based in powerful mythological narratives that are codified in sacred texts and subsequently transmitted to each generation by a socially acquired learning process. Sacred texts also provide models of interpretation for future events, and therefore an eschatology.

According to Sundén, we may identify with characters in biblical stories, or the individual can imagine himself interacting with God as if he were participating in the story. The behavior of the biblical God-image structures the Bible-reader's perception of her own behavior. The Bible-reader assumes that God will deal with him the way God dealt with biblical characters with whom the reader identifies; he imagines that he is in a similar relationship with God. The myth then structures the person's perception of the world. The Bible-reader thus develops a latent psychological propensity to experience his world in a religious manner, while prayer and ritual reinforce a specific religious framework. The myth becomes a living reality for the person when he experiences a life situation that corresponds to the mythic story.

Scholarly interest in Sundén's approach has declined since the 1990's, even though it fits well within the social constructivist and narrative psychological movements. However, it fails to account for the ways in which numinous experiences arise before they are contextualized and interpreted by the individual's social frame of reference. Numinous experience arises from the autonomous levels of the psyche and may have little to do with the subject's immediate social setting.

In summary, the ways in which religious traditions talk about their God-image and the human relationship to it are often colored by typical patterns of human relations and human psychology in general. However, this similarity does not show that God is nothing but a projection of human psychology, as Feuerbach and Freud suggested; the presence of such projections reveals the limitations of anthropomorphic imagery.

A Punitive God-image and its Relationship to Personal Psychology: Martin Luther

Martin Luther (1483-1546) provides us with an example of the relationship between an individual's personality, developmental dynamics, and his God-image. This kind of psychohistory[ix] or psychobiography does not have a good reputation, because of skepticism that we can make an accurate psychological assessment of a complex character who lived long ago, based purely on published material, some of which is speculative. However, a good deal of Luther's writing, speeches, and some examples of his behavior have been preserved. Although there remains the problem of the bias of his editors and translators, Luther had a gift for language, and his writing is often emotionally intense and does not seem edited.

Nevertheless, a degree of speculation is inevitable when discussing his psychology, which can only be based on the available textual evidence.

Despite the problems involved in psychological interpretation of historical personalities, modern research such as that of Rizzuto (1979) makes it clear that an individual's development history influences his or her God-image. To completely ignore this history, or to ignore the relationship between a person's character structure and his theology, would be as mistaken as using psychological theory to explain too much, which was an important critique of Erikson's 1958 biography, *Young man Luther*. Psychological theory has advanced considerably since that book, especially in our knowledge of trauma and in the development of relational psychoanalytic theory.

It is possible to draw parallels between some of Luther's religious beliefs and what is known about developmental factors in his childhood, because a good deal of information about Luther's inner life is available. However, we do not know how reliable this information is, or how much weight to give any particular datum. For example, it seems clear that Luther's relationship to his father had an important influence on his personality and his religious beliefs, but this relationship was only one among other factors that influenced his theology, which also has to be understood in its historical, social, and religious context.

Luther was melancholic. He suffered from spiritual despair and persistent brooding sadness, which seem to have a psychologically understandable origin, although some biographers believe his depression was endogenous, and some barely mention it, yet it was a formative influence in his theology. In fact, he believed that sorrow is "the essence of human existence" (Haile, 1980, p. 301) and sorrow is the place where God is hidden. Luther tried to make sense of his melancholy in religious terms, seeing it as a spiritual sickness—for instance, he thought that Satan causes us to dwell on our sins, which produces melancholy. Luther also says that he was driven by various fears and the need to control them. He had a great fear of death, and he struggled with the question of whether God could really raise us from the dead. He asked himself why, if he had faith in God, would he be afraid of death? He suffered from periodic attacks of terror that filled him with dread. The misery produced by these terrors caused him to practice extreme asceticism, which he thought might pacify an angry God (Schwiebert, 1950). His discovery of the gospel of grace (the justification of sinners through Christ) removed the need for his ascetical practices, but nevertheless, his depressions persisted for the rest of his life (Steinmetz, 2002).

Most biographers say that Luther felt so unworthy that his sins kept him from God and made God angry with him. Luther felt a deep sense of sinfulness, and at least for the first part of his life he understood Christ to be a punitive, angry judge. When he said his first mass after his ordination in 1507, he was so afraid of God that he panicked and had to be persuaded to finish the mass. He was in constant doubt about his salvation and about whether God would forgive him. This harsh God-image can at least in part be understood in terms of his early object relations and in terms of our modern understanding of trauma in childhood.

One possible source of Luther's melancholia was that as a child he was regularly and severely beaten by his father. Some Luther specialists report this story while others deny it, but there is evidence for it in his *Table Talk*, notes taken by his followers during meals. For example, discussing his childhood, Luther says: "My father once whipped me so severely that I fled from him and it was difficult for him to win me back again to himself" (Smith, 2016, p. 1). On at least one occasion he reported that his mother beat him "till the blood flowed" for stealing a nut (Haile, p. 242).[x] Corporal punishment of this kind was common among the child rearing practices of the time, but Luther may have been a particularly sensitive child. Erikson (1958) says that Martin was afraid of his father and hated him, but he also felt deep sadness about the way he was treated. Martin could not get close to his brutal father but also could not get away from him. Erikson thinks that Martin's father's behavior and Martin's rage at his father was a source of Martin's doubt about divine righteousness. At age 7, Martin went to Latin school where he was beaten for speaking German instead of Latin or for speaking out of turn—there was no verbal freedom. Later, it became important for him to speak his mind against what he saw as papal abuses, and it was important to feel that his words were divinely sanctioned. In school, each occasion on which he acted against the rules was counted and recorded in a secret ledger, and he was beaten for bad behavior. Some of Luther's biographers discount the importance of all this beating, but it clearly is the kind of abuse that would produce emotional damage. Erikson refers to the beatings Martin experience as "the mutilation of the child's spirit; for such mutilation undercuts the life principle of trust" (p. 70), and modern theory would see this kind of trauma as a form of soul murder in Shengold's (1991) sense.[xi] Perhaps Luther's experience of childhood abuse contributed to his feelings of terror, which felt as though he was being attacked by God himself. He was constantly judged as a child, and he was afraid of the judgment of God.

Both Luther's early selfobjects were unempathic to a traumatic degree—his experience of recurrent abuse and their chronic failure to be empathically responsive ruptured his selfobject tie to them, with no opportunity for repair. This kind of betrayal predisposes children to depression, partly because it violates the bond of trust between parent and child (Bacal et al, 1990). Such a failing selfobject milieu in childhood leads to internal emptiness, feelings of hopelessness, despair, and damage to the child's sense of self. Given his traumatic selfobject surroundings, Luther's spiritual search can be seen in part to be an attempt to find an unfailing selfobject.

Capps (1997) suggests another approach to Luther's chronic sadness. Capps believes that male melancholia is related to early experiences of the actual or perceived loss of mother's unconditional love. This is likely to occur when mother withdraws in a cruel, traumatic manner. According to Capps, such early loss leads to the search for a new (religious) object that the individual can trust. Luther's mother is reported by most biographers to have been a harsh disciplinarian, and Capps suggests that Luther's disappointment in his mother was a source of both melancholia and also a deep sense of self-hatred. Capps believes that the Bible restores his connection to his mother because it offers Luther solace and reassurance. Erikson also suggests that rather than a focus on Mother Church, the Bible was a kind of maternal voice for Luther. Erikson believes that prayer means surrender to God the Father, but it also means to be reborn out of the matrix of the scriptures. The scriptures are the perfect or ideal mother, because they reduced Luther's deep despair and anxiety. That is why Luther insists on their importance for salvation; *sola scriptura* is his doctrine that the Bible contains everything we need for salvation and holiness. From the point of view of self-psychology, the scriptures provided an important idealized selfobject function for Luther.

Not surprisingly, given the story of his parents' and teachers' harsh treatment of him, Luther had a strong sense of sinfulness and a guilty conscience, which predisposed him to religious scrupulousness and obsessional ruminations during periods of stress. Luther struggled for years to feel that he was worthy of God's grace but was never sure that he was sufficiently contrite. He was plagued by uncertainty about his worthiness. Consequently, he stressed humility and the idea that we can claim no merit in ourselves because we are worthless—which sounds like a self-esteem problem projected into his theology, hardly surprising given the radical failure of affective attunement in his childhood. He eventually found solace in the idea that God's acceptance is based on who one is, not on what one does. Justification is given by grace (underserved divine acceptance), and is not achieved by human work—that is one reason he rejected indulgences; they mean that instead of dependence on God's grace, salvation is something one could buy.

Nothing was ever good enough for Luther's teachers or for his father; it was hard to please them. Their harshness is reflected in Luther's belief that it was impossible to obey God's law; the law is intended to show us our sinfulness—an idea that seems to be related to a sense that he could not do right, no matter how hard he tried. His was a theology of human helplessness and divine omnipotence. If nothing we can do will save us, we are so guilty that we are only saved by faith—an idea that seems to arise from his harsh superego. Luther asserted that we have no righteousness, that righteousness comes only from the righteousness of Christ attributed to us vicariously, through faith. This is a typical comment of his:

> For I hated that word 'righteousness of God,'… by which God is righteous and punishes sinners and the unrighteous. Though I lived as a monk without reproach, I felt I was a sinner before God with a most disturbed conscience. I could not believe that he was placated by my satisfaction… I hated the righteous God who punishes sinners. Secretly, if not blasphemously, certainly murmuring greatly, I was angry with God. (Spitz, 1960, p. 336)

It took Luther a long time to find a God-image that was a mixture of both wrath and compassion, until he could "forgive God for being a Father" (Erikson, p. 222). It seems clear that entering the monastery against his father's wishes had been a major act of rebellion, and rebellion also shaped Luther's later theology. Erikson claims that Luther was able to split his experience of paternal authority by submitting to the father God while rebelling against the authority of the Pope.

Luther's anxiety had an obsessional quality about it. He was extremely scrupulous about practices such as prayer, and he was concerned about getting things exactly right in relation to God. He was also preoccupied with cleanliness. He suffered from chronic constipation and sometimes used scatological language to describe his enemies. He strained to obey the monastic rules and prayers in an obsessional way; he prayed, fasted, kept vigils, and almost froze to death in cold rooms (Nichols, 2002). Some \win back the approval of his parents (or the divine parent) by being good. Unfortunately, however, religious practices could not sooth his melancholia and his obsessional anxiety. He was helped by his discovery of the idea of justification by faith alone, based on Romans 1:17, "He who through faith is righteous shall live." This idea allowed him some peace. He discovered that the righteousness of God is not in fact punitive but is a gift through faith in Christ. However, despite this discovery, and despite his idea that although we cannot achieve righteousness, God freely gives it, Luther continued to suffer from anxiety. For example, he was disturbed by the thought that he might have made a mistake in his theology and led people astray. After the period of the 1527 Reformation, he constantly heard a haunting inner voice asking him again and again *"Du bist allein klug?"* roughly meaning "are you the only smart one?" This sounds like an obsessional rumination, and such self-doubt kept him in despair. At times he was afraid he would go to hell. He saw these periods as tests from the devil that strengthened his faith. He had a lifelong belief in the concrete reality of the devil, who might even make him question the existence of God. However, his belief in the literal reality of the devil cannot be judged by modern standards. We do not know to what extent he was affected by his belief that he was living in the last days before the apocalypse, or that a contest was going on between God and Satan. This belief may explain why Luther was an advocate of the burning of witches.

This discussion would not be complete without acknowledging Luther's bitter anti-Judaism, which in some ways contributed to the Holocaust. Cultural anti-Semitism was an endemic part of Luther's Europe. Early in his life, Luther had been tolerant of the Jews and he advocated their kind treatment, but his later writing is particularly and unusually vituperative, reaching a climax in his 1543 *On the Jews and Their Lies*, in which he castigates them for rejecting Jesus and repeats medieval superstitions about their killing Christian children and poisoning wells. He calls for the destruction of Jewish schools, synagogues, and houses, and urges that Jews should become slaves of Christians. Luther scholars sometimes attribute his anti-Jewish polemics to ill health, and possibly even dementia, since they occurred late in his life. He was disappointed and frustrated by the Jews' failure to convert to Christianity, which he seems to have taken very personally because he had hoped they might embrace his new approach to religion. He was also angered by the disagreement by the rabbinical authorities with Christian interpretation of biblical passages that he believed refer to Jesus. He was angry about reports of the Jews' proselytizing activities among Christians (Edwards, 1983). Luther may have simply been reflecting the anti-Semitic values of his society, but the virulence of his personal anti-Semitism reveals a remarkable capacity for hatred. Luther's anti-Semitism offers further insight into his psychology.

The usual psychodynamic explanations for anti-Semitism include projection of the personal shadow combined with the displacement of frustrated aggression and hatred onto Jews, defenses that reduce anxiety (Ackerman et al, 1950). As well, the more precarious are one's own beliefs, the more one might displace doubt onto non-believers who can then be attacked in projection. Anti-Semitism is often found among people with authoritarian personalities, which are typically produced by harsh parental discipline and dominance. In his *Moses and Monotheism*, Freud suggested that Jews evoke envy because of their assertion that they are chosen by God, and they are the people who transmitted the moral law, which causes resentment, so that anti-Judaism is actually a disguised form of anti-Christian feelings. Perhaps the Gospel's attempt to substitute faith in Jesus for the practice of the Torah was a way of coping with envy, since this substitution made the Torah unnecessary. Or, the idea that God's covenant was transferred to the Gentiles may have been a way of overcoming envy. If anyone can be saved, not just the exclusive members of a group, there is no need for envy. One can be saved rather than chosen.

Rubin (1990) has also noted that since Jesus was Jewish, unconscious hatred of God and the ethical demands of Christianity might be displaced onto the Jews. That is, the Jews represent the superego and so attract attacks. Jesus is unconsciously hated for his compassion, love, and forgiveness of others, producing standards it is difficult to meet. It seems to be safe to victimize Jews since they do not believe in Jesus' divinity, so that God might be pleased with the attack on people who rejected his incarnation. Luther therefore felt morally justified in his attack on the Jews, feeling that he was obeying the will of God. He also justified his actions by saying he was practicing "a sharp mercy" by trying to save them from "the glowing flames" (Luther, 1971, vol. 47, p. 268) thus blaming the victims.

One source of Luther's capacity for hatred seems to have been his father's harshness, in which case his hatred of his father was displaced onto the Jews. The Jews rebelled against the Gospels and rejected their authority, so Luther may have projected his own guilt about rebellion, and his need for punishment, onto them. Luther often referred to the Jews as devils, which was a common medieval attribution. Preoccupation with the devil is now understood to represent the projection of the individual's own shadow material, thus tending to confirm the idea that the Jews represented a projective device for him.

I should note here that Luther's anti-Semitism was formally repudiated by the Lutheran Evangelical Church in 1994. I would also like to reiterate that although we could see Luther's theological development as a process of trying to solve some of his psychological difficulties, a psychological understanding of his theology tells us nothing about the truth of his views about divine grace and the doctrine of salvation. His work as a theologian is more important to the faithful than his psychological attributes. Furthermore, the theologian can claim that God works through or by means of human psychology, an important dimension of which is the human imagination.

God and the Imagination

The imagination is an important source of our ability to create something entirely new, a product that may be independent of what we can perceive by means of the five senses. This capacity includes the development of new religious ideas, including new images of God. The imagination is a factor behind the work of much theological speculation; doctrine and dogma begin as creative, imaginative hypotheses that are gradually accepted as eternal truths. The writers of scripture were radically affected by the ways they imagined God and God's actions in the world. Every biblical story or parable engages the reader's imagination, or it has no effect. Reading scriptural stories affects the believer's imagination about what God is like or why God does what he does.

Many religious traditions prescribe the correct ways in which a believer is supposed to imagine God. Concern with having the wrong image of God is expressed in the biblical prohibition against making graven images of God or worshipping idols, which would be a misuse of the religious imagination. Each tradition prescribes their own official imaginative metaphors and images when talking about God, since God is not otherwise perceptible. Hence the use of terms such as "king" or "shepherd." At the time of the Council of Nicaea, the dominant image of God used analogies from the power of the Roman emperor—Jesus was imagined as a pantocrator, a powerful emperor rather than the Shepherd of the Psalms, and the Church was increasing seen as part of the divine kingdom. One can imagine God abstractly as pure spirit, or one can imagine God in terms of a specific religious notion such as a savior or celestial father figure. The particular way we imagine God plays a part in the way we are affected by God. These metaphors are often deployed during prayer. When people pray, they often have some idea or image in mind about the object of their prayer. This image might be based on a combination of scripture, family dynamics based on the projection of parental imagoes, personal numinous experience, and idiosyncratic features unique to the individual.

The Christian sees Jesus Christ as an image of God, and when Christians talk about a personal relationship with Jesus, they may be using their imagination or inner vision, but they would not accept the idea that this makes their relationship unreal. The imagination influences the way they experience or talk about spiritual reality. The imagination can therefore be thought of as "the point of contact between divine revelation and human experience" (Green, 1989, p. 4), so that the imagination is spiritually important. The spiritual exercises of Ignatius of Loyola[xii] are a good example of the use of the imagination for spiritual purposes.

We often express the products of the imagination in terms of metaphor, which is now understood to be an essential way of speaking about concepts that cannot be described literally. Some scriptural imagery is clearly mythic, and the only meaningful way we can read it is to see it as metaphorical rather than literal and historical. However, we need new metaphors, because the imagery that appealed to people in antiquity or to fourth century bishops in the Levant is no longer meaningful to many moderns. Emphasizing this point, Campbell (2001) distinguishes between what a religious image denotes, its literal meaning, and the spiritual connotation of the image that reveals its contemporary vitality and relevance. He uses the example of the Virgin Birth, which he suggests does not refer to the biological birth of Jesus but to the birth of the spirit that we can all experience within us. Similarly, he suggests that the Promised

Land does not refer to a geographical location but to "a spiritual place in the heart that can only be entered by contemplation" (p. 7), but which anyone can enter. In this vein, the incarnation is seen as a metaphor for the emergence of the eternal into time, an example of the break-up of the unitary level of reality as it enters our time and space. If we mis-read this kind of imagery as only referring to tangible facts, the spiritual signal "becomes ever fainter" (p.7). Campbell believes that when we see the metaphorical meaning of such imagery it gives us a sense of the transcendent reality to which it is pointing.

Not surprisingly, the imagination or imaginative metaphors may not be trusted by conservative religionists who prefer to think of God-images only in terms of received authority and scripture. They believe that the imagination is too subjective and may not be consistent with revelation, which they think is objective and independent of individuals. At times, the Christian tradition has seen the imagination as intrinsically perverse, as if it would interfere with the pure contemplation of the Incarnation. Evangelicals in particular tend to be suspicious of the imagination, perhaps because of St. Paul's warning about people becoming "vain in their imaginations" (Romans 1:21, KJV) that might lead to false religion. However, to take the Bible too literally is to deny its metaphorical and symbolic level; literalizing its imagery inhibits the imagination. But at the same time, there is a risk that the imagination could produce material that is heretical, so the imagination is a potential threat to the tradition. For traditionalists, it is risky to imagine the divine in ways not sanctioned by scripture and tradition. However, the meaning and use of scripture has been re-imagined multiple times during the history of Christianity, with no general agreement about which of these re-imaginings is acceptable. Debates about the proper way to imagine God led to major splits, such as the division of the Church into Eastern and Western branches in 1054 CE, which was partly the result of conflict about who had the power to control the tradition's way of imagining God. The "official" position has often been enforced using power. Theologians have frequently insisted that their ideas are normative for everyone.

The process of re-imagining proper doctrine and dogma has continued, leading to the development of innumerable branches of the tradition, *pari passu* accompanied by heresy hunters. Jung's notion of the Self, or the intra-psychic God-image, is a re-imagining of the traditional way of thinking about God, and it too gave rise to objections from traditionalists, who forget that Christianity itself arose as a way of re-imagining God. Now that science has displaced God as an explanation for the processes of the natural world, and heaven is no longer literally "above," Jung has re-discovered the manifestations of the divine within the psyche in the form of the Self. Spontaneously arising God-images are ways in which the Self makes images or imagines itself.

Green (1989) points out, that in the Bible, the word "heart" (referring to our emotional life) is also used in the sense of the imagination. Metaphorically, the heart can be deceitful, foolish, sad, glad, or wise. Green offers multiple examples; the heart is where the word of God lives (Deuteronomy 30:14) and it is the organ of faith (Romans 10:10). Jesus says: "Blessed are the pure in heart, for they shall see God" (Matthew 5:8). Green therefore sees the heart as another point at which the human and the divine come into contact: "the place where the image of God is newly impressed on the human being is the heart" (p. 110). This is consistent with Corbin's (1969) statement that in Sufism the heart is thought to be the organ that receives knowledge of God and perceives the divine mysteries. The heart and the imagination are then both loci of revelation.

Although the imagination can be a source of illusion, the imagination does not only refer to mere wishful fantasy, something unreal; it may also be one of the means by which reality is mediated to us. Corbin (1976) points out that our inner vision, which he refers to as the *mundus imaginalis* or the imaginal world, is ontologically as real as the world of the senses and that of the intellect. This world can give us veridical information; it is the perception of another dimension of reality. However, it is important to distinguish between what the alchemists referred to as true imagination; imagery that arises spontaneously from the unconscious, and simple day-dreaming that arises from the ego, based only on wish-fulfilling fantasies that are completely unsurprising. The Self is the source of the imagination when images arise from the unconscious during the creative process, or in the case of authentic active imagination in Jung's sense. This process always produces a sense of otherness or wonder within the ego, and it becomes a form of prayer. In some ways active imagination is the opposite of repression, since it allows material to emerge from the unconscious rather than being forced into it.

Forms of Revelation: Dreams and Visions Sent by the Gods

Theistic religions commonly assert that the divine has revealed itself in history. Sometimes this is reported to occur through an event such as the revelation at Mt. Sinai, while sometimes revelation is said to occur by a process of divine inspiration or possession by a god. The words of the priestess of Apollo at his oracle at Delphi were thought to be inspired by the god himself. Prophets such as Zarathustra, Mohammed, or the prophets of ancient Israel proclaim messages that they believe were given to them by their God. Subsequent theology, doctrine, and dogma arise out of the interpretation of such messages. Often, these ideas are clarified or become definitive doctrine and dogma in debates between orthodox believers and those thought to be heretics. As ethical systems develop, they are retrospectively attributed to the founder of the tradition or to his God, and they are claimed to have been part of the original revelation. For example, the Hebrew prophets claimed that the biblical Yhwh demands or prohibits certain behavior, and they insist that these standards have always been the case.

Dreams have long been associated with the voice of a deity and can be a source of religious experience and personal revelation (Bulkeley, 2001, 2008; Corbett, 1996, 2006). Sometimes this kind of dream is associated with prophecy; God appears to Abram in a deep sleep (Genesis 15:12) and tells him what will befall his descendants. His grandson Jacob had a dream in which angels ascend and descend a ladder to heaven; God stood above the ladder and promised to give the land to Jacob's descendants (28:12-15). This dream comforted Jacob and reassured him that his descendants would spread all over the earth. These dreams became important to the Jewish tradition, both religiously and politically. Dreams appeared to King Solomon (1 Kings 3:5) and to the prophet Daniel (Daniel 7:1). The biblical Yhwh announced that although he would speak directly to Moses, he would reveal himself in a dream or vision to the prophets (Numbers 12:6-8). However, Moses warns against the possibility of dreams leading people astray (Deuteronomy 13:1-3). Accordingly, throughout the Hebrew Bible there is a thread of both skepticism about dreams—such as Jeremiah's warning about deceitful dreams (23:25-28)—and also a sense of benefit from dreams. Viewed positively, dreams are seen as an important source of divine guidance and inspiration. The rabbinical tradition continued this ambivalence about dreams, suggesting that some are sent by heaven while others have the potential for being misused.

Dreams were important in ancient Greece, at least as far back as the Homeric period. The gods communicated with mortals by means of dreams in both the *Iliad* and the *Odyssey*. Socrates had a dream that predicted the date of his death (*Crito*, 44b). Plato and Aristotle were both interested in dreams, and so were the Greek playwrights such as Sophocles and Aeschylus. Dreams were a vital component of the temples of Asclepius, the Greek god of healing, where dream incubation was practiced in the hope that the god would visit in the form of a healing dream. The second century work on the interpretation of dreams by Artemidorus of Ephesus, a third century diviner, was part of a long tradition that can be traced back to the Assyrian and ancient Egyptian civilizations.

In the New Testament, an angel tells Joseph in a dream that Mary is conceived of the Holy Spirit (Matthew 1:20-21), and he is given a prophecy about Jesus' future. Joseph is warned about Herod's intention to kill male babies in a dream and told to escape to Egypt (2:13). Because of a dream, the wife of Pontius Pilate tries to persuade him not to condemn Jesus (27:19). Saint Paul reports several dreams, which were taken to be divine messages (Acts 16:9). The Apostle Peter has dream or a vision of animals being lowered from heaven, accompanied by a voice that tells him to kill and eat, which he interprets as God commanding him to eat hitherto unclean animals and preach to the gentiles (10:11). There is a possibility that after the resurrection Jesus appeared to the disciples in dreams or visionary states, although in the Gospel of Luke when Jesus appeared to his disciples, he insists that he not a spirit. Dreams and visions of Jesus are still experienced.

The conversion of the Emperor Constantine has been attributed to a dream image of a cross of light in the sky that predicted a victory, thus convincing him to worship the Christian God. Nevertheless, the early Church fathers were skeptical about the value of dreams, which they felt might tempt people to stray. Dream interpretation in the Christian tradition fell out of favor at the end of the fourth century CE, when St. Jerome translated the prohibition against augury in Leviticus 19:26 as a prohibition against attending to dreams. This seems to have been a deliberate mistranslation, based on a terrifying dream of his own, in which he was taken before a heavenly court and punished for reading pagan authors. St. Augustine was also ambivalent about dreams because they could be too sexually stimulating and too difficult to interpret. St. Aquinas believed that dreams might be forms of divine revelation, although some could be from the devil. Martin Luther struggled with his dreams but largely rejected working with dreams in favor of trust in the Scriptures. For him, the validity of a dream depended on whether it agreed with the Bible. Suspicion about dreams continued in the Christian tradition, for example when the Inquisition listed dreams as a source of demonic temptation. In Islam, the importance of dreams has long been stressed, although this tradition too acknowledges that dreams may come from God or from the devil. In the Buddhist tradition, the future Buddha's mother is said to have dreamed that she was carried to the Himalayas, dressed in heavenly garments and anointed with perfumes and flowers. The future Buddha appeared to her as a superb white elephant holding a white lotus in his trunk. He gently struck her right side and entered her womb.

Many religious traditions have begun with the dream or vision of a founder (McNamara, 2016). Zoroaster, the founder of the influential religion of Zoroastrianism, was said to have received a vision from Ahura Mazda, the Lord of Wisdom and the high god of ancient Iran, which turned him against the tradition in which he had been raised and authorized him to preach a new truth. This event began one of the world's oldest monotheistic traditions.

Reports of revelation by means of dreams have continued. In 1823, Joseph Smith experienced either a dream or a vision of an angel named Maroni, who appeared in a white robe "beyond anything earthly I had ever seen…His whole person was glorious beyond description, and his countenance truly like lightening" (Smith, 1981, p. xiii). Smith reports that Moroni directed him to the recovery of buried scriptures that became the founding documents of the Mormon Church. There are other analogous examples in the history of religion, but it is difficult or impossible for the psychologist to assess such experiences retrospectively, without first-hand discussion with the subject of the experience.

Visionary experiences, in which the subject has a dream-like experience while awake, are controversial. Depending on the observer's metaphysical commitments, visionary experiences may be considered to be authentic numinous encounters with the sacred dimension, or they may be reduced to hysteria, hallucinations, temporal lobe epilepsy, or the eruption of REM sleep mechanisms into waking consciousness. These reductive explanations deny that such visions could be the perception of anything veridical. For skeptics, religious phenomena of various types, including numinous dreams and visions, can always be reduced to purely psychogenic phenomena or to aberrant brain mechanisms. However, a numinous dream or vision may be mediated by the brain but not generated by the brain; that is, the brain may act as an organ of reception of the spiritual dimension. Knowing the brain mechanisms involved does not necessarily solve the problem of the source of the experience. Or, for idealist philosophers, brain states are localizations of phenomena that occur within consciousness, but the brain is not the source of these phenomena (Kastrup, 2019). In any case, understanding the brain mechanisms involved in dreaming does not necessarily help us to understand the content of the dream, which often seems to come from a superior intelligence to that of the dreamer, bringing information to which the ego had no access. A purely neurological explanation of dreaming would not account for prospective dreams of events yet to happen. These types of dream have been well documented in many cultures since antiquity. The skeptic can easily dismiss such dreams as coincidences, but for Jung they indicate that the psyche has dimensions that are outside of time and space. This is a far cry from theories of dreaming that reduce it to the random by-products of brain activity during sleep. At the moment, such purely reductive explanations of dreams only indicate a physicalist metaphysical commitment.

The Bible as Mythic Truth

The great events of the Hebrew Bible, such as the stories of the Exodus from Egypt or the conquest of Canaan, may not have happened the way they are traditionally described; they may be embellished tribal legends, exaggerated though multiple repetitions over time. Some stories, such as the Garden of Eden, are clearly mythic. However, such stories have become important features of worship and group identity; they are helpful to those who can identify with their themes. Repetition of the stories expresses devotion, while stories such as Noah's flood and the subsequent rainbow bring hope. Some of the Bible's mythic imagery is so powerful that religious doctrine and dogma have been based on its interpretation. These stories and their interpretations have been repeated and transmitted so often that they are taken to be factual. Like all mythic imagery, these stories may express spiritual or psychological truths, and they can be seen as the attempt of the psyche to reveal itself. They can also be seen as mythic examples of the encounter between the ego and the Self. The stories tell us what their writers believed about their God. Even if the Bible is not reliable as history, parts of it have the power of great literature, which in itself can be spiritually, morally, and psychologically valuable.

The resurrection story of the New Testament is a serious problem; either it is historically true, or it is purely mythic. Either Jesus actually rose from the dead or he did not, and for Christianity everything hinges on the truth of that historical question, even if it cannot be decided. For the Christian to have faith in Christ and to have a relationship with him, he must be alive. For Judaism as well, the question of whether God actually entered into history in events such as the Exodus is a central issue; these events may be purely mythic. For these two traditions therefore, the historical truth of at least some of the Bible is crucially important. However, the Bible cannot be read solely as a historical text; the reader's understanding of scripture is partly a matter of what he or she brings to it; passages that are incompatible with the reader's beliefs tend to be forgotten, ignored, reinterpreted, or rationalized.

For non-believers, the Bible's mythic imagery can be seen to make psychological rather than historical statements. For example, Genesis 22 tells the story of Abraham about to sacrifice his son Isaac when an angelic messenger tells him to stop. This can be understood symbolically to mean that Abraham's conscience, or an inner voice, stopped him. The idea that an angel stayed his hand is then purely projective. When Jesus was tempted by the devil in Matthew 4, one could see the devil as an aspect of Jesus' psyche struggling with the temptation of his power shadow. One could also see these kinds of stories as examples of the dark side of the Self, prompting these individuals to enact shadow material. That is, without taking the stories literally, they may nevertheless be psychologically and spiritually significant, so much so that Campbell (2008) believes that the mythic power of biblical stories is even greater than their historical truth. He suggests that the hero of any myth is relevant to each of us because each mythic story tells us about our own quest for salvation, and this quest is ultimately a search for the unity of the person and the divine. This is a somewhat Eastern approach, verging on non-duality. Christianity would prefer to see the Bible's mythic imagery as illustrations of individual relationships with a personal God who is distinct from the individual.

Religious Narcissism, Intolerance, and the Resulting Violence

Intolerance and murderous persecution of heretics and non-believers are common features of religious traditions. This violence may either result from an attempt to suppress challenges to religious authority, or it may be an attempt to project personal doubt onto external unbelievers. The individual's sense that his particular religion is superior to all others may simply be a component of a narcissistic personality. Each of the Abrahamic traditions insists on the truth of its own holy book, and each of these scriptures has justified the killing of non-believers. In the Christian tradition, St. Paul began a tradition of the burning of the wrong kind of books (Acts 19:19), and Constantine and later Christian authorities persecuted pagan priests. These were precursor steps to the *Index of Forbidden Books*[xiii] in the sixteenth century and the medieval Inquisition, which led to the burning of heretics or those who proposed a cosmology of which the Church disapproved.

Both Judaism and Christianity have their own view of their specialness; the Jews consider themselves to be chosen, while the Christians believe they are God's elect or saved, or that they are the new chosen people. The belief that one is chosen or saved may lead to a sense of entitlement, to the sense that other religions are less worthy of divine favors, or that other groups may be mistreated. God is then appropriated for the sake of religious narcissism, which at the same time may enhance individual self-esteem. Orthodox Jews believe God gave their ancestors the land of Israel, and some Americans believe that God has a special relationship with the USA, an idea that goes back to the days of the Pilgrims.[xiv] Fervent commitment to such belief systems is common to all religions. Not only do such religious beliefs allow a sense that life is meaningful, and one will be saved beyond the grave; belonging to a group of like-minded people promotes a powerful type of narcissistic self-enhancement and a variety of other narcissistic needs. Being surrounded by like-minded people produces a twinship or alter-ego relationship that bolsters the individual's sense of self. At the same time, group members are mirrored by each other and they idealize the group ideals and its heroes, all of which enhance the cohesion of the self. In these ways, group membership consolidates and confirms the individual's identity. A common sense of mission and direction allows a feeling of belonging. These dynamics are all enhanced by the sense that God blesses the group's beliefs, in which case the individual can feel superior to non-believers. A charismatic, idealized group leader who can embody and focus the group's ideology also helps to sustain the group identity. Unfortunately, the shadow side of these group phenomena is hostility to non-believers and the projection of negative traits onto other groups, sometimes leading to the need for an enemy onto whom one's own doubts can be projected (Meissner, 1978a). Devaluing the religious beliefs of others helps to sustain the individual's own beliefs and consolidates in-group cohesion. When primitive splitting and projective mechanisms dominate the individual's psyche, his or her group is seen as all good and the others become all bad. If these processes are combined with an intolerance of otherness, which is rooted in primitive mechanisms such as stranger anxiety, xenophobia and other forms of intolerance develop. When such attitudes towards others are colored by projected aggression, the enemy becomes a threat to the group and in the extreme is dehumanized or seen as an agent of Satan or the Antichrist.

The Hebrew prophets all stressed the importance of ethical behavior towards others, including outsiders. Given the evidence of history, it looks as if the prophets' ethical message failed to be implemented, for several reasons. One is that giving good spiritual advice does not deal with narcissism or with unconscious complexes that produce self-interest, rage, and hatred, not to mention deeply rooted individual and cultural shadow material such as racism. Religious traditions foster tribalism, which may be intrinsically in tension with the traditions' ethical teaching. God is easily invoked in the service of one's own prejudices, especially when the sacred texts themselves contain morally objectionable material.

We commonly see violence and fanaticism as components of religion (Kimball, 2002). One approach to these phenomena is to see them as a manifestation of intrapsychic splitting and projected aggression that color the believer's theology. Thus, the biblical *Revelation of John* describes an extraordinary split between the followers of Jesus, who are marked with a seal on their foreheads, and evil people, those who fornicate with the "Whore of Babylon," who are marked with the sign of the beast. The author includes the Jews in this latter group. According to this book, the righteous individuals will enter an eternal heavenly Jerusalem, while the rest will suffer violent punishment and a range of sadistic tortures.[xv] Traditional interpretations of this text suggest that "Babylon" refers to the Roman Empire (Thompson 1990), so that the book's violence and hatred represents the projection of the author's inner world onto the political situation of his time. The book contains some imagery, such as the marriage of the Lamb and his bride (19:7) that suggests an attempted reconciliation of this severe splitting, but the overall imagery is so bizarre that it is difficult to read the text without seeing it either as an intense active imagination or even as delusional. From a Kleinian standpoint, the book illustrates the intrapsychic good-bad splits of the paranoid-schizoid position. It may depict an unconscious phantasy that destruction of badness will bring about the restoration of an original paradise, but it does not offer much hope. Everything negative is projected onto the non-believers, while only the saints, dressed in white, enter heaven. If "Babylon" does refer to Rome and its eventual destruction, the book proved not to be prophetic, since the Church eventually entered into a long relationship with Rome. However, contemporary believers in millennialism still take the book literally, as an anticipation of an apocalypse to come, perhaps because its violence and splitting resonates with their own intrapsychic structures.

The story of Abraham being told to sacrifice his son Isaac is an instance of what seems to be divinely inspired violence. Abraham's willingness to accede to God's command is usually seen as a model of piety and devotion, although to modern ears this command is completely horrifying. The fact that Isaac is spared at the last moment is traditionally seen as an act of compassion, or as a teaching against the practice of child sacrifice, but it ignores the pain that Abraham and Sarah must have endured at the prospect of this sacrifice, and the grief that would have ensued at its consummation. This is not to mention the traumatic effect on Isaac, who grew up in the knowledge that his father agreed to kill him. Abraham's agreement to follow God's order ignores its cruel and immoral nature, illustrating how devotion to God, or "God intoxication," can lead to hideous behavior and an abandonment of ordinary moral judgment. If taken at face value, this story exemplifies the way in which attention to what the individual believes to be a divine commandment may take precedence over ordinary human decency. The skeptical psychologist will wonder whether Abraham was expressing his hostility to his son and mistaking this impulse for a divine commandment.

Jung's Critique of the Christian Tradition

Jung (1975, p. 7) criticized the theologian Rudolph Bultmann's attempt to demythologize Christianity (described on p. 306), because Jung felt that this process was overly rational and would lead to an impoverishment of Christian symbolism. If this process went too far, it would get rid of essential elements such as the Resurrection. Rather, Jung believed that our understanding of the Christian myth needs further development; our interpretation of the story has become obsolete in the face of the current world situation and requires renewal, yet: "The advocates of Christianity squander their energies in the mere preservation of what has come down to them, with no thought of building on to their house and making it roomier" (CW 9, ii, para. 170). Jung thought that although traditional interpretations of Christianity had become antiquated, "[t]he Christian symbol is a living thing that carries in itself the seeds of further development" (CW 10, para. 542). Christian symbols have to be understood anew in the face of our developing consciousness. For Jung, the mythic levels of the Christian story are of lasting value; the question of its historical accuracy is less so (Jung, 1973, p. 568).

Jung thought that the Protestant Reformation, whose iconoclasm eliminated much Christian imagery, resulted in a poverty of symbols that had previously "expressed important unconscious factors," while the loss of ritual was important because it had previously been "a safe way of dealing with the unpredictable force of the unconscious" (CW11, para. 82). Some Protestant traditions lost touch with their symbolic connections to the unconscious and succumbed to excessive rationalism; all that remained was faith in a transcendent God and belief in the Bible. In contrast, Jung felt that the Roman Catholic tradition retained a connection to the unconscious by preserving its rituals and symbols, which express archetypal themes.

Jung was repelled by one aspect of the Christian myth, namely the idea of killing a human victim "to placate the senseless wrath of a God who had created imperfect human beings unable to fulfill his expectations" (CW18, para.1643). This is a critique of the classical Christian theory of atonement, in which Jesus' self-sacrifice reconciles God with sinful humanity. Jung pointed out that contemporary people have heard more than enough about how sinful we are. The modern individual "is sorely beset by his own bad conscience, and wants rather to know how to reconcile himself with his own nature—how he is to love the enemy in his own heart" (CW 11, p. 431). Jung also believed that Christian teaching has the potential to avoid the shadow.[xvi] We see this tendency in St. Paul's comment that anyone who belongs to Christ is a new creation: "the old has passed away, the new has come" (2 Corinthians 5:17). The word "old" here may include shadow material that has never been dealt with, but this cannot be simply waved away or eradicated by belief in Christ. The shadow can be concealed under a spiritual persona, or we can try to avoid or conceal the shadow using spiritual practices. Furthermore, Jung thought that the Christian emphasis on human sinfulness tends to depreciate our humanity. We have to find a way to deal with shadow material rather than project it onto unbelievers, which leads to moral crusades. Or we can avoid the shadow by projecting it onto the Devil or the Antichrist. Jung points out that Sunday sermons help us recognize the shadow but do not help us deal with it (CW 9, ii, para. 35). For Jung, Christian moral categories are therefore "a dangerous inheritance, because they are the instruments by which we make it impossible to integrate the shadow. We condemn it and therefore we suppress it" (Jung, 1960, p. 1479). Jung believed that the traditional "imitation of Christ" is no longer sufficient because it only deals with the good and light side of human nature, and lacks awareness of the shadow. Jung (1960, p. 1477) points out that Jesus' exhortation to attend to "the least of these" (Matthew 25:40) also applies to shadow qualities within ourselves, not only to people in the outer world.

Jung (1960) was critical of the Christian depreciation of the body, and he was suspicious of the Christian notion of perfection that Jesus spoke of in his Sermon on the Mount (Matthew 5:48, KJV). Jung thought that this was an impossible goal and was responsible for the harsh repression of the shadow, which only leads to its intensification in the unconscious. (But see note? on the translation of the word "perfect.") Without the shadow, human nature would lack richness and vitality, not to mention creativity and the increased consciousness that arises from engaging with the shadow. Thus, instead of reaching for the ideal of perfection, Jung believed it would be better for the individual to content himself or herself with "the more accessible goal of approximate completeness" (CW 14, para. 616). One could also call this state approximate wholeness, since complete wholeness would encroach on perfection.

Jung was dubious about the historical validity of the story of the Resurrection. He felt that such miracle-stories were ways of demonstrating spiritual or psychological truths to the people of the time, who needed a concrete event for this purpose. The Resurrection story can be understood symbolically rather than literally; it belongs to the myth of the hero or the dying and resurrecting god who conquers death.[xvii] For Jung, the psychological, symbolic importance of the idea of resurrection is that it means we are not "completely subjected to the powers of annihilation because our psychic totality reaches beyond the barrier of space and time" (CW18, para.1572).

Jung was not happy with attempts to reduce the figure of Christ to a historical personality. Jesus was able to carry the projection of the Self by his followers, so that: "At a very early stage, therefore, the real Christ vanished behind the emotions and projections that swarmed about him from far and near; immediately and almost without trace he was absorbed into the surrounding religious systems and molded into their archetypal exponent" (CW 11, para. 229). The archetypal projections onto Jesus made the concrete person almost disappear. Jung also felt that to reduce Christ to a historical figure would divest him of his archetypal significance and thus of his redemptive power, which is the power of the divinity of the Self that he expressed. "The Christ of the doctrine is perfect, complete, whole, and therefore not individual at all, but a collective mythologem, viz. an archetype" (1975, p. 165). This is why "it is so difficult for researchers into the life of Jesus to construct from the gospel reports an individual life divested of myth" (CW 11, para. 146). For a psychological rather than theological point of view, the mythic projections onto Jesus are more important than seeing him historically.[xviii] If we were to simply see him as a great spiritual teacher whose messianic or apocalyptic expectations were mistaken, we would then not understand his historical effect, which was based on his ability to carry emotionally powerful archetypal projections. Similarly, Jung believed that historical biblical criticism and the attempt to demythologize the Bible might reduce its numinosity.

Jung makes the important point that Christ would not have made such an impression on his contemporaries if he had not expressed something important in their unconscious, and Christianity would not have spread throughout the pagan world "had its ideas not found an analogous psychic readiness to receive them" (CW 11, para. 713).

Evidently, the Christian story was, and still is for many people, able to contain an enormous range of human needs, partly because it offers powerful consolation and an explanation for suffering and death.

Some Psychosocial and Political Dimensions of Religion

Religions may be one of the factors that hold societies together and help to maintain social structures because of a shared set of beliefs and values. However, some societies do well without much organized religion, and different religions also cause friction between and among communities. It is also noteworthy how often certain theologies are attached to specific political ideologies. For example, Black theology and Womanist theology[xix] both claim to be supported by process theology[xx] (discussed on p. 309) and liberation theology. It is sometimes argued that certain modern political concepts of social justice are secularized versions of traditional theological ideas. However, societies with very different religions may have similar standards of behavior, so the connection between religion, social standards, and morality may not be particularly close. In fact, some (much debated) research suggests that religious faith is not highly correlated with moral conduct, and in fact might predispose to prejudice. Religious leaders of all kinds are often caught up in political debates and ideologies, sometimes supporting oppressive regimes. This suggests that traditional God-images do not necessarily have a psychologically beneficial effect on behavior. On some socially important issues, conservative faith leaders cling to attitudes that belong to a bygone era. Social advances may then occur despite religious opinion.

The Value of the Psychological Approach to the God-image

Religions differ radically from each other, raising the issue that competing, often mutually exclusive, God-images cannot all be valid unless they reveal different manifestations of the Self. By taking this position, the psychological approach to spirituality by-passes arguments about which of these competing God-images is correct. Since all the gods and goddesses arise from the autonomous psyche, no image is more or less valid than any other. Accordingly, unlike approaches based on holy books, the psychological approach to spirituality does not lead to conflict.

There are approaches to the God-image through revelation and scripture, approaches through philosophy, and approaches based on personal experience. Each of these has advantages and drawbacks. Revelation requires belief in sacred stories such as the story of Moses at Mt. Sinai, and today many people see such stories as purely mythic, not to be taken literally. Scripture is open to a wide variety of interpretations and questions about its reliability and historical truth. Philosophical approaches rely on reason, but they may be very abstract, and they are notoriously open to disagreement.

The psychological approach to our understanding of the God-image is largely based on experience, and so does not require a leap of faith. Nevertheless, it is inevitably colored by language and the cultural and psychological make-up of the subject. The psychological approach has the drawback that the source of an experience claimed to be of the divine cannot be proved; human beings are prone to error and misinterpretation. Furthermore, some individuals report few or no experiences of the numinosum. But the psychological approach is personal, it is convincing to the subject, and it often produces original imagery not derived from existing doctrine and dogma. This is important because we cannot possibly express all aspects of the divine in a single God-image. Jung's approach frees us from the tyranny of an exclusively monotheistic God-image, which implies a single center of value, since there are in fact many archetypal centers in the psyche. It is no longer necessary to transform experiences of the archetypal psyche into doctrine and dogma.

For a long time, people have believed that they must turn to scripture to hear the voice of God, even though the Bible contains so much that is objectionable, inconsistent, self-contradictory, and obviously unreliable. Scripture is not always a good guide to behavior. Much of the Bible has little to do with God but is a projection of human psychology and even psychopathology. The notion of a heavenly being who favors, saves, or choses a particular group of people has become irrelevant, if not dangerous. In contrast, Jung's emphasis on relationship with the Self, implemented by means of attention to the psyche, offers an experiential form of revelation not based on books written by people in the Bronze Age and later antiquity, who had a very different consciousness than our own. The projection of their own psychology onto their God-image is no longer relevant to us, and neither is the tribalism their fantasies continue to inspire. While is it comforting and narcissistically enhancing to belong to a tribe of like-minded believers, such adherence is also detrimental to individual thinking and the development of consciousness. Religious tribalism invariably promotes hostility to other groups, allowing atrocities that are attributed to the will of God rather than understood to be the projected shadow of the group.

The myth of a transcendent deity living in a metaphysical realm is no longer relevant to us, yet it is difficult to let go of a cherished God-image, in which so much has been invested by so many people for so long. The final burial of the monotheistic God-image is long overdue, perhaps due to denial of the inevitable grief that would entail. It has now been over a hundred years since William James (1902/1982, p. 447) pointed out that it is time to "bid a definitive good-bye to dogmatic theology, because the God-image of that theology is 'an absolutely worthless invention of the scholarly mind'" (p. 448).

Jung's approach to the Self offers an alternative to such theology; a new myth of God that locates the divine in the depths of the psyche, accessible via dialog with the transpersonal level of the unconscious, which provides a personal sacred text. Jung's work is radical, and currently lives only at the fringes of mainstream psychology. However, it is well known in the history of ideas that new thought often arises from the margins, and not simply as a development of established ideas.

[i] Naturalism is the doctrine that there are no supernatural events or beings; scientific laws can account for all phenomena.

[ii] The group selection theory is controversial because human groups do not behave as if they were single organisms the way anthills do. Nevertheless, there may have been an evolutionary predisposition to sacrifice for family members—so called kin selection.

[iii] A spandrel is an architectural term that refers to V-shaped spaces that that arise where two rounded arches meet. They are only the result of the design features of a building; spandrels have no function in themselves.

[iv] Although cognitive psychologists typically attribute religion to such encoded cognitive processes, if we were to say these processes are archetypal, we might imply that the archetypes are reducible to the brain, which I do not believe to be the case, since the archetypes are spiritual principles. The relationship between our archetypal endowment and our brain structure remains mysterious.

[v] Freud thought that the Oedipus complex resolves when the child identifies with the parent of the same sex, internalizes the parent's morally critical values, and in this way acquires a superego.

[vi] For the original guilt to be transmitted across generations, Freud postulates a "collective mind" that allows the continuity of psychological processes. This sounds like a Lamarckian view in which acquired characteristics are inherited.

[vii] Winnicott's view of illusion was therefore different than that of Freud. For Winnicott, illusion does not mean a distortion of reality; it refers to a form of play. He has a more realistic approach to human nature than Freud's overly rational idealization of reason.

[viii] A selfobject is Kohut's term for an individual or an object or belief that enhances the sense of cohesion or vitality of the self.

[ix] Psychohistory is the attempt to inform the study of history using psychological theory to explain historical figures.

[x] I'm assuming that these are what Kohut referred to as telescoped memories, which collapse multiple experiences of the same type into a single narrative.

[xi] Shengold uses the term "soul murder" to refer to the willful abuse and neglect of children to an extent that the child's subsequent emotional development is negatively affected. Such individuals often feel compelled to repeat the cruelty they experienced by identifying with the abusive parent. This abuse often leads to traumatic anxiety and rage, leading to defensive efforts to deaden affect. One can imagine how these dynamics could color one's God-image and lead to religious asceticism.

[xii] These are meditations on scriptural passages, prayers, imaginative mental exercises, and other contemplative practices.

[xiii] This index is a list of books that the Church authorities believed to be dangerous to the faith or morals of Roman Catholics. Its use was ended in 1966.

[xiv] Some members of the Mormon Church believe that Jesus Christ rose from the dead following his crucifixion and came to America, which he designated the new Promised Land. Some Christian nationalists wish to make the USA a Christian country, using the Bible to dictate behavior and political decisions. This movement is often seen to be not really Christian in its values, but essentially a religious disguise for conservative, sometimes racist, politics.

[xv] A partial list of the tortures of the damned includes hailstones from heaven, locusts that sting like scorpions, and being thrown alive into a sulfurous lake of fire that burns forever. The damned will be killed by plagues, earthquakes, and famine, and their flesh will be eaten by birds.

[xvi] Here Jung is ignoring the spiritual practice of the examination of conscience in the light of the moral law.

[xvii] Many of the early mystery religions relied on the mythology of a dying and resurrecting god, which is an archetypal theme found in various traditions. Orpheus, Heracles, and Jesus all performed miracles, descended to the underworld and suffered cruel deaths. They

were later raised to heaven by their divine fathers, from where they were thought to benefit their followers. The Orphic mystery tradition offered the prospect of union with the divine, deliverance of the soul from the prison of the body, and the achievement of new life by means of purification and sacramental rituals. Mystery religions typically impart information about the divine realm and offer direct contact with it.

[xviii] The archetype of the god-man was frequently seen in antiquity. The Pharaohs were considered to be divine, and the god Horus was thought to live within the Pharaoh, who would become entirely divine after his death. The Greeks had many heroic figures who achieved divine status, and Roman emperors were also deified.

[xix] Black theology views Christianity as a theology of liberation, a study of God in the light of the oppressed. Womanist theology tries to integrate theology with the experiences of women of color. It cultivates a God-image free of white supremacy.

[xx] In process theology, God participates in the suffering of humanity, including those who are oppressed, and works for their liberation. God guides people to the greater good.

References

Ackerman, N., & Jahoda, M. (1950). *Anti-Semitism and emotional disorders: A psycho-analytic interpretation.* New York: Harper.

Allegro, J.M., & Irvin, J. R. (1970). *The sacred mushroom and the cross: A study of the nature and origins of Christianity within the fertility cults of the ancient Near East.* London: Hodder and Stoughton.

Altizer, T. J. J. (1956). *The Gospel of Christian atheism.* Philadelphia, PA: Westminster Press.

Alston, W. P. (1991). *Perceiving God: The epistemology of religious experience.* Ithaca, NY: Cornell University Press.

Anderson, P. S. (2014). "Why feminist philosophy of religion? An interview with Pamela Anderson." *Logoi: A publication of the Center for Philosophy of Religion at Notre Dame, 1,* 11-13.

Appenzeller, T. (2018). "Europe's first artists were Neandertals: Spanish cave paintings date to before modern humans arrived in region." *Science, 359*(6378), 852-853.

Armstrong, K. (1994). *A history of God.* NY: Ballantine Books.

Asher, C. (2014). How becoming is the divine Self. *Jung Journal, 8*(2), pp. 8-19.

Aslan, R. (2013). *Zealot: The life and times of Jesus of Nazareth.* NY: Random House.

Atran, S. (2002). *In gods we trust.* NY: Oxford University Press.

Atwood, G. E., & Stolorow, R. D. (2001). *Faces in a cloud: Intersubjectivity in personality theory.* Lanham, MD: Jason Aronson.

Bacal, H., & Newman, K. (1990). *Theories of Object Relations: Bridges to Self Psychology.* New York: Columbia University Press.

Banerjee, K., & Bloom, P. (2013). *Trends in Cognitive Sciences, 17*(1), pp. 7-8.

Barnhart, B. (2007). *The future of wisdom: Toward a rebirth of sapiential Christianity.* NY: Continuum.

Barth, K. (1958). *Church Dogmatics iii.2: The doctrine of creation*. H. Knight (trans.). Edinburgh: T. & T. Clark.

Beitman, B. D., Celebi, E., & Coleman, S. L. (2009). Synchronicity and healing. In D. Monti & B. D. Beitman (Eds.), *Integrative psychiatry* (pp. 445-483). NY: Oxford University Press.

Benson, P., & Spilka, B. (1973). God image as a function of self-esteem and locus of control. *Journal for the Scientific Study of Religion, 12*(3), 297-310.

Berkovits, E. (1973). *Faith after the Holocaust*. NY: KTAV Publishing House.

Bering, J. (2012). *The belief instinct*. NY: W.W. Norton.

Blumenthal, D. R. (1993). *Facing the abusing God: A theology of protest*. Louisville, KY: Westminster John Knox Press.

Bohm, D. (1980). *Wholeness and the implicate order*. NY: Routledge and Kegan Paul.

Bollas, C. (1999). *The mystery of things*. NY: Routledge.

Bomford, R.W. (1990). The attributes of God and the characteristics of the unconscious. *International Review of Psycho-Analysis, 17*(4), 485-491.

Borg, M. (1994). *Jesus in contemporary scholarship*. Philadelphia, PA: Trinity Press International.

Bouchard, T. J., & McGue, M. (2003). Genetic and environmental influences on human psychological differences. *Journal of Neurobiology, 54*, 29-31.

Bourgeault, C. (2013). *The Holy Trinity and the Law of Three*. Boston, MA: Shambhala.

Boyer, P. (2001). *Religion explained: The evolutionary origins of religious thought*. NY: Basic Books.

Boys, M. C. (2013). *Redeeming our sacred story: The death of Jesus and relations between Jews and Christians*. NJ: Paulist Press.

Brandon, S. G. E. (1968). *The trial of Jesus of Nazareth*. London: Batsford.

Bridgman, L. P. & Carter, J. D. (1989). Christianity and psychoanalysis: Original sin—Oedipal or pre-Oedipal? *Journal of Psychology and Theology, 19*(1), 3-8.

Brooks, R. M. (2011). Un-Thought-out metaphysics in analytical psychology: A critique of Jung's epistemological basis for psychic reality. *Journal of Analytical Psychology, 56*(4), 492–513.

Brown, J. C., & Bohn, C. R. (Eds.), (1989). *Christianity, patriarchy, and abuse: A feminist critique.* NY: The Pilgrim Press.
Brueggemann, W. (1997). *Theology of the Old Testament: Testimony, dispute, advocacy.* Minneapolis, MN: Fortress Press.
Buber, M. (1957). *Eclipse of God: Studies in the relation between religion and philosophy.* NY Harper and Row.
Bulkeley, K. (Ed.), (2001). *Dreams: a reader on the religious, cultural, and psychological dimensions of dreaming.* NY: Palgrave.
Bulkeley, K. (2008). *Dreaming in the world's religions: A comparative study.* NY: New York University Press.
Bultmann, R. (1987). *Rudolf Bultmann: Interpreting faith for the modern era.* Ed. Roger Johnson. Minneapolis: Fortress Press.

Campbell, J. (1964). *The masks of God: Occidental mythology.* NY: Viking Press.
Campbell, J. (2008). *The hero with a thousand faces.* Novato, CA: New World Library.
Campbell, J. (2001). *Thou art that: Transforming religious metaphor.* Novato, CA: New World Library.
Capps, D. (1987). Symposium on Hjalmar Sundén's role-theory of religion. (1987). *Journal for the Scientific Study of Religion, 26*(3), 366-412.
Capps, D. (1997). *Men, religion, and melancholia.* New Haven, CT: Yale University Press.
Capps, D. (2000). *Jesus: A psychological biography.* St. Louis, MO: Chalice Press.
Carella, M. J. & Sheres, I. (1988). Hebraic Monotheism: The evolving belief, the enduring attitude. *Judaism, 37*(2), 229-239.
Charet, F. X. (1990). A dialogue between psychology and theology: The correspondence of C. G. Jung and Victor White. *Journal of Analytical Psychology, 35*(4), 421-441.
Childs, H. (2000). *The myth of the historical Jesus and the evolution of consciousness.* Atlanta, GA: Dissertation Series, Society of Biblical Literature.
Chilton, B. D. & Evans, C. A. (1999a). (Eds.). *Authenticating the words of Jesus.* Leiden: E. J. Brill.
Chilton, B. D. & Evans, C. A. (1999b). (Eds.). *Authenticating the activities of Jesus.* Leiden: E. J. Brill.

Clack, B. (2015). Feminist approaches to religion. In O. Graham (Ed.), *The Routledge handbook of contemporary philosophy of religion* (pp. 7-19). London: Routledge.

Clark, K. J. (1990). *Return to reason: A critique of Enlightenment evidentialism and a defense of reason and belief in God.* Grand Rapids, MI: Wm. B. Eerdmans Publishing Co.

Christ, C. P., & Plaskow, J. (1992). *Womanspirit rising: A feminist reader in religion.* San Francisco, CA: Harper San Francisco.

Christie-Murray, D. (1976). *A history of heresy.* NY: Oxford University Press.

Citlak, A. (2019). The concept of "Cratism" and "Heteropathic Feelings" in the psychobiography of Jesus from Nazareth. In C-H Mayer & Z. Kovary (Eds.). *New trends in psychobiography* (pp. 381-403). Cham, Switzerland: Springer.

Clottes, J. (2008). *Cave art.* NY: Phaidon Press.

Cohen, J. M. & Phipps, J. F. (1979). *The common experience.* Los Angeles, CA: J.P. Tarcher, Inc.

Cohen, A. A. (1981). *The tremendum: A theological interpretation of the Holocaust.* NY: Continuum International Publishing.

Cole, R. (1990). *The spiritual life of children.* Boston, MA: Houghton Mifflin Co.

Colledge, E. & McGinn, B. (1981). *Meister Eckhart: The essential sermons, commentaries, treatises, and defenses.* Mahwah, NJ: Paulist Press.

Colman, W. (2006). The Self. In R. Papadopoulos (Ed.), *The handbook of Jungian psychology.* (pp. 153-174). NY: Routledge.

Coogan, M. D., & Smith, M. S. (2012). *Stories from ancient Canaan.* Louisville, KY:
Westminster John Knox Press.

Coogan, M. D., & Chapman, C. R. (2017). *The Old Testament: A historical and literary introduction to the Hebrew Scriptures.* NY: Oxford University Press.

Corbett, L. & Kugler, P. (1989). The Self in Jung and Kohut. In A. Goldberg (Ed.), *Dimensions of self-experience: Progress in self psychology, 5.* (pp. 189-208). Hillsdale, NJ: Analytic Press.

Corbett, L. (1996). *The religious function of the psyche.* NY: Routledge.

Corbett, L. (2006) Varieties of numinous experience. In A. Casement (Ed.), *The idea of the numinous* (pp. 53-67). London: Brunner-Routledge.

Corbett, L. (2007). *Psyche and the sacred*. New Orleans, LA: Spring Publications.

Corbett, L. (2011). Jung's *The Red Book* dialogs with the soul. *Jung Journal: Culture and Psyche, (5)*3, 63-77.

Corbett, L. (2011). *The sacred cauldron: Psychotherapy as a spiritual practice*. Wilmette, IL: Chiron Publications.

Corbett, L. (2015). *The soul in anguish: Psychotherapeutic approaches to suffering*. Asheville, NC: Chiron Publications.

Corbett, L., & Whitney, L. (2016). Jung and non-duality: Some clinical and theoretical implications of the self as the totality of the psyche. *International Journal of Jungian Studies, 8*(1), 15-27.

Corbett, L. (2018). *Understanding evil: A psychotherapist's guide*. NY: Routledge.

Corbin, H. (1969). *Creative imagination in the Sufism of Ibn Arabi*. R. Mannheim trans. Princeton, NJ: Princeton University Press.

Corbin, H. (1976). *Mundus Imaginalis: Or, the imaginary and the imaginal*. Ashuelot, N.H.: Gogonooza Press.

Cousins, E. (1999). The convergence of cultures and religions in light of the evolution of consciousness. *Zygon, 34*(2), 209-219).

Christ, C. P. (1982). Why women need the goddess: Phenomenological, psychological, and political reflections. In C. Spretnak (Ed.), *The politics of women's spirituality* (pp. 71-86). Garden City, NY: Anchor.

Crenshaw, J.L. (1984). *A whirlpool of torment*. Philadelphia, PA: Fortress Press.

Cross, F. M. (1973). *Canaanite myth and Hebrew epic*. Boston, MA: Harvard University Press.

Culotta, E. (2009). On the origin of religion. *Science, 326*(5954), 784-787.

Cupitt, D. (1988). *The sea of faith*. NY: Cambridge University Press.

Daly, M. (1973). *Beyond God the Father: Toward a philosophy of women's liberation*. Boston, MA: Beacon Press.

Davies, P. (1992). *The mind of God*. NY: Simon and Schuster.

Davies, P. G. (1999). *Goddess unmasked: The rise of neopagan feminist spirituality*. McClean VA: Spence publishing.

Dawkins. (2006). *The God delusion*. NY: Bantam Books.

Davis, S.T. (1997). *God, reason, and theistic proofs*. Grand Rapids, MI: Wm. B. Eerdman Publishing.

Davis, C. (2007). *Dating the Old Testament*. NY: RJ Communications.

Davis, E. B., Mauch, J. C., & Moriarty G. L. (2013). God images and god concepts: Definitions, developments, and dynamics. *Psychology of Religion and Spirituality*, 5(1), 51-60.

Dawkins, R. (1976). *The selfish gene.* NY: Oxford University Press.

Dawkins, R. (1988). *The blind watchmaker: Why the evidence of evolution reveals a universe without design.* NY: W.W. Norton.

Day, J. (2000). *Yahweh and the Gods and Goddesses of Canaan.* Sheffield, England: Sheffield Academic Press.

de Chardin, T. (2001). *The divine milieu.* NY: Harper & Row.

de Chardin, T. (2004). *The future of man.* NY: Doubleday.

Dein, S. & Littlewood, R. (2007). The voice of God. *Anthropology and medicine*, 14(2), 213-228.

de Moor, J. C. (1990). *The rise of Yahwism.* Leuven, Belgium: Leuven University Press.

Dennett, D. C. (2007). *Breaking the spell: Religion as a natural phenomenon.* NY: Penguin Books.

Doran, R. M. (1988). Jungian psychology and Christian spirituality. In R.L. Moore (Ed.), *Jung and Christian spirituality* (pp. 66-108). NY: Paulist Press.

Dourley, J. (1992). *A strategy for a loss of faith: Jung's proposal.* Toronto: Inner City Books.

Dourley, J. (1995). *Jung and the religious alternative: The rerooting.* Lewiston, NY: Edwin Mellen.

Dourley, J. (2001). Jung, mysticism, and a myth in the making. *Studies in religion* 30(1), 65-78.

Dourley, J. (2003). Archetypal hatred as social bond: Strategies for its dissolution. In J. Beebe (Ed.), *Terror, violence, and the impulse to destroy: Perspectives from Analytical Psychology* (pp. 135-160). Einsiedeln, Switzerland: Daimon Verlag.

Dourley, J. (2010). *On behalf of the mystical fool: Jung on the religious situation.* NY: Routledge.

Dourley, J. (2011). Jung's equation of the ground of being with the ground of psyche. *Journal Of Analytical Psychology* 56(4), 514-531.

Dourley, J. (2015). C.G. Jung and Pierre Teilhard de Chardin: Is there a Border between psychic and evolutionary energy? In F. Gustafson (Ed.), *Pierre Teilhard de Chardin and Carl Gustav Jung: Side by side* (pp. 98-114). Cheyenne, WY: Fisher King Press.

Durkheim, E. (1955). *The elementary forms of religious life.* Trans. K.E. Fields. NY: The Free Press. (Originally published in 1912).

Edinger, E. F. (1960). The Ego-Self paradox. *Journal of Analytical Psychology*, 5(1), 3-18.

Edinger, E. (1984). *The creation of consciousness: Jung's myth for modern man*. Toronto: Inner City Books.

Edinger, E. (1987). *The Christian archetype: A Jungian commentary on the life of Christ*. Toronto: Inner City Books.

Edinger, E. (1996). *The Aion lectures: Exploring the self in Jung's Aion*. Toronto: Inner City Books.

Edinger, E.F. (2000). *Ego and Self: The Old Testament prophets*. Toronto, Canada: Inner City Books.

Edinger, E.F. (2025). *The new God-image: A study of Jung's key letters concerning the evolution of the Western God-image*. Wilmette, Il: Chiron Publications.

Edwards, M. U. (1983). *Luther's last battles: Politics and polemics, 1531-46*. Ithaca, NY: Cornell University Press.

Ehrman, B.D. (2003). *Lost Christianities*. NY: Oxford University Press.

Ehrman, B.D. (2009). *Jesus, interrupted: Revealing the hidden contradictions in the Bible*. NY: HarperCollins.

Ehrman, B.D. (2014). *How Jesus became God: The exaltation of a Jewish preacher from Galilee*. NY: HarperCollins.

Ehrman, B.D. (2016). *Jesus before the Gospels*. NY: HarperCollins.

Ehrman, B.D. (2018). *The triumph of Christianity: How a forbidden religion swept the world*. NY: Simon and Schuster.

Eichrodt, W. (1967). *Theology of the Old Testament*. (J.A. Baker, trans.). Philadelphia, PA: Westminster John Knox Press.

Eliade, M. (1957). *The sacred and the profane: The nature of religion*. NY: Harcourt Publishing.

Eliade, M. (1978). *The forge and the crucible: The origins and structures of alchemy*. Chicago, IL: University of Chicago Press.

Ellenberger, H. E. (1970). *The discovery of the unconscious*. NY: Basic Books.

Ellens, H. (2004). From Christ to Jesus: The Jesus quest. In J. H. Ellens & W. G. Rollins (Eds.), *Psychology and the Bible: A new way to read the scriptures* (pp. 13-19). Westport, CT: Praeger.

Eller, C. (2001). *The myth of matriarchal prehistory: Why an invented past won't give women a future*. Boston, MA: Beacon Press.

Ellerbe, H. (1995). *The dark side of Christian history*. Orlando, FLA: Morningstar and Lark.

Elms, A.C. (1994). *Uncovering lives*. NY: Oxford University Press.
Ericksen, R. P., & Heschel, S. (1999). *Betrayal: German churches and the Holocaust*. Minneapolis, MN: Augsburg Fortress Publishers.
Erikson, E. (1963). *Childhood and society*. NY: W.W. Norton.
Erikson, E. (1964). *Insight and responsibility*. NY: W.W. Norton.
Erikson, E. (1977). *Toys and reasons: Stages in the ritualization of experience*. NY: W.W. Norton.
Erikson, E. (1993). *Young man Luther: A study in psychoanalysis and history*. NY: W.W. Norton.
Evans, C. S. (1996). *The historical Jesus and the Jesus of faith*. NY: Oxford University Press.

Faber, M. D. (1998). *Synchronicity: C.G. Jung, psychoanalysis, and religion*. Westport, CT: Praeger.
Faber, M. D. (2004). *The psychological roots of religious belief: Searching for angels and the parent-god*. Amherst, NY: Prometheus Books.
Fackenheim, E. L. (1970a). *God's presence in history: Jewish affirmation and philosophical reflection*. NY: HarperTorchbook.
Fackenheim, E. L. (1970b). The people Israel lives. *The Christian Century, 87*(18), 563-568.
Feierman, J. (2009). *The biology of religious behavior: The evolutionary origins of faith and religion*. Santa Barbara, CA: Praeger.
Feuerbach, L. (2004). *The essence of religion*. Trans. A. Loos. Amherst, NY: Prometheus Books. Originally published in 1851.
Finkelstein, I., & Silberman, N. A. (2002). *The Bible unearthed: Archeology's new vision of ancient Israel and the origin of its sacred texts*. NY: Simon and Schuster/Touchstone.
Friedman, R. E. (1995). *The hidden face of God*. San Francisco, CA: HarperSanFrancisco.
Fordham, M. (1976). *The self and autism*. London: Heinemann Medical.
Fordham, M. (1985). The Self in Jung's works. In M. Fordham, R. Gordon, J. Hubback, & K. Lambert (Eds.), *Explorations into the Self* (pp. 5-33). London: Academic Press.
Forman, K. C. (1990). *The problem of pure consciousness*. NY: Oxford University Press.
Fox, R. L. (1991). *The unauthorized version: Truth and fiction in the Bible*. NY: Alfred Knopf.

Fowler, J. W. (1981). *Stages of faith: The psychology of human development and the quest for meaning*. San Francisco: Harper & Row.
Francis, L. J., Gibson, H. M., & Robbins, M. (2001). God images and self-worth among adolescents in Scotland. *Mental Health, Religion & Culture*, 4(2), 103-108.
Frazer, J. G. (1922/2009). *The Golden Bough: A study in magic and religion*. NY; Cosimo.
Freud, S. (1910). Leonardo da Vinci and a memory of his childhood. In *Standard Edition*, vol. 11, 1957, pp. 57-137.
Freud, S. (1913). *Totem and taboo: Resemblances between the mental life of savages and neurotics*. NY: Moffat, Yard, and Company.
Freud, S. (1927/1964). *The future of an illusion*, trans. J. Strachey. NY: W.W. Norton.
Friedman, R. E. (1987). *Who wrote the Bible?* NY: Simon and Schuster, Inc.
Friedman, R. E. (1996). *The hidden face of God*. NY: HarperCollins.
Fromm, E. (1972). *Psychoanalysis and religion*. NY: Bantam Books.

Galambush, J. (2006). *The reluctant parting: How the New Testament's Jewish writers created a Christian book*. NY: Harper Collins.
Gaylor, A. L. (2004). *Woe to the women: The Bible, Female sexuality, and the Law*. Madison, WI: Freedom from Religion Foundation.
Galen, L.W., & Kloet, J. D. (2011). Mental well-being in the religious and non-religious: Evidence for a curvilinear relationship. *Mental Health, Religion & Culture*, 14, 673-689.
Geisler, N. L., & Roach, W. C. (2012). *Defending inerrancy: Affirming the accuracy of Scripture for a new generation*. Grand Rapids, MI: Baker Books.
Gerstenburger, E. (1996). *Yahweh the patriarch: Ancient images of God and feminist theology*. (F. J. Gaiser, Trans.). Minneapolis, MN: Augsburg Fortress.
Gimbutas, M. (1991). *The civilization of the goddess: The world of old Europe*. San Francisco: Harper.
Godwin, J. (1981). *Mystery religions in the ancient world*. San Francisco, CA: Harper and Row.
Goldbrunner, J. (1949). *Individuation: A study of the depth psychology of Carl Gustav Jung*. Trans. S. Godman. Notre Dame, IN: University of Notre Dame Press.

Goodenough, E. R. (1986). *An introduction to Philo Judaeus.* Landham, MD: University Press of America.

Gould, S. J. (2002). *Rocks of ages: Science and religion in the fulness of life.* NY: Ballantine Books.

Grant, J. (1989). *White women's Christ and Black women's Jesus: Feminists Christology and womanist response.* Atlanta, GA: Scholar Press.

Green, G. (1989). *Imagining God: Theology and the religious imagination.* Grand Rapids, MI: William B. Eerdmans Publishing Company.

Green, R. H. (1999). *Born again skeptic's guide to the Bible.* Madison, WI: Freedom from Religion Foundation.

Green, M., & Elliott, M. (2010). Religion, health, and psychological well-being. *Journal of Religion and Health, 49,* 149-163.

Greenberg, I. (1988). *The third great cycle of Jewish History: Voluntary covenant.* NY: The National Jewish Center for Learning and Leadership.

Greenway, A. P., Milne, L. C., & Clarke, V. (2003). Personality variables, self-esteem and depression and an individual's perception of God. *Mental Health, Religion & Culture, 6*(1), 45-58.

Griffiths, B. (1989). *A new vision of reality: Western science, Eastern mysticism and Christian faith.* Springfield, IL: Templegate.

Gruenwald, I. (2004). Jewish and Christian messianism: The psycho-analytic approach of Heinz Kohut. In J. H. Ellens & Wayne G. Rollins (Eds.), *Psychology and the Bible: A new way to read the scriptures. Vol. 1: From Freud to Kohut* (pp. 248-275). Westport, CT: Praeger.

Guntrip, H. (1956). *Mental pain and the cure of souls.* London: Independent Press.

Guntrip, H. (1961). *Personality structure and human interaction.* London: Hogarth Press.

Guthrie, S. E. (1993). *Faces in the clouds: A new theory of religion.* NY: Oxford University Press.

Haile, H. G. (1980). *Luther: An experiment in biography.* Princeton, NJ: Princeton University Press.

Handy, L. K. (1994). *Among the hosts of heaven: The Syro-Palestinian pantheon as bureaucracy.* Winona Lake, IN: Eisenbrauns Inc.

Hardy, A. (1979). *The spiritual life of man.* NY. Oxford University Press.

Harris, S. (2004). *The end of faith: Religion, terror, and the future of reason.* NY: W.W. Norton.
Hartshorne, C. (1984). *Omnipotence and other theological mistakes.* Albany, NY: SUNY Press.
Haley, J. (1986). *The power tactics of Jesus Christ and other essays.* NY: Grossman publishers.
Hayes, C. (2012). *Introduction to the Bible.* New Haven, CT: Yale University Press.
Hawking, S., & Mlodinow, L. (2010). *The grand design.* NY: Bantam Books.
Heiler, F. (1968). The Madonna as a religious symbol. In *The mystic vision: Papers from the Eranos yearbooks.* Trans. R. Manheim. Bollingen Series XXX, 6. (pp. 348-474). Princeton, NJ: Princeton University Press. (Originally published in 1934).
Helms, R. M. (1997). *Who wrote the Gospels?* Altadena, CA: Millennium Press.
Henderson, D. (2010). The coincidence of opposites: C.G. Jung's reception of Nicholas of Cusa. *Studies in spirituality, 20,* 101-113.
Henry, R. C. (2005). The mental universe. *Nature, 436*(7047), 29.
Heisig, J. W. (1979). *Imago Dei: A study of C.G. Jung's psychology of religion.* Lewisburg, PA: Bucknell University Press.
Hill, J. (2010). The changing images of God: An anticipatory appraisal of the Jung/White encounter. In M. Stein & R. A. Jones (Eds.), *Cultures and identities in transition: Jungian perspectives* (pp. 156-157). New York, NY: Routledge.
Hillman, J. (1971). Psychology: Monotheistic or polytheistic? *Spring,* 193-208.
Hillman, J. (1975). *Re-visioning psychology.* NY: Harper & Row.
Hitchins, C. (2009). *God is not great. How religion poisons everything.* NY: Hatchett Books.
Horsely, R. A. (1987). *Jesus and the spiral of violence.* Minneapolis, MN: Augsberg Fortress Press.
Hutch, R. A. (1990). *Religious leadership: Personality, history and sacred authority.* NY: Peter Lang.
Huxley, A. (2009). *The perennial philosophy.* NY: Harper Collins.
Hyde, K. E. (1991). *Religion in childhood and adolescence.* Birmingham, AL: Religious Education Press.

Jack, A. I., Friedman, J. P., Boyatzis, R. E., & Taylor, S. N. (2016). Why do you believe in God? Relationships between religious belief, analytic thinking, mentalizing and moral concerns. *Plos ONE, 11*(3), 1-21.

James, W. (1982). *The varieties of religious experience.* Harmondsworth, Middlesex, UK: Penguin Books.

Janes, J. (1982). *The origin of consciousness in the breakdown of the bicameral mind.* Boston, MA: Haughton Mifflin.

Jaspers, K. (1953). *The origin and goal of history.* Trans. Michael Bullock. New Haven, CT: Yale University Press.

Jaspers, K. (1960). *Way to wisdom: An introduction to philosophy.* New Haven, CT: Yale University Press.

Johnson, L. T. (1996). *The real Jesus: The misguided quest for the historical Jesus and the truth of the Gospels.* San Francisco, CA: HarperSanFrancisco.

Jonas, H. (1987). The concept of God after Auschwitz: A Jewish voice. *The Journal of Religion, 67*(1), 1-13.

Jones, R. P., & Cox, D. (2017). *America's changing religious identity: Findings from the 2016 American values atlas.* Washington, DC: Public Religion Research Institute.

Joseph, R. (2001). The limbic system and the soul: Evolution and the neuroanatomy of religious experience. *Zygon, 36*(1), 105-136.

Jung, C. G. (1960). *Nietzsche's Zarathustra: Notes of the seminar given in 1934-1939 by C.G. Jung.* Princeton, NJ: Princeton University Press.

Jung, C. G. (1965). *Memories, dreams, reflections.* NY: Vintage Books.

Jung, C. G. (1973). *Letters,* vol. 1. Ed. G. Adler and A. Jaffe. Trans. R.F.C. Hull. Princeton, NJ: Princeton University Press.

Jung, C. G. (1975). *Letters,* vol. 2. Ed. G. Adler and A. Jaffe. Trans. R.F.C. Hull. Princeton, NJ: Princeton University Press.

Jung, C. G. (1976). *The visions seminars.* Zurich, Switzerland: Spring publications.

Jung, C. G. (1977). *C.G. Jung speaking: Interviews and encounters.* Princeton, NJ: Princeton University Press, pp. 427-428.

Jung, C. G. (1978). *Psychological reflections.* J. Jacobi & R.F.C. Hull, (Eds.). Bollingen Series 31. Princeton, NJ: Princeton University Press.

Jung, C. G. (2009). *The Red Book, Liber Novus.* Ed. Sonu Shamdasani. NY: WW Norton Co.

Jung, C. G. & Neumann, E. (2015). *Analytical psychology in exile: The correspondence of C.G. Jung and Erich Neumann.* Ed. Martin Liebscher. Princeton, NJ: Princeton University Press.

Kakar, S. (1991). *The analyst and the mystic: Psychoanalytic reflections on religion and mysticism.* Chicago, IL: University of Chicago Press.

Kant, I. (1953). *Critique of pure reason.* Trans. Norman Kemp. London: Smith, Macmillan & Co.

Kastrup, B. (2019). *The idea of the world.* Washington, D.C.: iff books.

Kaufman, W. (1972). *Critique of religion and philosophy.* NY: Harper Torchbooks.

Kaufman, Y. (1972). *The religion of Israel: From its beginnings to the Babylonian exile.* Trans. M. Greenberg. NY: Schocken Books.

Katz. S.T., Biderman, S., & Greenberg, G. (Eds.). *Wrestling with God: Jewish theological responses during and after the Holocaust.* NY: Oxford University Press.

Kelly, E. F. & Kelly, E.W. (2007). *Irreducible mind: Toward a psychology for the 21st century.* Lanham, MD: Rowman & Littlefield Publishers.

Kelsey, M. (1991). *God, dreams, and revelation: A Christian interpretation of dreams.* Minneapolis, MN: Augsburg Publishing House.

Kille, D. A. (2001). *Psychological biblical criticism.* Minneapolis, MN: Fortress Press.

Kimball, C. (2002). *When religion becomes evil.* San Francisco, CA: HarperSanFrancisco.

King, T. M. (2007). Believers and their disbelief. *Zygon, 42*(3), 779-792.

Kirkpatrick, L. A. (2005). *Attachment, evolution, and the psychology of religion.* NY: Guilford Press.

Kirkpatrick, L. A. (2005). Evolutionary psychology as a foundation for the psychology of religion. In R.F. Paloutzian & C.L. Park, R.F. (Eds.), *Handbook of the psychology of religion and spirituality,* (pp. 118-137). NY: Guilford Press.

Klawans, J. (2014). Concepts of purity in the Bible. In A. Berlin & M.Z. Brettler, (Eds.), *The Jewish study bible,* (pp. 1998-2005). NY: Oxford University Press.

Kluger, R. S. (1995). *Psyche in scripture: The idea of the chosen people and other essays.* Toronto: Inner City Books.

Knox, J. (2003). *Archetype, attachment, analysis. Jungian psychology and the emergent mind.* NY: Routledge.

Kohut, H. (1977). *The restoration of the self*. NY: International Universities Press.
Kramer, S. N. (1969). *The sacred marriage rite*. Bloomington, IN: Indiana University Press.
Krishnamurti, J. (1992). *On God*. San Francisco: HarperSanFrancisco.

Lammers, A. (1994). *In God's shadow: The collaboration of Victor White and C.G. Jung*. Mahwah, NJ: Paulist Press.
Lang, B. (1983). *Monotheism and the prophetic minority: An essay in Biblical history and sociology*. Sheffield, England: Almond Press.
Lang, B. (2002). *The Hebrew God: Portrait of an ancient deity*. New Haven, CT: Yale University Press.
Lawrence, L. T. (1997). Measuring the image of God: The God image inventory and the God image scales. *Journal of Psychology and Theology, 25*(2), 214-226.
Leavy, S. (1990). Reality in psychoanalysis and religion. In J.H. Smith & S. Handleman (Eds.), *Psychoanalysis and religion: Psychiatry and the humanities* (pp. 43-55). Baltimore, MD: Johns Hopkins University Press.
Leidenhag, J. (2016). A critique of emergent theologies. *Zygon, 51*(4), 867-882.
Lerner, G. (1986). *The creation of patriarchy*. New York, NY: Oxford University Press.
Levin, J. (2002). Is depressed affect a function of one's relationship with God? Findings from a study of primary care patients. *The International Journal of Psychiatry in Medicine, 32*, (4), 379-393.
Levin, J. S. (2010). Religion and mental health: Theory and research. *International Journal of Applied Psychoanalytic Studies, 7*(2), 102-115.
Levinas, E. (1979). *Totality and infinity*. The Hague: Martinus Nijhoff.
Levine, A-J. (2006). *The misunderstood Jew: The Church and the scandal of the Jewish Jesus*. San Francisco: HarperSanFrancisco.
Lewin, B. D. (1950). *The psychoanalysis of elation*. NY: International Universities Press.
Lewy, G. (1964). *The Catholic Church and Nazi Germany*. NY: McGraw Hill.
Littell, F. H. (1975). *The crucifixion of the Jews*. NY: Harper and Row.

Luhrmann, T. M. (2012). *When God talks back: Understanding the American evangelical relationship with God.* NY: Alfred A. Knopf.

Luther, M. (1971). On the Jews and their lies. In F. Sherman (Ed.), *Luther's works (Vol. 47).* Philadelphia: Fortress Books (Original work published in 1543).

Maccoby, H. (1984). Christianity's break with Judaism. *Commentary, 78*(2), 38–42.

MacKenna, C. (2000). Jung and Christianity—Wrestling with God. In E. Christopher & H.M. Solomon (Eds.), *Jungian thought in the modern world.* (pp. 173-190). London: Free Association Books.

Mackie, J. L. (1982). *The miracle of theism: Arguments for and against the existence of God.* NY: Oxford University Press.

McDargh, J. (1983). *Psychoanalytic object relations theory and the study of religion: On faith and the imaging of God.* Lanham, MD: University Press of America.

McDargh, J. (1992). The deep structures of religious representations. In M. Finn & J. Gartner (Eds.), *Object relations theory and religion: Clinical applications* (pp. 1-19). London, England: Praeger.

McFague, S. (2008). *A new climate for theology: God, the world, and global warming.* Minneapolis, MN: Fortress Press.

McGrath, A. (2007). *The Dawkins delusion.* London, UK: Society for Promoting Christian Knowledge.

McGrath, A. E. (2017). *Christian theology: An introduction.* Chichester, UK: John Wiley and Sons.

McGuire, W. & Hull, R. F. C. (1977). *C. G. Jung speaking.* Princeton, NJ: Princeton University Press.

McNamara, P. (2009). *The neuroscience of religious experience.* NY: Cambridge University Press.

McNamara, P. (2016). *Dreams and visions: How religious ideas emerge in sleep and dreams.* Santa Barbara, CA: Praeger.

McKnight, S. A. (2007). Religion and Francis Bacon's scientific utopianism. *Zygon, 42*(2), 463–486.

Meier, J. P. (1994). *A marginal Jew: Rethinking the historical Jesus.* NY: Doubleday.

Meissner, W. W. (1978a). *The paranoid process.* NY: Aronson.

Meissner, W. W. (1978b). Psychoanalytic aspects of religious experience. *Annual of Psychoanalysis, 8:* 103-41.

Meissner, W. W. (1984). *Psychoanalysis and religious experience*. New Haven, CT: Yale University Press.

Meissner, W. W. (1995). *Thy kingdom come: Psychoanalytic perspectives on the messiah and the millennium*. Kansas City, MO: Sheed & Ward.

Meissner, W. W. (2013). Winnicott's legacy: On psychoanalyzing religious patients. *Psychoanalytic Inquiry, 33*:21–35.

Mettinger, T. N. D. (2001). *The riddle of resurrection: "Dying and Rising Gods" in the ancient near East*. Stockholm: Almqvist & Wiksell.

Metzger, J. A. (2009). Where has Yahweh gone? Reclaiming unsavory images of God in New Testament studies. *Horizons in biblical theology, 31*, 51-76.

Meyer, J. P. (1991). *A marginal Jew: Rethinking the historical Jesus*. New Haven, CT: Yale University Press.

Miles, J. (1996). *God: A biography*. NY: Vintage Books.

Miller, D. L. (1974). *The new polytheism: Rebirth of the gods and goddesses*. NY: Harper and Row.

Miller, J. H. (1965). *The disappearance of God*. Cambridge, MA: Harvard University Press.

Miller, J. W. (1997). *Jesus at thirty: A psychological and historical portrait*. Minneapolis, MN: Fortress.

Miller, P. D. (2000). *The religion of ancient Israel*. Louisville, KY: Westminster John Knox Press.

Monod, J. (1971). *Chance and necessity: An essay on the natural philosophy of modern biology*. NY: Alfred Knopf.

Neumann, E. (1959). The significance of the genetic aspect for Analytical Psychology. *Journal of Analytical Psychology, 4*(2), 125-137.

Neumann, E. (1963). *The great mother: An analysis of the archetype*. (R. Manheim, Trans.). Princeton, NJ: Princeton University Press.

Neumann, E. (1968). Mystical man. In J. Campbell (Ed.), *The mystic vision: Papers from the Eranos yearbooks*. Bollingen Series XXX; vol. 6. (pp. 375-415). Princeton NJ: Princeton University Press. Trans. Ralph Mannheim.

Newberg, A. B. (2018). *Neurotheology: How science can enlighten us about spirituality*. NY: Columbia University Press.

Nichols, S. J. (2002). *Martin Luther: A guided tour of his life and thought*. Phillipsburg, NJ: P & R Publishing.

O'Connor, T. (2012). *Theism and ultimate explanation: The necessary shape of contingency*. Malden, MA: Blackwell Publishing.

Oldenhage, T. (2002). *Parables for out time: Rereading New Testament scholarship after the Holocaust*. NY: Oxford University Press.

Otto, R. (1958). *The idea of the holy*. NY: Oxford University Press.

Pagels, E. (1979). *The Gnostic gospels*. NY: Vintage Books.

Parrish, J. W. (2006). It's all in the definition: the problem with "dying and rising gods." *The Council of Societies for the Study of Religion Bulletin, 35*(3), 71–75.

Patai, R. (1990). *The Hebrew goddess*. Detroit, MI: Wayne State University Press.

Peacocke, A. (2006). Articulating God's Presence in and to the World Unveiled by the Sciences, In A. Peacocke & P. Clayton, (Eds.), *In Whom We Live and Move and Have Our Being: Panentheistic Reflections on God's Presence in a Scientific World*. (pp. 137 – 155). Grand Rapids, MI: William B. Eerdmans.

Penchansky, D. (1999). *What rough beast? Images of God in the Hebrew Bible*. Louisville, KY: John Knox Press.

Persinger, M. A. (1987). *Neuropsychological bases of God beliefs*. NY: Praeger.

Persinger, M. A., Saroka, K. S., & Koren, S. A. (2010). The electromagnetic induction of mystical and altered states within the laboratory. *Journal of Consciousness Exploration & Research, 1*(7), 808-830.

Pinnock, C. H. (Ed.). (1994). *The openness of God: A biblical challenge to the traditional understanding of God*. Downers Grove, IL: InterVarsity Press.

Plaskow, J. (1990). *Standing again at Sinai: Judaism from a feminist perspective*. NY: HarperOne.

Platinga, A. (1983), Reason and belief in God. In A. Platinga & N. Wolterstorff, (Eds.), *Faith and rationality*, (pp. 16-93). Notre Dame, IN: University of Notre Dame Press.

Pollock, G. H. (1989). *The mourning-liberation process*. Madison, CT: International Universities Press.

Pyysiäinen, I., & Hauser, M. (2010). The origins of religion: Evolved adaptation or by-product? *Trends in Cognitive Sciences, 14*, 104–109.

Rahner, K. (1978), *Foundations of Christian Faith*. New York: Crossroad Publishing.
Ramachandran, V. S., & Blakeslee, S. (1999). *Phantoms in the brain: Probing the mysteries of the human mind.* NY: HarperCollins.
Rancour-Laferriere, D. (2003). The Moral Masochism at the Heart of Christianity: Evidence from Russian Orthodox Iconography and Icon Veneration. *Journal for the Psychoanalysis of Culture & Society,* 8(1), 12.
Raphael, M. (1997). *Rudolph Otto and the concept of holiness.* Oxford, UK: Clarendon Press.
Raphael, M. (2003). *The female face of God in Auschwitz: A Jewish feminist theology of the Holocaust.* NY: Routledge.
Rector, L. (2001). Mystical experience as an expression of the idealizing selfobject need. In A. Goldberg, (Ed.), *Progress in Self Psychology,* 17, (pp. 179-195). Hillsdale, NJ: Analytic Press.
Rieff, P. (1966). *The triumph of the therapeutic: Uses of faith after Freud.* NY: Harper & Row.
Rizzuto, A-M. (1979). *The birth of the living God: A psychoanalytic study.* Chicago, Il: University of Chicago Press.
Rollins, W. G. (1995). Psychology, hermeneutics, and the Bible. In D.L. Miller (Ed.), *Jung and the Interpretation of the Bible,* (pp. 113-117). NY: Continuum. pp. 9-39.
Rollins, W. (1999). *Soul and psyche: The Bible in psychological perspective.* Minneapolis, MN: Fortress Press.
Rubenstein, R. L. (1966). *After Auschwitz: Radical theology and contemporary Judaism.* Indianapolis, IN: Bobbs-Merrill.
Rubin, T. (1990). *Anti-Semitism: A disease of the mind.* NY: Continuum.
Ruether, R. R. (1974). *Faith and fratricide.* Minneapolis, MN: Seabury.
Ruether, R. R. (1996). *Woman guides: Readings towards a feminist theology.* Boston, MA: Beacon Press.

Shamdasani, S. (2005). *Jung stripped bare.* London: Karnac Books.
Schapp-Jonker, H., Eurlings-Bontekoe, E., Verhagen, P. J., & Zock, H. (2002). Image of God and personality pathology: an exploration among psychiatric patients. *Mental Health, Religion & Culture,* 5(1), 55-71.
Schellenberg, J. L. (2006). *Divine hiddenness and human reason.* Ithaca, NY: Cornell University Press.

Schleiermacher, F. D. E. (1996). *On religion: Speeches to its cultured despisers.* Trans. Richard Couter. NY: Cambridge University Press. (First published in 1799).

Schleiermacher, F. D. E. (2011). *The Christian faith.* Berkely, CA: Apocryphile Press. (First published in 1821).

Shengold, L. (1991). *Soul murder: The effects of childhood abuse and deprivation.* NY: Ballantine books.

Shermer, M. (2008). Patternicity. *Scientific American, 299*(6), 48.

Shlain, L. (1998). *The alphabet versus the Goddess.* NY: Viking Penguin.

Schweitzer, A. (2005). *The quest of the historical Jesus.* Mineola, NY: Dover Publications. (Originally published in 1906).

Schweitzer, D. (2010). *Contemporary Christologies: A fortress introduction.* Minneapolis, MN: Fortress Press.

Schwiebert, E. G. (1950). *Luther and his times.* St. Louis, MO: Concordia Press.

Siniscalchi, G. B. (2018). Contemporary Trends in Atheist Criticism of Thomistic Natural Theology. *Heythrop Journal, 59*(4), 689–706.

Sjöö, M., & Mor, B. (1987). *The great cosmic mother: Rediscovering the religion of the earth.* San Francisco: Harper & Row.

Skinner, B. F. (1971). *Beyond freedom and dignity.* NY: Alfred A. Knopf.

Smith, J. (1981). *The Book of Mormon: Another testament of Jesus Christ.* NY: Doubleday.

Smart, N. (1984). *The religious experience of mankind.* NY: Charles Scribner & Sons.

Smith, M. (1971). *Palestinian parties and politics that shaped the Old Testament.* New York, NY: Columbia University Press.

Smith, W. C. (1979). *Faith and belief: The difference between them.* Princeton, NJ: Princeton University Press.

Smith, M. S. (1990). *The early history of God: Yahweh and the other deities in ancient Israel.* San Francisco, CA: Harper & Row.

Smith, M. S. (2001). *The origins of biblical monotheism.* NY: Oxford University Press.

Smith, O. S. (2001). *Matthew, Mark, Luke, and Paul: The influence of the Epistles on the Synoptic Gospels.* Eugene, OR: Resource Publications.

Smith, P., & Gallinger, H. P. (2016). *Conversations with Luther: Selections from the recently published sources of the table talk.* (Originally published in 1915). Scotts Valley, CA: CreateSpace Independent Publishing Platform.

Smith, M. (2014). *Jesus the magician*. San Francisco: Red Wheel/Weiser.
Soelle, D. (1975). *Suffering*. Philadelphia, PA: Fortress Press.
Spero, M. H. (1992). *Religious objects as psychological structures: A critical integration of object relations theory, psychotherapy, and Judaism*. Chicago, IL: University of Chicago Press.
Spilka, B., Shaver, P., & Kirkpatrick, L. A. (1993). The structure of mystical experience in relation to pre-and post-experience lifestyle correlates. *International Journal for the Psychology of Religion, 2*, 241-257.
Spitz, L. W. (1960). Preface to the Latin Writings [1545], in *Luther's Works: Career of the reformer iv:* 34, pp. 336-37. Minneapolis, MN: Fortress Press.
Spitzer, R. J. (2010). *New proofs for the existence of God: Contributions of contemporary physics and philosophy*. Grand Rapids, MI: Eerdmans.
Spong, J. S. (1998). *Why Christianity must change or die*. San Francisco: HarperSanFrancisco.
Stanford, E.V. (1960). *Foundations of Christian belief*. Westminster, London: The Newman Press.
Stark, R. (1965). A taxonomy of religious experience. *Journal for the Scientific Study of Religion, 5*, 97-116.
Stark, R. (1999). A theory of revelations. *Journal for the Scientific Study of Religion, 38*, 286-307.
Stein, M. (2008) 'Divinity expresses the Self...' An investigation. *Journal of Analytical Psychology* 53:305-327.
Steinmetz, D. C. (2002). *Luther in context*. Grand Rapids, MI: Baker Book House Company.
Stroope, S., Draper, S., & Whitehead, A. L. (2013). Images of a loving God and sense of meaning in life. *Social Indicators Research, 111*(1), 25-44.
St. Clair, M. (1994). *Human relationships and the experience of God*. Mahwah, NJ: Paulist Press.
Stone, M. (1976). *When God was a woman*. NY: Harcourt Brace Jovanovich.
Strickling, B. L. (2007). *Dreaming about the divine*. Albany, NY: State University of New York Press.
Suler, J. R. (1993). *Contemporary psychoanalysis and Eastern thought*. Albany, NY: SUNY Press.

Suttie, I. D. (1932). Religion: Racial character and mental and social health. *The British Journal of Medical Psychology, 12*, 289-315.
Suttie, I. D. (1935). *The origins of love and hate*. New York, NY: Julian Press.
Swinburne, R. (1979). *The existence of God*. NY: Oxford University Press.

Tabor, J. D. (2007). *The Jesus dynasty: The hidden history of Jesus, his royal family, and the birth of Christianity*. NY: Simon and Schuster.
Tacey, D. (2004). *The spirituality revolution: The emergence of contemporary spirituality*. NY: Routledge.
Tacey, D. (2010). Jung: Rebuilding the temple. In M. Stein and R. A. Jones (Eds.), *Cultures and identities in transition: Jungian Perspectives*, (pp 126-137). NY: Routledge.
Taliaferro, C., & Meister, C. (2016). *Contemporary philosophical theology*. London: Routledge.
Taves, A. (2009). *Religious experience reconsidered: A building-block approach to the study of religion and other special things*. Princeton, NJ: Princeton University Press.
Theissen, G. (1987). *Psychological aspects of Pauline theology*. NY: Bloomsbury Publishing.
Thiering, B. (1993). *Jesus and the riddle of the Dead Sea scrolls*. San Francisco: Harper Collins.
Thompson, L. L. (1990). *The Book of Revelation: Apocalypse and empire*. NY: Oxford University Press.
Tillich, P. (1964). *Theology of culture*. NY: Oxford University Press.
Tillich, P. (1967). *Systematic theology, vol. 1*. Chicago, Il: University of Chicago Press.
Torrey, E. F. (2017). *Evolving brains, emerging gods: Early humans and the origins of religion*. NY: Columbia University Press.
Trinkaus, E., Buzhilova, A. P., Mednikova, M., & Dobrovolskya, M. V. (2014). *The people of Sunghir: burials, bodies, and behavior in the earlier Upper Paleolithic*. NY: Oxford University Press.

Van Buren, P. (1966). *The secular meaning of the Gospel*. NY: Macmillan.
Van Buren, P. (1980). *Discerning the way: A theology of the Jewish-Christian reality*. NY: Seabury Press.
Van Buren, P. M. (1983). *A Christian theology of the people Israel*. NY: Seabury.

Van de Beek, A. (2007). The person of Jesus. In G. Glas, M.H. Spero, P.J. Verhagen, & H. M. van Praag (Eds.), *Hearing visions and seeing voices*, (pp. 169-181). Dordrecht, The Netherlands: Springer.

Vass, G. (1985). *A Theologian in Search of a Philosophy: Understanding Karl Rahner*. London: Sheed & Ward.

Vedder, B. (2007). *Heidegger's philosophy of religion: From God to the Gods*. Pittsburgh: Duquesne University Press.

Vergote, A., & Tamayo, A. (Eds.) (1981). *The parental figures and the representation of God: A psychological and cross-cultural study*. The Hague, The Netherlands: Mouton. (pp. 133-151).

Vergote, A. (2007). Casting a psychological look on Jesus the marginal Jew. In G. Glas, M. H. Spero, P. J. Verhagen & H. M. van Praag (Eds.), *Hearing visions and seeing voices*, (pp. 133-152). Dordrecht, The Netherlands: Springer.

Vermes, G. (1981). *Jesus the Jew: A historical reading of the gospels*. Minneapolis, MN: Fortress Press.

Vetter, G. B. (1973). Magic and religion: Their psychological nature, origin, and function. NY: Philosophical Library.

Vitz, P. C., & Gartner, J. (1984). Christianity and psychoanalysis, part 1: Jesus as the anti-Oedipus. *Journal of Psychology and Theology, 12*(1), 4-14.

Vitz, P. C. (2008). The psychology of atheism. *Antimatters, 2*(4), 33-44.

Visala, A. (2016). *Naturalism, theism, and the cognitive study of religion: Religion explained?* NY: Routledge.

Von Franz, M-L. (1980). *Projection and re-collection in Jungian psychology*. La Salle, IL: Open Court Press.

Wallis, J. H. (1997). *Post-Holocaust Christianity: Paul van Buren's Theology of the Jewish-Christian reality*. Lanham, MD: University Press of America.

Weldon, C. (2007). *FR. Victor White, O.P.: The story of Jung's "White Raven."* Scranton, PA: University of Scranton Press.

White, V. (1960). *Soul and psyche*. London: Collins and Harvill Press.

Whitehead, A. N. (1929). *Process and reality*. NY: Cambridge University Press.

Wiesel, E. (1968). *Legends of our time*. NY: Holt, Rinehart and Winston.

Wink, W. (1973). *The Bible in human transformation: Toward a new paradigm for biblical study*. Philadelphia: Fortress Press.

Wink, W. (2004). The original impulse of Jesus. In J. Harold Ellens & Wayne G. Rollins, (Eds.). *Psychology and the Bible: Vol. 4, From Christ to Jesus,* (pp. 209-221). Westport, CT: Praeger.

Winter, P. (1974). *On the trial of Jesus* (2nd ed). T. A. Burkill & G. Vermes, (Eds.), NY: Walter de Gruyter.

Weinberg, S. (1993). *The first three minutes: A modern view of the origin of the universe.* NY: Basic Books

White, V. (1960). *Soul and psyche: An enquiry into the relationship of psychology and religion.* London: Collins.

Winnicott, D.W. (1964). Memories, dreams, reflections by C.G. Jung. *International Journal of Psycho-Analysis,* 45, 450-455.

Winnicott, D.W. (1989). Playing and culture. In: Winnicott C, Shepherd R, & Davis M. (Eds.), *Psycho-Analytic Explorations.* Cambridge, MA: Harvard University Press, pp. 203-206.

Young-Eisendrath, P. (1997). The self in analysis. *Journal of Analytical Psychology,* 42(1), 157-166.

Zinkin, L. (2008). Your self: did you find it or make it? *Journal of Analytical Psychology,* 53(3), 389-406.

Zock, H. (1990). *A psychology of ultimate concern: Erik H. Erikson's contributions to the psychology of religion.* Amsterdam: Rodopi.

Index

A
Aaron, 184
abandonment, 187, 315, 323, 388, 412
 early, 133
Abel, 127
Abraham, 61, 171, 173–75, 181, 183, 190, 222–24, 257, 269, 409, 412
Abrahamic traditions, 326, 410
Abraham sacrifice, 341
Abram, 173, 224, 405
absence of belief, 36
Absolute, 5–6, 17, 35, 130, 359–60
Absolute Spirit, 359
abstract theological notions of God, 380
abuse, 55, 294, 315, 325, 396, 419, 423
 drug, 382
 papal, 396
Ackerman, 400, 421
active imagination, 141, 206, 404
 authentic, 404
 intense, 412
Adam, 180, 186, 190, 224, 228, 237, 279, 281–82, 284–85, 287, 295, 297, 332
adherence, 30–31, 46, 52, 77, 97, 174, 181, 202, 207, 244, 250
 blind, 293
 outward, 52
 strict, 92
Adonis, 126, 155, 162
Advaita Vedanta, 35, 101
Aeschylus, 406

affective attunement, 85, 398
African Americans, 314
afterlife, 55, 126, 139, 147, 150, 157–59, 163, 250, 334, 361, 375
age, 10, 21, 43–44, 119–20, 126, 223, 230, 322, 331, 388, 396
 apostolic, 235
 belonged to a bygone, 190
 ice, 151
 messianic, 55
 new, 33, 61, 204, 322
 old, 119
 post-Christian, 16
 sheer, 11
 young, 322, 351
aggression, 41, 263, 367, 379
 frustrated, 400
 military, 41
 projected, 411
 unintegrated, 99
aging, 118–19
agnostics, 15, 36
agreement, 17, 247, 283, 294, 332, 335, 356, 403
 covenantal, 174
 second, 243
Agriculturalists, 151
Ahriman, 161–62, 238
Ahura Mazda, 161, 179, 407
 followed, 162
Akkad, 222
Albany, 431, 440
Albrecht Ritschl, 359
alchemy, 368, 427
Aldous Huxley, 59

Alexandria, 207, 268
Alfred North Whitehead, 309
alienation, 85
 human, 302
Allah, 124
Allegro, 320, 421
Alston, 27, 421
Altadena, 431
altars, 57, 150, 179, 186, 198, 204
Amalekites, 184–85
ambivalence, 186, 188, 381, 390, 406
 intense, 265
 theist's, 390
 unconscious, 386
Amenhotep, 160
Amen-Re, 30
America, 33, 301, 419, 430, 432, 435, 442
Amherst, 428
Amos, 18, 174, 193–97, 200, 203, 212, 223–24, 390
amplification, 76
Amsterdam, 355, 443
Anabaptism, 342
Anabaptists, 299
analogies, 45, 70, 135, 140, 236–37, 287, 291, 357, 381, 402
 mathematical, 291
 remote, 357
Analytical Psychology, 72, 422–23, 426–27, 433, 436, 440, 443
analytic third, 117
Anath, 181
anathema, 99, 273
Anaxagoras, 163

ancestors, 147, 150, 152, 154, 167, 222, 340, 372, 410
  early, 148, 372, 374
  prehistoric, 146
ancestor-worship, 163
Ancient Egypt, 30, 157–58
ancient Greece, 155–57, 164, 406
Ancient Iranian religion, 161
ancient Israel, 160, 179–81, 428, 436, 439
Ancient of days, 337
ancient Roman and Scandinavian myths of Gods, 156
ancient world, 104, 177, 183, 240, 429
Anderson, 326, 421
angelic messengers, 29, 61, 409
angel Lucifer, 238
angels, 61, 84, 180, 201, 221, 246, 263, 370, 377, 405–7, 409
  avenging, 107
  fallen, 280
anger, 98, 183–84, 190, 193, 195, 210, 217, 244, 284, 340, 343
  burning, 228
  the rod of my, 212
Anglican theologians, 307
anguished emotional reactions, 193
Aniela Jaffé, 133
animal bones, 150
animal entrails, 160
animal form, 11
animal heads, 158
animal husbandry, 151
animals, 146–49, 151, 155, 158–59, 161, 163, 167, 171, 185–86, 189, 276, 280
  hunted, 154
  mixed, 158
  pattern-seeking, 374
  powerful, 111
  sacrificial, 341

totem, 380
  traditional, 240
  unclean, 406
animal symbolism, 111
anima mundi, 348
animism, 146–47, 374
Animosity, 299
annihilation, 415
annual flooding, 158
Annunciation, 332
Anselm, 285
Answer to Job, 72, 98–99, 120–21, 141
anthropic coincidences, 8
anthropocentric attitude, 132
anthropological approach to religion, 380
anthropological descriptions, 305
anthropologist Edward Tylor, 146
anthropomorphic, 21, 191, 369
anthropomorphic biblical imagery, 208
anthropomorphic characteristics, 34, 374
anthropomorphic Greek deities, 17
anthropomorphic projection, 108
anthropomorphize, 151, 374
Antichrist, 103, 113, 411, 414
anti-Jewish indoctrination, 215
anti-Judaism, 400
  polemical Christian, 254
anti-Oedipus, 342, 442
antiquity, 11, 56, 115, 126–27, 145–67, 276, 342, 402, 408, 417, 420
  remote, 163
antireductionist, 371
anti-Semitism, 254, 315, 400, 421, 438
  combat, 264
  personal, 400
antithetical, 48, 62, 75, 123, 126, 142, 270, 292

anxiety, 187, 197, 265, 335, 338, 369–70, 383, 388, 390, 397, 399–400
  constant, 224
  depressive, 263
  eternal life allays, 390
  great, 159
  obsessional, 399
  paranoid, 263
  stranger, 411
  tradition's, 40
  traumatic, 419
Anxious/ambivalent attachment styles, 392
Aphrodite, 157, 336
apocalypse, 337, 399, 412, 441
Apocalyptic fantasies, 337, 338
Apollo, 157, 405
Apollonius, 336
apologetics, 212
apophatic tradition, long, 309
apostasy, 192, 207
  denounced religious, 200
Apostle Peter, 406
apostles, 29, 232, 242–43, 245–46, 256, 258–59, 262, 276, 279, 326, 338
apparitions, 246
Appeals to scripture and divine revelation, 47
appearance of Christ, 138, 243
appearance of monotheism, 160
Appenzeller, 148, 421
Aquinas, 61, 239, 254, 282, 286–88, 307, 329, 338, 342, 347
Aquinas's thinking, 288
Arabic philosophy, 283
Arab philosophers, 292
Archaic forms of religion, 145
archaic religions, 26, 56, 145–67
  animistic, 62
archeological evidence, 171, 222–23, 320
  definitive, 319

necessary, 172
archeology, 156, 331, 428
archetypal, 15, 53, 126, 274, 319, 324, 419, 426
archetypal accretions, 244
archetypal centers, 417
  multiple, 128
archetypal character, 324
archetypal component, 104
archetypal constituents, 129
archetypal contents, 87, 112
archetypal cores, 87, 121
archetypal depiction, 89
archetypal dimension, 67
archetypal dominants, multiple, 129
archetypal dynamics, 91
archetypal elements, 117
archetypal endowments, 84, 86, 419
  individual's, 86
archetypal exponent, 415
archetypal feminine, 143
archetypal forces, 91, 124
archetypal forms, 85
archetypal ground, 86
archetypal ground of consciousness, 86
archetypal imagery, 95, 114, 324
  discreet, 78
archetypal manifestations, 68
archetypal motifs, 172, 240
archetypal pattern, 341
archetypal predisposition, 376
archetypal processes, 127, 129, 325
  discreet, 128
archetypal projections, 319, 324–25, 415
  accrued, 247
  powerful, 415
archetypal reality, 94
archetypal representation, 157
archetypal role, 112, 325
archetypal shadow, 104

archetypal symbol, 272
archetypal themes, 126–27, 162, 234, 240, 413, 419
Archetypal themes in religions, 126
archetype of wholeness, 114
archetypes, 74, 78, 82, 85, 87, 109, 128–29, 132, 140–41, 324–25, 419–20, 433, 436
  individual, 78
  living, 143
Archimedean, 95
Areopagite, 282
Ares, 56
argument from desire, 39
arguments, 7–9, 11–12, 15, 19–24, 45–46, 50–51, 54–55, 294, 297, 341, 343, 357, 366–68
  ancient, 368
  cosmological, 19–20
  empirical, 136
  good, 55
  logical, 286
  metaphysical, 292
  moral, 358
  ontological, 19, 22–23
  philosophical, 19, 307, 351
  plausible, 10
  popular, 18, 211
  proponent's, 24
  rational, 51, 136
  teleological, 21
  theistic, 11
  traditional, 12, 358
Arianism, 269
Ariège, 148
Aristotelian philosophy, 283
Aristotelian physics, 288
Aristotle, 11, 163–64, 229, 283, 286, 288–89, 345, 406
Aristotle's deity, 11
Aristotle's Prime Mover, 164
Arius, 268–69
Armenian, 335

Armstrong, 220, 421
art, 50, 97, 149, 225, 332–33, 423
  early, 149
  mosaic, 332
Artemidorus, 406
Artemis, 154, 338
Articulating God, 437
asceticism, 266
  extreme, 395
  religious, 266, 419
Asclepius, 157, 336, 406
Asher, 118, 421
Asherah, 178, 181–82, 207
Asherah's daughter Anath, 181
Asheville, 425
Ashtoreth/Astarte, 154, 155, 338
Ashur, 179
Asia, 376
Aslan, 255, 421
assertions, 14, 40, 53, 105, 293, 318, 370–71, 377, 386, 390, 400
  basic, 292
  creedal, 2
  pure, 46
  theological, 76, 364
Assyria, 183, 195, 203
Assyrian Adonis, 151
Assyrian army, 193
Assyrian Empire, 196
Assyrian King Sargon II, 198
Assyrian lightening, 238
Assyrian pantheon, 179
Assyrians, 176, 184, 196–99, 205, 212, 221, 224, 406
Assyrian threat, 197–98
Astarte, 181
Aten, 160, 381–82
Athanasius, 269
atheism, 33, 36–39, 42–43, 46–47, 49–50, 300, 303, 346–47, 355–56, 359, 361, 364, 369
atheists, 15–16, 19, 23, 36–41, 43–44, 46, 48, 50, 354–56, 386, 392
  new, 41–42, 44

scientific, 45
Athena, 336
Athens, 155, 282
Atlanta, 423, 430
Ātman, 79, 101, 131
Ātman forms, 131
atonement, 174, 205, 258–59, 276–79, 295, 314, 380, 413
atoning power of Christ, 278
Atran, 372, 421
atrocities, 18, 37, 54, 184, 225, 418
attachment, 343, 391, 433
  avoidant, 392
  insecure, 191
attachment figures, 378, 391–92
attachment styles, 391–92
  attention, 67–68, 77, 83, 92, 96–97, 114, 118, 125, 138, 141–42, 412, 417
  constant, 67
  individual, 141
  paying, 97
  religious, 151
  selective, 219
  sustained, 117
Attis, 126, 155, 162
attributes, 15, 17, 20, 22–23, 27, 29, 47, 50, 56, 58, 165–66, 186–87, 190, 208–10, 302
  abusive, 217
  benevolent, 210
  borrowed, 179
  cosmic, 316
  definitive, 16
  dogmatic Christian, 112
  human, 112
  idealized, 228
  infinite, 350
  metaphorical, 190
  negative, 16, 104, 218
  particular, 157
  positive, 208, 218
  psychological, 401
  traditional, 9, 17, 312, 347
  traditional moral, 7

Atwood, 133, 421
Augustine, 40, 103, 239, 270, 280–82, 297, 329, 338, 341–42, 347
Auschwitz, 103, 211–12, 214, 432, 438
authority, 5, 8, 40–41, 76, 170, 173, 265, 268, 275–76, 297–99, 301, 303, 340, 401, 403
  abusive, 314
  complete, 267
  delegates, 186
  dominant, 326
  local human, 180
  mainstream, 276
  multiple, 52
  papal, 283
  paternal, 398
  personal, 250
  pious, 172
  rabbinical, 355, 400
  scriptural, 334
  social, 327
  special, 170, 285
  spiritual, 276, 339
  ultimate, 135
authority and scripture, 403
authority of scripture, 5
authorship, 198, 201, 209, 262, 304
Avebury, 152
Axial, 162

B

Baal, 177–79, 181, 197, 207, 223
  attributes of, 178, 224
  worship of, 178–79
Ba'als, 176
Babel, 172
Babylon, 175, 177, 179–80, 183, 196, 199–200, 203, 205, 223, 412
  ancient, 160
  captured, 202
Babylonian and Egyptian stories and Hammurabi's code, 219
Babylonian captivity, 221

Babylonian empire, 155
Babylonian exile, 177, 199, 201, 203, 206, 224, 433
Babylonian gods, 177
Babylonian mythology, 154
Babylonian Sin, 143
Babylonian stories, 172
Babylonian Talmud, 225, 319
Bacal, 397, 421
Bachofen, 167
Bacon, 347–48
Baker, 427
Banerjee, 61, 421
baptism, 241–42, 257, 267, 275, 281, 284, 296, 298, 332, 338, 360
  infant, 342
Bar Kochba, 205, 224–25
Barnabas, 241
Barnhart, 316, 338, 421
Baron, 356
Baroque era, 320, 333
Baroque-era image of God, 326
Barth, 61, 96, 305–6, 368, 422
Basel cathedral, 75, 106
Basilica, 274
basis, 37, 43–44, 46–47, 51–52, 54, 301–2, 307, 319–20, 347, 354, 358–59
  epistemological, 422
  historical, 53
  mythological, 126
  natural, 354
  neurological, 377
  non-rational, 19
  objective, 23
  philosophical, 309
  scriptural, 258
  final apocalyptic, 105
  final destructive, 338
  important, 230
Bauer, Bruno, 47
BCE, 148, 154–56, 160–61, 163–64, 167, 169, 173, 180, 193, 195–202, 204–6, 221–24, 376–77
  second millennium, 160, 223

INDEX | 449

third millennium, 154
Bede Griffiths, 338
behavior, 30, 32, 37, 39, 128–29, 159, 162, 164, 169–70, 183–85, 218–19, 297, 373–75, 391–94, 416–17
　abhorrent, 40
　abusive, 218
　altruistic, 372
　bad, 102, 396
　bizarre, 202
　callous, 217
　control, 49
　correct, 299
　destructive, 216–17
　good, 159, 192, 279
　hideous, 412
　humanitarian, 250
　immoral, 219
　motivated, 264
　nation's, 174
　negative, 217
　observable, 393
　people's, 187–88
　pro-social, 370, 375
　repeating, 262
　reprehensible, 194
　savage, 94
　sinful, 225
　superstitious, 392
Behavioral Approaches to Religion, 392, 393
being, 22–23, 28–29, 92–93, 96, 128–29, 131–32, 173–75, 182–83, 228, 270, 279–80, 287–88, 291–94, 310, 337–38, 340, 342–43, 365–66, 368–69, 419
　early human, 151
　finite, 307
　finite human, 31
　imaginary, 48
　individual, 365
　intelligent, 293
　intelligent human, 349
　spiritual, 36, 61, 179, 275
Bel, 143
Belgium, 426

belief, 5, 7, 19, 30, 36, 40, 47–48, 50, 77, 125–26, 136, 150, 310–11, 331–33, 369, 371–72, 374–76, 378, 389–92, 399–400
　adopted, 177
　common, 6
　contemporary, 317
　dogmatic, 298, 312
　earlier, 280
　group's, 411
　heretical, 267
　lifelong, 399
　local, 15
　metaphysical, 382
　monotheistic, 207
　mythological, 97
　popular, 274
　professed, 303
　reader's, 409
　real, 209
　rejected, 307
　repudiated, 310
　spiritual, 376
　theistic, 36
　true, 319
belief in Christ, 311, 414
belief in doctrine, 52
belief in doctrine and dogma, 77, 106, 125, 138, 332
belief in God, 36, 39, 41, 45, 47–50, 349, 356–58, 366, 369, 371, 378–79, 384, 386
belief in God constellates, 119
Belief in Jesus' resurrection, 245
belief in miracles, 310
belief in reincarnation, 376
belief in sacred stories, 417
belief in spirits, 147, 374
belief instinct, 422
belief in stories, 136
belief in supernatural entities, 375
belief in terms of evi-

dence, 319
beliefs and assumptions, 172
beliefs and consolidates in-group cohesion, 411
beliefs and prejudices, 231, 331
beliefs in hierarchies, 156
belief systems, 58, 410
　traditional, 311
believers, 7, 9–10, 12, 18–19, 28, 38, 40–41, 43, 45, 49, 51, 319, 337–39, 379, 390–91
　contemporary, 18, 412
　early, 235, 339
　erstwhile, 38
　like-minded, 418
　orthodox, 405
　pious, 219
　scientific, 361
　traditional, 12, 113, 206
　true, 299
benevolent God-image, 390
　traditional, 211
Benson, 391, 422
Bering, 167, 422
Berkeley, 355
Berkovits, 213, 422
Bernard, 285–86
Bethlehem, 336
Bhagavad Gita, 132
biases, 37, 60, 262, 394
　empirical, 156
　pre-existing, 386
Bible, 40–41, 96, 109–10, 125, 170–72, 176, 179, 190–91, 217–18, 296–307, 310–11, 314–15, 322, 330–32, 346–47, 354–55, 397, 407–9, 417, 427–31
Bible claims, 362
Bible in local languages, 296
Bible in psychological perspective, 438
Bible's anthropomorphic depictions of God, 208
Bible's authority, 332
Bible's dark images of God, 218

Bible's inconsistencies, 331
Bible's laws, 354
Bible stories, 30, 44
Bible worships, 353
biblical, 55, 61, 207, 301, 303, 411, 437
  earlier, 202
  traditional, 31
Biblical Anthropomorphic Projections, 191
biblical books, 351
biblical characters, 394
biblical comments, 390
biblical depictions, 219
biblical descriptions, 183
biblical God-image, 44, 96, 100, 183, 187, 199, 214, 217–19, 311, 374
biblical history, 172, 322, 434
  confirming, 171
biblical inerrancy, 330–31
biblical Job, 115, 120
biblical literature, 181, 423
  important, 175
biblical material, 172
biblical message, 296, 332
  true, 62
biblical miracle stories, 40
biblical monotheism, 439
biblical Moses, 57, 171
biblical myth, 153, 304
biblical myth of creation, 304
biblical narrators, 190
biblical obsession, 40
biblical passages, 51, 76, 345, 368, 400
biblical period, 213
biblical personalities, 171, 323
biblical phrases, 176
biblical prohibition, 401
biblical prophecy, 335
biblical reason, 161
biblical references, 239
biblical religion, 353
biblical research, 332
  historical-critical, 305
biblical revelation, 208, 297

biblical scholars, 176, 322
biblical scholarship, 322
Biblical Sources, 4
biblical stories, 52–53, 167, 170–72, 190, 198, 218, 224, 238, 323, 394, 401
  literalizing, 137
  mythic, 16
  traditional, 137
biblical story of Job, 98, 391
biblical study, 322, 442
biblical text, 13, 169–70, 178, 182, 185, 193, 219, 303, 314
biblical theology, 96, 436
  synthesize, 207
biblical tradition, 21, 224
biblical verses, 269
biblical writers, 161, 331
biblical Yhwh, 82, 109, 126, 138, 156, 176, 179, 181, 405
biblical Yhwh and Christ, 126
bicameral mind, 377
Big Bang, 9, 329–30, 367
Big Bang hypothesis, 20
bigotry, 41, 293, 384
biologists, 42, 362
  modern, 44
biology, 362, 428
  evolutionary, 22
  modern, 436
Bion, 384
birth, 86, 95, 153, 172, 186, 222, 256, 289–90, 336, 438, 441
  biological, 402
  hazardous, 324
  new, 242
  ordinary, 340
  physical, 270
birth of God, 95, 289
Bishop Berkeley, 355
Black Death, 290
Black Madonna, 157
Black theologies, 314, 420
Black theology and Womanist theology, 416

Black women's Jesus, 430
Blaise Pascal, 351
Blake, William, 333, 360
blessed Abram, 236
Blessed Virgin Mary, 157, 236, 238, 337, 391
blessings, 84, 179, 198
  father's, 221
  financial, 338
blinding light, 25
blindness, systematic, 95
blind watchmaker, 44, 426
blood, 57, 150, 160, 179, 184, 234, 236, 249, 254, 261, 276–77
  clad in a robe dipped in, 245
  eating, 40, 234, 261
  menstrual, 187
  sacrificial, 57
  saved by the, 277
  washed in the, 277
blood of Christ, 236, 284, 296
blood sacrifice, 152, 240, 259, 276–77, 341
blueprint, 86, 207, 222
Blumenthal, 217, 422
bodily shaking, involuntary, 30
body, 36, 42–43, 84, 87, 147, 150, 154, 157–58, 189, 224–25, 236–38, 259, 283–84, 329, 340, 352, 354, 361
  diseased, 204
  earthly, 275
  female, 367
  refined, 164
  spiritual, 246
  transfigured, 316
body and blood of Christ, 284, 296
body and soul, 113
body of Christ, 242, 265, 341–42, 381
body of death, 262
body of myth, 238
Boehme, Jacob, 141, 271, 291
Bohm, 127, 422

Bohn, 423
Bollas, 384, 422
Bomford, 61, 422
Bonaventure, 288–89
book of Acts, 230, 241, 255
book of Deuteronomy, 198, 221
book of Genesis, 170, 236–37
Book of Job, 106, 142, 175, 189, 225
book of Judges, 179
book of Leviticus, 160, 206
book of life, 188, 224
Book of Mormon, 439
Book of Nature, 346
book of numbers, 194
book of Proverbs, 181
book of Psalms, 107
book of Revelation, 105, 107, 228, 236, 251, 273, 311, 343, 441
book of Sirach, 182
book of Zechariah, 193
Borg, 320, 422
Bouchard, 53, 422
boundaries, 123, 238
  dissolving ego, 116
  legitimate, 123
  sharp, 151
Bourgeault, 271–72, 340–41, 422
Boyer, 373, 375, 422
Boyle, 7, 346, 356
brain, 45, 129–30, 145–46, 156, 349, 369, 372–78, 408, 419, 438, 441
  human, 362, 372–74
  normal, 339
  physical, 15
brain aberrations, 24
brain activity, 43, 408
brain mechanisms, 42, 408
brain processes, 371, 375
brain program, 373
brain states, 408
brain structures, 375, 419
brain systems, 373
brain to brain, 45

Brandon, 320, 422
bread, 202, 240, 284, 296, 341
  consecrated, 236
  true, 236
Breuggemann, 217
bride, 273, 412
  unfaithful, 193
bride of Christ, 273
Bridgman, 342, 422
Brill, 423
British monk Pelagius, 281
Bronze Age, 156, 417
Brooks, 422
brothers, 104, 155, 176
  hostile, 127
Brothers Karamazov, 38
Bruno, 293
Buber, 123–24, 423
Buddha, 82, 120, 162, 244, 274, 407
  tempted, 337
Bulkeley, 115, 405, 423
Bultmann, 53, 306, 368, 423
burials, 150, 158, 441
  final, 418
burial sites, 150, 171
burning bush, 25, 140, 185, 190
Byzantine emperor Justinian, 155
Byzantine empress Theodora, 341

C
Cain, 127
Calvin, 239, 243, 297–99, 338
Calvinist tradition, 231
Cambridge, 436, 443
Cambridge Platonists, 350
Campbell, 240, 402–3, 409, 423, 436
Camus, 41
  Albert, 49
Canaan, 18, 171, 173, 185, 222, 408, 426
  ancient, 424
Canaanite cult, 171
Canaanite deities, 276

  multiple, 138
Canaanite gods, 177, 238
Canaanite gods El and Baal, 177
Canaanite myth and Hebrew epic, 425
Canaanite mythology, 178
Canaanite Queen, 338
Canaanite religion, 178
Canaanites, 179, 181, 184, 196, 219, 222–23, 225
Canaanite society, 171
Canaanite temples, 181
Canaanite traditions and worshipping El, 171
Canaanite woman, 242
Canada, 427
canon, 41, 169, 231, 335, 345
  final, 169
Canterbury, 285
capacity, 26, 109, 137, 140–41, 145, 184–85, 193, 336, 341–42, 350, 400–401
  cognitive, 16
  defensive, 31
  given, 308
  human, 52, 287, 371
  increased, 384
  individual's, 383
  intellectual, 51
  intrinsic, 10
  marked, 263
  necessary, 98
  soothing, 383
  symbolic, 148
Capps, 27, 322, 393, 397, 423
captivity, 25, 194
caregivers, 51
  early, 370, 386, 391
  primary, 387, 391
Carella, 223, 423
Carmody, 153
Carter, 422
Carthage, 231, 281
Casement, 424
Çatalhöyük, 154
cathedrals, 152
  medieval, 274

Catholic Church, 298, 434
Catholic clergy, 62
Catholic philosopher Marin Mersenne, 348
Catholics, 62, 221, 294, 299, 346
causality, 20, 143, 352, 384
causation, 20, 302
cave art, 424
Caverne, 148
caves, 148–50
celibacy, 259
celibate priests, 274
censure, 195
  stresses divine, 389
centers of consciousness, 86, 93
Central Asian Iran, 161
central image of Christ, 278
centuries BCE, 162
  thirteenth, 171
century, 47–49, 222, 230–31, 274, 280, 282–83, 301, 303–5, 318–19, 338, 341, 356, 359, 361, 363
  eighteenth, 33–34, 209, 300–301, 303, 317, 356
  first, 11, 207
  mid-fifth, 221
  mid-twentieth, 288, 313
  second, 232, 332
  sixteenth, 292, 410
  thirteenth, 142, 209, 289–90
century BCE, 11, 154–55, 163, 167, 174, 177, 181, 192, 203, 222
  first, 30, 165
  third, 345
certainties
  old, 312
  traditional, 349
chain, 258, 342, 355
  great, 292
Chalcedon, 269
Cham, 424
change, 41, 43, 65, 67, 120–21, 151–52, 203, 205, 208, 280, 307, 388, 390

changeless, 13–14, 287, 306, 308, 312, 329, 360, 363
Changing God-images, 332
changing religious identity, 432
chaos, 160, 247, 375
  initial, 10
  order amid, 172
characteristics
  acquired, 419
  evolved, 182
  human, 15, 151, 159, 191, 371, 373
  important, 175
  opposite, 47
  personal, 306
  unique, 61
characterological masochism, 266
characters, 36, 55, 183, 190, 218, 377, 394
  complex, 394
  daemonic, 95
  eternal, 71
  moral, 173
Chardin, 313, 316, 342, 426
Charet, 121, 123, 423
chariot, 153, 201
charismatic, 57–58, 411
charismatic leader, 83
Charles Darwin's theory, 44
Charles V, 296
Chauvet cave, 150
Cheyenne, 426
chief deity, 171, 180
  particular tribe's, 223
child, 120, 125, 184, 235, 242, 319, 343, 383–84, 386–87, 390, 396–97, 419, 423
  dead, 232
  growing, 387
  inner, 119–20
  male, 380
  rebellious, 184, 218
  sensitive, 396
childhood, 85, 97, 370,

384, 386, 388, 395–98, 428–29, 431
childhood abuse, 397, 439
childhood and society, 428
childhood association, 373
childhood development, 52
childhood experience, 28
childhood image, 105
childhood indoctrination, 5
childhood residues, 388
childhood trauma, 28
  early, 85
children, 30, 38, 171, 180, 183–85, 251, 254, 386, 388, 419, 424
  betrayal predisposes, 397
  children's, 184
  human, 336
  innocent Egyptian, 217
  innocent first-born, 185
  killing Christian, 399
  male, 174
  protecting, 372
  young, 380
child sacrifice, 276, 412
  practiced, 178
Chilton, 320, 423
Christ, 75, 88–90, 103–5, 224–25, 235–40, 242–43, 256–57, 263–65, 268–70, 277–79, 289–90, 295–96, 298–99, 309–11, 313–14, 316–18, 332–34, 340–43, 380–81, 414–15
  cosmic, 316
  imitation of, 414
  light shining in, 227
  mystical, 316
  offering, 278
  real, 415
  rejected, 243
  the Rock was, 256
  symbolized, 332
  tempted, 88
  you are the, 337
Christ and God, 256
Christ and Mercurius, 113

INDEX | 453

Christ consciousness, 313
Christ-event, 338
Christian and Jewish thought, 224
Christian anti-Semitism, 215, 243
Christian apologists, 43, 229
Christian archetype, 427
Christian art, 332, 333
Christian ascetics and celibate priests, 274
Christian atheism, 421
Christian authoritarian approach, traditional, 315
Christian authorities, 254, 410
Christian belief, 53, 61, 244, 272, 283, 305, 440
  standard, 267
  traditional, 304
  true, 279
Christian believer dreams, 75
Christian certainties, traditional, 216
Christian charity, 333
Christian Church, 255
Christian churches, 155, 216, 251, 338
  early, 231
Christian claims, 254, 331
Christian commentators, 205
Christian community, 355
  emerging mainstream, 335
Christian concepts, traditional, 229, 248, 356
Christian country, 419
Christian denominations, 227, 304, 326, 335
Christian denominations focus, 77
Christian depreciation, 414
Christian doctrine, 48, 90, 142, 164, 238–39, 285, 361, 381
  traditional, 75
Christian doctrine evil, 107

Christian doctrine of existence, 333
Christian dogma, 236, 289
Christian emphasis, 48, 414
Christian era, 135, 345
Christian Eucharist, 261
Christian Europe, 293
Christian evangelism, 334
Christian faith, 305, 318–19, 346, 430, 438–39
Christian folklore, 336
Christian Fundamentalism, 180, 310
Christian God, 302–3, 333, 352, 406
Christian God-image, 18, 48, 54, 227, 229, 239, 300–301, 304, 312, 323, 332
  classical, 74
  original, 325
Christian heritage, 26
Christian history, 115, 229, 332, 427
Christian ideals, 34
Christian image of God, 227, 273, 323
Christian imagery, 413
  traditional, 75
Christian imperialism, 334
Christian insistence, 334
Christian institutions, 215
Christian interpretation, 390, 400
Christian interpretation of dreams, 433
Christian intolerance, 263
Christianity, 16–18, 32–33, 47–48, 59–61, 134–36, 157–59, 215–16, 227, 237–40, 242–43, 252–53, 276–77, 292, 303–7, 333–35, 346–48, 350–54, 409–10, 420–23, 440–42
  attacked institutional, 301
  changed Western, 294
  contemporary, 338
  demythologize, 413
  free, 368
  influenced, 36

  liberalize, 33
  mainstream, 269, 276
  modern liberal, 313
  phallocentric, 367
  promoted, 230
  revitalizing, 292
  stream, 239
  trinitarian, 351
Christianity and psychoanalysis, 422, 442
Christianity split, 341
Christian leaders, 251, 266
Christian literature, 142
Christian martyrs, 249, 333
Christian message, 240, 253, 309, 323, 332
Christian messianism, 430
Christian monarchs and popes, 215
Christian monks, 319
Christian morality, 48
Christian mystics, 290
Christian myth, 104, 413
Christian mythology, 238
Christian nationalists, 419
Christian nativity scene, 240
Christian New Testament, 221
Christian non-duality, 338
Christian opinion, 346
Christian orthodoxy, 279
Christian paradoxes, great, 247
Christian phenomenon, 215
Christian philosophy, 229–30
Christian Platonist, 279
Christian politics, 325
Christian purposes, 237
Christian religion, 304
Christian ritual of confession and atonement for guilt, 380
Christians, 38–39, 104–5, 114–16, 215–16, 228–30, 234–35, 239, 241–42, 252–54, 264–65, 268, 272–73, 276–77, 288–89, 332–35, 338–40, 360, 399–400, 402, 409–10

anonymous, 59, 309
authentic, 360
baptized, 296
committed, 232
contemporary, 243, 249, 276, 319
earlier, 319
fundamentalist, 338
gentile, 242
mainstream, 343
medieval, 163, 243, 283–84
persecuted, 343
pious, 293
progressive, 260
traditional, 18
Christian scholastics, 208
Christian spirituality, 426
Christian story, 79, 228, 238, 335, 413, 416
Christian story of Jesus' atonement, 156
Christian stress on correct belief, 334
Christian symbolism, 413
Christian symbols, 134, 332, 413
Christian teaching, 18, 266, 285, 289, 390, 414
orthodox, 232
Christian theologians, 108, 215–16, 225, 253, 269, 274, 277–78, 325, 334, 338, 341
medieval, 164
Christian theology, 48, 103, 108, 121, 142, 216, 233, 237, 283–84, 435, 441
Christian thinkers, 39, 230, 280, 342
original early, 279
troubled, 230
Christian tradition, 103, 105, 134–35, 237, 239, 267, 270, 273, 276–78, 306–7, 403, 406–7, 410, 413
charismatic, 77
emerging, 240
mainstream, 340
Christian traditionalists, 62

Christian Trinity, 20, 114, 124, 289
Christian writers, 228, 240
Christie-Murray, 267, 424
Christification of many, 87
Christ Jesus, 260, 336
Christ myth theory, 343
Christ of faith, 233, 317–18
Christopher, 435
Christ's atoning death, 257
Christ's followers, 257
Christ's miracles, 311
Christ's sacrifice, 277
Christ's side, 246
Christ's spirituality, 88
Christ who lives in me, 74
Chrysostom, John, 254
Church, 76, 125, 135, 138, 271, 283–84, 294, 296, 304, 308–9, 314–16, 334, 345–46, 385, 402–3
early, 232, 260, 266, 273, 318, 335, 337
father's, 125
official, 70, 234, 275
Pauline, 260
true, 298
Church and Bible, 94
Church anti-Judaism and cultural anti-Semitism, 254
church attendance, 312
routine, 53
church authority, 52, 254, 282, 291–92, 341, 356, 419
church councils, 231, 234, 270, 335
early, 320
churches, 77, 135, 140, 259–60, 274, 287, 292, 296, 301, 304, 315, 340, 360–61
early, 332
institutional, 37
medieval, 289
unified, 231
church fathers, 243, 285, 340
early, 228, 406

Church Father Tertullian, 51
church hierarchy, 62, 288, 298, 361
male, 271
churchmen, worldly, 294
Church Militant, 252
church practices, 294
Church's attitude, 259
Church's history of violent suppression of heretics, 53
Church's thinking, 290
Church teaching, 71, 286
central, 293
official, 76
circles, inner, 119
circularity, 50, 362
circumcision, 241–42, 258, 268, 334, 381
cities, 111, 153, 159–60, 195, 204, 217, 224, 248, 254, 290
conquered, 18, 290
destroyed, 171
important Canaanite, 223
Citlak, 322, 424
civilization, 41–42, 153, 379, 429
ancient Egyptian, 406
pacifist, 156
Clack, 327, 424
claims, 5–6, 9, 11, 24–25, 39–40, 132, 137, 156, 233, 240–41, 245, 282, 323, 337, 377–78
classical, 306
competing, 83
post-modern, 130
religious, 136, 309
claim superiority, 135
Clairvaux, 285
clan, 147
particular, 147
Clark, 7, 422, 424
classes, 153, 315
new merchant, 290
social, 297
classical form, 288, 369
classical Judeo-Christian image of God, 310

INDEX | 455

classical metaphorical descriptions, 6
Classical Prophets, 223
classical theistic descriptions, 139
clay carvings, 153
clergy, 40, 125, 294, 299
　self-serving, 393
clerical privilege, 300
clerical superstructures, 237
Clift, 108
climate, 145
　new, 435
　stable, 151
Clinical applications, 435
clinician, 29, 110, 192
Clottes, 148–49, 424
cloud of unknowing, 282
clouds, 110, 188, 201, 261, 321, 337–38, 373, 421, 430
　great, 110
code, 221
　moral, 11, 37, 159, 284
coexistence, peaceful, 292
cognition, 99, 190, 307
cognitive abilities, 375
　human, 162
cognitive assent to doctrine and dogma, 308
cognitive processes, 373–74
　encoded, 419
Cognitive Sciences, 42, 421, 437
cognitive study of religion, 442
cognitive systems, 44, 128, 374
Cognitive Theories, 371
cohabitation, 187
Cohen, 213–14, 424
Cohen & Phipps, 81
cohesion, 372, 410, 419
　consolidates in-group, 411
　increasing group, 376
　social, 148, 362
coincidentia oppositorum, 116, 142, 291
Cole, 30, 424

Coleman, 422
collective Judeo-Christian image of God, 120
collective myth, 77, 119, 138
　new, 97
Colledge & McGinn, 338
Colman, 141, 424
colonialism, 37
Colossians, 256, 260, 277, 325, 339–40
comes upon man spontaneously, 110
comfort, 38–39, 187, 193, 265, 369–70
comforted Jacob, 405
comforting, 379, 417
comforting fable, 39
comforting paternal overtones, 79
commandments, 39, 100, 138, 161, 176, 186, 218–19, 225, 242, 331–32, 388–89
　humanitarian, 218
commandments in Exodus, 161, 218
commands, 18, 52, 179, 184, 189, 225, 244, 278, 296, 412
commentaries, 173, 424
Commentary, 435
commentators, 249
　rabbinic, 225
commission, 201
　apostolic, 256
commitment, 16, 24, 50, 137–38, 214, 306–7, 360, 370
　metaphysical, 255, 407–8
　moral, 364
　personal, 360
　prior, 42, 369
　prior religious, 76, 320
　rejected religious, 43
　renewed, 180
Common Essence, 59
common experience, 424
communion, 117, 298, 383
communities, 30, 57, 91–92, 141–42, 151–53, 231, 233, 241, 248, 362, 372

　dedicated, 58
　national, 213
　orthodox, 212
　religious, 52, 76
　scientific, 7
companions, 108, 237, 339
company, 290, 429
　parted, 253
comparative iconography, 140
compassion, 39, 41, 190, 196, 223, 250, 278, 293, 390, 398, 400
compensatory activity, 143
competition, 180, 337
　sometimes-murderous, 80
completeness, 109
　approximate, 414
completion, 111, 132, 140
　mutual, 89
complexes, 74, 87–88
　cultural, 123
　negatively-toned, 121
　personal, 100
　powerful, 206
　unconscious, 411
complexio oppositorum, 142
complexity, 9, 24, 218, 362, 371–72, 393
　biological, 10
　inordinate, 42
　religion's, 382
complex life forms, 44
complex philosophical problem, 24
complex physicochemical system, 43
complex religious notions, 45
complex ritual processes, 160
complex symbol system, 332
complicity of Christian politics in acts of violence, 325
components, 56, 85, 92, 142, 183, 379, 406, 410–11
　important, 340

important spiritual, 86
non-rational, 43
projected, 137
rational, 62
religious, 162
components of religion, 411
Comte, 48
conceptions, 71, 287, 294
 human, 217
 metaphysical, 324
 undisguised alchemical, 75
concepts
 relative, 127
 traditional, 365
conceptual approach to evil, 122
conceptual difficulties, 18
conceptual Thought, 59
conceptual understanding, 78
condemnation, 297
 eternal, 306
conditioned contents of consciousness, 35
confessional, 238
confessions, 97, 124, 380
confirmation, 360
 reliable historical, 317
conflict, 88, 91, 134–35, 137, 141–42, 160, 227, 232, 250, 253, 262, 265, 323
 basic ideational, 128
 provoking, 343
conflicts, internal, 88, 206, 268
conformity, 308, 314, 389
conformity bias, 375
Confucius, 162
confusion, 3, 78, 129, 212, 216, 298
 conceptual, 141
connection, 27, 29, 74, 77, 90, 92, 119–20, 137–38, 324, 336, 339, 413, 416
 archetypal, 152
 causal, 23, 115
 conceptual, 172
 conscious, 114
 cosmic, 383

human, 283
indelible, 281
lost, 287
personal, 11, 30
personal symbolic, 109
potential, 343
symbolic, 413
unmediated, 29
valid, 367
conquest, 91, 160, 171, 206, 222, 324, 333, 408
 military, 192
 violent, 171
conquest of evil, 333
conscience, 350, 419
 bad, 413
 disturbed, 398
 pure, 286
 self-critical, 265
consciousness, 6, 15, 82–86, 88–89, 93, 99–101, 110, 113–14, 126, 130–31, 140–43, 146, 302, 366, 377, 408, 417–18
 bridge, 109
 collective, 109, 326
 developing, 413
 discriminating, 336
 ego's, 83
 ever-increasing, 87
 evolved, 377
consciousness, human, 79, 94
consciousness
 imageless, 101
 increased, 106, 414
 increasing, 101
 individual, 131, 141
 individual's, 89
 infinite, 131, 385
 new, 136
 patriarchal, 367
 personal, 83, 93
 pre-existent to, 71
 rather dim, 99
 reflecting, 89, 99
 self-reflective, 376
 separate, 141
 ultimate, 128
 universal, 128
Consciousness and world, 131

consciousness of being, 302
conscious religious orientation, 75
conscious tendencies, 72
consecration, 276
consensual reality, 81
consensus, 76, 169, 298, 319–20, 323
 common, 176
 social, 23
Conservative Christians, 59, 62
Conservative Protestants, 310, 332
conservatives, 252, 331
consolation, 46, 204, 392
 powerful, 416
consort, 155, 181, 184
 female, 178, 181
Constantine, 37, 230, 252, 268, 332, 410
Constantinople, 269, 272, 341
constant mirroring, 100
constructivism, 62–63
constructivist position, 129
contact, 24, 26, 31–32, 38, 40, 57–58, 90–91, 94, 96, 208–9, 402, 404
 direct symbolic, 138
 personal, 2
 result of, 32, 61
contact of humanity and divinity, 208
containment, internal, 140
contemplation, 288, 403
 pure, 403
contemporary accounts of religion, 147
contemporary apologists, 219
Contemporary neuroscientists, 377
contemporary philosophy, 208, 424
Contemporary preachers, 172
contemporary scholarship, 320, 422
contemporary spirituality, 441

content, 2, 6, 15–17, 27, 61, 66, 69–70, 86, 101, 408, 414
  conditioned, 35
  moral, 217
  perceiving unconscious, 92
  repressed, 134
  symbolic, 91
context, 11, 15, 62, 78, 87, 181, 189, 237, 241, 251, 260
  cultural, 30, 96, 323
  fixed mythic, 141
  historical, 172, 195, 320
  linguistic, 307
  psychotherapeutic, 68
  religious, 395
  social, 129, 206, 303, 321
contextualist position, radical, 130
contiguous events, 20
contradicting Jesus, 339
contradictions, 13, 61, 209, 283
  internal, 40
contrast, 2, 5, 50, 52, 79, 88–89, 121–23, 218–19, 340, 343, 365, 367, 369
control, 34, 40, 107, 135, 156, 159, 177, 336–38, 393, 395, 403
  final, 310
  human, 161
  ideological, 266
  muscle, 339
  sovereign, 330
  wrest, 255
controversy, 6, 33, 99, 201, 205, 222, 227, 259, 267, 273, 276–77
  historical, 4
  important early, 235
  scholarly, 231
  sectarian, 32
convergence of cultures and religions in light, 425
conversations, 206, 349, 439

conversion, 260, 264–65, 332, 338–39, 406
conversion of Constantine, 252, 332
conviction, 23, 43, 111, 206
  intense, 58
  pure, 46
Coogan, 181, 424
Coogan & Chapman, 171
Copernicus, 345–46
Coptic, 335
Corbett, 26, 30, 55, 61, 67–68, 75, 101, 107–8, 114, 142–43, 424–25
Corbin, 404, 425
Corinthians, 51, 53, 235, 238, 242, 245–47, 249, 256, 258–61, 263, 265–66, 323, 325
Cornett, 388
Corporal punishment, 396
corporeal spirit, 349
correct belief, 77, 97, 279, 299, 334
correct form of religion, 294
correlation, 53, 133, 390
  inevitable, 323
correspondence, 115, 227, 423, 433
  private, 140
correspondence style, 391
corrupt clerics, 293
corruption, 33, 107, 293, 339
  human, 296
Cosimo, 429
cosmic, 325, 348
cosmic accident, 10
cosmic ecology, 119
cosmic Oversoul, 301
cosmic powers of evil, 337
cosmogonic significance, 88
cosmological, 19
cosmologists, 9, 21
cosmos, 7, 43, 291
Council, 211, 224, 231, 268–69, 273, 281, 296, 298, 402

Council of Societies, 437
councils and theologians, 296
counter, 9, 31, 38, 76, 138, 347, 350
  important, 318
  skeptical, 378
counter-argument, important, 101
countered notions, 34
counterfactual, 372
counterintuitive, 128, 372–73
Counter Reformation, 298
Cousins, 425
covenant, 102, 135–36, 173, 175, 194, 196–97, 199, 202, 204, 206, 211, 213, 216, 221–22
  distinct, 311
  first, 243
  new, 201, 213, 243, 257–58, 261, 283, 335
  old, 243
  original, 213, 225, 257, 283
  special, 196
covenant theology, 243
cow-goddess, 154
Cox, 432
creation, 9–10, 13–14, 55, 102–3, 107, 154–55, 189–90, 207–10, 221–23, 229–30, 238, 275, 282–83, 287–89, 304, 316–17
  continuous, 279
  human, 285, 313, 368
  new, 258, 414
  original, 177
  permeated, 278
  suffering, 335
creation event, 9
creation mythologies, 155
creation myths, 173, 210
  earlier, 173
  earlier Babylonian, 172
  original, 224
creation of consciousness, 427
creation of memes, 45

creation story, 172
  second, 221, 238
creative confrontation, 49
creative influx, 29
creativity, 19, 48, 290, 383, 414
  human, 358
creator, 8–11, 14, 16, 19–20, 33–34, 43–44, 46, 55, 99, 157–58, 164–65, 189, 288–89, 356–57, 367
  benevolent, 362
  cosmic, 161
  infinite, 360
  intelligent, 10
  second, 132
creator God, 6, 13, 61, 267, 305
  infinite, 261
  separate, 35
creator of heaven and earth, 186
creature feeling, 25
creatures, 14, 25, 110, 208, 280–81, 286–87, 300
  conscious, 99
  human, 310
  incomplete, 47
  lowest, 342
  ordinary, 287
  outsize, 111
  separate, 354
creedal statements, 77
Crenshaw, 217, 425
Crete, 154
crisis, 31, 178, 204, 384
  emotional, 265
  moral, 215
  national, 38
critics, 20, 23, 35, 54, 61, 76, 115, 123, 286, 357
  hostile, 276
critique of emergent theologies, 434
critique of fundamentalism, 393
critique of Jung's approach, 116
critique of pure reason, 433

critique of religion, 41
critique of religion and philosophy, 433
critique of Thomism, 288
critiques, 41, 116, 124, 131, 325–26, 388, 393, 413, 422, 424, 434
  behaviorist, 393
  important, 382, 395
  satirical, 293
  traditional, 310
  trenchant, 117
Crito, 406
crops, 151–52, 155–56, 161
crowd, 241
crown, 210, 273
  indented, 119
crucifixion, 76, 105, 216, 245, 247, 275, 283, 314–15, 332, 335, 337
cruel, 55, 172, 397, 412
cruel consequences, 99
cruel deaths, suffered, 419
cruel dimensions, 219
cruel test, 100
cruel treatment of Job, 98
cruelty, 41, 98, 218, 254, 305, 363, 419
  grotesque, 365
Crusaders, 289
crusades, 252, 290, 292
  moral, 414
cryptograms, 111
Culotta, 374, 425
cult, 155, 162, 178, 181
  religious, 83
cult center, 154
cultivation, 36
cult leader, 58
cult object, 167
Cultural anti-Semitism, 254, 399
cultural background, 62, 130, 318
cultural circumstances, 169
cultural conditions, 323
cultural factors, 134
cultural support, 61
cultured despisers, 439
culture heroes, 62
cultures, 50, 53, 91, 126,

130, 156, 313, 315, 361, 363, 425, 441, 443
  androcentric, 156
  child's, 387
  contemporary, 167, 313
  first century Jewish, 253
  foraging, 146
  industrial, 305
  modern, 307
  monotheistic Jewish, 269
  patriarchal, 325
  popular, 61, 321
  religious, 30, 115, 240
  surviving, 146
  western, 125, 218, 378
cultures and religions, 425
Cupitt, 313, 425
cure of souls, 430
curses, 68, 174, 184, 201, 212, 259, 263, 335
Cusa, 142, 291, 431
Cybele/Attis, 273
cycle, 111, 152, 187, 213
  annual, 155
  crop, 151
cycles of nature, 152
Cynic philosophers, 164
Cyrus, 202–3
Cyrus's victory, 203

D
Daly, 224, 326, 425
damage, 85, 210, 224, 397
  emotional, 396
damaged ego-Self relationship, 86
Dame, 421, 429, 437
damnation, 297, 352
  eternal, 18, 261, 263, 277, 334, 379
dangers, 9, 42, 44, 68, 176, 223, 306, 348, 372, 391
  psychological, 323
  signal, 374
Daniel, 112, 161, 188, 191, 235–36, 245, 337, 351, 405
darkness, 103–4, 107, 111, 113, 148, 239, 282
  diffuse, 173

darkness predisposes, 148
dark paganism, 94
dark side, 38, 91, 98–100, 102–8, 113, 121–22, 134, 142, 183, 187, 215–18
dark side of Christian history, 427
dark side of God, 99, 105, 107, 142, 224, 295
dark son, 113
dark underworld, 159
Darwin, 34, 44, 304, 361–62
Darwinian quality, 310
Darwin's opponents, 62
David, King, 171, 173, 185, 195, 204–5, 221–22, 230, 248
David's dynasty, 174
Davies, 7, 425
Davis, 3, 12, 22, 156, 169, 425–26, 443
Dawkins, 44–45, 425–26
Dawkins delusion, 435
Dawkins' selfish-gene theory, 45
day-dreaming, simple, 404
Dead Sea, 180, 321
Dead Sea Scrolls, 169, 441
deaf ears, 47
death, 48–49, 150, 152–53, 158–59, 216–18, 240–43, 246, 248–49, 255, 257, 264, 277–78, 284–85, 295, 298–99, 318–19, 333, 336–38, 369–70, 372
  decreed, 257
  painful, 246, 249, 272, 324
  produced, 238
  tortured, 259
death anxiety, 373
  extreme, 390
death camps, 212, 214
death of God approach, 212
death penalty, 184, 218
defeat, 87, 179, 182, 196, 198–99, 204, 211, 245, 248, 294, 338
  avenge Israel's, 205
  disastrous, 205
  final, 314
  greatest, 207
  military, 199–200
  suffered, 174
defeat of evil, 338
defender, 301
  early, 347
  strong, 348
Defending inerrancy, 429
defense of reason and belief in God, 424
defenses, 54, 112, 116, 133, 175, 213, 312, 331, 379, 381–82, 424
  free-will, 211
  psychological, 42
defensive efforts, 419
defensive reaction, 52
definitive expression, 139
definitive good-bye, 418
degrees, 9, 20, 54, 58, 167, 176, 280, 286–87, 317, 330, 395
  decreasing, 35
  increasing, 36
  lesser, 54, 280, 291
  terrifying, 94
  traumatic, 397
deintegrate, 86
deism, 33–34, 301
  advocated, 354
Deist God-image, 32, 44
deist image of God, 32
deist luminary, 301
deists, 32–34, 301, 317
deities, 3, 8–9, 137–38, 150, 153–54, 159–60, 165, 167, 176–80, 191–92, 199–200, 206–7, 223–24, 267–68, 369–70
  all-powerful, 327
  ancient, 434
  eternal, 61
  external, 26, 138
  friendly, 55
  imaginary, 47
  imperfect, 275
  important, 165
  inferior, 164
  metaphysical, 124
  mountain, 176
  pagan, 333
  patron, 159
  personal, 228
  preferred, 224
  projected, 82
  resurrecting, 158
deliverance, 249, 314, 420
Delphi, 405
delusion, 30, 67
delusional, 7, 321, 412
demands atonement, 256
demands attention, 114
demands piety, 205
Demeter, 157, 159
demi-gods, 157
Demiurge, 164, 275
  eternal, 163
demon, powerful, 337
demon Mara, 337
demons, 26, 48, 56, 61, 79, 233, 244, 321
demythologize, 62, 415
demythologizing, 53, 306
denial, 6, 107–8, 116, 266, 338, 418
Dennett, 42, 426
denominations, 297, 312
departure, 141
  radical, 250
dependence, 100, 398
  reduced, 303
dependency, 48
  absolute, 302
depicted Jesus, 256, 332
depiction, 218, 233, 254, 321
depression, 31, 395–97, 430
Depressives, 383
deprivation, 439
  sensory, 148
depth psychology, 2–3, 73, 128, 429
depths, 8, 70–71, 91–93, 137, 209, 289, 303, 307–8, 377, 418

460 | THE GOD-IMAGE

Descartes, 348–50, 356
Descartes postulates, 368
descendants, 222, 257, 405
descendent, 153, 230, 248, 380
descent, 154, 201
Descriptions of God in scripture, 208
desert, 171, 173, 256
Desiderius Erasmus, 292
design, 6–10, 12, 16, 18, 21–23, 44, 345, 347, 352, 356–57, 426
  intelligent, 10
  pre-ordained, 10
design argument, 8–9, 21–22
designer, 9, 21, 347, 351, 354, 357, 368
  celestial, 9
  intelligent, 8, 362
  purported, 9
design features, 419
design in nature, 18, 21–22, 33, 347, 350, 354
design of complex mechanisms, 21
design phenomenon, 372
despair, 31, 49, 101, 214, 262, 285, 305, 323, 336, 397, 399
  human, 307, 363
  spiritual, 395
destiny, 84, 324
destruction, 104, 107, 171, 174, 180, 182, 202, 204–5, 213, 242–43, 412
  complete, 327
  eternal, 334
  painful, 180
destruction of evil, 390
destruction of humanity, 311
destruction of Jerusalem, 202, 253
destructiveness, 370
destructive trait, 327
determinants, important, 390
Determinism, 366
Deuteronomic, 221

Deuteronomic law commands, 176
Deuteronomistic editors, 224
Deuteronomists, 199
Deuteronomist source, 221
Deuteronomy, 174–76, 178, 180–81, 183–84, 186–87, 193, 198–99, 210, 212, 217–18, 221, 223, 404–5
devaluation, 40, 157, 276, 340
  harsh, 54
  traditional Christianity's, 75
development, 10–11, 22–23, 33, 84–86, 94–95, 135–36, 145–46, 151, 170–71, 175–77, 187, 192–93, 217–18, 227–343, 366, 385–86, 413, 418
  cultural, 136
  dialectical, 359
  emotional, 419
  ethical, 58
  fullest, 86
  human, 429
  important, 250, 273
  inspired, 49
  moral, 281, 356, 359
  precocious, 324
  progressive, 223
  psychological, 118, 383
  theological, 401
developmental factors, 395
developmental ground plan, 86
developmental Implications, 83
developmental stage, 361
development of agriculture, 151
development of consciousness, 418
development of devotion to Yhwh, 177
development of discriminating consciousness, 336
development of God-images, 386
development of human consciousness, 88, 104
development of intelligence and consciousness, 39
development of monotheism, 165
development of myths and religion, 145
development of new consciousness, 136
development of relational psychoanalytic theory, 395
development of religion, 146, 148, 151, 382
deviation, 212, 266
devil, 103–4, 244, 251–52, 254, 276, 283, 335, 338, 399, 401, 407, 409, 414
  mythic, 95
devotees, 103, 109, 162, 165, 187, 191, 199, 240, 393
  fundamentalist, 331
devotio moderna, 292
devotion, 177, 197, 266, 274, 341, 380, 408, 412
  religious, 381
  stresses, 209
diagnosis, 192, 339
dialog, 113, 345, 418, 425
  internal, 198
  new, 366
diamond, 94
Diel, 145
dietary habits, 175
dietary rules, 206
differences, 93, 141, 143, 146, 170, 173, 221, 227, 232, 234, 286, 336, 340–41
differences in Jesus' genealogy, 336
differentiation, 81, 89, 127, 157, 341
differentiation of consciousness, 157
difficulties for Jung's approach to religion, 50

INDEX | 461

diffusion, 162, 333
dimensions, 41, 78, 127, 143, 272, 340, 366, 404, 408
　complementary, 113
　hidden, 366
　human, 268
　important, 401
　metaphysical, 70
　mythic, 320
　new, 271–72
　pleromatic, 127
　possible, 93
　psychological, 423
　social, 328
　unseen, 145
dimensions of religion, 41
Dionysius, 282
Dionysus, 162
direct contact, 206, 290, 420
　unmediated, 123
direction, 110, 196, 264, 271, 281, 384, 392, 411
　given, 142
　moral, 208
disagreement, 121, 262–63, 294, 298, 313, 336, 400, 417
　early, 267
　irreconcilable, 121
disappearance, 190, 436
　gradual, 36
disappointment, 250, 381
disasters, 199, 202, 206, 306
　national, 174, 207
　natural, 21, 373
　new, 199
　predicted, 196
　prophesized, 192
disbelief, 5, 18–19, 433
disbelievers, 18, 228
discern, 146, 262, 320, 331, 339, 366
disciples, 232, 317, 336–37, 341, 406
disciples in dreams, 406
disciplinarian, harsh, 397
disciplines, 211, 345–46, 378

fragmented, 305
harsh parental, 400
hermeneutical, 313
discontinuity, 318
　radical, 287
discovery, 7, 49, 130, 134, 198, 345–46, 367, 376, 395, 399, 427
　individual's, 301
　scientific, 300, 351
discreet experiences and images, 128
discrepancies, 35, 170, 221, 336
discrimination, 41, 99, 141
disease, 99, 145–46, 159, 186, 357, 438
disenchantment, 50, 61
disobedience, 135, 161, 237, 239, 273, 284, 346, 354
disobedient, 183, 228
disobey, 175, 224, 379
disorder, 280, 339, 357
　borderline personality, 192
　skin, 102
disorder and evil, 280
disorientation, 112, 148
Dispensationalists, 311
dispensations, 294, 311
　first, 90
　new, 90
displace doubt, 400
disputation, 291
disputes, 190, 320, 385, 423
　theological, 230, 271
dissenters, 299
　ill-treating, 372
dissident factions, 267
distance, 254, 327
　implicit divine-human, 123
distinguishing feature of Jung's psychology, 104
distress, 310
　emotional, 385
　expressed, 215
diversity, 59, 232, 271–72
divination, 160
divine, 2–6, 24–25, 27–

32, 34–35, 59–61, 65–66, 69–70, 72–74, 76–77, 88–90, 93–99, 103–7, 116–26, 134–36, 139–42, 227–30, 267–73, 275, 340–42, 383–85
the divine, 327
divine
　all-seeing, 65
　born, 267
　inner, 135
　intrapsychic, 89
　resist, 264
　transcendent, 132, 305
the divine, expression of, 66
the divine and human nature in Christ, 90
divine architect, 346
divine attributes, 192, 210, 354
divine authority, 172, 244
　claimed, 252
divine beings, 180
divine brutality, 18
divine by nature, 233
divine capacity, 197
divine child, 93, 240
divine children, 120
　fathered, 336
divine commandment, 412
divine compassion, 30
divine conflict, 88
divine consciousness, 89
divine council, 179
divine couple, 223
divine creation, 362
divine creator, 9–10
divine delight, 187
divine depths, 307
divine design, 362
divine designer, 10, 21, 44, 313, 357, 362
　supposed, 357
divine element, 119, 208
divine engineer, 347
divine essence, 307, 343
divine eye, 66, 70
divine fathers, 324, 326, 420
divine feminine, 152

divine figure, 181, 319
  pre-existing, 233
divine generosity, 224
divine geometer, 346
divine gift, 52, 153, 295
  highest, 354
divine glory, 236
divine goodness, 252
divine grace, 70, 90, 237, 262, 282–83, 342, 348, 401
  promised, 333
divine ground, 59
divine guidance, 405
divine hiddenness, 39, 438
divine-human identity, 338
divine image, 172, 220
  new, 214
divine immanence, 73
divine impregnation, 274
divine inspiration, 219, 336, 405
divine intelligence, 21–22
divine intentions, 219, 346
divine intervention, 33, 62, 171, 173, 212, 214, 222, 264–65, 350, 366
  constant, 346
  saving, 29
divine intervention in history, 62, 212, 214
divine judgment, 284
divine justice, 212
divine King, 6, 310
divine Kingdom, 135, 402
divine kingship, 157
divine laws, 59, 157, 230
divine life, 139, 152
divine light, 92
divine Logos, 279
divine love, 14
  unconditional, 266
divine manifestation, 340
divine mercy, 185
divine messages, 56, 406
divine milieu, 316, 426
divine Mind, 7, 36, 208, 270, 375
divine mother, 180
divine mother-son traditions, earlier, 273
divine mystery, 55, 188, 291, 404
divine names, 177
divine nature, 15, 163, 267, 269, 272, 274, 287, 293, 354–55
divine non-duality, 338
divine omnipotence, 398
  glorifying, 327
  traditional, 214
divine opposites, 106
divine origin, 330
divine pair, 181
divine parent, 399
divine perfection, 143, 346
divine plan, 182, 217, 247, 261, 326
divine pneuma, 72
divine powers, 57, 341
divine predestination, 281
divine process, emerging, 317
divine protection, 197
divine providence, 216, 259, 346–47, 365
divine punish, 57
divine punishment, 30, 192, 390
divine purpose, 304
divine qualities, 316
divine realms, 233
Divine Reason, 223
divine rejuvenation, 119
divine response, 101
divine response to Job, 101
divine retribution, 37, 204, 211–12
divine revelation, 6–7, 47, 227, 264, 304, 307, 322, 351, 356, 402, 407
divine rewards, 207, 243
divine righteousness, 396
diviners, 161
divine ruthlessness, 218
divine sanction, 23, 50
divine Self, 29, 421
divine self-consciousness, 341
divine self-disclosure, 340
divine self-realization, 139
divine service, 88
divine silence, 282
divine source, 229
  purported, 7
divine spark, 164, 275, 301
divine spirit, 305, 363
divine status, achieved, 420
divine stillness, 271
divine substance, 269, 272, 354
divine substance iv, 354
divine support, 163
divine transcendence, 34, 122
divine transformation, 104, 120
divine transmission, 194
divine trinity, 126
divine truths, 51, 282
divine unity, 270
  final, 313
divine warrior, 183, 244
divine wisdom, 182
divine world, 157
divine world soul, 293
divinity, 6–7, 50, 68, 71, 73, 95, 98–99, 116, 118, 120, 152–53, 160, 162, 219–20, 366
  all-powerful, 165
  female, 181
  inferior, 275
  non-dual, 338
  pre-existing pagan, 239
  projected, 374
  remote, 11
  unqualified, 268
divinity of Christ, 272
divinized matter, 316
divinized status, 316
divinizing, 274
division, 135, 152, 403
  natural, 171
  radical, 263
DNA, 10
Docetism, 267
doctor, 114, 349
doctrinal correctness, tra-

INDEX | 463

ditional, 76
doctrine, 14–15, 30, 73, 77, 229, 267–72, 274, 276, 278, 280–81, 284, 289–90, 292–93, 297, 364–66
  church, 52, 285, 304
  definitive, 405
  fundamental, 310
  new, 289
  non-psychological, 95
  official, 71, 266, 269, 281, 284, 342
  philosophical, 284
  pre-existing, 2
  religious, 302, 364, 408
  superstitious, 350
  theological, 306
  traditional, 2
  uncomfortable, 18
doctrine and dogma, 30, 71, 76, 92, 95, 138, 308, 401, 403, 417
doctrine of evil, 121
doctrines of divine pre-destination, 281
documentary, 171
documentary hypothesis, 221
  controversial, 221
documents
  founding, 407
  original, 319
Dogen, 62
dogma, 2, 30–31, 71, 73, 76–77, 95, 113, 125–26, 138, 143, 273–74, 292, 308, 405, 417
dogma portray Jesus, 322
dogmatic, 41, 46, 292, 299
dogmatic assertions, 13
  repeating, 125
dogmatic assumptions, 138
dogmatic attitude, 74
dogmatic Christian attributes of God, 112
dogmatic elaborations, 15
domains, 11, 134, 288
  metaphysical, 71, 137
  real, 110
  spiritual, 45
domains of morality and

science, 11
domestication, 151
dominance, 156, 400
  cultural, 367
dominant opinion, 267
domination, 290, 294, 310, 314–15, 343
  male, 224
  traditional, 325
Dominicans, 283
Dominican scholar Victor White, 121
dominion, 185, 187, 337
Doran, 108, 426
Dostoevsky, 38
Doubting Thomas, 246
Dourley, 79, 90–91, 122–23, 141, 288, 316, 426
Doves, 332
drama, 120, 192, 264
dread, 25, 28, 395
  daimonic, 62
  fundamental, 84
dreamer, 66, 75, 114, 119–20, 408
dream imagery, 75, 94, 96, 110, 117
dream incubation, 406
dreaming, 408, 423, 440
dream interpretation, 406
dream material, 68
dream motif, 140
dreams, 65–66, 87, 94, 109–12, 114–15, 117–20, 124, 133, 138, 141–42, 147, 194, 405–8, 432–33, 435
  deceitful, 405
  listed, 407
  numinous, 75, 114, 118, 408
  prospective, 408
  terrifying, 406
  true, 142
dreams and synchronicities, 135
dreams and visionary experiences, 65
dreams and visions, 405–6, 435
dreamtime, 62

dream work, 97
dualism, 13
  absolute, 239
  body-soul, 167
  metaphysical, 103
dualistic, 131, 276, 327, 338, 342
Dumuzi, represented, 155
Durkheim, 48, 362, 426
duty, 358
  human, 210
dynamic All-oneness, 80
dynamic interplay, 272
dynamics, 204, 266, 381, 386, 411, 419, 426
  developmental, 394
  fundamental, 391
  projected human psychological, 182
dynamics of early relationships in childhood, 386

E
Ea, 143
Earlier Mythic Traditions
Early Christian, 239
early agriculturalists, 152
early attachment configurations, 3
early books, 218, 377
early Christian art, 332
early Christian God-image, 255
early Christian image of God, 229
early Christianity, 142, 271
  influenced, 240
early Christians, 155, 235, 244, 246, 252–53, 266, 314, 320, 333, 335, 337
early Church leaders, 231
early concept, 158
Early Controversies, 266
early death, 125
Early Developers, 279
early docetists, 267
early followers, 237, 245, 318, 325
Early Goddess Traditions, 153

Early Greek, 163
early hominins, 145, 372
early humans, 145, 153, 373–74, 380, 441
early infant-mother symbiotic relationship, 385
early intimation, 105
early Israel, 186
early Israelites, 175, 181
early loss, 397
early losses, experienced, 385
early lost object, 370
early maternal care, 370
Early Mesopotamian religion, 159
early mingling of politics and religion, 159
early modern scientists, 345
early mosaics, 332
early object relationships, 388
early pagan goddess traditions, 273
early psychological experience, 387
early relationships in childhood, 386
Early Scientists, 345–46
early selfobjects, 397
early stage, 415
early studies, 321
early temples, 152
early twentieth century psychiatric studies, 321
early twenty-first centuries, 317
early works, 377
early years, 39, 83, 135, 273, 317, 335, 378
earth, 44, 140, 152–54, 158–59, 161, 182, 184, 186, 188, 203–4, 207, 237, 248–50, 283, 345–46
  immobile, 345
earth goddess, 280
earthly goods, 243
earthly Jesus, 318
earthly masters, 225

earth mother, 153
earthquakes, 55, 162, 178, 183, 419
Eastern, 6, 29, 35, 93, 101, 111, 135, 141, 166, 169, 223
Eastern and Western religions, 59
Eastern approach, 409
Eastern Church, 339, 341
Eastern city-states, 178
Eastern material, 320
Eastern mysticism, 430
Eastern Orthodox, 268
Eastern Orthodox Church, 341
Ebionites, 268
Ecclesiastes, 210
ecclesiastical authority, 300–301
  absolute, 334
Ecclesiasticus, 142
Eckhart, 80, 95, 289
Eclipse, 423
ecological sensibility, 328
ecstatic states, 30
  experienced, 194
Ecumenical Movement, 304
ecumenical statement, 326
Eden, 2, 39, 102, 182–83, 190, 219, 221, 228, 287, 336, 408
Eden story, 339
Edinger, 85, 89–90, 120, 142, 201, 427
editing, 170
editorial additions, 197
editorial opinion, 232
editors, 133, 140, 169–70, 176, 180, 193, 222, 224, 262, 394
  final, 221
  multiple, 322
Edomites, 176
Edwards, 400, 427
effect of religion, 370
effects, 20, 67, 71, 147, 151, 286, 289, 318–19, 322–23, 325, 327, 366, 370–72

  calming, 112
  important, 350
  largest, 387
  powerful, 72, 222, 302
egalitarianism, radical, 315
egg, 155, 173
ego, 28–29, 31, 56, 58, 67–72, 74, 80–81, 83–90, 92–94, 101, 115–16, 127–29, 140–42, 404, 408–9
  absolute, 359
  differentiated, 385
  discreet, 101
  dominant, 120
  human, 88
  personal, 253
ego and self, 83, 85, 141, 427
ego-consciousness, 84, 141, 385
ego consciousness, isolated, 137
ego development, 141
ego functions, 141
ego in scope and intensity, 84
ego loss, 101
ego nuclei, 86
ego's activity, 87
ego-Self axis, 85, 141
ego-Self paradox, 85, 427
ego-Self relationship, earliest, 85
egotistic motivation, 115
ego world, 82
Egypt, 154, 160, 171, 173, 175, 177, 185, 222, 235–36, 381, 406, 408
  left, 171, 177
  prehistoric Upper, 154
  ruled, 222
Egyptian Amen-Re, 179
Egyptian and Graeco-Roman religions, 240
Egyptian aristocrat, 381
Egyptian empire, 222
Egyptian family, 18
Egyptian gods Set and Osiris, 240
Egyptian myth, 240

INDEX | 465

Egyptian mythology, 158
Egyptian origins, 161
Egyptian Osiris, 143
Egyptian pharaohs, 241
Egyptian practice, 381
Egyptian pyramids, 152
Egyptian Ra, 157
Egyptians, 158, 167, 173, 185, 205, 236, 238, 240, 258, 336, 372
   ancient, 162
Egyptian stories, 219
Egyptian Thoth, 368
Egyptian tombs, 158
Ehrman, 231, 233, 246, 268, 333–34, 427
Eichrodt, 217, 427
eighteenth-century America, late, 301
eighteenth century materialism, 358
eighteenth-century philosopher David Hume, 165
eighteenth-century philosophers, 300
eighteenth century thinking, 46
El, 173, 177–78, 181, 224
   qualities of, 178, 224
elephant, white, 407
Eleusinian mysteries, 162
Eleusis, 155, 338
Eliade, 152–53, 427
Elijah, 110, 209, 223, 236, 248
Elijah's invocation of Yhwh, 223
elite, 33, 206
   educated, 343
Ellenberger, 358, 427
Ellens, 238, 427
   Harold, 443
Ellerbe, 53, 427
Elms, 133, 428
Elohim, 179, 221
El Shaddai, 223–24
emanations, 141, 209
   progressive, 291
embarrassment, 18, 271
embodiment, 87
   progressive, 85

embryonic form, 176
emergence, 12, 44, 61, 97, 109, 129, 136, 138, 147, 180, 317
   worldwide, 162
emergence of anthropomorphic gods, 147
emergence of contemporary spirituality, 441
emergence of life and morality, 12
emergence of religion, 61
emergence of Yhwh, 180
emergent mind, 433
emergent new reality, 317
emerging God-image, 134
emerging gods, 441
emerging Mythic Image, 97
Emerson, 301
emissaries, 242, 341
emotional appeal, 33, 42
emotional disorders, 421
emotional effect, 66
emotional life, 404
emotional quality, 26
   powerful, 2, 65
emotional turmoil, 206
   personal, 264
emotional upheaval, 188
emotional vulnerabilities, 55, 312
emotion in religion, 34
emotions, 34, 42, 54, 112, 183, 208, 302, 355, 358, 375, 378
   human, 208
   powerful, 362
   religious, 375
   unbearable, 211
emotions and projections, 415
empathy, 11, 384
emperor, powerful, 135, 402
Emperor Constantine, 155, 230, 268, 338, 406
emperor Decius, 230
emperor Justinian, 338
Emperor Leo, 341
Emperor Theodosius, 155

empire, 441
   divided, 268
   powerful, 195
empirical evidence, 44, 46, 130, 148, 392
   unassailable, 27
empirical investigation, 12
empirical psychological facts, 121
empirical reality, 95
empirical standpoint of analytical psychology, 72
emptiness, 29, 32, 66
   internal, 397
   painful, 340
Endless Light, 210
enemies, 102, 187, 196, 203, 207, 224, 250–51, 327, 335, 411, 414
   love your, 216
   people's, 195
   traditional, 176
   worst, 51
energy, 7, 28, 72, 266, 352, 357, 372, 413
   creative, 359
   evolutionary, 426
   releasing divine, 155
energy field, 62
   impersonal quantum, 366
England, 152, 298–99, 426, 434–35
English King Arthur, 222
enlightened state of consciousness, 251
Enlightenment, 7, 16, 141, 300, 302, 330, 333, 350, 353, 356, 360
   eighteenth-century, 46, 300
enlightenment attitude, 356
enlightenment materialism, 351
Enlightenment principles to religion, 301
enormity of evil, 102
enslavement, 248
enthusiasts, 45

entities, 12, 78, 92, 103, 114, 129, 143, 291, 358, 364–65
  bounded, 83
  discreet, 83, 93, 109, 127, 141
  ever-smaller, 366
  independent, 93
  isolated, 131
  multiplying, 131
  political, 343
  remote, 103
  separate, 90
  unobservable, 32
entitlement, 410
Enuma Elish, 154
environment, 50–51, 84, 86, 116, 151, 321, 362, 369, 374–75
  social, 322
Ephesians, 225, 228, 239, 242, 244, 259–60, 273, 331, 339–40
Ephesus, 273, 338, 406
Epicureans, 164
epilepsy, 27
  putative, 339
  temporal lobe, 61, 407
epileptic, 61, 255, 339
episodes, 224, 242, 339
  multiple, 175
epistemology, 421
epistemology of religious experience, 421
epistles, 135, 295, 339, 439
era, 97, 348
  bygone, 416
  first, 213
  medieval, 127
  new, 213
  post-exilic, 207
  rabbinic, 189
Erasmus, 292–93
Erasmus Darwin, 34
Ericksen, 215, 428
Erikson, 28, 51, 383, 395–98, 428, 443
Erikson claims, 398
error and evil, 353
errors, 33, 37, 44, 99, 289, 311, 330–31, 336, 353, 417
  human, 330
  logical, 22
erudite Cambridge Platonist, 351
eruption, 96, 189, 251, 363, 408
  directionless, 67
Esau, 176
escape, 68, 140, 275, 319, 360, 406
escape Herod, 235
eschatology, 393
  apocalyptic, 207, 260
essentialist, 130
establishment, 249, 296, 343
  religious, 135
estrangement, 122
eternity, 15, 18, 65, 152, 191, 210, 227, 269–70, 289, 342
ethereal spirits, 119
ethical behavior, 39, 411
ethical demands, 400
ethical life, 50
ethical message, 411
ethical precepts, 39
ethical systems, 304, 350, 405
ethics, 40, 42, 312, 355, 358, 387
Ethiopians, 258
ethnic cleansing, 40
ethnic inclusion, facilitated, 258
ethnocentrism, 316
ethnological parallels, 146
Eucharist, 29, 234, 246, 284, 296, 298, 341, 381, 384
Euhemerism, 163
Euhemerus, 11
Europe, 33, 62, 150, 152, 366, 421
  medieval, 239
  ravaged, 290
European colonialism, 294
European countries, 299
European wars of religion, 294
Eusebius, 230
Evangelicals, 77, 278, 299, 342–43, 403
  conservative, 311
evangelists, 320
Evans, 319, 423, 428
Eve, 39, 190, 228, 237, 273, 281, 284, 332, 390
event of Christ, 317
events
  ancient, 382
  concrete, 415
  decisive, 360
everlasting life, 188, 261
everlasting love, 218
everlasting salvation, 203
evidence, 7–10, 21, 23–24, 36, 38, 45, 50–51, 53, 112–13, 146–47, 318–20, 346–47, 356–57, 360–61, 382
  artistic, 332
  basic, 245
  controversial, 181
  earliest, 150
  experiential, 45
  geological, 304
  good, 54
  historical, 337
  independent, 50
  insufficient, 36
  physical, 319
  resist, 379
  textual, 181, 262, 395
evidence of design, 21
evidence of evolution, 426
evidence of history, 348, 411
evidence of universal goddess worship, 167
evidence of unresolved father-son difficulties, 123
evidential information, 319
evil, 37–38, 40, 54–56, 88, 102–8, 121–22, 142, 161–62, 187–88, 214, 216, 225, 238–39, 275–76, 279–80, 314, 327, 337–38, 353, 357
  collective, 121

INDEX | 467

committing, 211
ego attributes, 104
grant, 102
human, 262
moral, 353
natural, 55
project, 104
pure, 280
redeems, 323
resist, 251, 314
social, 314
world's, 44
evil and apostasy, 192
evil behavior, 23
evil Demiurge, 275
evil eye, 153
evil in terms, 40
evil on human sinfulness, 390
evil powers, 239, 337, 341
evil results, 105
evil spirit from God afflicts Saul, 224
evil spirits, 239
evil to human beings, 56
evolution, 7, 10, 44, 218–19, 287–88, 304, 313, 316–17, 359, 362–63, 368, 371, 373–75, 426–27, 432–33
attributing, 22
biological, 11, 45, 316
cultural, 376
divine force guides, 362
gradual, 170
historical, 34
human, 23, 371–72
making, 34
social, 11, 45
Evolutionary accounts of religion, 375
Evolutionary biologists, 371
evolutionary development, 138, 177
important, 375
Evolutionary explanations, 45, 372
evolutionary heritage, 39
evolutionary mistake, 44

evolutionary origins of religion, 422, 428
evolutionary step, 165
evolution of church doctrine, 304
evolution of consciousness, 423, 425
evolution of divinized matter, 316
Evolved adaptation, 437
evolved brain pathways, 378
exaltation, 273, 427
Excavations, 222
exclusiveness, 276
exclusivism, 137
excommunicating, 341
exemplars, 74, 289, 293
good moral, 372
exhortations, 55, 193, 216
exile, 174, 177, 179–80, 199–200, 202–4, 206–7, 212, 223, 339, 433
existence, 5–63, 73, 110–11, 131, 136, 139–40, 145–47, 163, 208–10, 214, 287–89, 300–302, 318–19, 346–47, 349–52, 355–56, 361–62, 392
daily, 49
difficult, 162
earthly, 81
independent, 280, 313, 355, 361
literal, 276
meditating Jung's, 141
necessary, 20
objective, 132
projects Jung's, 141
pure, 34
simultaneous, 127
stable, 21
symbolized, 150
existence and design, 12
existence and essence, 287
existence and nature of religion, 146
existence of beings, 365
existence of biblical personalities, 171

existence of evil, 21, 24, 37–38, 54–55, 162, 164, 280, 353, 357
existence of folkloric figures, 378
existence of God, 5–7, 12, 16–17, 19–20, 22–24, 38–39, 49–50, 52, 73, 136, 214, 285–86, 300, 307–8, 346–51, 356–58, 361, 440–41
existence of goodness, 20
existence of humanity, 10
existence of intrapsychic God-images, 136
existence of life, 8
existence of miracles, 33
existence of moral values, 21
existence of multiple authorities, 52
existence of numinous symbols, 113
existence of other gods, 176, 197
existence on other, 287
existential anxieties, 306–7
existential grievances, 46
existentialist orientation, 368
existentialists, 49
religious, 306, 363
ex nihilo, 9, 280
Exodus, 18, 25, 171, 174, 176, 178–79, 183–86, 188, 218, 222–24, 235, 241, 408–9
Exodus story, 199–200, 222
exorcisms, 239, 252
expectations
apocalyptic, 247, 415
high, 389
messianic, 225, 247, 249, 325, 384
expecting, 242, 247, 249
expense, 48, 133, 156
experience, 22–32, 61–63, 66–71, 73–74, 80–82, 86–87, 104–8, 113–16, 123–28, 130–32, 140,

142–43, 263–66, 284, 307–8, 338–40, 376–78, 383–87, 407–8, 417
authentic, 30
belies, 116
changing, 120
clinical, 388
conscious, 141
conversion, 255
cumulative, 131
daily, 163
direct, 2, 5, 24, 27, 73, 77, 102, 121, 124–26, 288, 290, 369, 371
discreet, 128
early, 369, 387, 397
ego's, 87, 95, 127
imageless, 80
individual's, 32, 50, 94
infantile, 28, 383
inner, 77
intrapsychic, 61
irrefutable, 139
lived, 393
meditative, 101
mystic's, 80
necessary, 117
non-rational, 62
ordinary, 308
road, 339
satori, 102
sensory, 300, 361
spiritual, 30, 289, 378
subject, 28
subjective, 27, 74, 109, 220, 288
symbolic, 71
traumatic, 102
unique, 31
visionary, 65–66, 110, 114, 140, 194, 385, 407
vivid, 25, 82
experience conflict, 265
experience freedom, 355
experience God, 28, 288, 388
experience illusions, 24
experience of archetypes, 82
experience of being, 81
experience of God, 15, 30, 32, 53, 69, 71, 74, 93, 123, 306, 309
experience of God results, 90
experience of Job, 121
experience of levels, 93
experience of nature, 308, 343
experience of paternal authority, 398
experience of recurrent abuse, 397
experience of synchronicity, 116
experience of transcendence, 74
experience of unity, 80
experiences in terms, 123
experiences of contact, 32
experiences of pure Consciousness, 63
experiences of women of color, 420
experiential form of revelation, 417
experiment, 84, 328, 366, 430
  double slit, 128
experimenter, 366
explanations, 5, 9, 11–12, 19, 23, 43, 45, 61, 145, 148, 331, 336
  anthropomorphic, 373
  causal, 374
  force-fit, 45
  materialistic, 19
  naturalistic, 32, 265, 339
  neurological, 376, 378, 408
  paternal, 385
  physical, 375
  possible, 10, 27, 162, 353
  psychodynamic, 400
  reductive, 28, 369, 408
  religious, 371, 392
  spiritual, 351
  teleological, 61
  theological, 211
exploitation, 47, 305, 314, 363
  economic, 315
exploration, 428, 438
exponent, 338
  ardent, 351
  early, 165
externalization, 140, 359
extra-psychic Being, 123
Extreme immanence, 229
extremes, 92, 266
eyewitnesses, 231, 335
Ezekiel, 110, 155, 178, 187, 193, 201–2, 248, 337, 339, 390
Ezekiel's vision, 110
Ezra, 202, 221

F

Faber, 116, 369, 428
Fackenheim, 214, 216, 428
failure, 3, 30, 38, 85, 121, 129, 174, 202, 211, 247–50, 305
  chronic, 397
  maternal, 133
  parental, 391
  people's, 174
  radical, 398
  traumatic, 85
faith, 16, 19, 36, 45–46, 49–53, 124–25, 138–39, 285–86, 292–93, 295–96, 298–300, 305–8, 317–20, 332–33, 347–48, 360–61, 363–65, 398–99, 428–29, 437–39
  common, 91
  exclusive, 257
  individual's, 138
  mature, 52, 383
  new, 242
  personal, 294
  primordial, 33
  religious, 41, 43–44, 52–53, 313, 371, 376, 416
  stressed, 243
  strong, 77
  substitute, 400
  true, 352, 360
faith and belief, 275, 439
Faith and rationality, 437
faith and religion, 428

faith claims, 51
faithfulness, 98, 191, 216, 218, 266, 340
faith in atheism, 36
faith in Christ, 39, 256, 264, 399, 409
faith in Yhwh, 174
faith seeking understanding, 51
fallacy, 141
  genetic, 134
family dynamics, 386, 402
famine, 107, 173, 202, 389, 419
fanaticism, 263, 411
  religious, 87
fantasies, 41, 192, 335, 380, 383, 404, 417
  messianic, 343
  sadistic, 263
  wish-fulfilling, 404
fascism, 62, 91
fate, 72, 115, 154, 159, 198, 215, 245, 274, 281, 325
  tragic, 125
father, 79, 124–25, 133, 140, 184–85, 230, 239, 244, 251, 267–72, 274–75, 277–78, 281, 322–23, 326–27, 332–34, 340–41, 379–81, 385–87, 395–98
  angry, 278, 387
  brutal, 396
  child's, 379–80, 387
  domineering, 379
  exalted, 379
  forgive God for being a, 398
  loving, 6, 139, 256
  minister, 106
  murdered, 380–81
  offended, 277
  original, 382
  primal, 380, 382
  strict, 256
  suffering, 134
  Father Almighty, 326
Father God, 265, 342, 379, 382, 398

father image, 382
  child's, 379
  missing, 385
Father's love, 270
fear, 37–38, 50, 52, 55–56, 210, 223, 225, 349, 351, 355, 357, 370, 379, 389–90
  constant, 203
  displaced, 380
  great, 395
  human, 5, 165
  sacred, 145
  soothe, 370
feature of archaic religion, 151
Feierman, 373, 375, 428
female deities, 181
  powerful, 181
feminine, 113, 120, 142, 157–58, 166, 271, 276, 327, 367
  dark, 157
feminine aspect, 116, 142, 181–82, 223, 273
feminine characteristics, 223
feminine deities, 181
feminine element, 113, 182
  missing, 273
feminine language, 327
feminine principle, 143
feminine qualities, 367
feminine role, 100
feminine wisdom, 100, 271, 327
feminine wisdom emanation, 157
feminist alternatives, 367
feminist Critiques, 325, 423
feminist philosophy of religion, 421
feminist reader, 424
Feminist writers, 326
fertility, 145, 152, 154–55, 157–60, 174, 177–78, 181, 223
  grant, 207
  sexual, 181

fertility cults, 421
fertility goddesses, 223
fertility icons, 154
fertility rites, 181
fetal position, 150
feudal system, 284
Feuerbach, 47, 112, 192, 313, 371, 373, 394, 428
Ficino, 291
fideism, 19, 23, 364
figure of Christ, 113, 318, 415
figures
  absent father, 50
  ancestral, 62
  ancient pagan goddess, 75
  archetypal, 152
  carved, 167
  celestial father, 402
  cosmic father, 333
  cosmic parent, 154
  early, 391
  female, 153–54
  folkloric, 378
  geometrical, 291
  historical, 227, 317–19, 324, 343, 415, 419
  horned anthropoid, 148
  idealized, 265
  mysterious, 282
  mythic, 318
  mythological, 368
  parental, 442
  positive, 83
  public, 83
  religious, 370
  semi-divine, 336
  servant, 205
  spiritual, 256
  supernatural parent, 304
figures in dreams, 110
figurines, 150, 153
  female, 223
Finkelstein, 171, 222, 428
first Adam, 243
First-century Palestine, 247, 320
first century worldview, 239
first Eve, 273

First Isaiah, 203
First Mover, 20
  purported, 20
First Principle, 275
five ways, 286
fixed symbol system, 92
flaming eyes, 236
flaming fire, 263
flesh, 142, 152, 160, 189, 227, 249, 259, 284, 340, 419
  burning animal, 179
  thorn in the, 339
  with us in the, 329
flood, 71, 159–61, 172, 186, 224
Flüe, 32, 76
focus on Jesus' love for humanity, 278
folkloric stories and legends, 325
followers, 232–33, 236, 241–42, 245–49, 252, 255, 260–61, 264, 266, 274, 323, 339–40, 411
  devoted, 264
  inspired, 321
food, 40, 145, 171, 179, 237, 266, 374
  burying, 150
  hazardous, 375
Forbidden Books, 293, 346
force of evil and death, 257
forces
  autonomous, 72
  brute, 100
  cosmic, 354
  creative, 302
  daemonic, 324
  demonic, 153, 252
  electromagnetic, 8
  energetic, 17
  gravitational, 8
  mightiest, 72
  nuclear, 8
  opposite, 271
  physical, 346–47
  political, 296
  psychic, 82
  spiritual, 48, 147, 149, 309, 363
  third, 271
  unpredictable, 413
forces of nature, 169, 173, 189
Fordham, 85–86, 428
foreign alliances, 197
forgive, 188, 339, 396
forgiveness, 190, 197, 203, 244, 250–51, 255, 277, 315, 317, 328, 335
forgiving, 186, 200, 251, 258, 370, 387
Forman, 63, 428
formation, 131, 170, 383, 387
formless spirits, 157
forsaken, 212, 253
fortunes, 142, 195
  bad, 147
foundational truths of religion, 20
foundations, 178, 210, 245, 293, 348, 358, 433, 438, 440
founders, 60, 162, 255, 321, 346–47, 358, 368, 405, 407
  charismatic, 299
Fowler, 52, 429
Fox, 299, 336, 428
fragmentation, 129, 299
fragments, 94, 104, 121, 127, 221, 232, 335
France, 148, 154, 299, 301
Francis, 390, 429
Franciscans, 283
Francisco, San, 424, 428–29, 432–34, 439–41
Franco, 62
Franklin, Benjamin, 34
Franz, 56, 99, 115, 126, 140, 442
fratricide, 438
fraud, pious, 198
fraudulent, 195, 200
Frazer, 126, 155, 156, 167, 240, 429
Free discussion, 33
freedom, 33, 48, 237, 286, 292, 314, 350, 358, 429–30, 439
  human, 49, 213
  human creative, 48
  intellectual, 301
  verbal, 396
free will, 18, 39, 43, 210, 279, 330, 353, 355
  given, 14, 281
  human, 280
free will defense, 54–55
French biologist Jacques Monod, 44
French medical materialist Julien Offray, 42
French philosopher Lucien Lévy-Brühl, 151
Frères, 148
Freud, 11, 148, 160, 192, 378–82, 384–87, 394, 400, 419, 429–30, 438
Freud attributes, 380
Freudian reduction, 140
Freudians, 336
Freud misunderstands Christianity, 381
Freud postulates, 419
Freud's ambivalence, 379
Freud's approach to religion, 382
Freud's concept, 342
Freud's emphasis, 379
Freud's focus, 382
Freud's Oedipal and paternal explanations for religion, 385
Freud's superego, 224
Friedman, 190, 221, 224, 428–29, 432
Friedrich Schleiermacher, 301
fruits, 266, 340
fulfillment, 172, 175, 204, 247, 249, 307, 335, 339, 363, 379
fullness, 143, 210, 256, 271, 275, 313, 341
  emotional, 28
function, 9, 11, 106, 109, 112, 153, 156, 161, 373, 375, 377, 419, 422
  defensive, 112
  epistemological, 109

important idealized self-object, 397
innate moral, 141
particular, 375
psyche's transcendent, 104
psychological, 90
religious mandalas, 112
self-regulating, 112
social, 362
true symbolic, 109
wave, 366
functional disadvantages of religion, 372
fundamental doctrines of Christianity, 310
fundamentalism, 41, 304, 311–12, 393
fundamentalist attitude, 45
fundamentalist circles, 339
Fundamentalist clergy, 75
Fundamentalist insistence, 312
fundamentalist-inspired terrorism, 311
fundamentalist preachers, 18
fundamentalists, 16, 61, 92, 116, 170, 172, 240, 310–12, 330–31, 343
contemporary, 40
fundamental laws of nature, 21
fundamentals, 211, 310
Funeral, 303
funerary decorations, 332
fury, 245, 264
raging, 263

G
Gaiser, 429
Galambush, 253, 429
Galatians, 255–61, 263–65, 74, 339–40
Galen, 36, 429
Galilean rabbi, great, 320
Galilee, 427
Galileo, 7, 345–46
Gallinger, 439
gap, 6, 24, 43, 298, 307, 320, 335

growing, 241
garden, 2, 39, 172, 182–83, 190, 219, 221, 228, 237, 336, 339
garments, 236, 407
mixing, 40
Gaylor, 326, 429
Geisler, 330, 429
Gellert, 182, 221
gender, 13, 156, 326
gender bias, 271
gender imbalance, 271
gender-relations, 326
gender stereotypes, 167
genealogies, 221
generations, 170, 222, 238, 254, 276, 279, 286, 316, 380, 382, 393
earlier, 305
from generation to, 184
generosity, 250, 293
genes, 11, 44–45, 84, 130
responsible, 372
Genesis, 170, 172–74, 176, 179–80, 183, 185–87, 189–90, 221, 224, 233, 236–37, 405, 409
genesis of religious experience, 377
Genesis story, 172, 224
genetic aspect for analytical psychology, 436
genocide, 216, 331
Gentiles, 256, 258, 260, 263, 268, 400, 406
win obedience from the, 258
Gentile world, 264
geologist Charles Lyell, 44, 304
German churches, 428
German theologian, 47
Germany, 154, 215
Gerstenberger, 177, 179, 181, 206
Ghost Theory, 147
giant eye, 66, 68
gift, 51, 152, 281, 346, 394, 399
gigantic clock, 345
Gilgamesh, 224
Gimbutas, 156, 429

Gimbutas' theory bridges, 156
Giordano Bruno, 293
Glas, 80, 442
glorification, 40, 327, 339
theological, 315
glory, 110, 188, 201, 205, 246, 260, 266, 273, 317, 321, 339
crowning, 238
get, 185
gnosis, 275–76
Gnostic God-image, 275
Gnostic gospels, 437
Gnosticism, 161, 276
gnostic leanings, 123
Gnostics, 123, 143, 164, 275–76, 335
gnostic sensibility, 122
goads, 264
goal of evolution, 313
goal of history, 432
goal of individuation, 116
goals, 36, 85, 87, 116, 141, 313, 316, 384, 393, 432
accessible, 414
final, 61, 256
impossible, 414
Göbekli Tepe, 151–52, 167
God, 5–41, 47–62, 68–77, 89–93, 95–109, 111–15, 119–26, 134–36, 138–43, 156–67, 169–80, 182–225, 227–30, 233–63, 265–73, 275–317, 325–43, 345–80, 384–407, 420–42
absolute, 90, 124
all-good, 54, 77, 107
angry, 395
anthropomorphic, 147, 380
believe, 287
believed, 192, 219
benevolent, 77, 214, 353
born, 120
caring, 214
change, 13
conceptualize, 291
covenant with, 174
dangerous, 387

INDEX | 471

depict, 221, 327, 333
deprive, 119
designed, 357
disembodied, 24
disobey, 237
displaced, 136, 404
dying and rising, 436–37
earlier, 240
earlier Homeric, 56
enemies of, 263
establishing, 248
ethical, 192
ethnic, 242
experienced, 239
external, 82, 95
false, 202
family, 176
foreign, 176
frustrate, 238
fulfilled, 257
good, 32, 267
grain, 126, 151, 240
hidden, 38
high, 275
highlight, 56
human-like, 373
I am, 267
the idea of, 112
identifying, 343
imagined, 120, 301, 314, 401
immanent, 13, 229
immaterial, 317
immortal, 284
impersonal, 360
incorporeal, 225
infinite, 31, 272, 277
innumerable, 109
interpreted, 280
invisible, 176, 256, 325
killed, 278
knowing, 14, 306
lesser, 157, 160–61, 165–66
a little less than, 185
local, 160, 176, 178
local nature, 193
loving, 105, 227–28, 258, 298, 342, 389, 392, 440
making, 34, 303

male sky-father, 156
omnipotent, 12, 17, 327
omniscient, 54
paradoxical, 106
personal, 7, 9, 12, 35, 307, 312, 355, 359, 364, 375, 379
postulate, 38
pre-Christian, 240
punitive, 390
remote, 121, 239
storm, 156
suffering, 214, 239
supreme, 36, 180, 275
timeless, 329
transformed, 117
trinitarian, 272
triumphant war, 389
true, 275, 334
tyrannical, 360
unchanging, 272
unconscious, 99
understanding, 288, 347
universe, 291
vegetation, 155, 159
ways, 135, 191
word, 3, 12, 355
the word of, 170
the wrath of, 228
God acts, 39, 92, 105, 114, 298, 345, 366
God and evil, 314
God and nature, 354–55
God and personality pathology, 438
God and Satan, 399
God-as-Father, 379
God blesses, 411
God cares, 195, 345
god-concept, 163
God constellates, 119
God delusion, 425
God demands, 341
goddess, 109, 113–14, 153–57, 159–60, 162, 167, 178, 180–82, 367, 425–26, 429, 436, 439
bloodthirsty, 181
great, 153
moon, 159
multiple, 154

pre-Christian, 274
goddess Aphrodite, 155
goddess Astarte, 181
goddess Demeter, 155
goddess imagery, 181, 367
Goddess Inanna, 155
goddess Nintu, 160
goddess nurtures, 189
goddess Nut, 154
goddess religions, 154
goddess Tiamat, 154
goddess traditions, earlier, 189
Goddess Ua Zit, 154
goddess worship, 156, 180–81, 367
  suppressed, 338
  universal, 167
God disciplines, 390
God exacerbates, 328
God experiences, 70, 101
God experiences re-birth, 119
God forgives sin, 263
God frees, 306
God guides, 362, 420
Godhead, 119, 142, 180, 269, 289
  rejuvenated, 118–19
  unified, 340
God idealizes, 280
GOD-IMAGE, 2–62, 66–143, 145–67, 169–225, 228–434, 436, 438, 440, 442
all-good, 103, 108
angry, 298
anthropomorphic, 16, 112, 221
anthropomorphize, 166, 371
archetypal, 73
brutal, 278
canonical, 120
cherished, 120, 418
classical, 10, 49, 96
classical theistic, 6
collective, 121, 135
competing, 416
conscious, 31
empirical, 70

INDEX | 473

harsh, 396
human, 107
idealized, 55, 102
incomplete, 105
innate, 5, 50, 65, 369
intrapsychic, 18, 66, 72, 116, 136
intra-psychic, 79, 136, 403
long-standing, 389
male, 224
masculine, 113, 119, 143, 156
naive, 102
narcissistic, 388
new, 78–79, 97, 109, 177, 214, 239, 427
particular, 137
patriarchal, 389
primitive, 218
private, 388
punitive, 265, 295, 389–90, 394
scientific, 347
single, 417
traditional, 12–13, 16, 37, 47, 134, 213, 300–301, 303–4, 307, 309, 312
traditional theistic, 12, 24, 37, 47, 97
unconscious, 110
unique, 109
God-image and parental images, 390
God-image Buber, 124
God-image During the Nineteenth Century, 359
God-image in Archaic Religions, 145
God-image in Jung's Psychology, 65
God-image in mind, 362
God-image in Process Theology, 309
God-image in Relation, 132, 262
God-image in Relation to Kant, 132
God-image Jung, 98
God-image of childhood, 388

God-image of Christianity, 354
God-image of local religions, 113
God-image of pantheism, 34
God-image of revelation, 15
God-imagery, 327, 386
  traditional, 97
  traditional theistic, 116
God images, 391, 422, 426, 429
  new, 92
God-images and numinous experiences, 136
God in Auschwitz, 438
God in Christ, 239
God in Christian art forms, 333
God in history, 311
God in scripture, 208
God interpenetrates, 34
God intoxication, 412
God in traditional terms, 308
God in twentieth century culture, 365
God-is-dead theologians, 312
God is love, 364
God is nothingness, 80
God language, 327
God-language
  male, 326
  traditional, 312
god-man, 247, 285, 325, 373, 420, 429
  archetype of the, 227
  mediating, 324
God-meme, 45
God-module, 376
God obsolete, 9
God of everyday religion, 6
God of Genesis, 164
God of history, 199, 204
God of philosophy, 365
God of scripture, 361
God of theology and philosophy, 6

God of universal love, 254
God oversaw history, 182
God punishes children, 202
God-realized soul, 253
God-representation, 387, 391
God rewards faith, 338
gods and devils, 136
gods and goddesses, 126, 153, 416, 436
Gods and Goddesses of Canaan, 426
gods and heavens, 124
gods and religious beliefs, 160
gods and spirits of animistic archaic religions, 62, 96
gods in charge of activities, 159
gods in rational terms, 11
gods of agriculture and fertility, 160
gods of animals, 159
gods of invaders, 160
gods of Israel's oppressors, 207
gods of Mesopotamia, 159, 372
gods of metals, 153
gods of metals and metallurgy, 153
gods of polytheistic traditions, 157
Gods of Theistic religions, 405
God substitute, 71
God-term, 93
God traits, 302
God transcend time, 329
God wills, 306
God within, 121–22
God within us, 65
  the, 130
God works, 401
gold, 65, 75, 153, 236
Goldbrunner, 116, 429
Golden Bough, 126, 155, 167, 429
golden calf, 184, 224

Golden Rule, 244
Goodenough, 207, 430
Good Shepherd, 332
Gospel accounts, 234
gospel message, 263, 279
Gospel narratives, 337
gospel of grace, 395
Gospel of Mark, 233, 241–42, 246, 335–36
Gospel passages, 247
gospels, 47, 53, 229, 231–36, 241, 244–46, 251, 253–54, 276–77, 306, 324–25, 333–37, 400–401, 431–32, 441–42
independent, 335
Gospels' anti-Judaism, 215
Gospel stories, 29, 79, 233–34, 237, 246, 250, 254, 317–18, 322
Gospel texts, 237, 321
Gospel tradition, written, 231
Gospel writers, 231, 253, 274, 306, 319
Gottfried Leibniz, 352
Gould, 11, 375, 430
governor, 203, 327
grace, 61, 121, 257, 277, 281, 287–88, 295, 308, 352, 395, 397–98
act of, 52, 111, 308
gift of, 77, 298
special, 342
grace of God, 239, 281
Graeco-Roman religions, 240
grain, 152, 159, 341
resurrected, 158
grand design, 43, 357, 431
Grand Inquisitor, 38
grandiosity, 206
grandparents, 126, 387
grave, 365, 410
grave goods, 159
graven images, 332
making, 401
Graves, Robert, 167
gravity, 122, 129, 225, 285, 346

gravity of evil, 122
Great Britain, 301
great mother, 153, 436
single, 154
great mother archetype, 157
Greco-Roman Egypt, 163
Greco-Roman world, 239
Greece, 283, 292, 354
classical, 155
Greek astronomer Aristarchus, 345
Greek Bible, 292
Greek civilization, 154
Greek concept, ancient, 162
Greek earth goddess Gaea, 155
Greek god-images, 162
Greek gods, 11
Greek Hermes, 368
Greek manuscripts, 232
Greek pantheon, 154, 274
Greek philosophers, 207
Greek philosopher Xenophanes, 11
Greek philosophical, 164
Greek philosophical term, 340
Greek philosophy, 36, 142, 207, 229
classical, 290
Greek playwrights, 406
Greek root, 335
Greeks, 161, 163, 207, 229–30, 232, 250, 269, 292, 336–37, 340, 406
neither Jew nor, 258
Greek term, 230, 339
Greek texts, 221
Greek thinkers, 56
Greek traditions, 229
Greek word, 225, 326, 332, 335
Greek writers, 292
Greek Zeus, 161
Greenberg, 213, 430, 433
Greenway, 390, 430
grief, 155, 183, 196, 312, 385, 412
inevitable, 418

unconscious, 312
grip, 91, 124, 262, 311
relentless, 68
ground, 6, 59, 79, 128, 302, 307, 338–39, 343, 356, 359, 367
hidden, 271
necessary, 352
rational, 33
soul's, 338
spiritual, 91
timeless, 302
uncaused, 367
ground and unity of life, 359
ground of being, 213, 426
ground of God, 289
ground of personality, 343
ground of psyche, 426
group ideals, 410
group identity, 408, 411
group members, 410
group phenomena, 411
groups, 44, 91, 146–48, 180, 184, 222, 297, 299, 312, 372, 380–81, 410–11, 418
competing, 267
eliminated non-Christian, 252
hate, 41
human, 419
particular, 417
size, 146
social, 372
splinter, 171
group thinking, 375
group worships, 166
growth, 111, 151, 159, 161, 283, 316
moral, 187
grudge, long-standing, 184
Gruenwald, 204, 384, 430
guidance, 30, 77
spiritual, 142
guide, 16, 208, 296, 321, 345
good, 417
internal spiritual, 75
reliable, 70

INDEX | 475

unreliable, 24
guided tour, 436
guilt, 40, 48, 56, 198, 262–63, 265, 328, 338, 341, 379–82, 389–90
  excessive, 389
  historical, 254
  inducing, 37
  inherited, 339
  intense, 266, 340
  nation's, 194
  original, 419
  unconscious, 343, 389
guilt-inducing effect, 339
guilty Christian believers, 324
guilty conscience, 397
Guntrip, 382, 383, 430, 116
Guthrie, 373, 430

H
Habiru, 222
habit, 20, 35, 109, 377, 392
Hades, 251
Haile, 395–96, 430
hair, 191
  snow-white, 236
Haley, 322, 431
hallucinations, 24, 29, 383, 407
  auditory, 376
hallucinatory, 224
Hammurabi, 186
Hammurabi's code, 219
Handy, 178, 430
happiness, 351, 355, 357
  based, 42
  human, 55
hardships, 266, 353
  great, 262
Hardy, 30, 303, 430
Hardy's subjects, 31
harlots, 204, 224, 331
  played the, 202
harmony, 38, 111, 145, 292, 350, 352–53
  absolute, 119
  basic, 292
  complete, 237

cosmic, 351
pre-established, 352
Harris, 41, 431
harshness, 217, 250, 398
  father's, 401
Hart, 10, 46
Hartshorne, 309, 431
harvest, 147, 159, 178
  good, 152
harvesting festivals, 152
Hasidic movement, 209
hate, 441
Hauser, 437
Hawking, 9, 431
Hayes, 223, 431
head-god, old, 180
healing, 29, 154, 157, 163, 239, 244, 383, 406, 422
  frequent, 252
  miraculous, 240
healing dream, 406
healing effect, 27, 31, 68, 119
healing factor, 105
healing grace, 342
health, 102, 430
  ill, 399
  physical, 186, 382, 392
  social, 441
heart, 26, 28, 114, 190, 264, 273, 293, 297, 323–24, 403–4, 414
  deceased's, 158
  first hardens Pharaoh's, 185
  radical change of, 264, 338
  sinful, 282
heart of Christianity, 324, 438
heart of Christian theology, 323
heart of religion, 26
heaven, 88, 94–96, 111, 113, 136, 140, 153–54, 184, 235–39, 249–51, 334, 336–38, 340–41, 404–6, 419–20
  external, 135
  keys of the kingdom of, 296

light from, 255
linked, 283
the man of, 256
new, 204
ruled, 154
Heaven kingdom of, 322
Hebraic Monotheism, 423
Hebrew and Christian scriptures, 297
Hebrew and Greek Bible, 292
Hebrew Bible, 40, 169–72, 176, 189–90, 217, 219, 221, 223–24, 372, 377, 380, 405, 408
Hebrew Bible and ancient Greece, 156
Hebrew Bible's approval of slavery, 225
Hebrew children, 235
Hebrew epic, 425
Hebrew God, 177, 239, 434
Hebrew goddess, 437
Hebrew image of God, 239
Hebrew monotheism, 223
Hebrew mythology, 161
  pre-existing, 267
Hebrew patriarchs, 142
Hebrew prophetic texts, 235
Hebrew Prophets, 155, 191, 193, 230, 247–48, 405, 411
  important, 192
Hebrews, 135, 177, 181, 196, 222, 228, 236, 243, 277, 341, 390
Hebrew Scriptural, 283
Hebrew Scriptures, 18, 107, 169–225, 228–31, 233, 235–37, 239, 246–48, 252–53, 258–59, 261, 267, 275–77, 325–27, 335–37
Hebrew tradition, 154, 239, 267
Hebrew word, 179, 210, 337
Hegel, 49, 359

Hegel's belief, 360
Hegel's image, 360
hegemony, 31, 77, 81
Heidegger's philosophy of religion, 442
heights, 77, 93, 196, 289, 348
Heiler, 274, 431
Heinemann Medical, 428
Heinz Kohut, 430
heir, 257
  male, 248
Heisig, 140, 431
hell, 18, 40, 55, 88, 136, 238, 251, 294, 389, 393, 399
  deepest, 99
Hellenistic mystery cults, 261
Hellenistic Seleucid, 203
Hellenized Jews, 241
Helms, 231, 338, 431
helpless, 145, 163, 257
helplessness, 16, 379
  human, 398
hemisphere
  left, 156, 376–77
  right, 156, 376–77
Henderson, 142, 431
henotheism, 165–66
henotheists, 333
Henry, 128, 431
Heracles, 274, 336, 419
Herbert Spencer's theory, 163
heresy, 135, 231, 263, 267, 270, 279, 283, 289, 293, 348, 424
  early, 267
heresy hunters, 135, 403
heretical, 39, 76, 231, 267, 269, 280, 290, 335, 338, 355, 403
heretics, 53, 252, 276, 292, 405, 410
Hermann Reimarus, 317
hermeneutics, 438
Hermes, 241
Hermes Trismegistus, 351, 368
hero, 58, 110, 172, 222, 409, 415, 423

Herod, King, 336
Herod's intention, 406
heroes, 274, 410
hero Heracles, 157
Heschel, 428
Hestia, 157
Heteropathic Feelings, 424
heuristic purposes, 141
Hezekiah, King, 221
hidden, 428–29
hidden contradictions, 427
hiddenness, 39, 190, 213, 295
  increasing, 190
hid his face, 225
hierarchical power structures, 315
hierarchy, 36, 138, 153, 156–57, 159, 162, 271, 280, 291, 298, 342
  earthly, 268
  fixed social, 62
  human political, 165
  religious, 76
hierarchy of goddesses, 162
hierarchy of goddesses and gods, 162
hierophanies, 152
High Middle Ages, 286
High Priest, 236
Hill, 123, 431
Hillman, 128, 134, 431
Himalayas, 407
Hindu, 114, 239, 338
Hindu deity Krishna, 336
Hinduism, 379
Hindu Kali, 167
Hindu tradition, 131
hints, 110, 142, 187, 262, 280
Hippo, 232
with his stripes we are healed, 277
historical, 169, 424
historical accuracy, 170, 310, 413
historical associations, 57
historical basis of Christianity, 53
historical claim, 33

historical consequences, 184
historical credibility, 319
historical-critical method, 322
historical curiosity, 198
Historical Development, 229
historical difficulties, 250
historical distance, 206, 262
historical effect, 325, 415
historical events, 13, 29, 122, 143, 275, 382
  unique, 89
historical incarnation in Christ, 309
historical Jesus, 235, 256, 306, 317–21, 325, 337, 423, 428, 432, 435–36, 439
historically warrantable, 238
historical method studies, 320
historical portrait, 436
historical process, long, 170
historical question, 409
historical reading, 442
historical reality, 311
historical record, 320
historical remnants, 218
historical reputation, 254
historical research, 319–20
historical statements, 409
historical study, 306
historicity, 171, 234
historicize, 136
history, 36–37, 62, 136–37, 198–99, 203–4, 210, 212–16, 232–34, 237–38, 305, 311, 316–20, 328–29, 359–60, 363, 409, 418–19, 428, 431–32
  ancient Mesopotamian, 159
  early, 199, 439
  early attachment, 392

INDEX | 477

hidden, 441
human intellectual, 359
inbuilt, 352
literal, 16, 92, 137, 238
personal, 67
reliable, 171
religious, 7, 374
symbolic, 67
violent, 323
history and biography, 232
history and revelation, 174
history and sacred authority, 431
history change, 359
history in events, 409
history of biblical texts, 303
history of Christianity, 255, 403
history of God, 421
history of heresy, 424
history of humanity, 359
history of religion, 407
Hitchens, 41
Hitler, 62, 83, 214
Hjalmar Sundén's role-theory of religion, 423
Hobbes, 303, 349, 350
hoc signo vinces, 230
Holbach, 356–57
holiness, 26, 56–57, 175, 186, 217, 221, 397, 438
Holiness Code, 40
Holiness Code in Leviticus, 40, 186
Holocaust, 105, 107, 175, 210–17, 225, 365, 422, 424, 428, 433, 437–38
Holocaust Christian, 215
Holocaust in terms of Christian theology, 216
holocaustos, 225
Holocaust studies, 215
Holocaust's victims, 211
holy, 17, 25–27, 56–58, 61, 66, 75, 175, 183, 186, 189, 320
show myself, 184
site, 57
holy books, 410, 416

Holy Child, 333
Holy Ghost, 139, 272
Holy Infant, 320
Holy Land, 57
Holy Mystery, 309
holy object, 151, 186
Holy Roman Emperor, 296
holy seed, 202
Holy Spirit, 29, 230, 251, 259, 269–71, 273–74, 281, 289, 333, 335–36, 340
Holy Trinity, 422
holy warrior, 252
holy women, 181
home, 8, 133, 173, 184, 197, 243
woman's, 154
Homeric period, 406
hominin ancestors, 371–72
early, 67, 145
homogeneous, 62
homoousia, 90
homoousios, 269, 340
Homo sapiens, 145, 150, 167
homosexuality, 18, 40, 45, 260
male, 184
hopelessness, 298, 397
Horeb, 221
Horizons, 436
horrible fights, 99
horrors, 39, 124, 277, 305, 312, 353
Horsely, 320, 431
Horus, 120, 143, 240, 420
Hos, 195
Hosea, 174, 181, 185, 190, 193, 195, 197–98, 200, 203, 212, 217, 223
Host, 236
hostility, 200, 251, 253, 263, 299, 379, 411–12, 418
long-standing murderous, 215
Host symbolizes, 341
house, 152, 222, 242, 399, 413

household, 159, 176
human abilities, 234, 290, 303, 347, 375
human act, 95
human actions, 163
human activities, daily, 157
human activity, 48
human affairs, 163, 182, 214, 349, 353
human awareness, 127
human behavior, 13–14, 45, 102, 183, 373
ethical, 213
human beings, 12–14, 17–18, 34–35, 37, 42–44, 54, 59, 99, 102–4, 106, 132, 158–59, 185, 275–82, 292–93, 295–96, 299–300, 302–4, 307–8, 374
human beings authority, 186
human beings color, 192
human beings experience, suffering, 101
human beings inflict, 54
Human beings invent, 37
Human belief in God, 47
human bodies, 158, 164, 342
human capacity to experience, 287
human comprehension, 209
human condition, 49, 257, 307–8, 348, 351, 371
human connection to God, 283
human consciousness, 23, 88–89, 93, 98–99, 101, 104, 117, 122, 132–33, 359, 368
human document, 307
human effort, 212, 262, 303
human endeavors, 362
human ethical choices, 106
human existence, 307–8, 369
the essence of, 395
human experience, 5, 8, 26, 229, 287, 359, 402

direct, 229
observable, 69
human experience of belief, 5
human faces in clouds, 373
human faculties, 348
human favorites, 163
human forms, 110, 158, 190, 201, 233, 238, 332
human history, 47–49, 135, 137, 145, 214, 228, 307, 327, 359, 363
human history attests, 17
Humani Generis, 316
human interaction, 130, 430
human interrelate, 123
humanists, 49, 292
humanitarian, 49, 199
humanity, 7–8, 89, 95, 98–101, 106–7, 172–73, 207–8, 229–30, 237–39, 245, 257, 261, 272–74, 276–79, 284–85, 287–88, 295, 297–98, 311–14, 358–63
  condemned, 295
  debt, 277
  fallen, 121
  free, 267
  guides, 208
  left, 295
  redeem, 257, 269
  redeemed, 274
  sinful, 142, 295, 298, 413
  taint, 281
humanity and nature, 358
humanity's goodness, 305
Humanity's purpose, 159
Humanity's sin, 277
human Jesus, 109, 230, 341
human life, 49, 59, 87, 156, 227, 272, 285, 315, 328, 358
human mental immaturity, 361
human mind, 15, 17, 32, 53, 112, 146, 208, 282, 286, 313, 342

Human moral standards, 219
human nature, 45, 47, 52, 56, 227–28, 269, 273–74, 285, 287–88, 295, 414, 419
human notions, 293
humanoid, 167
human opinion, 11, 301
human passions, 34
human personality traits, 186, 192
human productions, 357
human psychological constitution, 112
human psychological differences, 422
human psychology, 107, 191, 371, 394, 401, 417
human race, 237, 279
human reason, 20, 164, 288, 348, 438
human relations, 394
human relationships, 327, 343, 392, 394, 440
human rights, 301, 313
humans, 15, 47, 152, 162–63, 167, 185–86, 233, 330, 336, 373, 376
  modern, 421
human sinfulness, 37, 103, 190, 228, 297, 390, 414
  innate, 103
  intrinsic, 103
  universal, 390
  unredeemed, 237
human soul, 103, 289, 352, 361
human systems, 96
human timing, 250
human traits, 151, 192, 373
  projected, 374
human transformation, 442
human understanding, 16, 37, 87, 188, 219
human welfare, 37, 244, 250
human wickedness and disobedience to God, 161
Hume, 20, 34, 357–58

humility, 32, 243, 246, 250, 292–93, 330
  intellectual, 386
  stressed, 398
hundred years, 131, 170, 200, 203, 272, 418
hunt, 146, 148–51
  witch, 348
Hunter-gathering, 151
hunter-gathers, 146
husbands, 185, 197, 259, 333
  admonished, 260
Hutch, 387, 431
Huxley, 59, 431
Hyde, 388, 431
Hyksos, 222
hymns, 277
  singing, 387
hypostatize, 131
hypothesis
  man-as-machine, 43
  two-Source, 336
hysterical, 31, 255, 321

I
I am Brahman, 338
I am that I am, 270, 280
I am the bread of life, 233
I am the light of the world, 233, 252
I am who I am, 222, 241, 365
Ibn Arabi, 425
iconoclastic, 194, 264
iconoclastic reaction, 341
icons, 223, 296, 341
Icon Veneration, 438
idealization, 58, 83
  massive, 323
  rational, 419
idealize, 83, 410
idealized selfobjects, 384
idealized transference, 110
idealizing transference, 85
ideals, 372
  human, 393
  human spiritual, 313
  nationalistic, 249
Ideas
  eternal, 164

rejected Plato's, 288
identification, 87, 261, 265, 343, 370, 381
  projective, 151
identity, 80, 107, 129, 147, 151, 173, 198, 205, 311, 431, 441
ideological, 320
  important, 319
ideologies, 19, 50, 416
  dehumanizing, 314
  group's, 411
  political, 416
idolatrous, 31, 116, 269, 299
idolatrous worship of gods, 192
idolatry, 178, 194, 198, 312, 340
idols, 159, 200, 307
idol worship, 200, 223
  condemned, 197
Ignatius, 402
Ignatius Loyola, 298
ignorance, 41, 91, 349–50
  learned, 291
Iliad, 162, 377, 406
illegitimacy, 324
illegitimate, 322, 343
illness, 31, 81, 252
  mental, 252, 338
illogicalities, 61, 371
illumination, 106, 282
  inner, 28
  interior, 194
illusion, 35, 47, 95, 355, 378–79, 383, 404, 419, 429
  comforting, 48
illusory, 285, 370, 377, 378
illustrations, 410
image of Christ, 88, 227
Image of God and personality pathology, 438
image of Yhwh, 3, 98, 100
image points, 123
imagery, 66, 68, 70–71, 75, 79–80, 97, 110, 112, 114, 124–25, 141, 143, 236, 402–4, 412
  anthropomorphic, 6, 137, 225, 394
  demonstrable, 72
  earliest feminine, 273
  intrapsychic, 70, 73
  male, 325
  male sky-God, 157
  masculine, 271
  mythic, 29, 136, 141, 161, 236–37, 408–9
  original, 417
  prophetic, 205
  religious, 56, 74, 140
  sacred, 28
  scriptural, 402
  theriomorphic Self, 111
  traditional, 76, 139
  traditional androcentric, 327
images, 3, 65–66, 69–70, 72–73, 92–94, 109–14, 116–17, 119–21, 123–24, 139–40, 148–49, 156–60, 182–83, 185–87, 191, 325–27, 386–87, 389–92, 401–2, 404
  abstract, 120
  ambivalent, 188, 379
  amoral, 101
  archetypal, 81, 85, 270, 272
  central, 278
  child's, 379
  classical Christian, 49
  classical Judeo-Christian, 310
  collective, 114
  collective Judeo-Christian, 120
  complete, 112
  deist, 32
  dominant, 135, 402
  dream, 66, 68, 70, 79, 112, 138, 406
  earliest, 148
  early Christian, 229
  embellished Jesus,' 255
  enhanced Jesus,' 335
  enlarged Jesus,' 265
  favorite, 332
  human, 73, 136
  idealized, 112, 228
  idolatrous, 341
  idyllic, 167
  innate, 22
  innumerable, 112
  internal, 386
  intrapsychic, 69–70, 72, 96, 110, 117, 136
  let us make man in our, 180
  loving, 392
  making, 182
  mental, 6, 386
  mythic, 100, 126, 179, 187, 219, 222, 256, 273
  mythologized, 325
  naïve, 103
  negative, 388
  new, 305, 401
  numinous, 65, 76
  old, 120
  original, 167
  particular, 91, 136, 139
  people's, 192
  possible, 109
  powerful, 392
  pre-existing Hebrew scriptural, 239
  primitive, 388
  psychic, 140
  punitive, 258
  quaternity, 113
  religious, 383, 402
  rudimentary, 386
  separate psychological, 73
  traditional, 89, 122, 212, 214, 327, 329
  traditional Christian, 62, 280
  tradition's, 251
  tradition's patriarchal, 224
  unsavory, 55
images of divine ruthlessness and cruelty, 218
images of God in Christian art forms, 333
imaginal, 425
imaginary, 31, 425
imagination, 28, 79, 142,

190, 227, 358, 360, 401–4
  believer's, 401
  child's, 383
  human, 229, 401
  individual's, 114, 387
  infinite, 360
  over-heated, 27
  popular, 47
  reader's, 401
  spiritual, 79
  true, 404
imaginative hypotheses, 401
imaginative mental exercises, 419
imaginative metaphors, 403
  official, 402
Imagining God, 135, 403, 430
imago, 66, 83, 94, 431
Imhotep, 163
imitation, 30, 45, 59, 186
Immaculate Conception, 274, 341
immanence, 33, 307, 363
  pure psychic, 123
immanent, 13, 17, 59, 61, 96, 283, 287, 293, 302, 305, 312, 359
immanent aspect, 270
immanent destruction, 301
immanent in nature, 49
Immanuel Kant, 358
immaterial soul, 164
immersion, total, 157
immoral, 104
immorality, 37, 124
immortal, 159, 371
immortality, 23, 147, 152–53, 289, 340, 355, 358
immortal life, 172, 333
immortal soul, 291
impassibility, 272
imperfect, 21, 346, 351, 353–54, 413
imperfections, 106, 353
imperfect world, least, 353
imperial decree, 268
imperialistic, 327

impersonal, 5–6, 79, 111, 328, 343, 346–47, 359
Impersonal God-images, 355
impersonal universe, 44
implicate order, 127–28, 422
implications, 21, 70, 107, 140, 189, 216, 240, 296, 303, 326
  important, 95, 148
  metaphysical, 83
  not-so-subtle, 343
  ontological, 9
  political, 278, 335
  social, 116
  spiritual, 116
  theological, 70
  theoretical, 425
important opponents of belief in God, 366
important source of evil, 103
imposition, 37, 218, 282
impoverishment, 315, 413
impregnation, 126, 240
impression, 28, 192, 224, 231, 282, 415
  strong, 149
imprisonment, 266
impulses, 112, 412, 426
  original, 315, 443
  religious, 2, 15, 44, 137
impure, 57, 186
impurities, 40, 202, 340
  personal, 40
inaccuracies, 330
  well-documented historical, 234
Inanna's consort, 155
incarnating, 94, 101, 117, 283
incarnation, 13–14, 86–90, 94, 141, 270, 272–73, 285, 287, 335, 338, 360, 400, 403
  historical, 309
incarnation in Christ, 89, 101, 287, 360
incarnation of Christ, 317
incest, 380
incompleteness, 16

incomprehensibility, 16–17, 108
inconsistencies, 103, 290, 330
  internal, 41
incontrovertible scientific support, 130
indeterminacy, 366
index of forbidden books 293, 346, 410, 419
India, 152, 337
Indianapolis, 438
individual existence, 117
individual in dreams, 114
individual matter, 104
individuals, 23–24, 29–30, 58, 62, 92, 97, 104, 106, 284, 288, 389–90, 392, 403
  charismatic, 58, 206
  mythic, 39
  rebellious, 389
  righteous, 411
individual's identity, 411
individual's life, 57, 86, 129, 386
individual's life choices, 290
individual's position, 290
individual's religions tradition, 387
individual symbolic representations, 85
individuation, 86–87, 95, 116–17, 139, 141, 341, 429
  reciprocal, 115
individuation and enlightenment, 141
Individuation and individual existence, 117
individuation process, 85–87, 89, 94–95
Indo-European patriarchal warrior societies, 156
Indonesia, 148
Indulgences, 342
indulgencies, 342
Indus Valley, 154
inerrancy, 310, 331
inerrancy of scripture, 310

INDEX | 481

inerrant, 331, 340
infallible word, 340
infancy, 31, 41, 51, 85, 369, 382
infant, 129, 383
infantile, 370, 378–79, 382
infantile residues, 370
infantile symbiotic experiences, 370
infant-mother relationship, good, 383
infidelity, 187, 200
  king's, 193
infinite aspect, 13
infinite cognitive ability, 350
Infinite Horizon of human consciousness, 309
infinite number, 293, 352
infinity, 65–66, 93, 140, 291, 350, 353, 434
inflation, extreme, 68
inflicted discomfort, 266
inhabitants, 188
inheritance, dangerous, 414
inherited Jewish concept of God, 240
iniquities, 184, 390
initiation, 108, 338
  baptismal, 338
injury, 343
  narcissistic, 204
injustice, 38, 49, 134, 163, 196, 305, 363
  world-wide, 103
innate mental categories, 20, 61
innate mental processes, 132
innocent women, 218
innumerable gods and goddesses, 109
Innumerable religious groups, 58
Inquisition, 77, 284, 384, 407
  medieval, 410
inscribed in the book of life, 167
inscription, 223, 230
insecurity, 187, 191, 388

insertions, 29, 251, 260
insistence, 19, 97, 131, 182–83, 225, 266, 268, 279, 313
  church's, 287
  positivistic, 12
insistence on monotheism, 183, 268
institutions, 57, 78, 135, 215, 260
  cultural, 2
  father's, 140
  political, 33
  single, 284
instructions, 40, 158, 225, 242, 275
instruments, 142, 195, 199, 207, 212, 287, 393, 414
  musical, 148
integration, 68, 117, 128
Integrative psychiatry, 422
intellect, 36, 163, 282, 288, 404
intellects, greatest, 351
intellectual assent, 74
  voluntary, 52
intellectual curiosity, 285
intellectual defenders, 279
intellectual difficulties, 12, 43
intellectual dismissal, 116
intellectual exercise, 324
intellectual heritages, 123
intellectual integrity, maintaining, 304
intellectualize, 383
intellectuals, 33
intelligence, 15, 21, 36, 39, 185, 300, 357, 385
  artificial, 43
  creative, 44
  human, 7, 357
  pure, 164
  spiritual, 266
  superior, 408
intelligence and consciousness, 39
intensification, 414
intensity, 34, 84, 206, 211–12, 246, 294

affective, 68, 140
emotional, 17, 206
highest, 66
irresistible, 206
intentions, 72, 93, 117, 151, 170, 193–94
  human, 393
  original, 257
interaction, 117, 314, 352, 366
  creative, 118
  direct, 25
  divine-human, 296
interactive field, 129
intercessor, 274
interconnection, 352
intercourse, 155
  sexual, 184
interdependence, mutual, 89
interiority, 74
inter-marriage, prohibited, 202
intermediaries, 210, 361
intermediate area, 383
internalized early caregiver, 116
internal object relationship, 141
interpenetrate, 90, 351
interpenetration, mutual, 338
interpersonal, 14
interpersonal field, 117
interpretation, 76, 227, 232–33, 297, 299, 307, 320, 323, 342–43, 347, 405, 408, 413
  correct, 52, 298
  human, 306
  psychological, 264, 395
  rabbinic, 173
interpretation and testimony, 233
interpretation of scripture, 2, 76, 298
interpreted Jesus, 313
interpreters, 60, 296, 320, 331
Interpreting faith, 423
interpretive framework, 330

Intersubjectivity in personality theory, 421
intertwining of religion and politics, 153
interventions, 190, 292
  direct, 337
  miraculous, 34
  miraculous divine, 309
interview, 106, 421, 432
intimacy, 79, 85, 95, 197
  total, 123
intimate relationship, 58, 360
intolerance, 41, 165, 183, 296, 410–11
intolerant, 41, 47, 263, 266, 297, 300, 361
intrapsychic, 412
intrapsychic appearances, 115
intrapsychic manifestations, 79, 96
intrapsychic material, 95
  demonstrable, 70
intrapsychic relation, 95
intrapsychic relationship of consciousness, 89
intrapsychic splits, 134
  reconciled, 133
intrapsychic structures, 143, 412
intrinsic capacity for randomness and evolution, 10
introjection, 388
introspection, 348, 377
intuition, 5, 54, 145, 156, 291, 301–2, 308, 358
  mystical, 35
invaders, 156, 160, 389
invasion, 156, 192, 224
invention, 69, 156, 283, 296–97, 418
invisible reality, 223
invocation, 219, 355
I pommel my body and subdue it, 266
Iran, ancient, 161, 407
Iraq, 153
Irenaeus, 279
iron, 153
  with a rod of, 244

irreconcilable differences, 59
Irreducible mind, 433
irreducible spiritual core, 129
irreligious, 44
Isaac, 174, 212, 223–24, 381, 412
Isaiah, 107, 109–10, 175, 183–85, 187–88, 190, 193–95, 203–5, 212, 224–25, 235–36, 238, 246–47, 249, 258
Isaiah's prophecy, 246
Isaiah's superego, 224
Isaurian, 341
Ishtar, 143, 154–55
Ishvara, 83
Isis, 143, 154–55, 240, 338
Isis/Horus, 273
Islam, 3, 60, 124, 283, 352, 407
Islamic life, contemporary, 142
island, central, 111
Israel, 170, 173, 175–76, 178, 180, 182, 192–93, 195–203, 205, 207, 212–14, 222–24, 235–36, 242–43, 389–90
Israelite baby boys, 185
Israelite monotheism, 177
Israelite prophets, 162
Israelites, 18, 25, 171, 174, 176–80, 187, 196, 198–99, 202–3, 206, 218–19, 222–25, 236
  ancient, 181
  exiled, 199
  fellow, 242
  unite, 222
Israelites and God, 236
Israelites' bloodthirsty characteristics, 225
Israelites' idolatry, 224
Israelites' neighbors, 218
Israelites' numbers, 173
Israelites to return to Jerusalem and rebuild, 196

Israelite Tradition, 175
Israel's apostasy, 174
Israel's enemies, 183–84, 248
Israel's faithlessness, 198
Israel's Messiah, 258
Israel's oppressors, 207
Ithaca, 421, 427, 438
itinerant evangelist, 321
itinerant Jewish sage-healer, 337
it is finished, 336

J

Jack, 432
Jacob, 174, 176, 223–24, 381
Jacob/And hate, 194
Jacobi, 432
Jacob's descendants, 405
Jacob's sons, 173
Jacob steals, 221
Jaffe, 432
Jahoda, 421
Jairus, 232
James, William, 25, 29–32, 53–54, 268, 295, 338, 418, 432
Jamnia, 224
Janes, 377, 432
Jaspers, 162, 432
  Karl, 162
Jaynes, 376–77
jealous, 170, 222–23, 380
jealous husband, 197
jealous of Job, 100
jealousy, 183, 222, 340
Jean-Paul Sartre, 49
Jefferson, 34, 301
Jehoiakim, King, 200
Jephthah, 184
Jeremiah, 178, 183, 187–89, 193–95, 199–200, 206, 218, 225, 243, 248, 255, 339
Jeremiah's anguish, 201
Jeremiah's warning, 405
Jericho, 222
Jerome's translation, 142
Jerusalem, 111, 179, 187, 195–96, 198–99, 202,

204–5, 236, 242, 248, 253
captured, 200
conquer, 289
conquered, 196
Jerusalem priests, 180
Jerusalem temple, 57, 174, 198, 202, 242, 260, 326
first, 180
Jesus, 47, 51, 227, 229–61, 263–70, 272–79, 281–84, 303–4, 306–7, 312–26, 333–43, 384, 400, 402, 406, 409, 414–15, 421–24, 427–28, 440–43
Jésus, 47
Jesus
eclipsed, 249
embodied, 252
given, 241
Jesus' admonition, 244
Jesus' ascension, 306
Jesus' atonement, 156
Jesus atones, 323
Jesus' background, 335
Jesus' behavior, 321–22
Jesus' birth, 234
Jesus' body, 267
Jesus' boldest claims, 241
Jesus Christ, 90, 205, 229, 256–57, 283, 298, 305, 337, 360, 431, 439
Jesus' comments, 251
Jesus' compassion, 250
liberal politics stresses, 278
Jesus' contemporaries, 319
Jesus curing epilepsy, 338
Jesus' death, 156, 231–33, 245–47, 249, 254, 259, 261, 277–78, 315–17, 335–36
demanded, 254
Jesus' death and resurrection, 314
Jesus' death Mary Magdalen, 245
Jesus' divine nature, 272
Jesus' Divinity, 237, 266, 400

Jesus dynasty, 441
Jesus' effect, 325
Jesus' exhortation, 414
Jesus' family, 321
Jesus' family flees, 235
Jesus' followers, 241, 246, 249, 254–55, 264
persecuted, 259, 264
Jesus' genealogy, 336
Jesus' humiliating crucifixion, 248
Jesus' illegitimacy, 323
Jesus' insistence, 55
Jesus' Jewish, 261
Jesus' Jewishness, 253, 319, 321
Jesus' Jewish tradition, 255
Jesus' life, 227, 232–33, 317
Jesus' love, 278
Jesus' ministry, 247, 252
Jesus' miracles, 319
Jesus' mission, 281, 315
Jesus' mother, 260
Jesus movement, 255
Jesus' Non-dual Sensibility, 252
Jesus' opponents, 343
Jesus' origin, 336
Jesus' parents, 336
Jesus' post-resurrection appearance, 322
Jesus' psyche, 409
Jesus' psychology, 322
Jesus' resurrection, 233, 245, 261, 314, 336
Jesus' sacrifice, 265, 277, 298
Jesus' sacrificial death, 309
Jesus' self-sacrifice, 413
Jesus Seminar, 337
Jesus shares, 261
Jesus' supporters, 248
Jesus' teachings, 244, 250–52, 256, 318, 338
transmit, 265
Jesus' trial, 234
Jesus' Values, 250
Jesus.vi, 231
Jesus' voice, 255, 264

Jesus' work, 314
jewelry, 150, 153
Jewish, 114–15, 211, 213–14, 216, 224–25, 229, 253–54, 258–59, 264, 268, 277, 283
average, 35
orthodox, 181
Jewish affirmation and philosophical reflection, 428
Jewish and Christian messianism, 430
Jewish authorities, 254
Jewish background, traditional, 241
Jewish Bible, 221
Jewish canon, 221
Jewish-Christian audience, 335
Jewish-Christian reality, 441–42
Jewish Christians, 242, 268
Jewish codes, traditional, 250
Jewish communities, 241, 335, 355
Jewish concept, 205
inherited, 240
Jewish contemporaries, 248
Jewish covenant, 213
Jewish establishment and accusations of blasphemy, 253
Jewish Father-God, 265
Jewish feminist theology, 438
Jewish followers, 270
early, 253
Jewish God, 248
Jewish God-image, 365
traditional, 214
Jewish History, 213, 430
Jewish Jesus, 434
Jewish juridical procedures, 254
Jewish kinsmen, 264
Jewish law, 234, 241–42, 254, 264–65

traditional, 256
Jewish literature, 335
Jewish messianic expectations, 258
Jewish mystical tradition, 182, 201, 209
Jewish nationalism, 261
Jewishness of Judas, 215
Jewish origins, 263
Jewish philosopher, important, 208
Jewish population, 242
Jewish practices, 318
Jewish preacher, 427
Jewish precepts, pre-existing, 244
Jewish prohibitions, strict, 234
Jewish prophetic, 320
Jewish refusals, 253
Jewish rejection, 216
Jewish response, 225
Jewish schools, 399
Jewish survival, 214
Jewish system of theology, 212
Jewish taboo, 234
Jewish temple, 277
Jewish theologians, 212
Jewish thinkers, 210
Jewish Thought, 210
Jewish tradition, 167, 169, 205, 207, 210, 217, 236, 253, 256, 260, 327
 orthodox, 29, 175
Jewish voice, 432
Jews, 182, 210, 212–13, 215, 225, 241, 247–48, 253–56, 258, 263–65, 335–36, 381, 399–401, 410–11, 434–35
 fellow, 242–43
 fundamentalist, 255
 misunderstood, 434
 observant, 212
 saved, 62
 sheltered, 215
 victimize, 400
Jews and Christians, 422
Jews and Gentiles, 268
Jews and Gentiles to belief, 268

Jews and Muslims, 290
Jews of Europe, 62
Job, 72, 98–102, 106, 120–21, 134, 141–42, 175, 188–89, 191, 225, 391
 integrity, 98
 servant, 101
 suffering, 134
Job myth, 98
Job's capacity, 121
Job's experience, 102, 107
Job's piety, 102
Job's position, 121
Job story, 100–101
John, 105, 107, 229–31, 233–34, 236, 241–48, 250–52, 254, 334–37, 340, 343
John claims, 229
John Duns Scotus, 286
John Scotus Erigena, 283
Johnson, 318, 337, 432, 423
Jonah, 62, 332
Jonas, 214, 432
Jones, 431–32, 441
Jordan river, 268
Joseph, 222, 274, 336, 377, 406, 432
Josephus, 222, 319
Josephus's work, 319
Joshua, 18, 171, 176, 183, 216, 222, 224, 368
Josiah, 198–222
Josiah's court, 198
Josiah's Reforms, 198–99
Josiah's reforms Israel, 200
joy, 25, 31, 187, 210, 266, 340
Judah, 195, 198, 200, 203, 223
 intimidating, 203
 invaded, 199
 kingdom of, 177, 204, 206
 likened, 204
 southern kingdom of, 198, 203
Judah's captivity, 202
Judah's elite, 199

Judaism, 17–18, 136, 157, 161, 208, 211, 214–16, 253, 255, 409–10, 435, 437, 440
 attacked, 353
 first century, 318
 mainstream, 242
 post-exilic, 337
 rabbinic, 213
 reinvent, 253
 superseded, 243
 supplanted, 215
 traditional, 208–9, 244, 253, 256, 338
Judas, 215
Judeans, 199
 fellow, 200
Judeo-Christian, 39, 125, 159, 242
Judeo-Christian form, traditional, 26
Judeo-Christian forms of revelation, 70
Judeo-Christian God, 26, 136
Judeo-Christian God-image, 39, 68
 traditional, 366
Judeo-Christian model of God, 367
Judeo-Christian theists, 12
 traditional, 14
Judeo-Christian tradition, 157, 389
Judeo-Christian tradition fades, 126
to judge the living and the dead, 233
judgment, 55, 107, 159, 162–63, 180, 183, 198, 223, 243, 252, 295
 eschatological, 224
 final, 260
 necessary, 225
 ordinary moral, 412
 parental, 390
 preached, 203
 soften Amos's, 197
judgmental, 228, 310
judgmental Father God, 274

INDEX | 485

Judgment Day, 390
Julian, 290
Jung, 22–23, 26–27, 31–32, 56, 60–61, 65–96, 98–117, 119–28, 130–34, 136, 138–43, 209, 214–15, 323–25, 341–42, 403–4, 413–15, 422–26, 432–35, 441–43
Jung & Neumann, 141
Jung Christ, 113
Jung claims, 27
Jung credits, 88
Jungian analysis, 89
Jungian commentary, 427
Jungian literature, 3, 141
Jungian Perspectives, 431, 441
Jungian psychology, 121, 128, 424, 426, 433, 442
Jungians, 29, 70, 83, 85, 93, 95, 239
Jungian Studies, 425
Jungian terms, 272
Jungian thought, 435
Jungian work, 141
Jung Journal, 425
Jung's Aion, 427
Jung's appeal, 76
Jung's approach, 2–3, 18–19, 60–61, 90, 93, 96, 103, 105, 108–9, 116, 122–24, 132–33, 135–39
Jung's approach frees, 417
Jung's approach to God, 108
Jung's approach to religion, 124, 133, 138
Jung's approach to spirituality, 26
Jung's belief, 86, 101, 122
Jung's childhood vision, 75
Jung's Collected Works, 140
Jung's concept, 115, 131
Jung's critics, 67, 96
Jung's Critique, 413
Jung's Disagreement, 121

Jung's emphasis, 93, 95, 105, 288, 417
Jung's failure, 133
Jung's father, 125, 134, 140
Jung's image, 99
Jung's italics, 68, 90
Jung's key letters, 427
Jung's life, 125
Jung's life situation, 111
Jung's model, 138, 141
Jung's myth, 99, 427
Jung's position, 54, 74
Jung's preoccupation, 133
Jung's proposal, 92, 102, 136, 139, 220, 426
Jung's Psychology, 2, 65–143
Jung's psychology of religion, 431
Jung's reception, 431
Jung's recognition, 106
Jung's stress, 117, 139
Jung's vision, 75, 140
Jung's words, 68, 87, 325
Jung's work, 73, 133–34, 384, 418, 428
  links, 118
Jung/White, 431
Jung-White letters, 123
Jupiter, 224
justice, 102–3, 154, 158, 186, 190, 193, 203–4, 210, 217, 219, 246, 252, 314
  perverted, 196
  social, 41, 199, 244, 314, 416
justification, 40, 54, 242, 257, 319, 331, 361, 395, 398–99

K
Kabbala, 209–10, 213
Kakar, 385, 433
Kansas City, 436
Kant, 20, 22–23, 68, 132, 140, 300, 302, 342, 358–59, 433
Kant and Jung, 132
Kant's approach, 132, 358
Kant's approach to religion, 358

Kant's epistemology, 61
Kashmir, 337
Kastrup, 408, 433
Katz, 211, 433
Kaufman, 173, 177, 433
Kaufmann, 51, 54
Kelly, 130, 433
Kelsey, 142, 433
Kepler, 345–46
  Johannes, 346
Keter, 210
Khnum, 158
Kierkegaard, 357, 360–61
Kierkegaard's emphasis, 361
Kille, 322, 433
killing, 18, 183–84, 217, 252–53, 380, 382, 410, 413
  initial, 380
  occasion, 184
killing in battle, 184
Kimball, 411, 433
kin
  close, 11
  departed, 150
kindness, 55, 98, 184, 210, 250, 266–67, 340
king, 110, 112, 153, 155, 159, 161, 178–79, 181, 184–85, 190, 192, 194, 200, 223–24, 248
  all-powerful, 328
  anointed, 337
  celestial, 346
  great, 163, 184
  long-ago, 11
  puppet, 199
  righteous, 248
  sacral, 247
  supreme, 212
  triumphant, 320
  unpredictable, 139
  wicked, 198
kingdom, 88, 120, 196, 198, 210, 221, 243, 248–50, 260–61, 343, 436
  earthly, 311
  northern, 193, 196–98, 203, 221
  physical, 243

southern, 221
kingdom of God, 215, 243–44, 246–47, 249, 251, 337, 343
Kingdom of God on earth, 321
kingdom of heaven, 120, 322, 341
Kingdom of Heaven in terms of social progress, 361
the kingdom of heaven is at hand, 249
kingdom on earth, 248
King James translation, 235
King Jeroboam II, 196
King of Judah, 198
Kings Saul, 195
kinship, 147, 362
Kirkpatrick, 373, 391, 433, 440
KJV, 74, 238, 403, 414
Klawans, 186, 433
Klee, Paul, 365
Kleinian standpoint, 412
Kloet, 429
klug, 399
Kluger, 433
Knight, 422
knowledge, 51, 54, 59, 61, 197, 285–86, 290–91, 296–97, 299, 301, 308, 347–48, 350
astronomical, 346
destroyed by lack of, 197
direct, 275
esoteric, 275
historical, 337
human, 123, 346
innate, 279
modern, 305
new, 25, 304
rational, 354
reliable, 319
religious, 23, 348
scientific, 348
secret, 275
special, 57
superior, 98

true, 305
verifiable, 51
knowledge and love of Yhwh, 197
knowledge of nature, 347
Knox, 129, 433
Koan, Zen, 120
Kohut, 85–86, 100, 143, 265, 419, 424, 430, 434
Koren, 437
Kovary, 424
Kramer, 155, 434
Krishna, 120
Krishnamurti, 60, 434
Kristallnacht, 62
kritisch bearbeitet, 47
Kurgan nomads, 156

L
labor, 152
  hard, 237
ladder, 405
Lady, 154
Lady of Guadalupe, 274
laity, 299
lake, 223–24
  sulfurous, 419
Lamarck, 34
Lamarckian, 419
lamb, 105, 185, 236, 333, 412
  original, 236
  paschal, 236
lamentation, 18, 155, 183, 390
Lammers, 121, 434
land, 57, 158, 171, 173, 177, 182, 200–201, 204, 403, 405, 410
  dry, 161
  people's, 255
Lang, 30, 155, 161, 176–77, 180–81, 267, 434
  Andrew, 165
  Peter, 431
language, 2, 14, 25, 30, 35, 96, 125, 140, 308, 313, 363–64
  extreme, 195
  human, 146
  metaphysical, 306

modern, 309
ordinary, 60, 366
particular, 146
personal, 363
prophetic, 206
scatological, 399
theological, 308, 364
vernacular, 290
language games, 364
language redolent, 181
Lao-Tzu, 162
large number of universes, 9
last days, 247
Last Judgment, 244
Last Supper, 234, 332, 341
Latin, 142, 283, 296, 396
Latin poet Lucretius, 11, 165
Latin school, 396
Latin Vulgate translation, 293
Latin word, 335
Latin Writings, 440
Laurence, 390
law, 32–33, 173–75, 198–200, 202, 205, 212, 236–37, 244, 253, 257, 262, 265, 271, 283, 379, 398
  canon, 76, 288, 296
  dietary, 174, 186, 244, 258, 268, 334
  fundamental, 21
  moral, 23, 358, 400, 419
  oral, 173
  racial, 62
  scientific, 347, 419
  spiritual, 359
Law and biblical prophecy, 335
law code, 178
lawgiver, 154, 178, 186
Lawrence, 434
Laws Book, 11
laws of nature, 21, 367
laws of Yhwh, 198
Lazarus, 332
  raised, 233
leaders, 58, 83, 161, 187, 215, 252
  first-century church, 326

INDEX | 487

human, 197
idealized group, 411
military, 205, 248
political, 252
religious, 83, 416
tribal, 147
leadership, 198, 260, 337, 430
leadership positions, 259
senior, 315
learning theory, 392
Leavy, 134, 388, 434
Leben Jesu, 47
legacies, 299, 327, 340
legends, 47, 163, 219, 325, 381, 442
embellished tribal, 408
legitimize, 278, 367
Leibniz, 352–53, 356
Leidenhag, 317, 434
lens, 206
psychodynamic, 386
Leon, 209
Lerner, 156, 434
lethal rage attacks, 191
let him be accursed, 258
letters, 68, 72, 94, 98–99, 106, 114, 120, 124–25, 228, 232, 258–60, 339–41, 432
first, 245
important, 117
lower-case, 140
upper-case, 3
letters Jung, 72
letter to Buber, 124
Levant, 402
level, 8–9, 26–27, 53, 56, 67, 69, 79–80, 93, 95, 97, 101, 115, 135–36, 208–9, 212
absolute, 20, 127–28
archetypal, 58, 77, 80, 91, 96, 117, 135, 143, 188
autonomous, 394
collective, 88
complex, 371
conceptual, 85
conscious, 132
deepest, 80, 87
empirical, 83

fundamental, 127–28
high, 8, 21, 101, 182, 191
historical, 319
human, 90, 131, 138
individual's, 125
infinite, 16, 94
instinctual, 111
irrational, 379
lower, 36
metaphorical, 125
moral, 101
mythic, 413
mythopoetic, 29, 56, 126, 137
new, 45, 272
non-dual, 101
non-ego, 67–68, 74
non-egoic, 57
noumenal, 132
ontological, 143
personal, 78, 88, 104, 361, 384
psychological, 319
quantum, 366
symbolic, 403
unitary, 81, 403
unknowable, 209
level of consciousness, 135
level of evil, 54, 105, 216
Levin, 392, 434
Levinas, 39, 211, 434
Levine, 253, 335, 434
Leviticus, 18, 40, 142, 175, 178–79, 183–84, 186–87, 189, 218, 234, 244
Leviticus chapters, 40
Lévy-Brühl, 151
Lewin, 385, 434
Lewis, 43
Lewis-Williams, 149
Lewy, 216, 434
LGBTQ rights, 278
Liberal Christians, 18, 330–31
contemporary, 252, 338
liberals, 252, 310
liberal theologians, 18, 53, 302, 310
liberating effect, 138

liberation, 101, 278, 314, 420
gay, 314
women's, 425
liberation theologians, 314
licentiousness, 340
life, 7–10, 12, 30–31, 39–40, 43–44, 47, 49, 83–84, 118–20, 145, 150, 152–54, 158–59, 187–89, 324–25, 359–60, 364–65, 370–71, 383–84, 387–88
life and fertility, 152
life and history change, 359
life and morality, 12
life and worships, 328
life cycles, 152
life exigencies, 197
life immobile, 342
life-long preoccupation for Jung, 142
life of Christ, 89, 427
life principle, 111, 396
life situation, 394
individual's, 392
subject's, 68
lifetime, 125
author's, 282
light, inner, 111, 299
Light Bearer, 238
lightening, 146, 162, 238, 407
lightening flashing, 201
light of Christ, 299
like a master workman, 181
likeness, 241
lost, 285
Lily, 236
limbic lobe, ancient, 377
limbic system, 432
Limbo, 342
limbs, multiple, 159
liminal, 142
limitations, 9, 14, 16, 49, 82, 94–95, 140, 190, 262, 347–48, 360
human, 371
Lisbon earthquake, 353

literalism, 138, 271
literalizing, 91, 403
literalness, 240
literal reality, 238, 399
literal word, 331
literary conventions, 221
literary introduction, 424
literary styles, 232
Littell, 216, 434
liturgy, 315, 325
  empty, 196
  entered Christian, 277
Liverpool dream, 111
living God, 228, 438
Local cultures, 30
local economy, 153
localizations, 408
local languages, 140, 296
local names, 65, 146
local princes, 296
local religions, 113
local tribal chieftains, 222
local volcano, 381
local warrior-god, 177
location, 45
  geographical, 403
loci, 404, 422
Locke, 33, 349, 350, 356
locked doors, 246
logic, 29, 45, 61, 67
  circular, 330
  tortured, 265
logical difficulties, 16–17, 19
logic of consciousness, 61
Logoi, 421
logos, 164, 207–8, 229, 271, 279, 340
  eternal, 267
Loisy, Alfred, 304
longing, 308
  human, 2
Lord, 109–10, 176, 187–88, 193–94, 196–97, 201, 210, 212, 235, 245, 249, 261, 264
  build the temple of the, 248
Lost Christianities, 427
lost sheep of Israel, 215
Lost Tribes, 198

lotus, 112
  white, 407
Louisville, 422, 424, 436–37
love, 18–19, 45–48, 98–99, 105, 190–91, 197–99, 209–10, 238, 242–44, 266, 270–71, 278, 295, 306, 309–11, 314–15, 334–35, 342, 387–88, 392–93
  advocated, 255
  human, 287
  intellectual, 355
  maternal, 392
  mother's, 382
  overflowing, 228
  parental, 369–70
  practiced, 241
  pure, 287
  sacrificial, 239, 245
  spontaneous, 223
  unconditional, 397
love God, 242, 244, 286
love of self, 238
love of Yhwh, 197
love one another, 216
loving, 34, 37, 223, 228, 251–52, 259, 305, 310, 383, 386–87, 390–92
loving deity, 55
Loving God-images, 390, 392
loving image of God, 392
loving kindness, 210
loving mother, 28, 369
loving relationship, 392
loving society, 342
Lower Egypt, 154
loyalty, 187
  citizen's, 162
  reciprocal, 199
Lucifer, 237–38
  equated, 238
Lucifer myth, 238
Lucretius, 165
Ludwig Feuerbach, 47
Luhrmann, 29, 435
Luke, 53, 74, 205, 231, 234, 238, 241–43, 246–47, 249–52, 335–38, 343

Luria, Isaac, 210
Luther, 51, 215, 239, 294–97, 299, 338, 394–401, 427–28, 430, 435, 439–40
Lutheran Evangelical Church, 401
Luther's anti-Semitism, 400–401
Luther's anxiety, 398
Luther's belief, 398
Luther's biographers discount, 396
Luther's bitter anti-Judaism, 399
Luther's capacity, 401
Luther scholars, 399
Luther's disappointment, 397
Luther's Europe, 399
Luther's experience of childhood abuse, 397
Luther's melancholia, 396
Luther's mother, 397
Luther solace, 397
Luther sounds, 295
Luther specialists, 396
Luther's relationship, 395
Luther's stress, 296
Luther's teachers, 398
Luther's theory, 295
Luther's Works, 435, 440
Lyons, 279

M
Maat, 158
Maccoby, 215, 435
machine, 42–43, 48, 358
  complex, 345
  ghost in the, 43
MacKenna, 99, 133, 435
Mackie, 24, 435
Madonna, 332, 431
Magi, 240
magic, 368, 429, 442
  sympathetic, 149
magical, 58, 339
Magic and religion, 442
magician, 58, 320, 440
magisterium, 298
Maimonides, 208–9

INDEX | 489

mainstream Protestant denominations, 310
mainstream religions, 2, 58, 385
  contemporary, 82
maker of dreams, 114
making images of God, 182, 401
Malachi, 248
Malden, 437
malevolent, 17, 217
malice, 238, 357
Mama, 160
Mamre, 190
mandala imagery, 112
  idealized, 112
mandalas, 111–12, 120
  extraordinary, 66
mandala symbolism, 111, 127
Manichaeism, 161, 341
Manichean, 104, 239
manifestations, 59–60, 66–67, 70, 72, 77–78, 80, 82, 91–92, 97, 114–15, 117, 131–32, 138–39, 270–71, 341–42
  collective, 130
  terrifying, 213
  total, 131
manifests, 13, 36, 39, 78, 80, 94–96, 106, 108, 114, 122, 131
  unmanifest divine, 271
mankind, 90, 92, 257, 278, 360, 379, 439
manna, 236
  true, 236
manufacture, 91
manuscripts, 232, 246, 320
  early, 246, 335
  original, 232
Marcion, 267
Marduk, 154, 160, 199, 203, 224
  grandson, 224
Marduk of Babylon, 179
marginal Jew, 321, 435–36, 442
Mark Gundry, 335, 341
Mark Rothko, 365
Mark's Gospel, 338

Mark's story, 233
Maroni, 407
marriage, 100, 133, 155, 197, 259, 333, 412
  forced, 218
marriage bond, 160
Marsilio Ficino, 291
Martin, 396
martyrdom, suffered, 247
marvels, 324
  promised, 187
Marx, 47, 361
Marxism, 47–48, 50
Mary, 53, 113, 122, 142–43, 238, 269–70, 273–74, 276, 332, 336, 341
Mary's position, 273
Mary's role, 274
masculine, 120, 156, 158, 166, 181, 223, 271, 274, 326–27
Masculine Christian God-image, 325
masculine concepts, 367
masculine God-imagery, 326
masculine modes, 156
masculine noun, 146
masculine pronouns, 3, 325
masculine superiority, 326
masculinity, 367
masochistic, 324
massacres, 185, 254
masses, 216, 236, 396
  first, 396
mass hallucination, 322
mass killings, 184, 225
mass-mindedness, 91
mass murder, 107, 185
mass slaughter, 216, 255
material, 70, 76, 116, 118, 169–70, 221, 232–33, 238, 331–32, 335, 349–50, 355, 403–4
  borrowed, 336
  conscious, 124
  contemporary, 171
  folkloric, 62
  genetic, 45
  historical, 40, 133, 171

inserted, 193
  objectionable, 411
  parental, 205
  prophetic, 193
  psychological, 126
  rejected Gnostic, 279
  religious, 74
  unsubstantiated, 323
materialism, 42, 46, 355
  combat, 351
materialistic belief system, 116
materialists, 8, 21–22, 24, 27, 32, 34, 43, 129–30, 145
  dogmatic, 356
materialization, 366
materialize, 193, 203
material reality, 300
material universe, 348, 358
material world, 115, 275, 350–51, 357, 367
maternal accounts of religious experience, 385
maternal containment, missing, 385
maternal role, 193
mathematical, 351
mathematical descriptions, 9
mathematical necessity, 355
mathematical value, 8
mathematician, 7, 346
mathematics, 346
matriarchal prehistory, 427
matriarchal society, 167
  goddess worshipping, 167
matrilineal, 154
matrix, 397
  maternal, 383
Matte Blanco, 61
matter, 42, 44, 46, 113, 134, 140–42, 189, 274, 276, 280, 291, 293, 298, 348–52, 354–56
matter Kuan Yin, 109
Matthew, 231–36, 241–46, 249–51, 253–54, 321, 323, 331, 335–36,

338–39, 404, 406, 409, 414
matures, 390
  individual, 388
Mauch, 426
McClean, 425
McDargh, 31, 386, 388, 435
McFague, 327–28, 435
McGrath, 41, 318, 435
McKnight, 348, 435
McNamara, 145, 407, 435
meals, 234, 261, 396
  ancient totemic, 381
  traditional Passover, 234
meaninglessness, 2
meant to be, 115
measure
  final, 300
  large, 255
measurement, 366
  quantitative, 360
mechanical systems, 43
mechanical universe, 351
mechanics, 345
  classical, 366
mechanisms
  biological, 45, 376
  blind, 8
  complex, 21
  physical, 43, 61
  primitive, 411
  projective, 411
  psychological, 373
  random, 362
mediation, 103, 290
  institutional, 77
  necessary, 271
mediation of Christ, 103
mediator, 77, 84, 92, 274
  potential, 29
mediators of religious experience, 77
mediatrix of all graces, 273
medicine, 42, 147, 426, 434
medicine-man, 58
medieval focus, 284
medieval superstitions, 399
medieval William, 13
meditation, 29, 81, 272,
284, 288, 370, 419
Mediterranean, 255
Mediterranean agrarian cultures, 156
Mediterranean religion and Christianity, 159
medium, 68, 90, 92, 113, 194, 279, 307, 355
  powerful, 332
megalithic ceremonial sites, ancient, 151
Megalithic structures, 152
Meier, 321, 435
Meissner, 52, 204, 388, 390, 411, 435–36
Meister, 330, 441
Meister Eckhart, 80, 95, 289, 338, 424
melancholia, 322, 397, 399, 423
  male, 397
melancholic, 322, 395
Melanesian and Polynesian religion, 58
Melchizedek, 236
members, 41, 83, 142, 147, 253, 262, 272, 309, 333, 337, 341
  exclusive, 400
  offends, 59
membership, 298
  communal, 117
membership consolidates, 411
memes, 44–45, 62
  particular societal, 44
memories, 42, 81, 129, 133, 141, 231, 285, 349, 429, 432, 443
  autobiographical, 372
  circulating, 319
  collective, 233
  repressed, 380–81
  telescoped, 419
  unconscious, 369–70
menstruating, 40
menstruation, 187
mental apparatus, 143
mental health, 434
mentalizing, 432
mental life, 74, 429
Mental pain, 430
mental parasites, 45
mental representations, 386–87
mental universe, 431
Mercurius, 113
mercy, 7, 15, 18, 30, 204, 210, 212, 218–19, 285, 295, 297
  a sharp, 400
merger of gods, 177
merit, 223, 342, 398
  human, 295
Mersenne, 348
Mesopotamia, 153–55, 159
  ancient, 161
Mesopotamian city-state, 159
Mesopotamian god-images, 160
Mesopotamian gods, 186
Mesopotamian kings, 159
Mesopotamian mythology, 161
Mesopotamian politics, 160
Mesopotamian religion, 159
  earlier, 169
Mesopotamians, 158–59, 372
Mesopotamian stories, 161
Mesopotamian traditions, earlier, 173
Mesopotamian traditions, pre-existing, 172
Messene, 163
messiah, 95, 162, 174, 204–5, 212, 247–48, 256–60, 317, 321, 325, 336–37
  crucified, 258
  defeated, 258
  expected, 248, 258
  false, 225
  humiliated, 265
  promised, 242, 247, 261, 320
  suffering, 248
messiahship, 249
messianic, 247, 415
messianic era, 207
metadivine, 173
metallurgists, 153

INDEX | 491

metallurgy, 153
 early, 153
metals, 153
metaphor for individuation, 341
metaphorical, 183, 191, 261, 402–3
metaphorical references, 79
metaphors, 6, 70, 94, 187, 190, 192, 236, 245, 327–28, 340–41, 402–3
 anthropomorphic, 6
 behavioral, 194
 bodily, 178
 key, 328
 a language of, 79
 new, 79, 402
 oppressive, 328
 parental, 370, 389
 primary, 327
 scriptural, 79
 spatial, 96
metaphysical essence, 93
metaphysical Jung, 143
metaphysical nature of God, 218
metaphysical notions, traditional, 364
metaphysical position, 19, 375
metaphysical question, 73, 130
metaphysical realism, 366
metaphysical reality, 128
metaphysical scheme, 342
metaphysical statements, 364
metaphysical systems, 46
metaphysics, 46, 66, 271, 364–65
 speculative, 341, 363
 spiritual, 351
metapsychology, 133
meteorites, 153
Mettinger, 240, 436
Mettrie, 42
Metzger, 54–56, 436
Meyer, 318, 436
Micah, 223, 248, 336
Michelangelo's painting, 332

Middle Ages, 33, 208, 271, 282–84, 290, 320, 341
 early, 273
Middle East, 176, 181
Middle Paleolithic Period, 167
Midianite Moses, 381–82
mighty acts, 185
Miles, 187, 218, 221, 436
milieu, 241
 cultural, 326
militaristic, 252
military insurgent, 255
Military success, 174
millennialism, 412
Millennialism, 301
Miller, 36, 128, 177, 322, 436, 438
mind, 20–22, 24–25, 42–43, 59–61, 93–94, 131–32, 167, 182–83, 189, 242, 262, 288–89, 349–51, 354–59, 361–62, 375–76, 385–86
 believer's, 56
 bicameral, 376, 432
 collective, 419
 finite, 94
 individual's, 5, 29
 intelligent, 9
 matrix, 93
 modern, 304
 out of his, 321
 scholarly, 418
minds and hearts, 245
Mineola, 439
ministers, 96, 125, 133, 140, 239
ministry, 244, 309, 336, 338
Minoan Crete, 154
minority opinion, 177
miracles, 23, 29, 32–33, 47–48, 62, 79, 194, 219, 301, 310–11, 317
 performed, 244, 419
miracle-stories, 415
miraculous deeds, 324
miraculous portents, 240
misapplication, 374

misapprehension, 35
mis-attunement, 85
Mishnah, 173
misinterpretations, 234, 236, 417
misogyny, 259, 326, 331
missionaries, 146
mistranslation, 235
 deliberate, 406
Mistress, 154
mistrust priesthoods, 33
Mithra, 240
Mithraic tradition, 240
Mithraism, 240
Modalism, 270
models, 45, 137, 214, 291, 293, 298, 328–29, 339, 342, 345, 393
 classical theistic, 328
 compensatory, 391
 convergence, 367
 deist, 367
 deistic, 328
 dialogic, 328
 new, 328, 367
 organized, 393
 pantheistic, 329
 patriarchal, 214
 quaternity, 142
 subjective, 3
 traditional, 328
moderate asocial behavior, 372
modern bibles, 169, 232
modern chemistry, 346
modern ears, 216, 412
modern empiricism, 347
Modern English translations, 246
modern era, 423
modernist attitudes, 304
Modernist movement, 304
modernity, 146, 303, 343
modernize, 304, 317, 363
modern political concepts, 416
modern sensibilities, 172
modern understanding of trauma in childhood, 396
modes of existence, 270
modified Jung, 133

Mohammed, 405
Moloch, 276
monads, 352
  perfect, 352
monarchical, 327
monarchic Israel, 180
monarchies, 223, 298
  united, 195
monasteries, 58, 398
monastic rules, 399
money, 293
  making, 294
moneylenders, 335
monistic, 34, 90
Monkey Trial, 310
monks, 342, 398
Monod, 44, 436
monogenes, 340
monolatrism, 179
Monolatry, 223
monophytism, 267, 274
monotheism, 79, 82–83, 128, 136–37, 159–60, 165–66, 176–77, 180, 183, 223, 268, 270, 272, 381–82
  competing, 135
  ethical, 203
  pure, 340
  strict, 177
  traditional, 61, 80, 138
monotheistic, 32, 176, 230, 431
monotheistic biblical tradition, 181
monotheistic God-image, 169, 417–18
  emerging, 172
monotheistic revisionists, 181
monotheistic system, 93
monotheistic traditions, 7, 73, 79, 82, 137, 407
monotheists, 172, 180, 266
  first, 163
moon, 83, 146, 158, 249, 273, 293, 368
moral awareness, 98
moral behavior, 23, 191, 196, 301, 350

human, 37, 372
moral categories, 414
moral conduct, 416
moral crisis for Christianity, 215
moral effort, 281
moral framework, 300
moral influence, 313
moral integrity, 7
moralism, 380
morality, 11–12, 18, 23, 37, 42, 48–49, 192–93, 354, 356, 358, 370, 375
  given, 34
  human, 45, 182, 391
  individual, 278
  personal, 219
moral judgments, making, 37
moral masochism, 324, 343, 438
moral masochists, 343
moral order, 6, 11, 370
  objective, 139
  pre-existing, 11
moral preferences, 300
moral qualities, 8, 106, 354, 357
  idealized, 391
morals, 419
moral standards, 217, 251
  contemporary, 219, 225
  modern, 18
moral teaching, 106, 354
  necessary, 215
moral values, 21
  objective, 11, 23
More, Henry, 350
Mormon Church, 407, 419
Moroni, 407
mortality, 87, 237
  human, 339
mortals, 47, 101, 163, 273, 371, 406
Mortification, 284
Mortimer Adler, 43
Mosaic authorship, 354
Mosaic covenant, 173
Mosaic Law, 177, 236, 242, 257

mosaics, 274, 332
Moses, 25, 27, 161, 172–75, 183, 185, 198–99, 207–9, 222–24, 236–37, 241–42, 257, 279–80, 381–82, 405
Moses's monotheism, 382
Moses's vision, 140
Most High, 182, 267
mother, 85–86, 129, 133, 154, 268, 273, 323–24, 328, 380, 383, 385, 397
  child's, 387
  ideal, 397
  individual's, 385
  nurturing, 367
  pre-oedipal, 387
  subject's, 28
  virgin, 274
Mother Church, 397
Mother Earth, 153
  impregnated, 153
mother figure, 273
mother goddess, 152, 154, 181–82, 189, 273
  nurturing earth, 189
mother goddess Cybele, 155
motherhood, 159, 284
mother-imago, powerful, 387
mothering, 387
  good, 370
mother Mary, 245
motif, 127
  important religious, 363
motion, 11, 33, 164, 209, 229, 286, 347, 350
motivated behavior and experience, 264
motivations, 231
motivator, important, 322
mountains, 59, 111, 161, 178, 236
Mount Sinai, 173, 236, 339
mourning-liberation process, 437
Mouton, 442
movements, 146–48, 245, 251, 253, 312, 314, 318,

337, 342, 346–47, 352, 358, 374
charismatic, 29
cosmic, 358
cultural, 300
emancipation, 225
failed messianic, 258
mental, 314
messianic, 247
narrative psychological, 394
new, 242, 260
new religious, 290, 301, 303
political, 91
social protest, 320
mover, 84
unmoved, 11, 286
Müller, 146
Max, 146
Müller's Naturism, 146
multicultural, 242
multiplicity, 128, 176–77, 271
multitude, 227
multitude of gods, 157, 165
multiverse, 9
mummification, 158
mundane, 52
objective, 238
mundane reality, 82
mundus imaginalis, 404, 425
murderous, 105, 196, 252
murders, 140, 204, 380
original father, 381
putative, 382
music, 26, 81, 149, 284
Muslims, 290
Mussolini, 62
mutations, 10
random biological, 10
mutilation, 99, 396
mysteries, 2, 8–9, 12, 25, 27, 58, 132, 139, 145, 211–12, 308
impenetrable, 212
inexpressible, 141
innermost, 130
life's, 279
ultimate, 105
mysterious background, 145
mysterious decision, 295
mysterious plans, 103
mysterious ways, 78
mystery of existence, 362
Mystery religions, 162, 240, 420, 429
early, 419
mystical, 46, 436–37
mystical branches, 82
mystical experience, 25, 32, 62–63, 66, 80, 82, 130, 255, 384–85, 438, 440
mystical fool, 426
mysticism, 32, 290, 385, 426, 433
mystics, 29, 32, 59, 80, 82, 99, 101, 141, 288, 290, 385
mystic vision, 431, 436
myth and literal history, 238
mythic elements, 46, 240
mythic examples, 107, 409
mythic form, 143
mythic statement, 143
mythic status, 233
mythic stories, turning, 92
mythic system, 238
Mythic Truth, 408
Myth of Sisyphus, 49
mythologem, 39, 158
collective, 415
mythological, 140, 306
mythological heroes, 324
mythological instances, 336
mythological motifs, 324
mythological narratives, powerful, 393
mythologies, 87, 97, 149, 151, 155–56, 160, 169, 234, 238, 240, 274–75
ancient, 233
associated, 153
earlier pagan, 219
mythologizing, 306
myths, 47, 73–74, 145, 153, 237–38, 393–94, 409, 415, 418, 423, 426–27
explanatory, 87
guiding, 364
living, 120
new, 97, 138, 418
oriented, 380
personal, 77, 97, 119
religious, 387

N
Nag Hammadi in Egypt, 321
naïve image of God, 103
Nanna, 159
narcissism, 100, 137, 185, 342, 411
religious, 266, 312, 410
narcissistic element, 338
narcissistic equilibrium, 204
narcissistic fragility, 191
narcissistic isolation, 99
narcissistic self-enhancement, 410
narcissistic vulnerabilities, 186, 263, 384
human, 100
narratives, inherited, 73
national aspirations, 247
national identity, 206
nationalism, 194
nationalistic aspirations, 256
National Jewish Center for Learning and Leadership, 430
nations, 170, 174–75, 180, 194, 196, 203–5, 207, 242, 246, 248, 258
defeated, 199
as a light to the, 203
ruling, 244
surrounding, 194, 206
victorious, 199
natural constants, 8, 43
natural forces, 7, 145, 177, 304, 374
destructive, 146
Naturalism, 46, 419, 442
scientific, 46

naturalistic approach to religion, 370
natural law, 8, 13, 17, 32, 34, 43, 207, 288, 346
natural phenomena, 8, 12, 27, 48, 111, 147, 164–65, 169, 371, 373–74, 426
natural physical processes, 24
natural processes, 10, 136, 138, 157, 304, 307, 309, 357, 366, 373
  long, 317
natural reasoning powers, 361
natural selection, 10, 21, 44, 362, 372
  result of, 44, 375
natural truths, universal, 34
natural world, 17, 151, 154, 159, 165, 189, 244, 290, 348, 350, 404
nature, 7, 16–18, 21–22, 59–62, 70–71, 145–46, 167, 169, 189–90, 228, 268–70, 300–302, 308, 342–43, 346–48, 350, 354–55, 357–59, 361–63, 367–68
  anthropomorphic, 47
  biological, 10
  defective, 189
  depraved, 284
  eternal, 306
  finite, 17
  forgiving, 274
  immoral, 412
  imperishable, 152
  inauthentic, 282
  indestructible, 153
  individual's, 353
  infinite, 357
  invisible, 358
  metaphysical, 218
  moral, 11
  mysterious, 365
  often-violent, 187
  orderly, 21
  psychic, 69
  psychological, 442
  radical, 139
  rational, 32
  religious, 137
  self-cancelling, 17
  sinful, 52
  special, 234
  third, 316
  unique, 352
  unitary, 35, 80, 130
  unreasonable, 34
  warlike, 37
nature and humanity, 301
nature and origins, 421
nature loving, 11
nature of divinity, 60, 98, 219
nature of God, 14–15, 17, 22, 32, 36, 70, 76, 286, 289, 350, 357, 359
nature of human beings, 259
nature of love, 99
nature of reality, 10
natures of Christ, 340
Naturism, 146
Naturphilosophie, 358
Nazareth, 267, 336, 421–22, 424
Nazi Germany, 434
Nazi movement, 91
Nazi persecution, 215
Nazis, 62, 212, 215
Neandertals, 148, 150, 421
Nebuchadnezzar, King, 199
negativa, 16, 282
negative images of God, 388
negative self-images, 31, 279
negative traits, 47, 217, 411
Nehemiah, 224
neighbors, 169, 177–78, 203, 242, 244
Nekhebt, 154
Neolithic, 156
Neolithic period, 152, 167
  emerging, 151
Neolithic site, 154
neo-orthodox theologians, 61, 305
neo-paganism, 167
Neoplatonic, 289
Neo-Platonic, 291
Neo-Platonic form, 36
Neoplatonic thinkers, 35
Neo-Platonists, 292
neo-Reformation position, 305
neo-Reformation position of theologians, 305
Neo-Thomists, 288
Nero, 335
nervous system, 42–43
Netherlands, 442
Neumann, 67, 85–86, 152, 433, 436
neural networks, 129, 377
neural schemata, 373
neuroanatomy, 432
neuroanatomy of religious experience, 432
neurological basis of religion, 377
neurological explanation of dreaming, 408
neurological explanations for religion, 376, 378
neurological structures, 373
Neuropsychological bases, 437
neuroscientists, 376
Newberg, 377, 436
New England, 298
new level of consciousness, 108, 142
new myth supervenes, 56
New religious strictures, 206
New Testament, 224, 228, 231–32, 235, 239, 254, 306, 317–19, 331–32, 335, 339, 406, 409
New Testament scholars, 264, 337
New Testament studies, 55
new theory of religion, 430
Newton, 7, 48, 347, 350–51, 354, 356–57, 361

INDEX | 495

Newtonian science, 360
Newton's contemporaries, 347
new tradition, 239
  emerging, 235
New trends, 424
Nicaea, 268–69, 402
Nicene, 327
  original, 269
Nicene-Constantinopolitan Creed, 326
Nicene Creed, 237, 268
Nicholas, 291, 431
Nicholas's term, 342
Nichols, 399, 436
Nickolas, 77
Nicolaus Copernicus, 345
Nietzsche, 41, 48, 303, 361
Nietzsche's Zarathustra, 432
nihilo, 209
Nile, 158
Noah, 190, 224
Noah's ark, 311
Noah's drunkenness, 221
Noah's flood, 408
nomadic hunters, 150
nominalists, 284–85, 342
non-believers, 8, 19, 41, 250–51, 263, 265, 339, 352, 361, 400, 409–12
  consigns, 263
non-committed reader, 233
non-dual, 6, 35, 82–83, 90, 140, 252
non-dual Eastern, 101
non-dual event, 338
nonduality, 338
non-duality, 166, 338, 367, 409, 425
non-dual level of consciousness, 101
non-dual perspective, 132
non-dual sensibility, 80, 140, 253, 338
non-dual spirituality, 79, 253
non-dual tradition focus, 29
non-existent, 208, 311

non-Israelites, 202
Non-Narcissist, 342
non-patriarchal, 326
nonpurposive, 362
non-rational understanding, 291
non-religious background, 307
non-religious households, 38
Norwich, 290
nothingness, 25, 29, 32, 99, 213
no-thing-ness, 80
not-other-than-not-other, 291
noumenal reality, 132, 140
numinosity, 50, 58, 66, 73, 87, 109, 111, 116, 272, 415
  projected, 56
numinosum, 26, 29, 31, 52, 56, 61–62, 66–68, 71, 75, 325, 369
numinous, 25–26, 67–68, 70, 91, 106, 324, 424
  longer, 94
numinous center, 111
numinous contact, 82
numinous dimension, 26
numinous dimension of religion, 26
numinous dream image, 114, 116
numinous dreams and visions, 408
numinous ego-nucleus, 141
numinous eruption, 188
numinous experiences, 26–28, 30–32, 61–62, 66–69, 75–76, 80, 82, 106, 110, 127, 131, 136, 393–94
  direct, 82
  given, 28
  important, 75
  individual, 391
  personal, 67, 136, 402
  source of, 26
  toned, 28
Numinous experiences and images, 370

numinous imagery, 67, 69
  shared, 91
  unexpected, 32
numinous manifestations, 67, 96
numinous material, 76, 136
numinous phenomena, 67
numinous symbols, 109, 113
numinous vision, 102
numinous visionary experiences, 185
numinous vision of God, 102
Nuremberg, 62

O
obedience, 102, 141, 173, 175, 184, 194, 265, 278, 379, 384, 390
  absolute, 388
  demanded unquestioned, 283
  loyal, 328
objections, 8–9, 20, 22, 55, 131, 403
  greatest, 353
  horrified, 136
  important, 21
  theological, 317
objective evidence, 16, 143
objective factors, 52
objective form, 81
objective methods, 24
objective moral judgments, making, 300
objective reality, 56, 98, 376
objective reality transcendent, 140
objective spiritual realities, 130
objective status, 102
objective world, 56
object relations, 87, 421
  early, 134, 389, 396
object relationship, good, 382
object relations theory, 391, 440
Object relations theory and religion, 435

objects, 15, 17, 22, 56–58, 61, 100, 151, 154, 270, 306–7, 326, 328, 354–58, 383, 385
  celestial, 158
  early, 378, 385, 387
  given, 373
  inanimate, 147, 151
  internal, 50
  metaphysical, 308
  non-existent, 39
  ordinary, 27
  parental, 387
  particular, 12, 274
  physical, 12, 167, 280, 300, 351
  prehistoric, 167
  sacred, 57, 178
  transitional, 383–85
observable facts and experience, 308
observation of nature, 33, 61, 348
observations, 67, 73, 95, 128, 132
  empirical, 66
  incontrovertible, 136
  meticulous, 221
  phenomenological, 132
observers, 45, 67, 131, 379, 407
  skeptical, 31, 213
  strict, 255
obsessional disorders, 378
obsessional neurosis, universal, 378
obsessional ruminations, 397, 399
obsessionals, 265, 388
Obsessive Actions, 378
obsessively, 102, 262
occasions, 107, 166, 191, 201, 233, 396
  innumerable, 107
  religious, 148
  thirty-five, 244
Occidental mythology, 423
occupations, 18, 189
oceanic feeling, 385
Ockham, 13

O'Connor, 12, 437
Odyssey, 162, 377, 406
Oedipal, 386, 422
Oedipal father, 380
Oedipal material, 382
Oedipal rage, 140
Oedipal rebellion, 336, 342
Oedipal roots, 379
Oedipal situation, 382
Oedipal structure, 342
Oedipal theme, 380
Oedipal theory, 342, 380
Oedipus, 379–80, 386, 419
Oldenhage, 215, 437
old form of consciousness, 377
Old Testament, 207, 423–25, 427, 439
Omega Point, 316
omnipotence, 17–18, 202, 208, 213, 303, 312, 327, 342, 373, 380, 431
  idealizing, 327
  projected infantile, 110
omnipotence and moralism, 380
omnipotent King, 281
omnipotent permit, 328
omnipresent, 38, 228
omniscience, 14, 208
omniscient, 6, 17–18, 99, 208, 228, 310, 350, 381
only begotten Son, 270, 326
ontological reality, 140
ontological status, independent, 74
ontotheology, 365
openness, 308, 437
opinion of theologians, 96
opponents, 297, 312
  defeated, 218
  important, 366
opposite qualities, 16–17, 116
  co-existing, 183
opposites, 88–89, 104, 106, 109–11, 122, 134, 142, 271–72, 291, 295, 336
  balanced, 272

coincidence of, 142, 291, 431
  constellates, 104
  irreconcilable, 76, 103
  possible, 88
  tension of, 88, 142, 341
  undifferentiated, 104
  unite, 110
opposites manifest, 88
oppositions, 89, 106, 161, 163, 165, 291, 295
  church's, 287
  direct, 387
  internal, 88
opposition to monotheism, 165
oppression, 49, 173, 255, 278, 314
oppressive political regimes, 315
oppressive regimes, 416
oppressive superego structure, 102
oppressors, 189, 248, 301
optimism, 305
  spiritual, 353
oracles, 157, 405
oral sadism, 112
oral transmissions, 169, 320
orbits, consistent, 129
order, 7–8, 10, 16, 21, 112, 207–8, 287, 349, 351, 354–55, 357, 369, 373
  cosmic, 158
  explicate, 127
  intelligent, 16
  natural, 32–33, 288
  new, 301
  religious, 227, 283
  social, 177, 367
ordering principle, 129, 291
  intelligent, 287
order in nature, 342, 357
order of nature, 355
ordinances of councils and theologians, 296
organ, 68–69, 92, 160, 376, 378, 404, 408
  complex, 44

psychic, 114
organisms, 10
  living, 362
  pattern-seeking, 373
  single, 419
organization, 152
  effective social, 333
orientation, new, 362
Origen, 279–80
origin, 28, 32, 36, 231, 238, 372, 376, 421, 427–28, 432, 439, 441–43
  human, 362
  immaterial, 267
  infantile, 383
  psychological, 134, 387
original sin, 274, 281, 287, 295, 341–42, 361, 380, 422
  inherited, 274, 316
origin of religion, 146, 165, 369–70, 376, 378, 382, 425, 437, 441
origins of biblical monotheism, 439
Orpheus, 419
Orphic mystery tradition, 420
Orthodox church, 276, 341
orthodox exponents, 82
Orthodox Jews, 211–12, 410
orthodox religious believer, 31
Orthodox traditions, 173, 341
Osiris, 155, 158, 240
other, 56, 95, 141
  wholly, 26, 79
other gods, 100, 176, 194
no other gods before me, 176
otherness, 28, 404, 411
Otto, Rudolph, 25, 213, 438
ousia, 269
Outer Darkness, 238
Outer World, 115
outlook, 290
  religious, 78
outsiders, 174, 222, 411

P

pagan anxieties, ancient, 239
pagan gods, 162, 176, 230, 283, 333
  pre-biblical, 173
paganism, 16, 230
  rational, 354
pagans, 202, 241–42, 263, 333, 406
pagan traditions, 177
  contemporary, 276
  surrounding, 240
Pagels, 268, 276, 437
pain, 9, 22, 56, 72, 237, 373, 412
  extraordinary, 251
Paine, 33, 301, 303
Paleolithic, 146
Paleolithic cave art, 149
Paleolithic practices, 150
Palestine, 338
Palestinian parties, 439
Paley, 21, 368
Panentheism, 34
Panentheistic Reflections, 437
pantheism, 34, 229, 359, 367
pantheist, 163, 355
pantheon, 61, 95, 153, 159, 162, 165–66, 177, 199
  mythic, 75
  religious, 109, 124
  traditional, 161
pantheon of gods, 199
pantocrator, 135, 402
papal encyclical, 316
Papal infallibility, 341
papal tiara, 333
parables, 232, 354, 437
paradise, 241
  imagined pre-genital, 385
  original, 412
paranoid, 192, 321
paranoid process, 435
paranoid-schizoid position, 412
parapsychological research, 116
parental images, 121

parental imagoes, 3, 387–90, 402
parental projections, 121, 175, 188, 386
parenting, harsh, 389
parents, 30, 120, 126, 133, 184, 384, 387–90, 392, 397, 399, 419
  abusive, 390, 419
  guilt-inducing, 390
  miserable, 343
  narcissistic, 388
  primal, 237
  self-sacrificing, 343
  wished-for, 387
parishioners, 332
Parousia, 341
Parrish, 240, 437
Parthenon, 155
participation, 87, 162, 338, 358
  conscious, 137
  symbolic, 277
  unconscious, 384
participation mystique, 101, 151
partner, 120
  dominant, 155
Pascal, 351–52
passion, 48, 266, 284
  intense spiritual, 140
Passover, 234
  second, 236
Passover pilgrims, 255
pastoral counselors, 115
pastor Dietrich Bonhoeffer, 215
Patai, 181, 437
paternal explanations for religion, 385
path, 59, 72, 288, 317
  lonely, 92
  negative, 16
  spiritual, 250
path of Christ, 317
pathologies, 68, 137
  narcissistic, 135, 142
patience, 107, 266, 293, 340
patient, 77, 112, 130, 205
  primary care, 434

psychiatric, 438
religious, 436
patriarchal, 326–27
patriarchal attitude, 142
patriarchal concept, 326
patriarchal emphasis, 113
patriarchal era, 222
patriarchs, 175, 177, 204, 223, 341, 429
patriarchy, 156, 315, 326, 423, 434
Paul, 232, 235, 241, 245, 247, 255–67, 323, 333, 338–40, 439, 442
Pauline corpus, 262, 337
Pauline letters, 268
Pauline theology, 441
Paul's attitude, 259
Paul's authorship, 340
Paul's capacity for splitting, 264
Paul's conversion, 265
Paul's conversion experience, 264
Paul's experience, 255, 338–39
Paul's followers, 262
Paul's influence, 255
Paul's Jewish tradition, 259
Paul's letters, 260, 262, 297, 339
Paul's messianic eschatology, 260
Paul's mission, 258
Paul's movement, 266
Paul's rage, 265, 339
Paul's rigidity, 263
Paul's state of mind, 262
Paul's teaching, 242, 255
Paul's Theology, 256
Paul's visionary experience, 255
peace, 28, 30, 37, 112, 179, 185, 203, 248, 257, 264, 266
  achieved, 322
  symbolized, 332
  universal, 204
Peacocke, 317, 437
Pelagianism, 281

Pelagius, 281
Penchansky, 54, 103, 142, 217, 224, 437
Pentateuch, 221–22
Pentecost, 29, 230
Pentecostal emphasis, 29
people's apostasy, 224
people's attitude, 53
people's attitude to religion, 53
people's faithlessness, 206
people's image of God, 192
perception, 24, 27, 61, 68, 93, 132, 140, 315, 319, 404, 408
  individual's, 430
  mystical, 27
  person's, 394
perceptual strategies, 373
perceptual systems, 35
perennial philosophy, 59, 431
  transcultural, 62
perfectibility, 305, 342, 363
  human, 299
perfection, 13–14, 22, 35, 100, 105, 281, 287, 291, 353, 363, 414
  final, 342
  infinite, 354
  intended, 282
  mathematical, 349
  utopian, 348
period
  annual, 155
  darkest, 282
  historical, 130
  liminal, 108, 118
  medieval, 288–90
  middle, 142
  modern, 300
  mythic, 62
  transitional, 16
persecution, 41, 175, 200, 239, 254, 264, 266, 292, 335
  earlier, 256
  murderous, 410
persecutory objects, internal, 279

Perseus, 336
Persia, 203
Persian empire, 196
Persian King Artaxerxes, 203
Persian King Cyrus, 201–2, 222
Persinger, 377, 437
person, 29, 31, 82–83, 114–15, 117–18, 164–65, 230, 269–71, 275, 277, 294–96, 338, 343, 373, 389
  co-equal, 269–70
  concrete, 415
  disfigured, 186
  distinct, 284
  first, 341
  idealized, 57
  large-scale, 6
  real, 368
  religious-minded, 77
personal attitude, 364
personal choice, 141, 361
personal communication, 120, 341
personal doubt, 410
personal elements, 27
personal experience, 2, 31, 52, 71, 76–77, 79, 125, 276, 299, 313, 417
  emphasized, 356
personal form, 138, 290
personal God-image, 114, 262, 347, 386
  traditional, 355
  transformed, 118
personality, 31, 34, 67, 72, 84–89, 94, 124, 128–29, 183–84, 218, 221, 339, 343
  authoritarian, 400
  conscious, 111
  developing, 86, 94
  empirical, 3, 35, 94, 128, 141
  fragile, 81
  historical, 395, 415
  human, 89
  idealization-hungry, 58
  individual's, 394

INDEX | 499

integrated, 129
mana, 58
narcissistic, 410
objective, 110
paternalistic, 186
separate, 141
superior, 15, 182
supraordinate, 110
supreme, 5–6, 14
personality development, 391
personality fragmenting, 129
personality integration, 133
personality pathology, 438
personality structure, 430
personality traits, 355
personal language of faith, 363
personal life, 78, 256
  human, 307
personal metaphysical convictions, 371
personal opinion, 293
personal priorities, 76
personal profession, 342
personal profession of faith, 342
personal relationship, 5–6, 15, 34, 173, 256, 278, 299, 402
personal self, 3, 25, 83, 85, 129, 132, 140, 143
personhood, 129, 307
personification, 6, 82, 104, 126, 146, 158, 169, 181–82
personify, 11, 78, 358, 374
person of Christ, 277
person's life, 68, 117, 360
perspectives, 55, 170, 238, 320, 352, 375, 426
  common Jungian, 84
  ego's, 116
  evolutionary, 374
  feminist, 214, 437
  historical, 171, 331
  multiple psychological, 323
  one-ness, 82
  personal, 315

social science, 331
Pétain, 62
Peter, 230, 276, 278, 335, 337
Peter's denials, 336
pharaoh, 25, 158, 185, 222, 420
Pharaoh Akhenaten, 160, 165
pharaoh Ikhnaton, 381
pharaoh's body, 158
pharaoh's death, 158
Pharisees, 254
phenomena, 20, 23, 31–32, 45, 50, 56–57, 146–47, 151, 375–76, 408, 411
  anomalous, 45
  cultural, 375
  emergent, 129–30, 317
  macroscopic quantum, 366
  merely a psychic, 123
  mysterious, 162
  observable, 20
  personifying, 177
  produced, 162
  psychogenic, 408
  religious, 376, 408
  subjective visual, 148
  transitional, 385
phenomenal reality, 132
phenomenological approaches to religious experience, 313
phenomenologist, 66
phenomenology, 25, 324
phenomenology of religion, 324
Philemon, 339
Philippians, 339
Philo, 207–8
philologist, 146
philosopher, official, 286
philosophers, 11, 15–16, 33, 35, 46, 163, 285, 342, 348, 350, 364–65
  contemporary, 12
  enlightenment, 356
  idealist, 408
  important, 356

logical positivist, 364
  religious, 7
philosophical alternatives to religion, 41
philosophical attacks, 303
philosophical categories, 25
philosophical conundrums, 13
philosophical idealist, 140
philosophical invention, 142
philosophical investigation, 208
Philosophical Library, 442
philosophical naturalism, 46
philosophical objections, 38
Philosophical Problem, 11, 207
  important, 12
  intractable, 17
philosophical reasoning, 297, 363
philosophical reflection, 428
philosophical speculation, 288, 301, 313, 316
philosophical theologians, 312
philosophical thinkers, 312
philosophy, 43, 46–47, 132, 134, 292–93, 305, 354, 363–65, 421, 423, 425, 432–33, 440, 442
  anti-religious, 42
  classical, 292
  comprehensive spiritual, 59
  dominant Roman Catholic, 288
  feminist, 421
  materialist, 43
  natural, 436
  non-dual, 141
  official, 142
  rational, 360
philosophy of Aristotle, 283
philosophy of Kant, 132

philosophy of language, 363
philosophy of nature, 358
philosophy of women's liberation, 425
Phipps, 424
Phoebe, 260, 326
Phrygian Attis, 151, 158
physical constants, 8, 21
  natural, 10
physicalism, 366
physicalist, 12, 408
physicalist position, 46
physicalist solution, 43
physicality, 36
physical laws, 10
physical sciences, 32, 45
physical structure, 42
physical universe, 10
physical world, 13, 75, 191, 275
physicists, 46, 361
physics, 46, 127, 207, 345, 366
  classical, 366
  contemporary, 9, 440
  new, 33
  quantum, 62, 128, 366
piety, 102, 188, 292–93, 302, 412
  overt, 250
  personal, 30
  popular, 274, 325
Pilate, 254
pilgrimage, 230, 370
Pinnock, 218, 437
Pinochet, 62
Pivotal age, 162
plagues, 183–84, 224, 236, 419
  bubonic, 290
plant life, 152
Plaskow, 224, 326, 424, 437
Plato, 11, 163, 207, 292, 406
Platonic, 289, 291
Platonic God, 164
Platonized Christian thinking, 350
Plato's Demiurge, 164

Plato's Forms, 36
Plato's Idea, 229
Plato's image, 163
Plato's work, 163
Pleistocene era, 372
Pleroma, 127, 143, 275
Plotinus, 35–36, 291
ploughshares, 248
poem, 236
  mournful, 303
poisoning wells, 399
polemics, 343, 427
  anti-Jewish, 254, 399
political activists, contemporary, 260
political alliances, 177
political decisions, 419
political device, 337
Political Dimensions, 416
political divisions, 41
political independence, 301
political instability, 247
political manifesto, 222
political power, 154, 199
  domestic, 194
political reflections, 425
political rivalry, 88
politicians, 351
politico-social delusional systems, 137
politics, 50, 153, 159, 318, 343, 419, 425, 427, 439
  justified republican, 34
  right wing, 278
politics of women's spirituality, 425
Pollock, 365, 385, 437
Polynesian religion, 58
polytheism, 48, 157, 165, 169–70, 175–76, 180, 198–200, 223, 347
  ancient, 381
  earlier, 177
  early, 147
  early Hebrew, 170, 181
polytheistic, 161, 198, 200, 206, 431
Pontius Pilate, 406
Pope, 83, 124, 215, 290, 294, 296, 298, 398

Pope Leo IX, 341
Pope Pius, 62
Popular atheism, 46
possession, 91, 102, 124, 252, 405
  own, 175
  unconscious, 137
Post-biblical Jewish Tradition, 191, 207
Post-biblical Judaism, 169–225
post-exilic, 222
Post-Holocaust Christianity, 442
Post-modern Approach, 129
postmodernism, 363–64
postmodern readings focus, 330
postmodern understanding, 314
postmortem appearance, 246
post-mortem effects, 324
postpartum women, 40
postulate, 15, 20, 43–44, 50, 130–31, 304, 347
postulated agency detection device, 374
potentials, 85–86, 94, 310
  spiritual, 86
poverty, 252, 304, 314, 338, 413
power, 27–28, 57–58, 135, 151–52, 156–60, 164–65, 178–79, 195–96, 207–8, 239, 247–50, 283–84, 290, 310, 314, 322, 327, 343, 402–3, 415
  absolute, 290, 327
  active, 348
  alien, 204
  animating, 150
  archetypal, 137
  atoning, 278
  cosmic, 337
  demonic, 207, 279
  dominant, 155, 203
  emotional, 27, 56, 116
  external, 31

female, 367
foreign, 203
great, 175
impersonal, 33
infinite, 357
magical, 57
military, 205
mythic, 409
nature's, 146
real, 239
redemptive, 415
sacred, 146, 153
special, 157
spiritual, 83, 351
superior, 25
power-drenched concept of God, 310
powerful King, 110
power shadow, 185, 409
power tactics, 431
practices
  ancient burial, 150
  ascetical, 266, 396
  child rearing, 396
  common, 177
  contemplative, 419
  correct, 334
  family child-rearing, 387
  forbidden, 40
  legitimate magical, 348
  observing cultic, 196
  pagan, 178
  psychotherapeutic, 27, 112
  shamanic, 167
praise, 18
  child's, 139
  demands constant, 100
  extraordinary, 266
  propitiating, 139
prayer, 29, 35, 174–75, 183, 204, 213, 369–70, 393–94, 397–99, 402, 404
  authentic, 193
  childhood bedtime, 31
  direct, 248
  important, 221
  petitionary, 33, 373
preach, 200, 203–4, 243, 255–56, 258, 263–64, 406–7

preaching, 53, 133, 200, 204, 262, 306, 318
  harsh, 196
  inspired, 29
preconceptions and projections, 172
precursor, 153, 163, 176, 297, 352
  necessary, 136
precursor of monotheism, 176
predators, 374
  avoiding, 372
predecessors, 12
predestination, 281, 297
predisposition, 302
  evolutionary, 419
  innate, 374
Prehistorians, 146
prejudices, 37, 42, 95, 231, 331, 411, 416
premillennialists, 311
preoccupation, 125, 401
  important, 360
  life-long, 142
pre-Oedipal elements, 382
pre-ordained events, 161
pre-rational awareness, 302
president, third, 301
pressure, 176, 192
  internal, 195
prestige, 293, 300
price, 175, 278, 336
  grotesque, 211
pride, 194, 238, 258, 266, 350
priest Caiaphas, high, 254
priestesses, 155, 184, 405
  high, 155
priesthood, 33, 57, 224, 276
priests, 155, 161, 179, 186, 194–95, 221, 223, 236, 240, 248, 292, 296
  female, 326
  high-ranking, 202
  persecuted pagan, 410
  post-exilic, 221
  primal, 336

original, 380
primal horde, 382
primal murder, 381
primary narcissism, 342
  lost, 385
Prime Mover, 11, 229
  space-less, 164
primeval Sumerian goddess Nammu, 154
Primitive Culture, 146
primitive image of God, 388
primordial form of religion, 146
primordial sea-Goddess, 224
Princess Diana, 83
Princeton, 425, 430–33, 435–36, 439, 441
principle, 10, 18, 42–43, 113, 147, 161, 291, 342–43, 352, 364
  ancient metaphysical, 271
  animating, 146
  anthropic, 8–9, 21
  basic, 272
  cosmic, 161
  enlightenment, 301
  ethical, 358
  life-giving, 160
  manifesting, 271
  maternal, 154
  mathematical, 345–46
  physical, 347, 359
  traditional Christian, 308
  ultimate, 104
  unifying, 166
  universal, 20, 313
  un-manifest, 59
principle of evil, 142, 161
a priori existent, 85
a priori God-image, 388
a priori predisposition, 26
priority, 124, 253
prisca theologia, 351
Priscilla, 260, 326, 340
private form of religion, 117
privatio boni, 103, 121–22, 142, 280

Probing, 438
problem, 13–14, 16–17, 49–50, 77–78, 105, 189–90, 207, 215, 277–78, 284, 328–30, 338–39, 342–43, 352–53, 394–95, 408–9
  ancient, 128
  central, 189
  logical, 278
  long-standing, 13
  metaphysical, 19
  mind-body, 43
  narcissistic, 100
  new, 188
  particular, 340
  perennial, 175
  persistent, 272
  social, 304
  special, 211
  unsolved, 140
process, 44–45, 61–62, 85–89, 94, 104, 108, 117–19, 127–29, 137–38, 141–42, 159, 270–71, 312–13, 341, 403–5, 413
  all-inclusive, 310
  bodily, 356
  continuous, 141
  cosmic, 310
  creative, 404
  developmental, 380
  dialectical, 85
  evolutionary, 376
  grief, 120
  historical, 127
  integrative, 129
  orderly, 67
  psychological, 73, 126, 140, 419
  quantum, 128
  redemptive, 216
  self-healing, 112
  seven-stage, 340
  sociological, 362
  spiritual, 86
  therapeutic, 68
  trinitarian, 340
processes of nature, 350, 363

process of divine rejuvenation, 119
process of evolution, 10, 44, 304, 316–17, 359
process of literalizing biblical stories, 137
process of mutual redemption, 89
process philosophy, 309
process theologians, 13, 54, 218, 309–10, 312
process theology, 363, 420
process theology perspective, 214
proclamations, 122, 244
procreation, 160
  physical, 340
Prodigal Son, 251
Professional diviners, 161
progress, 49, 138, 281, 303, 305, 342, 363, 424, 438
  gradual, 363
  historical, 48, 363
  human, 48
progress of history, 363
prohibition, 39–40, 142, 182, 244, 332, 380, 406
  strict, 261
  traditional, 341
project, 47, 56, 82, 93, 126, 140, 151, 234, 391, 410, 414
projected outward, 95
projection, 56–58, 82–83, 99–100, 126, 170, 172, 191–92, 222, 224, 277–78, 382, 384, 400–402, 411–12, 415
  external, 126
  human, 137, 191, 219
  idealized, 137
  messianic, 247
  mythic, 415
  paranoid, 338
  personal, 323
  theoretical, 322
projection and personification, 6
projection of elements of human psychology, 191
projection of human narcissistic vulnerabilities, 100
projection of human personality traits, 186, 192
projection of human psychology, 107, 394, 417
projection of human violence, 277
projection of Isaiah's superego, 224
projection of negative traits, 411
projection of non-egoic levels, 57
projection of Oedipal material, 382
projection of parental imagoes, 402
projection of pre-Oedipal elements, 382
projection of psychological material, 126
projections and fantasy, 192
projections of levels, 56
projection theory, 384
projective device, 401
promiscuous, 200
Promised Land, 221
  new, 419
prone, 37, 192, 266, 374, 417
proofs, 19–20, 22, 24, 207, 245, 305, 337, 349, 358, 368
  indubitable, 27
  intellectual, 287
  ontological, 285
proofs of God, 305
prophecies, 29, 142, 157, 193, 196, 206, 230–31, 235, 237, 248–49, 405–6
  ancient, 244
  messianic, 193, 247
prophecies in dreams, 142
prophecy obscure, 301
prophesies, 236, 260
prophet Daniel, 405
prophet Ezekiel, 179, 194, 201

prophet Hosea, 197
prophetic, 236, 412
prophetic books, 224, 311
prophetic messages, 195
prophetic minority, 434
prophetic warnings, 198
prophetic word, 253
prophet Isaiah, 248–49, 267
prophet Jeremiah, 180–81, 199
prophet Joel, 230
prophets, 174, 178, 182, 184, 187, 192–96, 199–200, 203, 205–7, 218–19, 244–45, 279, 339–40, 405
  false, 7, 142, 263
prophet Haggai, 206
prophet Zarathustra, 165
propitiation, 156
proponents, 61, 292, 296, 330, 339
  important, 347
propositions, 43, 136, 357
  basic, 292
  religious, 41
proselytizing, 255
proselytizing activities, 400
prosperity, 174, 189, 196
prosperity gospel, 252, 338
prostitutes, 181, 197
prostitution, 187
protection, 30, 257, 373, 391
protector, 102
  benevolent celestial, 369
protein molecule, 10
protest, 31, 49, 107, 422
Protestant and Roman Catholic Church leadership, 215
Protestant churches, 268
Protestant clergy, 346
Protestant denominations, 334
Protestant heresies, 298
Protestantism, 297, 299
Protestant Reformation, 293–94, 346, 413

Protestant reformers, 243
Protestants, 169, 273–74, 294, 298–99, 330, 341
  contemporary, 315
  liberal, 304
  rationalist, 350
Protestant traditions, 141, 284, 413
Protestant work ethic, 297
prototype, 176, 392
prove, 5, 9–12, 22, 70, 73, 143, 147, 300, 347–48, 356–58, 367
provenance, unknown, 236
Proverbs, 181, 235, 339
providential, 214, 346
provider, 369
  good maternal, 369
province, 70–71, 371
  exclusive, 349
  particular, 259
province of religion, 371
provocative challenges to religion, 49
pruning hooks, 248
Psalmist, 188
Psalms, 107, 135, 178–79, 183–86, 191, 210, 225, 235, 263, 389–90, 402
pseudepigraphal, 259
Pseudo-Dionysius, 282
psilocybin mushrooms, 320
psyche, 26–27, 56–58, 60–61, 65–74, 77–78, 80, 82–83, 85, 90–97, 101, 103–4, 109–10, 112–16, 121, 123–26, 128–32, 135–38, 140–41, 417–18, 424–26
  archetypal, 417
  autonomous, 82, 416
  individual, 79–80, 94, 104, 128, 130–31, 381
  individual's, 411
  objective, 27, 32, 61, 90, 96, 123, 137–38, 188, 194, 272
  religious function of the, 26

  transpersonal, 79, 131
  unconscious, 71
Psyche in scripture, 433
Psychiatric Study, 321
psychiatry, 134, 434
psychic, 69, 426
psychic catastrophe, 68
psychic content, 123–24
  autonomous, 123–24
psychic facts, 67
psychic readiness, 415
psychic reality, 422
psychic structures, 73
psychoanalysis, 378, 422, 428–29, 434–35, 442
psychoanalysts, 182, 279, 324, 369, 385
  contemporary, 384
  early, 382
  personalistic, 117
  skeptical, 265
psychoanalytic circles, 131
psycho-analytic interpretation, 421
psychoanalytic reduction, 378
Psychoanalytic self-psychologists, 143, 384
psychoanalytic study, 438
Psychoanalytic Theories, 378
psychoanalytic theory, 384
  relational, 395
psychobiography, 262, 322, 394, 424
psychodynamic explanations for anti-Semitism, 400
psychodynamic factors, 264, 385
psychodynamics, 323, 371
  human, 137
  individual, 390
  personal, 99
psychohistory, 262, 419
psychological approaches, 69, 71, 74, 140, 205, 321–22, 324, 331, 369–419
psychological approach to spirituality, 69, 416
psychological assessment, 394

psychological biography, 423
psychological contents, 128
  projected, 95
psychological conviction, 23
psychological difficulties, 42, 383, 401
psychological disaster, 245
psychological dispensation, 90
psychological effect, 69
psychological equivalent, 127
psychological event, 71
psychological experiences, 69
  observable, 66
psychological explanation, 50, 206, 227, 382
  plausible, 264
psychological exploration, 74
psychological factors, 377
  unconscious, 331
psychological literature, 141
psychological make-up, 417
psychological manifestations, 83
psychological maturation, 86
psychological parallels, 385
psychological phenomena, 110, 393
  observable, 123
psychological powers, represented, 56
psychological propensity, 394
psychological propensity to experience, 394
psychological purposes, 69, 116
psychological realities, 95, 382
psychological reductionism, 324
psychological reflections, 432
psychological relationship, consistent, 69
psychological rule, 115
psychological structures, 389–90, 440
  embedded, 370
psychological studies, 322
psychological theory, 5, 76, 108, 322, 395, 419
  contemporary, 262
psychological understanding, 401
psychologism, 61, 123
psychologist faces, 262
psychologist Gustav Fechner, 361
psychologists, 3, 11, 76, 83, 124, 128, 179, 194, 322–23, 371, 373
  cognitive, 419
  depth, 61
  evolutionary, 372–73, 375
  skeptical, 29, 412
psychologist's comments, 323
psychology, 66, 69–70, 72–73, 123, 125, 391, 395, 422–23, 427, 429–31, 433–34, 438, 442–43
  evolutionary, 42, 45, 433
  individual's, 75, 115
  infantile reward-punishment, 79
  mainstream, 418
  nothing but, 322
  personal, 27, 76, 133, 259, 262, 394
  pure, 134
  subject's, 66
psychology and religion, 443
psychology-as-religion, 91
psychopathology, 388, 417
psychosis, 29, 68, 87
  transient, 27
Psychosocial and Political Dimensions of Religion, 416
psychosomatic symptom, 107
psychotherapeutic work, 115
Psychotherapeutic work on parental images, 121
psychotherapists, 108, 130, 136
psychotherapist's guide, 425
psychotherapy, 68, 77–78, 90–91, 106, 108, 118, 130, 141, 382, 389, 425
psychotherapy repairs, 85
psychotic, 81, 202
Ptah, 158
Ptolemy, 345
punish, 183, 189, 199, 217, 379, 390
punish dissenters, 346
punishment, 30–31, 174, 177, 180, 182, 184, 187, 195, 198, 200, 204–5, 207, 373, 389–90, 392–93
  deferred, 188
  delayed, 198
  eternal, 370
  harsh, 187, 217
  violent, 412
punitive image of God, 258
Pure Being, 289
pure Consciousness, 6, 35, 63, 101, 131, 428
pure reason, 23, 433
Purgatory, 342
Puritans, 298
purity, 40, 221, 250, 274, 433
putative transcendental object, 73
Pyysiäinen, 37, 437

Q
Quaker movement, 299
qualifications, 337
qualified aspect, 13
qualities, 3, 15–17, 22, 25, 27–28, 43, 45, 47–48, 55–57, 61, 153–54, 206, 209, 391

INDEX | 505

altruistic, 250
compassionate, 158
destructive, 103
discreet, 88
extra-special, 373
good, 16
human, 15
idealized, 391
important, 318
medieval, 308
mythic, 232, 339
negative, 98, 102
new, 159
noetic, 25
numinous, 67–68, 71
objective, 58
obsessional, 398
parental, 370
particular, 16, 342
positive, 208
quasi-spiritual, 83
religious, 30, 339
special, 56, 373
spiritual, 29
tribal, 252
universal, 192, 284
violent, 18
quality of attachment, 391
quantum, 128
quantum mechanics, 366
quantum vacuum, 62
quaternity, 140, 142, 271–72
queen, 110, 154, 181, 199, 223, 273, 367
Quelle, 336
Qumran, 180
Qumran sect, 320

R
Rabbi Hillel, 244
rabbis, 174, 213
Rabbi Shimon Bar Yohai, 209
Racial character, 441
racism, 41, 108, 314, 411
radiant, 236
radiant divine child, 110
Radical theology and contemporary Judaism, 438
rage, 48, 102, 121, 184–85, 228, 263, 411, 419

destructive, 55
murderous, 184
narcissistic, 184, 187
promised divine, 194
Rahner, 308–9, 438
 Karl, 59, 308
ram, 341
 aggressive, 105
Ramachandran, 339, 438
Ramakrishna's felicitous metaphor, 108
Ramses, 222
Rancour-Laferriere, 324, 438
random accidents, 373
random by-products, 408
random conglomeration, 44
random genetic mutation, 10
Random House, 421
random mechanical process, 374
randomness, 8, 10, 366
randomness and evolution, 10
random universe, 7
ransom, 277, 281
Raphael, 61, 214, 438
Rapture, 311, 343
Ras Shamra, 223
rational form of religion, 349
rational ground for religion, 33
rationalism, 34
 excessive, 413
rationalistic concepts, ignoring, 293
rationalists, 33, 245, 302
rationality, 326, 437
 human, 42, 347
rationalizations, 55, 103, 105, 218, 247, 249, 266, 331
 painful, 213
 theological, 212
 for your own good, 390
rationalize, 18, 26, 62, 165, 175, 180, 205, 357
rational methods, 32

rational spirit, 359
raw matter, 163
reader's understanding of scripture, 409
Realism, 284
Realist position, 284
realists, 342
realities
 final, 256
 harsh, 39
reality, 5–6, 9–10, 24–25, 45, 80–81, 122–23, 127–28, 132, 140, 335–36, 340–41, 354, 359, 366, 378–79, 403–4
reality conflict, 5
Reality in psychoanalysis and religion, 434
realization, 28, 85, 87, 318, 326
real Jesus, 432
real message, 53
realm of existence, 67
realm of religion, 324
realms, 99, 328
 human, 89
 mythic, 88
real power of darkness and evil, 239
reappearances, 152, 159, 324
reappraise Jung, 134
reason, 15–16, 19–20, 23, 32–37, 50–51, 53–54, 61–62, 74–75, 102–3, 151–52, 207–9, 245–46, 285–88, 291–92, 300–301, 342–43, 348–51, 354, 356–58, 424–25
 possible, 156
 suggested, 190
 traditional, 190
 unknown, 213
reason for belief in God, 50
reason to believe God, 287
reassurance, 397
rebel, 217, 265, 392
rebellion, 105, 187, 265, 398, 401
 instigate, 255

political, 255
recurrent, 299
wicked, 295
rebelliousness, 379
rebellious son, 217
rebirth, 150, 155, 292, 421, 436
receptivity, complete, 273
reciprocity, 152, 328
  mutual, 140
  redemptive, 122
recognition, 28, 142, 180, 278
recognized biblical form of revelation, 31
reconciliation, 51, 104, 106, 109, 195, 197, 245, 298, 314, 412
  complete, 295
reconstruction, 89, 203, 221, 318
  hypothetical, 382
recorded story of creation, 154
recourse, 2, 9, 22, 67, 92, 163
recourse to doctrine and dogma, 92
Rector, 384, 438
Redactor, 221
Red Book, 92, 143, 425
redeem, 138, 140, 228, 305, 310, 337
redeemer, 185, 227, 324
  personal, 227
redeem sinners, 295
redemption, 211, 214, 216, 223, 228, 237, 273, 275, 277–79, 295, 298
  mutual, 89, 122
redemptive act, 278
redemptive effect, 105, 323
redemptive value, observable, 55
Redfearn, 112
reductionism, 358, 366
reductionist, 371, 378
reductive explanations of dreams, 408
reductive psychoanalytic, 116

reductive psychodynamic accounts of belief in God, 50
Reductive Psychological Approaches to Belief in God, 369
Reformation, 48, 221, 296, 298–99, 333, 399
reformers, 296–98, 301, 440
Reform Jewish tradition, 223
reform movements, 137, 292
  international, 297
reforms, 92, 198, 222, 292, 294, 299
  authentic, 294
  producing, 294
regions, 154, 160, 176, 201, 203, 421
  necessary brain, 376
regress, 341
  infinite, 20, 357
regression, 101, 385
regressive return, 385
reign, 160, 195, 200, 204, 250, 301
reign of Christ, 301
re-imaginings, 135–36, 403
reincarnation, 120, 152, 376
reinforcement conditions behavior, 393
reinterpret, 134, 304, 308, 319
reiterate, 112, 331, 401
rejected indulgences, 398
rejected Jesus, 253–54, 258
rejected metaphysical notions, 365
rejecting Jesus, 399
rejection, 187, 194, 253, 312
  maternal, 85
rejuvenation, 119
relational dynamics, 133
  early, 390
relationship, 103, 114–15, 117, 120–21, 123, 128,
132–33, 174–75, 185–86, 222–23, 236, 317–18, 328–29, 360–61, 367–68, 385, 391–92, 394–95
  alter-ego, 410
  asymmetrical, 213
  child's, 85, 379
  curvilinear, 429
  direct, 103
  disturbed, 133
  divine-human, 276
  early, 133, 383, 386, 388, 391
  eternal, 340
  exact, 73, 230
  individual's, 361
  internal, 269
  interpersonal, 116
  intrapsychic, 89
  long, 412
  making, 250
  mother-child, 85
  original, 379
  psychotherapeutic, 78
  reciprocal, 89–90, 310
  reconciled, 257
  right, 295, 297
  saving, 309
  special, 410
  therapeutic, 108
  unique, 340
relationship of psychology and religion, 443
relationship to Christ, 360
relationship to time and history, 329
relative absence of God in twentieth century culture, 365
relativity of God, 89
relaxation, 241
  extreme, 241
relentless travelling, 262
reliance, 220, 301, 348
  total, 327
religion, 25–26, 38, 40–42, 44–47, 49–50, 61–62, 123–26, 138, 140–41, 145–48, 292, 299–303, 347–52, 354–58,

362–64, 369–86, 392–93, 416, 421–37, 439–43
  ancient Greek, 372
  ancient Israelite, 179
  attribute, 419
  based, 302
  change, 338
  collective, 91–92
  common, 372
  contemporary, 150
  defined, 156
  defining, 362
  derided, 357
  developed, 374
  dogmatic, 386
  early, 145–47, 165
  false, 403
  institutionalized, 361
  mainstream theistic, 2
  making, 137
  matriarchal, 189, 382
  national, 241
  nationalistic, 174
  natural, 33, 62
  new, 90, 240, 253, 335
  official, 37
  organized, 41, 301, 416
  original pure, 351
  particular, 410
  patriarchal, 367
  personal, 30
  pre-Christian, 234
  primitive, 157
  rational, 34
  reducing, 383
  right, 348
  routinized, 315
  single, 268
  third century Persian, 341
  traditional, 78–79, 91–92, 109, 124, 138, 161, 290, 300, 349
  true, 352
religion and science, 367
Religion for Freud, 379
religionists, 135, 137, 308
  conservative, 172, 219, 403
  conservative Christian, 52
  traditional, 28, 103, 134, 220, 361
religion of ancient Egypt, 30
religion of Aten, 381–82
religion of consolation, 46
religion of nature, 355
religion of Yhwh, 174
religion of Zoroastrianism, 407
religion poisons, 431
religion results, 376
religions and mythologies, 156
religions by rationalists, 33, 302
religiosity, 53
religious absolutes, 137
religious activity, 362
religious alternative, 426
religious attitude, 91
  dominant, 33
  new, 56, 126
religious authorities, 31, 47, 52, 293, 299, 302, 323, 327, 356, 359, 363
  traditional, 33
religious awe, 378
religious behavior, 392, 428
  human, 392
  observable, 393
  persistent, 393
religious beliefs, 50, 53–54, 147, 150, 371–72, 375, 377–79, 383, 389, 393, 395, 410–11, 428
  irrational, 371
  traditional, 30
religious believers, 22, 37, 44, 162, 356, 363
  traditional, 71
religious centers, 153
religious ceremonies, 196
religious certainties, traditional, 304
religious commitments influence, 55
Religious conflicts, 299–300
religious consciousness, 90
  human, 62
religious convictions, 234
religious disguise, 419
religious ecstasy, 377
religious education, 386, 389
  early, 4
religious emphasis, 370
religious existentialism, 307
religious experience, 30–31, 42, 67, 70, 77, 80, 92, 95, 377, 382–83, 385, 432, 435–36, 439–41
  direct, 297
  generating, 378
  human, 302
  intense, 31
  original, 76
  personal, 52
  spontaneous, 138
religious experience and practices, 377
religious experience of mankind, 439
religious expression, 332
religious feeling, 54, 302
religious forms, 140, 313
religious foundation, 157
  strong, 153
religious framework, 394
religious function, 94, 97, 125, 424
  authentic, 67
  innate, 114
  intrinsic, 97
religious iconography, 389
religious ideas emerge in sleep and dreams, 435
Religious illusions, 379
religious imagination, 402, 430
religious institutions, 215, 393
religious intolerance, 300
  extreme, 346
religious laxity, 197
Religious leadership, 431
religious life, 371, 426
religious literature, 290
religious martyrdom, 343

religious message, 194, 206
religious narcissists, 105
Religious objects, 440
religious opinion, 416
religious pluralism, 34
religious practices, 67, 173, 223, 378, 380, 399
  denounced orthodox, 195
  formal, 197
religious preferences, 58
religious questions, 292, 360
religious reality, 68
religious representations, 435
religious ritual and beliefs, 147
Religious Role Taking, 393
religious scrupulousness, 397
religious stories, traditional, 137
religious symbols, 74, 94, 431
  traditional, 138
Religious syncretism, 161
religious system, traditional, 52
religious systems, 149, 361
  surrounding, 415
Religious texts, 125, 331
  inspired, 170
religious thought, 422
religious toleration, 292
religious traditions, 29–30, 40, 56, 59, 62, 65–67, 69, 111, 114, 176–78, 386, 407, 410–11
  conservative, 390
  particular, 39, 130
  single, 109
Religious traditions and texts, 393
Religious tribalism, 418
religious value, 74
  individual, 360
remorse, 380–81
  transcendental, 293
REM sleep mechanisms, 408

Remus, 127
re-mythologize, 328
Renaissance, 33, 290, 292–94, 332, 348, 368
Renaissance humanists, 292
Renaissance naturalism, 348
Renan, Ernest, 47, 304
renew, 145, 149, 197, 202
renewal, 78, 120, 185, 202, 338, 413
renewed commitment to monotheism, 180
renounced worldly power, 246
renunciation, 180, 182
repentance, 188, 192, 202, 243, 339
repents, 183, 195, 213
repercussions, important, 356
repetitions, 170, 408
  multiple, 408
replaced Adam, 243
representation, 29, 134, 155, 224, 386, 388, 442
  abstract, 149
  individual's, 384
  symbolic, 88, 113, 360
represented Jesus, 321
repression, 53, 102, 105, 339, 382, 404
  harsh, 414
repression and projection of doubt, 53
reprisals, 62, 255
repudiation, 6, 140
rescue, 22, 74, 324
resented Jesus' success, 255
residue, 218, 326, 369, 387
resistance, 92, 134, 137–38, 153, 156, 165–66
  great, 107
  inevitable, 136
resistance to monotheism, 166
resolution, 379
  potential, 341

symbolic, 88
resources, 352
  costly, 372
responsibility, 39, 45, 48, 178, 199, 205, 215, 260, 298, 428
  human, 39
  new, 139
  personal, 52, 277
  shared, 328
responsibility for evil, 205
restitution, 281
restoration, 198, 412, 434
restore connection, 57
restrictions, 291, 327, 334
  degrading, 224
  dietary, 241
  ordered, 174
  traditional Sabbath, 244
result of evolution, 288
result of experiences, 284
result of visions, 246
resurrected Jesus, 340
resurrecting, 126, 415, 419
resurrecting grain gods, 151
resurrection, 156, 159, 235, 245–47, 257, 260–61, 275, 311, 314, 317, 335, 337–38, 340, 413, 415
resurrection story, 409, 415
retribution, 146, 194, 212, 224
reunion, 204, 378
  human, 289
revelation, 6–7, 13–15, 31–33, 49–50, 52, 62, 69–71, 76, 80, 96, 124, 228, 245, 305–8, 311–13, 348, 350–51, 358–59, 403–5, 417
  ancient, 351
  authoritative, 218
  continuous, 71, 80
  direct, 61, 97
  emphasized, 312
  hidden, 295
  individual, 71

new, 71, 75
original, 405
personal, 75, 114, 119, 405
private, 70
scriptural, 71
special, 91
revelation and belief in God, 356
revelation and grace, 121
revelation and scripture, 417
revelation in Christ, 136
revenge, 48, 200, 335, 338
reverence, 17, 210
  human, 56
revisionists, 222
re-vitalization, 134
revival, 348
  occult, 167
  spiritual, 294
revoking Judaic law, 265
revolt, 205, 224–25, 320
revolutionary, 313
revolutionary break, 177
revolutions, 301, 312
  agricultural, 151
  cultural, 252
  earth's, 84
  internal, 171
  political, 301
  religious, 301
reward, 102, 164, 174, 205, 289, 354, 358, 361, 390, 392–93
  posthumous, 40
Rieff, 117, 140, 438
righteous, 205, 212, 228, 259, 340, 398–99
righteous Branch, 248
righteous judgment, 263
righteousness, 15, 194, 196, 210, 218, 295, 398–99
righteousness of Christ, 398
righteousness of God, 212, 398–99
ritual impurity, 186
ritual initiation, 275
ritualization of experience, 428

ritual mourning, 155
ritual pollution, 375
ritual practices, 30, 53, 146, 149, 262
ritual purposes, 148
ritual re-enactment, 381
rituals, 29, 57, 62, 141, 148, 152–53, 155, 160, 369–70, 384, 387, 393–94, 413
  cultic, 192
  observing, 58
  observing sacrificial, 102
  primitive scapegoat, 40
  private, 378
  religious, 124, 147, 374, 378, 382
  sacramental, 420
  temple sacrificial, 224
ritual sacrifices, 174, 184
ritual sex, 178
ritual site, 167
rivals, 178, 222, 380
  early, 240
Rivkah Kluger, 157
Rizzuto, 3, 133, 384, 386–88, 395, 438
Roach, 429
Robertson Smith, 147
Rollins, 125, 322, 427, 438
Romain, Rolland, 385
Roman audience, 335
Roman authority, 256
Roman Catholic and Anglican theologians, 307
Roman Catholic Church, 142, 254, 286, 296, 298, 304, 337, 342, 346
Roman Catholics, 59, 75, 114, 268, 274, 296, 298–99, 308, 334, 341, 392
  traditional, 295
Roman Catholic tradition, 92, 141, 273, 330, 363, 413
Roman Church, 293, 341
Roman Emperor Domitian, 343
Roman emperors, 39, 135, 241, 402, 420

Roman Empire, 37, 231, 247, 253, 282, 343, 412
  stratified, 260
Roman galleon, 114
Roman gods, 39
Roman Jupiter, 161
Roman occupation, 247, 249, 317
Roman occupiers, 255
Roman oppression, 320
Roman Romulus, 222
Roman rule, 247, 249
Roman rulers, 252
Romans, 203, 205, 230, 247–50, 253, 255, 257–58, 260–63, 295, 297, 326, 339–40, 403–4
  ancient, 156
Roman society, 260
Romanticism, 358
Romantic painters, 333
Romantics, 358
Romantic writers, 360
Rome, 155, 224, 231, 254, 268, 283, 292, 294, 335, 354, 412
  imperial, 250
  overthrow, 256
Romulus, 127, 336
root of religion, 147
roots, 120, 141, 147, 263, 295, 383
  developmental, 389
  earliest, 383
  psychological, 428
  unconscious, 31
roots of religious experience, 383
royal dynasty, worldly, 321
Rubenstein, 212–13, 438
Rubin, 400, 438
rudimentary image of God, 386
Rudolf Bultmann, 306, 423
Ruether, 215, 325, 438
rulers, 58, 160, 222, 324, 327, 349
  human, 179, 327
Russel, Bertrand, 321

Russia, 150, 154
  southern, 156
Ruth, 187

S
Sabbath, 18, 174, 184
sacraments, 62, 109, 285, 287, 290, 296, 298, 308, 342
  true, 296
sacred, 56, 58, 425, 427
sacred authority, 387, 431
sacred cauldron, 425
sacred center, 336
sacred core, 384
sacred dimension, 57, 407
sacred enclosure, 57
sacred marriage, 113, 155
sacred marriage rite, 434
sacred mushroom, 421
sacred prostitutes, 181
sacred reality, 52
sacred secrets, 162
sacred stories, 97, 167, 417, 422
sacred texts, 2, 56, 67, 137, 240, 393, 411, 428
  personal, 418
sacred traditions, pre-existing, 240
sacrifice, 57, 152, 179, 184, 195, 197, 221–22, 236, 240–41, 257, 259, 372, 374, 409, 412
  animal, 159, 179, 182, 277, 283, 341
  atoning, 255
  bloody, 277
  human, 18, 138, 256, 341
  personal, 370
  substitute, 278
  terrible, 228
sacrifice of Christ, 236
sacrificial, 223, 278
sacrificial purposes, 148
sacrosanct unintelligibility, 74
sadness, 396
  chronic, 397
  persistent brooding, 395

sadomasochism, 279
Saint Anselm, 285
Saint Jerome, 142
Saint Paul, 406
Saint Paul's influence, 255
saints, 58, 245, 299, 332, 337, 342, 412
Salle, 442
salvation, 58–59, 241–42, 256–57, 274–78, 280–82, 292, 294–95, 297–98, 306, 308, 314–15, 396–98, 401
  eternal, 240
  personal, 256
  universal, 227
salvific, 315, 332
Samuel, 183, 185–87, 217, 224
Sanhedrin, 254–55, 265
Sarah, 412
Sargon, King, 222
Sartre, 41, 49
satan, 98, 100, 104, 142, 188, 224, 238–39, 252, 337, 395, 399
satanic, 217, 360
Saul, 25, 66
Saul's experience, 61
saving death, 227
saving word, 296
savior, 95, 158, 223, 247, 249, 274, 281, 292, 389, 402
  cosmic, 324
  external, 93, 276, 304
  mysterious, 204
  special, 91
savior figure, 110
scalpel, critical, 324
Scandinavian myths of Gods, 156
scapegoating, 278
scapegoats, 102, 205
scenario, 100, 380
Schaap-Jonker, 388–89
Schellenberg, 38, 438
Schelling, 358–59
schizoid, 383, 388
schizophrenia, 29, 377

Schleiermacher, 302, 439
Scholarly interest, 394
scholars, 171, 176, 179, 181, 217, 221–23, 233, 235, 240, 316–17, 319
  contemporary, 235
  medieval, 16
  textual, 335
scholarship, 41, 337
  modern, 339
scholasticism, dry, 290
Scholastic philosophers, 288
Scholastics, 284, 291–92
school, 214, 342, 358, 396
  childhood Sunday, 215
Schucman, Helen, 62
Schuster, 425, 427, 429, 441
Schuster/Touchstone, 428
Schweitzer, Albert, 313, 318, 321–22, 337, 439
Schwiebert, 395, 439
science, 5–63, 134, 136, 288, 290, 300, 302–4, 306, 308, 311, 345–48, 356–58, 363–64, 367, 436–37
  atheistic, 10
  emerging, 348, 350
  modern, 7, 331
  natural, 13
  new seventeenth century, 347
  rejected deterministic, 358
science and philosophy, 47
science and religion, 7, 44, 345, 347, 367, 430
scientific approach, 8, 347
scientific approach to religion, 347
scientific conclusions, 347
scientific descriptions, 366
scientific explanations, 8
  modern, 331
scientific inquiry, 42, 358
scientific method, 19, 32, 42, 45–46, 346–47
scientific orientation, 309

INDEX | 511

Scientific Revolution, 7, 61, 345–67
Scientific Study, 302
Scientific Study of Religion, 422–23, 440
scientific utopianism, 435
Scientific World, 437
scientist, great, 123
scientists, 7, 11–12, 21, 42–43, 61, 300, 345, 364, 376
  contemporary, 7
  greatest, 356
  important, 346
  materialistic, 9
scintillae, 128
Scopes trial, 343
Scotland, 298, 429
Scottish philosopher Duns Scotus, 286
scourging, 112, 266
scribes, 170, 246
scribing, 62
scriptural, 231, 296, 363
scriptural passages, 225, 248, 419
scripture and tradition, 403
scriptures, 2–3, 5–7, 76–77, 207–8, 279, 296, 298–99, 304–5, 324–25, 330, 343, 397, 401–3, 409–10, 417, 429–30
  buried, 407
  earlier, 200
  interpreting, 92
  old, 237
scriptures to guide, 296
scrupulous, 264, 389, 398
scrutiny, 160
  increasing, 300
  scholarly, 331
  withstood, 362
search, 133, 146, 160, 163, 190, 317–21, 323, 325, 337, 384, 397
  historical, 317, 320
  honest, 38
  spiritual, 397
  unconscious, 83
search for mystical experience, 384

second Adam, 238, 325
second century followers, 251
second coming of Christ, 105, 310
Second Council, 272
second Eve, 238, 273
Second Isaiah, 203, 205
Second Temple, 213
Second Vatican Council, 254, 304
Second World War, 365
secret attraction, 264
secret ledger, 396
secret of existence, 110
sect, 233
  new, 249, 253
  new Christian, 255
sectarian, 232, 251
sectarian disputes, 331
secular, 47, 195, 300, 356, 361
  attacked abusive, 293
  powerful, 296
secular age, 312
secular existentialism, 363
secularization, 311, 378
secular Zionism, 211
security, 30, 162, 211
  emotional, 391
  religion-based, 38
sedition, 196, 249, 254–55
seeds, 138, 254, 413
Seeds of Paul's change of heart, 264
selection, 141, 439
  kin, 419
selective arrangement, 133
self, 18–19, 50, 56–58, 60, 65–72, 74–75, 77–97, 101–24, 126–43, 302, 338, 360, 369–71, 376–77, 388–89, 403–4, 409–10, 415–19, 424–25, 427–28
  archetypal, 54
  false, 102
  intrapsychic, 70
  noumenal, 132
  original, 86

separate, 35
term, 78, 83
Self and disagreements, 121
Self and ego consciousness, 84
Self and other, 19
Self and traditional theistic notions of divinity, 71
self-assertion, 48
self-authenticating, 27
self-awareness, 35, 162, 271, 341, 377
self-cognition, 99
self-cohesion, 343
self-consciousness, 359, 377
  clearest, 359
self-contained points, 352
self-control, 266, 340
self-criticism, 262
  intense, 262
self-deception, 24
  a manual of, 54
self-denial, 259
self-discovery, 275, 290
self-doubt, 100, 399
self-esteem, 100, 204–5, 343, 390, 392, 422, 430
  individual, 410
  low, 31, 85, 338, 390
  people's, 175
self-esteem problem, 398
self-examination, 104
self-experience, 424
Self for Jung, 74
self-healing, 133
self-illuminating, 35
self-image, 391
  individual's, 390
self in analysis, 443
Self in Jung, 131
Self in Jung's works, 384, 428
self in Kohut, 143
self in Kohut and Jung, 143
Self in Mystical Experience, 80
self-interest, 352, 411

selfish gene, 44, 426
selfishness, 340
self-knowledge, 276, 285
self-limitation, voluntary, 14
self-loathing, 262
Self manifests, 106, 110, 112
selfobject, 100, 331, 384, 419
  idealizing, 438
  unfailing, 397
selfobject in childhood, 384
selfobject milieu in childhood, 397
self-psychologist, 384
self psychology, 421, 424, 397, 438
self-punishment, 266, 383
self-realization, 48, 89
self-reflection, 98, 100, 336, 341
self-revelation, 293, 297, 309
self-sacrifice, 278
  voluntary, 324
self-soothing, 385
self-sufficiency, 306, 312
Self-symbols, 94, 111–12
  incomplete, 122
Self-symbols reminds, 109
Self to infinite Consciousness, 131
semen cause pollution, 187
sensitivity, 53, 187, 324
  special, 323
separation, 81, 85, 347, 385
  distinct, 345
  divine-human, 338
separation of science and religion, 347
Sephirot, 210
  lower, 210
  lowest, 210
sequence, 169, 221, 286, 335
  aperiodic, 127
  temporal, 329

seraphim, 110, 204
Serapis, 161
sermons, 143, 236, 251, 414, 424
serpent, 102, 237
servant, 158, 175, 246, 340
  promised, 343
Servant Songs, 205
service, 99, 104, 177, 411
  selfless, 278
Settled agricultural villages, 152
settlements, 151, 222
seventeenth, 303
Seventeenth- and Eighteenth-Century Philosophers, 348
seventeenth centuries, 7, 33, 231, 290, 294, 298–99, 348, 350–51, 356
  early, 348
  late, 300
seventeenth century astronomers, 346
sex, 186, 419
sexuality, 40, 187, 259, 262, 281, 379
  human, 181
  normal, 339
  renouncing, 342
sexual promiscuity, 197
shadow, 41, 98, 104, 113, 121, 124, 251, 414, 434
  cultural, 192
  individual, 105
  personal, 100, 104, 121, 400
  projected, 418
  violent, 183
shadow impulses, 112
shadow in dreams, 124
shadow material, 104, 401, 409, 414
  cultural, 411
shadow qualities, 414
shadow side, 104, 411
shamanic practitioners, 146
shamans, 148
Shamash, 143, 169, 186

Shamdasani, 133, 438
shame, 194, 389
shared set of beliefs and values, 416
Sharon, 236
Shaver, 440
Shechinah, 327
sheep, 179, 332
  lost, 242
Shekinah, 157, 182, 223
Shengold, 396, 419, 439
shepherd, 6, 135, 185, 196, 390, 402, 443
shepherd Adonis, 155
Shermer, 375, 439
Shia, 59
Shinto Amaterasu, 167
Shiva, 82
Shlain, 156, 439
shrines, 154, 195, 198, 230, 252, 274
sickness, 48
  spiritual, 395
side effects of monotheism, 165
signs and wonders, 333
Silberman, 222, 428
silence, 26, 29, 215, 304
  pure, 29
  a sound of sheer, 190
  stunned, 211
Simon Bar Kochba, 224
simplicity, 24
  highest, 286
sin, 202, 204, 257–59, 262–65, 276–78, 281, 285–86, 295, 297–98, 309–10, 314–15, 333–34, 341–42, 389–90, 395–96
  earlier, 202
  eternal, 335
  heinous, 178
  human, 265, 277–78, 295, 323
  inciting, 265
  mortal, 342
  particular, 196
  people's, 225
  permit, 353
  ultimate, 238

INDEX | 513

venial, 342
Sinai, 90, 136, 173, 177, 188, 190, 200, 213, 219, 221, 236
Sinai desert, 222
Sinai experience, 96
sin and evil, 249
sincerity, 337, 342
sinful, 195, 263, 279, 285, 305, 383, 389, 413
sinful nature of humanity, 52
sinfulness, 228, 308, 340, 370, 396–98
humanity's, 277
sinners, 250, 284, 294, 297, 395, 398
punishes, 398
Sinope, 267
Sirach, 182
Sistine Chapel, 333
Sisyphus, 49
sitting on an ass's colt, 248
situation, 37–38, 49, 77, 79, 84, 87, 108, 112, 117, 120, 122, 373, 375
complex emotional, 112
contemporary, 138, 307
difficult, 225
given, 182
hopeless, 352
human, 298
infantile, 370
inner, 115
political, 192, 247, 255, 412
religious, 426
social, 391
therapeutic, 138
situation by finding, 77
Sixteenth Century Reformation, 294
Sjöö & Mor, 152–53
Skeptical biologists, 10
skepticism, 116, 301, 317, 394, 405
accelerating cultural, 138
skeptics, 5–7, 9, 11, 50–51, 55–56, 130–31, 205–6, 224–25, 234–35, 237, 247, 249, 293, 331, 408

religious, 347
skeptic's guide, 430
skeptics question, 7
skin, 148
reddish, 119
skin diseases, 186
Skinner, 392–93, 439
skulls, 131, 150
sky-God, male, 367
slavery, 40, 217–18, 225
sanctions, 18
slaves, 222, 225
obedient, 331
recalcitrant, 251
sleep, 86, 150, 160, 266, 405, 408, 435
Smith, 52, 153, 170, 177–81, 231, 320, 396, 407, 424, 433–34, 439–40
snake-goddess, 154
snakes, 111
poisonous, 183
social approval, 393
social benefits, 241
social change, radical, 314
social conditions, 272
social conflicts, 88
social constructivist, 394
social constructivist approach to religion, 393
social factors, 30, 47
social forces, 362
supported, 47
social frame, 394
social function of the Self, 115
Social Indicators Research, 440
social injustice, 194, 314
increasing, 196
social malaise results, 91
social manifestations, 108
Social Origins of Religion, 393
social outcasts, 323
social position, 260
social pressures, 24, 393
social progress, 47, 361
social safety net, inadequate, 38
social security systems, best, 38

social solidarity, 362
social structures, 178, 416
social success, 183, 225
social transmission of beliefs, 376
social values, changing, 191
societal factors, 148
societies, 48–49, 134, 137, 157, 159, 161, 192, 250, 290, 297, 300, 362, 391, 393, 416
bond, 362
civil, 348
contemporary, 2
developed rational, 48
early, 57
early pre-technological, 146
feudal, 290
goddess-worshipping, 154
hunter-gatherer, 150
ideal, 348
organized, 152
patriarchal, 326
prehistoric, 167
ruled, 167
traditional monotheistic, 40
sociological approach to religion, 376
sociologist Emile Durkheim, 362
Socrates, 406
Sodom, 215
Soelle, 216, 440
Sof, 209–10, 213
soil, 152, 189
fertile, 215
solace, 250, 398
sola fides, 295
solar system, 345
sola scriptura, 296, 397
somatic experience, intense, 30
somatic manifestations, 87
son, 155, 176, 178–79, 202, 227–28, 235–36, 239–40, 261, 268–72, 274, 276, 278–79, 337, 340–41, 380–81

Songs, 236
son Isaac, 173, 409, 412
son-lover, 155
　dying, 155
son-lover Attis, 155
son of God, 179, 241, 261, 277
Sophia, 100–101, 157, 181–82, 271, 275, 326–27
Sophia's divinity, 182
Søren Kierkegaard, 360
sorrow, 264, 395
soteriology, 314
soul, 36, 42–43, 84, 92–95, 103, 147, 163–64, 278–80, 289–91, 340, 349, 352, 355–56, 358–59, 425, 442–43
　living, 377
Soul and psyche, 438, 442–43
soul family, 115
soul in anguish, 425
soul murder, 396, 419, 439
soul's deepest, 79
source, 5–7, 26–28, 93–94, 122–24, 138–39, 208, 221, 228–29, 273–74, 289–91, 299, 302–3, 307–8, 310–11, 335–36, 349, 353, 382–83, 404, 407–8
　common, 80, 129, 137
　complex, 393
　important, 103, 142, 378, 401, 405
　medieval, 293
　possible, 267, 396
　psychological, 371
　real, 317
　reliable, 233
　true, 29, 92
source material, 231
source of religious experience, 95, 377, 405
South American, 62
Southern Baptists, 340
sovereigns, 223, 249, 330
　male, 325

sovereignty, 268
space, 13, 19, 81, 127, 130, 132, 209–10, 213, 403, 408, 415
　sacred, 66, 149
　safe, 111
　transitional, 383
Spain, 148, 154, 209
spandrels, 372, 419
Spanish Armada, 294
Spanish cave paintings
　date, 421
specialists, 262
　religious, 152
Specialized members, 146
specialness, 56, 410
specie aeternitatis, 82
species, 10, 41, 44–45, 371–72, 374
　human, 145
　new, 10
spectrum, 5, 378
speculate, 96, 323
speculation, 23, 33, 59, 73, 222, 264, 302–3, 363, 395
　metaphysical, 69–70, 140, 300, 305, 358–59, 368
　scientific, 361
　theological, 72, 142, 290, 401
speeches, 218, 394, 439
　free, 45
spell, 42, 426
　dangerous, 42
Spencer, 147
Spero, 385, 440, 442
spheres, 74, 111, 117, 140, 157–58, 291
　political, 223
Spilka, 31, 391, 422, 440
Spinoza, 14, 163, 303, 354–55, 368
spirit of Chardin, 316
spirits
　pure, 275, 402
　supreme, 356
spirits and gods, 165
spiritual attainment, 101
spiritual awareness, 316

spiritual center, 2, 111
spiritual concept of God, 112
spiritual connotation, 402
spiritual development, 55, 94, 388
　private, 275
spiritual dimension, 5, 29, 32, 41, 48, 362, 366, 369, 371, 376, 378
spiritual directors, 115
spiritual effect, 53
spiritual element, 135
spiritual essence, 130, 163, 275
spiritual exercises, 28, 402
spiritual influence, 30
spiritual interest, 115
spirituality, 69, 75, 78, 82, 137, 139, 141, 145, 416, 426, 431, 433, 436
　goddess-centered, 367
　individual's, 77
　neopagan feminist, 425
　non-theistic, 50
　personal, 135
　sincere, 244
spirituality revolution, 441
spiritualization, 182, 294
　extreme, 75
spiritualizing, 92, 145
spiritual level, 5
spiritual life, 114, 424, 430
spiritual notions, 392
spiritual persona, 414
spiritual practices, 68, 97, 108, 115, 370, 372, 414, 419, 425
　intense, 81
spiritual principles, 36, 108, 120, 129, 348, 376, 419
　common, 359
spiritual purposes, 402
spiritual questions, 80
spiritual reality, 27, 116, 285, 402
spiritual signal, 403
spiritual source, 139, 152
　internal, 83

spiritual structure, 272
spiritual teachers, 29, 175
　great, 415
　idealized, 58
spiritual traditions absorption, 101
spiritus rector, 94
Spitz, 398, 440
Spitzer, 7, 9–10, 440
Splendor, 210
split, 57, 75, 103–4, 113, 134–35, 154, 157, 182, 276, 398, 403
　extraordinary, 411
　good-bad, 412
　growing, 44
splitting, 103, 122, 251, 262–64, 412
　all-bad, 192
　intrapsychic, 411
　primitive, 411
splitting and projection, 263
splitting defense, 251
　wish-fulfilling, 108
splitting mechanism, 56
Spong, 237, 440
squared circle, 120
squares, 65, 111, 140
　elongated, 118
standardized religious package, 3
standards, 37, 107, 219, 364, 405, 416
　ethical, 333
　high, 388
　liturgical, 31
　modern, 40, 399
　producing, 400
　social, 416
　traditional, 102
standing stones, 152
Stanford, 52, 440
St. Anselm, 22, 51, 277
St. Aquinas, 407
Stark, 30, 440
stars, 94, 111–12, 160, 249, 273, 345
　morning, 238
　worn yellow, 216
state, 42, 44, 99, 101, 103,
143, 145–46, 162, 212–14, 292, 295, 298, 385, 388
　enlightened, 251
　human mental, 364
　infantile, 385
　initial, 173, 304
　intense affective, 288
　mystical, 385
　original, 80
　paradisiacal, 336
　particular psychic, 72
　permanent, 237
　prelapsarian, 348
　psychological, 93, 115
　regressive, 385
　spiritual, 67
　trance, 29, 148
　transformed, 341
　visionary, 272, 339, 406
state church, 342
state gods, 253
state law, 343
state of consciousness, 343, 385
statues, 159, 176, 178, 223, 296
St. Augustine, 104, 215, 259, 280, 314, 407
　xlvi, 340
St. Bernard, 285
St. Bonaventure, 288
St. Clair, 386, 440
Stein, 66, 431, 440–41
Steinmetz, 396, 440
Stephen, 264, 340
Stephen Hawking, 43
Step Pyramid, 163
　traditional Christian, 215
St. Ignatius, 28
St. Jerome, 406
St. John Chrysostom, 215
St. Louis, 423, 439
St. Nickolas, 32
　century, 76
Stoics, 164
stone, 152–53, 181, 217, 223, 337, 367, 440
　heavy, 150
　inscribed, 222
　precious, 112
　red-hot, 163
　sacred, 152
Stone Age, 146
Stonehenge, 152
stone structures, large, 152
stone tablets, 189
stone tools, 150
stoning, 266
　public, 218
stories, 12–13, 61–62, 126–27, 161, 170–72, 190, 205, 219, 221–23, 231–32, 234–38, 240, 246–49, 281, 319, 335–38, 396–97, 408–9, 412–13, 417
　consistent, 337
　earlier, 172, 174, 176
　flood, 221
　folkloric, 325
　miracle, 222
　miraculous, 233, 235
　mythic, 394, 409
　original, 234
　scriptural, 401
stories of Jesus' birth, 234
storms, 99, 145, 177–78, 224
　powerful, 111
story of Christ, 205, 236, 380
story of Jesus' death, 156, 231
story of Jesus' death and resurrection, 156
story of satan, 238
Stoughton, 421
St. Paul, 27, 225, 231, 234, 237, 239, 241–42, 249, 255, 325–26, 332, 410, 414
St. Paul's opinion, 284
St. Paul's warning, 403
St. Peter's church, 294
Strachey, 429
Strauss, 47
strength, 8, 20, 107, 194, 247, 265, 380
stress, 51–52, 74, 77, 81, 83, 128, 252, 259, 266, 273, 278, 377, 379

agriculturalist's, 154
biblical writers, 190
extended Jesus,' 258
gnostic, 123
great, 261
intense, 31
modern Christian, 251
tradition's, 192, 224
stress divine transcendence, 305
stress on belief, 77
stress randomness, 10
Strickling, 115, 440
Stroope, 392, 440
structures of existence, 10
St. Thomas Aquinas, 16, 20, 142, 286
study, 32, 205, 213, 346, 384, 387, 419–21, 423, 426–29, 431, 434
study and prayer, 213
study in magic, 429
study in magic and religion, 429
study in psychoanalysis, 428
study in psychoanalysis and history, 428
study of God, 420
study of history, 419
study of humanity, 42
study of human opinion, 301
study of mathematics, 346
study of mathematics and geometry, 346
study of matter, 356
study of nature, 62, 348
study of other, 32
study of Torah, 29, 222–23
style, 170, 340, 388, 391
early attachment, 391
style of attachment, 391
subject, 25, 27–28, 30, 32, 62, 67–68, 72, 110, 115–16, 231, 234, 407, 417
intense, 284
obedient, 281
supraordinate, 87

subjective convictions, 292
subjectivity, 2, 43, 77, 319
child's, 383
human, 26, 366, 393
individual, 76
subjectivity and consciousness, 43
submission, 40, 306, 373, 379
subordinate role, 260
subordination, 325
subservient, 224
substance, 6, 107, 268–69, 284, 340, 354, 368
substitute, 77, 223, 277, 295, 382, 385
substitute attachment figure, 391
succession, 10, 276
apostolic, 337
Suetonius, 319
suffering, 12, 31, 37–39, 54–57, 74–75, 87–89, 101, 103–8, 174–75, 189, 205, 216, 223–25, 265–66, 277–79, 314–15, 323–25, 335–36, 388–89
Suffering Servant, 205, 212, 235, 246, 249, 266
Sufism, 404, 425
suicide, 249, 382
Suler, 143, 440
Sumer, 153, 155
Sumerian, earlier, 172
Sumerian Anu, 143
Sumerian gods, 160
Sumerian pantheon, 153
Sumerians, 153, 155, 159
Sumerian Tammuz, 151
Summum Bonum, 102, 122
sun, 36, 61, 81, 84, 146, 157–60, 163, 169, 236, 273, 345–47
Sundays, 360
Sunday sermons, 414
Sunday services, 366
Sundén, 394
Sungir, 150

sun-gods, 146, 157
sunlight, 111, 143
Sunni Islam, 59
superego, 379, 390, 400, 419
harsh, 279, 398
punitive, 389
tyrannical, 205, 265, 295
superficiality, 299
superimposing, 67, 320
superimposition, 134
theological, 237
superiority, 156, 175, 203, 223, 343, 354
condemned racial, 316
supernatural, 36–37, 46, 62, 88, 210, 288, 293, 300, 337, 374
generic, 3
supernatural abilities, 159
supernatural agents, 374
supernatural audience, 167
supernatural backdrop, 23
supernatural background, 116
supernatural beings, 17
supernatural claims, 53, 317
traditional, 317
supernatural domains, 348
supernatural elements, 53, 300
supernatural entities, 358, 375
supernatural events, 419
supernatural experiences, 24, 30
supernatural explanation, 43
supernatural forces, 46
competing, 161
invisible, 374
supernatural healings, 306
supernatural manifestations, 57
supernatural order, 145, 288
supernatural origin, 305
supernatural origin of scripture, 305
supernatural power, special, 58

supernatural powers, necessary, 146
supernatural redeemer, 318
supernatural revelation, 328
supernatural stories, 47
super-psychic Being, 123
supersessionism, 215
superstition, 57, 59, 293, 348, 351, 356–57
Supporters, 260
support slavery, 260
suppression, 77, 180, 339, 367
 complete Roman, 261
supraordinate, 71, 141
supraordinate field of consciousness, 131
supremacy, 100
 national, 248
 white, 420
Supreme Being, 191
surrender, 238, 265, 342–43, 397
 total, 210
surroundings, 237
 traumatic selfobject, 397
survival, 150, 214, 216, 362, 372, 374–76
 fostered, 372
 group's, 372
surviving hunter-gatherer, 146
suspicion, 100, 407
 arousing, 299
 theologian's, 324
sustained attention to dreams and synchronicities, 117
Suttie, 382, 441
Swinburne, 23–24, 441
swords, 76, 202, 248
 sharp, 245
symbolic acts, 202
symbolic analog of consciousness, 65
symbolic appearances, 130
symbolic associations, 150
symbolic cannibalism, 234
symbolic expression, 72–73
symbolic form, 141

symbolic history of humanity, 67
symbolic manifestations, 70, 74, 108, 142
symbolic material, 322–23
 individual, 135
symbolic pointers, 275
symbolism, 66
 traditional patriarchal theism stresses goddess, 367
symbolize, 179, 202
symbolize matter, 273
symbol of Christ, 75, 104, 113
symbol points, 132
symbols, 68, 74–76, 82, 92, 94, 108–10, 113, 140, 142, 240, 245, 413
 ancient, 65, 140
 classical Self, 66
 collective, 93
 complete, 113
 earthly, 140
 incomplete, 104, 113
 intrapsychic Self, 73
 novel, 114
 particular, 109
 personal, 94
 personified, 145
 possible, 122
 valid, 109
symmetrical gardens, 112
Symmetrical geometrical figures, 111
synagogues, 340, 399
synchronicity, 68, 79, 115–17, 127, 135, 138, 162, 352, 422, 428
 important, 96, 115
 negative, 107
 powerful, 115
synchronistic meetings, 117
Synod, 232
Synoptic Gospels, 336, 439
Syriac, 335
Syrian Adonis, 159
Syro-Palestinian pantheon, 430

T
Table Talk, 396
taboo, 26, 56, 58, 148, 153, 180, 380–82, 429
 incest, 182
Tabor, 321, 441
Tacey, 2, 140, 441
Tacitus, 319
Taliaferro, 329
Talmud, 173
Tamayo, 442
Tammuz, 155, 158, 179
 dying, 155
Tao, 28, 131
Taoist tradition, 28
Taoist yin-yang symbol, 111
Tarsus, 255
taste, 302
 personal, 12
tautology, 8, 22
Taves, 24, 441
teachers, 181, 397
 enlightened, 313
 enlightened moral, 318
 great, 325
 high school, 343
 human, 245
 human Galilean, 269
 important, 301
teaching authority, 298
teaching evolution, 343
teachings, 172–73, 227, 229, 232, 239, 242, 244, 250–51, 253, 295, 298–300, 340, 351, 354, 389–90
 apocalyptic, 249, 317, 320
 classical, 313
 deemphasize Jesus' harsher, 252
 ethical, 58, 411
 important, 315
 important moral, 40
 official, 272
 oral, 275
 orthodox religious, 250
 radical monotheistic, 200
 theological, 288, 388
 traditional, 52, 304

traditional Roman Catholic, 316
teach universals, 284
technology, 45, 303
Teilhard, 316, 342
Teillard, 313
Tel-Dan, 222
teleological, 19
teleology, 287, 362
teleology in nature, 287
teleology in nature and order, 287
telos, 84
templates, 370, 373
  brain's, 373
  mental, 373
temple, 152–53, 155, 179–80, 182, 193, 195–96, 199, 202, 221, 223–24, 242–43, 252, 256–57, 338, 340–41
  ancient, 155
  building, 159
  first, 195
  new, 236
  original, 206
Temple Mount, 224
temple sacrifices, 174, 200, 223, 283
temple worship, 222
temporal lobes, 376–77
temporal relations, 329–30
temporary blindness, 339
temporary effect, 262
temporary necessity, 257
temptations, 244, 340, 409
  demonic, 407
tension, 35, 76, 84, 88, 96, 183, 207, 224, 266, 281, 283
  internal, 262
  muscle, 87
  traditional theological, 73
terms, 6–7, 12, 15–17, 24–26, 39–40, 58–59, 61–62, 66–67, 141–42, 180–81, 190–93, 206–8, 222, 306–7, 311–14, 335, 337–39, 358–59, 382–84, 402–3

abstract, 17
architectural, 419
atheistic, 43
behavioral, 393
common, 207
cosmic, 194
important plural, 179
medieval, 282
metaphysical, 87, 365
modern, 207
naturalistic, 24, 38
negative, 16
neutral, 327
ordinary human, 318
ordinary logical, 270
ordinary mythic, 177
ordinary physical, 336
philosophical, 312
plural, 180
psychic, 69
psychological, 70
rational, 11
religious, 395
societal, 11
subjective, 306
terrifying, 25, 107, 158
territory, 133, 340
  particular, 137
terror, 188, 295, 395, 397, 426, 431
testament, 335, 439
testimony, 174, 233, 319, 423
text, 3–4, 55–58, 169–72, 180–81, 204–5, 209–10, 217–19, 221, 224–25, 231–32, 262, 307, 314–15, 320–24, 330–31, 334–37, 412
  ancient, 219, 225, 246
  coherent, 169
  de-mythologized, 332
  earlier, 169, 171, 198
  earlier Hebrew, 235
  eschatological, 251
  final, 170, 221
  historical, 172, 409
  literary, 331
  original, 293, 331, 335
  original Hebrew, 242
  post-biblical, 207

primary, 62
prophetic, 193
scriptural, 384
separate, 231
traditional, 3
textual differences, 336
theism, 11–12, 17, 23–24, 37, 44, 61, 69, 72, 435, 437, 442
  classical, 34–35, 312
  rational, 356
  scientific, 7, 345
  traditional, 3, 69, 74, 99, 363
theism and atheism, 356
Theissen, 322, 441
theistic, 66, 109
  traditional, 39
Theistic God-image, 24, 36, 73
  classical, 7, 46
theistic image, 13
  traditional, 54
theistic image of God, 13
theistic philosophers, 13
theistic proofs, 23, 425
theistic religion, 391
theistic response, 37
theistic traditions, 14, 16, 29, 57, 59, 61, 69, 73, 109, 345, 360
  mainstream, 69
theists, 9–15, 17, 19, 23, 36–37, 39, 50, 55, 74, 287
  classical, 13, 329
  traditional, 6, 11–12, 34, 116, 189, 329, 348, 391
themes, 126, 161–62, 240, 274, 277, 290, 332, 408
  ancient, 314
  central psychological, 4
  common, 107, 336
  common background, 153
  dominant, 311
  mythic, 127, 172
  recurrent mythological, 126
  sacred marriage, 155
  spiritual, 365

INDEX | 519

theodicies, 54–55, 105, 211, 353
xliv, 225
Theodosius, 338
theologian Rudolph Bultmann, 413
theologians, 31, 53–54, 66, 70, 73, 76, 96, 124, 207, 305, 307–9, 312–13, 347, 364–65, 367–68, 401
Theologians and ministers of religion, 96
theologians and philosophers, 365
theologian's descriptions, 50
theologians over-idealize, 55
theologian's suspicion of psychology, 324
theological accounts, 5
separate, 317
theological beliefs, pre-existing, 30
theological claims, 79
theological contrivance, 272
theological correctness, 359
theological descriptions, 3, 60
theological edifice, 237
theological interpretations, 217, 424
theological mistakes, 431
theological notions, 79
abstract, 380
theological notions of God, 79
theological questions, 218
theological statements, 98, 122, 364
theological superstructure, 234
theology, 69–70, 72–74, 122–25, 217, 290–92, 295–97, 300–301, 304–6, 308–9, 313, 316–17, 328, 342–43, 364–66, 395, 398–99, 418, 420, 422–23, 441–42

believer's, 411
divided, 348
dogmatic, 418
emergent, 434
emerging, 231
existential, 307
father-knows-best, 217
liberal, 305, 311
liberation, 62, 314, 328, 416
making death-of-God, 386
modern, 303
mystical, 350
natural, 21, 61, 115, 307–9, 343, 348
negative, 16
neuro, 378
new, 198
philosophical, 308
rational, 32
scholastic, 288
single, 351
speculative, 293
systematic, 288, 441
traditional, 95, 99, 292, 303, 316
theology and philosophy, 6, 365
theology is anthropology, 47
theology of human helplessness and divine omnipotence, 398
theology of nature, 316
theology of personal salvation, 256
theorists, 5, 34, 61, 133, 148, 156, 372
cognitive, 374
theory, 44–45, 49, 146–48, 151, 156, 222, 224, 337, 342, 361–62, 382, 434, 440
biological, 376
classical Christian, 413
controversial, 181
developmental, 86
dual-inheritance, 375
evolutionary, 375
group selection, 419

isolated mind, 131
modern, 396
preconceived, 133
quantum, 366
spandrel, 375
traditional, 283
theory of evolution, 7, 10, 21, 44, 287, 316, 342, 362, 368
Theory of Mind, 167, 375
theory of revelations, 440
therapeutic couple, 117
therapeutic couple study, 138
therapeutic field, 117
therapeutic tool, 112
therapy, 46, 68
individual psycho, 97
real, 68
Thessalonians, 254, 261, 263, 334, 339–40
Thiering, 320, 441
thinkers, 14, 59, 61, 211, 293, 300, 348, 350, 353, 361
contemporary, 8
enlightenment, 46, 300, 317
important, 36
medieval, 283
thinkers contend, 7
thinking, 41–42, 93, 96, 135–36, 167, 172, 327–28, 342, 349, 356, 365–66
analytic, 432
apocalyptic, 251, 338
circular, 46
deist, 34
human, 67
individual, 418
left-over archaic, 9
magical, 39, 57
mature, 48
messianic, 338
modern, 288
original, 282
pre-logical, 151
produced, 349
rational, 351
religious, 151
scientific, 7–8

thinking types, 33
third thing, 117
thirteenth century Kabalistic book, 223
Thomas, 246, 335
Thomism, 142, 288
Thomism splits, 288
Thomistic, 307, 363
Thomistic concept, 308
Thomistic Natural Theology, 439
Thomistic theologians clung, 308
Thomists, 312
Thompson, 412, 441
thread, 405
  common, 351
  important, 214
threats, 18, 192, 196, 275–76, 279, 316, 318, 330, 334, 346, 352
  constant, 388
  harsh, 198
  political, 268
  potential, 403
throne, 75, 105, 109–10, 184, 201, 204, 242
  empty, 332
  glorious, 246
  rule upon his, 248
Tiamat, 224
Timaeus, 11, 163
time, 59–60, 85–87, 126–27, 154–55, 162–63, 169–71, 177–79, 193–97, 209–10, 221–25, 233–34, 251–56, 286–88, 323–26, 328–29, 335–36, 348–52, 355–56, 371–72, 402–3
timeless, 82, 164, 329
timelessness, 28, 32, 61, 93
time of extreme religious intolerance, 346
Timothy, 233, 330, 340
title, 158, 337
Titus, 259
tolerance, 41, 187, 249, 293
tolerance of religion, 41

tombs, 152, 158, 245, 336
  empty, 245–46
tone, 113, 278
  polemical, 41
toned complexes cause, 75
tongues, 29, 202
  long, 148
tools, 140, 153
tooth, 187
topic, 209
  controversial, 171
Torah, 29, 173, 196, 205, 208–9, 222–23, 255–57, 261, 339, 343, 400
  written, 173
Torah scroll, 56
torment, 18, 425
  eternal, 334
Toronto, 426–27, 433
Torrey, 372, 441
totality, 71, 78, 81–83, 85, 108–9, 111, 113, 116, 120, 128, 131, 141
  nameless, 35
  psychic, 415
Totality and infinity, 434
totality of consciousness, 80, 83, 88
totality of existence, 34
totality supraordinate, 71
totality supraordinate to consciousness, 71
totalizing, 130, 165
total manifestation of consciousness, 131
Totem, 148, 380–82, 429
Totem and taboo, 148, 380–82, 429
totem god-animal, 382
Totemism, 26, 148, 380, 382
  theory of, 147, 380
Tower, 172
traces, 46, 180–81, 369, 415
traditional beliefs, 46, 122, 125, 304
  making, 208
Traditional Biblical Story, 173

Traditional Christian God-image, 89, 228, 303
Traditional Christianity, 46, 75, 103
traditional Christian stereotypes of Jews, 215
traditional concept of God, 365
traditional figure of Christ, 103
traditional forms of religion, 78
traditionalists, 31, 122, 136, 167, 170, 278, 289, 307, 403–4
Traditional metaphors of God, 79
traditional metaphysical notions of God, 364
traditional models of God, 328
Traditional monotheists object, 34
traditional moral attributes of God, 7
traditional pantheon of gods, 161
traditional pantheon of gods of ancient Iran, 161
traditional terms, 308
traditional theistic descriptions of God, 65
traditional theistic image of God, 54
traditional theistic notions, 71
Traditional theologians, 96
Traditional Thomists, 52
traditions, 31–32, 35, 57–62, 80, 96–97, 119–20, 124–26, 140–42, 172–75, 191–92, 221–23, 227–30, 237–39, 252–53, 273–76, 313–15, 325–27, 329–31, 402–3, 409–11
  ancient, 113, 219, 253, 258, 291
  church, 296

INDEX | 521

cultural, 169
developing, 268
earlier, 240, 324, 336
ecclesiastical, 31
emerging, 241–42
esoteric, 209
folk, 273
gnostic, 276
historical, 323
individual's, 389
inherited, 97
liberal, 390
local, 50
long, 25, 263, 406
long-standing, 137, 234, 251
mainstream, 82, 230, 276, 326
matriarchal, 155, 382
multiple, 130
mystery, 162
mystical, 385
mythic, 97, 222
mythological, 190
neo-orthodox, 312
non-dual, 131, 338
occult, 368
oral, 231, 233
particular, 299
patriarchal, 157, 382
personal, 32
polytheistic, 157
pre-Christian, 327
prophetic, 79, 182–83, 192
rabbinic, 182, 222–23
rabbinical, 335, 405
scriptural, 71
single, 80
spiritual, 35, 83, 88, 90, 93, 101, 111, 166, 252
subject's, 63
theological, 55
tradition's patriarchal image of God, 224
trans-archetypal, 81
transcendence, 33, 48, 73–74, 93, 95, 124, 229, 308
absolute, 74
increasing, 190

transcendent, 11, 13–14, 209, 211, 229, 270, 272, 287, 306, 308–9, 312, 328, 341, 354, 356
transcendental background, 95
Transcendentalists, 301
transcendental realities, 69
transcendental remoteness of God, 293
transcendent background, 366
transcendent cause, 21
transcendent deity, 74, 82, 92, 312, 418
transcendent dimension, 52, 305
transcendent divinity, 141
transcendent form, 96
transcendent God, 61, 68–70, 78, 80, 96, 103, 121, 123, 272, 280, 359
transcendent God and belief, 413
transcendent mode, 13
transcendent of nature, 169
transcendent purpose, 212
transcendent reality, 20, 162, 238, 296, 363, 403
transcendent supernatural, 302
transcendent to nature, 354
transcription, 336
transfiguration, 236, 339
transfigured body of Christ, 316
transformation, 14, 89, 117–21, 142, 389
apocalyptic, 348
gradual, 67
transformation of God, 117
transformative effect, 27
transformed state of consciousness, 341
transgressions, 243
transition, 142, 156, 300, 431, 441
conceptual, 269

translation, 2, 69, 161, 232, 249, 283, 330, 340, 414
early Latin, 335
modern, 170
multiple, 320
original, 180
translators, 176, 193, 394
transmission, 26, 53, 60, 68, 194, 287, 330
cultural, 44, 375
genetic, 53
social, 376
written, 232
transmitter, 92
transpersonal, 27, 56, 66–67, 80, 93, 97, 138
transpersonal component, 130
transpersonal depths, 92, 138
transpersonal dimension, 2, 5, 109, 135, 137, 339
transpersonal level of psyche, 80
transpersonal levels, 26–27, 29, 32, 56, 60, 65, 80, 82, 93, 123, 136
transpersonal principle, 78
transpersonal reality, 28
transpersonal referent, 324
transpersonal Self, 3, 35, 65, 83, 129–30
transubstantiation, 296
trappings, traditional, 299
trauma, 38, 199, 211, 323, 389, 395–96
early, 133, 388
traumatic failure of affective attunement in childhood, 85
traumatic life event, 389
treatment
harsh, 397
unconscious, 120
unequal, 97
treatment of Job, 98
trees, 39, 75, 81, 147, 154–55, 172, 178, 181, 190, 237–38, 259

magnolia, 111
  sacred, 156
tree symbolism, 336
tremendum, 213, 424
Trends, 363, 421, 437
Trent, 298
trial, 234, 422, 443
  biological, 44
triangles, 291, 332
tribalism, 41, 137, 411, 417
  reinforced, 137
tribal war-deity, 192
tribes, 148, 222, 242, 380, 418
  distinct, 171
  local desert, 176
  particular, 137
tribulation, 311
Trinitarian doctrine, 270
Trinitarian God-image, 113, 142, 272
trinitarian system, 271
trinity, 15, 73–74, 113, 142, 180, 269–72, 284–85, 292, 340–41, 347
Trinkaus, 150, 441
Triple Goddess, 167
triumph, 247, 295, 334, 427, 438
triumphant, 183, 258
true source of religious experience, 92
trust, 51, 70, 120, 197, 258, 372, 378, 383, 392, 396–97, 407
  basic, 51, 383
  complete, 295
  new, 303
trust in Yhwh, 197
truth, 51–52, 56, 59, 123, 126, 158, 233–34, 285–86, 288–89, 297, 299–300, 315, 358, 360, 409–10
  absolute, 219, 364
  complete, 23
  eternal, 163, 401
  final, 80
  foundational, 20
  highest, 361
  historical, 325, 409, 417
  literal, 53
  new, 407
  objective, 313
  private, 76
  psychological, 409, 415
  rational, 354
  religious, 356
  spiritual, 238, 325
  subjective, 379
  transcendental, 46
  universal, 33
truth claims, 315, 382, 385
turd, 105
  giant, 75
Turkey, 151, 154
  modern, 152
turmoil, 33
  intense inner, 192
twentieth century, 43, 49, 287–88, 304–6, 308, 310–13, 315, 318, 320–22, 342, 345–67
  early, 309, 362
  late, 317
twentieth century approach, important, 321
twentieth century approaches, 307, 314
twentieth century artists, 365
twentieth century culture, 365
twentieth century ethicist, important, 43
twentieth century philosophers, 363
twentieth century theologians, 306, 309, 313–15, 365
Twentieth Century Thinkers, 363
twinship, 410
  intense, 266
twinship transference, 384
Tyana, 336
Tylor, 147
typological preference, 342
typology, 323, 342
U
UFO, 141, 201
Ugarit, 223
Ugaritic documents, 223
Ugaritic elements, 223
ultimate, 73, 102, 139, 443
ultimate cause, 164
ultimate determinant, 316
ultimate explanation, 437
ultimate goal, 84, 289
ultimate manifestation, 80
ultimate purpose, 59
ultimate reality, 25, 29, 35, 166, 307, 364, 384
  experienced, 25
  unknowable, 6, 133
ultimate realization, 286
ultimate retribution, 390
ultimate scapegoat, 323
ultimate Subject, 71, 80, 83, 142
ultimate subject of experience, 80
unanswerable question, 73, 339
unanswered questions, 126
unavoidable ambiguities, 78
unbelievers, 252, 352, 414
  external, 410
  persecuted, 263
  rejected, 260
uncaused First Cause, 20
unclean spirits, 239, 338
unconscious, 427
unconscious attitude, 137
unconscious condition, 98
unconscious factors, 323
unconscious life, 76
unconsciously stamped, 125
unconscious matter, 349
unconsciousness, 101
  state of, 81
unconscious oedipal problem, 182
unconscious phantasy, 412
unconscious prefiguration, 85
unconscious treatment of Job, 120
underserved divine acceptance, 398

underworld, 149, 158, 238, 419
undisguised alchemical conception of Christ, 75
unexamined superstitions, 300
unflattering and unsavory images of God, 55
unfolding, 49, 305, 317, 340
  ordered, 9
unfolding processes, 359, 363
unfolding revelation, 233
unicorns, 22, 285, 364
unify, 104, 160, 198, 268
unifying factor, 128
union, 75–76, 80, 140, 142, 223, 279, 285–86, 289, 291–92, 378, 385
  blissful, 385
  ecstatic, 209
  individual experiences, 385
  mystical, 36, 81
  real, 284
unitary document, 221
unite, 75, 109, 134, 142, 148, 197–98, 362
United States, 38, 225, 301
uniting, 272, 340
unity, 32, 35, 80, 115, 122, 127–30, 271–72, 279–80, 287, 338, 358–60
  absolute, 143
  ego-Self, 141
  eternal, 271
  eternal cosmic, 354
  highest, 358
  indissoluble, 358
  initial psychosomatic, 86
  original, 279
  reconciling, 291
  total, 209
  undifferentiated, 341
  undivided, 88
unity of humanity and nature, 358
universalize, 160
universal love, 254

Universal Mind, 93
universals, 284
universe, 6–13, 16, 18–22, 34, 43–44, 46, 48–50, 128, 163–64, 228–30, 283, 286, 288, 291, 293, 302, 316–17, 345– 47, 352–57, 366–67
universe and cares for humanity, 7
universe and ruled heaven, 154
universe by making evolution, 34
universe demands, 23
universities, 342
unknowable metaphysical background, 73
unknowable reality, 139
unknowing, 93
unlimited ability, 210
unnamed disciple, 335
unprovable assumption, 26
unqualified divinity of Christ, 268
unreasonable nature of human beings, 34
unresolved father-son difficulties, 123
unseen spirit, 372
Unspeakable, 73
untold numbers, 227
unus mundus, 127–28
Upanishadic Ātman, 83
Upanishadic tradition, 79, 101
Upanishads, 35, 131, 162
updated earlier laws, 199
Upper Paleolithic Period, 150, 167
  earlier, 441
Ur, 159, 173
Uranus, 155
utensils, 150, 186
Utnapishtim, 161
utopian, 167
Utu, 159
Uzzah, 186, 217
Uzziah, King, 204

V
vacancy, 66
vain, 53, 355
validity, 6, 53, 62, 79, 132, 136, 235, 323, 339, 375, 407
  historical, 415
Valley, 236
value of dreams, 406
value of religion, 382
values, 6, 8, 10, 22, 24, 31, 33, 35, 37, 250–52, 307, 313–14, 382, 412–13, 416–17
  absolute, 23
  anti-Semitic, 400
  critical, 419
  cultural, 41, 332
  establishment, 62
  gentle, 252
  great, 246
  highest, 72
  historical, 171
  human, 47
  original, 237
  particular, 366
  permanent, 193
  political, 34
  positive, 37
  possible, 8
  psychological, 379
  soteriological, 101
Van Buren, 216, 312, 441
variations, 335–36, 362
  textual, 40
Vass, 308, 442
Vatican, 62, 92, 142, 295, 298, 316
Vedantic, 83, 131
Vedder, 365, 442
Veneration, 150
vengeance, 183, 185, 187, 244, 263, 334
  wreak, 216
Venus, 75, 153
  pre-Christian, 114
veracity, 40, 337, 378, 382
verbal constructs, 130
Vergote, 386–87, 390, 442
veridical information, 404
verification, 7, 46
Vermes, 253, 321, 442–43

verses, 18, 235, 246
Vetter, 392, 442
victim of evil, 55
victims, 55, 211–12, 216, 218, 401
   human, 413
victims of Auschwitz, 211
victory, 182, 184, 198, 203, 223–24, 248, 309, 314, 406
   final, 338
   military, 183
   posthumous, 214
   resurrection symbolizes, 105
   theological, 200
   ultimate, 311
Vinci, 429
vindicate, 189, 205
vindication, final, 207
vindictive attitudes, 263
vindictiveness, 18
vine, true, 236
Vintage Books, 432, 436–37
violence, 137, 165, 167, 185, 323, 325, 339, 341, 410–12, 426, 431
   book's, 412
   human, 277, 335
   inspire, 219
   inspired, 41, 412
   religious, 370
   sacred, 316
   valorize, 341
violent history of Christianity, 323
violent suppression, 53
virgin, 162, 167, 223, 235, 274
virginal, 274
virginal conception, 53
virgin birth, 126, 234, 240, 274–75, 281, 306, 310–11, 317, 336, 402
Virgin Mary, 269
virtuous behavior, 39
virtuous life, 164, 192
virus, 45
   smallpox, 44
Visala, 378, 442
visibility of God in Christ, 239
vision of animals, 406
vision of God, 204
vision of perfection, 326
visions, 75–77, 109–10, 123, 138, 194, 201, 204, 337, 339, 342, 405–8
   beatific, 282, 342
   extraordinary, 201
   inner, 402, 404
   messianic, 204
   partial, 315
   particular, 58
   single, 364
   terrifying, 76
visions of reality, 123
visions seminars, 432
visualization, 28
vitality, 147, 414, 419
   contemporary, 402
Vith, 50
Vitz, 342, 442
vocation, 28, 67–68, 200, 206
voice, 25, 29, 111, 119, 170, 172, 193, 201, 376–77, 405–6, 442
   authoritative male, 118
   dominant, 289
   hallucinatory, 376
   inner, 111, 194, 224, 301, 399, 409
   internal, 62
   maternal, 397
   progressive, 276
   still small, 110, 190
voice of gods, 376
volcanic action, 178
Voltaire, 33, 342, 353–54
Voluntary covenant, 430
vulnerability, 249

W

wager, 100, 188, 352
Wallis, 216, 442
wall niches, 150
walls, 222
   thick, 112
Walter, 443
war, 37, 40, 107, 166, 176–78, 181, 183, 305–6, 311, 384, 391
   civil, 299
   first world, 61
   incited, 160
   judges and makes, 245
   religious, 17, 300
   terrible, 47
warrior, 248
   apocalyptic, 274
warrior goddess Athena, 154
warrior king, 327
Washington, 432–33
water, 80, 171, 173, 196, 233, 243, 256
   bath, 62
   living, 236
way-station, 223
way-stations pointing, 256
weakness, 49, 247, 266, 295
   love values, 48
   made perfect in, 247
wealth, 71, 76, 164, 250, 294, 297
   amasses, 361
   valued, 194
wealthy elites, 62
weather, 159, 176, 374
weather-God, 178
weight, 17, 62, 142, 324, 395
   behaviorism lent, 43
Weinberg, 7, 443
Weldon, 121, 442
wellbeing, 31, 343
Wellhausen, Julius, 221
Western branches, 135, 403
Western Church, 339
Western God-image, 121, 138, 349, 427
Western history, 282
Western intellectual tradition, 7
Western liberal values, 313
Western psyche, 120
Western religions, 59
Western religious traditions, 106, 367
Western scholars, 283
Western science, 430
Western society, 309

INDEX | 525

Western thinking, 282
Western tradition, 103
Westminster, 440
Westminster Confession, 231
Westport, 427–28, 430, 443
whale, 62, 332
wheels, 110, 153, 201
  potter's, 158
whirlpool, 425
White Goddess, 167
Whitehead, 440, 442
White Raven, 442
White women's Christ, 430
Whitney, 425
wholeness, 65, 69, 109, 111, 113–14, 127, 140, 324, 341, 422
  approximate, 414
  complete, 414
  immature, 336
  pleromatic, 127
  unbroken, 127
  unconscious, 341
Whore of Babylon, 411
wickedness, 194, 239, 301
  human, 161
Wiesel, 212, 442
wilderness, 40, 236, 337
Wiley, John, 435
Willendorf, 75, 114, 153
Wilmette, 425, 427
wind, 111, 140, 147, 374
  calmed storm, 232
wine, 80, 233–34, 284, 296
winged snake, 110
wings, 110, 159, 201, 204, 307, 375
  conservative, 252
  liberal, 306
Wink, 315–16, 322, 442–43
Winnicott, 133, 383–84, 419, 443
  Donald, 383
Winnicott's legacy, 436
Winona Lake, 430
Winston, 442
winter, 111, 151, 254, 443

wisdom, 51, 154, 177, 194, 205, 208, 210, 265, 270, 350–51, 357
  ancient, 351
  human, 312
wisdom and design in nature, 350
wisdom figure, 181
wisdom literature, 142
wisdom teacher, 320
wisdom teacher and holy, 320
witches, 18, 22, 224, 239, 285, 399
withdrawal, 95
  parental, 388
witness, 12, 108, 133, 244, 288, 333, 339
  public, 275
witnessing, 211, 303
witness miracles, 190
Wittgenstein, 364
Witwicki, 322
wives, 259, 333
  human, 179
  love your, 260
Wolff, 356
  mathematician Christian, 356
Wolterstorff, 437
woman, 116, 118, 120, 224, 240, 260, 339, 440
  human, 126
woman's name Junia, 326
womb, 150, 152, 155, 158, 200, 238, 287, 407
women, 40, 154, 157, 160, 180–81, 224, 259–60, 273–74, 276, 315, 325–27, 333, 336, 340, 367
  assigned, 260
  belittles, 326
  directed, 259
  human, 336
  silenced, 331
  young, 259
women and children, 171, 325
Women's bodies, 340
women's spirituality, 425
women weeping, 179
wonder-worker, 321

wool, 40
  pure, 191
word begotten, 340
word hominid, 167
word hominin, 167
word love, 133
words
  inadequate, 96
  true, 234
work, good, 295
workings, 7, 328
work of God in history, 311
Work on dreams, 115
work values, 141
world, 13–14, 32–36, 48–51, 54–56, 127–29, 131–32, 162–65, 207–10, 213–14, 228–29, 256–61, 280, 282–83, 286–87, 308–10, 327–29, 336–38, 349–55, 357–59, 361–63
  external, 116
  fallen, 302
  finite, 359
  human, 133
  ideal, 249
  imaginal, 404
  inner, 56, 86, 115, 133, 151, 384, 412
  macroscopic, 366
  mundane, 58
  mythological, 306
  one, 127
  pagan, 415
  phenomenal, 358
  possible, 353
  social, 328
  spacetime, 127
  spiritual, 151, 252
  temporal, 207, 329
world axis, 111
World Council, 304
world creating significance, 88
world-destruction, 190
world events, 312
worldliness, 294
world manifests, 23
world of gods and spirits, 96
world order, 250, 287, 301

new, 207, 257
world religions, 162
world situation, 413
world soul, 11, 36, 348, 359, 361
world's religions, 59, 423
World Unveiled, 437
World War, 83, 305, 307, 363
World War II, 312
worship, 150, 152–55, 166–67, 170, 176, 180–82, 184, 191, 193, 197, 206–7, 273, 299, 406, 408
　ancestor, 57, 147, 154
　associated, 240
　civic, 162
　exclusive, 100, 138, 197, 333
　idolatrous, 192
　monotheistic, 160, 206, 381
　public, 162
worship Babylonian gods, 199
worship God, 334
worship goddesses, 167
worship Jesus, 266, 269
worship of gods, 197
worship of local nature gods and goddesses, 193
worshippers, 109, 159, 179, 199, 341
　early, 183
worshipping, 82, 176, 180, 184, 199, 253, 362
worshipping Canaanite gods, 176
worshipping El, 171, 178
worshipping idols, 401
worshipping pagan gods, 197
worship services, 26
worship Yhwh, 180
wound, 201, 246
wrath, 18, 217, 239, 245, 263, 290, 341, 389, 398
　senseless, 413
the wrath of God rests upon him, 251
Wrestling, 433, 435

wretched man, 262
writer Pliny, 319
writers, 36, 41, 190, 192, 211–12, 214, 216, 219, 223, 231–35, 313–14, 320, 386–87
　early, 253
　particular biblical, 190
writers of scripture, 401
wrote of me, 242
Wu, 28
Wuji, 28

X
Xenophanes, 163

Y
Yahweh, 72, 79, 120, 141, 426, 429, 436, 439
Yahwism, 426
Yhwh, 98, 100–101, 106, 170, 173–81, 183–93, 197–200, 202–7, 217–18, 221, 223–24, 275, 381
　adopted, 178
　angry, 267
　apple, 180
　betrayed, 197
　exclusive worship of, 175–76, 180, 200, 203, 206
　figure of, 98, 182
　followers of, 176, 199
　name, 221–22
　south preferred, 178
　temple of, 205–6
　transform, 217
　worship of, 199, 223, 381
　worshipped, 171, 198
Yhwh afflicts, 224
Yhwh and Elohim, 221
Yhwh demands submission, 184
Yhwh murders, 185
Yhwh projects, 98, 100
Yhwh replies, 222
Yhwh's adherents, 182
Yhwh's atrocious behavior, 102
Yhwh's demands, 186

Yhwh's followers, 184
Yhwh's image, 190
Yhwh's laws, broken, 199
Yhwh's loving characteristics, 218
Yhwh's mixture of attributes, 187
Yhwh's punishment, 179
Yhwh's Relationship, 174
Yhwh's self-awareness, 121
Yhwh's temple, 202
Yhwh's threats, 202
Yhwh's unconsciousness, 100
Yhwist, 224
yogi, 141
Young, 395, 428
Young-Eisendrath, 129, 443
younger, 104, 119–20, 197, 319
youth, 125, 155, 190, 200, 295

Z
Zarathustra, 84, 162, 405
　tempted, 337
Zarathustrax, 161
zealot, 255, 421
zealous, 333
　extremely, 264
zealous anger, 339
Zechariah, 193, 206, 248–49, 260
Zedekiah, 199
Zero Point Field, 62
Zeus, 11, 82, 106, 162, 241, 336
Zinkin, 129, 443
Zock, 383, 438, 443
Zohar, 209, 223
Zoroaster, 162, 223, 244, 407
Zoroaster's mother, 223
Zoroastrian deity, 179
Zoroastrianism, 174, 223, 407
Zoroastrian myth, 238
Zoroastrian religion, 177

www.ingramcontent.com/pod-product-compliance
Lightning Source LLC
Chambersburg PA
CBHW021132230426
43667CB00005B/85